Young people who sexually abuse

Building the evidence base for your practice

Edited
by

Martin C. Calder

Child Protection Co-ordinator, City of Salford Community and Social Services Directorate;
Independent Child Protection Trainer and Consultant

Russell House Publishing

First published in 2002 by:
Russell House Publishing Ltd.
4 St George's House
Uplyme Road
Lyme Regis
Dorset DT7 3LS

Tel: 01297-443948
Fax: 01297-442722
e-mail: help@russellhouse.co.uk
www.russellhouse.co.uk

British Library Cataloguing-in-publication Data:
A catalogue record for this book is available from the British Library.

ISBN: 1-898924-89-9

Typeset by TW Typesetting, Plymouth, Devon

Printed by Antony Rowe, Chippenham

Russell House Publishing
Is a group of social work, probation, education and
youth and community work practitioners and
academics working in collaboration with a professional
publishing team.
Our aim is to work closely with the field to produce
innovative and valuable materials to help managers,
trainers, practitioners and students.
We are keen to receive feedback on publications and
new ideas for future projects.

Contents

To Janet, Stacey Laura and Emma Anne.

You are my world.

In loving memory of Walter, Rita and Charles.

Acknowledgements

Leigh library for all the material they continue to supply for me.

To the staff at Russell House Publishing for their perseverance with such lengthy manuscripts.

To all the contributors for producing manuscripts of such high quality.

To Judith Unsworth for her creative IT skills.

The contributors

Kamran Abassi LLB (Hons), Certificate in Counselling has been working as a Criminal Justice Development Officer on the South Asian Offenders Project in partnership with the National Probation Service – Greater Manchester, for over four years. He provides training and consultancy on cultural and religious aspects pertinent to the South Asian Community. He also provides a mentoring service to young South Asians. Seen as one of the pioneers in the field of sex offending within the South Asian community, Kamran is currently producing a manual to work with South Asian sex offenders. He can be contacted by e-mail at **offenders@pakistani-resource.org.uk**

Dr Tony Baker is a Consultant in Child and Family Psychiatry at Ashwood Centre, Brookwood, Surrey. Ashwood Centre was established in 1991 as an independent child and family consultancy practice offering a range of assessment, consultation and therapeutic services. Baker and Duncan have been providing specialist asessment and therapeutic services in Child Protection including work with adult sex offenders, their partners and families, adolescent male sex offenders, and we are also developing services for teenage women whose development of sexuality has been compromised by an abusive background. This could include early pregnancy, abusive behaviour, recurrent victimisation and involvement in the sex industry.

Nick Bankes BEd (Hons), Dip ASS, CQSW, CMS has worked for various Social Services Departments in the UK since 1984. He has been instrumental in developing assessment and treatment facilities for adult and adolescent perpetrators of sexual abuse both within Local Authority and Voluntary sectors since 1989 and is currently Team Manager of A.C.T., a specialist Local Authority therapeutic service for young people with sexual behaviour problems. He is chair of the NOTA South East branch and is a member of the NOTA research committee. Nick is also undertaking a part-time doctoral research degree.

Carol Barnes BSc, ClinDip (Family Therapy) was a member of the Psychology Department at Feltham Young Offender Institution until recently when she took up a post as Family Therapist at SWAAY (Social Work with Abused/Abusing Youth). She continues to work, albeit in a different milieu, with the families of young sexual abusers, and victims. This study was supported by a Cropwood Fellowship Award at the Institute of Criminology, Cambridge.

Dr Arnon Bentovim MB, BS, FRCPCH, FRCPsych, BPAS, DCH is Honorary Consultant Child and Adolescent Psychiatrist at Great Ormond Street Hospital for Children and the Tavistock Clinic; Honorary Senior Lecturer at the Institute of Child Health; and Director of The London Child and Family Consultation Service. He is involved with SWAAY, a nationally available residential service for adolescent boys who have sexually abused.

Sarah Boettner LSW is a licensed Social Worker at The Twelve Inc., TASC programme with Masters level training in the area of criminal justice. She has worked with youth sexual abusers in Forensic Foster Care over the past two years. You may contact Ms Boettner by e-mail at **swkr2@aol.com**

Mark A. Buehler CSW is a Certified Social Worker in the State of New York. He has worked in private practice and has worked extensively with individual psychotherapy and with supportive group psychotherapy. His interests include writing on self-help topics. He currently works at the Capital District Psychiatric Center in Albany, New York. Fax (518) 465 7714.

Martin C. Calder MA, CQSW is a Child Protection Co-ordinator with City of Salford Community and Social Services Directorate. He has particular interests in the area of sexual abuse and has written books on adult male sex offenders, young people who sexually abuse and mothers of sexually abused children. He also has an interest in the development of effective policy, procedure and practice guidance and child protection theory. He is available as an independent trainer and consultant on all child protection matters and can be contacted at **martinccalder@aol.com**

Peter Clarke MA has been working as a trainer, consultant and clinical practitioner for over fifteen years. He is currently working as Clinical Director at Glebe House Therapeutic Community where he oversees assessment and treatment programmes designed to offer relapse prevention strategies for adolescents who have sexually abused. Peter continues to work with other professionals and organisations supporting their efforts to create meaningful interventions for vulnerable and dangerous teenagers.

David O'Callaghan BA (Hons), CQSW qualified as a social worker at Lancaster University in 1982 and has worked as a child care practitioner and guardian ad litem in the West Midlands and the North West. He is currently the Programme Director of G-MAP, an independent project providing assessment and therapeutic services to young people who sexually abuse. G-MAP works with young people across the ability spectrum though it is noted for the development of service to young people with learning disabilities. David has published internationally on a number of aspects of work with young abusers and provides staff consultancy and training nationally.

Curtis R. Grant majored in social work at Virginia Union University in Richmond, Virginia. He has been a Juvenile Correctional Officer for the Virginia Department of Juvenile Justice since 1983. He served as a trainer, and presented at conferences in the United States and Canada on working with juvenile sex offenders. Mail address: HJCC, P.O. Box 507, Hanover, VA, 23116, USA. E-mail: **gunngrant@yahoo.com**

Simon Hackett is Lecturer in the Centre for Applied Social Studies at the University of Durham. Having previously worked for NSPCC, Simon was involved in the retrospective investigation of allegations of institutional abuse in North Wales children's homes, arising from the Waterhouse Inquiry. A co-founder and a former Programme Director of G-MAP, he has substantial practice and training experience in sexual aggression work and an ongoing practice base at Kaleidoscope, a specialist community-based programme in the North East of England. He is an active researcher in the field and has published variously in relation to sexual aggression, including the comprehensive practice manual (2001) *Facing the Future: A guide for parents of young people who have sexually abused others*, Lyme Regis: Russell House Publishing. Simon is a NEC member of the National Association for the Treatment of Abusers (NOTA) and is currently Convenor of NOTA's Policy and Practice Committee. A range of Simon's publications and resources relating to young people who sexually abuse can be accessed through his website: **www.sexualaggression.com**. E-mail: **simon@sexualaggression.com**

Colin Hawkes is the Consultant Social Worker at the Young Abusers Project, a specialist, multi-agency team providing assessment and treatment of children with sexual arousal problems. He has been involved in developing clinical practice, with both adults and children who abuse, for more than fifteen years and has a particular interest in research and education linked to this problem.

Charles E. Hodges Jnr LCSW, CSOTP holds a Master of Divinity and a Master of Clinical Social Work. He is a licensed Clinical Social Worker (VA), Certified Sex Offender Treatment Provider (VA), and a Juvenile Forensic Evaluator (VA). He has many years experience as a treatment programme administrator, sex offender clinician, and staff trainer. He regularly presents at regional and international conferences. Work settings include both community and residential sexual offender treatment. E-mail: **Chodge40@aol.com**

Dr Gareth Hughes is Head of Psychological Services at Kneesworth House Hospital and a Research Fellow at The Institute of Criminology, University of Cambridge. As a Chartered Clinical and Forensic Psychologist and an accredited (BABCP) Cognitive Psychotherapist, he has experience working with sex offenders. Research interests include psychopathy, treatment and evaluation, risk assessment and gender identity disorders.

Shabana Jamal BA (Hons), CQSW qualified as a Social Worker in 1990. She worked for two local authorities over a five-year period on the children and families team. She has been employed on the South Asian Offenders and Families Project for five years. Shabana is also a Practice Teacher in Social Work and carries out Independent Social Work Comprehensive assessments for court and family proceedings.

Andrew Kendrick is Professor of Residential Child Care in the Department of Social Work at Strathclyde University. He completed a PhD in Social Anthropology at the London School of Economics in 1984. Since then he has carried out research on a range of child care issues, including decision-making in child care and residential child care. He contributed literature reviews to the Skinner review of residential child care in Scotland and the Kent and Utting Children's Safeguards Reviews. He can be contacted at **andrew.kendrick@strath.ac.uk**

Robert E. Longo MRC, LPC is the Corporate Director of Special Programming and Clinical Training for New Hope Treatment Centers in Summerville, South Carolina. He also serves as a consultant, educator, trainer, and author dedicated to sexual abuse prevention and treatment. He was a co-founder and first President of the Association for the Treatment of Sexual Abusers and was previously Director of the Safer Society Foundation, Inc. and the Safer Society Press from 1993 through 1998. He has published more than 35 chapters and articles in the field of sexual abuse treatment and pioneered the Safer Society Press sexual abuser workbook series.

Ranald Mair qualified as a social worker and practiced in both fieldwork and residential settings. For five years he was a social work lecturer at Sheffield Hallam University. In 1988, he took up his current position as Principal of Geilsland Residential School. He has been closely involved with the Scottish Centre for Residential Child Care and its successor the Scottish Institute for Residential Child Care, and has contributed to a number of Scottish Executive Working Groups. E-mail: **rmair@geilsland.bosr.org.uk**

Sue Maskell MA is Head of Childcare at Conwy Social Services. She has a particular interest in the sexual abuse field and in research which brings worker and clients voices to the fore when considering policy. She is currently researching childrens attendance at child protection conferences for the National Assembly for Wales.

Michael H. Miner PhD is Assistant Professor in the Department of Family Practice and Community Health, Medical School, University of Minnesota. Mike currently directs sex offender treatment at the Programme in Human Sexuality, is the editor of the Forum, the newsletter for the Association for the Treatment of Sexual Abusers, and co-editor, with Dr Eli Coleman, of Sexual Offender Treatment: Biopsychosocial Perspectives. He is a Vice President of the International Association for the Treatment of Sexual Offenders and has published numerous papers and book chapters on Relapse Prevention, sex offender treatment outcome, and forensic assessment. His current research focuses on the causes of sex offending in adolescents and adults.

Lucinda A. Rasmussen PhD is an Associate Professor at the School of Social Work at San Diego State University. She co-authored a book on treating children with sexually abusive behaviour problems and has published four articles on treatment issues in the Journal of Child Sexual Abuse and Sexual Abuse: A Journal of Research and Treatment. She may be contacted at: San Diego State University, School of Social Work, 5500 Campanile Drive, San Diego, CA 92182-4119. (619) 594-6459 or **rasmuss2@mail.sdsu.edu**

Keeley Slack is a Child Protection Officer with NSPCC currently working in a Specialist Investigation Service in Newcastle. With a background in local authority child protection, Keeley worked at Kaleidoscope for two years and was part of the Parents' Groupwork Programme.

Paula Telford CQSW, PQ in Child Protection has 26 years experience in the child protection field. For the last six years Paula has been involved at the Kaleidoscope project in Sunderland in specific work with children and young people who have harmed others as a result of their sexual behaviour, both as worker and more recently as Children Services Manager. With colleagues at Kaleidoscope, Paula co-authored '*Work with adolescent females who sexually abuse: similarities and differences*' in Erooga M. and Masson H. (Eds.) (1999), *Children and Young People Who Sexually Abuse Others. Challenges and Responses*. Paula is currently Chair of NOTA's North East Branch.

Eileen Vizard FRCPsych is a Consultant Child and Adolescent Psychiatrist with the Young Abusers Project in London. She is Clinical Director of the Young Abusers Project, an assessment and treatment service within Camden and Islington Community Health Services NHS Trust and supported by the NSPCC. Dr Vizard has published, researched and taught widely within the field of child care and child abuse.

Ineke Way PhD, ACSW has treatment experience with children who have been sexually abused, non-offending parents, adolescents with sexual offending behaviours, and adult survivors of incest. She co-authored two books on treatment with sexually abusive adolescents and co-developed a cycle of offending behaviours. Her dissertation research examined the relationship between childhood maltreatment and empathy for victims of abuse and other traumas in adolescents with sexual offending behaviours. She is an Assistant Professor at the School of Social Work, Western Michigan University. Dr Way can be contacted at the School of Social Work, 1903 W Michigan Ave, Western Michigan University, Kalamazoo MI 49008-5354, (616) 387 3195 or **wayi@wmich.edu**

Edward Wieckowski holds a Masters of Clinical Psychology, and is Psychologist Senior for the Virginia Department of Juvenile Justice. He is a Certified Sex Offender Treatment Provider in Virginia. He regularly presents at regional and international conferences, and has published papers in areas of juvenile sexual offenders and sex offender classification systems. He served on legislative and agency committees, and consulted on programme development and modification. E-mail: **Webwie@aol.com**

Dr Darlene Williams has Forensic and Clinical Psychology practices in Tampa and Palm Harbor, Florida, specialising in adolescent, couples, and family therapy. She provides consultation services, is a part-time graduate instructor in psychology, and conducts workshops and presentations on relaxation therapy. Dr Williams has published articles in forensic and developmental psychology. She is also a board member for PACE Center for Girls, the Team Psychologist for Children's Medical Services Craniofacial Clinics in Tampa and St Petersburg, Florida, USA, and is an active member in Big Brothers/Big Sisters of Pinellas County, Florida. Dr Williams can be reached at (727) 772-0038, 2843 Alternate 19, Palm Harbor, FL 34683.

James Worling is the psychologist and co-ordinator of research at the SAFE-T Program (Sexual Abuse: Family Education and Treatment) in Toronto. Dr Worling has written a number of articles regarding adolescent sexual offenders, and his present research interests include the heterogeneity among adolescent sexual offenders, sexual recidivism risk estimation, and treatment approaches and outcome. For correspondence, please write to Dr James R. Worling, Psychologist, SAFE-T Program, Thistletown Regional Centre, 51 Panorama Court, Toronto, Ontario, Canada M9V 4L8.

James Yokley PhD is a Clinical Psychologist on the Medical Staff in the Department of Psychiatry at MetroHealth Medical Center in Cleveland, Ohio and an Assistant Professor at Case Western Reserve University School of Medicine. He developed The Twelve Inc., TASC programme that treats multiple abuser youth referred for sexual abuser treatment in Forensic Foster Care and has been the Supervising Psychologist in that programme over the past seven years. Dr Yokley has numerous professional publications and presentations in the area of abuse behaviour treatment. You may contact Dr Yokley at P.O. Box 538, Hudson, Ohio USA 44236 or by e-mail: **jimyokley@aol.com**

Introduction

Martin C. Calder

This book represents a sequel to *Working With Young People who Sexually Abuse: New Pieces of the Jigsaw Puzzle* (Calder, 1999) and endeavours to build on the growth of research material and practice developments in the intervening period. This book does not replace the jigsaw puzzle text, rather it attempts to build on the foundation blocks that it set down. This book is organised into several sections to help the reader in being able to access relatively easily, the particular information they need. These sections include research and practice developments, impact issues, broad practice issues, assessment, treatment, management and outcomes. Whilst the book can be read alone, it is best read in conjunction with my other works: *Juveniles and Children who Sexually Abuse: A Guide to Risk Assessment* (Calder, 1997); *Working With Young People who Sexually Abuse: New Pieces of the Jigsaw Puzzle* (Calder, 1999), and *Juveniles and Children who Sexually Abuse: Frameworks for Assessment. (2nd edn.)* (Calder, 2001). In this way, the reader will be able to grasp the individual and tailored responses now being advocated by referring back to where we started and why we have reached our current state. The books aim to stimulate thought and discussion, identify areas where further research is needed and hopefully will guide practice, policy and procedure development.

In an attempt to meet the above objectives, I have assembled contributions from England, Scotland, Wales, America and Canada and the authors draw from a combination of practice experience, research, programme evaluation and academic review. A couple of issues arise as an editor from such a wide audience catchment. Firstly, there is a wide range of terms used to refer to young people who sexually abuse, and I have not standardised those chosen to highlight why we continue to have basic obstacles to evidence-based practice in this field, especially comparative work. I am very clear about the choice of the term 'young people who sexually abuse' and Simon Hackett (2001) has articulated this especially well. He recognises that the term 'young person who has sexually abused' is quite clumsy and long, but he avoids using the shorter 'young abuser' or 'adolescent offender' as these terms describe the child only by what they have done wrong. They are terms that do not offer much hope to the young person concerned. It is important not to downplay what a young person has done or make it seem less serious by using language which does not fit with the abuse. However, we should always consider the messages that might be communicated beneath the words we use. Consider the following statements in the table below.

Secondly, there are some clear differences in spelling between the UK and America and I have chosen to keep the vocabulary as set down by the author. In doing so, I hope that this does not detract from its appeal and use.

The terms:	The messages that might be communicated beneath the terms to a young person:
'You are a sexual abuser'	• All you are is an abuser • You are still an abuser • You will always be an abuser • I am only interested in you as an abuser
'You are a young person who has sexually abused'	• You are a young person first and foremost • You have done something wrong in the past but this doesn't mean to say that you will always be an abuser • You could change • I am taking your behaviour seriously – it is abuse but I am interested in you as a young person as well

In the first section, O'Callaghan argues for more developmentally-sensitive intervention and provides us with a useful framework for developing any research-informed service to this group.

Ineke Way reviews the childhood maltreatment histories of males with sexually offending behaviours as she recognises the centrality of such trauma in the development of sexually abusive behaviour. She does so by reviewing and critiquing 37 American and Canadian studies as well as summarising their findings and setting out some of the implications for practice and research. The issue of critically examining the available literature and research is central to any move towards evidence-based practice as required by central government in the UK (see DoH, 1999) and critiqued by Hackett (forthcoming). Way highlights the varied methodology, focus, detail and specificity of the research that highlights the need for an integrative (ecological) model (see Calder, 2001) that accepts that each study and/or theory is only going to provide one small piece of the jigsaw puzzle (see Calder, 1999). Way recommends the move towards prospective data collection that is however time-consuming, costly and yields results slowly. This issue has been successfully addressed (and reported on in Chapter 22) by Arnon Bentovim and colleagues at the Institute of Child Health.

In the second section, Nick Bankes reports on his doctoral research into the unconscious processes in those professionals who work with young people who sexually abuse. This is an important area of work as it explores the impact of the work on the workers and how this affects their practice. It also highlights important issues when thinking about engaging the young person in their work. He notes the importance for workers of being conscious of their motivation for doing this work, particularly so they are not preoccupied with meeting their own needs. Bankes reports on practitioner recognition of several unconscious processes and how they impact upon their work and contaminate their personal lives. They may fall into one or more of three categories: feeling victimised, feeling persecutory and a need to rescue, and he analyses the observations made by practitioners in these domains. He concludes by making recommendations to workers before undertaking such work.

Simon Hackett explores the impact of the work on the worker, both the gains as well as the costs, setting out the key areas and explains them in detail on affective, cognitive and behavioural levels. He moves on to consider the professional context in which the work is done, embracing the wider socio-political context, providing a model to explain the interactional dynamics of any impact. He concludes with some pointers as to how to survive and then thrive in this area of work.

Finally, Sue Maskell explores how parents, carers and social workers cope in the midst of managing young people who sexually abuse and in so doing identifies just how they are central to the creation of understanding and potential solutions. She did so by adopting a narrative approach to the research, thus minimising the chances of researcher bias.

In the third section, Peter Clarke opens by setting out a model of effective intervention within a therapeutic community utilising a 5-stage process. The context this provides offers a real opportunity to reframe previous learning experiences and to increase the range of life experiences in order to build a lifestyle that includes the potential to live in non-abusive ways.

Kendrick and Mair report on the development of a focused residential unit for sexually aggressive young men in Scotland. They concentrate on the development of a core programme emphasising a safe, secure and nurturing environment which at the same time acknowledges and addresses the issue of sexual aggression. The centrality of the living environment is again noted and highlights the need to address both the sexually abusive behaviour as well as the holistic needs of the young person in question. The preliminary data highlights that treatment outcome is linked to the continued willingness of the young person to engage in the work and how the legal process can often act as a barrier to engagement.

Colin Hawkes then explores the important issue of accreditation of both the work and the workers involved in providing a service to children and young people who sexually abuse. This is an extension of the very real public and professional concern that young people removed into the care system continue to be abused by the same staff as are charged with protecting them and hopefully helping them on their journey to recovery. Hawkes explores the problems encountered in the specialist project where he works and then moves on to review the existing or planned legislation, pointing out the deficits when applied to this particular group, making recommendations for future consideration. He does acknowledge, however, that there is currently no consensus on the need for a system of accreditation let alone the means of establishing a system to monitor practice.

Longo then reports on the development of standards of care for residential treatment of young people who sexually abuse in the US. This initiative was grounded in concerns about the mushrooming number of emerging treatment programmes and with it a need to analyse the chosen interventions, staffing and outcome measurements. The consequences of treatment failure for this group are serious and include future victims. Thus, in an attempt to encourage the highest quality treatment, standards relating to the residential care environment were deemed an essential starting point. A working group produced 28 standards addressing the standard, the rationale for the standard and evaluation measures for the standard. The adoption of such standards does have the effect of promoting standards whilst also providing ammunition for anyone wishing to take legal action for those programmes who do not operate by them. It is hoped that they are disseminated widely and will serve as a benchmark for 'best practice'.

Simon Hackett, Paula Telford and Keeley Slack then look at some lessons from parents of young people who sexually abuse who have attended a groupwork programme.

In the section addressing assessment, Lucinda Rasmussen presents an intervention strategy that addresses the specialised needs of children with sexual behaviour problems. She describes how the Trauma Outcome Process Model can be used to create an integrated treatment approach for assessing children with sexually abusive behaviour problems and treating their perpetration and victimisation issues. She considers interventions that are directed towards enhancing the self-awareness and are geared towards the child being able to express and cope with their feelings in a constructive, rather than a self-victimising or abusive way. Eileen Vizard explores in detail the process and content of assessments conducted by her specialist service and this includes attention to such points as continuing casework responsibility that has the potential to drag on throughout the process from the point of referral unless resolved.

Jamal and Abassi report on their work with South Asian young people who sexually abuse and raise important cultural, religious and linguistic issues in our approach to the work. They explore professional and young person barriers to the work, communication issues, culture, religion, perceptions towards victim and offending, second and third generation South Asians, gender and race, the relevance of offence-focused work, and then explore the issues raised through two case studies.

Simon Hackett then goes on to consider work with young people who have a dual abuse experience. This has been a contentious area for some time, with concerns existing when their own victimisation is prioritised over their abusive behaviour. Hackett charts the course through the arguments and provides some useful practical guidance on how to address both the victim as well as the abuser in any intervention programme.

In the treatment section, Longo explores the need for a holistic approach to the work based on some concerns about existing treatment models. He addresses ways of blending traditional sex offender treatment models and modalities with holistic approaches that incorporate developmental issues and humanistic approaches. This represents ground-breaking material that warrants careful attention and widespread application.

Barnes and Hughes review their family therapy work with young people who sexually abuse and their families in a Young Offender Institution. They highlight the central role of parents offering a source of support in motivating the young person to successfully engage in the work, desist from future offending and play a part in the successful implementation of relapse prevention plans.

Wieckowski, Grant and Hodges then examine the need to anticipate, identify, and avoid wherever possible but where necessary manage the programme pitfalls in the treatment of young people who sexually abuse. They provide us with a concise and systematic four-step model to identify and manage ten common pitfalls, then provide us with an analysis of each pitfall accompanied by warning signs and suggested intervention factors.

Williams and Buehler outline the special characteristics of the young female who sexually abuses and contrast how these characteristics differ from female adult offenders and from male juvenile offenders. They then propose a community-based treatment programme that addresses assessment, group therapy, multi-family, family and couples therapy, individual therapy and case management intervention.

In the next section I provide a critical overview of the structural changes introduced in the UK that has set our work back significantly given the confusing, contradictory and misinformed guidance issued by the Department of Health and the Home Office. I then move on to try and propose some potential solutions, including a proposed procedural framework for local adaptation.

Yokley and Boettner explore many issues raised and lessons learned from their forensic foster care system for young people who sexually abuse, including foster parent selection and retention. This system represents another level in the advocated continuum of care for this group, in between residential and outpatient treatment for those young people whose behaviour management requires gradual re-introduction into the community under supervised conditions.

Tony Baker very eloquently and persuasively describes the community management approach adopted within his community-based therapeutic service. He introduces the concept of safe-enough uncertainty as an achievable goal rather than having unrealistic expectations about risk reduction or management. To do this requires us to identify as closely as possible the context in which the risk may be heightened as well as creating a safety net if such risk looks likely to materialise. Baker describes the assessment process with the young person, their carers, the therapeutic programme and outcome assessment and risk management issues.

In the final section on outcomes, Arnon Bentovim reports on some recently completed research on the development of sexually abusive behaviour in sexually abused males and then goes on to consider what the implications may be for any subsequent treatment. He explores very usefully both the risk as well as the protective factors that are central to looking at whether victims are destined to become abusers or not.

Michael Miner explores factors associated with recidivism of young people who sexually abuse who have committed serious sexual offences. He does so by reviewing the relevant literature on risk prediction in juvenile sex offenders, adult sex offenders and non-sexual juvenile delinquents. Using the findings from

these populations, he presents a study that extends the available literature by testing the applicability of identified risk factors for recidivism in the adult and non-sexual juvenile delinquency literature to a sample of adolescent sex offenders. James Worling also provides us with a framework for assessing risk of sexual recidivism in young people who sexually abuse that was used in the development of the ERASOR (Estimate of Risk of Adolescent Sexual Offence Recidivism) document: an empirically-guided, clinical risk prediction tool (reproduced in Calder, 2001).

Charles Hodges examines a 5-step family therapy protocol that can be used to guide the clinician's work toward healthy family reunification in families that have experienced sibling-on-sibling sexual abuse. In doing so, it promotes family healing by encouraging victim recovery, enhancing offender treatment and developing a new paradigm for future family interactions.

I hope you enjoy the read and find that it provides stimulus for practice development, research projects, and better outcomes for young people who sexually abuse and their victims.

References

Calder, M. C. (1997) *Juveniles and Children who Sexually Abuse: A Guide to Risk Assessment*. Lyme Regis: Russell House Publishing.

Calder, M. C. (Ed.) (1999) *Working With Young People who Sexually Abuse: New Pieces of the Jigsaw Puzzle*. Lyme Regis: Russell House Publishing.

Calder, M. C. (2001) *Juveniles and Children who Sexually Abuse: Frameworks for Assessment*. (2nd edition). Lyme Regis: Russell House Publishing.

DoH (1999) *Working Together to Safeguard Children*. London: HMSO.

Hackett, S. (2001) *Facing the Future: A Guide for Parents of Young People who Have Sexually Abused*. Lyme Regis: Russell House Publishing.

Hackett, S. (forthcoming) Evidence-based practice: A critique. In Calder M. C. and Hackett S. (Eds) *Assessments in Childcare: A Comprehensive Guide to Frameworks and Their Use*. Lyme Regis: Russell House Publishing.

Part 1: Research and Theoretical Developments

Chapter 1: Providing a Research Informed Service for Young People who Sexually Abuse

David O'Callaghan

In comparison to the relatively wide ranging development of treatment services both in prison and community settings for adults who sexually offend (Mann and Thornton, 1998; Allam and Browne, 1998) the last decade has seen a much less consistent pattern in terms of such services for young people. The reasons for this have been much commented upon and clearly include many structural issues relating to poor interagency working and inadequate commitment of resources (O'Callaghan and Corran, 2001; Masson and Morrison, 1999). Services to adults have developed with an integrated research and evaluation process, leading to increased refinement and service development (Beech et al., 1998). Provision for young people has however been dependent more upon local initiatives and partnerships with a lack of centrally co-ordinated services (HM Inspectorate of Probation, 1998). Although many projects developed across the UK and Eire through the 1990s (McKeown and McGarvey, 1999; Will et al., 1994) the nature of the services provided appears to be influenced primarily by the resources available and particular theoretical bias of the practitioners concerned. This chapter aims to provide a description of a service model, which has attempted to respond to the evolving pattern of research in this and allied areas of practice.

G-MAP is an independent provider that offers a range of services for young people who sexually harm others (see O'Callaghan, 1999; Print and O'Callaghan, 1999; Print and O'Callaghan, in Press). This includes:

- assessment
- individual therapy
- groupwork programmes
- family programme
- specialist residential care (in conjunction with a local authority care provider)
- training and consultancy

The service is accessible on a national basis and inevitably has a disproportionate number of more complex cases, for example around 80% of the young people we see are in some form of substitute care or secure setting.

In the last twelve or so years (the duration of the service) we have seen a profound shift in focus and orientation concerning interventions with sexually abusive youth, perhaps the most significant being the recognition that work with this group of young people has more similarities than differences with other young people who have significant emotional and behavioural disorders (Rich, 1998; Ryan, 1998). One major advantage of this more inclusive orientation has been the ability to draw upon the more extensive literature base (e.g. Loeber and Farrington, 1998; Rutter et al., 1998) in addition to research on young people and adults who sexually abuse. Whilst this does not compensate for the relative paucity of outcome and evaluation research specific to young people who sexually harm it does appear to provide us with important signposts to service development.

What then are some of the main themes emerging from these research areas and how might these help us to begin to frame intervention with young people who sexually harm others?

1. Interventions should be ecologically orientated and aim to promote systemic change

The multi-systemic therapy (MST) model has been developed over the past fifteen years and has an impressive body of studies to demonstrate its effectiveness (Henggeler et al., 1998). MST aims to promote change at the level of the young person's social ecology and thus engage the young person's network in the task of managing negative behaviours and promoting positive adaptations. MST advocates contend that such an approach fits closely with the known causal mechanisms of severe anti-social behaviour.

MST treatment principles

- The primary purpose of assessment is to understand the fit between the identified problems and their broader systemic context.
- Therapeutic contacts emphasise the positive and use systemic strengths as levers for change.
- Interventions are designed to promote responsible behaviour and decrease irresponsible behaviour among family members.
- Interventions are present focused and oriented, targeting specific and well-defined problems.
- Interventions target sequences of behaviour within and between multiple systems that maintain the identified problems.
- Interventions are developmentally appropriate and fit the developmental needs of the youth.
- Interventions are designed to require daily or weekly effort by family members.
- Intervention effectiveness is evaluated continuously from multiple perspectives with providers assuming accountability for overcoming barriers to successful outcomes.
- Interventions are designed to promote treatment generalisation and long-term maintenance of therapeutic change by empowering caregivers to address family members' needs across multiple systemic contexts.

Borduin et al. (1990) evaluated the impact on sexual and non-sexual recidivism of a small sample of abusive adolescents who were randomly assigned to an MST service or more traditional individual counselling. Although modest in scope, with a total of only sixteen participants, results over a three-year follow-up were striking, with 1:8 MST participants versus 6:8 of the individual counselling group re-offending. Additionally, the frequency of non-sexual re-offending was significantly lower amongst the MST group. In considering the development of the MST model in work with juveniles who sexually offend, Swenson et al. (1998) suggest that whilst MST can integrate the framework of a more traditional cognitive-behavioural approach in working with sexually abusive youth, there are three major differences in the implementation:

1. Individual (as opposed to systemic) inputs are viewed as part of rather than the primary treatment component.
2. These individually delivered components should take account of the young person's social system.
3. When possible they should be delivered via caregivers and family.

Such integration of the individual's treatment goals into their community and social systems appears to have broad support in the literature on intervention with offending/anti-social youth more generally (Hollin, 1999; Rutter et al., 1998); the literature on effective relapse prevention (Barber, 1992) and the increasing developmentally and holistically orientated approaches to work with young people who sexually abuse (Rich, 1998; Ryan and Associates, 1999). Worling and Curwen (2000) have recently provided perhaps the most substantial evaluation study to date. Based on a six year evaluation period the treatment sample were provided with a programme of specific groupwork and interventions aimed at promoting family strength and social functioning. The comparison group received no treatment or dropped out at an early stage. They found that the treatment group had a 5% sexual recidivism rate compared with 18% for the non-treated sample. Non-sexual offences, both violent and non-violent were significantly lower for the treated sample. The authors commented that the MST approach has many similarities with their programme and provides further support for holistic/systemic intervention approaches.

2. Programmes should aim to promote both cognitive and behavioural change and develop new skills and competencies

Hollin (1999) identifies effective treatment design as attempting to effect both change at the individual's social system and their personal functioning. Evaluation of programmes for anti-social youth has consistently found social-skills training to be a key component (Rutter et al., 1998; Hollin, 1999). In a meta-analysis of 200 programmes for serious juvenile offenders Lipsey and Wilson (1998) found programmes providing social skills and behavioural change interventions demonstrated the most significant treatment effects.

An increasing emphasis on developing social competence can be seen in many adult sex offender programmes (Fisher et al., 2001; Marshall et al., 1999). The evaluation of the UK prison programme for sex offenders (Beech et al., 1998) found that offenders in the 'High Deviancy' sample continued to be relatively socially incompetent at the end of the programme. A recommendation was for the extended programme to specifically target self-esteem, social skills and assertiveness.

Whilst programmes for adolescent and adult sexual offenders had traditionally aimed to promote attitudinal change, Ward and Keenan (1999) suggest the specific nature of the cognitive schema being targeted requires more precise identification within such a heterogeneous client group.

The potential value of addressing distorted cognitions (expectations and attributions) and improving problem solving and social skills is consistently identified in the literature relating to young people presenting severely challenging and offending behaviours (Chapman and Hough, 1998; Hollin, 1999; Jones, 2000).

3. Programme delivery should employ a variety of delivery methods (multiple modalities)

Increased impact appears to be achieved by use of multiple techniques e.g. individually focused interventions; groupwork; family interventions; educational inputs and expressive therapies (Chapman and Hough, 1998; Hollin, 1999).

4. Programmes should be structured to address factors, which contribute to the maintenance of all forms of criminal and anti-social behaviours

It has been a consistent finding that adolescents who sexually offend are more likely to re-offend non-sexually than sexually (Prentky et al., 2000; Rasmussen, 1999; Worling and Curwen, 2000) which supports a view that programmes cannot work on sexual issues in isolation of other high risk and problematic behaviours by young people (O'Brien, 2000; Rasmussen, 1999; Ryan and Associates, 1999).

5. Programmes should aim to actively involve families and carers

Progress in all forms of therapy appears most significantly influenced by the degree of support available to the individual. Young people engaged in treatment services for sexually abusive behaviours appear to do better if supported by either family (Sheridan et al., 1998; Sheridan and McGrath, 1999) or substitute carers (Farmer and Pollock, 1998), findings which connect with general support for the role of interventions targeting the families of problematic youth (Blechman and Dryan, 2000; Kumpfer and Alvarado, 1998).

6. The design of interventions should be informed by those factors seen to promote resilience and positive outcomes for young people

Rutter (1999) reviews the complex interactive process of multiple risk and protective factors which appear to influence the outcomes for children subject to adverse life experiences. Rutter suggests the available research indicates:

- Vulnerability derives from a combination of genetic predispositional and environmental factors.
- The impact of adverse life experiences can be mediated by the promotion of new opportunities.
- The effective and cognitive processing of experiences is critical to the individual mitigating their impact.

Reliance can be considered in terms of the individual's personal qualities (Rutter, 1999); family resilience (Gilgun, 1999; Walsh, 1996) and community factors such as education and social and leisure activities (Daniel, Wassell and Gilligan, 1999).

7. Programmes need to consider how to promote the engagement of non-co-operative and poorly motivated clients

Given that treatment dropout appears to be associated with increased risk of recidivism (Hunter and Figueredo, 1999), we have recognised that resistance and denial is a normative reaction for young people being asked to address their abusive behaviours (Jenkins, 1998; Blanchard, 1995) and that services need to integrate motivational strategies (O'Reilly et al., 2001; Print and O'Callaghan, in press) into their models of working.

8. Treatment for more deviant, problematic and poor functioning client requires significant intensity and duration of delivery

The STEP research projects evaluation of the UK Prison Programme (Beech et al., 1998) found that a minimum of 160 hours of treatment was required to produce a treatment effect with individuals in the high deviancy group and recommended that extended provision be made available to men assessed in this spectrum in both prison and the community based programmes. The ability to provide programmes of sufficient pace or length for individuals with learning difficulties and/or developmental delays (Lindsay et al., 1998: O'Callaghan, 1998) is essential if they are not to be excluded from services.

9. More effective programmes are characterised by high treatment integrity

Research suggests that programmes are more effective if they display the following qualities (Allam and Browne, 1998; Beech et al., 1998; Chapman and Hough, 1999; Hollin, 1999;):

- Have a clear theoretical and research basis.
- Assess specific clients' needs.
- Fit intervention to assessed need.
- Deliver service through written protocols.
- Have formalised methods for evaluation.

Monck and New (1996) in their study of services for child victims and young abusers in the UK suggested that more focused assessment processes, systematic record keeping and integrated evaluation procedures should be consistently incorporated into therapeutic programmes.

What are the principal questions that services to young people who sexually harm need to address?

Any service needs to consider a set of central themes, which will in turn inform the specific design of the provision. These can be seen as providing both the set of individual considerations as a young person progresses through an intervention process and more broadly as forming the philosophical/theoretical basis upon which the service is based (see Figure 1 overleaf).

- *What are the origins of sexually abusive behaviour?*

- *What characteristics are associated with the persistence of sexually harmful behaviours?*
- *How do we best assess individual need?*
- *What characterises an individually and developmentally sensitive service?*
- *How do we maximise participation?*
- *What are the characteristics of an effective service?*
- *How do we best evaluate progress, change and impact?*

Further to these core questions Rich (1998) suggests four principles of treatment:

1. Flexibility and responsiveness to the individual.
2. To address general patterns of behaviour in the young persons life which parallel and interrelate with sexually harmful behaviours.
3. To provide a comprehensive service which encompasses the young persons whole functioning.
4. To integrate treatment goals into the young persons everyday living.

Finally, Ryan and Associates (1999) propose that all therapeutic work with young people who sexually harm should have three overarching goals:

1. To develop positive communication skills.
2. To enhance empathic skills.
3. To promote accurate attributions of responsibility.

Key themes in work with young people who sexually abuse

Whilst our belief is that each young person has a very individual set of life experiences and developmental concerns our clinical experience and the literature would suggest a number of common themes.

Attachment

The role of negative attachment styles as a key variable in the subsequent development of problematic behaviour in children has been extensively documented (Crittenden, 1995; Happe and Frith, 1996; Levy and Orlans, 1998). Marshall first began to consider the potential role that attachment may have in terms of sexual offending by highlighting the connection with subsequent intimacy skills (Marshall, 1993, 2000). This theme has been increasingly explored by other researchers, for example Smallbone and Dadds (1998, 2000) who have reported that poor relationships with mothers

Figure 1: Research sensitive service delivery model.

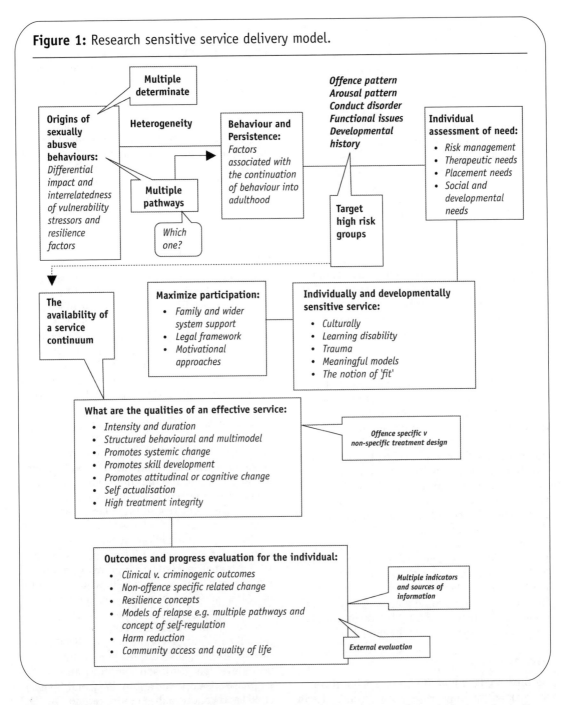

was a predictor (in their sample) of general anti-social behaviour and that poor paternal attachments predicted sexual coercion in adulthood. Ward and Hudson have recently attempted to identify more precisely the developmental process by which certain experiences of attachment may relate to interpersonal sexual violence for some males by applying the concept of 'theory of mind' (Keenan and Ward, 2000; Ward et al., 2000).

Trauma

Estimates of the proportion of young abusers who themselves have experienced sexual victimisation ranges from 30–50%, though histories including physical and emotional abuse, exposure to violence and neglect appear almost universally present (Beckett, 1999; Manocha and Mezey, 1998; Ryan et al., 1996). Increased disclosure of abuse during treatment appears a common feature (Worling, 1995; Yager et al., 1999), with boys appearing to find disclosure more difficult (Friedrich, 1995). Additional factors clearly mediate the impact of sexual trauma (Skuse, 1998) and whilst there is support for a view that a history of sexual victimisation is a significant risk factor for the persistence of sexually abusive behaviours (Burton, 2000; Johnson and Knight, 2000), this was not a finding replicated by Worling and Curwen (2000). The need to integrate treatment for sexual abuse into the overall intervention process where a young abuser has experienced sexual trauma is increasingly seen as essential (Bentovim, 2000) and the model of Abuse Focussed Therapy (Finkelhor and Berliner, 1995) provides a multi-dimensional treatment approach.

Non-sexual behavioural problems

Whilst a number of surveys of sexually abusive young people have suggested that their sexual behaviour is part of a broader pattern of delinquent or challenging behaviour (Dolan et al., 1996; Ryan, 1996) this appears likely to depend upon the nature of the sample, with two British samples finding that the majority of young abusers had no previous history of non-sexual offending (Beckett, 1999; Vizard, 2000). This may be indicative in particular of the differences between young people who victimise peers and those who abuse children, with O'Brien (2000) suggesting that the group he terms 'pervasive anti-social offenders', may require a different form of intervention from those young people who have profound social impairments and a predominant problem around predatory sexual behaviour.

Healthy sexuality

As Brown (2000) identifies, there is a danger of work with young people who sexually harm focussing on the negative aspects of sexuality. Young people whose personal and familial histories in which sexuality is associated with coercion, exploitation and manipulation of others require our support to envisage future sexual relationships as potentially mutual, caring and a positive part of life experience (Perry and Ohm, 1998).

Social functioning

Poor social competence has been a relatively consistent finding in the literature on young people who sexually harm (Vizard et al., 1995) and Barbaree et al. (1998) provided an integrated model to explore the interrelationship between early childhood experiences and the ongoing and interactive consequences on the development of inadequate models of interpersonal behaviour. They suggest the concept of a *syndrome of social disability* to illustrate the difficulty of the individual adolescent to adapt to evolving social and interpersonal demands.

Management of risk

The relapse prevention concept as originally applied to those who sexually offend by Pithers and colleagues has adapted and developed considerably over the last two decades (see Carich et al., 2001 for a review). Re-evaluation has critiqued the models deterministic view of the re-offence process, its complexity of language and concepts, and negative 'avoidance strategy' orientation (Marshall, 2001). Latterly, interest has focussed on a number of themes such as, whether offenders who do re-offend follow a number of alternate pathways (Ward et al., 1995); the application of 'approach goal' concepts to enhance motivation (Schofield and Mann, 1999) and the importance of teaching effective coping skills as the foundation of self-management and self-regulation (Marshall et al., 2000).

The relapse prevention model has been adapted for work with adolescents (e.g. Steen, 1993; Thomason, 2001), though many of the issues raised concerning adults would seem to have a greater weight when considering work with young people.

In work with adolescents the 'cycle of sexually abusive behaviour' (Ryan, 1989) has proved an influential approach and this has been developed with some sophistication to emphasise 'escape routes' by Way and Spieker (1997) and conceptualised more recently by Gail Ryan as a 'high-risk cycle', to emphasise the commonality with a variety of problematic and dysfunctional behaviours in youth (Ryan, 1999). Whilst these models are useful in analysing patterns of behaviour and considering specific interventions, our experience mirrors that of other practitioners (Rich, 1998) in that overly complex or elaborate models are difficult for

Figure 2: The progress of a young person through the service.

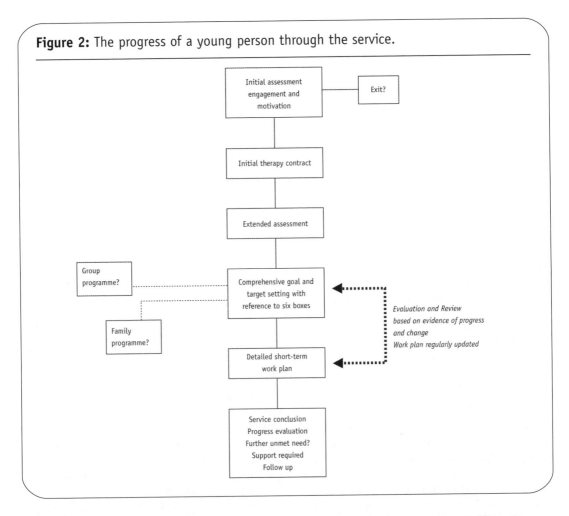

young people to retain and generalise into key learning points.

For many of our most concerning young people we are providing treatment in the context of totally managed and supervised lives. The process by which we can move to graduated reduction and greater independence in the community is complex and involves an effective inter-agency working and a sharing both of information and decision making.

The rest of this chapter will describe G-MAP's attempt to develop a service framework, and is informed by the currently available literature base and models of best practice.

The G-MAP service structure

The process through which young people progress through the service is depicted in Figure 2.

Initial assessments of young people

Whilst there are no currently available validated models to assess risk in adolescents who sexually harm, two recent models have been proposed (Prentky et al., 2000; Worling and Curwen, 2000). These assessment tools focus primarily on the issue of attempting to categorise the risk of *sexual* re-offence. The model of assessment recently developed by Print and colleagues (Print et al., 2001) provides a broader, though primarily evidenced based, approach by outlining a continuum both of strengths and concerns. The model draws both upon outcome and recidivism research concerning adolescents who sexually offend and known factors concerning the persistence of problematic and offending behaviours in young people, combining these with existing national assessment frameworks for young offenders, (ASSET, Home Office, 2000) and children in need (DoH, 2000). This initial assessment aims to identify the level of service required by a young person ranging from advice and guidance to family/carers to specialised residential placements. At this point in the process we may be forming a preliminary hypothesis as to the factors influencing the emergence of sexually problematic behaviours.

Engagement and motivation

Perhaps the most significant shift in thinking in work with both adult and adolescent sexual abusers has been the recognition that motivation is an interactive and variable construct and that certain approaches may be more successful than others in engaging the individual in a process of change (Miller and Rollnick, 1991). We recognise that there are a number of influences on motivation, primarily these are: the attitudes of parents and carers; the presence/absence of a mandate and the style and approach taken by the therapeutic practitioners. The approach to engaging young people employed within G-MAP is most significantly influenced by the work of Alan Jenkins (1998). Jenkins' draws upon narrative therapy (White and Epstom, 1990) to explore the social construction that has developed around the young person and their family, developing an alternative to the problem or deficit saturated narrative previously dominant. With engagement as the overriding goal the practitioners' tasks in the initial phase of the therapeutic process is to:

- Establish a sense of fairness and interest
- Explore the young persons views, experiences and relationships
- Identify injustices and individual strengths
- Identify positive personal qualities
- Enhance motivation to address problems

The young persons positive personal qualities are seen as providing the basis of an alternative construction to that of the young person as problematic and abusive. These include:

- strengths gained in coping with adversity
- the wish to protect others
- a sense of justice or injustice
- a willingness to face up to problems
- the abilities to protect himself
- concern for others

It is our experience that by approaching the early stages of the work with young people

from this perspective rather than a focus on their abusive or offending behaviour we increase the likelihood of successful engagement.

Therapeutic Contracting

Levy and Orlans (1998) suggest three elements around which a therapeutic contract may be organised. We have found it helpful to apply this model to generate a clear but positive focus for our work with young people.

1. Define the problem

e.g. Why we are working together:

Michael has a problem with his sexual behaviour. This has meant that Michael has sexually touched younger children including his cousin Andrew. Michael was arrested and told the court he did sexually touch Andrew on a number of occasions. The court placed Michael on a two-year Supervision Order during which time he has agreed to work with G-MAP.

2. Reframe problems as goals

e.g. What we want to achieve. We have agreed the following list as the main areas of work for us:

- *Michael's life and what he has experienced growing up.*
- *What Michael knows about sexual development and sexual behaviour.*
- *How we decide whether sexual behaviour is OK or not OK.*
- *What way was Michael's sexual behaviour not OK.*
- *Understanding why Michael sexually abused.*
- *Michael gaining more control over his sexual behaviour.*

3. Identify concrete targets

e.g. Work over the next six weeks:

- *Meet weekly at G-MAP*
- *Michael to complete questionnaires*
- *Michael to complete homework on 'our bodies' and puberty*
- *G-MAP staff to visit mum*
- *Begin work on timeline*

As the work progresses therapeutic goals are framed within the standard format of an ongoing work plan (see overleaf). We ask young people to actively contribute to the recording and goal process by completing a brief

Figure 3: The G-MAP Six Box Model

Abuse specific	Family	Influences on participation
Social functioning	Sexuality	Non-sexual behavioural problems

session evaluation sheet identifying the themes of the session; considering how difficult the session may have been and noting any decisions as to work in the next session.

Extended assessments

An extended assessment is undertaken over a period of 12–16 weeks and aims to provide a detailed understanding of the young persons familial and developmental history; social functioning; psycho-sexual history and current presentation; general behaviour; issues of communication and motivation; current networks; family support and placement issues. A key organising feature is a timeline undertaken with the young person that locates significant life experiences and explores recurring themes (loss; unfairness) and aims to begin the preliminary process of drawing connections between life experiences, unhelpful models, and abusive behaviour. Throughout the emphasis remains on promoting engagement and motivation. When we have reached a point at which, we consider that we have a detailed understanding of the young persons needs we draw upon our detailed framework for therapeutic goals to produce an individualised work plan.

The Six-Box Model

The six themes contained in the model assist in framing our holistic approach to the individual young person (see Figure 3). The model is then sub-divided into a series of specific themes for the work (see Figure 4 overleaf) with concrete and measurable targets for the work to be undertaken. The framework outlined depicts the goals and targets specific to the direct therapeutic work but as described below overall evaluation is based additionally on measurable behavioural change and

competencies across the young persons life and differing contexts.

Detailed work-plans

Work-plans provide the basis upon which sessions with the young person are structured (see Figure 5 pages 15–19) and subsequently evaluated. They assist the young person to experience the process as planned and predictable, and ideally are formed with active involvement by the young person and significant others.

Family work

Despite the frequent references to the critical importance of family work in the literature on young sexual abusers we have limited examples of practice models, with Jerry Thomas providing a notable exception (Thomas, 1991; Thomas and Wilson Viar, 2001). We recognise that parents are a critical influence on young peoples participation, have important information and may have management responsibilities for some or most of the young person's supervisory needs. The consequences of not engaging families are numerous and include:

- families being left isolated
- resentment or resistance towards professionals
- lack of family involvement in planning
- minimisation or denial of the problem
- compounding of crisis: rejection
- lack of protection of victims
- constricted assessment
- compromised care plans
- restricted services
- limited therapeutic gains
- increasing risk of drop: leading to increased risk of recidivism

Figure 4: Michael's workplan

Name: Michael **Date workplan completed: xx2001** **Date review due: xxx2001**

G-Map workers: xxxxxxxxxxx

Area we want to work on	Things we might discuss	What we want to achieve
Michael to better understand his feelings in himself and those of others.	How has Michael seen other people show their feelings as he has been growing up? What has been helpful and what unhelpful? How has Michael felt about different things in his life?	Michael practising communicating his feelings in a more helpful way. Michael practising recognising others feelings. Michael practising responding in an appropriate manner.
Michael expressing his feelings about things now and in his past.	How did he show his feelings? How does Michael show feelings now?	
Making sense of Michael's abusive sexual behaviour.	Using the four steps and lifeline. Looking at other peoples stories. Does this explain why it happened? If not, what else do we need to do.	Making sense of the abuse starting and continuing. What was true about Michael at the time. How things have changed.
Michael taking responsibility for his harmful sexual behaviour.	How do we know if a person genuinely takes responsibility: is it words and actions? What might Andrew see as sufficient? How might it involve Michael's parents? Does it involve honesty?	Being clear about what we mean by 'taking responsibility'. Michael taking responsibility for producing an honest account of his behaviour. How can this be shared? What does it mean about being different in the future?
Being sexual: interests, thoughts, feelings and behaviour.	What is true about Michael's sexual feelings now? How does Michael see this part of his life in the future? What rules are important? What are the difficult parts?	A way for Michael to communicate about sexual interests and feelings. Looking at future relationships. What is important in personal and intimate relationships? How can Michael work on the difficult bits?

We have found considerable benefit in establishing a family service as a stand-alone programme with dedicated staff. The G-MAP Family Programme provides a framework to explore parents own histories, explore their understanding of their child's behaviour and identifying strengths upon which a working relationship can be based (Morrison and Wilkinson, 2001). As with our contact with the young person the emphasis is on engagement and a key message to parents is that they are not to blame for the child's abusive behaviour. We see that parents bring common themes; such as their expectation of criticism, feelings of guilt and shame, the need for reassurance and search for explanation as to why their child has abused. Key assessment areas are:

Figure 5: Therapeutic goals.

Programme Block A Abuse behaviour specific	Therapeutic goals
Behaviour analysis	1. The young person can provide an active account of their thoughts, feelings and behaviours regarding their abusive conduct.
Pathway into abuse	1. The young person can understand the four-step/pathway model. 2. The young person can apply the four-step/pathway model to his own behaviour.
Accountability and responsibility	1. The young person is able to identify the factors that make them accountable for their behaviours. 2. The young person is able to take full responsibility for his abusive behaviour.
Sexual interests and responsiveness	1. The young person is able to explore his sexual thoughts and interests with workers. 2. Young person can identify problematic thoughts and feelings. 3. Young person can identify appropriate non-abusive sexual expression. 4. Young person can identify appropriate coping strategies.
Consequences for the young person if they continue sexually abusive behaviours	1. The young person is able to identify negative consequences of further abusive behaviours that are meaningful to him and appear to have a deterrent impact.
Understanding of impact of sexual abuse on victims	1. The young person is able to identify the impact of sexual abuse on victims. 2. He is able to apply this understanding to his victims. 3. His understanding includes a meaningful emotional component.
Management of risk	1. The young person is motivated to avoid future abusive behaviour. 2. Is communicative and apparently open as to issues of risk. 3. The young person can identify risky thoughts, feelings, mood states, behaviours and situations. 4. He has realistic strategies to deal with risk, including use of others.

Programme Block B Family and Personal History	Therapeutic Goals
Developing timeline work and identifying key learning experiences	1. The young person can identify significant people and events in his life, including positive and negative experiences. 2. The young person's account is congruent with known facts? 3. He is able to comment on the emotional significance of specific life experiences?
Family behaviour models and coping styles	1. The young person understands the messages and models he has learnt from his family regarding how to deal with stress, problems and conflict. 2. He is able to critically appraise these and identify unhelpful models and messages. 3. He is able to identify alternatives to these unhelpful models/messages.

Figure 5: *Continued.*

Attachment experiences: losses, moves and rejections	1. The young person is able to identify key relationships throughout his life.
	2. The young person is able to recognise the influence of these relationships in the way he thinks, feels and behaves?
	3. The young person can identify positive qualities in current relationships with significant others.
Exposure to trauma	1. The young person can identify and discuss significant traumatic events.
	2. He can identify how these events have affected his thoughts, feelings and behaviours.
	3. The young person can appropriately attribute responsibility for these events.
	4. The young person is able to recognise and employ appropriate coping strategies to deal with continuing consequences e.g. intrusive memories, anxiety or avoidance, sexual functioning problems.

Programme Block C **Sexuality**	**Therapeutic Goals**
Sex education	1. The young person has an appropriate developmental level of understanding of sexual behaviours, terminology, legal or illegal sexual behaviours, the meaning of consent and safe sex.
Sexual relationships and sexual scripts	1. The young person can identify his expectations and needs in sexual relationships with others.
	2. The young person has a reasonable understanding of how to negotiate safe and respectful sexual relationships with others.
	3. He is able to appropriately interpret the cues and responses of others.
	4. He is ready to accept a negative as well as a positive response.
Masculinity	1. The young person has a healthy view of masculinity and can recognise superficial gender roles or stereotypes.
	2. The young person is able to demonstrate positive attitudes to females, children and vulnerable others.
Orientation	1. The young person has a positive and confident view of his sexual identity.
	2. He can recognise oppressive and discriminatory views.
	3. He is able to accept that others may have different sexual orientations.
Own victimisation	1. Young person is able to recognise any sexual abuse he has experienced.
	2. Young person is able to communicate the nature and impact of negative sexual experiences.
	3. He is able to appropriately attribute responsibility for the abuse.
	4. He has developed healthy coping strategies to deal with the impact of the abuse.

Figure 5: *Continued.*

Programme Block D Influences on participation	Therapeutic Goals
Contracting and goal setting	1. The young person has actively participated in the construction of a therapeutic contract and work plan. 2. He is able to acknowledge that his sexual behaviour problems are a central focus for the work plan. 3. The young person can recognise and accept the validity of the components that contribute to his work plan. 4. The young person is motivated to make progress in his work plan.
Support and external influences	1. The young person has at least one adult (preferably a family member or carer) who is willing and able to actively support the young person through the therapeutic work. 2. He can identify the reasons why he is motivated to engage in the work. 3. He is able to agree on the method and nature of information sharing with his supporters. 4. He actively uses the support offered by others. 5. He has identified realistic and achievable life goals for himself outside of the therapeutic programme.
Methods	1. A range of work methods have been tried with the young person and the most positive and productive modalities have been identified. 2. He is able to communicate consistently and effectively via the methods employed. 3. The methods used offer the young person a reasonable degree of variety and appear to maintain a positive level of involvement. 4. The methods used take account of the young person's developmental and learning needs.
Pace and timetabling	1. The young person is generally able to work at a consistent pace. 2. The work plan is reasonably adhered to. 3. Progress is measurable, demonstrable and recognised over reasonable timescales.
Health issues	1. The young person is physically and psychologically able to cope with the therapeutic work.
Programme Block E **Social functioning**	**Therapeutic Goals**
Core social skills	1. The young person has basic competence in conversational and listening skills, such as he is not socially disadvantaged, relative to age and developmental status. 2. He can adhere to commonly expected social conventions to the degree that he is not restricted in social activities. 3. He is able to appropriately communicate his wishes and feelings.

Figure 5: *Continued.*

Relationship skills	1. The young person is able to understand what constitutes healthy relationships. 2. He recognises the value of healthy relationships with others. 3. He can evaluate his strengths and deficits in forming relationships and is willing to work to improve necessary skills. 4. The young person has the ability to form and sustain healthy relationships with peers and others.
Empathic concern	1. The young person can understand emotion and affect in self and others. 2. He is able to correctly evaluate other's cues and feelings in a social setting. 3. He is able to consistently appreciate and appropriately display responses.
Assertiveness	1. Young person understands the difference between aggressive, assertive and passive behaviours. 2. He appreciates the potential benefits of assertiveness. 3. He is able to demonstrate negotiation skills and expression of feelings. 4. He is able to identify and employ assertive strategies when necessary.
Self esteem	1. The young person is able to identify positive personal qualities. 2. He is able to recognise skills and talents and take pride in his achievements. 3. He is able to acknowledge and accept praise from others.
Problem solving	1. The young person can employ task based rather than emotion focused or avoidance strategies. 2. In difficult situations the young person is able to consider options and make rational decisions. 3. He has the ability to reflect on and learn from experience. 4. He is willing and able to invite advice or opinions from others.
Self-care and independence	1. The young person is able to identify the skills and resources he will require to progress towards greater independence. 2. Views this as a positive and normative life goal. 3. Has a realistic appreciation of the challenges and difficulties involved in this transition.
Education and vocational goals	1. That the young person has positive and realistic life goals concerning education and employment.
Social and leisure activities and pursuits	1. The young person can identify appropriate social and leisure activities and has motivation to attempt these. 2. The young person can share anxieties involved in new situations and experiences.

Figure 5: *Continued.*

Programme Block F Non-sexual behavioural problems	Therapeutic Goals
Aggression	1. The young person can recognise the emotional impact and learnt messages he has received concerning aggression and expression of anger. 2. The young person can differentiate anger and aggression and recognise the negative consequences of aggression. 3. He can control and manage his aggressive behaviours via constructive strategies.
Oppositional or challenging behaviours	1. That the young person is prepared to explore current or historical examples of oppositional and challenging behaviours. 2. He is able to consider what might be the relationship between learnt behaviour; external circumstances; mood states; physical sensations and attributions (distorted perceptions/thinking). 3. He is able to consider what might be the function of these behaviours (avoidance, control, displacement, communication). 4. He is able to consider the costs or negative consequences for himself and others of such behaviours. 5. He is able to consider adopting alternative strategies to achieve the same function.
Emotional self-regulation	1. Young person is able to recognise the links between feelings, thoughts and behaviours. 2. He can recognise the patterns he has learnt from his life experiences. 3. That the young person is able to manage difficult emotions and express feelings in an appropriate way.
High risk and impulsive behaviours	1. That the young person can identify the relationship between circumstances; mood states; behaviours and decisions that have been involved in previous negative and high-risk behaviours. 2. He can identify motivations (heightened arousal; social acceptance etc.) and distorted or permissive thinking involved in high-risk or impulsive behaviours. 3. He can identify previous and future consequences. 4. He can identify potential connections with heightened risk of sexually abusive behaviours. 5. He can identify realistic coping strategies to manage circumstances/mood states associated with high-risk and impulsive behaviours.

- response to the discovery of abusive behaviour
- family history
- boundaries
- stresses and needs
- family organisation and dynamics
- attachment styles and parents own attachment experiences
- emotional responsiveness and deprivation
- cultural values and needs
- community embeddedness and social support
- leisure pursuits

- parental motivation and capacity to address issues

There are degrees of parental involvement in the therapeutic process which range from that of simply sharing information; the family supporting the young person whilst having limited direct involvement themselves; to the family being full participants in the therapeutic process. Even when practical or emotional constraints inhibit families participation we aim to at least maintain contact on the basis of information sharing and continue to promote more extensive links.

Group Work Programmes

Whilst groups for adults who sexually offend have become the primary treatment modality (Allam and Browne, 1998) their development for adolescents has been much more limited and inconsistent (HM Inspectorate of Probation, 1998). Whilst the concept of cognitive-behavioural groups may have been somewhat uncritically accepted (Lab et al., 1993), as a therapeutic medium for troubled children and young people, several advantages have been cited for groupwork techniques (Carrell, 1993; Duboust and Knight, 1995; Dwivedi, 1997; Malekoff, 1995). A summary of their findings includes:

- For young people who have difficulties in expressing emotions and experiences the group offers a potential to learn from others whilst developing competency in self-disclosure.
- Groups can reduce a sense of isolation, particularly for young people whose problem has a degree of social stigma.
- The group environment can become a safe psychological space in which to explore difficult or anxiety provoking issues.
- Important interpersonal and social skills can be rehearsed in a group setting.
- Groups allow a range of experiential activities which actively engage children and young people that are not practical within an adult-child interaction.
- Peer education and reinforcement is seen as particularly effective for adolescents.

G-MAP has a consistent history of groupwork with young people who sexually abuse (Print and O'Callaghan, 1999) and currently operate two groupwork programmes, one for young men of mainstream educational abilities and one

for young men with a degree of learning difficulties or intellectual impairment.

Both groups operate a modular structure of eight programme blocks as described below:

1. communication
2. relationships with others
3. sexual development
4. how sexual behaviour problems start
5. the consequences of sexual abuse
6. managing risk
7. being assertive and managing anger
8. problem solving

The delivery of the modules is designed to meet the specific learning needs of the young men participating in either group, but both are structured to identify learning points and behavioural targets that are enacted and reviewed outside of the group setting. Neither programme is considered sufficient as a stand-alone service and all participants will have concurrent individual and family work.

Evaluation of progress

In evaluating the extent to which a young person has made progress over the course of treatment, emphasis is on multiple sources of information, particularly from carers, and our ability to identify demonstrable new skills and behaviours that are both transferable and generalised across settings. The detailed therapeutic goals identified in Figure 5 are complimented by a broader evaluation framework that emphasises behavioural change. Particularly important themes are:

- a coherent sense of personal history
- concrete and realistic personal goals
- improved social competence
- enhanced problem solving skills
- better self-regulation, particularly in terms of managing difficult emotional states
- healthy attitudes to sexuality

Whilst Worling and Curwen's (2000) recent research provides evidence in support of a significant treatment effect for programmes that emphasise individual strengths and promote family and systemic change, we have as yet a limited evidence base upon which to draw when developing services. Brown and Kolko (1998) outline a series of recommendations concerning more effective clinical evaluation of service to young sexual abusers which include the more precise assessment procedures and greater specificity both of the treatment components delivered and the changes measured.

References

Allam, J. A. and Browne, K. D. (1998) Evaluating Community-based Treatment Programmes for Men who Sexually Abuse Children. *Child Abuse Review.* 7: 13–29.

Barbaree H. E., Marshall, W. E., and McCormick, J. (1998) The Development of Deviant Sexual Behaviour Among Adolescents and its Implications for Prevention and Treatment. *The Irish Journal of Psychology.* 19: 1–31.

Barber, J. G. (1992) Relapse Prevention and the Need for Brief Social Interventions. *Journal of Substance Abuse Treatment.* 9: 157–68.

Beckett, R. (1999) *The Latest Research on Young Abusers.* Presentation to an Infolog Conference, *Young abusers: the hidden crime of children who sexually abuse children.* Royal Over-Seas House, Park Place, London, 5th Oct.

Beech, A., Fisher, D. and Beckett, R. (1998) *STEP3: An Evaluation of the Prison Sex Offender Treatment Programme.* London: Home Office.

Bentovim, A. (1995) *Trauma Organised Systems: Physical and Sexual Abuse in Families.* London and New York: Karnac.

Bentovim, A. (2000) Working with the victimisation experiences of young people who have sexually offended. Paper presented at *Working with Adolescent Sex Offenders.* Pavilion Conference, London, Nov.

Blanchard, G. T. (1995) *The Difficult Connection: The Therapeutic Relationship in Sex Offender Treatment.* VT: Safer Society Press.

Blechman, E. A. and Dryan, K. D. (2000) Pro-social Family Therapy: A Manual for Preventive Intervention for Juvenile Offenders. *Aggression and Violent Behaviour.* 5(4): 343–78.

Borduin, C. M., Hengeller, S. W., Blaske, D. M. and Stein, R. J. (1990) Multisystemic Treatment of Adolescent Sex Offenders. *International Journal of Offender Therapy and Comparative Criminology.* 34(2): 105–13.

Bourke, M. L. and Donohue, B. (1996) 'Assessment and treatment of juvenile sex offenders: an empirical review', *Journal of Child Sexual Abuse,* 5 (1): 47–70.

Brown, E. J. and Kolko, D. J. (1998) Treatment Efficacy and Program Evaluation With Juvenile Sexual Abusers: A Critique With Directions for Service Delivery and Research. *Child Maltreatment.* 3(4): 362–73.

Brown, S. M. (2000) Healthy Sexuality and the Treatment of Sexually Abusive Youth. *Siecus Report.* 29(1) Oct/Nov.

Burton, D. L. (2000) Were Adolescent Sexual Offenders Children With Sexual Behaviour Problems? *Sexual Abuse: A Journal of Research and Treatment.* 12(1): 37–48.

Carich, M. S., Gray, A., Rombouts, S., Stone, M. and Pithers, M. (2001) Relapse Prevention and The Sexual Assault Cycle. in Carich, M. S.. and Mussack, S. (Eds.) *Handbook of Sexual Abuser Assessment and Treatment.* Vermont: Safer Society Press, 77–103.

Carrell, S. (1993) *Group Exercises for Adolescents: A Manual for Therapists.* London: Sage.

Chapman, T. and Hough, M. (1998) *Evidence Based Practice: A Guide to Effective Practice.* HM Inspectorate of Probation. London: Home Office.

Crittenden, P. M. (1995) Attachment and Psychopathology. in Goldberg, S. Muir, R. and Kerr, J. (Eds.) *Attachment Theory: Social, Developmental, and Clinical Perspectives.* Hillsdale, NJ: Analytic Press.

Daniel, B., Wassell, S. and Gilligan, R. (1999) It's Just Common Sense isn't it? Exploring Ways of Putting the Theory of Resilience into Action. *Adoption and Fostering.* 23(2): 6–15.

DoH (2000) *Framework for the Assessment of Children in Need and their Families.* London: TSO.

Dolan, M., Holloway, J., Bailey, S. and Kroll, L. (1996) The Psychosocial Characteristics of Juvenile Sexual Offenders Referred to an Adolescent Forensic Service in the UK. *Medicine, Science and the Law.* 36: 343–52.

Duboust, S. and Knight, P. (1995) *Group Activities for Personal Development.* Bicester: Winslow Press.

Dwivedi, K. N. (1997) Groupwork with Violent Children and Adolescents. in Varma, V. (Ed.) *Violence in Children and Adolescents.* London: Jessica Kingsley.

Farmer, E. and Pollock, S. (1998) *Sexually Abused and Abusing Children in Substitute Care.* Chichester: John Wiley and Sons.

Figueredo, J. and Hunter, J. A. (1999) Factors Associated with Treatment Compliance in a Population of Juvenile Sexual Offenders. *Sexual Abuse: A Journal of Research and Treatment.* 11(1) 49–67.

Finkelhor, D., and Berliner, L. (1995) Research on the Treatment of Sexually Abused

Children: A Review and Recommendations. *Journal of the American Academy of Child and Adolescent Psychiatry*. 34: 1408–23.

Friedrich, W. (1995) *Psychotherapy with Sexually Abused Boys*. Thousand Oaks. CA: Sage.

Gilgun, J. F. (1999) CASPARS: Clinical Assessment Instruments That Measure Strengths and Risks in Children and Families. in Calder, M. C. (Ed.) *Working with Young People Who Sexually Abuse: New Pieces of the Jigsaw Puzzle*. Lyme Regis, Dorset: Russell House Publishing, 49–58.

Happé, F. and Frith, U. (1996) Theory of Mind and Social Impairment in Children With Conduct Disorder. *British Journal of Developmental Psychology*. 15, 385–98.

Henggeler S. W., Schoenwald S. K., Borduin, C. M., Rowland, M. D., and Cunningham P. B. (1998) *Multisystemic Treatment of Antisocial Behaviour in Children and Adolescents*. NY: Guilford Press.

HM Inspectorate of Probation (1998) *Exercising Constant Vigilance: The Role of the Probation Service in Protecting the Public from Sex Offenders. Report of a Thematic Inspection*. London: Home Office.

Hollin, C. (1999) Treatment Programs for Offenders: Meta-analysis, 'What Works,' and Beyond. *International Journal of Law and Psychiatry*. 22(3–4) 361–72.

Home Office (2000) *The ASSET Form*. London: Youth Justice Board.

Hudson, S. M., Ward, T. and Laws, D. R. (2000) Whither Relapse Prevention? in Laws, D. R., Hudson, S. M. and Ward, T. (Eds.) *Remaking Relapse Prevention With Sex Offenders: A Sourcebook*. Thousand Oaks, CA: Sage.

Hunter, J. A. and Figueredo, J. (1999) Factors Associated With Treatment Compliance in a Population of Juvenile Sexual Offenders. *Sexual Abuse: A Journal of Research and Treatment*. 11(1): 49–67.

Hunter, J. A., Hazelwood, R. R., and Slesinger, D. (2000) Juvenile-perpetrated Sex Crimes: Patterns of Offending and Predictors of Violence. *Journal of Family Violence*. 15(1): 81–93.

Jenkins, A. (1998) Invitations to Responsibility: Engaging Adolescents and Young Men Who Have Sexually Abused. in Marshall, W., Fernandez, Y., Hudson, S. and Ward, T. (Eds.) *Sourcebook of Treatment Programmes for Sexual Offenders*. NY: Plenum.

Johnson, G. M., and Knight, A. K. (2000) Developmental Antecedents of Sexual

Coercion in Juvenile Sexual Offenders. *Sexual Abuse: A Journal of Research and Treatment*. 12(3): 165–78.

Jones, D. (2000) Cognitive, Behavioural and Systemic Approaches to Coping With Emotional and Behavioural Difficulties in Children. in Cooper, P. (Ed.) *Understanding and Supporting Children with Emotional and Behavioural Difficulties*. London: Jessica Kingsley Publishers.

Keenan, T. and Ward, T. (2000) A Theory of Mind Perspective on Cognitive, Affective, and Intimacy Deficits in Child Sexual Offenders. *Sexual Abuse: A Journal of Research and Treatment*. 12: 49–60.

Kumpfer, K. L., and Alvardo. D. R. (1998) Effective family strengthening interventions. *Juvenile Justice Bulletin*, U.S. Department of Justice, Office of Juvenile Justice and Delinquency Prevention (NCJ 171121) November.

Lab, S. P., Shields, G. and Schondel, C. (1993) Research Note: An Evaluation of Juvenile Sexual Offender Treatment. *Crime and Delinquency*. 39(4): 543–53.

Laws, D. R., Hudson, S. M., and Ward, T. (2000) The Original Model or Relapse Prevention With Sex Offenders: Promise Unfulfilled. in Laws; D. R., Hudson, S. M. and Ward, T. (Eds.) *Remaking Relapse Prevention With Sex Offenders: A Sourcebook*. Thousand Oaks, CA: Sage.

Levy, T. M. and Orlans, M. (1998) *Attachment, Trauma, and Healing: Understanding and Treating Attachment Disorder in Children and Families*. Washington DC: CWLA Press.

Lindsay, W. R., Neilson, C. Q., Morrison, F. and Smith, A. H. (1998) The Treatment of Six Men With a Learning Disability Convicted of Sex Offences Against Children. *British Journal of Clinical Psychology*. 37, 83–98.

Lipsey, M. and Wilson D. B. (1998) Effective intervention for serious juvenile offenders. in Loeber, R. L. and Farringdon, D. P. (Eds.). *Serious and violent juvenile offenders: risk factors and successful interventions*. Thousand Oaks, CA: Sage, 313–45.

Loeber, R. and Farrington, D. P. (Eds.) (1998) *Serious and Violent Juvenile Offenders: Risk Factors and Successful Interventions*. Thousand Oaks. CA: Sage.

Malekoff, A. (1997) *Group Work with Adolescents: Principles and Practice*. New York, Guilford Press.

Mann, R. and Thornton, D. (1998) The Evolution of a Multi-site Offender Treatment Program.

in Marshall, W., Fernandez, Y., Hudson, S. and Ward, T. (Eds.) *Sourcebook of Treatment Programs for Sexual Offenders.* NY: Plenum.

Manocha, K. F. and Mezey, G. (1998) British Adolescents Who Sexually Abuse: A Descriptive Study. *The Journal of Forensic Psychiatry.* 9(3): 588–608.

Marshall, W. L. (1993) The Role of Attachment, Intimacy, and Loneliness in the Aetiology and Maintenance of Sexual Offending. *Sexual and Marital Therapy.* 8: 109–21.

Marshall, W. L. (2001) Enhancing Social and Relationship Skills. in Carich, M. S. and Mussack, S. (Eds.) *Handbook for Sexual Abuser Assessment and Treatment.* Brandon, VT: Safer Society Press, 149–62.

Marshall, W. L., Barbaree, H. E. and Fernandez, Y. M. (1995) Some Aspects of Social Competence in Sex Offenders. *Sexual Abuse: A Journal of Research and Treatment.* 7: 113–27.

Marshall, W. L., Serran, G. A. and Cortoni, F. A. (2000) Childhood Attachments, Sexual Abuse, and their Relationship to Adult Coping in Child Molesters. *Sexual Abuse: A Journal of Research and Treatment.* 12(1): 17–26.

Marshall, W. L., Anderson, D. and Fernandez, Y. (1999) *Cognitive Behavioural Treatment of Sexual Offenders.* Chichester: John Wiley and Sons.

Marshall, W. L. and Anderson, D. (2000) Do Relapse Prevention Components Enhance Treatment Effectiveness? in Laws, D. R., Hudson, S. M. and Ward, T. (Eds.) *Remaking Relapse Prevention with Sex Offenders: A Sourcebook.* Thousand Oaks, CA: Sage.

Masson, H. and Morrison, T. (1999) Young Sexual Abusers: Conceptual Frameworks, Issues and Imperatives. *Children and Society.* 13: 203–15.

McKeown, L. and McGarvey, J. (1999) A Psycho-educational Support Group for a Neglected Clinical Population: Parents/ Carers of Young People Who Sexually Abuse Children. in Calder, M. C. (Ed.) *Working with Young People Who Sexually Abuse: New Pieces of the Jigsaw Puzzle.* Lyme Regis, Dorset: Russell House Publishing, 185–206.

Miller, W. R. and Rollnick, S. (1991) *Motivational Interviewing: Preparing People to Change Addictive Behaviours.* NY: Guilford Press.

Monck, E. and New, M. (1996) *Report of a Study of Sexually Abused Children and Adolescents, and of Young Perpetrators of Sexual Abuse who were Treated in Voluntary Agency Community Facilities.* London: HMSO.

Morrison, T. and Wilkinson, L. (2001) *The G-MAP Family Service: A Manual of Assessment and Intervention.* Manchester, UK: G-MAP.

O'Brien, M. (2000) *A Typology of Adolescent Sexual Offenders.* Paper presented to Positive Outcomes Conference, Manchester Airport, 11–13th Jul.

O'Callaghan, D. (1998) Practice Issues in Working With Young Abusers Who Have Learning Disabilities. *Child Abuse Review.* 7: 435–48.

O'Callaghan, D. (1999) Young Abusers With Learning Disabilities: Towards Better Understanding and Positive Interventions. in Calder, M. C. (Ed.) *Working with Young People who Sexually Abuse: New Pieces of the Jigsaw Puzzle.* Lyme Regis, Dorset: Russell House Publishing, 225–49.

O'Callaghan, D. and Corran, M. (2001) The Inter-agency Management of Children and Young People Who Sexually Abuse. in Bailey, S. and Dolan, M. (Eds.) *Handbook of Adolescent Psychiatry.* London, Blackwell Scientific Press.

O'Reilly, G., Morrison, T. and Carr, A. (In press) A Group Based Module for Adolescents to Improve Motivation to Change Sexually Abusive Behaviour. in Marshall, W., Beckett, R., and O'Reilly, G. (Eds.) *Handbook of Clinical Intervention with Juvenile Sexual Abusers.* Chichester: John Wiley and Sons.

Perry, G. and Ohm, (1998) The Role Healthy Sexuality Plays in Modifying Abusive Behaviours of Adolescent Sex Offenders: Practical Considerations for Professionals. *Canadian Journal of Counselling.* 33(2): 157–69.

Prentky, R., Harris, B., Frizzell, and Righthand, S. (2000) An Actuarial Procedure for Assessing Risk With Juvenile Sex Offenders. *Sexual Abuse: A Journal of Research and Treatment.* 12(2) 71–93.

Print, B. and O'Callaghan, D. (1999) Working in groups with young men who have sexually abused others. in Erooga, M. and Masson, H. (Eds.) *Children and Young People who Sexually Abuse Others: Challenges and Responses.* London: Routledge. 124–45.

Print, B. and O'Callaghan, D. (in press) Essentials of an Effective Treatment Programme for Adolescents Who Sexually Abuse Others: Offence Specific Treatment Tasks. in Marshall, W., Beckett, R. and O'Reilly, G. (Eds.) *Handbook of Clinical Intervention with Juvenile Sexual Abusers.* Chichester: John Wiley and Sons.

Print, B., Morrison, T. and Henniker, J. (2001) An Inter-agency Assessment Framework for

Young People Who Sexually Abuse: Principles, Processes and Practicalities. in Calder, M. C. *Juveniles and Children Who Sexually Abuse: Frameworks for Assessment (2nd edn)* Lyme Regis, Dorset: Russell House Publishing. 271–81.

Rasmussen, L. A. (1999) Factors Related to Recidivism Among Juvenile Sexual Offenders. *Sexual Abuse: A Journal of Research and Treatment.* 11(1) 69–85.

Rasmussen, L. A. (1999) The Trauma Outcome Process: An Integrated Model for Guiding Clinical Practice With Children With Sexually Abusive Behaviour Problems. *Journal of Child Sexual Abuse.* 8(4): 3–33.

Rich, S. A. (1998) The Developmental Approach to the Treatment of Adolescent Sexual Offenders. *The Irish Journal of Psychology.* 19(1): 102–18.

Rutter, M. (1999) Resilience Concepts and Findings: Implications for Family Therapy. *Journal of Family Therapy.* 21: 119–44.

Rutter, M., Giller, H. and Hagel, A. (1998) *Antisocial Behaviour by Young People.* Cambridge: Cambridge University Press.

Ryan, G. and Associates (1999) *Web of Meaning: A Developmental-Contextual Approach in Sexual Abuse Treatment.* Brandon, VT: Safer Society Press.

Ryan, G., Miyoshi, T. J., Metzner, J. L., Krugman, R. D. and Fryer, G. E. (1996) Trends in a National Sample of Sexually Abusive Youths. *Journal of the American Academy of Child and Adolescent Psychiatry.* 33: 17–25.

Ryan, G. (1999) Treatment of Sexually Abusive Youth: The Evolving Consensus. *Journal of Interpersonal Violence.* 14: 422–36.

Ryan, G. D. (1989) Victim to Victimiser: Rethinking Victim Treatment. *Journal of Interpersonal Violence.* 4(3): 325–41.

Ryan, G. (1998) What is so Special About Specialised Treatment? *Journal of Interpersonal Violence.* 13(5): 647–52.

Schofield, C. and Mann, R. (1999) A Goal Oriented Approach to Relapse in Sexual Offenders. Paper presented at *Conference of National Organization for the Treatment of Abusers,* University of York, Oct.

Sheridan, A. and McGrath, K. (1999) Adolescent Sex Offenders: Characteristics and Treatment Effectiveness in The Republic Of Ireland. in Calder, M. C. (Ed.) *Working With Young People Who Sexually Abuse: New Pieces of the Jigsaw Puzzle.* Lyme Regis, Dorset: Russell House Publishing, 295–309.

Sheridan, A., McKeown, K., Cherry, J., Donohhoe, E., McGrath, K., O'Reilly, K., Phelan, S. and Tallon, M. (1998) Perspectives on Treatment Outcome in Adolescent Sexual Offending: A Study of a Community-based Treatment Programme. *The Irish Journal of Psychology.* 19(1): 168–80.

Skuse, D., Bentovim, A., Hodges, J., Stevenson, J., Andreou, C., Lanyado, M., New, M., Williams, B. and McMillan, D. (1998) Risk Factors for Development of Sexually Abusive Behaviour in Sexually Victimised Adolescent Boys: Cross Sectional Study. *British Medical Journal.* 317: 175–9.

Smallbone, S. W. and Dadds, M. R. (1998) Childhood Attachment and Adult Attachment in Incarcerated Male Adult Sex Offenders. *Journal of Interpersonal Violence.* 13: 555–73.

Smallbone, S. W. and Dadds, M. R. (2000) Attachment and Coercive Sexual Behaviour. *Sexual Abuse: A Journal of Research and Treatment.* 12(1): 3–15.

Steen, C. (1993) *The Relapse Prevention Workbook for Youth in Treatment.* VT: Safer Society Press.

Swenson, C., Henggeler., Schoenwald, S., Kaufman, K. and Randall, J. (1998) Changing the Social Ecologies of Adolescent Sexual Offenders: Implications of the Success of Multi-systemic Therapy in Treating Serious Antisocial Behaviour in Adolescents. *Child Maltreatment.* 3(4): 330–8.

Thomas, J. (1991) The Adolescent Sex Offender's Family in Treatment. in Ryan, G. and Lane, S. (Eds.) *Juvenile Sex Offending; Causes, Consequences and Correction.* Lexington, Mass; Lexington Books.

Thomas, J. and Wilson Viar III, C. (2001) Family Treatment of Adult Sexual Abusers. in Carich, M. and Mussack, S. (Eds.) *Handbook of Sexual Abuser Assessment and Treatment.* Vermont. Safer Society Press, 163–92.

Thomason, P. (2000) *Focussed Work with Adolescents who Sexually Abuse.* Brighton: Pavilion Publishing.

Vizard, E. (2000) Characteristics of a British Sample of Sexually Abusive Children. *Keynote presentation to the BASPCAN National Congress,* University of York, Sep.

Vizard, E., Monck, E. and Misch, P. (1995) Child and Adolescent Sex Abuse Perpetrators: A Review of the Research Literature. *Journal of Child Psychol. Psychiat.* 36(5): 731–56.

Walsh, F. (1996) The Concept of Family Resilience: Crisis and Challenge. *Family Process.* 35: 261–81.

Ward, T., Londen, K., Hudson, S. M. and Marshall, W. L. (1995) A Descriptive Model of the Offence Claim for Child Models. *Journal of Interpersonal Violence.* 10: 452–72.

Ward, T., Hudson, S. M. and McCormack, J. (1997) Attachment Style, Intimacy Deficits, and Sexual Offending. in Swartz, B. K. and Cellini, H. R. (Eds.) *The Sex Offender; New Insights, Treatment Innovations, and Legal Developments.* Kingston, NJ: Civic Research Institute.

Ward, T., Keenan, T. and Hudson, S. M. (2000) Understanding Cognitive Affective, and Intimacy Deficits in Sexual Offenders: A Developmental Perspective. *Aggression and Violent Behaviour.* 5(1): 41–62.

Way, I. F. and Spieker, (1997) *The Cycle of Offence: A Framework for Treating Adolescent Sexual Offenders.* Notre Dame. IN: Jalice.

White, M. and Epstom, D. (1990) *Narrative Means to Therapeutic Ends.* London/New York: WW Norton.

Will, D., Douglas, A. and Wood, C. (1994) The Evolution of a Group Therapy Programme for Adolescent Perpetrators of Sexual Abusive Behaviour. *The Journal Of Sexual Aggression.* 1(2): 69–82.

Worling, J. R. and Curwen, T. (2001) The ERASOR. in Calder, M. C. *Juveniles and Children Who Sexually Abuse: Frameworks for Assessment (2nd Edn)* Lyme Regis, Dorset: Russell House Publishing.

Worling, J. (1995) Sexual Abuse Histories of Adolescent Male Sex Offenders: Differences on the Basis of the Age and Gender of their Victims. *Journal of Abnormal Psychology.* 104: 610–3.

Worling, J. R., and Curwen, T. (2000) Adolescent Sexual Offenders Recidivism: Success of Specialized Treatment and Implications for Risk Prediction. *Child Abuse and Neglect.* 24(7): 965–82.

Yager, J., Knight, L., Arnold, L. and Kempe, R. (1999) The Discovery Process. in Ryan, G. and Associates *Web of Meaning: A Developmental-contextual Approach in Sexual Abuse Treatment.* Brandon, VT: Safer Society Press.

Chapter 2: Childhood Maltreatment Histories of Male Adolescents with Sexual Offending Behaviours: A Review of the Literature

Ineke Way

Many adolescents with sexual offending behaviours grew up in families where violence of some sort was perpetrated against family members. Theoreticians and researchers have long questioned the role of one form of violence, childhood maltreatment, in the aetiology of sexual offending behaviours in adolescents. One theory of sexual offending, victim-to-victimiser theory, suggests that unresolved childhood traumatic experiences, including childhood maltreatment, may lead to ineffective coping strategies, which may include sexually offending against others (Ballantyne, 1993; Rasmussen, Burton, and Cristopherson, 1992; Ryan, 1989; Ryan, Lane, Davis, and Isaac, 1987). Many questions remain about the relationship between prior victimisation histories and sexual assaultive behaviour, and whether there is another unidentified, yet more critical, factor that helps explain this phenomenon. Watkins and Bentovim (1992) suggest that while the victim-to-victimiser process clearly does not account for all adolescent sexual offending behaviour, the hypothesis should not be ignored because it offers a framework for intervention (e.g., with sexually abused children) and offers guidance for helping prevent subsequent sexual offending behaviour by adolescents.

This chapter is written on the premise that it is clinically important for us to understand the childhood histories of adolescents with sexual offending behaviours. We need to know more about the types and degree of traumatic experiences these adolescents have experienced, not to excuse their offending behaviour but to effectively plan intervention that resolves their pressing issues and helps prevent further offending that harms children. The purpose of the present literature review is to detail what we know about prior maltreatment in this population, and to examine the implications of this knowledge for practice and further research.

While a large number of studies have examined maltreatment histories of adolescents with sexual offending behaviours, these studies differ in the way they define key concepts. They also use differing research methodologies, which makes comparisons among studies difficult. This chapter reviews and critiques existing studies of prior maltreatment of sexually abusive adolescents, and summarises their findings. The chapter concludes with discussion of critical methodological issues in conducting this research, and implications for practice and research.

Criteria for inclusion

Extensive efforts were made to locate studies of adolescents with sexual offending behaviours, including published and unpublished investigations. A literature search was conducted using PsycInfo and Dissertation Abstracts databases, and examining the reference lists of all studies located. Studies were included in this review if they met the following criteria:

- The study reported data on prior childhood victimisation.
- The study sample included male adolescents with sexual offending behaviours.
- The study findings were reported in English.

Studies were excluded if the sample was a general population, e.g. retrospectively asking young adults in college about their adolescent and childhood experiences (e.g. Fromuth, Burkhart, and Jones, 1991; Fromuth and Conn, 1997). The literature search described above resulted in 37 studies. These included one study project report, 25 journal articles and 11 dissertations. These studies included findings from the United States and Canada.

Table organisation and study characteristics

Table 1 presents a comparison of the studies included in this review. These studies are listed

Table 1: Studies of childhood victimisation of adolescent sexual offenders

Study	Sample	Timing of data collection	Data collection method	Operationalisation of maltreatment	Extent of detail
Longo, 1982	adult court, adolescent sexual offenders (N=17)	point in time	self-report questionnaire	sexual abuse	gender of perpetrator, age at first sexual experience, age of perpetrator
Gomes-Schwartz, 1984	outpatient, child molesters (N=18)	intake	diagnostic evaluation interview; case record review	sexual abuse	yes/no
Becker, Kaplan et al., 1986	outpatient, incest offenders (N=22)	not stated	structured clinical interview	sexual contact between family members physical abuse non deviant sexual experience = 'non coercive sexual interaction with a peer'	relationship to perpetrator
Fehrenbach et al., 1986	offenders with hands-on and hands-off offending (N=297)	intake	intake: client, family	sexual abuse, physical abuse, both	yes/no
Ryan et al., 1987	residential and outpatient, nationwide survey, treatment providers (N=559)	throughout treatment	therapist report of case record review	sexual abuse, physical abuse	reported, adjudication for perpetrator, relationship to perpetrator, perpetrator gender
DeMartino, 1988	outpatient, sexual offenders (N=30)	point in time	interview	sexual abuse, physical abuse	type of sexual abuse, age at first sexual experience
Fagan and Wexler, 1988	court, sexual offenders/ violent offenders (n=34/174)	point in time	interview; official records	molestation physical abuse ='hit by an object' witness parental violence	severity

Table 1: *Continued*

Fahlberg, 1988	outpatient, sexual offenders/community comparison group (n = 21/21)	point in time	interview	sexual abuse	yes/no
Smith, 1988	outpatient, sexual offenders (N = 450)	intake	interview client, family	sexual abuse, physical abuse, sexual abuse of sibling/family member, physical abuse of sibling/family member	yes/no
Awad and Saunders, 1989	outpatient, child molesters (N = 29)	intake assessment	interview; clinician completed questionnaire, case record review	history of sexual abuse based on disclosure by adolescent/parents or reports from CPS/past therapists	family history of incest, family history of sexually deviant behaviours
Brannon et al., 1989	residential, sexual offenders (N = 63)	point in time	structured interview	molestation = 'being tricked, seduced, or manipulated into sexual relations (touching through intercourse) without being intimidated by verbal threats and/or physical coercion' abuse = 'being forced into participating in a sexual relationship (touching through intercourse) by another individual's use of verbal threats and intimidation, or physical abuse and violence'	relationship to perpetrator perpetrator gender and age perpetration acts, age at first abuse
Rowe-Lonczynski, 1989	outpatient, child molesters/non sexual offenders (n = 20/16)	point in time	clinical record review	sexual abuse, physical abuse	yes/no
Abbott, 1990	outpatient, minimally aggressive sexual offenders/violent sexual offenders/non violent delinquents (n = 20/20/20)	point in time	interview	sexual abuse, physical abuse, witness family violence, emotional abuse	yes/no

Study	Sample	Timing	Method	Abuse type / definition	Dimensions measured
Hsu and Starzynski, 1990	outpatient, child molesters/assaulters (n=17/15)	intake	interview; case record review	sexual abuse, physical abuse	yes/no
Arundell, 1991	outpatient and inpatient facilities, abused sexual offenders/abused adolescents (n=30/30)	point in time	interview, 10-item instrument developed by author	sexual abuse = 'reported or self-reported sexual contact (fondling to intercourse) experienced by the male before age 15, initiated by someone 5 years or more their senior' perceived family violence	type of sexual abuse, age at abuse, told parent, abuse reported to authorities, abuse frequency, relationship to perpetrator, perpetrator gender, perpetrator's use of force/threat, treatment following abuse
Awad and Saunders, 1991	outpatient, child molesters/assaulters/delinquents (n=45/49/24)	intake assessment	interview; clinician complete questionnaire	sexual abuse, physical abuse	yes/no
Bagley and Shewchuk-Dann, 1991	residential, sexual offenders/controls (n=60/322)	throughout treatment	case record review	sexual abuse, severe physical abuse	relation to perpetrator
Becker et al., 1991	outpatient, sexual offenders (N=246)	intake	structured clinical interview	sexual abuse, physical abuse, both	yes/no
Benoit and Kennedy, 1992	residential, child molesters/assaulters/violent offenders/non violent offenders (n=25/25/25/25)	not stated	case record review	sexual abuse non intense physical abuse = 'no broken bones or severe burns'	frequency, intensity (yes/no)
Gilchrist, 1992	residential, sexual offenders/violent offenders/non violent offenders (n=34/42/46)	point in time	self-report survey	sexual abuse = items from the Reddon-Jackson Social History (1990)	yes/no
Zgourides et al., 1994	juvenile facility, sexual offenders/high school students (n=47/109)	not stated	anonymous completion of written survey	touched or grabbed by an adult in a sexual way	yes/no

Table 1: *Continued*

Ford and Linney, 1995	residential, child molesters/rapists/violent delinquents/status offenders (n = 21/14/26/21)	not stated	case record review; structured interview; Conflict Tactics Scale	sexual abuse, child abuse, witness/experience parental violence in the home, exposure to hard-core pornography	witness versus experience violence
Kobayashi et al., 1995	outpatient, sexual offenders (N = 117)	intake	structured clinical interview; self-report questionnaire	sexual abuse, physical abuse	relationship to abuser, frequency, coercion/physical force
Worling, 1995a	outpatient, child molesters/assaulters with female victims (n = 29/27)	during treatment	Assessing Environments III Scale (Berger et al., 1988)	sexual abuse = 'any unwanted sexual contact (touching/penetration) prior to onset of offending, or sexual contact before age 12, with someone at least 13, and 4 years older' (p282) physical abuse	perpetrator gender
Worling, 1995c	outpatient, child molesters/assaulters (n = 60/27)	during treatment	analysis of data from assessment, treatment contacts	sexual abuse = 'any unwanted sexual contact (touching/penetration) prior to onset of offending, or sexual contact before age 12, with someone at least 13, and 4 years older' (p612)	frequency
Capozza, 1996	correctional settings, sexual offenders/non sexual offenders (n = 57/54)	point in time	analysis of data from individual interviews	sexual abuse = 1 item from the SONE Sexual History Background Form (Maletky and McGovern, 1991)	yes/no
Clark, 1996	outpatient, adolescent sexual offenders who denied/admitted their offending behaviour (n = 50/89)	intake	case record review	sexual abuse = 'subject, subject's parent, or guardian reported that the subject was victimised by an act that would be considered a sexual offence which could be legally prosecuted' (p58)	yes/no

Study	Sample	Timing	Method	Definition	Variables
Cooper et al., 1996	outpatient, abused/non abused sexual offenders (n=134/156)	intake	structured clinical interview; self-report questionnaire: client, family, official records	sexual abuse = 'hands on/off involving clear age difference of at least 5 years, clear indication of coercion' physical abuse = 'non accidental physical injury by parent, guardian, caretaker'	yes/no
Kaufman et al., 1996	incarcerated, abused/non abused (n=77/100)	not stated	anonymous self-report questionnaire	sexual abuse = 'detailed definition' (not provided)	yes/no
Napolitano, 1996	residential, sexual offenders/conduct disordered (n=18/18)	first week of placement	self-report questionnaire	sexual abuse, physical abuse	age at time of abuse, duration, severity, relationship to perpetrator, perpetrator age
Ryan et al., 1996	residential and outpatient, nationwide survey, treatment providers (N=1600)	throughout treatment	therapist report of case record review	sexual abuse, physical abuse, neglect witness family violence	adjudication status of perpetrator
Agee, 1997	juvenile court, adolescents charged with a sexual offence (N=122)	intake	case record review	sexual abuse	relationship to perpetrator, victimisation reported to authorities
McClellan et al., 1997	psychiatric hospital, abused/non abused males ages 5–18, with inappropriate sexual behaviours (n=125/189)	total treatment period	case record review	sexual abuse = 'confirmed report from CPS or child or witness/evaluator' physical abuse = major injury … skeletal injury or internal organ damage' neglect = 'gross lack of provision of basic needs, failure to thrive'	severity, type of sexual abuse, age at abuse, frequency/chronicity, relationship to perpetrator, number of perpetrators

Table 1: *Continued*

Way, 1999	training school and outpatient, child molesters, assaulters (n=67/29)	point in time, minimum 1 month in current treatment program	structured interview Childhood Trauma Questionnaire completed during interview	responses to questions on CTQ (sexual abuse, physical abuse, physical neglect)	severity, duration, number of perpetrators, relationship to perpetrator, age at first incident of each type, frequency, use of force
Burton, 2000	incarcerated, adolescents who offended early, late, continually (n=48/130/65)	point in time	anonymous survey Sexual Abuse Exposure Questionnaire Childhood Trauma Questionnaire	responses to CTQ: sexual abuse, physical abuse physical neglect, emotional neglect, emotional abuse	perpetration acts, severity
Johnson and Knight, 2000	inpatient treatment centres, juvenile sexual offenders (N=122)	not stated	self-report questionnaire	sexual abuse, physical abuse	type, frequency
Veneziano et al., 2000	residential, sexual offenders (N=74)	assessment following placement	Adolescent sexual offender Packet (Gray and Wallace, 1992)	sexual abuse	age at first victimisation, gender of perpetrator

in chronological order, and the table outlines the source for the sample, sample size and composition, method and timing of data collection, how maltreatment was operationalised, and the extent of detail provided regarding maltreatment history.

Study samples were obtained from such diverse sources as court settings, sexual offender residential treatment programmes, outpatient sexual offender treatment programmes, psychiatric institutions, and hospital emergency rooms. Many studies used convenience samples, which limits generalisability of findings. Studies also varied in the composition of their samples. Samples ranged in size from early small exploratory studies (N = 17, Longo, 1982; N = 18, Gomes-Schwartz, 1984) to a nationwide survey of treatment providers (N = 1,600, Ryan, Miyoshi, Metzner, Krugman, and Fryer, 1996). Fifteen studies used sexual offender samples smaller than 50, and another nine had samples smaller than 100, which limits generalisability of findings, particularly when subgroup comparisons are made. Of the 37 studies, 22 used a comparison group, and 13 of these used a non-offender comparison group. This allows more detailed examination of how adolescents with sexual offending behaviours differ from other adolescent populations.

Studies differed in the timing of data collection. Thirteen studies collected these data at the time of intake, while six studies collapsed data collected throughout treatment, and 12 selected a point in time for data collection. The remainder did not specify this information. This variation makes comparison across studies problematic, as it is expected that data collection at disparate points in treatment may garner differing data.

History of maltreatment or other victimisation was collected variously through structured interviews, reviews of official records, anonymous self-report, or reviews of case records. Standardised self-report instruments used in these studies included the Conflict Tactics Scale (Straus, 1979), Assessing Environments III Scale (Berger, Knutson, Mehm, and Perkins, 1988), Sexual Abuse Exposure Questionnaire (Ryan, Rodriguez, Anderson, and Foy, 1992), the Childhood Trauma Questionnaire (Bernstein and Fink, 1998), the Adolescent Sexual Offender Packet (Gray and Wallace, 1992), and author-developed questionnaires. Several studies collected data as a part of the treatment process, while others

collected data specifically for research purposes. Two studies also collected data from family members (Cooper, Murphy, and Haynes, 1996; Fehrenbach, Smith, Monastersky, and Deisher, 1986).

Studies differed in the types of maltreatment included in the study. All studies included in this review collected data on prior sexual abuse victimisation, while 19 also collected data on prior physical abuse, four included data on neglect (Burton, 2000; McClellan, McCurry, Ronnei, Adams, Storck, Eisner, and Smith, 1997; Ryan et al., 1996; Way, 1999), four collected data on witnessing violence (Abbott, 1990; Fagan and Wexler, 1988; Ford and Linney, 1995; Ryan et al., 1996), and one collected data on exposure to pornography (Ford and Linney, 1995).

Studies also differed in how specific types of maltreatment were operationalised. Several studies used standardised instruments and incorporated the operationalisation provided by these instruments (Burton, 2000; Ford and Linney, 1995; Veneziano, Veneziano, and LeGrand, 2000; Way, 1999; Worling, 1995a). Some studies used existing data from official records (Cooper et al., 1996; Fagan and Wexler, 1988). Others developed a detailed operationalisation specifically for the study. None of the studies specified data on maltreatment that adolescents may have experienced while in out-of-home placement (e.g., while in residential treatment, boarding school, etc.)

Examples of operationalisation of sexual abuse history varied, and included:

> Molestation defined as 'being tricked, seduced, or manipulated into sexual relations (touching through intercourse) without being intimidated by verbal threats or physical coercion,' and abuse defined as 'being forced into participating in a sexual relationship (touching through intercourse) by another individual's use of verbal threats and intimidation, or physical abuse and violence'
> (Brannon, Larson, and Doggett, 1988, p163)

> '(a) experiencing any unwanted sexual contact (i.e., sexual touching or penetration) prior to onset of his offences, or (b) sexual contact while under the age of 12, with someone who was at least 13 years of age, and four years older'
> (Worling, 1995c, p612)

> 'hands-on offences involving either a clear age difference of at least five years between the offender and the patient or where there was clear indication of the use of coercion'
> (Cooper et al., 1996, p111)

'touched or grabbed by an adult in a sexual way'
(Zougrides, Monto, and Harris, 1994, p1042)

'sexual contact between family members'
(Becker, Kaplan, Cunningham-Rathner, and Kavoussi, 1986, p87)

Examples of operationalisation of physical abuse included:

'non accidental physical injury afflicted on a child by a parent, guardian, caretaker'
(Cooper et al., 1996, p111)

'major injury ... skeletal injury or internal organ damage'
(McClellan et al., 1997, p960)

Examples of operationalisation of neglect included:

'gross lack of provision of basic needs, failure to thrive'
(McClellan et al., 1997, p960)

The largest group of studies, however, did not provide an operationalisation of types of maltreatment. This lack of detail makes it difficult to compare findings across studies.

In considering the type of data that may be collected on childhood maltreatment histories of sexually abusive adolescents, it is instructive to turn to research on maltreated children. In addition to the presence of specific types of maltreatment, research on sexually abused children typically measures a wide variety of variables (e.g., pre-abuse functioning, age at molestation, use of force or weapon, relation to perpetrator, gender of perpetrator, number of perpetrators, duration, severity, number of incidents, to whom disclosure was made, family and Child Protective Services (CPS) response to disclosure, perceived support from non-offending parent following disclosure, legal consequences for offender, or system's response following disclosure). This detail enables a greater contextual understanding of the maltreatment under examination, as well as the possible effects of experiencing this maltreatment.

The extent of this detail also provides insight on the breadth of data that could potentially be collected on victimisation histories of sexually abusive adolescents. In contrast, however, existing studies have provided limited detail about the childhood maltreatment experienced by abusive adolescents. Fifteen studies provided no detail beyond the simple presence (yes or no) of prior maltreatment. In the 37 studies examined for this review, the

most frequent detail provided was about maltreatment severity/use of force (7 studies), followed by the adolescent's relationship to the perpetrator (10 studies), frequency/chronicity/ duration (8 studies), age at victimisation (8 studies), and perpetrator gender (6 studies) Only six studies collected detail on four or more characteristics of prior childhood maltreatment (Arundell, 1991; Brannon et al., 1989; McClellan et al., 1997; Napolitano, 1996; Ryan, Davis, Miyoshi, Lane, and Wilson, 1987; Way, 1999). This lack of detail severely limits our ability to understand these maltreatment histories in detail.

In summary, studies have varied greatly in their methodology, focus, detail, and specificity. This means that each study may provide only a small piece of the puzzle, and studies are likely to provide apparently contradictory findings because they differ so widely in their methodology and detail. Given this caveat, findings from studies of childhood maltreatment histories for adolescents with behaviour problems are reported in the following sections. These findings are reported separately for sexual abuse, physical abuse, neglect, and witnessing family violence.

Maltreatment Histories of Adolescents With Sexual Offending Behaviours

Childhood sexual abuse

This section examines what we know about prior sexual abuse of adolescents with sexual offending behaviours. The sections below report findings on prevalence, victimisation characteristics, and perpetrator characteristics (see Table 2).

Prevalence. Estimates of childhood sexual victimisation histories among adolescent sexual offenders vary widely and range from 4% (Awad and Saunders, 1991) to 75% (Worling, 1995a), depending on sample characteristics and timing of data collection. Some studies examine adolescents with sexual offending behaviours as a homogeneous population, while others examine between-group differences. A number of studies that did distinguish offender subgroups found a higher prevalence of prior sexual abuse for child molesters than for sexual assaulters (Awad and Saunders, 1991; Ford and Linney, 1995; Way, 1999). Ford and Linney (1995) found that child molesters reported much higher rates of sexual abuse history (52%) than sexual assaulters (17%), violent non-sexual delinquents (17%), and status offenders (13.04%, $\chi^2 = 12.85$, $p < 0.005$) These findings were supported by Way (1999), who found that child molesters in residential treatment reported higher rates of childhood sexual abuse than sexual assaulters (80% versus 50%, $\chi^2(1,74) = 7.53$, $p < 0.01$). In contrast, Worling (1995c) reported nearly equal rates of sexual abuse for these samples (24% of child molesters and 26% of sexual assaulters).

Given the frequently reported disparity in rates of childhood sexual victimisation between offender subgroups, studies that combine child molester and assaulter samples are difficult to interpret. Those studies that combine statistics for child molesters and assaulters report varied prevalence rates for childhood sexual abuse, ranging from 9% (Fagan and Wexler, 1988) to 70% (Brannon et al., 1989). Thus, these combined samples may obscure the between-group differences found in studies that do distinguish offender subgroups.

Differences in the sexual offender's relationship to the victim and gender of the victim also produce differing prevalence rates. Intrafamilial offenders in residential treatment report a higher rate (54%) of prior sexual abuse than extrafamilial offenders (31%, Bagley and Shewchuk-Dann, 1991). Seventy-five percent of adolescents who sexually abused a male had themselves been sexually abused, compared with 25% of those who molested a female (Worling, 1995a). This suggests that there may be different developmental pathways for these offender subgroups.

In summary, adolescent sexual offenders consistently report a higher prevalence of childhood sexual abuse victimisation (21% to 92%) than males in the general population (10% to 16%, Faller, 1993). These studies suggest differing aetiology for differing types of offending patterns, and the limited detail in existing studies indicates the need for further research. It is not clear whether the actual prevalence of childhood victimisation for this population is higher or lower than that self-reported by adolescent sexual offenders. Some researchers suggest that sexual offenders may exaggerate this history in an attempt to excuse their offending behaviour (Rezmovic, Sloane, Alexander, Seltser, and Jessor, 1996), while others contend that males tend to under-report victimisation histories (Watkins and Bentovim, 1992). The studies included in this review that report the lowest rates of victimisation collected these data either at the time of intake (Awad and Saunders, 1991; Fehrenbach et al., 1986) or in a court setting (Fagan and Wexler, 1988) rather than during treatment. This may result in reduced honest reporting given the lack of treatment progress and limited treatment relationship development (Becker et al., 1986; Cooper et al., 1996; Worling, 1995a).

Victimisation characteristics. The previous section reported sexual abuse victimisation as a dichotomous (yes/no) variable. Victim-to-victimiser theory suggests that it is important to distinguish abuse history *characteristics* to better understand the level of trauma experienced by adolescents with sexual offending behaviours. Existing studies provide differing levels of detail on the childhood sexual abuse experienced by adolescents with sexual offending behaviours.

Studies of adolescents with sexual offending behaviours indicate that their sexual abuse began when young and often continued over time. Studies have found that they were first molested at an average age of 8 to 10 (Arundell, 1991; Brannon et al., 1989; Longo, 1982; Napolitano, 1996), and that this initial sexual contact is reported to include 'consensual sex' (Longo, 1982). Way (1999) found that respondents reported their sexual abuse victimisation began at an average 5½ years old (SD = 2.9), and continued a little over 3 years (SD = 3.7). These findings indicate that these youths were sexualised early in their development, and that a number of developmental stages were disrupted during this extended victimisation.

Increased frequency and severity of abuse are likely to increase trauma for the child (Beitchman, Zucker, Hood, DaCosta, Akman, and Cassavia, 1992). A high proportion of adolescents with sexual offending behaviours reported severe levels of sexual abuse. Arundell (1991) found that 80% of sexually abused offenders had been molested up to 15 times as children, and 72% reported verbal abuse concurrent with that sexual abuse. Napolitano (1996) reported that 91% of the offenders in his study reported 'serious' sexual abuse (e.g., cunnilingus, fellatio, analingus, penile penetration). Veneziano et al. (2000) analysed the relationship between the sexual victimisation experienced by adolescents with their sexual offending behaviours and patterns. They found a significant relationship between

Table 2: Studies of childhood sexual abuse history

Study	Sample	Prevalence	Victimisation characteristics	Perpetrator characteristics
Abbott, 1990	outpatient, minimally aggressive sexual offenders/violent sexual offenders/non violent delinquents (n = 20/20/20/20)			
Agee, 1997	juvenile court, adolescents charged with sexual offence (N = 122)	70%	64% molested by a family member 42% of victimisation reported to authorities	25% abused by female equal proportion of intra- and extrafamilial
Arundell, 1991	outpatient and inpatient settings, abused sexual offenders/abused adolescents (n = 30/30)		average age at abuse: 8 72% of abuse included verbal threats 80% abused up to 15 times	
Awad and Saunders, 1989	outpatient, child molesters (N = 29)	26% of child molesters		
Awad and Saunders, 1991	outpatient, child molesters assaulters delinquents (n = 45/49/24/)	21% of child molesters 4% of assaulters		
Bagley and Shewchuk-Dann, 1991	residential, sexual offenders/controls (n = 60/322)	54% of intrafamilial offenders 31% of extrafamilial offenders 3–5% of controls		
Becker et al., 1991	outpatient, sexual offenders (N = 246)			
Becker, Kaplan et al., 1986	outpatient, incest offenders (N = 22)	23% of incest offenders		

Study	Sample			
Benoit and Kennedy, 1992	residential, child molesters/assaulters/violent offenders/non violent offenders (N = 100)	26% of child molesters	100% penetration	100% >1 perpetrator
Brannon et al., 1989	residential, sexual offenders (N = 63)	70% of offenders	50% of all abuse was intercourse; 33% of all abuse was fellatio; mean age at abuse: 8	perpetrators 42% male, mean age 28; 58% female
Burton, 2000	incarcerated, adolescents who offended early, late, continually (n = 48/130/65)			
Capozza, 1996	correctional settings, sexual offenders/non sexual offenders in (n = 57/54)	35% of sexual offenders vs. 7.4% of non offenders (x^2 (1, N = 111) = 12.54, $p < 0.001$)		
Clark, 1996	outpatient, adolescent sexual offenders who denied/admitted their offending behaviour (n = 50/89)	45% overall; 48% of deniers vs. 41% of admitters		
Cooper et al., 1996	outpatient, abused/non abused (n = 134/156)	33% of offenders; 45% sexual or physical		
DeMartino, 1988	outpatient, sexual offenders (N = 30)	40% of offenders	50% of these experienced intercourse, first sexual experience at age 10–12	
Fagan and Wexler, 1988	court, sexual offenders/violent offenders (n = 34/174)	9% of offenders		
Fahlberg, 1988	outpatient, sexual offenders/community comparison group (n = 21/21)	38% of offenders		
Fehrenbach et al., 1986	offenders with hands-on and hands-off offending (N = 297)	11% of offenders; 7% both sexual and physical abuse		

Table 2: *Continued*

Study	Sample	Prevalence	Findings
Ford and Linney, 1995	residential, child molesters/rapists/violent delinquents/status offenders (n=21/14/26/21)	52% of child molesters / 17% of assaulters / 18% of violent delinquents / 13% of status offenders	
Gilchrist, 1992	residential, sexual offenders/violent offenders/non violent offenders (n=34/42/46)	38% of sexual offenders vs. 5.5% of non offenders (χ^2 (1, N=122)=20.66, p<0.001)	
Gomes-Schwartz, 1984	outpatient, child molesters (N=18)	38% of child molesters, plus 18% suspected	
Hsu and Starzynski, 1990	outpatient, child molesters/assaulters (n=17/15)	'most abused'	
Kaufman et al., 1996	incarcerated, abused, non abused (n=77/100)	44% of offenders	
Kobayashi et al., 1995	outpatient, sexual offenders (N=117)	20% of offenders	sexual abuse by males more coercive than by females poor bonding to mother predictor of sexual offence ($t=-4.13$, p<0.01) / abuse by males predictor of sexual offence ($t=3.83$, p<0.01) 74% had extrafamilial perpetrators
Longo, 1982	adult court, adolescent sexual offenders (N=17)	47% of offenders	average age 9 at first sexual experience abuse often not reported
McClellan et al., 1997	psychiatric hospital, abused/non abused males ages 5–18, with inappropriate sexual behaviours (n=125/189)	40% of male offenders	24% molested by mother stepmother 37% molested by father stepfather
Napolitano, 1996	residential, sexual offenders/conduct disordered adolescents (n=18/18)	61% of offenders vs. 5 of non offenders (χ^2 (1, N=36)=12.50, p<0.001)	91% <10 when abused 91% reported severe abuse / 46% abused by family member

Study	Sample	Rate		
Rowe-Lonczynski, 1989	outpatient, child molesters/non sexual offenders (n=20/16)	20% of sexual offenders, plus 30% suspected vs. 0% of comparison group		
Ryan et al., 1987	residential and outpatient, nationwide survey, treatment providers (N=559)	33%	37% reported the abuse	33% of those reported were adjudicated
Ryan et al., 1996	residential and outpatient, nationwide survey, treatment providers (N=1600)	34% (self report) 39% (case records)		22% abused by female 51% of offenders were <5 years older 37% of abusers were adjudicated
Smith, 1988	outpatient, sexual offenders (N=450)	19% of sample 1 31.9% of sample 2		
Venzeniano et al., 2000	residential, sexual offenders (N=74)	92%		
Way, 1999	training school and outpatient, child molesters/sexual assaulters (n=67/29)	75% of child molesters vs. 52% of assaulters ($p<0.03$) 69% of residential sample vs. 61% of outpatient (ns)	19% moderate abuse; 80% severe mean age: 5.5 (SD=2.9) duration: 3.4 years (SD=3.7) 19% daily abuse; 21% weekly; 19% monthly; 40% yearly or less; 21% threat w/weapon; used; 21% hit w/object; 62% hit with hand; 10% tied down; 77% held down	58% abused by males; 9% abused by females; 33% abused by both males and females 67% intrafamilial perpetrator
Worling, 1995a	outpatient, child molesters/assaulters with female victims (n=29/27)	43% of offenders 25% of offenders against females 75% of offenders against males		86% of abused child molesters against females were abused by males 71% of abused assaulters against females were abused by females ($s^2=4.67$, $p<0.05$)

Table 2: *Continued*

Worling, 1995c	outpatient, child molesters/assaulters (n = 60/27)	24% of child molesters 26% of assaulters
Zgourides et al., 1994	juvenile facility, sexual offenders/high school students (n = 47/109)	62% of offenders; 19% of non offenders

severity of prior sexual abuse (molestation before age 5, molestation by a family member, and molestation acts including intercourse) and the later repetition of these characteristics in the adolescents' sexual offending.

Perpetrator characteristics. Of the 37 studies that examined prior sexual abuse of adolescents with sexual offending behaviours, just over a third reported data on the characteristics of the perpetrators of this sexual abuse, and these studies found that adolescent sexual offenders report a high frequency of female perpetrators. Figures range from 22% to 25% for those in combined outpatient and residential settings (Arundell, 1991; Ryan et al., 1996), while Way (1999) found that 42% of a combined residential and outpatient sample reported molestation by females or by both males and females. This high rate is supported by Brannon et al. (1989), who found that 58% of those in residential treatment settings had been molested by a female. These two studies did not distinguish between child molester and sexual assaulter subgroups. In contrast, Worling (1995a) found that 71% of abused adolescents with female peer/adult victims had been molested by a female while 86% of those with a female child victim had been molested by a male ($\chi^2 = 4.67$, $p < 0.05$).

The female perpetrators reported by adolescents with sexual offending behaviours tended to be as much as 10 years younger than male perpetrators (Brannon et al., 1989) and were frequently less than five years older than the male victim (Ryan et al., 1996). It is possible that this smaller age difference contributes to the male child's ambiguity about whether the sexual interaction was sexual abuse or consensual sexual relations; this may also lead to reduced reporting.

These findings have striking implications for early intervention because overall, boys are less likely than girls to disclose their sexual victimisation (Finkelhor, Hotaling, Lewis, and Smith, 1990), and female perpetrators are less likely to be reported than male perpetrators (Jennings, 1993). Thus, boys who are molested by females may be less likely to disclose their victimisation, and therefore less likely to receive treatment after being victimised, and may be more at risk to inappropriately act out their unresolved issues in ways that harm themselves or others.

Studies provide limited, and often conflicting, data on the relationship to perpetrators of prior sexual abuse. Some studies indicate a high rate of intra-familial perpetrators (67%, Way, 1999; 61%, McClellan et al., 1997). Other studies found an equal proportion of intra and extra-familial perpetrators (Arundell, 1991) or a majority of extra-familial perpetrators (74%, Kobayashi, Sales, Becker, Figueredo, and Kaplan, 1995). While these studies provide some data on relationship to the perpetrator, they do not offer detail on the context of these relationships nor on the relative effects of these differing relationships.

Summary. In summary, the high rate of childhood sexual abuse and the severity of that maltreatment indicates that these sexually abused adolescents may have experienced a high rate of traumatic sexualisation. At the same time, it appears that there are 10% to 60% of sexually abusive adolescents (depending on the study) who report no childhood sexual abuse. It may be that there is another developmental pathway for these youths. The next section discusses findings on another form of childhood maltreatment, physical abuse.

Childhood physical abuse

The actual prevalence of childhood physical abuse is difficult to determine because many studies do not examine this phenomenon (see Table 3). A number of other studies report concurrent physical abuse and sexual abuse histories (Cooper et al., 1996; Fehrenbach et al., 1986; Johnson and Knight, 2000; Smith, 1988; Way, 1999). Extensive attention has been given to the compounded effects on children of experiencing more severe maltreatment (Lebowitz, Harvey, and Herman, 1993; Rutter, 1989). Prevalence of childhood physical abuse is examined below, first for offender subgroups and then for sexually abusive adolescents in comparison with other adolescent groups.

Offender subgroups. Studies have found conflicting data on the rate of physical abuse victimisation for those who molested a child (child molesters) versus those who assaulted a peer and/or adult (sexual assaulters). Awad and Saunders (1991) found that 27% of child molesters in outpatient treatment had been physically abused as children, in contrast to 33% of sexual assaulters. These findings are supported by Worling (1995a), who found that assaulters of female peers or women reported significantly more physical punishment as children than molesters of girls ($t = 2.09$,

$p < 0.05$), while intra-familial offenders reported greater physical punishment as children than extra-familial offenders ($t = 2.22$, $p < 0.02$, Worling, 1995b). In contrast, Way (1999) found that sexual assaulters reported a higher (though non-significant) history of childhood physical abuse (86% versus 81%). Though these studies all show differing victimisation rates for offender subgroups, within studies these differences are not large. This suggests that differing rates may be due to differences in research methodology rather than actual differences in prevalence.

Comparison with other adolescent groups. Studies have also compared sexual offenders with other adolescent groups. These studies indicate that adolescents with sexual offending behaviours have a higher rate of prior physical abuse victimisation than other delinquents (Awad and Saunders, 1991; Fagan and Wexler, 1988) and than psychiatric inpatients have experienced (McClellan et al., 1997). One study (Napolitano, 1996) found no difference between adolescents with sexual offending behaviours and other conduct-disordered youths, but the small sample ($N = 36$) limits generalisability of these findings. The remainder of the studies summarised in Table 3 combine data for offender populations and treatment settings.

Victimisation characteristics. While 23 studies examined the presence of prior physical abuse in adolescents with sexual offending behaviours, only a third provided research data on the *nature* of that victimisation, and these studies vary widely in operationalisation and the detail provided. Studies indicate that these adolescents experienced more severe abuse (28% versus 13%), more chronic abuse (61% versus 38%), and more harsh and/or inconsistent discipline (22% versus 13%) than other adolescents (Bagley and Shewchuk-Dann, 1991; McClellan et al., 1997). One study (Way, 1999) suggests that physical abuse began early (M = 6.4 years, SD = 3.8), continued for years (M = 5.8 years, SD = 3.8), and was rated as severe by a majority of the respondents (58%). This study also found that this abuse frequently included force; 33% had a weapon used, 40% were threatened with a weapon, and 82% were hit with an object. However, this study's small sample ($N = 96$) and lack of a non-offender comparison group limit the generalisability of these findings. The study also does not distinguish characteristics for offender subgroups. Burton (2000) found no difference

Table 3: Studies of childhood physical abuse history

Study	Sample	Prevalence	Victimisation characteristics	Perpetrator characteristics
Abbott, 1990	outpatient, minimally aggressive sexual offenders/violent sexual offenders/non violent delinquents (n=20/20/20/20)	15% of minimally aggressive sexual offenders vs. 25% of aggressive sexual offenders and 28% of delinquents (ns)		
Awad and Saunders, 1991	outpatient, child molesters/assaulters/delinquents (n=45/49/24)	27% of child molesters abused 33% of assaulters abused 12% of delinquents abused		
Bagley and Shewchuk-Dann, 1991	residential, sexual offenders/controls (n=60/322)		28% severe abuse vs. 13% for controls 32% inconsistent discipline vs. 25% 22% consistently harsh discipline vs. 13%	
Becker et al., 1991	outpatient, sexual offenders (N=246)	physically abused offenders more depressed (z=2.62, $p<0.01$)		
Becker, Kaplan et al., 1986	outpatient, incest offenders (N=22)	14%	father used a belt	
Benoit and Kennedy, 1992	residential, child molesters/assaulters/violent offenders/non violent offenders (n=25/25/25/25)	40% of all sexual offenders no difference between groups		
Burton, 2000	incarcerated, adolescents who offended early, late, continually (n=48/130/65)		no difference in severity between offender subgroups	
Cooper et al., 1996	outpatient, abused/non abused (n=134/156)	9% physical abuse only 12% physical and sexual abuse		

Study	Sample	Finding	Additional finding
DeMartino 1988	outpatient, sexual offenders (N=30)	53% of offenders	
Fagan and Wexler 1988	court, sexual offenders/violent offenders (n=34/174)	25% of offenders vs. 15% of delinquents	hit by an object
Fehrenbach et al., 1986	offenders with hands-on and hands-off offending (N=297)	16% of offenders abused 7% both physical and sexual abuse	child molesters had more early memories of abuse (23 vs. 3 for rapists, 0 for other groups)
Ford and Linney, 1995	residential, child molesters/rapists/violent delinquents/status offenders (n=21/14/26/21)	child molesters more total child abuse ($p<0.05$)	
Hsu and Starzynski, 1990	outpatient, child molesters/assaulters (n=17/15)		2 subjects had sustained multiple fractures as the result of physical abuse
Johnson and Knight, 2000	inpatient treatment centres, juvenile sexual offenders (N=122)	much covariation of physical abuse and sexual abuse	childhood physical abuse predicted peer aggression ($b=.19$, $p<0.05$) and alcohol abuse ($b=.26$, $p<0.01$), which then predicted sexual coercion
Kobayashi et al., 1995	outpatient, sexual offenders (N=117)	36% abused	most frequent abuse was by mother (71 incidents vs. 50 incidents by father) abuse by father predictor of sexual offence ($t=3.07$, df=116, $p<0.01$)
McClellan et al., 1997	psychiatric hospital, abused/non abused males ages 5–18, with inappropriate sexual behaviours (n=125/189)	73% of male offenders abused vs. 53% of non offenders	61% chronically abused vs. 38% of non offenders

Table 3: *Continued*

Napolitano, 1996	residential, sexual offenders/conduct disordered adolescents (n = 18/18)	11% of offenders vs. 22% of non offenders (ns)		
Rowe-Lonczynski, 1989	outpatient, child molesters/non sexual offenders (n = 20/16)	35% of offenders vs. 0% for comparison group		
Ryan et al., 1987	residential and outpatient, nationwide survey, treatment providers (N = 559)	40% abused		10% of complaints were adjudicated
Ryan et al., 1996	residential and outpatient, nationwide survey, treatment providers (N = 1600)	45% abused (by self report) 42% abused (by case records)		17% of perpetrators adjudicated
Smith, 1988	outpatient, sexual offenders (N = 450)	25% of sample 1 (35% with or without sexual abuse) 38% of sample 2 (56% with or without sexual abuse)	abuse history predicted more serious offences ($p < 0.01$) abuse history predicted younger victims ($p < 0.03$)	
Way, 1999	residential, outpatient, child molesters/sexual assaulters (n = 67/29)	81% of child molesters vs. 86% of assaulters (ns) 89% of residential sample vs. 59% of outpatient ($p < 0.003$) 77% had multiple forms of maltreatment	25% moderate abuse; 58% severe mean age: 6.4 (SD = 3.8) duration: 5.8 years (SD = 3.8) 18% daily abuse; 34% weekly; 22% monthly; 26% yearly or less 33% weapon used; 40% threat w/weapon; 82% hit w/object; 89% hit with hand; 12% tied down; 41% held down	55% abused by males; 41% abused by males and females 75% extrafamilial perpetrator
Worling, 1995a	outpatient, child molesters/sexual assaulters with female victims (n = 29/27)		assaulters with female victims reported more physical punishment than child molesters with female victims ($t = 2.09$, $p < 0.05$)	

in severity of childhood physical abuse among sexually abusive youths who offended only at a young age, only at an older age, or continually.

Perpetrator characteristics. We have little data on those who physically abused the sexually abusive adolescents. Studies indicate that the majority of physical abuse was committed by males (Way, 1999), while mothers perpetrated more *incidents* of physical abuse than did fathers (Kobayashi et al., 1995). However, Way's finding that 75% of physical abuse perpetrators were extra-familial raises the question of comparability with other studies that use the CPS operationalisation of *intra-familial* abuse. Ryan and colleagues (1987; 1996) found that only a small proportion of reported abuse complaints had been adjudicated (10%–17%). They suggest that this may have implications for adolescents' learning about consequences and accountability.

Effects of victimisation. Some research has examined the effects of childhood physical abuse on adolescents with sexual offending behaviours. Becker, Kaplan, Tenke, and Tartaglini (1991) found that adolescents with prior physical abuse were more depressed than offenders with no such history ($z = 2.62$, $p < 0.01$). Kobayashi et al. (1995) examined types of childhood maltreatment perpetrated by mothers and fathers in their structural equation modelling analysis of the personal and family characteristics of adolescent sexual offenders. They found that only physical abuse by fathers was significantly related to adolescent sexual offending ($t = 3.070$, df $= 116$, $p < 0.01$)

Summary. In summary, one quarter to three quarters of adolescents with sexual offending behaviours report histories of childhood physical abuse, with outliers at both ends of this range. These rates may vary because of different operationalisation, measurement, sample composition, and/or timing of data collection. The higher rate (73%) is reported by psychiatrically hospitalised adolescent sexual offenders (McClellan et al., 1997), while the lowest rates are for adolescent sexual offenders in outpatient treatment who were interviewed at intake (16%, Fehrenbach et al., 1986) and for review of case records for adolescent sexual offenders in residential treatment (11%, Napolitano, 1996). These limited findings on prior physical abuse suggest an important direction for future research. Widom and Ames (1994; see also Widom, 1995) suggests that childhood physical abuse is a stronger predictor of arrests for sexual offending as an adult than is childhood sexual abuse, and Vizard, Monck, and Misch (1995) emphasise the need to examine the relationship between physical abuse victimisation and adolescent sexual offending.

Childhood neglect

Few studies of adolescent sexual offenders have examined childhood neglect (see Table 4). Studies that do examine neglect history frequently combine these findings with physical abuse data (e.g., Hsu and Starzynski, 1990). One of the few studies (McClellan et al., 1997) that measured neglect separately found that psychiatrically hospitalised sexually aggressive children and adolescents reported a higher rate of childhood neglect than did non-victimising children and adolescents (37% versus 26%). Another study of treatment providers found that 26% of adolescent sexual offenders had reported childhood neglect (Ryan et al., 1996). Way (1999) compared neglect histories for offender subgroups and found that sexual assaulters had a slightly higher rate of neglect than did child molesters (χ^2 (1, N=96)=6.3, $p < 0.01$); this difference held true when comparing subgroups in the residential sample (χ^2 (1, N=74)=3.6, $p < 0.006$). The study found a non-significant difference in neglect histories between respondents in residential and outpatient treatment (43% versus 26%). It appears that small cell size may have prevented detection of statistically significant differences.

Victimisation characteristics. In one of the few studies that examined characteristics of childhood neglect, Burton (2000) found no difference in severity of neglect among adolescents who began engaging in sexually aggressive behaviours as children and continued into adolescence, those who acted out sexually as children and stopped before adolescence, and those who began their sexually aggressive behaviour as adolescents. However, he did find that adolescents with a history of continual offending reported more severe emotional abuse histories (F (2, 240)=4.92, $p < 0.01$). In another examination of severity, Way (1999) found that 100% of neglected respondents experienced *moderate* or *severe* physical neglect. This neglect began young (M=5.53 years, SD=2.95), continued for multiple years (M=5.67, SD=3.89), and

Table 4: Studies of childhood neglect history

Study	Sample	Prevalence	Victimisation characteristics	Perpetration characteristics
Burton, 2000	incarcerated, adolescents who offended early, late, continually (n =48/130/65)		neglect: no difference in severity between groups emotional abuse: continuous offenders reported highest severity (F (2, 240) =4.92, $p<0.01$)	
McClellan et al., 1997	psychiatric hospital, abused/non abused males ages 5–18, with inappropriate sexual behaviours (n =125/189)	37% of males with sexual behaviours vs. 21% for those without		
Ryan et al., 1996	residential and outpatient, nationwide survey, treatment providers (N =1600)	26%		
Way, 1999	training school and outpatient, child molesters/sexual assaulters (n =67/29)	31% of child molesters vs. 59% of assaulters (^{s} (1, N =96) =6.3, $p<0.01$) 43% of residential sample vs. 26% outpatient (ns) 35% of child molesters in residential vs. 57% of assaulters (^{s} (1, N =74) =3.6, $p=.006$)	40% moderate neglect; 61% severe age: M =5.5 (SD =2.95) duration: M =5.7 years (SD =3.9) 69% daily neglect; 21% weekly; 3% monthly; 7% yearly or less	10% neglected by males 24% neglected by females 66% neglected by both 93% had intrafamilial perpetrator

Table 5: Studies of family violence history

Study	Sample	Prevalence
Abbott, 1990	outpatient, minimally aggressive sexual offenders/violent sexual offenders/non violent delinquents (n = 20/20/20/20)	15% of minimally aggressive sexual offenders vs. 20% of aggressive sexual offenders and 35% of delinquents (ns)
Fagan and Wexler, 1988	court, sexual offenders/violent offenders (n = 34/174)	sexual offenders reported less history of family violence and higher rates of parents incarcerated
Ford and Linney, 1995	residential, child molesters/rapists/violent delinquents/status offenders (n = 21/14/26/21)	33% of child molesters vs. 20% of rapists, 21% of violent offenders, 17% of status offenders (p < 0.05)
Ryan et al., 1996	residential and outpatient, nationwide survey, treatment providers (N = 1600)	63% had observed family violence

occurred daily or weekly for 90% of respondents, indicating chronicity and possibility of cumulative effects. Again, the small sample and lack of a non-offender comparison group limits generalisability of these findings, and further research is needed.

Perpetrator characteristics. We have almost no data on the characteristics of neglect perpetrators. Only one study reported any data; Way (1999) found that the majority (66%) of adolescent respondents reported being neglected by both males and females, and 93% of their perpetrators were within the family.

Summary. The sparse data on childhood neglect histories for this population is of concern given the growing awareness of the harm of childhood neglect on subsequent development (Dubowitz, 1999; Erickson, Egeland, and Pianta, 1989). The scant data that are available for childhood neglect in offender subgroups suggest the possibility of diverse developmental pathways. Research needs to examine this phenomenon in greater detail.

Witnessing family violence

Social learning theory suggests that early exposure to violence may lead children (especially boys) to conclude that aggression is an appropriate way to solve interpersonal problems (Staub, 1996). Only four studies have examined adolescent sexual offenders' histories of witnessing family violence (see Table 5). These studies vary widely, and indicate that 15% to 63% of sexually abusive youths have

witnessed family violence (Abbott, 1990; Ford and Linney, 1995; Ryan et al., 1996). These wide variations suggest that more research is needed in this area in order to understand the prevalence and characteristics of exposure to violence.

Summary. In summary, while more than 35 studies have examined prior maltreatment in adolescents with sexual offending behaviours, we do not have extensive detail on the characteristics of that history, and differing operationalisation of key concepts makes comparison among studies problematic. The next section discusses specific measurement issues in conducting research in this area and makes recommendations for future research.

Validity of Retrospective Data

A critical issue in examining the childhood maltreatment histories of adolescents is collecting accurate data. Most studies are retrospective and rely on self-report by adolescent or adult sexual offenders. The validity of retrospective data may be influenced by legitimate amnesia, fears about confidentiality/reporting consequences, inaccurate recall, and/or response bias (Briere, 1992; Laumann et al., 1994). These problems are exacerbated when criminals are asked to report retrospective data.

One particular threat to validity of retrospective data is the issue of self-report bias, or data that is inaccurate because the informant has intentionally or accidentally biased his or her report. For the purposes of this review, this phenomenon may occur whenever we ask individuals adjudicated for criminal behaviour to provide accurate and honest information about sensitive topics. The issue of self-report bias presents a dilemma. It is true that some data may not be available through sources other than self-report. Official records of child maltreatment can only provide data about maltreatment that had been reported to the CPS (Widom, 1988). In contrast, youths' self-report of child maltreatment may avoid this bias. However, self-report data, while extensive, may also be biased and cannot always be corroborated.

Reliance on self-report data presents a particular dilemma when sexual offender subjects perceive that there is a secondary gain for claiming a maltreatment history. For example, Hindman (1988) found dramatic differences in the rates of child sexual abuse reported by two groups of adult sexual offenders; one group was merely asked about a history of childhood sexual abuse while members of the other group were told they would be given polygraph tests to confirm their report. There was a significant difference in the rates reported by these two groups (67% without threat of polygraph versus 29% with that threat). However, the data were collected from two groups of adults and 8 years passed between the studies; thus the two samples are not necessarily comparable. Nonetheless, this study raises concerns about the validity of retrospective data, suggesting that sexual offenders may use reports of child sexual abuse to excuse their offences (Rezmovic et al., 1996). In contrast, a prospective study (Rubinstein, Yeager, Goodstein, and Lewis, 1993) found that a large number of adult sexual offenders had no recollection of childhood sexual abuse they had experienced (documented in childhood case records), and those who did recall their victimisation frequently minimised the effects. In another study using polygraph, Emerick and Dutton (1993) found that adolescent sexual offenders reported equally high rates of sexual abuse victimisation with interviews and polygraph tests, with a slightly higher (though non-significant) disclosure rate using polygraphy. Self-report data may be minimised or inflated due to social desirability response bias, which is discussed in the next section.

Social desirability response bias. Social desirability response bias is a specific form of self-report bias, and refers to the tendency of respondents to provide the answer they believe is most desirable or places them in the best possible light. This bias may result in over-reporting data that respondents believe enhances their presentation and underreporting data that they believe diminishes them. While social desirability response bias is a risk in any research, it presents a greater concern in research with criminal populations. These respondents may attempt to excuse their victimising behaviour by misreporting their own victimisation history, or they may portray themselves as, for example, more empathic, less hostile, more concerned, and less dangerous than they really are.

Several studies have measured self-report bias simply by comparing self-reports to reports of collateral sources. Forehand, Frame, Wierson, Armistead, and Kempton (1991) found that youths under-reported their externalising behaviour problems as compared with parent or caretaker and teacher reports. Children tended to reported more parent-to-child violence than did their parents, while parents report more child-to-parent violence than did their children (Kolko, Kazdin, and Day, 1996).

Strategies to reduce response bias. Researchers must resolve the dilemma of response bias in order to collect accurate data and gain credibility and legitimacy for their research findings. One methodological solution to the dilemma is to emphasise that there is no reward for either a negative or positive report of particular retrospective data (Briere, 1992). Other solutions to increase the validity of self-report data include the use of multiple measures and multiple items and using Likert response scales rather than dichotomous response scales. For example, Peters, Wyatt, and Finkelhor (1986) contended that asking multiple questions about sexual abuse history helps respondents become comfortable in discussing the topic, helps them become familiar with the terminology, and helps them cognitively scan their memory. The use of multiple items with multiple response items stands in sharp contrast to studies that measure sexual abuse victimisation history as a single dichotomous (yes/no) variable.

Another recommendation is to ask about experiences and behaviours rather than to label that experience, e.g., asking about early sexual *experiences* rather than, 'Were you sexually abused as a child?' (Black and DeBlassie, 1993;

Rubinstein et al., 1993). This is especially important when asking males about sexual abuse victimisation. Males may under-report this history because they are socialised to be self-sufficient and independent (Watkins and Bentovim, 1992), may view early sexual activity as non-abusive (Freeman-Longo, 1986), and are less likely to disclose sexual abuse victimisation (Ryan, Lane et al., 1987), especially when the perpetrator was female. Another strategy to reduce self-report bias is to use multiple data sources (Kaufman, Jones, Steiglitz, Vitulano, and Mannarino, 1994; Peters et al., 1986; Widom, 1988). These additional sources may include parents, legal records, and/or case records. This method can not only garner additional data, but can also increase the likelihood of honest responses from subjects who know their answers will be corroborated. Finally, researchers recommend collecting data from adolescent sexual offenders who are in treatment rather than at the time of intake in order to increase honest reporting (Becker et al., 1986; Cooper et al., 1996; Worling, 1995a). Still other recommendations include measuring multiple forms of childhood maltreatment separately, explicitly asking about both intra-familial and extra-familial perpetrators, and asking about detailed maltreatment characteristics such as severity and duration (Widom, 1988).

Discussion

A great deal of debate and controversy has arisen over whether a cycle of violence exists for sexually abusive adolescents. A strict correspondence of childhood sexual abuse and later sexual offending behaviour has been widely disputed and summarily discarded (Finkelhor, 1986; Garland and Dougher, 1990; Rezmovic et al., 1996; Widom, 1991). Yet, when we expand the definition of childhood maltreatment beyond sexual abuse, researchers and practitioners report that these adolescents recount high rates of childhood sexual abuse, physical abuse, neglect, and family violence. The current review found more than 30 studies that examined childhood maltreatment histories of sexually abusive adolescents. These studies span the past 18 years, and as a group, they suggest that adolescents with sexual offending behaviours have a high rate of prior childhood maltreatment. This maltreatment may have included sexual abuse, but also often

included physical abuse and/or neglect. Studies that examined severity found that this maltreatment took multiple forms, began at an early age, was severe, and often became chronic. What sense are we to make of these data?

On the one hand, the literature on developmental effects of childhood maltreatment suggests that with appropriate intervention, maltreated children can be helped to heal and resolve their victimisation, thus reducing the harm of their traumatic experiences. We know that most maltreated children do not act out against others and that the effects of maltreatment more likely look like depression and withdrawal than harming others. At the same time, we cannot deny that studies of adolescents with sexual offending behaviours find that there was a high proportion of prior childhood maltreatment and that this proportion is higher than for adolescents generally.

It may be that these maltreated sexually abusive adolescents are a subgroup of sexual offenders and that they are also a subset of those maltreated children who have not adequately resolved their victimisation and subsequently sexually offend against others. This possibility does not excuse their offending behaviour and it does not absolve these adolescents of responsibility for their actions. However, it does provoke us to determine how to respond to these clinical and empirical data.

In addition, we may need to learn more about how to effectively intervene with maltreated children, including those who are at higher risk to later engage in harmful acting out behaviour, in order to help provide early intervention and help them regain healthy functioning. This certainly does not mean that we view each child victim as a potential offender; this would be patently wrong. However, it may be that intervention with an eye to potential acting out behaviours may help address focus treatment in ways that help children regain healthy functioning and help prevent further trauma for themselves or others (Ryan, 1989).

The current review is an effort to understand what empirical data already exist to help direct clinical interventions and guide further research into the role of childhood maltreatment in adolescents' sexual offending. Unfortunately, prior childhood maltreatment histories in this population have been studied sporadically, inconsistently, and without great detail. This limits our ability to draw broad conclusions about the prevalence and severity of this history. A number of methodological challenges interfere with effective study of this phenomenon. Studies have differed in their methodology, operationalisation of key concepts, and the breadth of the data collected. This impedes comparison of findings across studies. Many studies were conducted with small clinical samples, which limits generalisation of findings. In addition, studies that rely only on retrospective self-report or only on official records risk reporting a fraction of the truth. Many examinations of childhood maltreatment in this population are limited to sexual abuse only, or collect only prevalence data rather than amassing detail on maltreatment severity. Few studies examine the effects of multiple forms of maltreatment.

Despite the limitations of the data, some preliminary implications exist for clinical practice and further research. First, clinicians may need to better understand the issues of both abused children and sexual offenders. The practice dichotomy between treating only victims or only offenders may block therapists from understanding and effectively intervening in the possible progression from victim to victimiser. Intervention with abused male children could include assessment, and intervention as needed, for empathy development (Feshbach, 1989), assertiveness training, anger management (Ryan, 1989), relationship skills, and acting out behaviours that injure themselves or others (including pets and other animals, Ascione, 1993). Clinicians could focus on risk and protective factors when they evaluate and treat abused boys and their families. Ryan (1989) suggests that intervention with abused children should help them manage their anger, powerlessness, and betrayal in ways that do not harm themselves or others.

This review also has implications for the assessment process with adolescent sexual offenders. The first implication of these findings is that when we ask, we will hear. Practitioners may need to frame assessment questions to include extensive investigation of childhood history, in addition to collecting detailed information about offending behaviour. Multiple questions that describe experiences rather than label abuse will garner the most detailed information. It also may not be adequate to inquire about childhood history only at intake; clients may become willing to disclose more information as they move through the treatment process. Clinicians may benefit from understanding the long-term effects of childhood physical abuse and its impact on subsequent functioning (Cornett, 1985; Dodge, Pettit, Bates, and Valente, 1995; Glod, 1993; Malinosky-Rummell and Hansen, 1993; Vizard, 1993) and may need to incorporate resolution of these effects into their treatment programmes.

As this awareness grows, it will be crucial to maintain a clear stance that prior maltreatment history does not supercede the offender client's accountability and responsibility for his offending behaviour. Most abused children do not go on to assault others; what is important is how *this* adolescent responded to and coped with his experiences that resulted in his harming others.

This review found a high rate of childhood maltreatment by family members. This indicates that clinicians need to understand the family context within which adolescent sexual offenders grew up. Social learning theory suggests that children learn about roles, interpersonal relationships, and coping styles through early models. An individual treatment focus that does not account for family dynamics and interactions will miss a large part of the adolescent's reality.

The few studies that examined age at first maltreatment started found that it began at a young age and was of long duration. This would suggest that multiple developmental stages were disrupted, which in turn suggests that practitioners should take a holistic approach in developing interpersonal and coping skills, rather than focusing only on offenders' assaultive offending behaviour (Marshall, 1993).

This review also suggests direction for future research on maltreatment histories of adolescents with sexual offending behaviours. Ideally, we would conduct prospective research which could focus on risk and protective factors, which would help identify personal, family, and community characteristics that moderate adjustment to childhood maltreatment (Mrazek and Mrazek, 1987; Widom, 1991; Zuravin, McMillen, DePanfilis, and Risley-Curtis, 1996). However, this type of research is costly and time-consuming, and yields results slowly. Because we know that only a small proportion of maltreated children become sexual offenders, this research would ideally examine sexual offending as one of many possible outcomes (including healthy adjustment).

A second alternative is to analyse existing data. Secondary data analysis is relatively inexpensive, recognises the voluminous data that already exist, and allows a longitudinal view of phenomena of interest. One obvious weakness of analysing existing data is that it limits the researcher to those variables already collected. Another limitation is that it precludes examination of maltreated children who never come to the attention of the CPS. It may be hypothesised that these children comprise a subgroup of maltreated children, who receive no intervention, and thus may be at higher risk to act out their unresolved conflicts.

As researchers examine further the phenomenon of prior maltreatment in sexually abusive adolescents, it will be important to plan the timing and method of data collection. Measurement during treatment could increase the likelihood of obtaining honest, detailed information on childhood maltreatment (Becker, Cunningham-Rathner et al., 1986; Cooper et al., 1996; Worling, 1995a). This review's findings suggest the importance of measuring multiple types of childhood maltreatment to more fully understand the early childhood experiences of adolescent sexual offenders.

Future research could examine the ecological context of childhood maltreatment in greater detail to learn more about risk and protective factors that influence adjustment for maltreated children. These factors may include whether the childhood maltreatment was disclosed, what the reaction was of the non-offending parent, the level of perceived parental support following the maltreatment, whether the perpetrator was prosecuted, and whether and for how long the respondent received treatment. Researchers could corroborate self-reported childhood maltreatment with CPS records or case record review, recognising that much maltreatment is never disclosed or reported (Finkelhor, 1984; Widom, 1988).

In summary, we have a large amount of data on prior maltreatment histories of sexually abusive adolescents, but there are a number of methodological problems and inconsistencies that prevent us from drawing broad conclusions. Further research is needed, and this review has made recommendations to strengthen the methodology of these investigations.

Lastly, while it is important to learn more about maltreated sexual offenders, we know very little about those sexually abusive adolescents who were not maltreated. Researchers should investigate the aetiology of sexual offending in greater detail to learn more about multiple developmental pathways. It may be that there are disparate developmental pathways for different offender subgroups (e.g., those who do/do not use force, those who offend against children/peers/adults, those who molest opposite-sex/same-sex victims). It may also be that other, unidentified variables play a crucial aetiologic role, such as predisposing factors, risk and protective factors (Widom, 1991) or societal factors (Herman, 1990; Staub, 1996). Understanding these developmental pathways could help prevent and intervene with sexual offending behaviours and help protect children.

References

Abbott, B. R. (1990) *Family Dynamics, Intergenerational Patterns of Negative Events and Trauma, and Patterns of Offending Behaviour: A Comparison of Adolescent Sexual Offenders and Delinquent Adolescents and their Parents.* Unpublished doctoral dissertation, San Francisco: California Institute of Integral Studies.

Agee, T. L. (1997) *Juvenile Sex Offenders: A Comparison of Demographic and Behavioural Data With the Adult Paedophile Population.* Unpublished doctoral dissertation. San Diego: United States International University.

Arundell, R. M. (1991) *The Relationships of Empathy, Social Support, Trauma Symptoms and Family Violence in the Victim to Victimiser Process in Adolescent Males.* Unpublished doctoral dissertation. Cincinnati: University of Cincinnati.

Ascione, F. R. (1993) Children who are Cruel to Animals: A Review of Research and Implications for Developmental Psychopathology. *Anthrozoos.* 6: 226–47.

Awad, G. A. and Saunders, E. B. (1989) Adolescent Child Molesters: Clinical Observations. *Child Psychiatry and Human Development.* 19: 195–206.

Awad, G. A. and Saunders, E. B. (1991) Adolescent Child Molesters: Clinical Observations. *Journal of Interpersonal Violence.* 6: 446–60.

Bagley, C. and Shewchuk-Dann (1991) Characteristics of 60 Children and Adolescents Who Have a History of Sexual

Assault Against Others: Evidence from a Controlled Study. *Journal of Child and Youth Care.* 6: 43–52.

Ballantyne, W. (1993) *A Cognitive Coping Model to Explain the Victim-offender Phenomenon in the Sexual Abuse of Males.* Unpublished doctoral dissertation, Keene, New Hampshire: Antioch University.

Becker, J. V., Kaplan, M. S., Cunningham-Rathner, J. and Kavoussi, R. (1986) Characteristics of Adolescent Incest Sexual Perpetrators: Preliminary Findings. *Journal of Family Violence.* 1: 85–97.

Becker, J. V., Kaplan, M. S., Tenke, C. E. and Tartaglini, A. (1991) The Incidence of Depressive Symptomatology in Juvenile Sex Offenders With a History of Abuse. *Child Abuse and Neglect.* 15: 531–5.

Beitchman, J. H., Zucker, K. J., Hood, J. E., DaCosta, G. A., Akman, D. and Cassavia, E. (1992) A Review of the Long-term Effects of Child Sexual Abuse. *Child Abuse and Neglect.* 16: 101–18.

Benoit, J. L. and Kennedy, W. A. (1992) The Abuse History of Male Adolescent Sex Offenders. *Journal of Interpersonal Violence.* 7: 543–8.

Berger, A. M., Knutson, J. F., Mehm, J. G. and Perkins, K. A. (1988) The Self-report of Punitive Childhood Experiences of Young Adults and Adolescents. *Child Abuse and Neglect.* 12: 251–62.

Bernstein, D. P. and Fink, L. (1998) *Childhood Trauma Questionnaire: A Retrospective Self-report Manual.* San Antonio: The Psychological Corporation.

Black, C. A. and DeBlassie, R. R. (1993) Sexual Abuse in Male Children and Adolescents: Indicators, Effects and Treatments. *Adolescence.* 28: 123–33.

Brannon, J. M., Larson, B. and Doggett, M. (1989) The Extent and Origins of Sexual Molestation and Abuse Among Incarcerated Adolescent Males. *International Journal of Offender Therapy and Comparative Criminology.* 33: 161–72.

Briere, J. (1992) Methodological Issues in the Study of Sexual Abuse Effects. *Journal of Consulting and Clinical Psychology.* 60: 196–203.

Burton, D. L. (2000) Were Adolescent Sexual Offenders Children With Sexual Behaviour Problems? *Sexual Abuse: A Journal of Research and Treatment.* 12, 37–48.

Capozza, M. V. (1996) *Psycho-Sexual Differences Between Sexual Offenders and Other Offenders in the California Youth Authority.* Unpublished Master Thesis, Long Beach: California State University.

Clark, M. W. (1996) *Characteristics of Juvenile Sex Offenders Who Admit Versus Those Who Deny Their Offences.* Unpublished Doctoral Dissertation, Malibu, California: Pepperdine University.

Cooper, C. L., Murphy, W. D. and Haynes, M. R. (1996) Characteristics of Abused and Non-abused Adolescent Sexual Offenders. *Sexual Abuse: A Journal of Research and Treatment.* 8: 105–19.

Cornett, C. (1985) The Cyclical Pattern of Child Physical Abuse From a Psychoanalytic Self-psychology Perspective. *Child and Adolescent Social Work.* 2: 83–92.

Demartino, R. A. (1988) *School Aged Juvenile Sexual Offenders: A Descriptive Study of Self-reported Personality Characteristics, Depression, Familial Perceptions and Social History.* Unpublished Doctoral Dissertation, Albany: State University Of New York.

Dodge, K. A., Pettit, G. S., Bates, J. E. and Valente, E. (1995) Social Information-processing Patterns Partially Mediate the Effect of Early Physical Abuse on Later Conduct Problems. *Journal of Abnormal Psychology.* 104: 632–43.

Dubowitz, H. (Ed.) (1999) *Neglected Children: Research, Practice, and Policy.* Thousand Oaks, CA: Sage Publications.

Emerick, R. L. and Dutton, W. A. (1993) The Effect of Polygraphy on the Self-report of Adolescent Sexual Offenders: Implications for Risk Management. *Annals of Sex Research.* 6: 83–103.

Erickson, M. F., Egeland, B. and Pianta, R. (1989) The Effects of Maltreatment on the Development of Young Children. in Cicchetti, D. and Carlson, V. (Eds.) *Child Maltreatment: Theory and Research on the Causes and Consequences of Child Abuse and Neglect.* Cambridge, MA: Cambridge University Press. 647–84.

Fagan, J. and Wexler, S. (1988) Explanations of Sexual Assault Among Violent Delinquents. *Journal of Adolescent Research.* 3: 363–85.

Faller, K. C. (1993) Child Sexual Abuse: Intervention and Treatment Issues. Washington, D.C.: U.S. Department of Health and Human Services.

Fehrenbach, P. A., Smith, W., Monastersky, C. and Deisher, R. W. (1986) Adolescent Sexual Offenders: Offender and Offence Characteristics. *American Journal of Orthopsychiatry.* 56: 225–33.

Feshbach, N. D. (1989) The Construct of Empathy and the Phenomenon of Physical Maltreatment of Children. in Cicchetti, D. and Carlson, V. (Eds.) *Child Maltreatment: Theory and Research on the Causes and Consequences of Child Abuse and Neglect*. Cambridge, MA: Cambridge University Press. 349–73.

Finkelhor, D. (1986) Abusers: Special Topics. in *A Sourcebook on Child Sexual Abuse*. Beverly Hills, CA: Sage Publications. 119–42.

Finkelhor, D. (1984) Implications for Theory, Research, and Practice. in *Child Sexual Abuse: New Theory and Research*. New York: The Free Press. 221–36.

Finkelhor, D., Hotaling, G., Lewis, I. A. and Smith, C. (1990) Sexual Abuse in a National Survey of Adult Men and Women: Prevalence, Characteristics, and Risk Factors. *Child Abuse and Neglect*. 14: 19–28.

Ford, M. E. and Linney, J. A. (1995) Comparative Analysis of Juvenile Sexual Offenders, Violent Non Sexual Offenders, and Status Offenders. *Journal of Interpersonal Violence*. 10: 56–70.

Forehand, R., Frame, C. L., Wierson, M., Armistead, L. and Kempton, T. (1991) Assessment of Incarcerated Juvenile Delinquents: Agreement Across Raters and Approaches to Psychopathology. *Journal of Psychopathology and Behavioural Assessment*. 13: 17–25.

Freeman-Longo, R. E. (1986) The Impact of Sexual Victimisation on Males. *Child Abuse and Neglect*. 10: 411–4.

Fromuth, M. E., Burkhart, B. R. and Jones, C. W. (1991) Hidden Child Molestation: An Investigation of Adolescent Perpetrators in a Non Clinical Sample. *Journal of Interpersonal Violence*. 6: 376–84.

Fromuth, M. E. and Conn, V. E. (1997) Hidden Perpetrators: Sexual Molestation in a Non Clinical Sample of College Women. *Journal of Interpersonal Violence*. 12: 456–65.

Garland, R. J. and Dougher, M. J. (1990) The Abused/Abuser Hypothesis of Child Sexual Abuse: A Critical Review of Theory and Research. in Feierman, J. R. (Ed.) *Pedophilia: Biosocial Dimensions*. New York: Springer-Verlag. 488–509.

Glod, C. A. (1993) Long-term Consequences of Childhood Physical and Sexual Abuse. *Archives of Psychiatric Nursing*. 7: 163–73.

Gomes-Schwartz, B. (1984) Juvenile Sexual Offenders. in Division of Child Psychiatry, *Sexually Exploited Children: Service and Research Project, Family Crisis Program for Sexaully Abused Children*. Boston, MA: Tufts New England Medical Center. 245–60.

Gordon, M. (1990) Males and Females as Victims of Childhood Sexual Abuse: An Examination of the Gender Effect. *Journal of Family Violence*. 5: 321–32.

Gray, A. S. and Wallace, R. (1992) *Adolescent Sex Offender Assessment Packet*. Orwell, VT: Safer Society Press.

Herman, J. L. (1990) Sex Offenders: A Feminist Perspective. in Marshall, W. L., Laws, D. R. and Barbaree, H. E. (Eds.) *Handbook of Sexual Assault: Issues, Theories and Treatment of the Offender*. New York: Plenum Press. 177–93.

Hindman, J. (1988) Research Disputes Assumptions About Child Molesters. *National District Attorneys Association (NDAA) Bulletin*. 7: 1, 3.

Hsu, L. K. G. and Starzynski, J. (1990) Adolescent Rapists and Adolescent Child Sexual Assaulters. *International Journal of Offender Therapy and Comparative Criminology*. 34: 23–30.

Jennings, K. T. (1993) Female Child Molesters: A Review of the Literature. in Elliott, M. (Ed.), Female Sexual Abuse Of Children (pp. 219–234) New York: The Guilford Press.

Johnson, G. M. and Knight, R. A. (2000) Developmental Antecedents of Sexual Coercion in Juvenile Sexual Offenders. *Sexual Abuse: A Journal of Research and Treatment*. 12: 165–178.

Kaufman, J., Jones, B., Steiglitz, E., Vitulano, L. and Mannarino, A. P. (1994) The Use Of Multiple Informants To Assess Children's Maltreatment Experiences. *Journal of Family Violence*. 9: 227–248.

Kaufman, K. L., Hilliker, D. R. and Daleiden, E. L. (1996) Subgroup Differences in the Modus Operandi of Adolescent Sexual Offenders. *Child Maltreatment*. 1: 17–24.

Kobayashi, J., Sales, B. D., Becker, J. V., Figueredo, A. J. and Kaplan, M. S. (1995) Perceived Parental Deviance, Parent-Child Bonding, Child Abuse, and Child Sexual Aggression. *Sexual Abuse: A Journal of Research and Treatment*. 7: 25–44.

Kolko, D. J., Kazdin, A. E. and Day, B. T. (1996) Children's Perspectives in the Assessment of Family Violence: Psychometric Characteristics and Comparison to Parent Reports. *Child Maltreatment*. 1: 156–67.

Laumann, E. O., Gagnon, J. H., Michael, R. T. and Michaels, S. (1994) *Formative Sexual*

Experiences in the Social Organisation of Sexuality: Sexual Practices in the United States. Chicago: The University of Chicago. 321–47.

Lebowitz, L., Harvey, M. R. and Herman, J. L. (1993) A Stage-By-Dimension Model of Recovery from Sexual Trauma. *Journal of Interpersonal Violence.* 8: 378–91.

Longo, R. E. (1982) Sexual Learning and Experience Among Adolescent Sexual Offenders. *International Journal of Offender Therapy and Comparative Criminology.* 26: 235–41.

Malinosky-Rummell, R. and Hansen, David J. (1993) Long-term Consequences of Childhood Physical Abuse. *Psychological Bulletin.* 114: 68–79.

Marshall, W. L. (1993) The Role of Attachments, Intimacy, and Loneliness in the Etiology and Maintenance of Sexual Offending. *Sexual and Marital Therapy.* 8: 109–21.

McClellan, J., McCurry, C., Ronnei, M., Adams, J., Storck, M., Eisner, A. and Smith, C. (1997) Relationship Between Sexual Abuse, Gender, and Sexually Inappropriate Behaviours in Seriously Mentally Ill Youths. *Journal of American Academy of Child and Adolescent Psychiatry.* 36: 959–65.

Mrazek, P. J. and Mrazek, D. A. (1987) Resilience in Child Maltreatment Victims: A Conceptual Exploration. *Child Abuse and Neglect.* 11: 357–66.

Napolitano, S. A. (1996) *Depression, Cognitive Characteristics, and Social Functioning in Adolescent Sex Offenders and Conduct Disordered Adolescents in Residential Treatment.* Unpublished Doctoral Dissertation, Austin: University of Texas.

Peters, S. D., Wyatt, G. E. and Finkelhor, D. (1986) Prevalence. in Finkelhor, D., Araji, S., Baron, L., Browne, A., Peters, S. D. and Wyatt, G. (Ed.) *A Sourcebook on Child Sexual Abuse.* Newbury Park, Sage Publications. 15–59.

Rasmussen, L. A., Burton, J. E. and Cristopherson, B. J. (1992) Precursors to Offending and the Trauma Outcome Process in Sexually Reactive Children. *Journal of Child Sexual Abuse.* 1: 33–48.

Rezmovic, E. L., Sloane, D., Alexander, D., Seltser, B. and Jessor, T. (1996) *Cycle of Sexual Abuse: Research Inconclusive About Whether Child Victims Become Adult Abusers.* Washington: General Accounting Office.

Rowe-Lonczynski, C. M. (1989) *Adolescent Sexual Offenders' Social Isolation, Social Competency Skills, and Identified Problem Behaviours.*

Unpublished Doctoral Dissertation, Canada: University of Windsor.

Rubinstein, M., Yeager, C. A., Goodstein, C. and Lewis, D. O. (1993) Sexually Assaultive Male Juveniles: A Follow-up. *American Journal of Psychiatry.* 150: 262–5.

Rutter, M. (1989) Pathways from Childhood to Adult Life. *Journal of Child Psychology and Psychiatry.* 30: 23–51.

Ryan, G. (1989) Victim to Victimiser: Rethinking Victim Treatment. *Journal of Interpersonal Violence.* 4: 325–41.

Ryan, G., Davis, J., Miyoshi, T., Lane, S. and Wilson, K. (1987) *Getting at the Facts: The First Report from the Uniform Data Collection System.* Interchange. 5–7.

Ryan, G., Lane, S., Davis, J. and Isaac, C. (1987) Juvenile Sex Offenders: Development and Correction. *Child Abuse and Neglect.* 11: 385–95.

Ryan, G., Miyoshi, T., Metzner, J. L., Krugman, R. D. and Fryer, G. E. (1996) Trends in a National Sample of Sexually Abusive Youths. *Journal of the American Academy of Child and Adolescent Psychiatry.* 35: 17–25.

Ryan, S., Rodriguez, J., Anderson, R. and Foy, D. (1992) *Psychometric Analysis of the Sexual Abuse Exposure Questionnaire (SAEQ).* Paper Presented at The American Psychological Association, Washington, DC.

Smith, W. R. (1988) Delinquency and Abuse Among Juvenile Sexual Offenders. *Journal of Interpersonal Violence.* 3: 400–13.

Staub, E. (1996) Cultural-Societal Roots of Violence: The Examples of Genocidal Violence and Contemporary Youth Violence in the United States. *American Psychologist.* 51: 117–32.

Straus, M. A. (1979) Measuring Intrafamily Conflict and Violence: The Conflict Tactics (CT) Scales. *Journal of Marriage and the Family.* 41: 75–88.

Veneziano, C., Veneziano, L. and LeGrand, S. (2000) The Relationship Between Adolescent Sex Offender Behaviours and Victim Characteristics With Prior Victimisation. *Journal of Interpersonal Violence.* 15: 363–74.

Vizard, E., Monck, E. and Misch, P. (1993) Child and Adolescent Sex Abuse Perpetrators: A Review of the Research Literature. *Journal of Child Psychology and Psychiatry.* 36: 731–56.

Vizard, E., Monck, E. and Misch, P. (1995) Child and Adolescent Sex Abuse Perpetrators: A Review of the Research Literature. *Journal of Child Psychology and Psychiatry.* 36: 731–56.

Watkins, B. and Bentovim, A. (1992) The Sexual Abuse of Male Children and Adolescents: A

Review of Current Research. *Journal of Child Psychology and Psychiatry*. 33: 197–248.

Way, I.F. (1999) *Adolescent Sexual Offenders: The Role of Cognitive and Emotional Victim Empathy in the Victim-to-Victimiser Process*. Unpublished Doctoral Dissertation, St. Louis: Washington University.

Widom, C. S. (1991) Avoidance of Criminality in Abused and Neglected Children. *Psychiatry*. 54: 162–74.

Widom, C. S. (1988) Sampling Biases and Implications for Child Abuse Research. *American Journal of Orthopsychiatry*. 58: 260–70.

Widom, C. S. (1995, March) Victims of Childhood Sexual Abuse: Later Criminal Consequences. *NIJ Research in Brief*. [On-Line] Doc. No. NCJ 151525. Available Http:// www.Ncjrs.Org/Txtfiles/Abuse.Txt.

Widom, C. S. and Ames, M. A. (1994) Criminal Consequences of Childhood Sexual Victimisation. *Child Abuse and Neglect*. 18: 303–18.

Worling, J. R. (1995a) Adolescent Sex Offenders Against Females: Differences Based on the Age of Their Victims. *International Journal of Offender Therapy and Comparative Criminology*. 39: 276–93.

Worling, J. R. (1995b) Adolescent Sibling-incest Offenders: Differences in Family and Individual Functioning When Compared to Adolescent Non Sibling Sex Offenders. *Child Abuse and Neglect*. 19: 633–43.

Worling, J. R. (1995c) Sexual Histories of Adolescent Male Sex Offenders: Differences on the Basis of the Age and Gender of Their Victims. *Journal of Abnormal Psychology*. 104: 610–3.

Zgourides, G., Monto, M. and Harris, R. (1994) Prevalence of Prior Adult Sexual Contact in a Sample of Adolescent Male Sex Offenders. *Psychological Reports*. 75: 1042.

Zuravin, S., Mcmillen, C., Depanfilis, D. and Risley-Curtis, C. (1996) The Intergenerational Cycle of Child Maltreatment: Continuity Versus Discontinuity. *Journal of Interpersonal Violence*. 11: 315–34.

Part 2: Impact Issues

Chapter 3: I'm Sorry I Haven't a Clue: Unconscious Processes in Practitioners who Work with Young People who Sexually Abuse

Nick Bankes

Just as the rigid authoritarian parent virtually creates a rebellious attitude in the child, the technique dominated analyst creates a great deal of resentment in the patient.

Reuben Fine (1985, p14–15)

Good therapy is an engagement of two people that leaves both changed. If only the patient changes, the therapy has been a failure.

Janis Robitscher (1980, p488)

Introduction

It is important for those of us who work in any field of social welfare to question why we are doing it, what the impact of the work is on ourselves and how this affects our practice. Bowlby (1977, 1979), Malan (1979) and others (see for example: Vincent, 1996; Wolgien and Coady, 1997) talk of 'compulsive care giving', the 'helping profession syndrome' or the 'wounded healer'. The notion behind these concepts is that unless practitioners are aware of their own motivation to help others they may simply be trying to heal themselves in their drive to help others. If this is true, then being unaware of what drives us to help others may result in practice which meets our own needs rather than those of the people whom we are trying to help. At best this can result in some good for some clients, at worst it can result in destructive practice. Most of us probably fall somewhere in the middle of that continuum. I suggest that the majority of social welfare practitioners are probably not wholly aware of what motivated them to enter their profession nor how these unconscious motivations can influence their practice (Bankes et al., 1999; Blanchard, 1995; Carr, 1989; Epstein and Feiner, 1979; Lewis, 1979; Menzies, 1970; Obholzer and Roberts, 1994; Preston-Shoot and Agass, 1990; Sayers, 1991; Sexton, 1999; Vincent, 1996). Practitioners who work therapeutically with

young people who sexually abuse are no exception to these unconscious processes.

In this chapter I will describe the research, which I have been undertaking for the past five years into unconscious processes in practitioners who are working therapeutically with children and young people who sexually abuse.

Background to the research

The research arose out of my professional role as a practitioner working in this field. I had been running an assessment and treatment service for this client group for a social services department in the UK and I began to have some misgivings about the way in which we undertook the work, particularly the way we treated the young people we were working with. There was an underlying pressure to get the client to disclose more than he had done so far. This was accompanied by a dynamic of rivalries between us as workers. Who was the most expert? Who would get the client to admit what he had previously denied?

We used the cognitive behavioural techniques, which we had learned from our work with adults who sexually abuse, including the use of assumptive questioning and confronting denial. These techniques seemed somewhat interrogative and punitive towards the young person and I began to question what my colleagues and I were getting out of it: what motivated us to do this work? We merely paid lip service to such questions, and I was aware of a reluctance in myself to raise my misgivings with my co-workers. My fantasy was that if I said 'don't you think we're being a little harsh with Peter, perhaps he has only done it once' it would be met with accusations that I was minimising Peter's offending, colluding with him or, at best that I had been 'groomed' by Peter. At a deeper level my fear was that by demonstrating any kindness, empathy or understanding towards Peter, this would be seen by my co-workers as an indication that I didn't think that what he had done was serious, that perhaps I colluded with sexual abuse per se, or worse still, that perhaps I was a child abuser myself.

These are powerful inhibitors to an honest disclosure of one's thoughts and feelings about the work and for me this had the effect of making me 'bury' such thoughts and feelings. It strikes me that there are some parallels or mirroring here between what we expect of our clients, but which they may be reluctant or unwilling to talk about, and what we should, but are perhaps reluctant or unwilling, to ask of ourselves and each other. In psychodynamic terms this known as a countertransference reaction.

So I became interested in what is going on for practitioners in this field at an unconscious or semi-conscious level. Are these unconscious processes emanating from the client, part of our own unresolved issues, or, more likely, a mixture of both? If they remain unconscious is there a danger that they will be acted out in the therapeutic relationship? If so, does this matter? Do unconscious processes exist at all? How do we address the misgivings, which I was becoming aware of in our work with Peter and others, in a way which would be helpful to both the clients and the workers in effecting a lasting change in their behaviour? These then are the questions that I have been addressing in my research.

Conscious and unconscious process and outcome research in psychotherapy

There is a now a substantial body of research that has explored the therapeutic process and compared how these processes produce successful or unsuccessful outcomes for the client in therapy (See for example: Beutler et al., 1994; Lambert and Bergin, 1994; Luborsky et al., 1975; McConnaughty, 1987; Wampold et al., 1997). A consistent finding in this research is that the single most predictive factor for a successful outcome in therapy is the nature of the therapeutic relationship. Therapists who are perceived, by the client, as warm, empathic, honest, respectful, non-judgmental and who maintain clear and safe boundaries produce the most successful outcomes irrespective of theoretical orientation. This is known as the 'Dodo Bird Effect' after the character in 'Alice's

Adventures in Wonderland' who declaims that 'everyone has won and all must have prizes' (Carroll, 1962: p412) when judging a race in which it was impossible to say who had won or even when the race had begun or ended.

There is also a considerable volume of literature and research which examines the impact, both conscious and unconscious, on practitioners working in the field of child sexual abuse (Anderson, 2000; Bankes et al., 1999; Bengis, 1997; Carr, 1989; Erooga, 1994; Farrenkopf, 1992; Furniss, 1983; Ganzarain and Buchele, 1986; Gil and Johnson, 1993; Hackett, 1999; Hackett, 2001; Hopkins, 1998; Justice and Justice, 1993; Kraemer, 1988; Little and Hanby, 1996; Loughlin, 1992; Mintzer, 1996; Mitchell and Melikian, 1995; Morrison, 1990; Pogge and Stone, 1990; Preston-Shoot and Agass, 1990; Reynolds-Mejia and Levitan, 1990; Woods, 1999). Common threads running throughout this body of literature are the high levels of stress and the 'contaminating' effect on practitioners who work in the field of child sexual abuse, often leading to professional 'burnout'.

Any research that purports to examine unconscious processes is beset with problems from the outset. How can we 'prove' that such processes exist if, by their very nature, they are not available to our conscious awareness? And if some thought or feeling enters our conscious awareness how do we know that it was previously stored in some other part of our mind out of conscious awareness? Shevrin et al. (1996) attempt to scientifically demonstrate the existence of unconscious processes drawing on psychodynamic, cognitive and neurophysiological methods, whilst Langs (1999), a prominent psychoanalytic practitioner, teacher and researcher in the USA, claims to have discovered scientific and mathematical verification for the existence of unconscious processes in psychotherapy.

Countertransference

A key concept to aid our understanding of how unconscious processes in therapy affect the therapist is that of 'countertransference'. The term was originally coined by Sigmund Freud (Freud, 1910) and developed by the psychoanalytic and psychodynamic movement throughout the 20th century. More recently other therapeutic disciplines have begun to acknowledge and incorporate the concept into their teaching, practice and research (Baron et al., 1992; Bentovim, 1998; Curtis, 1991; Epstein, 1994; Goldfried, 1982; Weiner, 1975).

In order to understand the concept of countertransference it might be helpful to explore the concept of 'transference', as they are essentially two sides of the same coin. Transference is what is going on, primarily at an unconscious level, for the client whereas countertransference is what is going on for the therapist, often, again, out of conscious awareness. Laplanche and Pontalis define transference as:

A process of actualisation of unconscious wishes. Transference uses specific objects and operates in the framework of a specific relationship established with these objects. Its context par excellence is the analytic situation. In the transference, infantile prototypes re-emerge and are experienced with a strong sensation of immediacy. As a rule what psycho-analysts mean by the unqualified use of the term 'transference' is transference during treatment. Classically, the transference is acknowledged to be the terrain on which all the basic problems of a given analysis play themselves out: the establishment, modalities, interpretation and resolution of the transference are in fact what defines the cure.

(Laplanche 1973 p455)

The term was originally used by Sigmund Freud in his work with Josef Breuer on the causes of hysteria (Freud and Breuer, 1895/1991) and he initially viewed it as a hindrance to therapy, something that needed to be eliminated before the real work of therapy could begin. The event, which prompted the discovery of transference was that during the course of the therapeutic treatment of Anna O, the patient had fallen in love with the physician, Breuer. Unlike Breuer, who decided to terminate his treatment of Anna O believing it to be unethical to continue, Freud wanted to understand this phenomenon as he was noticing that several of his female patients were demonstrating 'anxious affections' for him (Hinshelwood, 1989 p447). Freud reached the conclusion that these affections were being unconsciously transferred onto him from earlier figures in the patient's life (Freud, 1905).

Freud subsequently realised, through his 'unsuccessful' treatment with Dora, who had angrily withdrawn from therapy with Freud, that patients' transferences could be either positive (love/eros) or negative (hate/thanatos) and represented some kind of re-enactment in the therapist/patient relationship of earlier relationships or fantasies in the patient's life:

Freud could see how Dora's negative transference recapitulated certain feelings she had previously felt towards a certain Herr K. He (Freud) had in fact known that transference was linked to early traumas in the patient's history. Now he had a real lesson in how the trauma is relived, re-experienced, re-enacted, as real life – in the transference to the analyst.

(Hinshelwood, 1989 p448)

Throughout the 20th century psychodynamic and psychoanalytic researchers and practitioners have been examining, developing and redefining the concept of transference. Transference is generally held to be:

- An *unconscious* process emanating from a client in therapy whereby the client transfers to the therapist their way of relating to others.
- A resonance of childhood experiences.
- A significant part of the therapeutic process.

The 'classical' (Freudian) definition of countertransference is, according to Laplanche and Pontalis:

The whole of the analyst's unconscious reactions to the individual and especially to the analyst's own transference.

(Laplanche and Pontalis, 1973 p92)

Laplanche and Pontalis go on to acknowledge that there is a considerable amount of disagreement within the psychoanalytic community as to how broadly or narrowly the concept is defined and the consequent implications as to how to deal with it. This lack of agreement may be understood, in part, in the context of the fact that Freud never really fully developed the concept. In fact Freud made only four brief references to countertransference in all of his writings (Freud, 1910, 1915, 1931, 1937).

Towards the end of the 1940s and during the 1950s there was a surge of interest in the concept of countertransference. What is considered to be a landmark in the development of the concept was Paula Heimann's brief but concise paper (Heimann, 1950), where she stated that analysts feel afraid of, and guilty about, their emotional responses to their patients and attempt to overcome these feelings through detachment: by which she implied that psychoanalysts adhering to Freud's notion of maintaining an attitude of benign neutrality are demonstrating. Heimann supported the notion that:

The analyst's counter-transference is an instrument of research into the patient's unconscious ... my impression is that it has not been sufficiently stressed that it (the patient/analyst relationship) is a relationship between two persons.

(Heimann, 1950: p81)

Heimann suggested that the analyst's unconscious perception of the patient is 'more acute and in advance of his conscious conception of the situation' (Heimann, 1950: p82) but was cautious to stress the need not to 'impute to his patient what belongs to himself' (Heimann, 1950: p83) and advocated that the analyst works through his or her infantile conflicts and anxieties by means of their own analysis. The important point that Heimann was making and which departed from the traditional view is that the countertransference is not merely a phenomenon, which the analyst should be aware of and keep in check, but that it could offer useful insights into the patient's unconscious material. This echoes Freud's shift from initially seeing the client's transference as an obstacle to the therapy to coming to view it as central to the therapy.

Since Heimann's paper there has been a growing acknowledgement within the psychoanalytic and psychodynamic community (Epstein and Feiner, 1979; Gorkin, 1987; Little, 1951/1981; Maroda, 1991; Money-Kyrle, 1956 in Spillius, 1988; Racker, 1953/1968; Tsiantis et al., 1996; Winnicott, 1949/1958) that the narrow classical definition (Reich, 1960) of countertransference is less useful than the 'totalistic' definition: i.e. the totality of the therapist's response to the client including conscious and unconscious feelings, thoughts and behaviour. As Epstein and Feiner note:

> *We see, for instance, an increasing convergence and integration of the intrapsychic and interpersonal field orientations, points of view which were, some years back, evidently polarised.*
>
> (Epstein and Feiner, 1979 p19)

Figure 1, adapted from Marshall (1979: p416), depicts the 'totalistic' definition of countertransference.

In Figure 1 it can be seen that countertransference reactions can be broken down into four categories:

1. Countertransference which is an unconscious reaction to the client.
2. Countertransference which a conscious reaction to the client.
3. Countertransference which is unconscious but originates in the therapist.
4. Countertransference which is conscious but originates in the therapist.

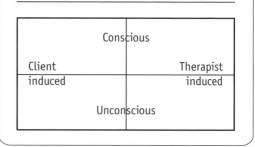

Figure 1: Totalistic definition of countertransference.

It is recognised that the divisions between unconscious and conscious or between therapist induced and client induced countertransferences are not so rigid as Figure 1 depicts. For example, when the client's transference originates in a childhood experience which is similar to that of the therapist then, although the countertransference will be primarily client induced, there may be elements of unresolved conflicts in the therapist which heighten their countertransference.

The totalistic definition of countertransference is, then, the total response of the therapist within the therapeutic frame. This includes the way the therapist decorates the consulting room; the conscious and unconscious elements which the therapist brings to the therapeutic relationship; those elements which are specific to each specific therapeutic relationship and those which are general such as attitudes, beliefs, values, mannerisms etc.

The concept has grown from being considered a hindrance to the therapeutic task to being viewed as a phenomenon that is a hindrance if it remains unconscious but that can enhance the therapy if it is brought into conscious awareness in the therapist (Curtis, 1991; Epstein and Feiner, 1979; Fox and Carey, 1999; Giovacchini, 1989; Glickauf-Hughes, 1997; Gorkin, 1987; Langs, 1992 and 1999; Maroda, 1991; Raichelson et al., 1997; Smith, 1991; Tsiantis et al., 1996).

Aims of the research

Work with young people who sexually abuse is a developing area of practice and research. The problem of young people who commit sexual abuse had received scant attention prior to the proliferation of interest in adults who

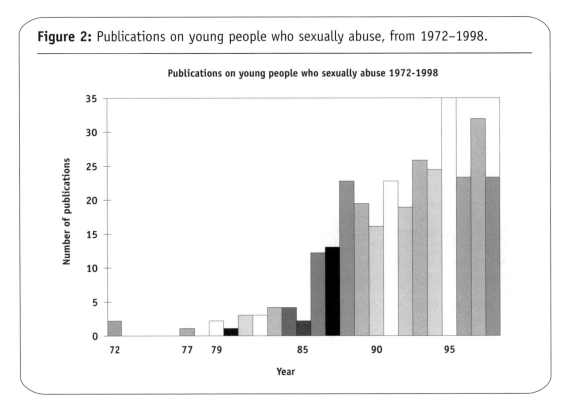

Figure 2: Publications on young people who sexually abuse, from 1972–1998.

Publications on young people who sexually abuse 1972-1998

sexually abuse in the United States and Canada in the early 1980's. The earliest study devoted specifically to young people who sexually abuse was Doshay's research (Doshay, 1943) over a six year period which examined the demographic and personality characteristics of 256 boys who came to his attention, as a forensic adolescent psychiatrist, by virtue of their appearance for sexual offences in the Juvenile Court in New York between 1928 and 1934. As part of his research Doshay also conducted a six year follow up study to determine the proportion of boys who were subsequently reconvicted or recharged with sexual offences. Previous studies had tended to subsume juvenile sexual offenders within larger samples of deviant youths/adults or had considered only small samples (Cook, 1934; Healy, 1917a, 1917b; Healy and Bronner, 1926; Healy et al., 1929: (quoted in Doshay 1943), Healy and Alexander, 1935; Healy and Bronner, 1936: (quoted in Doshay, 1943), Glueck, 1934; Waggoner and Boyd, 1941: (quoted in Barbaree et al., 1993)). Since the Doshay research and up until the 1980s there were few studies regarding young people who sexually abuse (Atcheson and Williams, 1954; Groth, 1977; Lewis et al., 1979: quoted in Barbaree et al., 1993; Markey, 1950;

Maclay, 1960; Reiss, 1960; Roberts et al., 1969, 1973; Shoor et al., 1966). However, as work with adult perpetrators of sexual abuse progressed, there was an increasing awareness that a significant proportion (over 50%) of these clients had begun their abusive behaviour as children or adolescents (Abel et al., 1986; Freeman-Longo, 1983; Ryan and Lane, 1991) and a complementary increase in studies into this client group took place. Craig et al. (1999) have compiled a comprehensive bibliography of research studies and literature about young people who sexually abuse from 1972 to 1998 (see Figure 2). They found that from 1972 to 1985 (13 years) there were only 22 published works in this field. From 1986 to 1998 (12 years), however, there were 292 (see Figure 3).

In the USA and Canada this is reflected by the burgeoning of therapeutic services for children and adolescents who sexually abuse. Fay Honey Knopp (1982) identified twenty-two specialist therapeutic services for young people who sexually abuse in the USA in 1982. By 1988 this had increased to 645 (Knopp and Stevenson, 1989; cited in Ryan and Lane, 1991: p21) and by 1992 to 755 (Knopp et al., 1992).

In Britain however, despite a similar increase in awareness that sexual abuse by children and

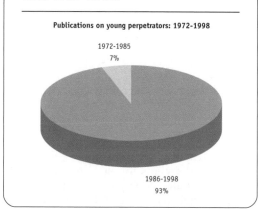

Figure 3: Percentage of publications on young people who sexually abuse, from 1972–1998.

Publications on young perpetrators: 1972-1998

1972-1985
7%

1986-1998
93%

adolescents was a significant problem (NCH, 1992, 1996), a similar burgeoning of therapeutic services for this client group has not occurred (Masson, 1997). In the USA these services are largely cognitive behavioural in approach (Araji, 1997; Barbaree et al., 1993; Ertl and McNamara, 1997; Gil and Johnson, 1993; Hoghughi et al., 1997; Hunter, 1995; Knopp et al., 1992; O'Donohue and Geer, 1992; Perry and Orchard, 1992; Ryan, 1999; Steen and Monnette, 1989) as are those services that do exist in Britain (Bentovim et al., 1991; Calder et al., 1997; Erooga and Masson, 1999; Leheup and Myers, 1999; Morrison et al., 1994). As Leheup and Myers state:

> *The abusive behaviour becomes the prime definer of that young person which can only be corrected through cognitive behavioural approaches.*
> (Leheup and Myers, 1999 p175)

Thus, breaking the 'cycle' of abuse, confronting and challenging the young persons' 'distorted cognitions' which have enabled them to justify the abuse, helping them to empathise with their victims, preparing a relapse prevention plan, all became the stock-in-trade for those practitioners working with this client group, normally within a group work context (Araji, 1997; Barbaree et al., 1993; Calder et al., 1997; Calder, 1999; Gil and Johnson, 1993; Hoghughi et al., 1997; Hunter, 1995; O'Donohue and Geer, 1992; Perry and Orchard, 1992; Ryan and Lane, 1991; Steen and Monnette, 1989). As with the adult population, little attention has been paid to the unconscious processes, which were taking place in the work. Exceptions

to this are Leheup and Myers (1999), Gil and Johnson (1993), and Bankes et al. (1999). As Gil and Johnson say:

> *Therapists may have a range of countertransference responses including fear, incompetency, arousal, overidentification, rescuing, helplessness, anger, overcontrol and victimisation. In addition, therapists working with child abuse may feel isolated, in despair and paranoid about abuse invading their own families.*
> (Gil and Johnson, 1993 p325)

To my knowledge no studies have been undertaken on the detailed analysis of practice in this field. My research therefore aimed to conduct such an analysis paying particular attention to the practitioner's experience of working therapeutically with these clients, focusing on their cognitive/attitudinal, affective/emotional and behavioural responses in the therapeutic situation, in an attempt to discover whether unconscious processes are present and if so how this might affect their practice.

Methodology

I adopted a descriptive, case study approach that is hypothesis generating as opposed to an empirical, theory generating approach. It is largely a qualitative study, though there is a quantitative aspect to it, and is based on Glaser and Strauss' grounded theory approach (Glaser and Strauss, 1968).

I used three methods to gather my data:

1. Each practitioner completed a questionnaire detailing demographic information such as gender, qualifications and experience.
2. I conducted a qualitative and quantitative analysis of one videotaped recording of 10 UK-based practitioners' therapeutic 1:1 sessions with young people who sexually abuse. (Only 9 have been completed at the time of writing.) In order to eliminate bias the videotape was one that the practitioner had not known was going to be used for research.
3. Following the analysis of the videotapes, each practitioner was interviewed. The interviews followed a semi-structured format and focused on the practitioner's views of the impact, on them, of working with young perpetrators in general and with the impact of working with the client in the videotape.

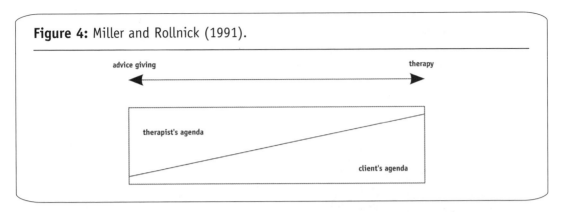

Figure 4: Miller and Rollnick (1991).

Findings

As previously stated in this chapter the most common approach used by practitioners in their therapeutic work with young people who sexually abuse is cognitive behavioural therapy. Most cognitive behavioural theoretical and practice guidelines, either generic or sex abuse specific, do not advocate an exploration of unconscious processes in the therapeutic relationship. Interestingly, however, the practitioners interviewed as part of this research, as well as other practitioners who I have discussed this with in my professional role, do not dispute the existence of these unconscious processes. They are, indeed, keen to acknowledge and explore these processes once the question has been raised with them. In the everyday practice of the majority of professionals in this field this is, however, the exception rather than the rule.

My concern is that this omission may lead to practice that meets the needs of the therapist rather than that of the client. The implication of this is that, if unconscious processes are not explored and brought to conscious awareness through clinical supervision, *any* approach, whether cognitive behavioural or otherwise, is, at best, not a therapeutic intervention but an educative one. This is demonstrated in Figure 4 by Miller and Rollnick (1991) who pioneered the use of Motivational Interviewing for addictive behaviours. At worst, it may provide a vehicle for the therapist to unconsciously abuse the client under the conscious guise of therapeutic imperatives.

The Sample

The practitioners in the research came from a wide variety of theoretical disciplines. Table 1 shows the participants' self-reported theoretical approaches to work with any type of client. Their approach to working with children and young people who sexually abuse is shown in Table 2. (Note: T3 did not complete a questionnaire and declined to be interviewed after the videotape had been transcribed. I

Table 1: Practitioners general theoretical approach

T1	Brief therapy
T2	Cognitive behavioural therapy
T4	Psychodynamic
T5	Cognitive behavioural therapy
T6	Cognitive behavioural therapy
T7	Eclectic: Psychodynamic; Person-centred; Gestalt
T8	Eclectic: Cognitive behavioural: Systemic; Psychodynamic
T9	Psychodynamic
T10	Systemic social constructionist
T11	Integrative

Table 2: Practitioners' theoretical approaches to work with young people who sexually abuse

T1	Non-directive play therapy
T2	Cognitive behavioural therapy
T4	Cognitive behavioural therapy
T5	Cognitive behavioural therapy
T6	Cognitive behavioural therapy
T7	Person-centred
T8	Eclectic: Cognitive behavioural: Systemic; Psychodynamic
T9	Psychodynamic
T10	Systemic social constructionist
T11	Integrative with a leaning towards cognitive behavioural

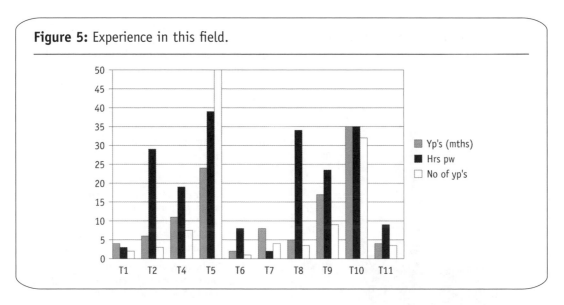

Figure 5: Experience in this field.

agreed, therefore, not to use the video transcription as part of the qualitative analysis of the research.)

The participants ages ranged from 29 to 59 with a mean age of 39.6. Three of them were men and seven were women. In terms of ethnicity nine of the participants were White European and one was Black African.

Eight of the participants worked in specialist community projects. Of the remaining two, one worked in a young offenders institution and the other worked in a specialist residential facility.

Figure 5 shows the degree of variation in the participants' experience in this field. The 1st column for each therapist represents how many months they had been working with this client group. The 2nd column indicates how many hours per week (including administration, recording and meetings) each participant spends on their work with this client group. The 3rd column shows how many of these clients the participant had worked with at the time the videotape had been made.

Quantitative results

Part of the analysis of the videotapes included a breakdown of how many words were spoken by the therapist and the client, how many times the therapist interrupted the client and how many times the therapist did not 'pick up' on a new theme introduced by the client. Robert Langs et al. (1991) have suggested that these aspects of the therapeutic encounter indicate

that unconscious countertransference reactions are operating. In other words, the more the therapist speaks, interrupts or does not pick up on the client's new themes, the greater the likelihood that the therapist is acting out a countertransference.

At the time of writing only the word count has been completed. Table 3 shows the percentage of words spoken by each therapist in their respective videotapes and Figure 6 shows how many words were spoken by each therapist and their respective client. Apart from T7, it is worthy of note that the therapists speak more than their clients indicating, according to Langs et al. (1991), the existence of unconscious countertransference reactions in the sessions. In the case of T7 it can be seen from Figure 6 that T7 speaks just over 4000 words (in a 60 minute session) and that the client speaks just over 6000 words. Given that

Table 3: Percentage of words spoken by each therapist.

T1	74%
T2	79%
T3	67%
T4	76%
T5	68%
T7	40%
T8	64%
T9	56%
T10	51%
T11	55%

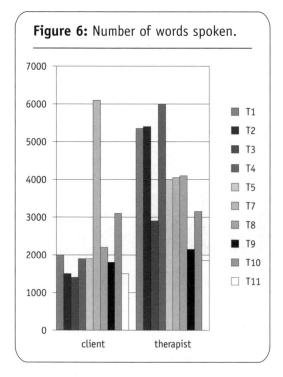

Figure 6: Number of words spoken.

the average amount of words spoken in all of the videotapes (in an equivalent 60 minute session) is 4010 by the therapists and 2376 by the clients, then it can be seen that T7 spoke the average number of words of all participants. T7's client by contrast speaks nearly three times the average of all the clients in the videotapes. Apart from T7 however, the fact that the therapists speak more than the client would tend to suggest that it is the therapists' agendas which are dominating in the sessions and that therefore, according to Miller and Rollnick (see Figure 4), these are educative rather than therapeutic sessions.

Qualitative results: recognition of unconscious processes

Firstly, did the practitioners that I interviewed believe that such processes exist and impact on their professional and/or personal lives? The short answer is yes.

All of the participants recognised their own unconscious processes operating in this work and how these were acted out in ways, which, to varying degrees, were unhelpful to the client. This was particularly evident when I asked the participant to comment on what they thought was going on for them in the short video clips of their session that I showed them

as part of the interview. In other words, inviting the practitioner to reflect on their own practice gave them an insight into how they could improve their practice by paying more attention to these unconscious processes. Some also acknowledged that the work had a contaminating effect in their personal lives.

The following comments made by the therapists during their interviews with me illustrate this point.

> *Who are these sessions for? That's the real question I think, I really need to think about that. You know I've missed quite a lot there, I've missed a hell of a lot of what Kevin was saying and I think the agendas that I was carrying into those sessions were the all important ones really. I need to check that.*

> *I think now that he was showing me a confused and fragmented part of himself but I missed that because I was too tied up in being brilliant.*

> *I thought at the time that I was beating my head against a brick wall but actually listening to the video again, listening to this bit with you, there was something in his voice, something quite strident. He was defending his position.*

> *I think it was definitely something that was going on very unconsciously, well actually just watching it, it's kind of like a real flirtation kind of thing going on here.*

> *Yeah I don't know why I said that. It was like you know, yeah probably I had my own little agenda there so I think I was going by that. Seeing the video, seeing the video now it's like 'oh no! I should have carried on talking about the girls.'*

> *. . . after a few weeks of working here my first son was coming to stay with us at weekends, you know? They always used to muck about in the bedroom and also mucking about in the bed . . . I said 'what are you doing on the bed?' and he looked at me and said 'playing'. I said 'no I don't want you to play on the bed, I don't want you to play with the bedroom door shut' you know? And afterwards I thought 'gosh this is work'.*

So, what are these unconscious processes and how are they acted out in the therapy? They seemed to fall into one of three categories:

- feeling victimised
- feeling persecutory
- a need to rescue

This can be understood as an example of Steven Karpman's model of the 'Drama Triangle' (Karpman, 1968, see Figure 7).

Karpman analysed fairy tales to highlight how these three 'roles' of victim, rescuer and

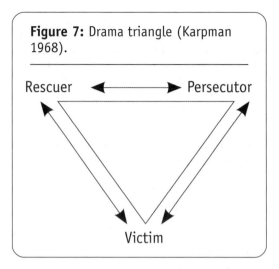

Figure 7: Drama triangle (Karpman 1968).

persecutor, are played out interchangeably in real life situations as well as in the therapeutic relationship:

> In the Pied Piper, the hero begins as Rescuer of the city and Persecutor of the rats, then becomes Victim to the Persecutor mayor's double-cross (fee withheld), and in revenge switches to the Persecutor of the city's children. The mayor switches from Victim (of rats), to Rescuer (hiring the Pied Piper), to Persecutor (double-cross), to Victim (his children dead). The children switch from Persecuted Victims (rats) to Rescued Victims, to Victims Persecuted by their Rescuer.
>
> (Karpman, 1968, p40)

Karpman proposed that we unconsciously 'act out' the roles in the drama triangle both in everyday life and the therapeutic situation. He also proposed that bringing these unconscious dynamics into conscious awareness through therapy enabled clients to step out of what he calls an 'errant life script' (Karpman, 1968 p39).

'Victimised' reactions

Typical of the countertransference reactions experienced by the participants were feelings of: anxiety, guilt, confusion, frustration, hurt, depression, helplessness, isolation, fear, incompetence, inadequacy, loss of control and, perhaps most significantly, an enormous sense of responsibility for ensuring that their client did not abuse again.

> I find that I feel devalued and I don't know where the root of that is other than myself.

> Probably the deeper part is about an insecurity to do with 'is this any good, is this having some effect?' And feeling responsible for having some dramatic effect on someone's behaviour, unrealistically but nevertheless a very real feeling.

> When he started his first session I thought, gosh, you know, he's really intimidating me.

> I think you can get shocked sometimes, like a real kick in the stomach.

As an unconscious attempt to defend themselves against these feelings of victimisation, the therapists experienced either persecutory or rescuing feelings.

'Persecutory' reactions

The persecutory feelings were irritation, resentment, anger, dislike and competitiveness. These would be acted out by the therapist being either:

- over-controlling:
  > In order to not let myself get too vulnerable I have to take charge and be directive.
- blaming:
  > I just thought 'how could you do this?' You know? 'How can you do this ... to a 7 year-old girl? She trusted you and you knew, you must've known what you were doing. There is no way you can blame the child for it, you are older and much wiser.
- or confrontational:
  > I was completely pissed off with the young person and I'd had enough and I thought 'I'm doing all the work here' ... thinking back on it, I know that I responded in exactly the way he had pushed and pushed and pushed to see how far he could push the boundaries. So I behaved like mum or I behaved like a teacher or any of these other people who have given him a negative response.

Rescuing reactions

The rescuing feelings were sadness and concern:

> I felt sadness when I first met him, I thought 'you poor boy'.

These were acted out by:

- collusion:
  > I think maybe I was anxious that he might end being upset and I don't want to hear him being upset.
- by overidentification:
  > Yes, I guess probably there is a bit of, you know, I could be John sitting there sometimes and getting quite angry (in professionals meetings). Perhaps I take some of his feelings with me.
- or by trying harder:
  > You become practically involved in their lives as well as emotionally, it's extra to the therapeutic relationship.

These reactions were frequently complemented by persecutory feelings towards social services or the client's parent.

> *What the hell have social services been doing? So let's rectify this terrible mistake that social services have made, you know, charge in on your white horse . . . do the business.*

> *I just felt a sense of who's guiding this kid, who is actually saying at this crucial time 'look, this is what you've got to do if you want to get anything decent out of your exams'? It felt like a precious moment and nobody was standing next to him helping him to appreciate how important the moment was. Cos that's why I'd asked about who is talking to you about this stuff and I guess there isn't anybody really.*

Specific to the client group

Most of the therapists felt that there were unconscious processes which were different to their experience of working with other clients.

> *Of course it impacts on your practice. I mean these are emotions that you have that are very negative ones.*

> *The sex offenders take more energy, it takes me longer to get into in my head, I have to do more preparation work before the session begins.*

> *To me it's the dangerousness of it, I think the issues are much more intense, I think the emotions are more intense.*

The most common countertransference reaction associated with working with this client group was a sense of feeling responsible for ensuring that the client does not sexually abuse again. This is demonstrated in the following case study.

Case study

'Joe' was a fourteen-year-old boy who had been sexually abused as a child. Joe had also been physically abused by his father. Joe began sexually abusing his five-year-old step-sister when he was ten and his sister and her friend, both aged 8 when he was eleven. He had been referred to a specialist project by social services for a risk assessment. Joe's attendance at the project had been very intermittent. The videotape I looked at was session five.

The therapist, 'Adam', qualified as a social worker five years previously and had worked as a social worker in a Child Protection team for approximately four years, prior to coming to work in the project. He had also, during the latter part of that period, worked therapeutically with adult perpetrators of sexual abuse. Adam had no formal qualifications in therapeutic work. He described his theoretical orientation to working with young people who sexually abuse as 'cognitive behavioural'.

From an analysis of the videotape three salient issues emerged:

- Adam is angry about Joe's intermittent attendance and acts this out punitively toward Joe.
- Adam appears to be very anxious to complete the assessment and hurries the process.
- Adam strongly imposes his agenda on the session leaving no emotional or therapeutic space for Joe.

From the interview with Adam it became clear that this analysis was accurate and had been operating largely outside of his conscious awareness. The interview enabled Adam and I to make some sense of this:

- Adam was fostered as a child causing him to feel, unconsciously, rejection and abandonment which has led to a need to prove himself professionally. He was experiencing an inordinate sense of responsibility to 'get it right' in this case.
- It has also led to a close identification with children who have been separated from their parents or who have been the victims of abuse.

So when the client, who had disclosed his own experience of being abused to Adam in their early sessions, began to miss sessions, this resonated with Adam at an unconscious level. He felt that Joe 'owes me one' and not honouring this caused Adam to feel let down (abandoned and rejected) by Joe:

> *In the second session he told me about him being abused, I've been supportive when he's told me that. And I don't know whether this is true Nick but I don't know whether I felt a sense of 'he owes me one'. I'd held his hand through the crap that he'd just told me, and I'd respected it, so where was the respect for me and my feelings in this?*

This, in turn, then activated Adam's fear that he is not a 'good enough' practitioner and that if Joe abuses again it will be due to Adam's failure as a therapist. Adam expands further on this theme of the enormity of the responsibility that he feels and the apparent impossibility of making a difference:

I'm angry because, all the things about the personal stuff and the professional stuff, all the things about my professionalism not being good enough, but there's also fear there for me. Fear that if this kid continues to abuse, but also the implications of that for my professionalism.

Adam described the feelings which this gave rise to as 'anxious', 'deflated', and then 'angry'. These feelings were largely unconscious in the videotaped session.

But also I talked about being punitive. I think when you're angry, particularly, or when there's this pressure to get something done, to get information almost, then you can come across as a bit punitive with young people. And I think that's specific to this work because very often the young people present as victims, and they may actually use that against you. So very often kids will come and will set themselves up as a victim first and foremost, without taking on any responsibility for their own role as a victimiser. And if there is something particularly sad that you've read about their lives, then you can fall into that trap. There may be things from your own personal life that you can identify with these young people. I'm particularly conscious of it because of my background because a lot of these kids are in foster-care.

So, for Adam, empathising with the client carries with it the danger of minimising the behaviour or being manipulated by the client. In order to defend against this Adam is conscious that he can become somewhat punitive towards his clients. Unconsciously, perhaps, Adam is also using his anger to defend against his own sense of abandonment, resulting from his own childhood experience of being taken into care by the social services department, that this client evokes in him.

Another source of Adam's anger was an intrusive thought which Joe had evoked in him. Adam recognised that this intrusive thought was so powerful for him because it involved a 'helpless' child and a neglectful and irresponsible mother. Unconsciously it seems likely that this is part of the cause of Adam's countertransference reaction and is linked to his own personal history of a neglectful parent figure and his sense of himself as a helpless child who is unworthy of the parent's love or protection. He experiences this in the present as a need to demonstrate his effectiveness as a professional. When this effectiveness is threatened by a client a sense of being 'out of control' and 'not good enough' kick in. In order to defend against these feelings he becomes

angry with the client and acts this out punitively:

. . . but I do recognise that in myself I have begun to become punitive and I don't think I should have been. Retrospectively I don't think I should have been. I think, thinking about it now, it's about my anger it's just struck me that I was carrying the responsibility but maybe unconsciously I was feeling that all the time.

Adam also began to connect this with his sense of needing to demonstrate his effectiveness:

You're constantly questioning your own abilities. Talking specifically about Joe, the times he wasn't turning up was, for me, about him. We're not engaging, in a way I'm not important.

By reflecting on unconscious processes in his work Adam was able to bring to conscious awareness the insight that certain issues from his own childhood experiences were being re-activated in his work with Joe. These were then being acted out by Adam, again unconsciously, in the way he carried out the work with his client to the likely detriment of the therapeutic task.

In terms of Karpman's drama triangle Adam was initially Joe's rescuer. When Joe began to miss sessions Adam felt victimised by Joe. He began to question his abilities as a therapist and to feel that if Joe abused again this would be partly, or even wholly, due to Adam's perceived inadequacy as a therapist. This in turn made Adam angry which he then acted out by becoming the persecutor of Joe.

Conclusion

The heightening of these dynamics in Child Protection teams has been described by Alan Carr (1989) and others (Justice and Justice, 1993; Lamb, 1996; Mintzer, 1996; Reynolds-Mejia and Levitan, 1990; Richardson, 1999; Sanders and Ladwa-Thomas, 1997). So it is not surprising that they also can be seen to be operating in work with children and young people who sexually abuse. What I believe is different though is the more acute sense of feeling victimised in the work and particularly the sense of an urgent need or responsibility to ensure that they don't abuse again. This leads, in my view, to an increased risk of the therapist unconsciously acting out these countertransferences. This could be by way of using somewhat over-controlling or persecutory interventions towards the client, the parents or professionals. Or it could be by way of colluding, trying harder or overidentifying with the client, the parents or professionals. In order to prevent this it seems to me that it is essential in this work that we:

- Question ourselves and each other as to why we are doing the work.
- Recognise and acknowledge what is going on for us as practitioners at an emotional level.
- Explore what this might mean for us or for our clients.
- Examine whether these processes are being replayed in our work with clients, in supervision, or with our colleagues.

Concepts such as splitting, projection, projective identification, transference and countertransference help us to evaluate whether our reactions to our clients (emotional, cognitive, behavioural and somatic) can be attributed to the client or ourselves or a mixture of both. For psychodynamic and psychotherapeutic practitioners an awareness of these processes is acknowledged to be crucial in order to prevent them from being acted out in the therapy in unhelpful, anti-therapeutic or dysfunctional ways as well as to assist the practitioners in their assessment of the client's 'inner world' and therapeutic needs.

Cognitive behavioural therapy can help the client to understand the pattern of their offending, the emotional triggers to their offending and a sense of how their offending impacts on their victims. What it does not address is the unconscious, habitual and dysfunctional ways of relating to others and the personal causes in their own histories that have contributed towards their offending. Including an understanding of these processes within a cognitive behavioural framework could assist both the therapist and the client towards successful therapeutic outcomes. These concepts are, however, complex. They should only be applied when they are fully understood, both intellectually and experientially, by the therapist and his or her supervisor.

Finally I would like to share an experience I had with a client recently where I suggested he listen to a comedy radio programme called 'I'm sorry I haven't a clue!' on his way home, as I was intending to do myself. I don't usually say this sort of thing to clients so I wondered why I'd mentioned it. I wondered why I wanted to give him something, why I wanted

him to like me. Then it struck me that the unconscious message was much more direct. This was a client who distrusted me, who wanted me to fail in the therapy (unconsciously) to prove to himself that he was right not to trust anybody. The following week I shared with him the feeling that he evoked in me – a sense of being unable to help him in any way: I'm sorry I haven't a clue. This turned out to be one of those pivotal moments in therapy. This client has, since my acknowledgement of how he made me feel, been able to trust, for the first time in his life, another human being and open up his deepest concerns and worries, which we have begun to work on. It seems to me that this is a good example of paying attention to, and understanding, that one's own countertransference can be used to beneficial purpose in the therapy.

Acknowledgement

I would like to take this opportunity to express my sincere thanks and appreciation to all of the practitioners who have been brave enough to let me scrutinise their work and for their openness and honesty in our interviews.

References

Abel, G. G., Mittelman, M. S. and Becker, J. B. (1985) Sex Offenders: Results of Assessment and Recommendations for Treatment. in Ben-Aaron, H., Hucker, S. and Webster, C. (Eds.) *Clinical Criminology: The Assessment and Treatment of Criminal Behaviour*. Toronto: M. and M. Graphics.

Anderson, D. (2000) Coping Strategies and Burnout Among Veteran CP Workers. *Child Abuse and Neglect*. 24(6): 869–78.

Araji, S. K. (1997) *Sexually Aggressive Children: Coming to Understand Them*. NY: Sage Publications.

Atcheson, J. D. and Williams, D. C. (1954) A Study of Juvenile Sex Offenders. *American Journal of Orthopsychiatry*. 111: 366–70.

Bankes, N., Daniels, K. and Quartly, C. (1999) Placement Provision and Placement Decisions: Resources and Processes. in Erooga, M. and Masson, H. (Eds.) *Children and Young People Who Sexually Abuse Others: Challenges and Responses*. London: Routledge.

Barbaree, H. E., Marshall, W. L. and Hudson, S. M. (Eds.) (1993) *The Juvenile Sex Offender*. NY: Guildford Press.

Baron, W., Eagle, M. N. and Wolitzky, D. L. (Eds.) (1992) *Interface of Psychoanalysis and Psychology.* USA: American Psychological Association.

Beckett, R. (1994) Cognitive-Behavioural Treatment of Sex Offenders. in Morrison, T. et al. (Eds.) *Sexual Offending Against Children: Assessment and Treatment of Male Abusers.* London: Routledge.

Bengis, S. M. (1997) Personal and Interpersonal Issues for Staff Working with Sexually Abusive Youth. in Edmunds, S. (Ed.) *Impact: Working with Sexual Abusers.* Vermont: Safer Society Press.

Bentovim, A., Vizard, E. and Hollows, A. (1991) *Children and Young People as Abusers: An Agenda for Action.* London: National Children's Bureau.

Bentovim, A. (1998) A Full Circle: Psychodynamic Understanding and Systems Theory. *Journal of Family Therapy.* 20: 113–22.

Beutler, L., Machado, P. and Neufeldt, S. (1994) Therapist Variables. in Bergin, A. and Garfield, S. (Eds.) *Handbook of Psychotherapy and Behaviour Change.* NY: John Wiley.

Blanchard, G. T. (1995) *The Difficult Connection: The Therapeutic Relationship in Sex Offender Treatment.* Vermont: Safer Society Press.

Bowlby, J. (1977) The Making and Breaking of Affectional Bonds. *British Journal of Psychiatry.* 130: 201–431.

Bowlby, J. (1979) The Making and Breaking of Affectional Bonds. London: Tavistock Publications.

Calder, M. C., Hanks, H. and Epps, K. J. (1997) Juveniles and Children Who Sexually Abuse. Dorset: Russell House Publishing.

Calder, M. C. (Ed.) (1999) *Working With Young People Who Sexually Abuse: New Pieces of the Jigsaw Puzzle.* Dorset: Russell House Publishing.

Carr, A. (1989) Countertransference to Families Where Child Abuse has Occurred. *The Association for Family Therapy.* 11(1): 87–97.

Carroll, L. (1962) *Alice's Adventures in Wonderland.* London: Penguin Books (originally published in 1865).

Cook, E. B. (1934) Cultural Marginality in Sexual Delinquency. *American Journal of Sociology.* 39: 493–500: cited in Barbaree, H. E., Marshall, W. L. and Hudson, S. M. (Eds.) (1993) *The Juvenile Sex Offender.* NY: Guilford Press. 10.

Craig, K. S., Smith, C. J., Hayler, B. and Pardie, P. L. (1999) *A Comprehensive Bibliography of Scholarly Research and Literature Relating to Juvenile Sex Offenders.* USA: Dept of Justice.

Curtis, R. (Ed.) (1991) *The Relational Self.* NY: Guilford Press.

Doshay, L. (1943) *The Boy Sex Offender and His Later Career.* NY: Grune and Stratton.

Edmunds, S. B. (Ed.) (1997) *Impact: Working with Sexual Abusers.* Vermont: Safer Society Press.

Epstein, S. (1994) Integration of the Cognitive Psychodynamic Unconscious. *American Psychologist.* 49(8): 709–24.

Epstein, L. and Feiner, A. (Eds.) (1979) *Counter Transference: The Therapist's Contribution to the Therapeutic Situation.* NY: Jason Aronson.

Erooga, M. (1994) Where the Professional Meets the Personal. in Morrison, T. et al. (Eds.) *Sexual Offending Against Children: Assessment and Treatment of Male Abusers.* London: Routledge.

Erooga, M. and Masson, H. (Eds.) (1999) *Children and Young People Who Sexually Abuse Others: Challenges and Responses.* London: Routledge.

Ertl, M. A. and McNamara, J. R. (1997) Treatment of Juvenile Sex Offenders: A Review of the Literature. *Child and Adolescent Social Work Journal.* 14(3): 199–221.

Farrenkopf, T. (1992) What Happens to Therapists Who Work with Sex Offenders. *Journal of Offender Rehabilitation.* 18(3/4): 217–23.

Fine, R. (1985) Countertransference Reactions to the Difficult Patient. in Strean, H. (Ed.) *Psychoanalytic Approaches to the Resistant Client.* NY: Haworth Press.

Fox, R. and Carey, L. (1999) Therapists' Collusion with the Resistance of Rape Survivors. *Clinical Social Work Journal.* 27(2): 185–201.

Freeman-Longo, R. E. (1983) Juvenile Sexual Offences in the History of Adult Rapists and Child Molesters. *International Journal of Offender Therapy and Comparative Criminology.* 27(2): 150–5.

Freud, S. (1905) *A Case of Hysteria.* Standard Edition 7.

Freud, S. (1910) *The Future Prospects of Psychoanalytic Therapy.* Standard Edition 11.

Freud, S. (1912) *Recommendations for Physicians Practicing Psychoanalysis.* Standard Edition 12.

Freud, S. (1914) *Remembering, Repeating and Working Through.* Standard Edition 12.

Freud, S. (1915) *Observations on Transference Love.* Standard Edition 12.

Freud, S. (1931) *Female Sexuality.* Standard Edition 21.

Freud, S. (1937) *Analysis Terminable and Interminable.* Standard Edition 23.

Freud, S. and Breuer, J. (1895/1991) *Studies on Hysteria*. London: Penguin.

Furniss, T. (1983) Mutual Influence and Interlocking Professional: Family Process in the Treatment of CSA. *Child Abuse and Neglect.* 7: 207–23.

Ganzarain, R. and Buchele, B. (1986) Countertransference When Incest is the Problem. *International Journal of Group Psychotherapy.* 36(4): 549–67.

Gil, E. and Johnson, T. C. (Eds.) (1993) *Sexualised Children: Assessment and Treatment of Sexualised Children and Children Who Molest.* USA: Launch Press.

Gil, E. and Johnson, T. C. (1993) Transference and Countertransference. in Gil, E. and Johnson, T. C. (Eds.) *Sexualised Children: Assessment and Treatment of Sexualised Children and Children Who Molest.* USA: Launch Press.

Glaser, B. and Strauss, A. (1968) *The Discovery of Grounded Theory.* London: Weidenfield and Nicholson.

Giovacchini, P. (1989) *Countertransference Triumphs and Catastrophies.* London: Jason Aronson.

Glickauf-Hughes, C. (1997) Teaching Students About Primitive Defences in Supervision. *The Clinical Supervisor.* 15(2): 105–13.

Glueck, S. S. (1934) *One Thousand Juvenile Delinquents.* NY: Harvard University Press.

Goldfried, M. (Ed.) (1982) *Converging Themes in Psychotherapy: Trends in Psychodynamic, Humanistic and Behavioural Practice.* NY: Springer Publishing Co.

Gorkin, M. (1987) *The Uses of Countertransference.* NY: Jason Aronson.

Groth, N. (1977) The Adolescent Sexual Offender and His Prey. *International Journal of Offender Therapy and Comparative Criminology.* 21: 249–54.

Hackett, S. (1999) Empowered Practice with Young People who Sexually Abuse. in Erooga, M. and Masson, H. (Eds.) *Children and Young People Who Sexually Abuse Others: Challenges and Responses.* London: Routledge.

Hackett, S. (2001) The impact of the Work on the Worker: The Personal Context to Work with Young People who Sexually Abuse Others. in Calder, M. C. (Ed.) *Young People Who Sexually Abuse: Building the Evidence-base for Your Practice.* Dorset: Russell House Publishing.

Healy, W. (1917a) *The Individual Delinquent.* Boston: Little, Brown and Co.

Healy, W. (1917b) *Mental Conflicts and Misconduct.* Boston: Little, Brown and Co.

Healey, W. and Alexander, F. (1935) *Roots of Crime.* NY: Knopf.

Healy, W. and Bronner, A. F. (1926) *Delinquents and Criminals.* NY: MacMillan.

Healy, W. and Bronner, A. F. (1936) *New Light on JuvenileDelinquency.* USA: Yale University Press.

Healey, W. et al. (1929) *Reconstructing Behaviour in Youth.* NY: Knopf.

Heimann, P. (1950) On Countertransference. *International Journal of Psychoanalysis.* 31: 81–4.

Hinshelwood, R. D. (1989) *A Dictionary of Kleinian Thought.* London: Free Association Books.

Hoghughi, M. S., Bhate, S. R. and Graham, F. (Eds.) (1997) *Working With Sexually Abusive Adolescents.* London: Sage Publications.

Hopkins, J. (1998) Secondary Abuse. in Bannister, A. (Ed.) *From Hearing to Healing: Working with the Aftermath of Child Sexual Abuse.* (2nd edn) Chichester: John Wiley and Sons.

Hunter, M. (Ed.) (1995) Child Survivors and Perpetrators of Sexual Abuse: Treatment Innovations. NY: Sage Publications.

Jenkins, A. (1990) *Invitations to Responsibility.* Australia: Dulwich Centre Publications.

Jenkins, A. (1995) *Engaging Adolescents Who Sexually Abuse: Workshop Notes Update #7.* (unpublished)

Justice, R. and Justice, B. (1993) Child Abuse and the Law: How to Avoid Being the Abused or the Abuser. *Transactional Analysis Journal.* 23(3): 139–45.

Knopp, F. H. (1982) *Remedial Interventions in Adolescent Sex Offences: Nine Program Descriptions.* Orwell, VT: Safer Society Press.

Knopp, F. H. and Stevenson, W. (1989) *Nationwide Survey of Juvenile and Adult Sex Offender Treatment Programs and Models: 1988.* Orwell, VT: Safer Society Press.

Knopp, F. H., Freeman Longo, R. and Stevenson, W. F. (1992) *Nationwide Survey of Juvenile and Adult Sex Offender Treatment Programmes and Models.* Orwell, VT: Safer Society Press.

Kraemer, S. (1988) Splitting and Stupidity in Child Sexual Abuse. *Psychoanalytic Psychotherapy.* 3(3): 247–57.

Karpman, S. (1968) Fairytales and Script Drama Analysis. *TA Bulletin.* 7(26): 39–43.

Lamb, S. (1996) *The Trouble with Blame: Victims, Perpetrators and Responsibility.* NY: Harvard University Press

Lambert, M. J. and Bergin, A. (1994) The Effectiveness of Psychotherapy. in Bergin, A.

and Garfield, S. (Eds.) *Handbook of Psychotherapy and Behaviour Change.* Chichester: John Wiley.

Langs, R., Badalamenti, A. and Bryant, R. (1991) A Measure of Linear Influence Between Patient and Therapist. *Psychological Reports.* 69: 355–68.

Langs, R. (1992) *Science, Systems and Psychoanalysis.* London: Karnac Books.

Langs, R. (1999) *Psychotherapy and Science.* NY: Sage.

Laplanche, J. and Pontalis, J. (1973) *The Language of Psychoanalysis.* London: Hogarth.

Leheup, R. and Myers, S. (1999) A Description of a Community-based Project to Work with Young People who Sexually Abuse. in Calder, M. C. (Ed.) *Working With Young People Who Sexually Abuse: New Pieces of the Jigsaw Puzzle.* Dorset: Russell House Publishing.

Lewis, E. (1979) Counter-transference Problems in Hospital Practice. *British Journal of Medical Psychology.* 52: 37–42.

Lewis, D. O., Shankok, S. S. and Pincus, J. H. (1979) Juvenile Male Sexual Assaulters. *American Journal of Psychiatry.* 136: 1194–6.

Little, M. I. (1951/1981) *Transference Neurosis and Transference Psychosis.* NY: Jason Aronson.

Little, L. and Hamby, S. L. (1996) Impact of a Clinician Sexual Abuse History, Gender and Theoretical Orientation on Treatment Issues. *Professional Psychology: Research and Practice.* 27(6): 617–25.

Loughlin, B. (1992) Supervision in the Face of No Cure: Working on the Boundary. *Journal of Social Work Practice.* 6(2): 111–6.

Luborsky, L. (1975) Comparative Study of Psychotherapies. *Archives of General Psychiatry.* 132:995–1007.

Maclay, D. T. (1960) Boys Who Commit Sexual Misdemeanours. *British Medical Journal.* 186: 186–90.

Malan, D. (1979) *Individual Psychotherapy and the Science of Psychodynamics.* London: Butterworth-Heinemann.

Markey, O. B. (1950) A Study of Aggressive Sex Misbehaviour in Adolescents Brought before the Court. *American Journal of Orthopsychiatry.* 20: 719–31.

Maroda, K. J. (1991) *The Power of Countertransference.* Chichester: John Wiley and Sons.

Marshall, R. J. (1979) Countertransference with Children and Adolescents. in Epstein, L. and Feiner, A. (Eds.) *Counter Transference: The Therapist's Contribution to the Therapeutic Situation.* NY: Jason Aronson.

Masson, H. (1997) Researching Policy and Practice in Relation to Children and Young People who Sexually Abuse. *Research, Policy and Planning.* 15(3): 8–15.

McConnaughty, E. (1987)The Person of the Therapist in Psychotherapeutic Practice. *Psychotherapy.* 23: 370–4.

Menzies, I. (1970) *The Functioning of Social Systems as a Defence Against Anxiety.* London: Tavistock Publications.

Miller, W. R. and Rollnick, S. (1991) *Motivational Interviewing: Preparing People to Change Addictive Behaviour.* NY: Guildford Press.

Mintzer, M. (1996) Understanding Countertransference Reactions in Working with Adolescent Perpetrators of Sexual Abuse. *Bulletin of the Meninger Clinic.* 60(2): 219–27.

Mitchell, C. and Melikian, K. (1995) The Treatment of Male Sexual Offenders: Countertransference Reactions. *Journal of Child Sexual Abuse.* 4(1): 87–93.

Money-Kyrle, R. (1956) Normal Countertransference and Some of its Deviations. in Spillius, E. B. (Ed.) (1988) *Melanie Klein Today Vol. 2.* London: Routledge (Tavistock).

Morrison, T. (1990) The Emotional Impact of Child Protection Work on the Worker. *Practice.* 4(4): 253–71.

Morrison, T., Erooga, M. and Beckett, R. C. (Eds.) (1994) *Sexual Offending Against Children: Assessment and Treatment of Male Abusers.* London: Routledge.

NCH. (1992) *Report of the Committee of Enquiry into Children and Young People who Sexually Abuse Other Children.* London: National Childrens Homes.

NCH. (1996) *Children and Young People Who Sexually Abuse Other Children* Unpublished, UK.

Obholzer, A. and Roberts, V. Z. (1994) *The Unconscious at Work: Individual and Organisational Stress in the Human Services.* London: Routledge.

O'Donohue, W. and Geer, J. H. (Eds.) (1992) *The Sexual Abuse of Children Vol 1 Theory and Research, Vol 2 Clinical Issues.* NY: Lawrence Erlbaum Associates.

Perry, G. P. and Orchard, J. (1992) *Assessment and Treatment of Adolescent Sex Offenders.* USA: Professional Resources Press.

Pogge, D. L. and Stone, K. (1990) Conflicts and Issues in the Treatment of Child Sexual Abuse. *Professional Psychology: Research and Practice.* 21(5): 304–16.

Preston-Shoot, M. and Agass, D. (1990) *Making Sense of Social Work: Psychodynamics, Systems and Practice.* London: MacMillan.

Racker, H. (1953/1968) *Transference and Countertransference.* London: Butler and Tanner Ltd.

Raichelson, S. H. et al. (1997) Incidents and Effects of Parallel Process in Psychotherapy Supervision. *The Clinical Supervisor.* 15(2): 37–48.

Reich, A. (1960) Further Remarks on Countertransference. *International Journal of Psychoanalysis.* 32: 135–40.

Reiss, A. J. (1960) Sex Offences: The Marginal Status of the Adolescent. *Law and Contemporary Problems.* 25: 309–30.

Reynolds-Mejia, P. and Levitan, S. (1990) Countertransference Issues in the In-home Treatment of Child Sexual Abuse. *Child Welfare.* 69(1): 53–61.

Richardson, S. (1999) Transforming Conflict: Mediation and Reparation in a Staff Team. *Child Abuse Review.* 8(2): 133–42.

Roberts, R. E., McBee, G. W. and Bettis, M. C. (1969) 'Youthful Sex Offenders: An Epidemiologic Comparison of Types'. *Journal of Sex Research* 5: 29–40

Robitscher, J. (1980) *The Powers of Psychiatry.* Boston: Houghton-Mifflin.

Ryan, G. D. (1999) Treatment of Sexually Abusive Youth: The Evolving Consensus. *Journal of Interpersonal Violence.* 14(4): 422–36.

Ryan, G. D. and Lane, S. L. (Eds.) (1991) *Juvenile Sexual Offending: Causes, Consequences and Correction.* NY: Lexington Books.

Sanders, R. and Ladwa-Thomas, U. (1997) Interagency Perspectives on Child Sexual Abuse Perpetrated by Juveniles.*Child Maltreatment.* 2(3): 264–71.

Sayers, J. (1991) Talking about Child Protection: Stress and Supervision. *Practice.* 5(2): 121–37.

Sexton, L. (1999) Vicarious Traumatisation of Counsellors and Effects on their Workplaces. *British Journal of Guidance and Counselling.* 27(3): 393–403.

Shevrin, H., Bond, J., Brakel, L., Hertel, R. and Williams, W. (1996) *Conscious and Unconscious Processes: Psychodynamic, Cognitive and Neurophysiological Convergences.* NY: Guildford Press.

Shoor, M., Speed, M. H. and Bartlett, C. (1966) Syndrome of the Adolescent Child Molester. *American Journal of Orthopsychiatry.* 122: 783–9.

Smith, D. L. (1991) *Hidden Conversations: An Introduction to Communicative Psychoanalysis.* London: Tavistock Routledge.

Steen, C. and Monnette, B. (1989) *Treating Adolescent Sex Offenders in the Community.* USA: Charles C Thomas.

Tsiantis, J. et al. (1996) *Countertransference in Psychoanalytic Psychotherapy with Children and Adolescents.* London: Karnac Books.

Vincent, J. (1996) Why Do We Ever Do It? Unconscious Motivation in Choosing Social Work as a Career. *Journal of Social Work Practice.* 10(1): 63–9.

Waggoner, R. and Boyd, D. (1941) Juvenile Aberrant Sexual Behaviour. *American Journal of Orthopsychiatry.* 11: 275–91.

Wampold, B. E. et al. (1997) A Meta-analysis of Outcome Studies Comparing Bona Fide Psychotherapies: Empirically, 'All Must Have Prizes'. *Psychological Bulletin.* 122(3): 203–15.

Weiner, M. L. (1975) *The Cognitive Unconscious: A Piagetian Approach to Psychotherapy.* USA: International Psychological Press.

Winnicott, D. W. (1949/1958) *Collected Papers.* London: Tavistock.

Wolgien, C. S. and Coady, N. F. (1997) Good Therapists' Beliefs About the Development of their Helping Ability: The Wounded Healer Paradigm Revisited. *The Clinical Supervisor.* 15(2): 19–35.

Woods, J. (1999) Professional Fragmentation in the Treatment of Young People who have Abused: A Review Article. *Clinical Child Psychology and Psychiatry.* 4(2): 281–300.

Chapter 4: Negotiating Difficult Terrain: The Personal Context to Work with Young People who Sexually Abuse Others

Simon Hackett

Introduction: the inevitability of a personal response to work with young people who sexually abuse

This chapter attempts to negotiate the difficult terrain associated with the personal context to work with young people who sexually abuse others. It examines practitioner impact issues; put simply, how practitioners can be affected by the work they undertake. It explores particularly the personal costs and personal gains involved in engaging in the therapeutic process with young people who have sexually abused. Managing the personal and professional context to this work is a crucial consideration. A personal response of some nature is an inevitable consequence of interpersonal engagement with other human beings. In relation to practice within the sexual aggression field, such responses, properly harnessed and appropriately managed, form the foundations for practice which is respectful to victims and accountable to communities. If we become emotionally immune to accounts of sexual abuse, and our sense of empathy and responsibility is eroded, we also lose the capacity to meet the needs of our clients. At the same time, the pain and trauma of sexual abuse can be contagious. As Ryan and Lane (1991) state, sexual abuse has enough causalities without workers experiencing the secondary traumatisation that can accompany sexual abuse work. At the time of writing, this is evidenced starkly by the award of significant amounts of financial compensation to two prison officers diagnosed with post traumatic stress disorder after spending four years working with sex offenders at Albany prison, on the Isle of Wight. One of the two men concerned is reported to have suffered nightmares, flashbacks, mood swings, guilt and loss of self confidence and had begun to see himself as an abuser. The other is said to have developed a phobia of children and his psychologist maintained that this man 'now irrationally tries to recognise children who may have been abused from accounts given by paedophiles' (reported in *The Guardian*, 6th June, 2001).

Whilst such accounts are evidence of the far-reaching difficulties that can accompany this work, at the same time, they can also promote a very negative sense of the work. A balanced view on impact should also recognise the potential positives of this field- what individuals can gain from the work. Negotiating this difficult terrain effectively is about ensuring that we remain emotionally responsive to the young people with whom we work, whilst not becoming emotionally 'disabled' by the experience of engaging with their accounts of abuse.

The impact of the wider socio-political context on the recognition of impact

Impact issues and practitioner emotional competence is an area which has received relatively little attention in the professional literature on sex offender work. Whilst there is limited attention to counter-transference issues and professional burnout, the psychological literature in general, and the sex offender literature in particular, has only rarely discussed what impact the prolonged exposure to abuse issues has on workers. Why could it be that accounts of therapeutic intervention with sex offenders have not always adequately addressed these issues? Is experiencing a personal response in work with sex offenders more shameful and difficult to talk about than it is in parallel fields, for example in relation to work with survivors of abuse? If the answer to this question is 'yes', this may in part be connected to the at times uneasy fit between sex offender work and the wider social care and health fields. Practitioners who work with sex offenders can be subject not only to boundary challenges from the clients with whom they work, but can also experience scepticism and scrutiny of their motivations on the part of colleagues who do not work with this client group. These questions can include the following:

Figure 1: The cycle of professional defensiveness in sex offender work (adapted from Hackett and Marsland, 1997).

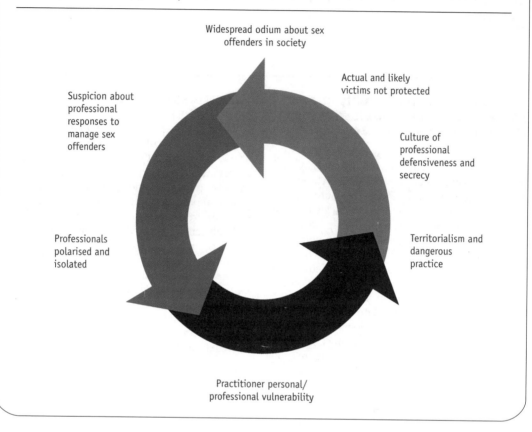

- *Why do you choose to spend your time talking to sex offenders?*
- *What is it about the work that interests you?*
- *How did you end up working with these people?*

At times, it can feel that we are also under siege by the wider socio-political context within which the work takes place. The general contempt within which sex offenders are held does not stop at adult 'paedophiles' in the community. All sex offenders- those who are children and young people included- are subject to a general sense of public odium. Where does this leave the practitioner who seeks to engage therapeutically with such people in order to promote change?

The risks of failing to engage with the personal context of this work include, at an individual level, personal vulnerability and burnout, as well as professional territorialism and defensive practice at a system level. At their worst, such processes can be represented as in Figure 1:

Answering the 'why' question: a personal account

In the face of such processes and issues, a number of difficult questions are raised, such as:

- Why would practitioners choose to put themselves in this difficult position?
- What are the long-term consequences of carrying out this work and engaging with offenders' distortions, fantasises, accounts of abuse, etc. within such a climate of societal mistrust and hostility?

These are, I suggest, fundamental debates for us to engage in as practitioners if we are to remain healthy, responsive and effective in our work with young people. Considering such questions involves us being clear about why we choose to carry out this work and what we gain from it.

For example, it was never my intention to make this area of practice such a core element of my own professional experience. Nevertheless, the experiences I have had in this field, have become one of the most defining parts of my personal experience, not just my professional work. Having come into social work with a clear commitment to work with those who had been victimised sexually, I was in fact initially even quite hostile and resistant to the notion of work with children and young people who had sexually abused. I thought that the whole notion of 'perpetrator work' was incongruent with my beliefs and my commitment to survivors. In the child protection team in which I practised, a colleague suggested that I might like to think about 'abuser work'. I was horrified. What did this say about how my female colleague viewed me? Did she, as a woman, think that I, as a man, was only fit to work with the perpetrators? And furthermore, in making this suggestion, was she not placing me in the abuser camp: aligning me with the perpetrator? This felt very uncomfortable indeed.

Now, although I do not like young people's sexually abusive behaviours, and I remain at times deeply disturbed and troubled by their accounts of these behaviours, I enjoy my work with such young people. At times, I find myself sharing a joke with young people, obviously in appropriate contexts and in appropriate ways. With notable exceptions, I feel a degree of fondness and empathic concern for the majority of my young clients. My sense of myself as a man and a male professional have grown and benefited as a direct consequence. I have probably learnt something about myself from all of the young people and families with whom I have worked. In many cases, their struggles have been embedded in pain and histories of multiple trauma and abuse, but I feel privileged to have been part of the resolution of these struggles nonetheless.

The journey I have undergone from my initial hostility to my current position has been one of great personal significance. It has taken a good deal of effort and reflection on my part. On the way, I have experienced a whole panoply of emotion; conflict, confusion, disappointment and frustration. At times, staying healthy and emotionally responsive to users in this field has been difficult. Whilst the initial journey was, indeed, unplanned, I am proud of where I have reached and pleased that this is an area of work into which I have dedicated my efforts. That the work has

fundamentally changed me as a person is beyond doubt.

This mixture of personal cost and personal gain through the experience of working with those who have perpetrated sexual abuse is not unique to me. Freeman-Longo says:

> There is no doubt in my mind that I look at the world through a very different set of glasses than my family, friends, and others who do not work with sexual abuse ... It felt like the loss of innocence. There were few, if any 'safe' places or people left in the world.
>
> (Freeman-Longo, 1997, p5)

But, he goes on to say that:

> My work has broadened my experience and enriched my life in numerous ways.
>
> (Freeman-Longo, 1997, p7)

The value of impact

I offer the above account of my own personal context not to be anecdotal. Indeed, writing in such a personal manner, as above, feels a little risky. I have thought about whether my comments about feeling a degree of fondness for many of my clients might make some people angry or feel that I am in downplaying young people's abuse, or that I am an apologist for abusive behaviour in some way. At the same time, I wonder how much of what I have briefly described of my experience mirrors or conflicts with other practitioners' personal stories and experiences in this field.

One of the points I hope to make is that acknowledging impact forces us to recognise and value the interpersonal aspect of the work we conduct, rather than to hide beneath this. For example, in the sex offender field, we talk about undertaking 'offence focussed' work. Young people may be asked to 'report' to us or be 'under our supervision'. We hand out the next chapter from the workbook, read the exercise from the groupwork manual, photocopy the cycle of abuse and ask the young person to fill in the gaps. This kind of professional language and approach, for me, runs the risk of masking the very basic fact that those young people with whom we work are, like us, people and that we, like them, have personal lives, our own histories and issues which can be brought into such sharp focus by the work. Just as the young people concerned are, we hope, amenable to our influence, so we are not immune, as people, to their influence. The likelihood that we are going to be influenced in a deeply rooted way by young people's thoughts, emotions and behaviours is of fundamental and vital importance to the field. Bengis offers us a clear account of the wide-ranging implications of this when he says:

> Once treatment providers have chosen to work in sex offender treatment, we enter what I can best describe as a 'twilight world.' This world alters our perceptions of daily events and, even more disturbingly, may change our inner lives- sometimes irrevocably. What we see when we walk down the street, what we think about in public places, what we fantasise, feel or fear often differs markedly from the experiences of others who do not experience the worlds in which we immerse ourselves.
>
> (Bengis, 1997, p31)

If such discussions and debates are largely missing from the developing literature and intervention orthodoxy of sexual abuser work, I wonder if they are also missing from the daily lives of practitioners, from their supervisory relationships and discussions in team meetings too? How much of this is constrained in the organisations in which we work and by the wider socio-political context within which these organisations are located?

So, what does this work mean to you? How do you conceive of it? Why do you do it? What do you feel about the work you do? How has this work changed you? These are fundamental questions that all practitioners in this field should be able to ask and answer in respect of their work. To deal with the longer-term impact of the work we need to know why we do the work, what we gain from it and we need to be aware of the demands the work places upon us.

Imagine for a minute the senior Social Services manager who, in the course of a research interview with me on the subject of gender issues in the sexual abuse field, became embarrassed and haltingly recalled a time he was asked to read a report which went into detail about an adult man's abuse of his daughter. To his absolute horror, as he read this in his office, the man concerned began to feel sexually aroused. He was confused about this. He was a father with small children. He had nowhere to go with the pain and confusion that this incident caused him. He could not tell his wife, nor could he tell his colleagues for fear of being perceived as an abuser. 'This kind of mud sticks', he said. Several years on he recounted this incident for the very first time to me, a person he had never previously met. He admitted that this incident, which was

not based in any kind of direct practice experience but was merely a response to a written account, had not left him and had preoccupied him, interfering in his work on a number of occasions. It is clear that if we do not create the organisational or team cultures where debate about the impact and the personal context of this work can take place, we run the risk of replicating this man's experience, mirroring his isolation and limiting the efficacy of our own interventions.

Connecting with impact issues

This section examines in more detail the range of potential impact issues that may arise in the course of work with young people who sexually abuse. Although many of these are focused on 'negative' issues, impact issues can also work positively and the notion of impact should be regarded as a hopeful concept (Hackett, 1999). As a term it concerns not only the range of difficulties that may arise as a consequence of the work, but also embraces the optimism that difficult, problematic or dysfunctional impact issues may be harnessed positively to enrich us as practitioners and people. The challenge is to not so much rid ourselves of impact issues, as this would be to minimise our response to human pain and distress, but to ensure that we develop sufficient awareness of our responses and healthy coping strategies to continue to function in our work:

> We should not be untouched, nor on occasions untroubled, by our work. At the same time, the work should challenge us, inspire us, fire our creativity and lead us to new and positive personal and professional understandings.
>
> (Hackett, 1999, p226–7)

In order to deal constructively with impact in this field of practice then, it is my view that workers need to consider three distinct elements, which I deal with in brief below:

- The first is to examine the common impact responses described in relation to this work.
- The second is for practitioners to develop a working model for considering their own responses and impact issues: something which helps move an individual from a position of merely acknowledging a particular feeling, to being able to understand where it comes from and what its implications are.
- The third is to develop appropriate ways of dealing with these issues.

One of the problems in relation to identifying impact is the lack of empirical research. There are, however, some descriptive accounts from individuals, including some from the UK. What research there has been is largely North American and, even then, there are methodological problems. In the absence of control groups, it is difficult to conclude from surveys of sex offender workers what might be distinct impact issues in sex offender work, as opposed to, say work with physically abusive men, or other trauma related or psychotherapy fields. What seems to be unique in the sex offender field is: *'The need to repeatedly address and evaluate the disturbing thoughts and behaviours of sexually abusive people'* (Bird Edmunds, 1997, p12). There are also few accounts of impact issues specifically in relation to work with adolescents rather than adults who have sexually abused, many studies making general and global comments about work with sex offenders without looking into the particular demands of working with children and young people. Ostensibly, the additional issue facing practitioners working with young sex offenders is the degree to which they are forced to make an associative link between sex, aggression and children as aggressors.

Despite the relative lack of empirical research, some important signposts of others' experiences emerge from the existing literature which we can use to check and better gauge our professional and personal responses. Secrecy, as we know, is a key issue in the aetiology of sexual abuse and breaking secrecy also means practitioners speaking out about their experience of the work. Although the organisational context within which practice takes place and, indeed, our professional training and identities may be different, our individual responses are not unique and should not simply be seen as a marker of our own problems, or inability to do the work, but can represent normative responses. Despite the difficulty of the work, this is something from which practitioners should take strength.

Common impact responses described in relation to work with young people who sexually abuse

Affective responses and burnout

The presence of difficult emotional responses are perhaps the most commonly acknowledged aspect of 'impact' in work with adolescent and adult sex offenders. A wide range of feelings are described, for example; anger and hatred (Haugaard and Reppucci, 1988), sadistic feelings and retaliatory impulses (Mitchell and Melikian, 1995), feeling psychologically victimised by young people who abuse, due to unresolved issues of victimisation from one's own past or the over-identification with victims (National Taskforce, 1993), fear and paranoia (National Taskforce, 1993), feeling 'dirtied' or sullied by the work (Hoghughi, 1997) and feeling powerlessness and desiring control (Erooga, 1994).

The concept of burnout seeks to link these affective responses with their behavioural consequences. In North America, Bird Edmunds collected data from 289 sexual abuser treatment professionals using a standardised questionnaire. Respondents were almost equally split in terms of gender and represented a wide range of professional disciplines and roles. Almost half of the subjects in the research had over fifteen years experience of mental health work and a similar number had worked with sexual abusers specifically between three and eight years. Although this group of respondents included those who work with adults as well as young people, 41% identified 10–20-year-olds as the user group they worked with.

Bird Edmunds' questionnaire focused particularly on factors known to be associated with professional burnout. She found that high numbers of these people (85%) retained a positive attitude towards their work and 97% perceived themselves to be effective. Despite this, she found that over half of the respondents reported increased fatigue, over a third reported an increase in cynicism, sleep disturbances and preoccupation with work outside of work time. Approximately one quarter said they had difficulties in making decisions, depression or depressive episodes, 20% said they had become more insensitive to others, 10% had misused drugs or alcohol to cope with the emotional demands of the work. Interestingly all of these findings were in almost equal measure for men and women.

Workers' own abuse experiences

A number of other interesting factors emerge from Bird Edmunds' research. The first concerns respondents' own victim experiences. The questionnaire asked workers to self identify their own experiences of abuse and, in total, 56% of respondents indicated that they themselves had been physically, sexually or emotionally abused at some point in their lives (of these, 22% reported psychological abuse, 11% physical and 21% of sexual abuse). Bird Edmunds analysed her findings on impact and burn-out for survivors and non-survivors and found that the survivor group appeared to experience less fatigue and sleep disturbance, but more frustration and depression than the non-survivor group. Whilst these findings in no way suggest a causal link, the important message that emerges is the degree to which sexual abuser work can connect with workers' prior experiences and therefore how important it is for us to be sensitive to our own life experiences, whatever these are. As indicated by the high prevalence of own abuse experiences, survivors play a major role in this field of work and should not be seen as vulnerable or unable to do this work by dint of their experiences, as is sometimes suggested or implied (see for example, Barter, 1997). Indeed, some workers appear to have derived skills and strength in having survived their own abuse experiences which may help them to cope better with some facets of professional burnout than non-survivors. On the other hand, that 82% of those who reported depression as a result of the work came from the survivor group has major implications for staff and organisational care.

Frequency of abuser contact and impact issues

Another finding from Bird Edmunds' research is the relationship between frequency of burnout symptoms and the amount of sexual abuser contact. It would seem logical perhaps that those who are exposed the most to sexual abusers, their accounts and distortions, would be most vulnerable to stress and negative personal responses, however this was not the case in her study. Respondents reporting the greatest increases in cynicism (43%) frustration (62%) and fatigue (67%) worked on average 11–20 client contact hours a week, with these figures dropping for those who have more client contact. This would appear to suggest that some workers may experience stress and incongruence between the different aspects of their work if they are not working routinely with abusers. We might conclude from this that it is difficult to work with the occasional adolescent sexual abuser on a caseload of non-sexual offenders, or general child welfare

cases. This finding may therefore have important implications for organisational service delivery, allocation of work and staff supervision.

Power and powerlessness

As power and powerlessness is a theme which is central to the issue of sexual abuse, it is perhaps not surprising that this is also a core area of impact in relation to work with sexual abusers. This can take place on an affective level, including the development of feelings of helplessness or disempowerment, or a cognitive level including the development of irrational thinking as a result of being exposed to issues of control and the abuse of power in respect of young people who abuse (National Taskforce, 1993). Morrison also highlights how we can develop distorted thinking about issues of responsibility, including thinking that we are overly-responsible for our clients' behaviour (Morrison, 1997). Sometimes, workers can over-compensate in their behaviour for feelings of relative powerlessness with aggressive attempts to exert our power over young people. We may distort and misdirect this to those in our own families or find ourselves behaving in impatient, 'over-the-top' or aggressive ways with our own children or partners.

Sex and sexuality

Another major area of potential impact relates to sex and sexuality. This is perhaps the most difficult area of impact to acknowledge. As Bengis says:

> Few practitioners work with sex abusers without becoming aware of the presence of new ideas, feelings, fantasies, impulses and urges related to this work. In spite of ourselves, we may discover inner imagery that simply will not go away or fantasies that parallel the acts described to us by our clients.
> (Bengis, 1997, p31)

Bengis suggests that for the most part we live with these the occupational hazards of our work in isolation. We can worry about our own sexual identification, we can become too sensitised on sexual matters and we can become hyper-vigilant about the safety of our own or other children. Common sexual responses (Hackett, 1999) can include:

- Mistrust of others' sexual behaviour or motivations, especially those with access to children.

- Seeing sex in everything: projecting a sexual dimension onto non-sexual interactions.
- Hyper-awareness of one's own arousal patterns and fantasises leading in some cases to sexual dysfunction and interference in sexual relationships, or heightening the importance of sex in personal relationships.
- An inability to talk to one's partner about sex, about work or about the connections between the two.
- Over-sensitisation to sex; with sex becoming a way of self-soothing, coping with the stress of the work or 'ridding oneself' of particularly distasteful images from casework.
- Intrusive flashbacks to details of case work whilst engaged in sex.
- Feelings of sexual corruption; a sense of being dirtied by hearing and having to listen to such 'sordid' sexual material.

Gender and personal identity issues

A final major area of impact is that of gender and personal identification. As a result of the constant struggle to encourage young people to look critically at their masculinity or femininity, both men and women can experience feelings of loss and grief regarding aspects of their gender. I have talked elsewhere (Hackett, 1999) of how male practitioners in particular can experience a gender crisis, including feelings of gender shame or guilt. This kind of personal reappraisal can be a painful process, but can also lead to new levels of positive personal awareness. Related to these issues is the theme of boundary setting and maintenance. Ellerby et al. (1993) found that 84% of the women therapists in their research felt that their boundaries had been invaded by clients, and 42% described feeling sexualised by abusers. Male therapists reported these invasions much less frequently, 34% and 16% respectively. 58% of therapists said that they had felt 'unclean' after a session with a sex offender. In the same study, 73% of female and 63% of male practitioners reported having felt endangered or threatened by a client.

Distinguishing impact on affective, cognitive and behavioural levels

The list of impact issues touched on above suggests that we should accept the inevitability of a personal response of some nature (Morrison, 1990, 1997), yet one of the difficulties remains understanding why some individuals respond in certain ways to aspects of the work with adolescents who abuse and others in vastly different ways. One of most difficult aspects of my own practice experience has been the unpredictability of negative personal responses. Why is it that I can hear all kinds of very deviant and abusive sexual material in the work and this has little impact on me, but a relatively minor or insignificant matter or detail or look or gesture from a young person can have a profound and inexplicable influence?

Previously, I have described a model (Hackett, 1999) which seeks to help practitioners understand impact issues arising from the work as *interactional* in nature, influenced (both heightened or lessened even) by a complex set of variables. This model, which I called the Interactional Dynamics of Impact Model draws upon Finkelhor and Browne's (1985) traumagenic dynamics model of sexual abuse. The model breaks down the issue of practitioner impact into its interactional components, namely:

- The existence of pre-existing factors.
- The dynamics of the young person- worker relationship and interpersonal exchange.
- The affective and cognitive impact upon the worker.
- The worker's behavioural responses.

This whole dynamic is set within the broader life and personal experiences that both the young person and worker bring to the exchange, as well as the environmental and agency context within which the work takes place, as depicted in Figure 2:

One of the implications of this model is that practitioners, and those who may be responsible for their welfare such as their supervisors or managers, should recognise and understand the connections between affective, cognitive and behavioural impact issues. The model promotes the following kind of questions (Hackett, 1999):

- In what way do my previous life and professional experiences influence my responses to young people and their families?
- How do my values, particularly in relation to sexuality and abuse, affect the way in which I conduct the work and make sense of my role in the task?
- What are my previous experiences of practice in this field? How do they influence my approaches and responses?

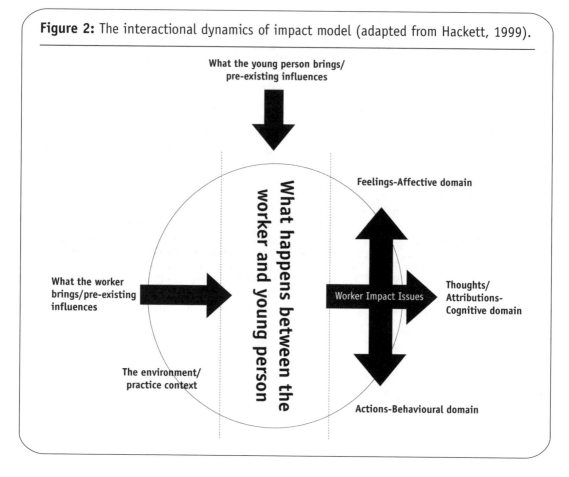

Figure 2: The interactional dynamics of impact model (adapted from Hackett, 1999).

- What is happening in my external life/ personal life currently?
- How does the environment I work in contribute to, or influence, the impact of my experience?
- What are the details of the interpersonal exchange I have with my clients?
- What are the particular themes and struggles associated with my direct contact with young people?
- What feelings are promoted in me as a consequence of the work about me, my work and my world view?
- What patterns and links can I trace in the web of feelings that emerge?
- What particular scripts and schemas are being projected upon me?
- In what ways are my thoughts, beliefs and attitudes being changed, eroded or strengthened through the experience of the work?
- What is different now about my behaviour than when I first engaged in this work?

- To what degree are my behaviours appropriate and effective ways of coping?
- To what extent are my behaviours, thoughts and feelings congruent to each other?

Table 1 seeks to highlight some of these connections with specific reference to the three impact areas I have described above:

Conclusions: Towards Effective Management of Impact Issues

There is a huge and often unspoken challenge for practitioners in this field to address the range of difficult impact issues discussed above. Just as impact works on cognitive, affective and emotional levels, so our self-care responses need to be multi-levelled and multi-dimensional.

Affectively, we should share emotional issues with others. We should offer colleagues, and be open to receive for ourselves, empathy and permission to express our feelings. As Ryan and Lane (1991) highlight, minimisation and

Table 1: Connecting impact on affective, cognitive and behavioural levels (Hackett, 1999).

Impact area	Dynamics	Affective domain	Cognitive domain	Behavioural domain
Sex and sexuality	• Worker is bombarded by sexual stimuli in the work • Worker listens to accounts of abusive sexuality • Worker subject to sexually deviant fantasies • Young person's sexual behaviours force the worker to make an association between sex, children and abuse	• Repulsion by sexual issues • Worker feels victimised sexually • Worker feels like an abuser • Fear of being perceived an abuser • Own sexual development and experiences highlighted • Unresolved feelings about own victimisation experiences resurface • Feeling that all sex is dirty and sordid	• Re-evaluation of sexual values • Distorted views of sexual normality (abuse = the norm, or all sex = abuse) • 'Reading sex into everything' Over-salience of sex in cognitive schema • Sexual imagery intrudes into sexual experiences- affective flashbacks to the work/an account of abuse, esp. during sex • Development of deviant fantasies	• Sexual abstinence • Questioning of sexual identity (positive and negative connotations) • Over-emphasis on sex • Sexual fixation and increased sexual drive • Arousal problems • Consensual sex becomes a behavioural fix- a way of 'cleansing' self from influence of work • Relationship strain and break-up
Gender and personal identification	• Worker subject to overwhelming accounts of male sexual and non-sexual violence • Abuser attempts to recruit workers into exaggerated gender stereotypes; e.g. men into collusion to distortions about women, women into submissive roles, etc.	• Feelings of gender confusion • Feelings of loss; of innocence, of self, of elements of gender socialisation • Anger at abusers for damaging own gendered identity and gender assumptions • Fear of being associated as an abuser through commonality of gender or other personal aspect • Self guilt and gender shame (men) • Pride in new gender awareness • Personal isolation	• Distorted sense of responsibility for actions of all men • Distorted view of masculine and feminine roles • Review of self and own socialisation, leading to negative or positive new self-awareness • Male worker experiences a 'gender crisis' • Sense of distance from members of same gender (esp. men)	• Career revision to cope with gender role strain • Exaggerated behavioural attempts to distance self from identification as 'abuser' • Reluctance to engage in certain professional or personal life activities/ roles; e.g. bathing children • Review of external life activities; e.g. protection of own children

Table 1: *Continued.*

Power and powerlessness	• Abuser engages worker in power struggle • Worker is required to exercise an uncomfortable level of power and control over young person • Young person projects overwhelming level of need upon worker	• Worker feels overwhelmed by extent of young person's unmet need • Feelings of exaggerated power- euphoria • Feelings of exaggerated powerlessness- depression • Deep cynicism about society and the denial of sexual abuse issues • Desire for revenge- wish to right wrongs of victim	• Distorted sense of own power • Increased self confidence and increased level of self esteem • Non-abusive relationships given added value	• Punitive behaviours towards others • Increased respectful behaviours within own relationships • New-found assertiveness

denial of feelings and affective responses in the work is a parallel process to the abuser's minimisation and denial and can lead to objectification of the worker.

Cognitively, we need to be aware of the dangers of adopting or being influenced by the distortions which are fed to us by those who commit sexual offences. Ryan and Lane (1991) talk of the need to monitor the subtle shifts that can take us away from notions of responsibility and accountability.

Behaviourally, we should reflect upon the way in which our behaviours may be adaptive and maladaptive responses to the experience of the work.

I would like to issue two challenges for every reader who is involved in this area of work. The first challenge is to think of one constructive thing you can do to acknowledge and manage negative impact issues in your work and to harness this in a positive manner to retain your optimism and positive outlook and to ensure that you are enriched by your work. Having done this, the second challenge is to share your idea with one other person who does this work. Here is my own six point guide to surviving and, indeed, thriving in this work:

• Retain your sense of balance. The world does not revolve around sexual abuse: it only feels like this sometimes.
• Check yourself regularly for distortions and if you are unsure about something you find, get someone else to have a look!
• Develop and use your supports. Do not be too proud or 'expert' to ask for support or to express your feelings. Break the silence on impact.
• Remember that you are not a limitless sponge which can soak up other people's problems.
• Remember that you are not alone. There are others out there who are similarly struggling with this terrain.
• Value the unique perspectives that the work brings to you. Not everybody is as privileged to have these personal learning opportunities. Make the most of them.

Bengis (1997) suggests that those of us with any degree of longevity in the field have probably learnt to cope with the litany of impact issues which I have touched on above. However, he suggests that we owe it to others who are new to the field to provide a context for working with these 'inner land mines'. Of course, we should not be intrusive or demand self-disclosure from others. But, by naming some of the above issues as I have attempted to do, we can 'normalise' their existence and leave the door open for future exploration. I hope that this is a hopeful and inspiring reason for what can be a difficult process. We can, I believe, negotiate the personal and professional issues inherent in work with young people who abuse. The terrain we inhabit will remain tough, exhausting, at times uncompromising and harsh, but perhaps the way will be safer and the supports we receive and give stronger. We might just move across this terrain a little easier.

References

Barter, S. (1997) Social Work Students with Personal Experiences of Sexual Abuse: Implications for Diploma in Social Work Programme Providers. *Social Work Education.* 16: 2 113–32.

Bengis, S. (1997) Personal and Interpersonal Issues for Staff Working with Sexually Abusive Youth. in Bird Edmunds, S. (Ed.) *Impact: Working with Sexual Abusers.* Brandon: Safer Society Press.

Bird Edmunds, S. (Ed.) *Impact: Working with Sexual Abusers.* Brandon: Safer Society Press.

Bird Edmunds, S. (1997) The Personal Impact of Working with Sex Offenders. in Bird Edmunds, S. (Ed.) *Impact: Working with Sexual Abusers.* Brandon: Safer Society Press.

Ellerby, L., Gutkin, B., Smith, T. and Atkinson, R. (1993) *Treating Sex Offenders: The Impact on Clinicians.* Poster presentation, 12th Annual Conference of the Association for the Treatment of Sexual Abusers, Boston, Massachusetts.

Erooga, M. (1994) Where the Professional Meets the Personal. in Morrison, T., Erooga, M. and Beckett, R. *Sexual Offending Against Children. Assessment and Treatment of Male Abusers.* London: Routledge.

Finkelhor, D. and Browne, A. (1985) The Traumatic Impact of Child Sexual Abuse: An Update. *American Journal of Orthopsychiatry.* 55: 530–41.

Freeman-Longo, R. (1997) A Personal and Professional Perspective on Burnout. in Bird Edmunds, S. (Ed.) *Impact: Working with Sexual Abusers.* Brandon: Safer Society Press.

Hackett, S. and Marsland, P. (1997) Perceptions of Power: An Exploration of the Dynamics in the Student-Tutor-Practice Teacher Relationship within Child Protection Placements. *Social Work Education.* 16(2): 44–62.

Hackett, S. (1999) Empowered Practice. in Erooga, M. and Masson, H. (1999) *Young People Who Sexually Abuse Others. Responses to an Emerging Problem.* London: Routledge.

Haugaard, J. and Reppuci, N. (1988) *The Sexual Abuse of Children: A Comprehensive Guide to Current Knowledge and Intervention Strategies.* San Francisco, CA: Jossey-Bass.

Hoghughi, M., Bhate, S. and Graham, F. (1997) *Working with Sexually Abusive Adolescents.* London: Sage.

Mitchell, C. and Melikian, K. (1995) The Treatment of Male Sex Offenders: Countertransference Reactions. *Journal of Child Sexual Abuse.* 4:1. 87–93.

Morrison, T. (1990) The Emotional Effects of Child Protection on the Worker. *Practice.* 4:4 253–71.

Morrison, T., Erooga, M. and Beckett, R. (1994) *Sexual Offending Against Children. Assessment and Treatment of Male Abusers.* London: Routledge.

Morrison, T. (1996) Emotionally Competent Child Protection Organisations: Fallacy, Fiction or Necessity. (Eds.) Bates, J., Pugh, R. and Thompson, N. *Protecting Children: Challenges and Change.* Arena Books.

Morrison, T. (1997) Where Have we Come from: Where are we Going? Managing Adolescents who Sexually Abuse Others. *NOTA News.* 21: 15–27.

The National Adolescent Perpetrator Network. (1993) The Revised Report from the National Task Force on Juvenile Sexual Offending. *Juvenile and Family Court Journal.* 44: 4.

Ryan, G. and Lane, S. (1991) *Juvenile Sexual Offending: Causes, Consequences and Corrections.* Lexington: Lexington Books.

Chapter 5: 'No one's Prepared for Anything Like This': Learning from Adults who Care for Children who Sexually Offend: A Narrative Study

Sue Maskell

Introduction

Working with children who sexually harm others is an area of practice which developed in the UK during the last decade. However, it has been difficult to establish an appropriate and consistent response to these children, as evidenced by Masson (1995) and observed in my own practice as an independent chairperson at Child Protection Case Conferences where I became aware of:

- The extreme level of distress experienced by families in such cases.
- The scarcity of appropriate placements and the struggle to identify other resources (including maintaining the child's basic education).
- The valiant efforts of Social Workers who attempt to practice in what can be an isolated environment.
- That formal assessments of the family were not usually completed and that children in these cases were invariably worked with in isolation from their families.
- That confusion abounded around thresholds for intervention, not least of all because of a lack of detailed, firm practice guidance about normal childhood sexual behaviour. It was clear that professionals struggle to define the nature of childhood sexual activity, for instance; is this sexually reactive behaviour, normal sexual experimentation, or sexually aggressive behaviour?

The scarcity of research into this area of practice has been criticised, as has its quality (Adler and Schutz, 1995; Araji, 1997; Vizard et al., 1996.). I found no research which focused exclusively on the adults involved. For these reasons this study focuses on the experiences of adults who influence the lives of sexually offending children. Throughout the study I use the term 'Child Sex Offender' to describe the children. I use this term, shortened to CSO, to avoid the pejorative associations of the words adolescent and juvenile and also because many offenders are not yet teenagers. Furthermore, the use of the word 'child' emphasises the fact that we are discussing children: dependent, vulnerable human beings who need care, support and nurture, whatever their offence may be. These children, however, can be dangerous to others and 'sex offender' recognises that despite the tender age of the offender, victims suffer serious harm. In fact, victims of CSOs are more likely to have suffered penetration than with many older offenders. So, this is a situation where dependent children seriously damage other vulnerable children.

There is nothing in the research literature which exclusively explores how the adults, social workers, carers and parents are coping in the midst of all the debates which surround them. In the end, real people must deal with real situations. In doing so, they often 'surface' answers which are unobtainable to those who are not directly involved. In studying the experiences of adults who are directly involved I attempted to discover how they managed their responsibilities; in an effort to see if they had developed 'answers' and to find how these fitted with the generally accepted knowledge and practice for working with CSOs.

Method

As an observer it would have been possible to have made assumptions about the experiences and problems of the adults. However, I felt that creating hypotheses and formulating questionnaires based on assumptions would be risky, my hypotheses would be based on hunches and these may well be inaccurate, leading to the exclusion of vital issues. I believed that, given the relative infancy of the practice and the scarcity of research into the experiences of adults involved with, or caring for children who sexually harm others, a constructivist approach would provide the richest and least biased data. In this I was influenced by Van Kaam (1966):

*Preconceived designs and statistical methods im-
posed on subjects are likely to restrict and prevent
disclosure of the full meaning and richness of human
behaviour.*

The study is therefore based on narrative
interviews with parents, social workers and
carers of children who sexually harm others.

Sample

The case for the purpose of this research is each
adult's experiences.

Carers

Sample: From the statutory and voluntary
sector, three foster carers and a manager of
children's units, all had cared for CSOs. The
children cared for by the aforementioned group
had only one child in common with the parents
group. There were five different children
discussed by the carers, and four out of the five
had learning difficulties.

Parents

Parents were selected by requesting social
worker's assistance in identifying possible
participants. The first four from the given list
were asked to participate, a fifth was asked after
one family did not wish to participate. Families
came from two authority areas.

Social workers

Four social workers were selected from workers
who had experience of dealing with such cases.
The workers were from two agencies, a national
voluntary organisation and a social services
department. Three of them had almost ten years
experience.

The interviews

Twelve interviews took place with fourteen
people; in two 'parent' cases the interview
involved both partners in the couple. The
questions were open ended and designed to
enable each of the participating groups to tell
about their own experience. The interviews
were recorded and full transcripts made. The
material selected, including full quotations and
the issues raised were fed back to each
participant after analysis and an opportunity
given to object, or disagree with the analysis of
their contribution.

Analysis

The time consuming nature of qualitative data
is much discussed, as is the fact that the
researchers self is integrated into any analysis
and this must be acknowledged. Glaser and
Strauss (1967) say that the material cannot be
left to speak for itself, and describes a voyage of
discovery, where the researcher is open minded
and free from rigid ideas. The task of
analysis was undertaken by memo writing,
reading and re-reading the texts and making
notes and eventually organising the findings
into categories. The categories emerged as the
memos from the data increased. There were
some exceptionally strong themes, which arose
again and again in the narratives. Although a
lengthy process, it was not difficult to
identify significant categories, particularly
because the power of expression emphasised
repeatedly those issues, which were important
to the narrators.

In analysis I made use of Reissman's (1993)
ideas about the poetic features of language.
Reissman demonstrated how stanzas lend
coherence to the narrative. I found that

Table 1: Characteristics of CSOs whose parents were interviewed.

Child characteristics	Family 1	Family 2	Family 3	Family 4
Gender of CSO; male/female.	M	M	M	M
Nature of criminal disposal for offence	Caution	None	Sup. Order	Sup. Order
Number of offences known.	Three	One	One	Two
Offended against siblings.	Yes	Yes	No	No
CSO has Learning Difficulties.	No	Mild	Moderate	No
Child remains in the family home.	In care.	Yes after temporary move.	Had moved to father's home.	Yes.

participants express important ideas and feelings with stanzas, and by looking for stanzas, themes emerged.

Another feature of speech is extreme case formulation, i.e. the repeated use of words, as described by Pomerantz (1986). This is used when the speaker is uncertain about whether their claims or ideas will be accepted. These are words like: always, extremely, very very, everyone. Repetition of the same word is also used to establish an issue or feeling. There is also a point well into the interviews where resolution is reached, (Labov, 1972). This resolution can sometimes be a painful and resigned conclusion.

Validity

Robson (1993) writes that if two sources give the same message, then to some extent they cross validate each other. I believe the narrators did substantially validate each other's experiences and so my findings. There must, though, be an acceptance that the stories are given from a point of view which will include the interests and values of the narrators. In the opinion of some people this may undermine the value of the data. For my purpose, in trying to understand what was happening for a group of adults, all involved in a similar enterprise, the values and points of view are as important and affect the behaviour of people as much as any historical fact of their experience.

Findings

The findings are summarised in the following three figures, which illustrate the issues on which participants agree or have congruent experience, (centre of diagram), and the issues which were more specific to their own milieu. These issues fall into three main areas: the child, the effects on the adults and views on service provision.

The parents

Given the nature of the interviews, which were non-directive, the amount of data collected is considerable. The findings are summarised under collective headings with commentary in the parent's own words.

Experiencing shock and denial

The parents all described the initial shock of discovering their child's offences. One father said:

Everything went sort of Whoomph! in the house.

A mother described her feelings: when telephoning Social Services to report her son's offending she felt terrified that the child would be removed from her care:

> *Crying, I was really really crying. I said 'I can't do it'. She said 'you're going to have to do it'. I said 'I know'. I knew I had to do it, I just couldn't bring myself to do it.*

All the parents described how initially they had experienced denial, one said:

> *When we first found out, . . . I didn't . . . couldn't, believe it was true . . . it was lots of denial in my head.*

Another said:

> *You see at first when he said he hadn't done it every man and his dog believed him.*

After attending a court hearing the shock of realisation was described:

> *So we knew then, he knew what he was doing. He knew exactly what he was doing. And that just turned everything upside down then, because up till then, for some strange reason, you could fathom why it happened.*

Following on from the discovery of the abuse families then experienced significant changes which amounted to loss. There may have been other losses, as this was not a direct question, the information below being given spontaneously.

In relation to a child leaving home one mother said:

> *He wants to come home, and he can't, he just can't . . . he can't come back, he's hurt too many people in this house.*

One father commented that although he told his employers about his problems he couldn't concentrate enough to work properly:

> *And I was going in to work and I didn't know what day it was . . . I couldn't . . . I kept going into work, and I didn't know what I was doing there. So I lost my job, and we very nearly lost this house.*

One mother talked about being too stressed to leave the child:

> *I was off work for seven months because I was petrified to let him out of my sight. Cos I was convinced he was going to do it again.*

The families described a variety of effects on functioning: crying, worrying, sleepless nights, lack of concentration, and their efforts to manage what could often be overwhelming

Figure 1: The child.

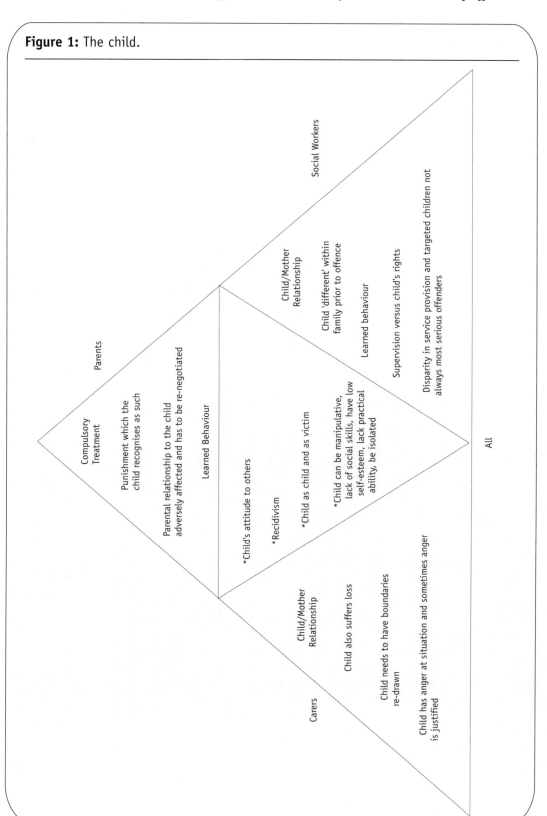

Figure 2: The effect on interviewees.

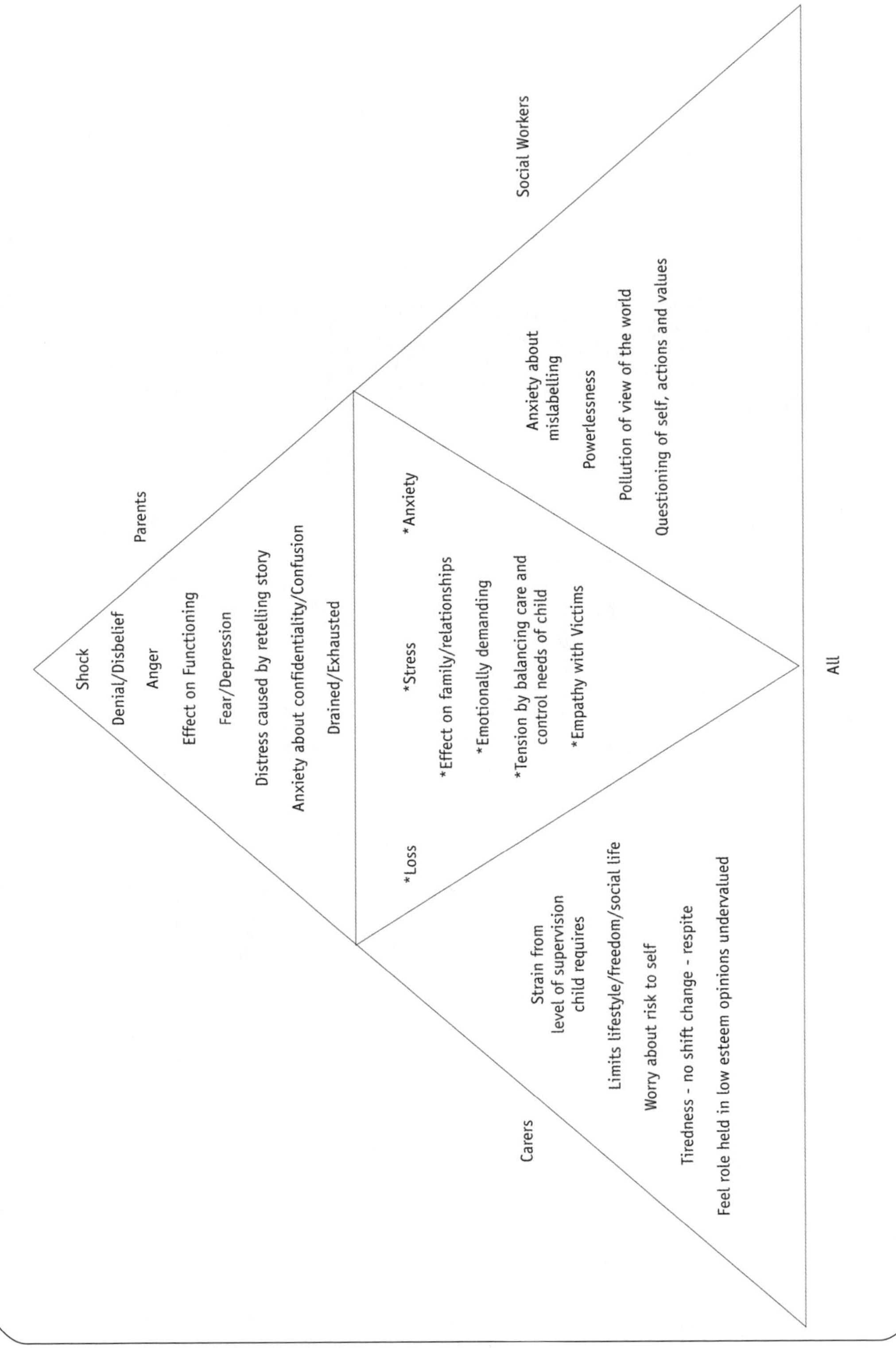

Parents
- Shock
- Denial/Disbelief
- Anger
- Effect on Functioning
- Fear/Depression
- Distress caused by retelling story
- Anxiety about confidentiality/Confusion
- Drained/Exhausted

Social Workers
- Anxiety about mislabelling
- Powerlessness
- Pollution of view of the world
- Questioning of self, actions and values

All
- *Loss
- *Stress
- *Anxiety
- *Effect on family/relationships
- *Emotionally demanding
- *Tension by balancing care and control needs of child
- *Empathy with Victims

Carers
- Strain from level of supervision child requires
- Limits lifestyle/freedom/social life
- Worry about risk to self
- Tiredness - no shift change - respite
- Feel role held in low esteem opinions undervalued

Figure 3: Views on what is needed to improve services to CSOs.

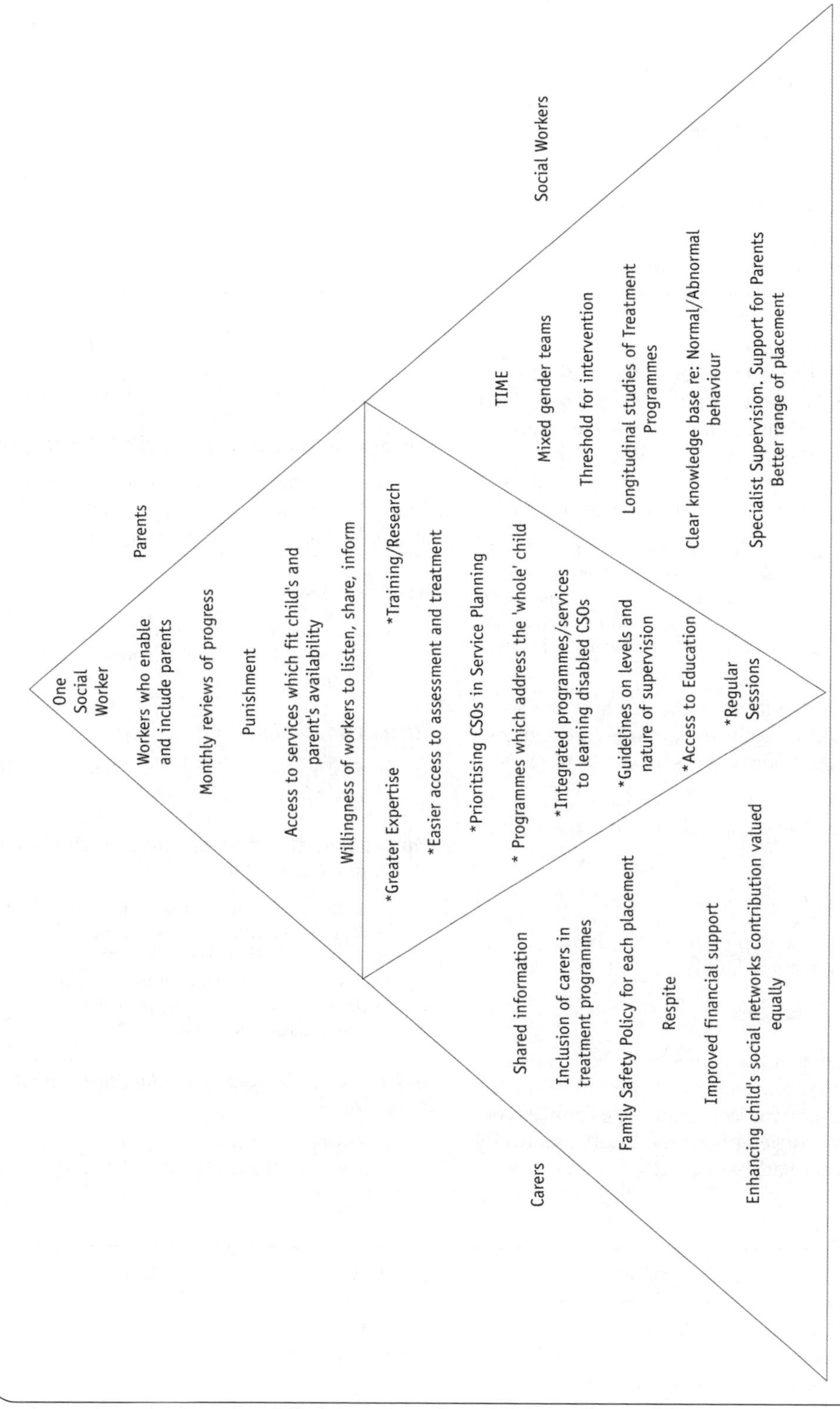

Table 2:

Losses	Families			
	1	2	3	4
Child Leaves Home temporarily/or permanently	✓	✓	✓	
Parental Job Loss			✓	
Ill Health/Effect on Functioning	✓	✓	✓	
Financial Loss			✓	
House Move		✓		
Loss of Friends		✓		✓
Sibling of abusing child moves out	✓			
Loss of Sense of Security/Stability	✓	✓	✓	

feelings in front of the children. One family had to move house in order to have the child returned to the home. Another family described staying up at night because they were afraid of attacks on the house, including arson.

Relationships were affected in every family and stress on the parents relationships was described:

> Because it added to my stress it added to O's (husband's) stress because he didn't want to think about it. But he had to because I couldn't just let it go. I couldn't just let him (son) fall by the wayside, because, then he could end up hurting a lot more people.

In one family the father talked of how the son's offending had brought the parents to the brink of divorce. Another father said about his loss of a friend:

> He was probably one of my best mates, but he cut all his ties . . . (silence).

Family disruption

Only one family experienced no change in the constitution of their family.

Fear

Fear was frequently expressed and related to various issues, but fear about the future for the offending child was common. One family were particularly worried about the local community knowing what had happened:

> I was frightened to death of something happening around here, because you know, then what's going to happen to him? What's going to happen to us?

Feelings and concerns about the offending child

The families all expressed concern about the child who had offended, some of these concerns are illustrated here in the parents own words:

Attitude to women

> That's a worry, when there isn't a man around, he treats women like absolute garbage. And when there is he's fine.

Attitude to victims

> He detests her, There's a hatred in there. . . . and it's really really deep and he won't speak her name.

Worry about the child not getting treatment or adequate treatment

> Yes and he's not getting any help. He's not being made to do any work to work this out. It's just there inside him. And I know it's there. And Social Services know its there. And the risk assessor knows its there, but nothings being done, because **nobody** knows what to do.

Anger about the fact that the punishment is insufficient

> It doesn't . . . It hasn't sunk in, no matter what anyone says. It hasn't sunk in how serious it was.

Table 3:

Family one	Family two	Family three	Family Four
CSO leaves the family 1/2 sibling returns to natural mother.	CSO leaves family home but returns after house move.	CSO joins natural father's household.	CSO remains within family.

Because it's just like (tutts) 'naughty boy, now go on' because there wasn't any punishment.

(NB. Child was subject to Supervision order)

Lack of compulsion to have treatment

Said of a son who would not engage in treatment:

I really, really believe that he shouldn't have a choice, I didn't have a choice when I was small, you know there's thousands of people who have lost the right to choose. What gives offenders the right to choose? 'I didn't wanna do it!' What gives them that right?'

. . . and again another parent:

Something's gotta be done. Something else has gotta be done. Something's gotta make him. Whether he's confronted with someone who's had the offence done to them. or whether, I don't know, I don't know how . . .

So, parents expressed considerable doubt that their child was wholly and effectively engaged in treatment which offered any significant hope of preventing further offending. Some parents experienced extreme stress and anxiety about this, feeling that the child was not sufficiently punished and therefore would re-offend. Parents felt that the child should be compelled to engage in treatment:

A lot of these young people will grow up and think, 'What happened?' Nothing. I'll do it again.

Parents suffered distress at having to repeat their stories to several workers, and consistency of social work staff was one of their firmest recommendations. Parents knew when workers were struggling in terms of their expertise and they were angry, confused and upset when given conflicting advice. Parents recognised the lack of investment in this area of work and felt ill informed about the process or progress of their child's treatment. Parents said that they needed inclusion and advice on how to manage the CSO on an incremental basis, and one couple felt that reviews of work should be at least monthly. One father said there should be:

More help for the families, rather than just centering on the person that done the thing. More help, because no one, no one's prepared for anything like this.

The level of distress was very considerable and long lasting, families struggled to come to terms with what had happened. Furthermore, the victim child is often a child of the couple, whereas the abuser may be a child of the mother only, thus mothers find themselves having to re-negotiate the basis upon which the family will function. A year after the event, describing how he couldn't sleep at night, one father said:

Cos it's really destroyed me, because I can't come to terms with what he's done, and I don't know whether I will ever be able to . . . (silence) . . . just . . . (silence).

Failure to offer parents adequate information, education, personal support and counselling, as well as inclusion in the treatment programme, will sabotage the work with the child. (Araji, 1997; Gil and Cavanagh Johnson, 1993; O'Brien, 1991). Parents need help so that they can help their children. Both parents need this support, and evidence from this study found that the women were often dealing with the situation alone because their partner could not cope with talking about it. We must recognise the trauma which parents suffer when their child abuses another. If services are not provided to support parents, they are unlikely to be able to respond appropriately to their children. Parents must be involved at every stage and need incremental guidance on managing the offending child, and in protecting siblings.

This study found that parents appreciated workers who made themselves available and who were enabling in their approach. They praised work with victims and the 'keep safe' work undertaken with siblings. In cases where the parent gains confidence and ability through involvement in 'keep safe' work the likelihood of further abuse of siblings is reduced significantly. However, 'keep safe' work is often done with the children alone and this will not be sufficient. The level of prior victimisation of mothers in these cases is high, such mothers need enabling to protect since they may never have received help themselves. One mother's report to me of the way in which the social worker empowered her, demonstrated her increased confidence and ability to parent her children. This ability extended beyond keeping safe into other parenting capacities, especially the ability to relate closely to her children and to 'listen' to them.

The carers

Again the issues raised are gathered under headings illustrated as much as possible in the carers' own words.

The children

The theme of loss was continued in the carers' stories. It was explained that children placed in care need time to build a relationship with their carer, and, recognising that the children had suffered the loss of being removed from their family, one carer commented:

> These children have offended, and they've often offended because of what's happened to them. And then when they come into care they lose their families. So more bad things happen to them. Well to them they go through, it's like a bereavement process.

It was observed that the history of children was not always fully known or understood and so the child's behaviour could be indicative of past undisclosed abuse. Therefore patience is required to enable children to feel that they can discuss both their offending behaviour and their own hurt.

One carer observed that CSOs were more compliant than many other children and that they worked hard to be liked, even to the extent of submerging their own personality in the personality of the object of their affection, but their compliance and need to be liked could be deceptive and dangerous. Another carer commented on a child who had a great need to be liked, but lacked the social skills to achieve this:

> He's a very difficult young man to get on with. When you first meet him, . . . or you've just had a few meetings with him, he comes across as very likeable . . . very intelligent. But when you get to know him he's very difficult. A very difficult young man. Very difficult, very secretive, very manipulative.

The emotional demands of caring for children who are not at a point where they can reciprocate in any way for the love shown to them was also mentioned:

> There's nothing, because you give and give and give, and sometimes get **absolutely** nothing back.

Carers explained that when a child is denied something, like freedom to come and go, or access to another child, then anger is usually directed to the carer, despite the child's awareness that the carer is not responsible for the decision. The children's anger in relation to injustice was also discussed:

> In his eyes he's been punished regardless of what's been done to him. The child is often punished, when their abuser is not.

Managing learning disabled children in placement

All four carers talked about the importance of working with the 'whole' child. The three carers who had experience of learning disabled children spoke of the need to work on the child's development in order to enhance their potential and to improve self esteem, which was recognised by carers to be an essential element in reducing offending. One carer summarised this in the following way:

> I think that these children **often** are so low in self esteem, so lacking in practical skills, that if you build up the practical side of them, then you can increase their self esteem, and one of the things you've got to develop is their personality, their self esteem, their confidence, to enable them to have other outlets in the community. rather than to seek out younger children to abuse them.
>
> If they don't build up those skills, even the basic ones like going shopping, they are not going to mix with their peers, they're not going to build relationships.
>
> They're going to be pushed back into . . . erm, furtive sexual relationships with vulnerable people.

Supervision

Supervision was a significant issue about which the carers had developed their own views. One carer talked about a particular child moving placement with a very restrictive supervision programme already in place, this included restrictions on TV viewing etc. The problem was that no-one could remember the reasons for some of these restrictions. So, carers felt that supervision had to achieve a balance between keeping others safe and developing the child's potential for growth and change.

> There is a danger in putting restrictions into place and not reviewing them.
> There is a risk of sanitising the child's world, so that he loses touch with reality, becomes institutionalised, and can never function in the community.

All the carers mentioned the importance of talking openly with the child about the carer's knowledge of his offences and discussing the carer's determination to protect others within the home, neighbourhood, or placement. However, it was acknowledged that the vigilance required is constant and demanding, this was especially true for the foster carers, who have no relief from shift changes as in a residential unit:

I find it really difficult the amount of supervision he needs. I find that really difficult. Cos I was given a set time to let him out you know. And it was difficult because I felt like a prison warder and not a carer. My role had suddenly changed and I couldn't quite deal with it. You know I felt like I was being cruel. I was in a way but to be kind. I was trying to protect him. But he is only a little boy at the end of the day. And we can't forget that you know. I found that awfully hard to do.

Carers were very concerned about children losing normal peer contacts. This is exacerbated by school exclusions, which are a frequent problem. When in school the child is often the subject of constant supervision by an adult and may be segregated from others during play and lessons, this leads to further isolation of the child, another factor the carers identified as a risk for further abusive behaviour. The carers felt that supervision is necessary but it should not be too intrusive. The following views were expressed by the carers:

- The child should be supported in different environments so they can experience normal activities. When the child knows that he is being monitored it gives him a sense of safety and inner control.
- The supervision needs to move along with the therapy the child receives and the child needs to gradually resume responsibility for their own behaviour.
- Although children may have special needs they can be manipulative and it is wise to bear this in mind, and make boundaries absolutely clear.
- It is important for children to participate in normal educational provision.

It is important to note that many CSOs are excluded from school after their offence. This puts further pressure on placements and on families and increases isolation.

Treatment as a daily activity

The carers felt that they should be thoroughly involved in and consulted about any treatment plans. Treatment was seen as a daily activity which is not confined to the therapeutic process and to treat the two as separate was likely to inhibit the child's progress. Carers stated that they had very significant information, which was not taken account of. This led to the problems described below in the carers' own words:

There is a problem with learning disability in that there is a tendency to overestimate a child's ability, because they are verbally very competent. Cognitive behavioural therapy has resulted in children repeating words, but not understanding what they are saying. This is dangerous. Carers are in a better position to know the child's limitations and to be able to comment on their difficulty in learning. Any therapy is useless unless it is targeted properly.

Another reason given for involving carers in the therapy is that they have to cope with the child both before and after therapy. Carers appreciated the opportunity to discuss the child with the therapist directly, but this did not always happen. One carer observed that a child in her care was compliant with an assessment rather than involved in it, the assessment took place many miles away, the carer never saw or spoke with the assessor.

Every carer had comments to make about meetings. Whilst all considered that they should be involved in planning meetings etc., they felt that their contribution was not as influential as the contribution of others and in this respect, the following comments were made:

I can participate in meetings, and give an opinion, but there is a sort of hierarchy of value given to opinions,depending on who holds them.

Another commented:

Meetings tend to be therapist led.
There is a tendency not to say, or know that things will not be valued, because the therapists were the most powerful contributors, in terms of their influence.
   It is important for everybody to work together, and to value each contribution, and this should be done face to face.
   Where this has been done the intervention is much more successful.

Two carers commented specifically on the influence which parents could have over the child's progress. One carer observed that when the child's mother did anything that was rejecting it influenced behaviour significantly. This child's parent had been alternatively accepting and rejecting of the child:

*I think that this, his mother specifically, **nobody else** ... his **mother**, when he gets this kind of treatment, or rejection, or this anger inside him it's to do with his mother, it comes out in these ... (silence), I'm almost certain it's the trigger with him.*

Another commented:

It is difficult to manage children when their parents also lack the mental capacity to understand the concerns and limits on behaviour. It may be necessary to closely supervise during contact when the parent puts the young abuser in risky situations. The young person may have been taught a relapse prevention strategy to remove himself from situations which the parents then set up, or are encouraging, during contact, e.g. close contact with a younger vulnerable child.

Impacts on the carers

Caring for these children does have particular impacts on carers, not least of all because of the nature of the concerns. However, the level of supervision required is onerous within a family home. The foster carers had only received basic level training on safe caring and no specialist training was provided, though one carer had support from an expert in this field.

Family safety policies were not routinely provided to guide the care of individual children and although carers described themselves as having 'safe care routines' these were related to general caring rather than to the specific needs of CSOs. One carer said she was afraid of allegations being made against her in the future:

I want to specialise, I want to do this, but at the same time, I want to make sure I'm safe.

Clearly caring for such children is time consuming, demanding and can create anxiety. For single carers in particular there is no relief. Respite is hard to find for such children and so the family life of the carers is restricted. Carers pointed out 'if you are ill, or tired, you must nevertheless maintain the same level of supervision and care and this is very hard to do'.

Providing a written family safety policy for each placement of a CSO, which is tailored to the individual child would provide a firm basis for managing the child in placement. The child's co-operation with the 'rules' around keeping safe could be reviewed as part of the treatment and risk assessment process. Tying these matters together would prevent the stultification, which appears to occur in relation to reviewing the quantity and purpose of the child's supervision.

There are only two studies which explore caring for sexually abused or abusing children in the UK. Farmer and Pollock (1998) and Macaskill (1991). Farmer's study discusses the carers' difficulties in managing the child's need

for affection with the need to keep themselves safe. The carers in her study were lacking in frameworks for understanding the child's behaviour and were excluded from therapy. In this study the residential unit and one carer (who also had access to a national expert) had direct involvement with the child's therapists, this was experienced as immensely valuable because of the opportunity to share information about the child and to collaborate in developing management strategies. One carer reported never meeting the child's 'risk assessor' and so being unable to express her view that the child was compliant with, but dismissive of, the work on his offending. It is essential that the views and observations of carers are given due consideration, failure to do so is dangerous.

O'Callaghan (1999) writes of the importance of involving carers in programmes for treating learning disabled CSOs. Only one 'looked after' child in this study was totally free of learning difficulties. Macaskill (1991) noted that carers were frustrated about their lack of involvement in planning and therapy, and this study found that carers are inconsistently involved. Professionals should note that carers were angry that their views were held in low esteem, and often dismissed by therapists, who only had limited contact with the child.

The social workers

As with other groups these interviews produced a large quantity of data and this has been collated under headings and described below. The interviews were characterised both by the workers' enthusiasm and commitment to the work and by their common difficulties and frustrations.

Parents

The social workers discussed the shock, anger and denial of parents and one worker observed that overcoming this could take weeks or months, meaning that parents would find it hard to adequately support their child during this time. Another worker said that it was no use feeling frustrated that parents didn't want to hear what social workers had to say:

It's very hard for them to recognise that this young person has gone and done something. You've got to understand where they're coming from. They've got to stand by their child, and they do love their child, . . . and if you do love somebody, you don't want to know the nasty part.

One worker discussed the embarrassment that both mothers and fathers feel, the fathers often avoiding contact with the social worker leaving the mothers to 'get on with it'. The mothers are torn between the need to protect other children, but not wanting to lose their son:

> *Both mothers were kind of evasive, but then I put that down to not really wanting to, basically, not really wanting to acknowledge what had happened.*

It is obvious that it is very hard to be the parent of an abusing child, because this involves a whole range of losses, and society is unlikely to be sympathetic to the parents plight. In some cases the parent cannot accept what has happened. One mother was described as being white with rage:

> *She just didn't want to talk about it and was disgusted by him, you know, so 'stay over there at arms length,' and I guess what I wonder is, with the shock of this, when this happens, how available are the mothers?*

There was a shared view that parents need time to overcome their initial hostility towards Social Work intervention. However, parental denial could be such that the child is prevented from accessing the treatment needed and so remains high risk, and this concern was expressed by all the workers in some way:

> *She was just so cross, so angry, and so upset at the time. She didn't want to give me access to 'Z' She didn't want me to talk to him at all. 'NO! no, I'm not interested!'*

Ultimately this family did not allow access to their child, and because of the tender age of his victim, no prosecution could be brought. He has remained untreated though his offence was serious.

Anxieties

Anxiety about this area of practice appears to decrease with experience, but, nevertheless, workers describe the reluctance of other workers to engage in practice with CSOs. One of the reasons given for this reluctance was that the work was described as isolating and too new to have tested standards. Another reason was thought to be concern related to making a wrong judgement and putting other children at risk, while some anxiety was about the possibility of making the child's behaviour worse. Workers expressed anxiety about mislabelling and the fact that 'labels can alter the whole course of a child's life'. The most experienced worker felt that anxieties would decrease if there was more research available into the efficacy of programmes.

Undertaking the work

Practice and resource issues are identified by the practitioner, see table below.

Impacts on workers

The work impacted on the workers in a variety of ways. One worker talked about the risk of 'burn out' if the emotional self is denied in order to deal with the work:

> A   *You're asking for problems, and if you don't have the problem, well either your work colleagues are going to have to deal with the problem, or your family are going to have to*

Table 4: Elements identified for good practice.

Working with child sex offenders	1	2	3	4
Working with more experienced workers increases confidence. Practice wisdom is generally gained from more experienced practitioners and developments in this area of work have been practitioner led.	✓	✓	✓	✓
The work should be undertaken in mixed gender pairs, but resources often mitigate against this.	✓	✓	✓	✓
There is a need for supervision from someone who has specific expertise in this work and such supervision is not usually available.	✓	✓	✓	✓
It is important to prepare for sessions and to reflect upon them, the time this takes is not always recognised.	✓	✓	✓	✓
More training, research and resources are needed for this area of practice which must have a multi disciplinary approach.	✓	✓	✓	✓

Table 5: Summary of resource issues.

Resource issues	1	2	3	4
SERVICES. There are problems in obtaining services for CSOs and sometimes this includes universal services i.e. education. 'Trying to get X into school, and saying, that he has behavioural difficulties, he has learning difficulties and he's dangerous. So you have lots of excuses.'	✓	✓	✓	
PLACEMENT. There is a lack of suitable placements and trained carers, or trained supporters of carers. Lack of respite and lack of ability to guarantee not placing victims with offenders.	✓		✓	
TREATMENT. There is an unevenness about provision of services provided and it is not always the most serious cases that get the input.		✓	✓	
ALLOCATION OF RESOURCES. When it comes to allocating resources they are more likely to go to victims. 'Other priorities take precedence, politically this work doesn't maintain a profile, victims attract funds, abusers don't.' 'Children who abuse don't have strong advocates in society do they?' 'People want them punished, they don't want to see them enabled to change'	✓	✓	✓	✓
TIME. Work with CSOs in fieldwork teams often measn having to cancel appointments because of other priorities and this is wrong because it gives the message to the CSO that. 'What you say is not that important, because I've found something more important to do.'	✓	✓	✓	✓

deal with the problem, because you'll lose that bit of humanity that keeps you sane.

S   *Do you think people do that?*

A   *Frightening isn't it, you deal with it all the time, and you become blasé, it's . . . to a certain degree you become immune.*

S   *mmm*

A   *And you should be angry if a three or four-year-old, or a fourteen-year-old has been abused. It's wrong. It's natural. I think a lot of these experiences which are harmful to people become like words on a page, and the emotional content of it gets forgotten.*

Another worker talked of the disgust felt at the incidents which had to be dealt with .The worker would then reflect on the impact of such an incident on their own family.

The sense of powerlessness in the case of an untreated offender was described:

Basically you think, he's tried to have sex with this five-year-old boy and there's nothing that anyone can do about it.

Another worker described the personal costs of the work, of a sort of tainting of the personality, which in summary he described as:

Workers may not always link the impact of what they're doing with the feelings and thoughts they have, but the work can make you suspect others, start to question everyone, even to question your own sexual behaviour. It impacts upon family and private life: What I have to do is constantly ground myself, because at times, it doesn't always seem like a minority of people.

The children

The workers identified a number of common features in the children with whom they worked. The children are often the oldest male child in the family, the product of a previous relationship and who has lived alone with his mother before the new relationship. There is often a history of sexual abuse of a parent, usually the mother in the family. Some parents describe their children as having significant behaviour problems prior to the offence:

What they're saying is that they've always been different, they've always been more difficult than the other children, actually they are both boys in a family of girls.

The worker then goes on to ask this question:

Its chicken and egg that kind of thing, I mean what comes first? The naughty behaviour, or the one that's naughty, I mean being labelled the one that's naughty in the family.

Some workers also discussed the children's' attitude to females:

I think he's very angry, very resentful of women, yeah, and I think that the idea he has of women, is that they . . . they are people who basically get beaten up by men.

The children's prior victimisation is sometimes, but not always known to the workers:

This child is a victim in his own right, he's had a hell of a bloody life, he's very little insight into what he's doing he's like somebody that has been wound up and then set off in motion.

Workers said that the children often lack victim empathy and do not acknowledge, or in some cases understand, the impact of their offence. Learning disability is also a feature in some of the children and the standard treatment programmes for CSOs do not work given the child's 'concrete' thinking.

Supervision of the children

One worker discussed how he had drawn up a comprehensive' Family Safety Policy' with a family, yet the child had abused again. He referred to local practice guidelines which state that ' It is very easy for professionals to overestimate the ability of parents to protect victims, whilst still in shock over the actual incident of abuse.' However, the supervision of some children was felt to be too extensive and amounted in practical terms to virtual house arrest. This raised human rights issues for the workers and fits with the observations of the carers group. The most experienced worker talked about how there is a need to move on, to take risks and to encourage those activities which are less risky and which would enhance life and recovery. This comment ties in with observations made about the limits of the responsibility of the worker:

There's something about taking clear control in the first place, which is about making it clear what you're responsible for, but there's a great deal about where that control ends, and about how you give it back.

Another worker recognised that some children will offend again, but that from a Child Protection point of view at least other children are protected during the period of treatment, or supervision.

Holistic approach

The necessity of working with the 'whole child' was asserted, since improved social skills and increased self esteem would mitigate against re-offending. Invariably though, requests for work are offence focused and this focus can cause a sort of blindness to the individual child, who can become defined by their behaviour. One worker summed this up as follows:

The guy I was working with said: 'The trouble is we get older every year, but the young people stay the same age.' I think that he was saying that unless you're careful you don't see the individuals, you just see the glue sniffer, the abuser, the thief. The label is about a particular behaviour, it's not about a particular person. But that's what you can get focused on, because that's what you're dealing with.

Finally, one worker talked about the inappropriateness of transferring models of working with adults to work with children. He believed that such models were not transferable but nevertheless, they still form the basis of most orthodox interventions. There is a need for models which are specifically designed for children and which have a more holistic approach.

Carers, parents and social workers

There were significant areas of agreement amongst the groups, that is, issues arising within one set of findings also emerged in the other two groups. Because of the very different roles of the participants there were bound to be themes specific to their own milieu. The narrative method provided a wealth of data, which there is little space here to explore but I believe the words of the participants are powerful and can speak for themselves. Below I will mention a few of the issues which arose from this study.

Cause and family treatment

Much of the literature in the review pathologises families, but it is dangerous to conclude that it is always the family environment which generates the abusive behaviour. In this study adults mentioned that some CSOs had suffered sexual harm themselves, sometimes within their family and sometimes by outsiders, for instance one child had been sexually abused by another school child. However, for many CSOs predisposing factors appeared more to do with their isolation and lack of social skills, and sometimes this was due to learning disability. This study's findings would support Bischof and Bosen's (1997) 'Ecological Perspective', which suggests that there may be other dimensions of the child's life, apart from or additionally to his family, which explicate the behaviour, and these should also be explored when making assessments. However, from the weight of findings in the literature it seems reasonable to conclude that the younger the child, the more likely it is that the cause lies within the family, or is directly connected to prior victimisation (Araji, 1997; Gil and Cavanagh Johnson, 1993; Smith and Israel, 1987). Therefore, the fact that so few families are involved directly in treatment is a cause for considerable concern.

Recidivism

All groups were concerned about recidivism. Notions about recidivism rates need to be constructed on the basis of longitudinal studies of CSOs rather than adult offenders, research into recidivism must include control groups and be informed by knowledge of normal adolescent sexual behaviour. Indications are that we are justly concerned with recidivism, but whilst we must deal with the emergence of sexual aggression in children, we cannot assume on the basis of current knowledge that they **will** become adult offenders. Our aim must be to prevent; not to predestine.

Learning difficulty

Learning difficulties were a frequent feature in the children discussed in this study. In the experience of the carers and social workers no formal assessment is made of a child's mental capacity prior to intervention. Therefore, I would question whether these children have their rights met at the initial police interview. Subsequently, treatment should be appropriately targeted and designed. The lack of an initial psychological assessment has resulted in cognitive behavioural therapy being undertaken with those who do not have the cognition to participate. It should be remembered that verbal ability can shroud intellectual inability and lead to over optimistic assessments of the impacts of treatment. Intervention with CSOs with learning difficulties is a long term task. At present a skill deficit exists and there is a failure to adequately meet either short or long-term needs.

Supervision

Guidelines on the purpose, extent and duration of day-to-day supervision must be part of any treatment programme. Treatment must include a gradual loosening of restrictions and a testing out of learning. Without this the child will increase their dependency and isolation and be unable to develop the skills which will support their adult existence, thus increasing the likelihood of re-offending.

Child mother dyad

The carers and social work group both commented on cases where they felt the mother/child relationship had significance in the development of abusive behaviour. In three cases in the 'parent' group the offender was the oldest male child from a previous relationship and lived with his mother prior to a new relationship, after which time other children had been born into the family. Bischof and Rosen (1997) suggest that the problem has to do with the child's displacement when a new male enters the household. The abuse is seen as an attempt to regain status over siblings. Gil (1993) suggests that it has to do with the loss of role and possible scapegoating as a child of the previous marriage. The victim is often the favoured child of the new marriage. So, literature suggests that the eldest male/mother relationship is significant in developing sexually abusive behaviour (Araji et al., 1993; Bischof, 1997; Gil, 1993; O'Brien, 1991; Sefarbi, 1990; Kaplan et al., 1990.) There is a suggestion that some kind of 'transmission' occurs which violates interpersonal boundaries, (O'Brien, 1991; Gil, 1993). It may be possible that the mother is in such a needy stage of her life that she does not recognise this. Two mothers in this study described how their children saw themselves as head of the household after their father had left. Three of the four children in the 'parents group' were the eldest male child of previous relationships.

Sgroi (1982), highlighted role reversal as producing vulnerability to sexual victimisation. Given that there is a tendency for girls to internalise behavioural manifestations of distress and for boys to externalise them, this role reversal for boys probably leads to vulnerability to become an abuser. Authors agree on two major social and relationship factors for predisposal to sexual aggression, isolation (including no best friend and lack of female friends) and poor social skills. Boys in the above situation have had their mother as their best friend and may well have failed to build the usual social networks, thus producing social isolation and a lack of ability to function within their peer group. This is an interesting phenomena and is worthy of further research.

Social workers

Social workers experienced many of the feelings mentioned by the other two groups. Although they had anxieties about the work itself and their management of it, there was evidence that experience reduces anxiety. All social work has personal costs, but working with offenders has been especially difficult to establish and maintain. Politically it has not attracted the level of funding which is allocated to other work. *Working Together* (NAW, 2000) removes CSOs from the child protection system and places them within the Criminal Justice System, this is symptomatic of society's need to blame rather than understand and invest in change. To dichotomise need and criminality is self-defeating. A worker said; 'People want to see them punished, not enabled to change.'

Parents felt that their children were sidelined by the system, and one mother said, 'You shouldn't have to fight, fight, fight, to get help for a child who abuses'. The feeling that these children were poorly provided for was expressed by all the narrators. The impact of keeping practice 'going' where there has been a lack of resources and political commitment is commented on by Dalgleish (1999), who says:

> 'If a worker perceives their agency taking less action than they want to, then the worker has high scores on emotional exhaustion and client depersonalisation as measured by the 'Masclach Burnout Inventory', that is, worker health is affected and burnout can occur'.

Workers with CSOs are likely to experience all the stresses of working in the area of sexual abuse, plus what appears to be a lack of societal sanction or support for their work.

Expertise

There was a strong desire for assistance in the form of greater expertise from each group. One parent said:

> There needs to be more in place and more experienced workers dealing with offenders.

. . . later she said:

> There needs to be the development of more expertise in this area.

The literature supports the views of the narrators, and many authors are critical of the quality of research which has been undertaken to date (Adler and Schutz, 1995; Araji, 1997; Vizard et al., 1996). There are certainly particular areas, e.g. normal/abnormal sexual behaviours, ideas about 'transmission' as a causal factor to mention only two, where the literature so far suggests the need for urgent further exploration. People search more for experts in times of uncertainty, yet 'expert' status is currently vested in very few practitioners in this field in the UK. The way forward is to follow Calder's suggestions and to encourage international co-operation and sharing of ideas and suggestions as well as research (Calder, 1997, 1999).

Holistic treatment

There is a need for holistic approaches to managing and treating CSOs, which takes account of their needs as children and is developmentally appropriate. Parents expressed despair that their children were not receiving adequate help and thus anxiety about re-offending was high. This anxiety may have been reduced had they been more involved in what was being done with their child. It should be borne in mind that the very fact that this group of parents were willing to be interviewed for the study indicates some insight and co-operation. Of course this will not be so in every case. However, the inclusion of parents, in terms of assessment, therapy and support is vital to success and this is stated repeatedly in the research (Araji, 1997; Vizard, 1996). Equally the child cannot wait for the parents to overcome their initial shock and denial and work needs to be offered without delay to the CSO.

This study and the literature show that these children suffer high levels of emotional, physical and sexual abuse, and frequently they have witnessed domestic violence. They often lose contact with their natural father. They are more likely to be isolated children who have poor, or non-existent peer relationships and do not have girlfriends. They may suffer from

PTSD or other serious psychological disorders, they may exhibit behavioural disturbance such as conduct disorder. Learning disability is a factor in many cases. Discovery of the abuse can lead to further loss, i.e. rejection by their family. They may also experience anger because they have been punished whereas the adult/s who harmed them have not. Yet few were receiving any treatment or therapy other than for the sex offending behaviour. Mullholland and McIntee (1999) write about the need to treat both trauma and offending behaviour. He emphasises that therapy and treatment are inseparable and a failure to treat the whole child will result in further maladjustment.

Research indicates that extensive intervention at the optimum time is the best hope of breaking the cycle of abuse. In summary, treatment needs to be regular, in sessions which do not suffer cancellation and are longer term than in the past, not less than a year. Treatment should be systemic and must address:

- The child with his needs for therapy, for treatment of offending behaviour, as well as practical, social and educational skills.
- The child's family.
- Siblings, whether victims or not.
- The placement, if any.
- The supervision of the child.
- The child's environment.

Conclusion

There is a tendency in all of us when overloaded with responsibility to regard other peoples' views as moans and irrelevant. The further down the professional hierarchy the more likely it is that views will not be listened to, where, for instance, carers complained about not being 'heard'. This study demonstrates the enormous contribution which parents and carers can make to our understanding. When exploring ways forward we must continue to include the experience and advice of our clients. Parents in this study were able to describe helpful enabling interventions, which should boost worker confidence. They were equally able to identify deficits in provision, they knew when workers were struggling, they were aware of the current limited skills and knowledge in this area of practice and they articulated their unmet needs and had clear ideas about how they could be met.

We should listen to them.

References

Adler, N. A. and Schutz, J. (1995) Sibling Incest Offenders. *Child Abuse and Neglect*. 19(7): 811–9.

Araji, S., Jache, A., Pfeiffer, K. and Smith, B. (1993) *Survey Results Describing Sexually Aggressive Children*. unpublished report. University of Alaska at Anchorage.

Araji, S. K. (1997) *Sexually Aggressive Children. Coming to Understand Them*. Thousand Oaks, Ca: Sage Publications.

Bischof, G. H. and Rosen, K. H. (1997) An Ecological Perspective on Adolescent Sex Offending. *Journal of Offender Rehabilitation*. 26(1/2): 67–88.

Calder, M. C. (1997) Young People Who Sexually Abuse, Towards an International Consensus. *Social Work in Europe*. 4(1): 36–9.

Calder, M. C. (1999) A conceptual framework for managing young people who sexually abuse. in Calder, M. C. (ED.) *Working with Young People Who Sexually Abuse: New Pieces of the Jigsaw Puzzle*. Dorset: Russel House Publishing, 109–50.

Dalgleish, L. I. (2000) Paper given at 13th International Congress on Child Abuse and Neglect, Durban, Sep.

Farmer, E. and Pollock, S. (1998) *Sexually Abused and Abusing Children in Substitute Care*. Chichester: John Wiley.

Gil, E. and Cavanagh Johnson. T. (1993) *Sexualised Children Assessment and Treatment of Sexualised Children*. Launch Press.

Glaser, B. and Strauss, A. (1967) *The Discovery of Grounded Theory*. Chicago: Aldine de Gruyter.

Kaplan, M. S., Becker, J. V. and Martinez, D. F. (1990) A Comparison of Mothers of Adolescent Incest Versus Non Incest Perpetrators. *Journal of Family Violence*. 5(3): 209–14.

Labov, W. (1972) The Transformation of Experience in Narrative Syntax. in Labov, W. (Ed.) *Language in the Inner City: Studies in Black and English Vernacular*. Thousand Oaks, Ca: Sage.

Masson, H. (1995) *Children and Adolescents who Sexually Abuse Other Children, Responses to an Emerging Problem*. University of Huddersfield.

Macaskill. C. (1991) *Adopting and Fostering a Sexually Abused Child*. Child care policy and practice series. London: B.A.A.F./Batsford.

Mullholland, S. J. and McIntee, J. (1999) The Significance of Trauma in Problematic Sexual

Behaviour in Calder, M. C. (Ed.) *Working with Young People who Sexually Abuse. New Pieces of the Jigsaw Puzzle.* Lyme Regis: Russell House Publishing.

National Assembly for Wales (2000) *Working Together to Safeguard Children.* NAW.

O'Brien, M. J. (1991) Taking Sibling Incest Seriously. in Patton, M. Q. (Ed.) *Family Sex Abuse: Frontline Research and Evaluation.* Newbury Park, Ca: Sage Publications, 75–92.

O'Callaghan, D. (1999) Young Abusers with Learning Disabilities: Towards Better Understanding and Positive Interventions. in Calder, M. C. (Ed.) (1999) op cit., 225–49.

Pomerantz, A. M. (1986) Extreme Case Formulations: A Way of Legitimising Claims. in Gilbert, N. (1993) *Researching Social Life.* London: Sage Publications, 298–9.

Reissman, C. K. (1993) *Narrative Analysis.* Thousand Oaks, Ca: Sage.

Robson, C. (1993) *Real World Research.* Oxford: Blackwell.

Sefarbi, R. (1990) Admitters and Deniers Among Adolescent Sex Offenders and Their Families: A Preliminary Study. *American Journal of Orthopsychiatry.* 60(3): 460–5.

Sgroi, S. (1982) *Handbook of Clinical Intervention in Child Sexual Abuse.* Lexington, M.A. Lexington Books.

Smith, H. and Israel, E. (1987) Sibling Incest: A Study of the Dynamics of 25 Cases. *Child Abuse and Neglect.* 11: 101–8.

Van Kaams, M. (1996) in Moustakis, C. (1994) *Phenomenological Research Methods.* London: Sage Publications. 12–3.

Vizard, E., Wynick, S., Hawkes, C. and Woods, J. (1996) Juvenile Sex Offenders: Assessment Issues. *British Journal of Psychiatry.* 168: 259–62.

Part 3: Broad Practice Issues

Chapter 6: Therapeutic Communities: A Model for Effective Intervention with Teenagers Known to Have Perpetrated Sexual Abuse

Peter Clarke

If you give a man a fish, he will have a single meal.
If you teach him how to fish, he will eat all his life.
(Kwan-Tzu)

Research indicates that approximately a third of all sexual offences are committed by teenagers (Grubin, 1998; O'Callaghan and Print, 1994). Furthermore, research into the offending history of adult sex offenders suggests that a significant number of adult paedophiles first offended during their teenage years (Abel et al., 1987). The increasing awareness in the last decade of this teenage sub-group of sexual abusers has resulted in both a significant increase in treatment programmes and research projects. Intervention with teenagers could therefore be considered to be appropriate in endeavouring to prevent individuals from developing habitual sexually abusive behaviour. This development in understanding has resulted in a significant increase in the number of specialist treatment programmes offering specific services to the sub-group of teenagers known to have perpetrated sexual abuse. In this chapter I will describe a model for residential intervention with teenagers known to have perpetrated sexual abuse.

The model adopted and developed at Glebe House is that of a specialist programme being delivered within the framework of a Therapeutic Community. Glebe House has run as a Therapeutic Community for over thirty years and for the last ten years offering a specialised programme for young men known to have perpetrated sexual abuse. The age range of residents is 15–19 years, and the average stay for completion of programme is two years. Various components of the programme will be discussed to demonstrate the workings of the interventions designed to offer young men an opportunity to move away from destructive choices they have made in the past. It is very much with the victims and potential future victims in mind that this work is undertaken.

Our experience of the young men that are referred to Glebe House is that they themselves have suffered significant trauma, often during their early years. It is within the framework of the Children Act (1989) that we undertake work with young men that we identify as being 'Children in Need' within legislation. All work with children and young people has been subject to a considerable shift in understanding and perception since the Children Act (1989). Intervention programmes for teenagers who have sexually abused have begun in recent years to begin to assess how these shifts might be incorporated in the ethos of offence specific work and intervention. The majority of intervention programmes established for teenagers who have sexually abused have their roots in the services developed for adults. In recent years the significance of addressing the young person's developmental and emotional needs has been highlighted (see Hackett and O'Callaghan, Chapter 1), especially in identifying and working with power issues as a means of preventing future offences (Jenkins, 2000). Therapeutic Communities can provide an intensive setting for this holistic work. Intervention during teenage years within the Therapeutic Community context offers a real opportunity to reframe previous learning experiences, and to increase the range of life experiences in order to begin to build a lifestyle that includes the potential to live in non-abusive ways.

Until recently, the principal model of understanding of the processes involved in the perpetration of sexual abuse has been derived from intervention programmes or research with adults. However, in recent years there has been a significant increase in work with teenagers who have sexually abused and this has been matched by a growth in research that has evidenced a shift towards a more holistic view of the needs of children and young people.

Within the field of work with perpetrators of sexual abuse there has been a re-evaluation of the essentially cognitive-behavioural approaches adopted by the vast majority of intervention programmes (Marshall et al., 2000). The fixed patterns that practitioners seek to elaborate into cycles might not be as prevalent for teenage sexual offenders as common orthodoxy suggests. In contrast to adult offenders, teenage abusers are less likely to have persistent sexual fantasy or to have engaged in elaborate planning. This suggests that alternatives to the structured intervention style used with adults might be more effective for teenagers. Recent shifts in understanding of issues in the work with teenagers who have sexually abused would reinforce this more eclectic position. Some assumptions that practitioners use as a matter of course are being challenged, for example that there are likely to be a significant number of unknown offences, or that there is likely to be overt or covert planning (Marshall et al., 2000). Additionally, there is a questioning of the concept that there is a clear offence pattern (Chaffin, 2000). For teenagers known to have perpetrated sexual abuse the potential for the index offence to be truly the first incident of abuse is greater than for adults. If there is a single known event, or even a small number of events, then the relevance of using a cycle of behaviour should be reviewed.

Beech and Fordham's (1997) study of community based treatment programmes with adult sex offenders noted that the therapeutic climate appears to be a significant indicator of treatment effectiveness. In this study the groups rating highest for negative environment and leader control scored lowest on level of positive change. Groups that are able to form cohesively and generate a sense of support and interdependence created the most positive change in members. This offers an encouraging message to Therapeutic Communities who historically have stressed the significance of the 'therapeutic relationship' within the community group as a means of promoting positive change.

The Therapeutic community ethos

At the core of the therapeutic community movement is a belief that the process of living together is itself a tool for therapeutic change. It is through the resolution of group issues within the 'living and learning environment' (Jones, 1968) that key changes in an individual's world view can be facilitated. Current thinking about the therapeutic community environment uses a model of human developmental sequence to conceptualise the value and meaning of the living experience. Haigh has identified what he terms a *secondary emotional development*, a five-stage process that offers an opportunity to re-experience and re-work issues that may have been left unresolved during primary (early years) experience (Haigh, 1999). The operation of a therapeutic community can therefore be understood through the concepts of:

- attachment
- containment
- communication
- involvement
- agency

This model is mirrored by the concept of the adolescent task being a second separation from carers. Second individuation suggests that the adolescent shift from childhood into adulthood is achieved through a re-working of the issues experienced in early childhood. If the parental figures and mental structures internalised in early childhood are founded on distorted and abusive relationships then this opportunity for reconstruction is crucial. These issues are made more complex due to physiological changes in the teenager but the solutions a teenager produces will form the foundation for the beliefs, attitudes and world view that will shape adult behaviour (Blos, 1962). Recent research with teenagers who have sexually abused is beginning to suggest that within the range of antecedents to the development of sexually abusive behaviours issues relating to attachment can be highlighted as significant (Harris and Staunton, 2000). A therapeutic community offers an opportunity to experience more secure forms of attachment with safer adults and therefore facilitates the reconstruction of healthier internal structures.

> *The experience of loss, rejection, lack of warmth or empathy from parental figures can set a template of insecurity upon which subsequent experiences at school, in the extended family and with friends can be superimposed ... Research ... has focused on understanding the possible links between disruptive attachment, intimacy-*

deficit and sex offending. Generally, such investigations have found a prevalence of insecure attachment, high levels of anxiety and social isolation in young male sex offenders.

(Harris et al., 2000, p59)

Approaching the possible treatment needs of teenagers who have perpetrated sexual abuse through a framework of human emotional development, with attachment issues forming a necessary starting point, may enable practitioners to make sense of the wide range of research findings relating to the abuser's own experiences of abuse. Understanding the impact upon abusers of having been subject to sexual victimisation will always present difficulties for researchers due to the secret nature of the experiences. Research studies looking at an abuser's own experiences of sexual victimisation have noted a vast range of prevalence from self reported experiences of sexual victimisation, typically between 30% and 70% of abusers stating that they themselves were victims of childhood sexual abuse (Vizard et al., 1995; and Ineke Way in Chapter two for a review). This makes the identification of experiences as a child of sexual victimisation as an antecedent to perpetration of sexual abuse problematic. Salter recently noted that the introduction of polygraph tests in the evaluation of her treatment programme reduced the self-report of childhood victim experiences from approximately 50% of the group to 30% (Salter, 1997). This raises questions about the validity and significance of reports of either being subject to or witnessing physical abuse within the family setting. Some research has suggested that boys who have been victims of sexual abuse are significantly more likely to go on to perpetrate sexual abuse themselves if they have a history of either being subject to, or witnessing, intrafamilial violence (Skuse et al., 1998). If this is viewed in relation to the resultant harmful effect upon the development of an attachment style in early childhood then a clear treatment pathway can be identified.

The following sections detail various elements of the Glebe House Therapeutic Programme. The different components are designed to address a range of needs presented by teenagers who have sexually abused using a holistic and emotional developmental model. Inherent within this is a psychodynamic understanding that identifies attachment issues as the starting point for therapeutic engagement.

Glebe House Therapeutic Programme

There are five key components to the therapeutic experience on offer at Glebe House. Milieu is the term used for the whole living environment. This is the core of the therapeutic experience and acts as the container for the more formal areas of input. It is in the Milieu that individuals have opportunities to experiment with alternative coping strategies. The Milieu is an intense emotional environment where transference and countertransference issues can be explored in real concrete ways. It places flesh onto the skeleton of structures adopted from other aspects of the Therapeutic Programme. This offers a real test to the effectiveness of the other aspects of the Therapeutic Programme and evidences the behaviours relevant to Risk Assessment. The five components are:

- milieu setting
- therapy programme
- offence focused programme
- community projects
- daily meetings

1. Milieu setting

(a) Milieu: attaching and understanding meaning

It is in the management of the environment, in the forming and reforming of relationships and the understanding of group dynamics that a young person has opportunities to learn skills that will assist in the development of a non-abusive lifestyle. This is the arena where individuals have a chance to rework the stages of emotional development, starting with attachment issues. It is in the referral and joining process that attachment issues usually begin to surface. For some young men in the community attachment might remain the primary therapeutic arena throughout their placement. For these young men attachment is usually connected with basic and powerful emotions. Attachment might be feared or experienced as threatening, or alternatively it may be sought in an overly demanding and suffocating manner. Attachment style is the foundation for all other therapeutic engagements within the community. It is the emotional language that interprets all human relationships into an individual's own understanding of the world.

Teenagers living in a Therapeutic Community have an opportunity to combine *secondary*

Figure 1: Therapeutic experience.

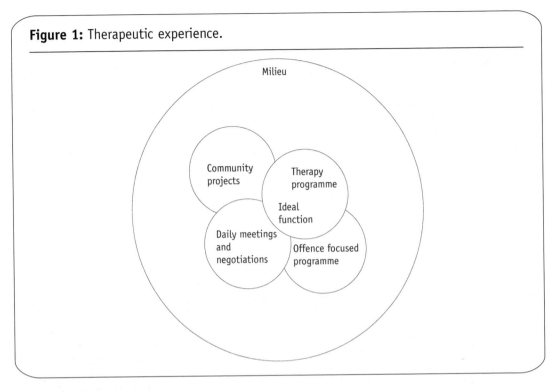

emotional development (Haigh, 1999) with the *second individuation* process. Basic early year's solutions to issues relating to attachment will shape the nature of all future relationships. In the teens young people revisit their early year experiences and have an opportunity to fix alternative solutions. The attachments formed during a teenager's placement within a therapeutic community can potentially counter destructive visions of the world.

Significantly, it is in the leaving process that the strength of attachments are truly tested. Leaving presents both practical and metaphorical issues. This can be accompanied with powerful emotions, such as anger, a sense of loss, abandonment, hope or fear. The loss of an important attachment will often generate a review of the nature and meaning of that attachment. This will usually involve heightened emotional experiences, such as intense fear of what the future may hold, and the dread of the impending loss of significant attachments. Interestingly, communities that have existed for many years report that at times previous clients will return to visit. Occasionally these returning clients will not meet any staff who knew them during their placement. It is the building that holds the significance for the young person. This acts as a very concrete

container for and symbol of the significant relationships experienced during their placement.

Assessment is a carefully staged process. Throughout referral and assessment the significance and meaning of the interactions is interpreted as a means of developing an understanding of the young person's ability to form a variety of attachments. The individual young person's needs may alter the process, but the model used as a starting point contains a number of benchmarks. These act as opportunities to review placement and to make overt statements about inclusion, or the wish for inclusion. Sometimes it is the first time that a young person has ever heard that adults actively want them around and that adults believe they are worth time and energy. This can be experienced as overwhelming for young people who have had problematic childhood experiences. The staging of the assessment process is designed to enable the young person to take small and manageable steps towards a more long term commitment.

Stages of assessment

- enquiry
- assessment visit
- five day assessment

- four week assessment
- review

During the enquiry stage it is the professionals that are communicating. After an initial contact is made reports are considered and discussions regarding the potential assessment are started. The first contact with the young person is usually an assessment visit. Ideally, staff from the Intake and Assessment Team will visit the young man in his current placement. This is an information-sharing visit. The young person is given information about Glebe House and offered opportunities to talk about himself and his understanding of his current situation. Progression through each subsequent stage of the assessment process is through mutual consent of the young person, Glebe House and the referring agency. The young man's first contact with Glebe House is usually at the start of a 'five day visit', although occasionally we suggest a single day visit. The five day visit is seen in terms of information sharing, when the young man is invited to attend parts of the programme. However, usually there is no offence specific work undertaken during this week.

At the end of the five day visit, ideally the young man leaves the community for at least a weekend. This reinforces the active choice that needs to be made in returning for a 'four week assessment' if the young person is to return. During the four week assessment, one to one sessions are usually directed at information gathering, including some offence specific information. At the close of the four week assessment a statutory review is held, and it is in that forum (if appropriate) that an offer of a placement is made. The therapeutic programme is designed to run for approximately two years.

Following the formal joining to the community a young person can then begin to engage in community life. This may signal a shift in the therapeutic task, from attachment to containment and possibly on to communication, involvement and agency (Haigh,1999).

(b) Milieu: containment

We don't have rules here, we have boundaries.

This description of the containing process was given by a resident to a young man on assessment. Boundaries are different from rules in a number of ways. A boundary is flexible,

it can move, just as the boundary between land and sea moves with the tides. Boundaries are jointly owned and negotiated by all members of the community. They're not imposed by the adults. Boundaries are essential to provide safety for individuals and for the group. They offer a forum in which to engage in discussion and negotiation about a range of power based issues. These negotiations must be held within a safe and containing environment where all members of the group can expect the group and its boundaries to maintain a reasonable level of physical and emotional safety while allowing true expressions of feelings.

The balance between maintaining a safe and containing environment, that also allows for free expression, requires significant input and structure. Within the Glebe House programme this is provided by regular group meetings. The resident group meet with the staff team three times a day for approximately two and a half hours in total. Each day opens with a community meeting to set the tasks for that morning and review recent events within the community's life. This meeting is chaired by a member of the resident group, and offers a forum for the group to attempt to make sense of the dynamics within the community. Individuals can be supported and challenged: often and most effectively by their peers.

After lunch there is a 'business meeting' again chaired by a resident. Once a week this has a particular focus on negotiation of proposals to change boundaries, either in the short or long term. Proposals can range from requests for reduced supervision for a specific activity to discussions regarding the operation of a particular boundary. The Director of the community reserves the right to veto any change in boundaries that is considered unsafe. Negotiation is a complex procedure, and the community seeks to gain mandates through consensus rather than through majority rule.

The final group meeting of the day is a review meeting marking the end of the 'work' day. Residents are asked to give a verbal account of their day. The group has an opportunity to give feedback regarding an individual's behaviour. Additionally, there is a planning element in the meeting to consider the approaching evening.

(c) Milieu: communication

All the aspects of the therapeutic programme should be interlinked and there will often be an overlapping of the developmental issues being addressed at any stage. Communication issues are explored in partnership between all members of the community group. Just as boundaries are necessary to provide a safe containing environment, communication is equally necessary to begin to think about how an individual might resolve power issues during the separation from the community and engage with the 'real world'. It is through addressing issues about communication that a 'culture of enquiry' can be established. The group can then begin to seek to understand behaviours, thoughts and feelings. The practice of scrutinising and questioning often provokes strong reactions, usually of anger or anxiety. It is an uncomfortable and challenging task. Within the Milieu and the structures of the daily meetings this potentially uncomfortable and challenging task can be directly undertaken.

In addition to regular daily meetings it is possible that at any time any member of the community can call a 'Communications Meeting'. This is a full group meeting that is intended to unpack potentially destructive dynamics. It offers individuals a platform where they can express themselves in a safe and contained manner. Conflict can then be resolved in non-abusive ways, and these alternative resolutions may be generalised out as coping strategies for the future. For example, one common statement made by the young people is 'He is annoying.' This can be personalised to 'He is annoying *me*' and possibly generalised out to explore how 'annoying people' might be coped with in the wider community in ways that are not abusive, or damaging to either party.

(d) Milieu: involvement

As a young person moves through the Glebe House programme they have an opportunity to make an input in the management of their physical environment, generating a sense of 'ownership' that furthers and consolidates the human attachment bonds created in the group. Involvement gives a young person an opportunity to identify what they are good at, and to take risks to learn new skills. Understanding the process of change recognises that a change *to* something is more sustainable than a move *away* from something. Community projects range from very practical tasks to taking some responsibility for the day-to-day

management of the group through the chairman role. Regularly throughout the year there are clearly defined community events, for example a holiday, bonfire night and various outward bound exercises. These, coupled with the daily tasks of running a large house in the country, offer many opportunities for the group to learn while working together.

The chairman role has a high status within the community. Residents are offered guidance and support within this role. This role offers opportunities to the young people to enable them to hold a position of power and status where there will be monitoring and feedback given. Learning how to exercise power and influence in non-abusive ways is a vital skill for long-term relapse prevention. Developing an understanding of the responsibility that accompanies positions of power and influence enables a young person to reflect in more general ways about the nature of power. Often offences and victim experiences have contained elements including an experience of powerlessness, learning how to hold power appropriately can act as a reparative experience that can have long-term benefits.

(e) Milieu: agency

In communities where members have agency . . . an asymmetry and difference between therapist and patient is accepted, but an automatic assumption of 'superiority' is rejected: members acknowledge that anybody in the group might have something valuable to contribute to any other member.

(Haigh, 2000, p254)

Agency reflects the culture of being empowered, either for the individual or for the group. Agency is the final expression of the process of developing a non-abusive but empowered community. Authority has been described as existing between people rather than within individuals (Haigh, 2000). Agency is the ability to hold responsibility and authority in non-abusive ways. If a young man can hold a position of agency within the community the final therapeutic task is to 'face him looking outside', facilitated by a move into independence.

At Glebe House independence is re-framed as *interdependence*. It is not the ability to live as an island that is the goal, rather the ability to form and maintain appropriate support networks, and identify when others might be needed to help solve a problem. Some young men coming towards the end of their placement, who may be living in the separate independence bungalow, negotiate a staged separation from the community. This is the final test within the Therapeutic Programme of the appropriate exercise of power. The goal for a placement for a young man known to have abused is to reduce risk of recidivism *in the long term*. The exercise of agency in the form of the appropriate use of personal power is a sustainable skill that will support the mechanics of risk reduction plans and relapse prevention strategies.

2. Therapy programme

Often the motive for referral to Glebe House is that the young man is known to have perpetrated sexual abuse. They remain, however, young men, with all the developmental needs other young men have. They have yet to resolve the adolescent task of moving from childhood into adulthood, and have many questions left unanswered. In addition to the chaos of this developmental stage, the young men at Glebe House are often contending with traumatic early year experiences. Attachment issues are common as are experiences of being a victim to abusive authority figures. These are young men who have specialist needs, and should be recognised as 'Children in Need' as detailed in the UK legislation.

To meet some of the identified needs of the young men Glebe House offers a wide range of group and one to one experiences. Some parts of this programme are elective, others not so, although it is made clear to the young men at the close of their assessment which elements are not negotiable for them. Psychotherapy is seen as appropriate for some of the young men and it is always elective. A young man must make an active choice to begin psychotherapy sessions.

I would particularly highlight three of the group experiences within the therapy programme to give a sense of the range of inputs on offer: the Film Group, Linkgroup, and Education.

The Film Group: offers the residents at Glebe House an opportunity to make a film. The dialogue is unscripted, with the group working from a set of story boards. Traditionally the film is shown to an invited audience as the start of the Christmas programme. This experience is held in high regard by the resident

group, and offers opportunities to build self-esteem and to explore aspects of human relationships in a non-threatening forum.

Linkgroup: consists of the entire resident community, with consistent facilitators from the staff team. It offers members opportunities to examine events from their formative years as well as day-to-day issues as they affect the life of the community. It uses both experiential and discussion based exercises to highlight links between past experiences and current behaviour. It suggests that all behaviour can be linked up, so understanding one aspect of a relationship might assist in unravelling another.

Education: Almost all the young men at Glebe House have had interrupted education, therefore education has become a core element of this programme. Due to the age of the group, education is usually not statutory. The young person's experience of the schooling system has often been negative, so, as a result, the education packages are presented in an adult form with emphasis on 'Lifelong Learning'. There is a particular emphasis placed on improving literacy and numeracy skills. This can increase self-esteem and facilitates the sense of developing agency.

3. Offence focused programme

Each young person within the Offence Focused Programme can expect a weekly one to one session, and at times they will form part of a small group. Additionally, the management of immediate risk is a task for the whole group as it affects the whole group. This has the effect of placing an individuals potential risk on the community agenda. If an individual wishes to negotiate for reduced supervision for a particular activity then that is the business of the whole group (with the added protection of the Director's veto).

The Offence Focused Programme is subdivided into four phases:

The first phase incorporates the formal assessment process, the primary task being information gathering. At this stage small group work would be unlikely. Supervision remains very tight (either no trips off site, or only with one to one staff supervision). At the close of the first phase an initial risk analysis will have been completed and subsequently supervision can be reviewed. Risk analysis is a complex process, which weighs static information against current factors (see Calder, 2000 and Calder, 2001 for a review of these concepts). The aim is to reduce risk of re-offending in the long term, containment during these early stages of a placement must be weighted against the knowledge that at some stage in the future each young man will be largely unsupervised. It is in the first phase that an initial assessment of treatment needs is made. It is our experience that only a small number of young men referred have already developed a strong fixation or have a strongly defined offence pattern. Young men who have a clear offence pattern, often accompanied by multiple known victims, will be offered a more cognitive behavioural approach.

In the second phase of the Offence Focused Programme a young person will often join a small group, they will also continue to receive weekly one to one sessions. The small group aims to begin to give ownership of the offence analysis back to the young person. Some (or all) known offences are discussed in detail, and the young person is asked to elaborate on particular aspects of their known offence, and factors that encouraged that abusive behaviour are explored. Working in small groups allows peers to challenge beliefs and attitudes, as well as offering a different perspective to assist in understanding risk. This close focus exercise will often be followed by offering some structures to the group to assist in the understanding of the abuse process. At times the group might be offered Finkelhor's Four Preconditions model (Finkelhor, 1984), at other times a step model is used. Using the idea of cycles of behaviour may be appropriate for some young men, although they are used with some caution. Sexually abusive behaviour may not be planned or fixed at this stage and an over emphasis on the repetitive nature of an offence cycle may encourage a worldview of abusive behaviour as inevitable.

The third phase of the Offence Focused Programme again usually consists of both one to one work and membership of a small group. The focus is shifted from analysis and understanding past behaviour to working in the 'here and now' and developing possible strategies for future situations. For some young men this may result in very concrete relapse prevention strategies, and for some the creation of a written folder with plans and exercises to divert the progression towards an incident. For others the work will remain more in the 'here and now' with the emphasis on developing an emotional vocabulary that will enable the young person to think through the consequences of their behaviours. There are often exercises aimed at creating the skills that will support relapse prevention in areas such as:

- problem solving
- anger management
- victim experiences
- victim empathy
- relationships
- consequences: 'seemingly irrelevant decisions'
- fantasy
- anxiety management
- social skills

In the fourth and final phase of the Offence Focus Programme the emphasis shifts to interdependence, as the young person is encouraged to begin to look outwards towards the wider community beyond Glebe House. The group work may be phased out, and the frequency of one to one work reduced. The emphasis for input will vary depending on treatment needs and on the move-on plan. Work is tailored to fit with the likely living environment post Glebe House. For some young men there may be a significant increase in family contact, and usually there will be opportunities to increase contact with the community the young person will be moving to. Thought is given to reinforcing internal inhibitors, and consideration is given to likely external monitoring. Advice is offered to professionals who will hold case responsibility regarding external monitoring and support as this is regarded as a vital element in the majority of relapse prevention plans. If non-professionals, either within or outside the family, are to be included as external protectors, then some thought must be given to supporting these individuals in that role.

One aspect of the Offence Focused Programme that intertwines with the other strands of the Therapeutic Community described in this chapter is that of supervision of residents when off site. There is a clear stepped supervision structure which ranges from young men being asked not to leave the grounds to various stages of off-site staff supervision to paired trust exercises with other residents, and finally, if the risk assessment allows, to trust exercises where young men are unsupervised for agreed periods of time. Risk levels are dynamic, and can alter significantly depending on situations. The static risk factors such as previous offence history are significant and are combined with more fluid factors such as an individual's current emotional state or the scenario. An individual who might be regarded as being of high risk in a shopping centre may be able to have a reduction of their supervision in another setting that presented a different environment. The day-to-day management of supervision levels presents one of the greatest challenges to the staff team, and to the community as a whole. The pressure to revert to a 'children's home response' can be seen clearly and needs to be resisted. By 'children's home response', I mean a response where the adults make decisions *for* the young people, rather than *with* the young people. It is not simply that non-inclusive decisions are more likely to be challenged or ignored, but rather that the process of making inclusive decisions reinforces the development of agency.

4 + 5. Supporting the staff

The structures described above form a complex organic system, and there is a clear vision as to how the various aspects are able to fit together constructively. However, this is a process that requires much thought and effort to maintain. The forces that seek to shift the community away from its core task are powerful. These include: transference, countertransference, projective identification, and practical or ideological influences. The reality is that the task is often great, and that there are tight time constraints. A creative and productive team can become overwhelmed by what appears to be a never-ending task. Measuring effectiveness has always been problematic in this field, recidivism rates can offer some benchmark but the numbers of young people in residential specialist care are too small for meaningful research into recidivism.

Acknowledging stresses and seeking to operate a service that is not abusive towards the adults employed requires a support network that can function on many levels. Clear and effective management, skilled staff supervision that enables individuals to think about their work in creative and supportive ways, and a robust appraisal system are essential tools in building a support network for the team

(Obholzer, 1994). Additionally, the team is given a range of opportunities to think about the dynamics they are working within. Both the Milieu Team and the practitioners who work in the Offence Focused Programme, are each offered fortnightly group supervision with external facilitators. In addition, the whole team meets with an outside facilitator alternate weeks. A number of staff have clinical supervision, or therapy, from practitioners outside the organisation. This intensive input is seen as essential for maintaining the community's task, and for encouraging the adults to think about the dynamics within the community in ways that are sustainable. An ethical organisation will recognise the need for this level of support both to meet the work task, but also to counteract the emotional effect of work in this field for individual practitioners.

Overview

There are some strong arguments, derived from research and theory, which suggest that a therapeutic community model is particularly suitable as an effective intervention strategy for teenagers who are known to have perpetrated sexual abuse. It seeks to combine a therapeutic experience that generates a *secondary emotional development* with the developmental stage of *second individuation*. The therapeutic community model allows for the specialist input contained within the Offence Specific Programme to be integrated with the holistic approach that offers assistance to young men who are negotiating the bumpy ride through adolescence. This model allows for a revisiting of early year experiences, at a time when new foundations are being put in place that will shape the future worldview of the individual. Glebe House offers structures for the young person to experiment with the appropriate exercise of power and to form and maintain human relationships within a safe environment. The two-year programme allows time and space for young people to integrate and then separate as they move into adulthood. It offers an environment of enquiry where attachments can be established, explored and understood.

Acknowledgements

I would like to acknowledge the support of Nina Neild and Pamela Atkinson in the preparation of this chapter.

References

Abel, G. Becker, J. and Mittleman, M. (1987) Self Reported Sex Crimes of Non-incarcerated Paraphiliacs. *Journal of Interpersonal Violence.* 2 3–25.

Beech, A. and Fordham, A. (1997) Therapeutic Climate of Sexual Offender Treatment Programs. *Sexual Abuse: A Journal of Research and Treatment.* 9: 219–37.

Blos. (1962) *On Adolescence.* London: Routledge.

Calder, M. C. (2000) *The Complete Guide To Sexual Abuse Assessments.* Dorset: Russell House Publishing.

Calder, M. C. (2001) *Juveniles and Children who Sexually Abuse: Frameworks for Assessment.* (2nd edition). Dorset: Russell House Publishing.

Chaffin, M. (2000) *Family and Ecological Emphasis in Intervention: A Developmental Perspective in Working With Children, Adolescents and Adults With Sexually Abusive Behaviours.* NOTA Presentation, Dublin.

Finkelhor, D. (1984) *Child Sexual Abuse: New Theory and Research.* New York, Free Press.

Grubin, D. (1998) *Sex Offending Against Children: Understanding the Risk.* London: Home Office.

Haigh, R. (1999) The Quintessence of a Therapeutic Community Environment: Five Universal Qualities. in Campling, P. and Haigh, R. (Eds.) *Therapeutic Communities: Past, Present and Future.* London: Jessica Kingsley Publishers.

Harris, V. and Staunton, C. (2000) The Antecedents of Young Male Sex Offenders. in Boswell, G. (Ed.) *Violent Children and Adolescents: Asking the Question Why.* London, Whurr Publishers.

Jones, M. (1968) *Social Psychiatry in Practice.* Harmondsworth, Penguin.

Jenkins, A. (2000) *Making it Fair: Creating a Context for Just Intervention With Disadvantaged Young People Who Have Sexually Abused.* Keynote address NOTA conference, Dublin.

Kwan-Tsu Chinese Proverb.

Marshall, W. and Serran, G. (2000) Improving the Effectiveness of Sexual Offender Treatment. *Trauma, Violence and Abuse.* 1(3): 203–22.

Obholzer, A. (1994) Managing Social Anxieties in Public Sector Organisations. in Obholzer, A. and Zagier, V. (Eds.) *The Unconscious at Work: Individual and Organisational Stress in the Human Services.* London: Routledge.

O'Callaghan, D. and Print, B. (1994) Adolescent Sexual Abusers: Research, Assessment and Treatment. in Morrison, T., Erooga, M. and Beckett, R. (Eds.) *Sexual Offending Against Children: Assessment and Treatment of Male Abusers.* London: Routledge.

Salter, A. (1997) NOTA presentation, Southampton.

Skuse, D., Bentovim, A., Hodges, J., Stevenson, J., Andreou, C., Lanyado, M., Williams, B. and McMillan, D. (1998) Risk Factors for Development of Sexually Abusive Behaviour in Sexually Victimised Adolescent Boys: Cross Sectional Study. *British Medical Journal.* 317 Jul. 175–9.

Vizard, E., Monck, E. and Misch, P. (1995) Child and Adolescent Sex Abuse Perpetrators: A Review of the Research Literature. *Journal of Child Psychology and Psychiatry.* 36:5 731–56.

Further Information

Peter Clarke can be contacted at: *training@glebehouse.org.uk*

Chapter 7: Developing Focused Care: A Residential Unit for Sexually Aggressive Young Men

Dr Andrew Kendrick and Ranald Mair

Introduction

. . . and then they come and telt me it was for sex offenders and I went 'Ah well, at least I'm not the only one'. That put a big bit off of me because now I ken it's not just me, the whole unit's part of it. So it took a lot off of me, kind of calmed me down a bit.
(young man)

In this chapter, we will review the first 12 months in the development of a focused residential unit for sexually aggressive young men. An important lesson to be learnt from this first 12 months concerns the development of a 'core programme' emphasising a safe, secure and nurturing environment which at the same time acknowledges and addresses the issues of sexual aggression. The work in the focused unit was developed on the basis of an integrated model, where residential care staff were involved in both the provision of individual work on sexual aggression; core residential tasks; and confronting and challenging the repertoire of background attitudes and behaviours which form the basis of the young men's sexual aggression. In addition to this, the work involved issues of victimisation and trauma. The experience of the unit suggests that individual personal change programmes cannot productively take place unless this is supported by a secure and stable care experience. As Farmer and Pollock state, ' . . . the *context* in which therapeutic help was offered seemed to be of considerable importance.' (Farmer and Pollock, 1998, p182).

The unit is part of Geilsland School which offers a residential care service for young men aged between 15 and 18 and operates as a Scotland-wide resource. It is managed by the Church of Scotland's Board of Social Responsibility; although it is non-denominational in its intake and staffing. The areas of need that it responds to include: alternative to custody; offending; learning difficulties; sexual behaviour; independent living; vocational training; developing life skills; and relationships. It provides 36 residential places in three recently completed, purpose-built, residential units on the campus. Education is provided on campus and links are also made to further education courses outwith the school.

The Context for the Development

Work with sexually aggressive young people has become an increasing priority. A significant proportion of sexual abuse is perpetrated by children and adolescents (Glasgow et al., 1994; Grubin, 1998; Hoghughi, 1997; Monck and New, 1996; National Children's Home, 1992, Ryan, 1991a). In England and Wales, criminal statistics show that 45 per cent of the individuals cautioned and 13.5 per cent of those found guilty of sexual offences were between 10 and 20 years of age (Masson and Morrison, 1999).

The Committee of Enquiry into Children and Young People who Sexually Abuse Other Children recommended a 'continuum of care' which would make available a range of services from child guidance clinics (working with children displaying pre-abusive behaviours) to secure accommodation. Within this continuum of care, the Committee stated a need for the establishment of more specialist residential treatment facilities for children and young people who have abused other children, who are assessed as being in need of this type of intervention (National Children's Home, 1992; see also Heinz, Ryan and Bengis, 1991). However, Fisher and Beech (1999) contrast recent developments with adult sex offenders, with the lack of progress for adolescents who abuse; 'the availability of assessment and treatment is . . . largely dependant on local developments, and these do not constitute a coherent service that requires a framework of resources and policies' (Fisher and Beech, 1999, p. 247; see also Masson, 1995; 1997; Morrison, 1999; Scottish Executive, 2000). Farmer and Pollock (1998), in their study of sexually abused and abusing children in substitute care, found that little work focused on the abusing behaviour (see also Lindsay, 1999).

Abuse by young people in care settings was highlighted in the Scottish Office 'Children's Safeguards Review' and Roger Kent recommended that further programmes for helping young abusers need to be initiated (Kent, 1997, p127). The Scottish Office guidance on inter-agency co-operation in child protection also stressed that 'perpetrators who are themselves children or young people, will need help, and, in particular, access to specialist assessment and services, such as personal change programmes and counselling to reduce the likelihood that they will continue to abuse children as they mature' (Scottish Office, 1998a, p. 49). Research in the UK and the United States 'lends support to personal change programmes which use a range of methods based on a core of cognitive-behavioural work' (Scottish Office, 1997; see also Vennard, Sugg, and Hedderman,1997; Worling and Curwen, 2000). The Government's response to the 'Children's Safeguards Review', acknowledged the Geilsland proposal to pilot a specialist residential service for sexually aggressive young men in the context of developments across the range of provision (Scottish Office, 1998b).

A number of important issues in the residential care of sexually aggressive young men have been highlighted in the literature and have had to be addressed in the development of the focused unit. There are important implications for placement policies, staffing levels, training and supervision, and access to external consultancy. There are also significant issues in relation to building design and structure, peer group characteristics, behaviour management and control, communication and decision-making, and confidentiality (Centre for Residential Child Care, 1995; Epps, 1997a, 1997b; Gil, 1993; National Children's Home, 1992; Skinner,1992). The issue of through-care and integration back into the community is also a particular problem in residential work with sexually aggressive adolescents (Greer, 1991; Hird, 1997; Knopp, 1982).

However, Epps states that one of the 'advantages of working in a residential context is that it allows for greater control over the environmental and situational variables that contribute to sexually abusive behaviour' (Epps, 1997a, p45).

History to the development of the unit

Since the early 1990s, Geilsland School has steadily developed its work with sexually aggressive young men. In April 1999, one-third of the young men in the school were specifically identified as sexually aggressive at the point of referral. At this time, the sexually aggressive young men were placed across all three of the residential units. This work was carried out in conjunction with specialist services such as the HALT project (a community based resource for adolescent sex abusers) in Glasgow and with appropriate external support, in particular involving a consultant psychologist with expertise in the field of sexual aggression.

During 1998, senior management at the school felt that it was important to review the work being undertaken in the school. Consultation took place, involving representatives from local authority social work departments, the Social Work Services Inspectorate of the Scottish Executive, the Centre for Residential Child Care; and agencies working with sexually aggressive young men. The potential benefits of having a focused unit were identified as:

- Identifying this work more clearly as an area of special provision.
- More scope to support dedicated programmes of intervention, risk assessment, relapse prevention, groupwork etc.
- Being able to organise the daily life and regime of the unit round the needs of this particular group without worrying about this restricting the living situation for others.
- Reducing the risk to other residents.
- Concentrating staff resources more effectively.
(Geilsland, 1998).

In June 1999, Geilsland School embarked on a three year pilot project to provide 'an integrated programme of care and intervention' with the overall aim 'to directly address the issue of sexual aggression whilst at the same time continuing to meet the holistic care needs of each young person' (Geilsland School, 2000). Funding from the Social Work Services Inspectorate of the Scottish Executive supports the development of this work.

The unit can accommodate nine young men in eight core places and one bedsit used for young men preparing to move on from the unit. The staffing resource was intended to provide a higher ratio of staff than applied in the other units of the school. As will be seen, the experience of the first 12 months has highlighted the need for this to be increased further to facilitate the work of the unit.

The criteria for admission to the unit are:

- *Conviction for a sexual offence or formal identification of involvement in sexual aggression.*

- *Acknowledgement by young person of problem.*
- *Willingness to participate in focused programme.*
                                            (Geilsland, 2000)

While these reflect a minimalist approach to suitability for involvement in the programme as suggested by Will (1999), they were also intended to avoid the unit being used simply as a holding facility for young men about whom there is concern and to establish the basis for focused work.

There has been a clear commitment to openness with the young men about the reason why they are all in the unit:

> *Without compromising the confidentiality surrounding individual circumstances there is openness within the Unit regarding the fact that all the young people have a common problem with sexual aggression. This acknowledgement is an important starting point in terms of encouraging young people to take responsibility for their behaviour and to believe that it can be worked on and changed.*
>   (Geilsland, 2000)

The unit has set out to provide a non-abusive environment for the young men, a safe and secure placement, which was considered a core aim of the unit (Centre for Residential Child Care, 1995; Epps, 1999). Within this core context of 'a safe and developmentally appropriate environment', the stated aims of the programme are to:

- Help the young person to avoid or reduce the risk of behaving in an abusive manner.
- Reduce the seriousness of the abusive behaviour.
- Encourage an increase in appropriate social interaction through understanding and being offered the opportunity to learn new skills and enhance those already acquired.
- Develop appropriate links with family and help the family understand the behaviour of their son.
- Assess risk in terms of planning for future placements/return to the community.
                                            (Geilsland 2000)

The research

The research was commissioned by Geilsland School and has aimed to provide a 'process evaluation' of the development of the work in the focused unit over its first year of operation. The research has focused on:

- Safe caring in working with sexually aggressive young males in a residential context.
- Outcomes for young people.
- Development of personal change programmes (e.g. Risk assessment, relapse prevention, groupwork).
- Confidentiality and individual's rights.
- Staff development and training issues.
- Inter-agency relationships.

Given the sensitive nature of the subject area, detailed discussions took place about consent, confidentiality, and procedures in the event of further suspicions of abuse raised by the research in general and interviews with the young men in particular (Alderson, 1995; Cleaver and Freeman, 1995). This information was gone through with the young men by key workers and the researcher. All the young men approached in the first phase of the research agreed to be interviewed.

Data collection consisted of four main methods:

1. Documentary analysis and case file analysis

Relevant school and unit documents have been identified and either collected for analysis or, where this is not possible, read on site and notes taken. Individual case files on the 14 young men included in the study have been read to provide background information.

2. Semi-structured interviews

35 face-to-face, semi-structured interviews have been carried out involving: 12 unit staff (5 having been interviewed twice); 3 other Geilsland staff; and 3 interviews with the consultant psychologist. Telephone interviews have been completed with 6 social workers. In addition, 8 young men were interviewed about their experience of living in the focused unit and undertaking work on their sexual aggression.

3. Structured questionnaires

26 structured questionnaires were completed for 13 of the young men in the unit by the young men's key workers and individual workers. The questionnaires focused on aspects of the young men's attitudes and behaviour at referral to the unit; progress in the placement in relation to attitudes and behaviour; and achievement of aims and objectives.

4. *Observation*

Fieldwork at Geilsland School consisted of 12 visits ranging from two to five days between July 1999 and August 2000. This allowed observation of groupwork (three sessions); staff team meetings (four meetings); unit meetings involving young men (three meetings). Importantly it also allowed time to be spent in the unit at different times of day, for example, mealtimes, recreation times, and night-time; an opportunity to chat with young men and staff informally; and attendance at school events. This provided a 'richness of qualitative data on everyday occurrences, interactions and problems' (Berridge and Brodie, 1998; Marshall and Rossman, 1989).

The Young Men

During the 12 months from July 1999 to June 2000, 15 sexually aggressive young men were placed in the unit. One young man, however, withdrew co-operation from the programme and very shortly moved out of the unit. Information in this chapter therefore relates to 14 young men. Four of the young men were 15 years old when they moved in to the unit, eight were 16 and the remaining two young men were 17 years old.

The young men had carried out a range of sexually aggressive acts which included indecent exposure; indecent assault of children or adult women; inappropriate touching; stalking; rape of younger children; and mutilation of animals involving a sexual element. The number of known victims ranged from one to over twenty. The victims of the abuse included family members (siblings, step-siblings and cousins); younger children (both male and female) in the community; other children and young people in residential, foster care or day school settings; female staff in residential settings; and adult women.

The young men frequently had complex histories of sexually aggressive behaviour. A significant number also had histories of involvement in the care system going back to early childhood. Exactly half of the young men had been in residential or foster care before their sexually aggressive behaviour came to light and most of these had abused victims in previous residential or foster care placements or in special educational establishments (Barter, 1997; Gibbs and Sinclair, 2000; Kendrick, 1997). Three other young men experienced other residential placements following the allegations of sexually aggressive behaviour that led to them being placed at Geilsland. Only four of the young men came into Geilsland School directly from their home community.

Half of the young men in the unit had moderate to significant learning difficulties (O'Callaghan, 1999) and all of these had attended special educational provision. Most had attended special education since primary age and two had been in special schools for all of their education. All but one had experienced residential special schools or residential care because of their challenging behaviour and all had been in care or been looked after. Most of the other young men, however, had exhibited problem behaviour in education, having been excluded from school, truanted or having involvement with educational psychological services.

The legislation under which the young men were placed in Geilsland varied widely. Partly this is due to the fact that in Scotland young offenders, for the most part, are dealt with by the Children's Hearings system. Established in 1971, Children's Hearings, consisting of three lay people, make decisions about the care and protection of children. The Children's Hearings system is based on a welfare principle, which does not distinguish children who offend and those who are offended against (Lockyer and Stone, 1998). Children up until the age of 16 will be dealt with by the Children's Hearings system except in the case of serious offences, such as sexual offences, which may be dealt with by the court system. Between the ages of 16-18, young people will be dealt with by the court system unless they are already subject to a supervision requirement from the Children's Hearing system when they may be referred back to a Children's Hearing. A court also has the option to refer a case to the Children's Hearing system for advice or for disposal.

The route by which a case is dealt with is important because of the long-term implications related to the Sex Offenders (1997) Act. Those convicted of a sexual offence by a court will be required to register with the police within 14 days. However, those young people dealt with by the Children's Hearings system are not required to register (this includes young people who, following conviction, are remitted by a Court back to the Children's Hearings for disposal).

Accordingly, some of the young men had come to Geilsland through the court system and were on the sex offender register; some had come through the children's hearings system and were not required to register. However, a small number who had initially come to Geilsland through the children's hearings system had to register because they had also been sentenced in court. The legislative route, however, was not determined by the seriousness of the offence and there appears to be a degree of arbitrariness about the decisions, which raises issues about consistency of approach and natural justice. Masson and Morrison (1999), discussing the Sex Offenders Act in the English context, argue that it lacks flexibility and that decisions on registration 'should be made on a case by case basis, through a process of multi-disciplinary decision-making' (Masson and Morrison, 1999, p212).

The young men's case histories also highlighted significant issues of trauma and disruption in their lives (Mulholland and McIntee, 1999; Scottish Executive, 2000). This reinforced the focus on their holistic care needs and the need to provide stability and security as the basis for individual work.

Assessment of issues at referral to the unit

Two of the criteria for inclusion in the programme were: conviction for a sexual offence or formal identification of involvement in sexual aggression; and, acknowledgement by the young person of a problem. There were still major issues in terms of the young men's acceptance of responsibility and the levels of their denial at the time of their referral to the programme. Most of the young men, even if they accepted their offence, accepted no, or little, responsibility and minimised their sexually aggressive behaviour.

As could be anticipated given the numbers of young men with learning difficulties, they fell into two groups in terms of their communication skills: some had very good communication skills while others had very poor skills. However, most of the young men had low self-esteem and tended to have poor assertiveness skills, poor personal and social skills and poor anger management skills.

In relation to their sexually aggressive behaviour at referral, the young men were considered to have very poor awareness of victim issues; very poor levels of understanding of the distinction between consensual and coercive relationships; very poor understanding of their own sexually aggressive behaviour; and poor levels of knowledge of sex and sexuality.

The development of the unit

Staff in the unit felt a great deal of anxiety at the start. They were very conscious of the high profile nature of the developments, with the involvement of the Scottish Executive and an external researcher. There was concern about the reaction of the young men to being told that the unit would be focusing work on sexual aggression. However, to a large extent, this proved unfounded and there appeared to be a visible sense of relief for some of the young men. The concern that the creation of the unit might lead to scape-goating of residents by other young men in the school also proved, for the most part, to be unfounded. Having the focused unit appears to have afforded the group a degree of normality, acceptance and protection.

The initial work in the unit did not, however, progress totally smoothly. The unit opened in June 1999 and the groupwork programme started well. However, the advent of the summer holiday period meant there was little time to consolidate the work of the unit. The testing out behaviour of certain of the young men resulted in some serious incidents of violence against other residents and staff. There was also an allegation of physical assault made by one young man against a member of staff. This resulted in a shaky period and with hindsight it was probably unwise to open the unit so close to the holiday period. With the start of the school term in August 1999, the life of the unit stabilised, the groupwork restarted and individual programmes of work with the young men were firmed up.

The core programme

Staff have three primary roles: to protect, to nurture, and to observe.

(Ryan, 1991b, p415)

As indicated the unit set out to provide a non-abusive environment for the young men, and this is reflected in the ground-rules of the unit.

The initial aim was to establish a culture (Brown et al., 1998; Epps, 1999; Lindsay, 1999)

Table 1:

<hr>

Residents' Rules

1. Residents will not be in another resident's bedroom.
2. Residents will not be out without staff supervision unless given permission e.g. upstairs in the unit, outside of the building.
3. Residents will be escorted to and from school and around the estate by staff.
4. Residents will not engage in physical contact i.e. playfighting.
5. Residents are not allowed in the staff office, unless invited to do so by staff.
6. Swearing and sexualised talk or gestures will not be acceptable.
7. Groupwork sessions are not an option, they are part of each residential care plan.
8. Attendance at unit meetings is expected.

Residents' Information

1. Each resident will be allocated a keyworker and teacher before or on admission.
2. Bullying of residents or staff will not be tolerated: refer to handbook.
3. Staff will use discretion on what TV programmes residents watch, what magazines, posters, computer games they have.
4. Residents will not be allowed to watch 18+ only videos.
5. Residents will not be allowed topless or pornographic posters to be displayed on their walls.
6. Sectarian posters or artwork will not be allowed to be displayed on walls.
7. Complaints by residents will be dealt with: refer to handbook.
8. The school handbook will give residents information on pocket money, bedtimes, clothing, money, birthday and Christmas money, toiletries, school times, chapel and assembly, reviews and panels, and key team meetings.

<hr>

and contract with the young men and to a large extent, staff feel that the unit has been successful in meeting the core task of providing a safe and secure environment, with appropriate levels of care and support.

> I think the kind of messages we are trying to get across, the ethos and the culture, and the way people treat each other, reiterated day-in and day-out. And that's the most important thing.
>
> (staff member)

> Safe boundaries, I think that is something that is reinforced every single day as to what is going on and why we are asking them to behave in a certain way. It is for their safety, it is for the other boys' safety, it is for ours . . . we are very clear.
>
> (staff member)

The local authority social workers interviewed were positive about the care provided and one commented on the 'very high standard' of care:

> I think they did a pretty good job, given (young man's) extremely difficult behaviour, they did an extremely good job . . .
>
> (social worker)

There was general consensus that the physical layout of the building was well suited for the purpose of the new unit.

> The . . . buildings, are ideal, purpose built, the physical surroundings are perfect . . . that's worked very, very well.
>
> (staff member)

Although there are high levels of supervision in the unit (Epps, 1999), Geilsland is an open setting. There has, however, been little absconding from the unit. For the most part, any absconding which has occurred has been linked more with general delinquency (for example, car theft) than with sexually aggressive behaviour. Similarly, there has not been a major issue with drugs and alcohol in the unit. This would seem to support the view that these young men can be accommodated safely in an open setting.

As far as is known, there have been no incidents of a sexually aggressive nature between the young men in the unit over the first year of its operation. There have, however, been a number of incidents of sexually aggressive behaviour targeted at female members of staff. This has taken two main forms; verbal abuse and inappropriate touching. In the context of the work within the unit, such behaviour has been confronted and addressed in direct work with the young men.

Perhaps the most significant issue relating to safe caring in the unit concerns bullying (Barter, 1997; Gibbs and Sinclair, 2000; Kendrick, 1997). The mixed abilities in the group was seen to contribute to this. It was acknowledged as a problem and was consistently confronted within the unit.

One issue, however, related to the consistency of approach in the unit and to a degree this was linked to the different approaches adopted in the different units. Unit ground rules stated that 'swearing and sexualised talk or gestures will not be acceptable'. An external consultant who was requested by the Board of Social Responsibility to provide an independent view of the culture of Geilsland identified the difference between units.

> *In one (unit) swearing was not acceptable. When boys swore in staff's presence they were checked and desisted. In the others staff made perfunctory attempts to discourage bad language but as if they were going through the motions; there was an air of inevitability about its use and the bad language continued ... What was noticeable was that in that Unit the general atmosphere was much calmer than the rest of the school. It appeared that the absence of swearing may have made a significant contribution to that.*
>
> (Confidential report, 2000)

From observation on the unit it was apparent that the regular staff more consistently addressed swearing and verbal abuse than did staff from other units who were providing cover. This lack of consistency was also identified by some of the young men.

> *... the staff that you see mostly in the unit, they are the ones that are dead strict. Whereas the ones that take you out in the van and out and about are quite lenient ... You find that with most of the (unit) staff compared with (staff from other units), they are a lot stricter ...*
>
> (young man)

Staff also identified differences between unit staff and other Geilsland staff, particularly education staff, in their attention to the level of supervision of the young men. Consistency of approach in regard to safe caring and stability has to be worked at over time and this was recognised by staff.

> *I think we've realised that we have to keep restating and re-negotiating the ground rules ... particularly if there are new young people coming in, but just even for an existing population ... you don't start relaxing or losing sight of things that have been*

> *negotiated and agreed ... maintaining a non-abusive environment.*
>
> (staff member)

However, the development of the core programme has also focused on the holistic care needs of each young man and on providing a nurturing experience. Getting the balance right between the emphasis on safe care and providing an environment within which the young men can thrive has been an important aspect of the core programme.

Integrated Model of Work

Individual programmes of work

Individual work with the young men is carried out either by the consultant psychologist or the unit manager in conjunction with a residential care worker (in male-female pairs). There is a separation, however, in the role of key-worker and individual worker; the key-worker focusing on the core task of care and support and the individual worker focusing on direct work related to sexually aggressive behaviour. Individual work begins with a six-week programme of assessment, after which a longer-term plan of work is drawn up (although staff did consider that the planning of individual work should be more rigorously formalised).

Involved staff felt that there was an issue relating to the consistency of the individual sessions with the young men. Too often, it was felt, weekly sessions did not take place, either because of staffing issues or because the young men were not available. It was also generally considered that too great a load of direct work fell on the consultant psychologist and the unit manager.

An important aspect of the individual work with the young men which was recognised to be an area for concern related to the provision of assessment reports and written feedback:

> *I think we are quite good in assessment, we assess everything constantly. What we have to be better at is formalising that. Actually writing reports ... and part of that is about actually finding the time to do that ... I think we are quite good at assessing the risk that somebody might pose, or what would be safe for somebody to do. But actually writing that down is the bit that, I certainly think, we are not so good at.*
>
> (staff member)

This was the main area of criticism made by the social workers interviewed.

Another issue related to the time-scale of work, particularly when dealing with young men with learning difficulties. Two of the young men who left the unit during the year had actually been in the unit for over two years and direct work on their sexually aggressive behaviour had been undertaken during the whole of this period, and to an extent, it was felt that this time frame was needed. However, for some of the young men the time-scales imposed by the courts was much less than this. Another issue raised by the legislative process concerns the length of time it can take a case for a final verdict to be reached, particularly if an appeal is lodged. It was apparent that for some of the young men, this process could be highly disruptive to the work they were doing in the unit because of the levels of anxiety created by court appearances (Scottish Executive, 2000).

Groupwork

As was seen from the unit ground-rules, attendance at groupwork is not optional. Cognitive skills groupwork takes place in weekly sessions for the whole group. Issues which have been addressed in groupwork have included: problem solving; social skills; anger management; values and beliefs; power and control; men and violence; consequences of behaviour; self-awareness. In addition to the cognitive skills group, task centred and time-limited groups have been run for smaller groups of young men focusing on sex education and social skills (Taylor, 1997). The decision at the outset was that offence specific groupwork would not be appropriate.

Staff acknowledged that the introduction of groupwork raised their anxiety levels. In part this may have been because groupwork took on a symbolic identification with the change in remit of the Unit. Staff in the unit had experience of individual work with sexually aggressive young men. Groupwork, however, was a new experience and although it started positively, there was a difficult period over the holidays.

Initially I think it went quite well, the first two or three sessions. We then had a major blip when we hit the summer holidays. And there were lots of reasons for that ... So over the summer, it didn't really work out, the boys weren't interested, the staff I think lost a bit of confidence ...

(staff member)

Following the summer, the head of school was involved in restarting the programme of groupwork and co-worked the group for a number of sessions but gradually withdrew from the group.

From March 2000, the cognitive skills groupwork was split into two groups because of the problems created by the mixed ability of the group. This was felt to have been a generally positive move and the more able young men were able to focus on the work better. Staff felt that the young men with learning difficulties were difficult to work with as a group, but it was important to persevere (O'Callaghan, 1999). While for both groups, some of the sessions were not very successful, one for example was described as 'shambolic for the most part', most brief summaries of the sessions described positive participation by the young men. Steinberg similarly describes the difficulties, 'chaotic disorder' but also 'minor triumphs' in groupwork with troubled adolescents (Steinberg, 1987).

The final session of the year was written up as follows:

All of the boys worked well during the session ... To mark the end of the session and indeed the group-working for the summer, all the boys congratulated themselves with a round of applause. A good humoured and enjoyable session to bring the term to a close.

(Groupwork notes, 29.6.00)

By the end of the 12 months, staff felt more confident and relaxed about groupwork and were developing plans to design groupwork material which they felt more directly addressed the needs of the young men in the unit.

The guys themselves talk. They are quite good about saying, 'We did that in groupwork'. They are working quite well; they are taking it on board ... It's amazing, they ... take part. You know, at first it was, 'I don't want to do it'. Now they are up for it and they take part.

(staff member)

So I've got a lot out of groupwork and it has helped me a lot. And the stuff I'm doing in groupwork at the moment contrasts with my individual work, so I know what to say in my groupwork and I know what to say in my individual work, because the two are helping each other, know what I mean.

(Young man)

Family work

Acknowledging the importance of work with families (Burnham et al., 1999), one of the stated aims of the programme is to: develop appropriate links with family and help the family understand the behaviour of their son. This was felt to be an aim, which had been achieved to a very limited extent.

> *We don't do family work. And again some of that is about distance, some of that is about families' inability . . . to be able to do that. Some of them are very angry about what has happened, they don't understand what has happened . . .*
>
> (staff member)

While there are instances of positive work with families, it is very costly in terms of staff time when the young men's families live on the other side of Scotland. The lack of effective family work impacts on the progress of individual work and on the planning for the young men's return to the community. Accordingly it is recognised as an important area for future development.

Issues of the integrated model

One of the main benefits of the integrated model of work is the way in which the work done with the young men in direct individual work and groupwork could be reinforced by discussion and work within the unit on a day-by-day basis. Similarly, issues arising in the unit, such as bullying or instances of sexually aggressive behaviour could be confronted openly and linked to work in individual sessions or in groupwork.

> *I think it is good, you know, if you are speaking to a guy in individual work and things are getting passed on, and you add that to groupwork and you add that to the culture . . .*
>
> (staff member)

However, this integration has also led to a high degree of stress on staff due to the intensive nature of the direct work on top of the expectations of the core task of caring and support.

> *'We're multi-roled now, as well. We've got key working; got individual work; we're group working. It's quite a load.*
>
> (staff member)

In addition, the young men have come to Geilsland from all over Scotland and issues of distance and travel have had a significant impact on resources in the unit, partly because of the levels of supervision which are needed for the young men in the unit.

Assessment of progress

Five of the six young men who initially took part in the programme left the unit over the next 12 months and the sixth left in July 2000. Of the eight young men who came in to the unit over the first 12 month period, all of them were still there at the end of the period, although one left in July 2000.

If we include those young men who left in July 2000, three young men returned to the community (one via a short placement in another unit in Geilsland); two moved on into other units in Geilsland; one moved on to a residential resource for adults with learning difficulties; and one was imprisoned following the failure of his appeal against a custodial sentence.

In terms of staff ratings of progress on the programme a clear distinction can be seen in terms of those young men who were considered to be willing to participate in the programme and those where participation was more problematic (either through the young men themselves not being willing or because external factors, such as court processes, hampered participation).

For those young men considered willing to participate in the programme (7 out of 13), in general it was thought that there was marked improvement in terms of them acknowledging their sexually aggressive behaviour, acceptance of responsibility and the extent to which they denied and minimised their sexually aggressive behaviour. There was also improvement in relation to awareness of victim issues; levels of understanding of the distinction between consensual and coercive relationships; understanding of their own sexually aggressive behaviour; levels of knowledge of sex and sexuality. However, this tended to be rated as slight improvement.

For two of the young men ongoing court processes hampered engagement with participation, and staff considered that there was little evidence of change (one of the young men moved on to custody). For three of the young men, there were problems in relation to their continued willingness to participate in the programme and again staff considered that there was little evidence of change. Two of the young men moved into other units in Geilsland, partly at least because of violent behaviour in the unit, and work continued in the other units.

However, this is not to say that the focused unit was necessarily considered an inappropriate placement and, for two of the young men, the placement was ongoing.

Overall, staff considered that for six of the thirteen young men there was a significant reduction in the risk of the young man behaving in a sexually abusive manner (it must be stressed that this assessment of risk was in the context of the young men in the residential setting). For four of the young men, staff considered there had been a slight reduction and for three young men, no reduction in risk.

> If it is about a reduction in sexually aggressive behaviour, who knows? Perhaps it is that the good work is being undermined by (the situation in the community). Whether he will offend again? . . .
> (social worker)

> . . . he's now got to the point where he actually understands . . . he truly, cognitively understands the theories about sexual offending, and he understands why he's done what he's done.
> (staff member)

> Very successful, I can't fault the unit in terms of the work with (young man).
> (social worker)

The unit has used the Adolescent Sexual Abuser Project (ASAP) profile in relation to some of the young men and it is anticipated that re-testing may provide clearer measures of outcome and change.

Conclusion

There has been major progress in the development of work in the focused unit over its first year. In particular, the development of the core ethos and tasks in the unit has produced positive results in ensuring an open, supportive and non-abusive environment for the direct work on sexually aggressive behaviour. This has led to the unit providing secure and stable placements to young men whose behaviour is extremely difficult.

There has also been significant progress in the development of groupwork for the young men in the unit and staff were reviewing the content and format of the programme to meet the differing needs and abilities of young men in the unit.

While there have also been positive developments in terms of individual programmes of work for the young men, a number of areas of concern have been identified. These relate to the consistency of the work and to formal recording of work. More generally the monitoring, analysis and review of progress of the young men needs to be further developed.

Work with families about the sexual aggression of the young men has not taken place to the extent hoped for. This has been due in part to the negative reactions of families and in part to the distance from the young men's homes.

Significant issues, then, have been identified in relation to staff resources for the work in the unit. It was felt that staff cover within the unit was for the most part adequate (although as we saw above issues of consistency of approach arise). Where the staff team was stretched was in covering the range of tasks now expected of them, particularly given the intensive nature of direct work with sexually aggressive young men. This issue of the resource base of the focused programme is obviously linked to the charges made for the service. A comparison with a similar service run by St Helen's Metropolitan Council, for example, showed Geilsland's charges to be less than half those of the English residential establishment.

There is, therefore, an important need to review the fit between the level of resources needed to further develop the focused programme and the aims, (and importantly, the expectations linked to the aims) of the programme. For example, an additional qualified, specialist worker to lead and co-ordinate individual work with the young men would relieve the pressure on the consultant psychologist and the unit manager (enabling more focus on management and planning for the unit and staff development and training). In addition, they would enable a more rigorous approach to planning, recording, monitoring and analysis of individual programmes of work. Additional staff in the unit could focus on particular tasks, which have been identified, such as social skills; bullying and aggression; and family work.

Parallel to considerations of the resource levels necessary to develop the work, there should be a review of the aims of the programme. This review should focus in particular on the way in which the broad aims of the programme are translated into individualised aims for the young men referred to the programme. This is important because of the impact that factors such as ongoing court proceedings or the length of sentences imposed by the court may have on the direct work with young men. There needs to be clarity about how the aims of the programme are expressed to placing agencies to ensure realistic expectations on both sides.

This being said, the positive features of the integrated model of work developed in the focused programme have been identified. It is therefore important that a balance is struck in relieving pressure on staff but also enabling them to continue to be involved in different aspects of the work and in the ongoing development of the programme.

> *I think we've achieved a huge amount. I think there's some things we beat ourselves up about unnecessarily . . . I think we've learned a lot in the first year. I think, there are things we now want to change but if we hadn't done it the way we have done, we wouldn't have known . . .*
>
> (staff member)

> *I think in the first year, it's been amazing. The progress that the boys have made, that the staff have made. Accepting the job of what we are doing, of what we are supposed to be doing . . . I think it's worked very, very well. And I'll be interested to see what happens in the next year or so.*
>
> (staff member)

Building on the start that has been made over the first 12 months, the aim of the unit is to use the remaining two years of the pilot to further develop and (through continuing evaluation) to demonstrate the effectiveness of focused care for this complex group of young men.

> *Well its helping me anyway and I probably, if I wasnae in here I'd probably be some place else I didnae want to be. These folk come to my rescue . . . All I can say is they have done all the best they can. And it is time to move on.*
>
> (young man)

References

Alderson, P. (1995) *Listening to Children: Children, Ethics and Social Research*. Ilford: Barnardos.

Barter, C. (1997) Who's to Blame: Conceptualising Institutional Abuse by Children. *Early Child Development and Care*. 133: 101–14.

Berridge, D. and Brodie, I. (1998) *Children's Homes Revisited*. London: Jessica Kingsley.

Brown, E., Bullock, R., Hobson, C. and Little, M. (1998) *Making Residential Care Work: Structure and Culture in Children's Homes*. Aldershot: Ashgate Publishing.

Buist, M. and Fuller, R. (1997) *A Chance to Change: An Intervention with Young People who have Sexually Abused Others*. Edinburgh: The Stationery Office.

Burnham, J., Moss, J., deBelle, J. and Jamieson, R. (1999) Working with Families of Young Sexual Abusers: Assessment and Intervention Issues. in Erooga, M. and Masson, H. (Eds.) *Children and Young People who Sexually Abuse Others: Challenges and Responses*. London: Routledge. 146–67.

Centre for Residential Child Care. (1995) *Guidance for Residential Workers Caring for Young People who have been Sexually Abused and Those who Abuse Others*. Glasgow: Centre for Residential Child Care.

Cleaver, H. and Freeman, P. (1995) *Parental Perspectives in Cases of Suspected Child Abuse*. London: HMSO.

Epps, K. (1997a) Managing Risk. in Hoghughi, M., Bhate, S. and Graham, F. (Eds.) *Working with Sexually Abusive Adolescents*. London: Sage. 35–51.

Epps, K. (1997b) Pointers for Carers. in Calder, M. with Hanks, H. and Epps, K. *Juveniles and Children who Sexually Abuse: A Guide to Risk Assessment*. Lyme Regis: Russell House Publishing, 99–109.

Epps, K. (1999) Looking After Young Sexual Abusers: Child Protection, Risk Management and Risk Reduction. in Erooga, M. and Masson, H. (Eds.) *Children and Young People who Sexually Abuse Others: Challenges and Responses*. London: Routledge. 67–85.

Farmer, E, and Pollock, S. (1998) *Sexually Abused and Abusing Children in Substitute Care*. Chichester: Wiley.

Fisher, D. and Beech, A. R. (1999) Current Practice in Britain With Sexual Offenders. *Journal of Interpersonal Violence*. 14(3): 240–56.

Geilsland School. (1998) *Developing the Service for Sexually Aggressive Young People*, June 1998, internal document.

Geilsland School. (2000) *Focused Care and Work with Sexually Aggressive Young People*. Internal document. Mar.

Gibbs, I. and Sinclair, I. (2000) Bullying, Sexual Harassment and Happiness in Residential Children's Homes. *Child Abuse Review*. 9: 247–56.

Gil, E. (1993) Out-of-home Care. in Gil, E and Johnson, T. C. *Sexualised Children: Assessment and Treatment of Sexualised Children and Children who Molest*. Rockville: Launch Press.

Glasgow, D., Horne, L., Calam, R. and Cox, A. (1994) Evidence, Incidence, Gender and Age in Sexual Abuse of Children Perpetrated by Children: Towards a Developmental Analysis of Child Sexual Abuse. *Child Abuse Review*. 3: 196–210.

Greer, W. C. (1991) Aftercare: Community Integration Following Institutional Treatment. in Ryan, G. and Lane, S. (Eds.) *Juvenile Sexual Offending*. Lexington: Lexington Books.

Grubin, D. (1998) *Sex Offending against Children: Understanding the Risk*. Police Research Series Paper 99, London: Home Office.

Heinz, J. Ryan, G. and Bengis, S. (1991) The System's Response to Juvenile Sex Offenders. in Ryan, G. and Lane, S. (Eds.) *Juvenile Sexual Offending*, Lexington: Lexington Books.

Hird, J. (1997) Working in Context, in Hoghughi, M., Bhate, S. and Graham, F. (Eds.) *Working with Sexually Abusive Adolescents*. London: Sage. 177–95.

Hoghughi, M. (1997) Sexual Abuse by Adolescents. in Hoghughi, M., Bhate, S. and Graham, F. (Eds.) *Working with Sexually Abusive Adolescents*. London: Sage. 1–19.

Kendrick, A. (1997) Safeguarding Children Living Away from Home from Abuse: Literature Review. in Kent, R. *Children's Safeguards Review*. Edinburgh: Scottish Office. 143–275.

Kent, R. (1997) *Children's Safeguards Review*. Edinburgh: Scottish Office.

Knopp, F. H. (1982) *Remedial Intervention in Adolescent Sex Offenses: Nine Program Descriptions*. Orwell: Safer Society Press.

Lindsay, M. (1999) Dilemmas and Potential Work With Sexually Abusive Young People in Residential Settings. in Calder, M. C. (Ed.) *Working with Young People who Sexually Abuse: New Pieces of the Jigsaw Puzzle*. Lyme Regis: Russell House Publishing, 282–93.

Lockyer, A. and Stone, F. H. (Eds.) (1998) *Juvenile Justice in Scotland: Twenty-five Years of the Welfare Approach*. Edinburgh: T and T Clark.

Marshall, C. and Rossman, G. (1989) *Designing Qualitative Research*. Newbury Park: Sage.

Masson, H. (1995) Children and Adolescents who Sexually Abuse Other Children: Responses to an Emerging Problem. *Journal of Social Welfare and Family Law*. 17(3): 325–36.

Masson, H. (1997) Researching Policy and Practice in Relation to Children and Young People who Sexually Abuse. *Research, Policy and Planning*. 15(3): 8–16.

Masson, H. and Morrison, T. (1999) Young Sexual Abusers: Conceptual Frameworks,

Issues and Imperatives. *Children and Society*. 13: 203–15.

Monck, E. and New, M. (1996) *Report of a Study of Sexually Abused Children and Adolescents, and of Young Perpetrators of Sexual Abuse who were Treated in Voluntary Agency Community Facilities*. London: HMSO.

Morrison, T. (1999) 'Is There a Strategy out There?': Policy and Management Perspectives on Young People who Sexually Abuse Others. in Erooga, M. and Masson, H. (Eds.) *Children and Young People who Sexually Abuse Others: Challenges and Responses*. London: Routledge. 19–35.

Mullholland, S. J. and McIntee, J. (1999) The Significance of Trauma in Problematic Sexual Behaviour. in Calder, M. C. (Ed.) *Working with Young People who Sexually Abuse: New Pieces of the Jigsaw Puzzle*. Lyme Regis: Russell House Publishing, 265–79.

National Children's Home. (1992) *The Report of the Committee of Inquiry in to Children and Young People who Sexually Abuse Other Children*. London: NCH.

O'Callaghan, D. (1999) Young Abusers With Learning Disabilities: Towards Better Understanding and Positive Interventions. in Calder, M. C. (Ed.) *Working with Young People who Sexually Abuse: New Pieces of the Jigsaw Puzzle*. Lyme Regis: Russell House Publishing. 223–49.

O'Callaghan, D. and Print, B. (1994) Adolescent Sexual Abusers: Research, Treatment and Assessment. in Morrison, T., Erooga, M. and Beckett, R. C. (Eds.) *Sexual Offending Against Children: Assessment and Treatment of Male Abusers* London: Routledge. 146–77.

Ryan, G. (1991a) Incidence and Prevalence of Sexual Offences Committed by Juveniles. in Ryan, G. and Lane, S. (Eds.) *Juvenile Sexual Offending*. Lexington: Lexington Books.

Ryan, G. (1991b) Creating an 'Abuse-specific' Milieu, in Ryan, G. and Lane, S. (Eds.) *Juvenile Sexual Offending*. Lexington: Lexington Books. 404–16.

Skinner, A. (1992) *Another Kind of Home: A Review of Residential Child Care*. Edinburgh: Scottish Office.

Steinberg, D. (1987) Innovation in an Adolescent Unit: The Introduction of Small Group Work. in Coleman, J. C. (Ed.) *Working with Troubled Adolescents: A Handbook*. London: Academic Press. 79–90.

Taylor, J. L. (1997) Educational Approaches to Treatment. in Hoghughi, M., Bhate, S. and

Graham, F. (Eds.) *Working with Sexually Abusive Adolescents*. London: Sage. 114–27.

Scottish Executive. (2000) *Managing the Risk: An Inspection of the Management of Sex Offender Cases in the Community. http:// www.scotland.gov.uk/library3/social/mtr-00.asp*, accessed January 2001.

The Scottish Office. (1997) *A Commitment to Protect: Supervising Sex Offenders: Proposals for More Effective Management*. Edinburgh: The Stationery Office.

The Scottish Office. (1998a) *Protecting Children: A Shared Responsibility: Guidance on Inter-agency Co-operation*. Edinburgh: The Stationery Office.

The Scottish Office (1998b) *The Government's Response to Kent Report on Children's Safeguards Review. http://www.scotland.gov.uk/library/ documents7/kent-ch4.htm*, accessed January 2000.

Vennard, J., Sugg, D. and Hedderman, C. (1997) *The use of Cognitive-behavioural Approaches With Offenders: Messages from Research. Changing Offenders' Attitudes and Behaviour: What Works?* Home Office Research Study 171 Part I, London: Home Office.

Will, D. (1999) Assessment Issues, in Erooga, M. and Masson, H. (Eds.) *Children and Young People who Sexually Abuse Others: Challenges and Responses*. London: Routledge. 86–103.

Worling. J. R. and Curwen, T. (2000) Adolescent Sexual Offender Recidivism: Success of Specialized Treatment and Implications for Risk Prediction. *Child Abuse and Neglect*. 24(7): 965–82.

Chapter 8: Accreditation of Work and Workers Involved in Providing a Service to Children and Young People who Sexually Abuse

Colin Hawkes

Introduction

This chapter considers the need for a consistent system of accreditation of treatment methods and of professionals who work with children and young people who sexually abuse. Definitional issues in relation to child sexual abuse and accreditation will be discussed and the wider context of accreditation established. Evidence of problems will be outlined and reference made to relevant literature and other sources of information. Existing and planned legislation is described and analysed. Finally a number of ways are suggested to incorporate clinical experience in the accreditation of individual workers and differing treatment regimes.

Definitions

For the purposes of the chapter 'accreditation' is defined as a system of authorising an individual or a treatment method as ethical, safe, effective and accountable. 'Child Sexual Abuse' is used as an inclusive term, which describes a wide spectrum of events, from aggressive, penetrative sexual assault against children to repetitive sexual acts which do not coincide with normative sexual behaviours. 'Children' and 'Young People' are terms that are used to describe males and females up to the age of eighteen years.

The issue is addressed from the clinical perspective of a social work practitioner involved in the assessment and treatment of young people with an established pattern of child sexually abusive or sexually aggressive behaviour. The observations and comments made are based primarily on experiences gained from working in the Young Abusers Project. This is a London situated, community-based project with an experienced multi-disciplinary team including specialist social workers, psychiatrists, psychologists and psychotherapists. It is managed by the NSPCC in partnership with Camden and Islington Health Trust and has a national catchment area.

Other influences on the content of the chapter have been, research evidence and the experiences of colleagues working in the adult criminal justice sphere, child psychiatry, child psychotherapy, clinical psychology, education and childcare.

The wider context

Accreditation of social workers and other professionals with regard to their capacity and suitability to work with children who sexually abuse is one element of a process by which society recognises and validates therapeutic and other efforts to achieve behavioural change. An exhaustive examination of this complex process is impossible in a short book chapter. It would amongst other things require a full analysis of the way in which childhood is defined and of our individual and collective attitudes to children's sexuality. However, in order to explain why clinical concerns should help to influence decisions about who should carry out such work and what should be regarded as acceptable work methods, it is necessary to share a view of the function which specialist practice with children who sexually abuse carries out within this process.

A static model of any aspect of society will fail to capture the dynamic, overlapping and concurrent character of constituent elements. The Theoretical Classifications Model described by Hawkes, Jenkins and Vizard (1997) is an example of an attempt to achieve an appreciation of the flux of influences that interplay in relation to understanding sexually abusive children and young people. This model can be adapted to represent social work and other interventions with children and young people who sexually abuse as taking place on the fifth level of a model that has seven interactive layers (see Figure 1). These may be represented as follows:

1. Societal perceptions of children and young people who sexually abuse. Expectations of

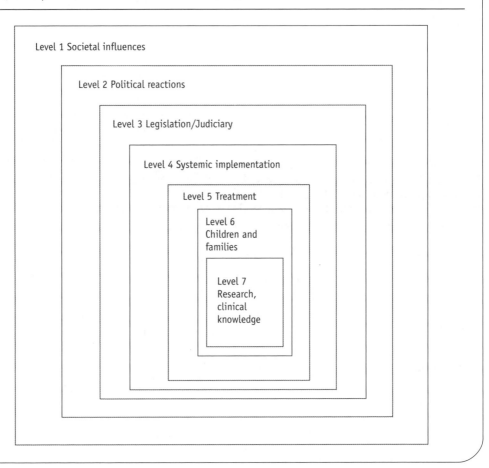

Figure 1: Adapted from 'The Theoretical Classification Model', (Hawkes, Jenkins and Vizard, 1997).

how they should be treated. Examples are direct action by members of the public, media campaigns etc.

2. Political reactions to manifestations of public perceptions. Party political debate and policy, pressure group lobbying.
3. Legislative and judicial representation of political will. For instance the Children Act 1989, Criminal Laws.
4. Systemic or organisational implementation of legislation.
5. Department of Health, Home Office, Department of Education, voluntary organisations (NSPCC), professional bodies representing psychotherapy and counselling etc.
6. Social work and other modes of intervention with children and young people who sexually abuse.

7. Children and young people who sexually abuse. Their families and carers.
8. Relevant research and clinical findings.

Some activities are widespread and may develop formal rules and regulations without being seen as requiring legislative or legal controls. The rules for many sports are examples of activities that have national prominence and may be the focus of heated debate but which are not subject in the most part to executive control by parliament or the courts. Others come to be seen as in need of external management. Occasionally problems enter the public arena, (Level 1 in the model above), often through the media, in sudden and dramatic fashion. When this happens without confidence in a recognised framework of adequate legislative and institutional response (Level 3) public anxiety may spiral and the essential nature of the problem becomes lost. This exaggerated public anxiety has been characterised as having an element of 'moral panic' by Cohen (1993).

There is powerful anecdotal evidence that an apparent disparity between the high level of public concern about child sexual abuse and child sexual abusers and perceived inadequacies of the response at other levels of the model has found expression in direct action by members of the public. One striking example is the action taken by residents of the Paulsgrove Estate in Portsmouth. In the summer of 2000, in the wake of a campaign by the News of the World newspaper to 'Name and Shame' convicted paedophiles they literally took the law into their own hands and attacked the persons and property of those they knew, or believed to be, child sexual abusers. Their actions received considerable national sympathy in the form of letters and telephone calls to the newspaper but also provoked expressions of concern that such action was counter productive, drove child sexual abusers underground and mistakenly targeted innocent families. The events attracted political attention and resulted in consideration of legislative change to enable greater public access to information about convicted child sexual abusers.

This example reveals the importance of gaining public understanding and confidence in the ability of social mechanisms to manage sensitive concerns. It also demonstrates the role that practitioners should play in informing public debate, political action and organisational systems so that open reliable treatment methods can be developed. It is dangerous for work with children and young people who sexually abuse to develop in the absence of an expressed knowledge and research base. Equally it is not safe for practitioners to adopt what may be seen as an arrogant belief that they are the only ones who understand the problem and should be left to get on with it. This is not to argue that practice should be slavishly populist and ignore clinical knowledge but that knowledge must be evidenced and brought to wider attention. Understanding of the nature of child sexually abusive behaviour brings with it a responsibility to contribute to the establishment of appropriate change throughout the system. In Figure 1 it is crucial that communication occurs between the different levels so that an informed debate can direct legislation and the construction of

reliable and authorised systems to address the problem.

Having made these general observations it is important to acknowledge that child sexual abuse is a phenomenon that for a number of reasons evokes unusually strong emotions. The desire to protect children is universal and is comfortably accepted. However, to a degree the strength of feelings about children is unconsciously and primitively determined. At best it reflects ambivalence and at worst cruel instincts as has been pointed out by de Mause (1974) amongst others. As a result the optimistic hope of achieving a consistent response in which congruence between public opinion, legislative and systemic response and research findings will occur is unlikely. Nevertheless, the effort to include work with children and young people who sexually abuse in the mainstream of acceptable child protection must persist and accreditation of workers and work methods is an important element of that effort.

The proposition that work with children and young people who sexually abuse should be effectively monitored and regulated is made in the recognition that this is a new and changing area of expertise. As the following section of the chapter will show, this is an aspect of work that, as is so often the case, has been dependent on the insight and expertise of committed practitioners who have started work in the absence of existing practice and policy guidelines. Accreditation systems must be responsive to new ideas and not act as a dead hand that prevents the incorporation of research, clinical evidence or indeed community concerns.

History of Work with Children and Young People who Sexually Abuse

What follows is a breakdown of the journey towards recognition of the study of the behaviour of children and young people who sexually abuse as a legitimate focus of attention. There are many useful analyses of this process, most of which incorporate a breakdown of the theoretical explanations that have emerged to explain the information about child sexual abuse that has come to light. In the UK, Calder (2001), Craissati (1999), Epps (1999), Hawkes, Jenkins and Vizard (1997) and Vizard, Monck and Misch (1995) are examples of such accounts.

One important early development was a challenge to the psychodynamic dismissal of the reality of child sexual abuse as a pathological resolution of childhood fantasy about sexual relationships with parents proposed by Sigmund Freud (1925). During the 1960s and 1970s feminist writers confirmed their own experiences of abuse as real and not a psychotic invention. Initially feminists typified child sexual abuse as one facet of the systematic abuse of women by a patriarchal and phallocentric society. Some of the most influential publications have been in the sphere of literature such as *The Bluest Eye* by Toni Morrison (1970) and Alice Walker's *The Colour Purple* (1983). As a consequence of this change in perspective the question arose. If we were abused as children and remained ignored and unheard, what is happening to the present generation of children? The resulting increase in ability to recognise and respond to evidence of sexual abuse-led to the beginning of more appropriate services for adult and child survivors.

The second step forward came as practitioners influenced by the disclosures made by women recognised that it was not sufficient to provide help for those victimised by child sexual abuse. Something had to be done to stop or change the behaviour of adults who carried out this abuse. In America treatment programmes developed in prison and in the community to achieve this child protection ambition. The experience of many of these practitioners raised fundamental questions about the characteristics and nature of child sexually abusive behaviour. Research, often practitioner led, indicated that many adult paedophiles began to perpetrate abuse in their adolescence or earlier. One such study, by Abel et al. (1987) obtained evidence to this effect from the self-report of a large sample of adult male child sexual abusers.

In the United Kingdom, as in America, treatment programmes had also begun to appear, usually as the result of the efforts of individual workers, such as Ray Wyre (in Albany Prison during the 1980s and subsequently the Gracewell Clinic). Small multi-disciplinary teams such as the North East London Probation Service Sex Offenders Project and the G-Map scheme in Greater Manchester also emerged. In the absence of existing management structures and guidelines for good practice these initiatives developed similar ideas about the importance of open confidentiality and an integrated approach, which incorporated child protection measures with treatment aims (Mezey, 1991).

It was the experiences of practitioners involved in adult sexual abusers treatment programmes together with the influx of information from research that led to the next step. This was the emergence of treatment programmes designed to meet the needs of adolescent abusers. As these services began to develop in America, in the UK and elsewhere, research attention was directed to these young abusers, their behaviours and their backgrounds. During the late 1980s and 1990s Becker (1986), Friedrich (1991) and Johnson (1993) have been amongst the most prominent Americans to consider the characteristics of children and and young people who sexually abuse, while in this country Skuse, Bentovim et al. (1998) have provided valuable insights into possible causal factors such as exposure to domestic violence, attachment problems and rejection (explored in detail by Calder in 2001).

We have now reached the point where acceptance of work with child sexual abuse as a child protection measure has entered the mainstream of social work, psychiatry, psychotherapy and psychology. Schemes have proliferated to meet this need. In the voluntary sector the NSPCC has adopted work with children and young people who sexually abuse as an integral part of an overall ambition to end abuse of children within a generation. These are all encouraging developments and yet there is worrying evidence that the speed with which work with child sexual abuse has expanded is in danger of outstripping the construction of a safe structure within which it can take place. Calder in Chapter 19 explores the current structural changes in the UK which arguably exit most young people who sexually abuse from the child protection system and relocates them either as children in need or the responsibility of the Youth Offending Teams.

Evidence of problems from a specialist practice perspective

Society has the right to expect that vulnerable children who have been removed from harmful or inadequate families are protected and nurtured by the professional care system. During the past ten years this expectation has been assaulted by revelations of the systematic physical and sexual abuse of those appointed and paid to care for them. The infiltration of residential homes and allied agencies in North Wales by large numbers of paedophiles was documented in the Waterhouse (2000) report. The climate of cover-up and secrecy surrounding the appointment of Mark Trotter to positions which allowed him to sexually abuse children (Barratt, 1998) demonstrated the failings in the appointment and supervision of staff, which continues today. Children and young people who sexually abuse are frequently the victims of such abuse. They are recognised as having 'dual status'. This definition acknowledges that they are children in need while concurrently being perpetrators of sexual harm who may be dealt with by the Criminal Justice system. Such children are at particular risk of further sexual exploitation because of their high level of arousal, passivity or compliance with adult instruction. These characteristics mean that any disclosures of sexual abuse that they make may be discredited because it is wrongly assumed that they invited their abuse in some way. It is because of the real dangers to these children that this chapter argues that measures are taken to make them and the settings in which they live and receive treatment as safe as possible.

Information gained from notorious cases, such as those quoted above, about the extent of problems with existing mechanisms to manage and treat children and young people who sexually abuse, is complemented by the experience of professionals engaged in this work on a day-to-day basis. The team at the Young Abusers Project has now assessed more than two hundred children from five up to twenty-one years of age. A number of themes have emerged in carrying out these assessments, which should not be ignored in the debate about good practice with this difficult and complex group. A quantitative evaluation is of course important in determining allocation of resources and in targeting training and management priorities. The following observations are intended to stimulate further direct research and the construction of sensible policies including accreditation of workers and work modes:

- **Absence of a thought out plan.** The decisions taken by social workers and others who refer children to the Young Abusers Project are subject to many powerful influences. The caring professions now exist in a world of restricted budgets, the need to justify expenditure and the commitment of the time of skilled practitioners. Specialist workers who can be perceived as occupying an ivory tower, insulated from the real world must understand these pressures. However, it is evident that the process of meeting the needs of these children and young people can be typified as reactive rather than carefully thought out. Most referrals come with a long history of their sexually abusive behaviour often dating back to pre-adolescence. Reading through the referral letter and the documents provided for us often brings the assessment team to the conclusion that sufficient information is already available for the network of professionals involved with the child to establish child protection and care plans, including identification of accommodation and treatment needs. However, what we observe is a pattern of piecemeal responses that seem to ignore past events and re-invent the wheel each time a sexually abusive act occurs.

    One worrying consequence is the frequency with which children and and young people who sexually abuse continue to live in unsupervised contact with younger siblings or other potential victims for years after the emergence of their abusive behaviour.

- **Delay in identification.** This characteristic and unhelpful pattern may be the result of lack of resources, inadequate training or lack of containing management. Whatever the cause, a failure to identify harmful sexual behaviour at an early stage means that child victims are not protected and the children who they abuse are not provided with a treatment service at an early point. This delay in recognition of the problem is even more pronounced in the cases of girls who abuse. The clinical impression of workers at the Young Abusers Project is that girls have to display even more disturbed and harmful behaviour for longer than their male counterparts.

- **Absence of a safe care context.** At the professionals meeting which precedes assessment the question will be regularly asked of visiting colleagues, 'Who is parenting this child?' The child in question will normally have an extensive history of victimisation by every kind of abuse in addition to a catalogue of documented perpetration without ever having been made subject to a Care Order or removal from the sources of abuse at home. Workers will explain to us that the parents have always co-operated with social work plans for the child and the local authority is acting in accordance with the Children Act philosophy to operate with 'a light touch' and without orders where that is possible. If asked to provide the evidence for deciding to work in this way, a lack of any comprehensive assessment of the parenting ability of the family or any formal assessment of risk frequently becomes apparent. Other elements of common sense practice such as a sensitive physical examination of siblings or other children who have been in unsupervised contact with the referred child tend also to be absent.

It is important to stress that the professionals referred to are normally capable and experienced and that the lack of properly planned work may not be characteristic of other elements of their practice. There are some problems in child rearing, education or delinquent behaviour that can be dealt with in isolation but childrens and and young peoples sexual behaviour is not one such problem. It is important to make a holistic assessment of their background, their behaviour and social context before reaching a conclusion. However, once identified the problem requires long-term planning which is difficult to achieve with rapid turnover of staff and short-term budget constraints.

- **Managerial uncertainty.** During the nine-year history of the Project we have come to recognise the importance of engaging with social work managers in assessment and treatment of children and young people who sexually abuse. Where intervention with these children and young people is not accorded a firm status in a social work department it is sometimes left to an inexperienced social worker often ill-acquainted with the history of the child/young person and their family to argue the case for action to be taken. It is a shared impression of staff at the project that unless a manager is involved in the process of assessment at an early stage, the momentum towards treatment will fall away. On several occasions a social worker has accepted recommendations for treatment and prerequisite child protection action but in the absence of a supportive manager these plans will fall away until a further episode of sexual abuse leads to an anxious telephone call asking for help.

- **Foster carers.** Foster care is a vital part in the jigsaw of provision for children and young people who sexually abuse. It is often important to move children and young people away from home either permanently or temporarily until it is safe for them to return. However, it is essential that foster care is a safe place for sexually abusive children and young people to live. In general this means that they cannot be accommodated where there are younger or in some other way vulnerable children. (For instance vulnerable through physical or mental impairment). It is essential that foster carers be provided with full information about the risk posed by an abusive child. The establishment of the principle that foster carers are entitled to compensation for abuse carried out by a child placed with them (Family Court Reporter, 1998), brings home the need for local authorities and foster care organisations to co-operate in the establishment of measures that prevent the recurrence of any such incident. Calder in Chapter 19 also highlights the need under Health and Safety legislation to conduct risk assessments of any child or young person in the home where an abuser is placed.

We have repeatedly dealt with referrals where it has proved impossible to find appropriate placements for this group of children and young people. As a consequence they may be placed out of the Borough, sometimes hundreds of miles from their families and communities. Unfortunately, the foster carers asked to look after them have not been provided with the training, information or ongoing support necessary to carry out their important task. Hackett (2001) has produced, however, an excellent workbook that will go some way to resolving this particular problem.

Existing and planned legislation and systemic implementation

In this chapter it will not be possible to deal with the steps which have or are planned to be taken in respect of every agency, organisation or individual therapist that provides a service for children and young people who sexually abuse. This section of the chapter will primarily concentrate on the state of play with regard to the two lead Ministries, namely the Department of Health and the Home Office and briefly comment on the position of other significant bodies such as the NSPCC and those representing psychotherapy.

Department of Health

The Social Care Act (2000) will bring with it substantial change in the way in which social work training and practice is regulated. The Act authorises the replacement of the Central Council for Education and Training in Social Work (CCETSW) with a Social Care Council for England that should be operative by October or November of 2001. This new Council will be empowered to define what constitutes good practice with regard to specific areas and to accredit post-qualifying training in social work. It is likely that a register of accredited child care practitioners will be created and that the necessary criteria for registration will be possession of a Post Qualifying Child Care Award (CCETSW, 2000).

One component of training courses that lead to this award is likely to be part of a module that addresses the subject of children and young people who sexually abuse. This session or sessions will give a general introduction to the work, in particular to recognition and assessment of risk essential to all experienced social workers. However, it is not known if a further level of training will be required for those intending to work in a specialised capacity with these young people.

At present the Advanced Learning Award courses would appear best suited to providing an appropriate vehicle for providing this higher level of training. However, there is concern amongst social work educators that the Advanced Learning Award may not survive the current re-organisation. £11 million have been made available to Social Services Departments through the Training Support Programme (TSP) in order to train 7,000 social workers to Post Qualifying award level during the years 1999 to 2003. There is no provision for funding for any other specialist training to be ring fenced. In a conversation on this matter Pat Walton, Social Work Lecturer at the University of Leicester School of Social Work (Waldon, 2000), expressed her concern that this might leave a worrying gap in the emerging framework of training and child protection measures surrounding and containing work with children and young people who sexually abuse.

A concurrent development to the creation of the Social Care Council is the establishment of the Social Care Institute for Excellence (SCIE), as described in *A Quality Strategy for Social Care* (DoH, 2000). This body will collect research and practitioner evidence and act as a feedback loop into the Council that will influence policy and practice advice. At present it is not known what advice will be given in relation to work with children and young people who sexually abuse. However, this will be an important conduit for clinical experience and practice into training courses.

As has been noted earlier in this chapter some convicted young people who sexually abuse will fall within the remit of Youth Offender Teams (YOTS) that are the responsibility of the Youth Justice Board. At present there is no national system of accreditation of treatment programmes for young people who sexually abuse to be provided by YOTS. Some teams are in the process of developing their own programmes and others are trying to create partnerships with specialist resources such as those provided by NSPCC. The system is in flux but may well move towards the model adopted by the Home Office for the accreditation of treatment services for adult sex offenders. This model is discussed in more detail below.

In addition to training, the Department of Health is also sensitive to the need for employers to exercise care in the recruitment and appointment of staff. The general duty of care to children incumbent on the Department means that guidelines have been created that advise on measures for assessing suitability of applicants to any position that gives access to children. The burden of responsibility is particularly weighty when the employment in question involves work with children such as young abusers, who are vulnerable. Specific recommendations on the process and mechanics of appointment are given in the Warner Report, *Choosing With Care* (DoH, 1992). More recently the Department commissioned a video and training pack *Towards Safer Care* (Cleaver Media and DoH, 1999) from the NSPCC. Further instruction was included in the revised *Working Together* (DoH, 1999). Taken together these guidelines help provide a general foundation for a safer approach to the selection and accreditation of staff. However, the system must be honed and made more sophisticated to meet the needs of specialist undertakings.

Home Office

Lines of responsibility for young offenders are not as straightforward as suggested above. The Probation Service, which falls under the ministerial aegis of the Home Office, has been identified as the lead agency in developing offender programmes for sex offenders within YOTS. However, it is not clear which agency has responsibility for providing similar services in young offender institutions.

The Home Office has established a clear system of accreditation for group treatment programmes for adult offenders, including sex offenders, in prison and in the community. All prison service or community based programmes, whether staffed by probation officers or operated by specialist units in partnership with the Probation Service must satisfy the criteria established by the Joint Accreditation Panel (2000). The criteria have been drawn up in accordance with the evidence-based ethos that governs the Home Office What Works Initiative Crime Reduction Programme. The ninth requirement of the criteria for the accreditation of programme design (p19 Joint Accreditation Panel, 2000) is that of Continuity of Programmes and Services. Within this requirement child protection and interagency networking are highlighted. These two elements are central to any service offered to children. If the framework of the Joint Accreditation Panel is used as a blueprint for accreditation of a service for young offenders in custody, supervised in the community or children in Local Authority Secure Accommodation it must be substantially amended to accord them greater priority.

The accreditation criteria do not include guidelines on child protection dilemmas. For instance it will be necessary to give instruction on the circumstances in which treatment may be provided to a child or young person who has sexually abused and who continues to live in the same family home (or other accommodation) as their victim or other vulnerable children.

A second area that is not fully covered by the accreditation criteria is that of staff suitability. Criteria 8, Engagement and Motivation (Joint Accreditation Panel, 2000), refers to the importance of staff training and approach of staff in the provision of group treatment. These are of course essential elements of accreditation but where the subject matter is the behaviour of young people who sexually abuse a more searching assessment of staff suitability is necessary. This issue is discussed at greater length later in this chapter.

The voluntary sector and other professional organisations

At the time of writing this chapter, Lord Allardyce's Psychotherapy Bill is awaiting parliamentary consideration. The Bill is intended to prevent anyone from describing themselves as a psychotherapist without an accredited qualification, and although the need for regulation is generally accepted the Act may never reach the statute book. There is substantial opposition mounted by those who fear that the fundamental aim to exclude unsafe, untrained or unscrupulous practitioners will not be achieved unless the remit of the proposed Act is widened to include counselling and other therapies. It is argued that the effect of the Act will be to establish an elite of accredited Psychotherapists leaving an unregulated mass within which competent and ethical practitioners would be indistinguishable from those motivated by sexual or other unacceptable intentions.

In addition to Social Services Departments the United Kingdom has a number of influential voluntary organisations that perform a significant child care function. NCH Action for Children, Barnados and the NSPCC amongst others have become involved in one way or another in work with children and young people who sexually abuse. The NSPCC includes this work as a component of their strategy to end the abuse of children within a generation (NSPCC, 1999) and now has sixteen specialist schemes offering assessment and treatment services. In a development which parallels the process now occurring in the wider social work arena the Society is using existing child protection legislation, lessons from other allied areas of work and specialist practice experience to define organisational policies to establish national guidelines for good practice.

The current picture is therefore one of structure beginning to appear. The foundations are in place although the detail of the end result is not clear. There is considerable political pressure to complete construction quickly but this task must incorporate information from research and practice.

Observations on Elements of Accreditation from a Specialist Standpoint

Appointment of staff to social work and other positions

The role of the Young Abusers Project in providing consultation and training to a variety of teams and departments has given us an insight into the problems that can emerge and persist when there is a lack of a reliable framework to manage the appointment, management and supervision of staff who have access to children. The following comments are intended to address problems that might occur with regard to appointing staff to work in a specialist capacity. However, they are also relevant to foster care, residential childcare and other appointments. Morrison (1997) amongst others has highlighted the importance of having systems and workers that realistically address the need to protect children.

Catherine Walden, the Human Resources Manager for the North West region of the NSPCC is evaluating a pilot scheme for appointments to childcare employment that makes use of the Warner Report (1992) recommendations. In conversation (Walden, 2000) she expressed the view that the particular recommendation from Warner regarding enquiring into 'the character and attitudes of shortlisted candidates' had posed dilemmas for many local authorities and voluntary organisations in terms of implementation. This recommendation appeared to be at odds with the equal opportunities approach adopted about 10 years ago, which was designed to be less subjective, more systematic and less discriminatory than the methods which tended to result in recruiting 'in our own image'. However, in our attempts to ensure equal rights and access, we have focused almost exclusively on examining the professional and technical abilities to do a particular job to the exclusion of the candidates' underlying values, beliefs and motivations to work in a particularly responsible, difficult and sensitive area of work. Walden believes that it is possible, indeed it is imperative, that we retain the philosophy and principles of equal opportunities whilst also endeavouring to explore the character, attitudes and motivations of candidates who seek to work with vulnerable children and young people. This is a challenging task for any recruitment process, but we owe it to children and young people, to embrace this challenge and make safer recruitment decisions.

Let us consider the worst case-scenarios. It is possible that an agency or professional network has been infiltrated systematically by paedophiles. Alternatively a culture of sexual abuse may have grown within a professional network. There have been instances where paedophiles have appointed others of like mind to positions of responsibility for children. Grievances have been dismissed or not acted on and changes in working methods opposed and delayed. Social work departments, foster care and residential organisations and police and education have experienced just such corrupting experiences (Waterhouse, 2000).

Alternatively individuals may apply for jobs who are ill equipped through personality or sexual attitude to children for work with sexually aroused young abusers. Given the history of sexual and physical abuse by male professional caregivers, it might be argued that being of the male gender is sufficient to ensure such a mismatch. However, the potential for female professionals to abuse children must not be ignored. The selection of an appointment panel is an important safeguard against mistaken employment of unsuitable workers. The panel should include workers from different but related disciplines and should regularly change in membership. Gender, race and cultural difference should be represented and at least one of the members must have experience of working with children and young people who sexually abuse.

Appointment panels must test the theoretical and practice skills of the applicants. It is unwise to appoint newly qualified staff to specialist posts of this kind. It is, for instance, essential that applicants have attended some form of reliable/accredited training. Those who work with these children must be capable of genuinely shared, and integrated work with fellow professionals. Panels must also assess an applicant's ability to demonstrate an appreciation of their own sexuality and how this will be affected by working with sexually abusive children.

Accreditation of therapy and group treatment options

The Home Office model for the accreditation of group treatment programmes provides a useful blueprint for designing a system for evaluating the academic and practice credentials of programme design. However, as stated earlier it does not cover some issues that we regard as important in providing a service for children and young people. First it is necessary to acknowledge that a reliable, holistic assessment of need must take place before any decision is made about treatment options. This is necessary especially when a child is very young and concerns may be more about displays of sexualised behaviour rather than repeated, overtly sexually abusive acts. Skilled assessment at this stage will help to support and advise individual children and their family before behaviours become more extreme. Once a child has begun to show an entrenched pattern of behaviour, which substantially deviates from normal peer-appropriate actions over a period of time, assessment will assist decisions about where a child can be safely accommodated, educated and treated. Researchers and clinicians have been working to produce reliable descriptions of normative sexual behaviour (Friedrich et al., 1991). This will assist the accurate delineation of problematic symptoms, as will reliable psychiatric diagnoses of sexual problems in children (Vizard, 1998). Secondly, an individual or organisation seeking to provide therapy must show an understanding of the elements of reliable assessment and require these elements to be adhered to by those referring patients to them for treatment. Our practice at the Project is to try and ensure that the following fundamental tasks are carried out in respect of each child referred to us:

- Lilac book assessment/risk assessment of family or caregivers.
- Individual assessment by specialist workers.
- Psychiatric assessment where mental health concerns exist.
- Clinical psychological testing.
- Physical examination by skilled paediatrician where contact sexual or physical abuse of the index patient has occurred.
- Reports from school.
- Additional relevant reports, for instance from foster carers.

Others have adopted different assessment methods and we are aware that in some cases assessment is carried out by single workers without access to other disciplines or by single discipline teams of social workers or health workers.

The basis for deciding on individual or group treatment is sometimes determined by the relative availability of local resource and in some cases by the lack of funds to pay for treatment.

Accreditation of individual therapy programmes

Any therapist who offers a treatment service to children and young people who have sexually abused should be required to meet the following basic requirements, which are derived from clinical experience and from the categories used by the Joint Prison and Probation Accreditation Panel (2000):

- Clear child protection strategies in place. A policy of open-confidentiality, which requires the sharing of information about previously undisclosed child sexual abuse to police, social work and other relevant bodies.
- Experience of specialist training.
- A reliable research or theoretical base on which therapy is based.
- Identifiable aims of treatment, both general and specific to each patient.
- Access to other disciplines.
- A physically safe setting for the therapist and subject, and agreed guidelines on how to maintain this.
- Supervision from a skilled source.
- Evaluation of outcome.

This chapter will not consider the merits of any one treatment-mode against another. Useful accounts of individual psychotherapy with children who have sexually abused can be found in publications by Vizard and Usiskin (1999) and Woods (1997). Others may rely on individual programmes based on behavioural or cognitive theories (Maletsky, 1991). Where more radical therapeutic approaches, such are body therapy are proposed as the preferred mode of treatment or as part of a treatment package, the theoretical and research evidence for employing them must be convincingly demonstrated. The risks inherent in any work that involves physical contact between child and adult are even greater than those present in a 'talking cure' and must be anticipated and carefully assessed.

The focus here is on what basic structure ought to be demanded before accreditation is merited. A child psychotherapist or counsellor working with a child or young person is in a position of trust but is also vulnerable. Individual treatment almost always depends on the establishment of a trusting relationship. The boundary of that relationship will be established at the outset. Even where a traditional child-centred approach to individual therapy is taken it is essential that agreement is reached between therapist and patient on the fact that only a limited degree of confidentiality can be provided. The limit should be that disclosure of hitherto unknown acts of abuse will result in the sharing of that information with relevant authorities. This perspective of good practice is not shared by all those who work with children and young people who sexually abuse. Some hold concerns that to work in such a way is to prevent patients from sharing the full extent of their victimisation or perpetration. This is one more matter for debate before guidelines for accreditation can be identified.

The practice at the Young Abusers project is to ensure that all patients have allocated social workers who make arrangements for the escorting of patients to and from therapy and with whom information about progress is shared on a regular basis. This provides a responsive structure should a patient disclose abuse or find that a session has caused distress, anger or perhaps arousal. The process of therapy will inevitable result in such reactions from time to time and it is ethically unacceptable to leave responsibility with a child to keep themselves and the public safe when they have a known history of causing sexual harm. Therapists should anticipate this and show that they have taken steps to protect against it in their treatment protocol. In our view these measures are fundamental even when referral comes direct from families or by self-referral.

The nature of child sexual abuse means that careful measures have to be taken to ensure that suitable individuals are allowed to carry out work with child perpetrators. There are publications that look at the general issue of therapist selection (O'Connell et al., 1990). It is certain that the boundaries of the therapeutic relationship will be tested as therapy progresses. As the prime focus of treatment is concern about the sexually abusive behaviour of the patient it is inevitable that the dynamics of transference, counter-transference and projective identification will be specifically sexual in nature. There are dangers of arousal and reaction to that arousal on both sides of the equation. Hackett (2000) used his experience of work with the G-MAP project as evidence for recognising this as an important facet in establishing a safe arena for work.

A number of important issues arise here, the first being risk of sexual abuse of the patient. Unless a therapist is appreciative of the sexualised nature of the therapeutic relationship this danger may well be overlooked. In a closed and unsupervised setting a replication of the patient's earlier experience of abuse can become manifest in concrete rather than a symbolic way. This danger is likely to be greatest with patients who are in their older teens but will not be restricted to this age group. Children and young people, who have been skilfully groomed by adult abusers, perhaps within their own family, will habitually respond to other adults in an aroused and arousing way. Although there is acknowledgement of this phenomenon in relation to the world of adult therapeutic relationships there is a powerful resistance to any admission that a child might evoke sexual feelings in a therapist. In the world outside therapy, for an adult to identify within himself or herself recognition of sexual arousal towards a child would probably be taken as a declaration of paedophilic interest in that child. Therapists have little reluctance in sharing vicarious understanding of the murderous feelings of violent patients, or of experiencing the projected terror of someone suffering a phobic reaction. However, it is far less common to read accounts of therapy with child survivors or perpetrators of sexual abuse that honestly discuss sexualised transferences and counter-transferences as well as the management of sexualised behaviour by children and young people in the therapy room.

It is important that a containing framework is in place for therapists working in this arena, where such feelings can be discussed with a skilled and experienced supervisor. In our view such a framework is an essential element of reliable individual therapy and would help reduce the risk of further abuse of vulnerable children.

The provision of supervision will also reduce the danger of false allegations of abuse made against therapists. Such allegations will occur from time to time, in particular with adolescent children. One factor in deciding whether a child is more suitable for group or individual therapy will be the degree to which they are aroused to adults and whether they have a history of making such allegations in the past. Sometimes children have a record of alleging abuse then retracting the allegations. The consequences for a therapist of being the focus of an investigation resulting from an allegation of sexual abuse of a child patient are profoundly damaging and it would be to their advantage to show that they have anticipated just such an eventuality and have discussed it in their supervision.

In some cases a decision may be made that individual therapy with a child is the only remedial option even though there is a danger that the child may struggle to control their actions and feelings in therapy. Such difficult choices arise frequently in work with the most disturbed children in secure units or other settings where the alternative may be that the child has no therapeutic input at all. In these cases an imaginative approach to providing active surveillance of the session may be necessary. This can be achieved by way of video or tape-recording the session. These steps may be regarded as intrusive and counterproductive by some therapists. We raise the issue as one for those considering the design of effective treatment with a view to accreditation.

It is entirely likely that the individual therapy offered to a child patient may be part of an over all package of therapies which could include separate work with parents, siblings or other family members. There may be concurrent programmes of intervention designed to complement individual therapy, such as body therapy or participation in a group programme. Attendance at a variety of sessions is commonplace in specialist residential settings but may also take place as part of the plan drawn up for an individual child in the community. Where this is the case it is always important that every part of the treatment package is aware of the aims, practice and progress of the others. Lines of communication and responsibility must be established in advance and systems put in place to deal with disagreement or breakdown in the professional network. We take the view that primary responsibility must rest with the Local Authority, working in co-operation with parents or alone where shared responsibility is not feasible. (For instance where the family is one where adults are sexually abusive or condone sexually abusive behaviour or the young person has no family context.) Where different

disciplines are involved in concurrent or conjoint work the local Area Child Protection Conference is a body that can discuss the establishment of a reliable system of management.

All modes of treatment including individual therapy should incorporate evaluation of the outcome of intervention. The assessment of adult therapeutic programmes required by the Joint Accreditation Panel is essentially by means of quantitative analysis. This is to be expected from a body which is part of the 'What Works' initiative. However, there is an argument to be made for a more qualitative approach to evaluation of individual therapy. Once again this is a matter for discussion and perhaps an acceptance of the validity of both approaches is the way forward. For small projects or for individual workers it would be difficult to produce a sufficiently large number of patients to give a meaningful statistical exploration of outcomes but a narrative account of therapy would be possible.

Accreditation of group treatment programmes

This chapter argues, for the reasons discussed earlier, that in order to meet the criteria for accreditation, Group Treatment Programmes should demonstrate accordance with a number of requirements. Some requirements mirror those suggested in the section dealing with individual therapy:

- Child protection framework.
- Links to or integration with other relevant disciplines.
- A credible theoretical framework.
- A programme which has identified, quantifiable aims, linked to the theoretical base.
- A safe arena for the work to take place.
- A reliable system of appointing staff.
- Effective supervision and management of staff.
- Access to skilled consultation.
- Evaluation of treatment outcome and practice.

Child protection is integral to the operation of a safe and supportive treatment programme. It is necessary to do as much as possible to safeguard the child participants but also to realistically take measures to protect potential victims from them. It is ethically wrong to embark on a therapeutic venture that carries with it a risk, that for a time at least, participants may become more depressed, angry or aroused without ensuring that those who might suffer the consequences are not informed or in some other way kept safe. It is an uncomfortable reality that a proportion of the children being treated for child sexual abusive behaviour will perpetrate further acts of abuse. The most disturbed may seriously harm or perhaps kill a child victim. It is necessary to use this knowledge to set up a system that will stand up in the wake of any subsequent enquiry into practice.

Child patients entering group treatment may not be subject to care, other criminal or civil law orders. Nevertheless the nature of their problem is such that treatment should never take place in isolation from social workers who have the authority to act should the need for investigative or child protection measures emerge.

Conclusion

This chapter is in essence a plea for the assumption of a more honest accountability of practice and practitioners involved in working with children and young people who sexually abuse. At present there is no consensus on the need for a system of accreditation let alone on the means of establishing a system to monitor practice. Improvements in the way that we identify child sexual abusers and their problematic behaviour will inevitably occur and new knowledge will require changes in those factors that validate treatment options. No system can remain rigid and unresponsive to research and clinical developments. Nevertheless, to adopt a laisser-faire policy and to allow the unfettered growth of untested modes of working is dangerous. We have seen the devastation caused to an extensive professional network by lack of control over harmful and perverse practices instituted by Frank Beck, a charismatic and persuasive social worker.

It will never be enough to rely on accreditation alone to achieve safe practice and to display the basis of safe practice to the public. It is inevitable that from time to time dangerous individuals and harmful work methods will occur. Lasting improvement will require substantial changes in our understanding and attitude towards children who sexually abuse and in the training provided to specialist

workers, but also to all those who enter the social work and health professions.

Acknowledgments

Dr Eileen Vizard for her invaluable advice and assistance. Tony Morrison, Catherine Walden, Pat Walton, Gwynne Jones at CCETSW, Trevor De Tute from the Seiff Foundation and Philip Hodson for their time and direction through areas new to me.

References

Abel, G. G., Becker, J. V., Cunningham-Rathner, J., Rouleau, J. and Murphy, W. (1987) Self-reported crimes of non-incarcerated paraphiliacs. *Journal of Interpersonal Violence.* 2: 3–25.

Barratt, J. K. (1998) *The Report of the 1997 Enquiry into the 'Trotter Affair':* Report by J. K. Barratt to the Council of the London Borough of Hackney, London: London Borough of Hackney.

Becker, J., Kaplan, M., Cunningham-Rathner, J. and Kavoussi, R. (1986) Characteristics of Adolescent Incest Sexual Perpetrators: Preliminary Findings. *Journal of Family Violence.* 1(1): 85–97.

Biaggio, M., Duffy, R. and Staffelbach, D. F. (1998) Obstacles to Addressing Professional Misconduct. *Clinical Psychology Review.* 18(3): 273–85.

Calder, M. C. (2001) *Juveniles and Children Who Sexually Abuse: Frameworks for Assessment.* (2nd edition). Dorset: Russell House Publishing.

CCETSW (2000) *Assuring Quality for Child Care Social Work.* Requirements for the post-qualifying Child Care Award and for the Approval, Review and Inspection of Child Care Programmes. London: CCETSW.

Cleaver Media and Department of Health. (1999) *Towards Safer Care.* Training and Resource Pack. London: Department of Health.

Cohen, S. (1993) *Folk Devils and Moral Panic: The creation of the Mods and Rockers.* Oxford: Basil Blackwell.

Craissati, J. (1998) *Child Sexual Abusers: A Community Treatment Approach.* Hove: UK. Psychology Press.

De Mause, L. (1974) *The History of Childhood.* New York: Psychotherapy Press.

Department of Health, Home Office and Department of Education and Employment (1999). *Working Together to Safeguard Children:*

A Guideline to Inter-agency Working to Safeguard and Promote the Welfare of Children. London: The Stationery Office.

Department of Health. (2000) *A Quality Strategy for Social Care.* London: Department of Health.

Epps, K. (1999) Causal Explanations: Filling the Theoretical Reservoir. in Calder, M. C. (Ed.) *Working with Young People who Sexually Abuse: New Pieces of the Jigsaw Puzzle.* Dorset: Russell House Publishing. 8–26.

Family Court Reporter. (1998) W and Others v Essex County Council and Another. *Family Court Reporter.* 2: 7.

Freidrich, W. N., Grambsc, P. and Bielke, R. L. (1991) Normative Sexual Behaviour in Children. *Paediatrics,* 83: 456–64.

Freud, S. (1925) An Autobiographical Study. in *Standard Edition 20* (translator Strachey, J.) (1959) London: Hogarth Press.

Hackett, S. (2000) *Impact on the Worker.* Keynote presentation to a national conference on working with Adolescent Sex Offenders. Ort House, Camden, London, 6–7 Nov.

Hackett, S. (2001) *Facing the Future: A Guide for Parents of Young People who Have Sexually Abused.* Dorset: Russell House Publishing.

Hawkes, C, Jenkins. J. A. and Vizard, E. (1997) Roots of Sexual Violence in Children and Adolescents. in Varma V. (Ed.) *Violence in Children and Adolescents.* London: Jessica Kingsley.

Johnson, T. C. (1993) Childhood Sexuality. in Gil, E. and Johnson, T. C. (Eds.) *Sexualised Children: Assessment and Treatment of Sexualised Children and Children who Molest.* Rockville, Launch Press. 1–20.

Joint Prison and Probation Accreditation Panel. (2000) *Joint Prison and Probation Accreditation Criteria:* Version 28.4.00. Home Office.

Maletzky, B. M. (1991) *Treating the Sexual Offender.* Newbury park, CA: Sage Publications.

Mezey, G., Vizard, E., Hawkes, C. and Austin, R. (1991) A Community Treatment Programme for Convicted Child Sexual Abusers: A Preliminary Report. *The Journal of Forensic Psychiatry.* 2(1).

Morrison, T. (1970) *The Bluest Eye.* London: Random House.

Morrison, T. (1997) Emotionally Competent Child Protection Organisations? Fallacy, Fiction or Necessity. in Bates, N., Pugh, S. and Thompson, N. (Eds.) *Protecting Children: Challenge and Change.* Aldershot: Arena.

O'Connell, M. A., Leeberg, E. and Donaldson, C. R. (1990) *Working with Sex Offenders: A Guide to Therapist Selection.* Newbury Park: CA. Sage.

Pope, K. S. (2000) Therapists Sexual Feelings and Behaviours. Research, Trends and Quandaries. in Szuchman, L. T., Muscarella, F. et al. (Eds.) *Psychological Perspectives on Human Sexuality.* New York: John Wiley and Sons. 603–58.

Skuse, D., Bentovim, A. J., Stevenson, J., Andreou, C., Lanyado, M., New, M., Williams, B. and McMillan, D. (1998) Risk Factors for Development of Sexually Abusive Behaviour in Sexually Victimised Adolescent Boys: Cross Sectional Study. *British Medical Journal,* 317, 18 Jul.

Vizard, E. (1998) *Operational Criteria for Sexual Arousal Disorder of Childhood.* Paper given in forensic session of the Residential Conference of the Child and Adolescent Psychiatry Faculty of the Royal College of Psychiatrists, Bristol, UK. 24–26 Sep.

Vizard, E., Monck, E. and Misch, P. (1995) Child and Adolescent Sex Abuse Perpetrators: A Review of the Literature. *Journal of Child Psychology and Psychiatry.* 36: 731–59.

Vizard, E. and Usiskin, J. (1999) Providing Individual Psychotherapy for Young Sexual Abusers of Children. in Erooga, M. and Masson, H. (Eds.) *Children and Young People who Sexually Abuse Others.* London: Routledge. 104–23.

Walton, P. (2000) Cited in Walden (2000).

Walden, C. (2000) Personal communication, 11 Oct.

Waterhouse, R. (2000) *Lost in Care: Report of the Tribunal of Enquiry into the Abuse of Children in Care in the Former County Council Areas of Gwynedd, Clwyd, since 1994: Summary of the Report with Conclusions and Recommendations in Full.* London: The Stationery Office.

Walker, A. (1983) *The Color Purple.* London: The Women's Press.

Warner, N. (1992) *Choosing With Care.* Department of Health: Stationery Office.

Woods, J. (1997) Breaking the Cycle of Abuse and Abusing: Individual Psychotherapy for Juvenile Sex Offenders. *Clinical Child Psychology and Psychiatry.* 2(3): ??.

Chapter 9: Residential Standards of Care

Robert E. Longo MRC, LCP

Introduction

Criminal sexual behaviour has been acknowledged as a human sexual behavioural problem for centuries, dating back to early civilisations. Sexual abusers and their potential to be treated have been addressed in the literature as far back as the 1800s according to Kraft Ebing's (1886) work *Psychopathis Sexualis*. The more recent attempts at treating sexual offenders in the United States of America date back to the 1940s in the state of Wisconsin (Brecher, 1978).

In the mid 1970s, juveniles who committed sexual offences were often diagnosed as *adolescent adjustment reactions*. More often than not, their behaviour was considered a result of an *emotional disturbance*, viewed as typical male adolescent *sexual experimentation*, or downplayed by seeing the behaviour as 'boys will be boys' (National Task Force on Juvenile Sexual Offending, 1993). The criminal justice response was often dismissive or sanctions were minimal. In many cases legal charges, if any, were reduced to non-sexual crimes.

For the purposes of this chapter, sexually abusive youth are defined as adolescents aged 13 to 17-year-olds who have been charged with a criminal sexual offence or have known histories of engaging in sexually abusive behaviour. It is important to note that, although both male and female adolescents engage in the sexual abuse of children and others, the majority of perpetrators are male, and that a number of clinical studies have identified prepubescent youth, and females, who engage in sexually abusive behaviour (Center for Sex Offender Management, 1999; Araji, 1997). As many as 40 per cent of the victims abused by these young persons are relatives of juvenile sexual abusers (American Academy of Child and Adolescent Psychiatry, 1999). Research has distinguished two groups of juvenile sex offenders:

- Sexually abusive youth who target peers and adults.
- Sexually abusive youth who target younger children and young children under the age of five.

(Barbaree et al., 1993)

Another problem identified in the field of working with sexually abusive youth has been the trickle down of assessment and treatment methods and models designed for adults being used on youthful sexual abusers. Adult sex offending focuses on deviancy, rape, child molestation, and other paraphilias. Sexually abusive behaviour by youth covers a broader range of sexual behaviour and includes a wide range of behaviour distinct from sexual intercourse and/or forced sex.

A growing problem

During the past decade there has been a growing concern regarding how we assess, treat, and manage children and adolescents with sexual behaviour problems. Many are concerned about how these young people are viewed and dealt with in the criminal justice system. These concerns have most clearly risen among professionals who work with or treat adolescents with sexual behaviour problems.

While there are many concerns, and too many to address in the limited scope of this chapter, one major area of concern is the problems associated with the downward extension of adult models to adolescent sexual abusers and in some cases young children with sexual behaviour problems. Clearly, many of these youths do not meet the diagnostic criteria to be diagnosed with a paraphilic disorder, however, this has not stopped many state laws, youth related agencies, and in many cases treatment programmes from looking at youth with sexual behaviour problems with a 'one size fits all' mentality.

When adult treatment modalities and models are extended to the assessment and treatment of adolescent sexual abusers, the end product is all too often excessive treatment or the wrong treatment that itself may sexualise vulnerable youth, or not be tailored to the needs of sub groups of youth with sexual behaviour problems, i.e., lower functioning sexually abusive youth, female sexual abusers, mentally ill youth with sexual behaviour problems, etc.

According to national surveys of programmes treating adult and juvenile sexual abusers (Knopp et al., 1986, 1989, 1992 and Freeman-Longo et al., 1995), many treatment programmes for youth are virtually no different in the treatment models and practices used than those programmes which treat adult sexual offenders. Unfortunately, treatment models and modalities for adult sex offenders include many controversial areas of practice, especially when used for juveniles. According to a preliminary report published by the Department of Justice, Office of Juvenile Justice and Delinquency Prevention;

> *'these include involuntary treatment ordered for public safety rather than rehabilitative reasons,[1] pre-adjudication evaluations,[2] phallometric assessment,[3] polygraph examinations,[4] arousal conditioning,[5] psychopharmacologic therapies.[6] These areas of practice are controversial because they may expose children and youth to a greater sexualisation than the original offence, and they also raise ethical issues that too closely blend treatment and rehabilitation with adjudication and attributions of criminal responsibility'*

(Development Services Group, 2000)

Another issue of growing concern has been a recent decrease in the number of programmes providing family treatment for adolescents with sexual behaviour problems. Family therapy is considered a key part of treating sexually offending youth because 'it is within the family context that many of the offender's beliefs, myths, and cognitive distortions about sexuality, aggression, and gender have been evolved and maintained' (American Academy of Child and Adolescent Psychiatry, 1999:25). According to unpublished data on sex offender treatment programmes (Burton et al. 2000), the reduction in the number of programmes treating juveniles who also do family treatment has decreased significantly. There is little question regarding the importance of family treatment in working with troubled youth and especially those with sexual behaviour problems. Treatment should emphasise reintegration into the family and the community (Borduin, 1990). As fears for community safety increase, a growing number of children are being removed from their families and placed in residential treatment centres. Many states do not have adequate resources to provide residential treatment, or services are lacking in rural areas. In these instances children are sent to out-of-state residential programmes. Often, the lack of community-based facilities, or the distances to travel to them, impedes visitation with the family and conducting family therapy.

Many of the myths and misconceptions about sex offending youth, the nature of their problems, and who they are as people has been the result of misinformation in the media. There is no doubt that there is a need for public education and information dissemination about new research findings on treatment and rehabilitation of juveniles adjudicated for sexual offences. In addition, the public, legislators and alike, need to better understand what constitutes sexual offending versus normal development. To date, there are few studies that adequately address treatment efficacy and outcome with adolescent sexual abusers (Worling, 2000). Despite these few studies and limited literature on juvenile sexual offending that can help guide policy making, policy changes are occurring in the absence of good information about treatment efficacy and public safety needs.

While it is important to understand and recognise that the majority of sexually offending youth won't recidivate, it is also incorrect to believe that all are treatable. Public safety remains an issue, despite the age of the sexual abuser, and the prognosis for successful treatment. As a result risk assessment has been a focal point within the field in recent years and research to look at a typology of adolescent sexual abusers as well as validation of risk scales is currently underway in the United States.

Risk assessment at this point is not a precise science, and the low base-rate of recidivism in current studies suggests that at this point in time all models of risk assessment will over-predict the risk of re-offending. Therefore we must be cautious in developing risk assessment scales. Risk assessment should include multiple areas for assessment and warning flags. To properly assess risk we must review and use information in criminal arrest records, listen to client self report, talk with informants, family members, significant others and friends, and look closely at clinical records and all materials in the official client record. Decisions about disposition and the level of care should be based on relativism and judgement, not absolutism.

Table 1: Comparison of treatment provider responses since 1986

Year	Adult	Juvenile	Child	Total
1986	297	346	n/a	643
1988	429	573	n/a	1,002
1990	541	626	n/a	1,167
1992	745	755	n/a	1,500
1994	710	684	390	1,784
1996	527	539	314	1,380

Growth of treatment programmes

As the highly specialised field of sexual offender treatment and specifically adolescent sexual offender treatment has grown, the criminal justice response to adolescent sexual offending has undergone dramatic changes. By the late 1990s, sexual offences committed by juveniles have been estimated to account for as much as 30 per cent of the reported cases of child sexual abuse (Finkelhor, 1994), including as many as a fifth of rapes and one-half of the cases of child molestation (Sinkmund et al., 1997, Freeman-Longo and Blanchard, 1998). The criminal justice response has been to develop tougher sanctions for sex offending youth, and holding juveniles accountable for their behaviour to the point where many states now consider waiving youth to adult court systems for sexual offending behaviour. In addition, sex offender registration laws and public notification of sex offender release laws have been applied to juvenile sexual offenders at an alarming rate (Freeman-Longo, 2000).

The Safer Society Foundation, Inc., (SSF) formerly the Safer Society Program and Press, began tracking the growth and development of specialised sex offender treatment programmes in the United States of America in the 1970s when its founder and then director, the late Fay Honey Knopp, recognised the need for these specialised programmes and assumed the role of networking programmes and professionals doing this work to facilitate the growth of the field. Just twenty-four years ago, the Safer Society had identified only a handful of programmes, and those programmes were described in Brecher, 1978.

The growth of identified specialised juvenile and adult sexual abuser programmes and treatment providers have mushroomed from 22 identified programs in 1976 to over 1,391 programmes in 1996 (see Table 1). Generally, and until recently, juvenile sexual abuser treatment services have grown less rapidly than adult programmes which now appear to be declining as more prison-based treatment programmes close their doors, diverting funds from programming to prison construction. The SSF has maintained files on identified programmes and clinicians providing such services to juvenile and adult sex offenders since 1976, and from the first national survey in 1986, the SSF's listings of identified specialised juvenile and adult sex-offender programmes and treatment providers increased dramatically.

The Safer Society national surveys recognised 'identified' programmes only as those programmes who filled out and returned the nationwide surveys. In 1994, the survey was lengthened and only 65 per cent of programmes returned to the survey. During the 1996 survey only an estimated 55 per cent of programmes receiving the survey questionnaire completed it and returned the survey to the Safer Society by the specified date. The 2000 survey, which has been underway since fall of 1999 is showing an even greater decrease in respondents (Burton, 2000) Thus the figures in Table 1 reflect only identified programmes who responded to the surveys and do not accurately represent the total number of specialised programmes in existence in the United States.

In recent years, experts have questioned whether the growth in the number of programmes treating juvenile sexual abusers have kept up with new knowledge and advances in treating juvenile sex offenders. For example, in 1998, the American Professional Society on the Abuse of Children published a special issue of *Child Maltreatment* and asked 'Have we gone too far in our response?' In 1999, the American Academy of Child and

Adolescent Psychiatry developed a set of practice parameters for the assessment and treatment of sexually abusive youth. Their findings suggest that adolescent offenders are more amenable to treatment than adult sex offenders, and that a 'significant percentage of juvenile sexual abusers will respond to therapeutic intervention' (1999:20).

During the 1990s other concerns began to grow in the field of treating youth with sexual behaviour problems. For example, programmes designed for teachers and professionals in schools and other child-serving institutions have also grown. Changes in state and national laws have resulted in institutions being held liable for children being abused or harassed by other children while in the care of the organisation[7]. Increased awareness of liability has led to greater identification of potential abusers (Development Service Group, 2000; Freeman-Longo and Ryan, 1990).

All of the above points to a need for both a continuum of care regarding the treatment of youth with sexual behaviour problems, and the need for standardisation of programme placement decisions. It is becoming more commonplace within the field to see children placed in secure facilities as a routine practice based upon community safety needs rather than the specific treatment needs of the individual child. As a result many youth are placed in high security facilities needlessly, instead of in facilities that will provide them with the optimal care they need in order to heal. Many children are bounced back and forth between facilities and foster care because they are not getting the appropriate treatment they need.

Background and history of the standards

Over the past two decades, an increasing number of programmes have begun offering offence-specific residential treatment or have started treating sexually abusive youth within heterogeneous residential environments. During this time, reports of abusive incidents against staff or other residents have increasingly come to light. In response to these revelations, state licensing agencies and residential providers have asked for consultation expertise to help improve the quality of these residential services.

The consequences of treatment failures for this population are serious. In many instances such failures result in new victims.

Additionally, due to changing social attitudes, the youth who fail in residential programmes and re-offend often face severe and lifelong consequences. The need for maximising successful treatment outcomes through provision of the highest quality treatment has never been more compelling. However, such quality is not likely to occur without the promulgation of offence-specific residential treatment standards. Several attempts to develop standards have been initiated in various parts of the country. One in particular became the starting point for the present effort, which will be described below.

In particular one major problem in developing programmes, among other concerns, that led to the formulation of standards has been the over-focus on 'sex' which is used to isolate sexually offending juveniles in sex offender treatment programmes to the exclusion of other or more primary treatment needs. Freeman-Longo and Blanchard (1998) speak of the harm and potential dangers of labelling for both sexual abusers and victims of sexual abuse. Clinicians and other professionals need to avoid over labelling. When there is the mention of sex offence in clinical and legal files, it is often the case that the juvenile will be shut out of appropriate psychiatric resources and put into exclusively sex offender treatment. This is not necessarily the appropriate system for these juveniles, and in many instances the most appropriate and necessary treatments are not afforded to the youth.

When assessing and evaluating youth with sexual behaviour problems for appropriate treatment, the following should be considered.[8]

- Interventions should be determined by individual needs and public safety, not the portal of entry. Treatment interventions should be based upon discussion and findings of programme treatment teams which include the input from an interdisciplinary team of professionals representing mental health, education and adjunctive treatment fields.
- Current models of risk assessment over-predict risk: risk assessment should be based on relativism and judgement, not absolutism. To date, although several risk assessment instruments have been developed for use with youth who sexually abuse and are being researched, none have been validated.
- Treatment and rehabilitation must go beyond 'sex' to focus on ways that juveniles re-offend.

This takes into account looking at a variety of aetiological models and developmental issues.

- Downward extension of adult models may itself over-sexualise vulnerable youth and result in improper and or problematic treatment.
- Treatment should stress re-integration into family, schools, and the community while monitoring peer relationships and interactions.

In 1996, as part of programme development consultations in Western Massachusetts, Drs Steven Bengis and Penny Cuninggim drafted a set of standards for use by their clients. Based on the positive experiences of these programmes in implementing these standards, the programmes encouraged Dr Bengis to consider a national standards development effort and agreed to provide seed funding.

In response to this support, Dr Bengis contacted several other colleagues with national reputations in the residential offence-specific field. These professionals recommended others and soon a core group of seven had agreed to volunteer their time in pursuit of the goal of developing national standards of care for residential treatment of juvenile sexual abusers. This core group became known as the National Offence-Specific Residential Standards Task Force[9]. The task force met in a two-day formal work session for the first time in 1996 and defined its mission to develop offence-specific standards of practice for residential treatment programmes balancing a commitment to quality and safety with an understanding of the practical realities of administering these programmes in a complex and multifaceted service-delivery system.

While the group felt that all programmes providing such services should be required to meet whatever standards would be created, the decision about how best to accomplish this goal (i.e. whether or not to formally accredit programmes) was put off for a future discussion.

Early in the process the group made the following decisions:

- To seek out an advisory board comprised of the top professionals in the offence-specific field to help guide the development of the standards work.
- To maintain the integrity of a small working group to maximise productivity.

- To use current research and existing literature to guide the work whenever possible.
- To format the document using several sections: a description of the standard; a rationale for the standard; a definition of relevant terms; and evaluative criteria by which to measure compliance with the standard.
- To encourage wide peer review of the final working draft of the document prior to dissemination of the final product.
- To seek peer approval from the field for the development of standards development through a questionnaire and workshops at national conferences of the Association for the Treatment of Sexual Abusers (ATSA) and the National Adolescent Perpetrator Network (NAPN).
- To share the work during the development stages only with colleagues who were involved in similar standards development efforts in other states.
- To seek legal advice regarding standards creation, dissemination, and possible accreditation.
- To explore the possibility of developing collaborative accreditation procedures through the Joint Commission on Accreditation of Healthcare Organisations (JCAHO) and the Council on Accreditation (COA).

Based on these decisions, the group began its work by reviewing the initial standards document created by Drs Bengis and Cuninggim. Work group members suggested additional standards. Assignments were made according to interest and expertise. The group operated primarily by consensus. Drafts were reviewed prior to meetings and any and all positions were discussed until all members agreed or accepted the majority view. Having reached agreement on an initial draft, the advisory board and additional readers were asked for input. As anticipated, that input proved invaluable and resulted in a significant re-write of major sections of the document.

During this time, selected members of the group visited JCAHO in Chicago and spoke at length with the Executive Director of COA. On the basis of those discussions, the group decided that a collaborative accrediting venture would not be the most effective way to maintain the integrity of the standards project. Subsequently, and after incorporating comments from the field received through questionnaires, the group decided against becoming an accrediting body. Rather, they decided that subsequent to publication of the final document, they would work with state agencies and licensing authorities to encourage them to incorporate the standards into their own oversight and licensing mandates.

By the Fall of 1998, the working group had completed a final draft which was prepared for dissemination both over the Internet and by mail to the professional field for peer review. The Task Force reviewed all comments, made revisions, and published a final document by Spring, 1999.

A driving force in developing the standards was a recognition that the Task Force participants overwhelmingly agreed that the rights of sex offending children and youth to be placed in the least restrictive environment should be maintained and quality best practice specialised treatment be offered by programmes treating this population. Civil commitment was cited as a problem in some States where youth are kept confined even after sanctions and treatment. While some small proportion is probably not treatable, most youth are. The Task Force members agreed that the needs of the community, the victim and the rights of the offender must be balanced. Another driving principle the Task Force agreed upon was that a focus on sex offender specific treatment alone was too narrow. Early intervention and primary and secondary prevention measures are to halt the development of sexual perpetration and victimisation. Part of this process includes developing standards for the field based upon age levels and concepts of healthy behaviour and normal development.

The standards

The now published standards (Bengis et al., 1999) consist of 28 standards. Each standard is addressed in three areas:

- The standard: a brief statement that embodies the overall purpose and target area of the standard.
- The rationale for the standard: the rationale provides more narrative to assist in developing an understanding of the background and intent of the standard.
- Evaluation measures for the standard: gives more detailed guidelines for assessing

compliance with, and implementing, the standards. This section is not meant to include all possible measures of compliance, but rather key examples for each standard.

The twenty-eight standards include four categories:
    Program related standards
    Staff related standards
    Residential safety standards
    Clinical intervention standards
    The individual standards in each of the four areas include under:

(a) Programme related standards

1. commitment of governing authority
2. admission and exclusion criteria
3. intake and informed consent
4. least restrictive setting
5. victim rights, resident rights and community safety

(b) Staff related standards

8. staff qualifications and competence
9. staff orientation and training
10. staff communication
11. staff supervision

(c) Residential safety standards

12. facility environment
13. staffing levels and patterns
14. prevention of sexual contact
15. programme response to sexual contact
16. mixed populations
17. residential risk management

(d) Clinical intervention standards

18. assessment and evaluation
19. treatment planning
20. use of intrusive methods
21. family involvement
22. programme milieu
23. case management
24. multicultural issues
25. community integration
26. discharge criteria
27. aftercare services
28. evaluating treatment effectiveness

The standards were written

- To increase programme and professional accountability for sex abuse-specific residential treatment.

- To provide residential service providers, placement personnel, licensing authorities, parents and other client advocates with a mechanism for evaluating the quality and appropriateness of sex abuse-specific residential programmes.
- To establish a common baseline of safety and competence in abuse-specific residential care.
- The document was designed to maintain programmatic quality and competence while supporting creativity and diversity and recognising the broad differences among programmes in physical site capacities, contracting requirements, licensing and oversight restrictions, and resource availability.

The standards are written for an adolescent population aged thirteen to seventeen years old. The evaluation measures allow for variances due to increased or decreased client risk levels. Therefore, the standards are as relevant to shelters and step-down group homes as they are to intensive residential treatment programmes. These residential standards represent the best knowledge currently available in the sex abuse-specific field at the time of their publication. The authors plan to update the document to reflect new information as future research and clinical experience alter the assumptions which form the foundation of the standards development.

Standards four and 16 below are examples of two of the actual published standards.

Standard Four: least restrictive setting

Each resident has the right to treatment in the least restrictive setting that maximises resident and community safety.

Rationale

Offence-specific residential treatment programmes must provide for the rights of residents in a manner that does not conflict with the obligation to maximise community safety. The programme should provide a continuum of services for sexually abusive or aggressive residents covering a range of treatment intensities and community access. Only residents who require severe restrictions in order to manage their level of risk to the community should be housed in restricted settings.

Offence-specific assessments should include recommendations regarding the environmental restrictions necessary to safely treat a resident, which may not always directly correlate with the severity of the youth's sexually abusive or aggressive behaviour. When a sexually abusive or aggressive youth is referred for admission to a programme with a level of restriction exceeding that needed to safely treat the youth, the programme should indicate that a less restrictive treatment setting is more appropriate.

Evaluation measures

The programme's mission, description of services, and treatment philosophy indicate adherence to the ethical concept of utilising the least restrictive treatment setting necessary to provide safe, effective treatment.

The programme maintains a list of alternative treatment programmes or has access to reputable referral services for youths who require referral to a more restrictive or less restrictive treatment setting.

The clinical records for each resident include written justification for the level of restriction in the treatment setting. This justification is reviewed with the same frequency as the individual treatment plan.

The programme's policies require the treatment team to recommend transfer to a less restrictive treatment setting when the youth no longer requires the current level of restriction.

Standard Sixteen: mixed populations

A programme with mixed treatment populations must demonstrate the ability to safely meet the treatment needs of all the residents.

Rationale

Realistically, it often is not possible to separate sexually abusive residents from other populations, or even to separate sub-populations of sexually abusive residents. Efficiency, economics, or practicality often dictate that resources be shared. Sexually abusive or aggressive youth are often housed, educated, or treated quite successfully in facilities with mixed populations. It is up to the programme to ensure that treatment needs are met and that safety can be assured.

The decisions about when, where, and how to mix populations need to be made by a multi-disciplinary treatment team after careful consideration. Factors to be considered should include but not be limited to: the number of sexually abusive youths to be served; concrete versus abstract thinking ability; treatment setting; age, maturity or developmental factors; criminal behaviours; psychiatric or medical problems; intellectual capacity; and developmental or learning disabilities.

It is essential to meet the individual treatment and safety needs of residents of all populations. In general, sub-populations should not be mixed where age, behaviour, intellectual functioning or developmental differences make it impossible to meet the clinical and safety needs of each youth.

Evaluation measures

The programme policies and procedures factor into the admission decision the safety of all populations. The resident's initial and ongoing assessment determines appropriate placement in a particular milieu, treatment track or unit.

The programme documents the clinical justification for combining populations in a treatment setting.

The programme follows a written description for each population that is served, where and how each is housed, and how interactions of populations are monitored.

The programme implements policies and procedures for the physical environment to reduce the risk of sexual or physical abuse. The programme requires that the environmental placement of individuals or groups is always a treatment team decision. Policies and procedures prohibit the placement of known sexual abuse victims who have not offended in the same bedroom with a youth known to have sexually abusive or aggressive behaviours. Policies and procedures require assessing the risk of victimisation in all placement decisions.

Policies and procedures clearly define the limits of confidentiality in order to foster open communication among staff and administration and minimise the secrecy that enables any form of abuse.

The programme follows clearly defined policies and procedures for the psychological, physical, and sexual safety of all populations.

Use of the Standards

The standards of care were developed and designed to be used in a variety of ways and at various levels. It was the hope of the Task Force that individual states would adopt the standards as a part of existing state standards regarding residential treatment centres for youth. Since their publication some states have expressed an interest in adopting them for sex-offender specific residential treatment programmes. In addition, with their publication, the Task Force has encouraged individual programmes to adopt and use them regardless of state use or interest.

The Task Force designed the standards in such a way as to not conflict with or overlap with other existing agencies that govern or accredit programmes, i.e., JCAHO, COA. The standards were designed to address only those areas that are unique to sex-offender specific treatment. Thus, for example, although the standards address safety and security issues, they do not set a standard as to how they should be met but rather that they be met to ensure staff, patient, and community safety.

The need for the development and use of standards in the residential care of juvenile sexual abusers is the first of many steps that must be taken in order to assure the quality care and treatment of youth with sexual behaviour problems. The Task Force considers this document as an evolving one that will be updated as changes within the field occur.

Since the publication of the standards, the Task Force has developed a process by which to evaluate programmes regarding their compliance with the standards and has developed a standardised evaluation form for use when conducting programme evaluations to insure uniformity and consistency in all programme evaluations.

Implications for the future

The fact that these standards have been developed, both peer and field reviewed, and subsequently published has implications for the future of programming. As recently as the year they were published, several suites and legal actions against residential programmes have occurred. In one case we were called by one of the Advisory Board members who had reviewed the document. This professional was involved as an expert witness in a suit and was asked if any such standards were in existence. This profession was then obliged to report that the standards document was in the final stages of development and she was asked to obtain a copy for the trial/review board and request a copy to use in the trial.

As of the writing of this paper several programmes and or states are using the standards as a guide to developing statewide standards or programme standards i.e., New York State is developing a set of statewide standards using the document as a foundation for their development. Many programmes have already requested their programme be evaluated using the standards. As the standards become more widely adopted or adapted to state or programme specific standards, others will see the standards as a hallmark for juvenile sex-offence specific residential care. As the standards become more widely adopted or used for programme or statewide adaptation, the potential for liability may increase for those programmes and states that do not develop some standard of care. The possible result will be the continuation and potential increase for programmes who do not operate by a set of standards to face legal challenges.

Litigation or tort liability is a reality for programmes and has been so since the time programmes to treat sexually abusive youth began to be developed (Freeman-Longo and Ryan, 1990). However, with the publication of these standards, programmes will no longer be able to claim there is not a written standard. The risk of such suits underscores the need for conscientious and purposeful practice; although state-of-the-art practice should be motivated by the desire to provide help and prevent harm, rather than the fear of litigation.

In tort liability the burden of proof is on the plaintiff to prove that the defendant did *not* act as a reasonable person. A 'reasonable person' may be defined somewhat differently in different states or countries but generally means a careful and prudent individual who adjusts to the situation at hand.

Litigation places the burden of proof on the plaintiff. Burden of proof requires that the plaintiff do the following:

- Prove that an obligation or duty was important.
- Prove that the duty was not met.
- Prove that the defendant was obliged to perform a duty by the standards of their profession.
- Prove that the consequences of nonfeasance or misfeasance were foreseeable.
- Prove that the plaintiff sustained injury.
- Prove that there is a close, casual relationship between the defendant's failure to perform

a specific obligation or duty and the resulting injury.

As of the publication of the standards, these issues become a force in the potential for tort liability especially when there is negligence. There are two areas of negligence, which might typically affect those who work with sexually abusive juveniles: nonfeasance and misfeasance. Negligence is alleged on the basis that a failure in performance has resulted in injury to another. Nonfeasance refers to a defendant's failure to perform a duty, which should have been performed. Misfeasance refers to the improper performance of a duty.

Most frequently, negligence suits relevant to juvenile sexual offending arise from:

- lack of treatment or lack of appropriate treatment
- malpractice
- inadequate or inappropriate services
- inadequate protection
- client suicide
- crimes committed during treatment on other patients
- abuse and neglect of clients
- violation of clients civil rights
- violation of clients patient rights

Informed consent for specific procedures, disclosures of programme goals and provider qualifications, and waivers of releases of confidentiality and information, are three practices which are basic to responsible practice with sexually abusive youth, as well as management of liability.

Informed consent should include:

- a definition of procedures
- the purpose in relation to treatment
- treatment or procedural specific details
- potential likelihood of benefits
- known potential negative side effects
- alternatives to the treatment or procedure
- voluntary participation
- option to withdraw without consequence
- signature of client and parent or legal guardian indicating they have read, and understood the informed consent
- signature of witness and date

Summary

The development and use of residential standards of care for juvenile sex-abuse specific programmes has been welcomed in the United

States by practitioners, professionals, programmes, and others who have believed the need for this type of guidance. Although the first of its kind and the first publication of them, the Task Force plans to periodically review and update the standards over time and win conjunction with developments in the field.

Any highly specialised field or practice risks the potential for professionals and others to operate outside of standard ethics and practices, and, within a new field, with new developments and ongoing research and developments, this potential is increased. The field of juvenile sexual-abuser treatment, and specifically residential treatment, has already witnessed the closure of programmes and legal intervention in programmes where there have been suicides, improper treatment, misuse of technology, and more. For-profit corporations have begun to take over smaller programmes with a primary interest in profit rather than patient care.

The now published *Standards of Care for Youth in Sex-offence Specific Residential Programmes,* provide the first opportunity for the field of juvenile sexual abuser treatment to work toward a standard of care in residential setting. With time it is anticipated that these standards will serve as a hallmark for providing 'best practice' in the assessment and treatment of juvenile sexual abusers.

Notes

[1] Juvenile justice is intended to rehabilitate. Involuntary treatment ordered for public safety reasons may be inappropriately applied to youth who do not meet legal criteria for involuntary treatment. Controversial areas of practice applied to youth may lack voluntary participation.

[2] Pre-adjudication evaluations raise ethical and legal issues because youth are asked to provide information which may be used against them in court. Youth may not be developmentally or intellectually capable of participating in such evaluations and may not readily understand the implications of their participation.

[3] Phallometric assessment (an intrusive and evasive biofeedback process/tool to measure sexual interest and arousal) presents erotic stimulii and assesses sexual arousal by measuring blood flow to the penis.

[4] Polygraph examinations are used to verify offender's veracity in terms of offence history and compliance with supervision and therapeutic requirements. In 1997, Texas began requiring this for juveniles released from the Texas Youth Commission. (Center for Sex Offender Management, 1999).

[5] Arousal conditioning involves pairing masturbation with physically or emotionally painful stimuli to reduce arousal related to sexual offending. Such procedures have been researched to some degree with adult sexual offenders but little research has been conducted in the use of these treatment modalities with youth who have sexual behaviour problems.

[6] Anti-androgens and hormonal agents, as well as anti-depressants (selective serotonin re-uptake inhibitors) are used to depress sexual arousal. Because of effects on growth and development, hormonal agents are controversial with youth treatment.

[7] Employers have been liable for sexual harassment under the 1964 Civil Rights Act, and a series of Equal Employment Opportunity Commission rulings and court cases since the 1980s. Schools are held liable under Title IX of the 1972 Higher Education Act. In 1999, the Supreme Court extended the liability of schools under Title IX in *Davis vs. Monroe County Board of Education* 97-843, which made deliberate indifference a criteria for liability for student-on-student harassment. In addition treatment programs can be held liable for the improper placement and housing of sexually abusive youth with other populations and for the actions of patients and clients within treatment programs.

[8] Adapted from: Development Services Group (2000) *Understanding Treatment and Accountability in Juvenile Sex Offending: Results and Recommendations From an OJJDP Focus Group.* Prepared for: Office of Juvenile Justice and Delinquency Prevention Training and Technical Assistance Division. Inc.7315 Wisconsin Avenue, Suite 700EBethesda, MD 20814.

[9] The task force includes Dr. Bengis, from Massachusetts; Art Brown, Ph.D. from Utah; Rob Longo, M.R.C., L.P.C. from Vermont; Bryon Matsuda, M.A. from Utah; Jonathan Ross, M.A. from South Carolina; Ken Singer, L.C.S.W. from New Jersey and Jerry Thomas, M.Ed. from Tennessee.

References

Araji, S. K. (1997) *Sexually Aggressive Children: Coming to Understand Them.* Thousand Oaks, CA: Sage.

American Academy of Child and Adolescent Psychiatry, Work Group on Quality Issues. (1999) Practice Parameters for the Assessment and Treatment of Children and Adolescents Who Are Sexually Abusive of Others: AACAP Official Action. *Journal of the American Academy of Child and Adolescent Psychiatry.* 38(12 *M*SupplementsN): 55S–76S.

Barbaree, H. E., Hudson, S. M. and Seto, M. C. (1993) Sexual Assault in Society: The Role of the Juvenile Offender. in Barbaree, H. E., Marshall, W. L. and Hudson, S. W. (Eds.) *The Juvenile Sex Offender.* 10–1.

Bengis, S., Brown, A., Freeman-Longo, R., Matsuda, B., Ross, J., Singer, K. and Thomas, J.(1999) *Standards of Care for Youth in Sex-offence Specific Residential Programs.* Holyoke, MA: NEARI Press.

Borduin, C. M., Scott, W., Henggeler, D., Blaske, M. and Sterm, J. (1990) *International Journal of Offender Therapy and Comparative Criminology.* 34: 105–13.

Brecher, E. M. (1978) *Treatment Programs for Sex Offenders.* Washington, DC. National Institute of Law Enforcement and Criminal Justice; Law Enforcement Assistance Administration; United States Department of Justice.

Burton, D., Freeman-Longo, R., Fiske, J., Levins, J. and Smith-Darden, J. (2000). *1996 Nationwide Survey of Treatment Programs and Models: Serving Abuse Reactive Children and Adolescent and Adult Sexual Offenders.* Brandon, VT: Safer Society Press.

Center for Sex Offender Management. (1999) *Understanding Juvenile Sexual Offending Behaviour: Emerging Research, Treatment Approaches and Management Practices.* Silver Spring, MD: Center for Sex Offender Management.

Development Services Group. (2000) *Understanding Treatment and Accountability in Juvenile Sex Offending: Results and Recommendations from an OJJDP Focus Group.* Bethesda. Office of Juvenile Justice and Delinquency Prevention Training and Technical Assistance Division.

Finkelhor, D. (1994) Current Information on the Scope and Nature of Child Sexual Abuse. *Future of Children.* 4(2), 31–53.

Freeman-Longo, R. E. (2000) *Revisiting Megan's Law and Sex Offender Registration: Prevention or Problem.* American Probation and Parole Association (http://www.appa-net.org)

Freeman-Longo, R. E., Bird, S., Stevenson, W. F. and Fiske, J. A. (1995) *1994 Nationwide Survey of Treatment Programs and Models: Serving Abuse-reactive Children and Adolescent and Adult Sex Offenders.*

Freeman-Longo, R. E. and Blanchard, G. T. (1998) *Sexual Abuse in America: Epidemic of the 21st Century.* Brandon, VT: Safer Society Press.

Freeman-Longo, R. E. and Ryan, G. (1990) *Tort Liability in Treatment of Sexually Abusive Juveniles.* Denver, CO: National Adolescent Perpetrator Network.

Knopp, F. H., Freeman-Longo, R. E. and Stevenson, W. F. (1993) *Nationwide Survey of Juvenile and Adult Sex Offender Treatment Programs and Models, 1992.* Orwell, VT: Safer Society Press.

Knopp, F. H., Rosenberg, J. and Stevenson, W. F. (1986) *Report on Nationwide Survey of Juvenile and Adult Sex-offender Treatment Programs and Providers, 1986.* Orwell, VT: The Safer Society Program.

Knopp, F. H. and Stevenson, W. F. (1989) *Nationwide Survey of Juvenile and Adult Sex-offender Treatment Programs and Models, 1988.* Orwell, VT: The Safer Society Program.

Knopp, F. H., Freeman-Longo, R. E. and Stevenson, W. F. (1992) *Nationwide Survey of Juvenile and Adult Sex-offender Treatment Programs and Models, 1992.* Orwell, VT: The Safer Society Program.

Krafft-Ebing, R. V. (1886) *Psychopathia Sexualis.* (Klaf, F. S. Trans.) (1965) New York: Stein and Day.

National Council of Juvenile and Family Court Judges. (1993) The Revised Report from the National Task Force on Juvenile Sexual Offending, 1993, of the National Adolescent Perpetrator Network. *Juvenile and Family Court Journal.* 44: 4.

Sinkmund, M., Snyder, H. N. and Poe-Yamagata, E. (1997) *Juvenile Offenders and Victims: 1997 Update on Violence.* Washington, DC: Office of Juvenile Justice and Delinquency Prevention.

Worling, J. R. and Curwen, T. (2000) Adolescent Sexual Offender Recidivism: Success of Specialised Treatment and Implications for Risk Prediction. *Child Abuse and Neglect.* 24: 965–82.

Chapter 10: Groupwork with Parents of Children who Have Sexually Harmed Others

Simon Hackett, Paula Telford and Keeley Slack

Setting a Family Context to Intervention

In the UK, there has recently been a proliferation of projects and agencies offering services to young people who have committed sexual offences or who have displayed aggressive or harmful sexual behaviours. Unlike in the adult sex offender field, the standardisation of intervention programmes for young people who have harmed others as a result of their sexual behaviour is still in its infancy. Within the range of services offered to adult sex offenders, groupwork has come to represent a core and central plank in service delivery (Beech et al., 1998), the theoretical orientation of such groups being overwhelmingly cognitive-behavioural (Allam and Browne, 1998). There are fewer specific groupwork programmes currently on offer for adolescents who have sexually harmed others, but those that are reported in the literature suggest an increasing consensus as to their theoretical basis and delivery (Print and O'Callaghan, 1999).

Nevertheless, alongside this growth in available services and the clearer theoretical framework within which to conceive the work (Hird and Morrison, 1996), a number of concerns are emerging about some elements of the developing orthodoxy. Increasingly, authors have argued that work with young people needs to be more developmentally sensitive (Rich, 1998; Ryan, 1999; Hackett and O'Callaghan, forthcoming; Chaffin, 2000; O'Callaghan and Hackett, 1999). Moreover, it is recognised that, in attempting to work with young people to change their sexually harmful behaviour, it is also essential to intervene to change their family systems (Bourke and Donohue, 1996; Hackett et al., 1998; Hackett, 2001). To an extent, this recognition is not yet mirrored in the development of comprehensive services for parents whose children have sexually harmed others, with many projects only able to offer limited services to families. Additionally, there remains a general shortage of UK services offering individual intervention for young

people who have sexually harmed others (Masson, 1995), let alone complementary programmes for parents of such children. In the literature, parents and families are discussed primarily in relation to the aetiology of young people's behaviours, typical family characteristics and an emphasis upon family 'dysfunction'. Parents' *influence upon therapeutic outcomes* or *how to work with parents* is otherwise given limited attention.

For practitioners struggling to make the best of limited resources in a climate of limited services, family work can slip off the agenda and parental involvement can all too easily become limited to their involvement in intermittent planning meetings or reviews. This tendency is not unique in the field of sexual aggression. In her review of the sexual abuse literature, Trotter (1998) found that discussion relating to parents was limited to their complicity in the abuse or their failure to protect. Other studies have indicated how the differing perspectives between social workers and parents often go unrecognised and parents sometimes feel that their views are pushed aside in favour of professionals' views (Thoburn et al., 1995; Cleaver and Freeman, 1995).

There may be a range of additional reasons why there has been limited attention to family work in the field of sexual aggression. Firstly, whilst parents often themselves would welcome closer links into the work (McKeown and McGarvey, 1999), an 'expert culture' has been promoted at times, which may limit parents' ability to offer their own concerns, views and contributions. Secondly, professionals may be anxious that involving parents too closely in intervention work with young people could negatively influence or undermine the work, particularly if there is a history of poor parenting or wider issues of abuse within the family system. Thirdly, there may be a misconception about the notion of 'individual abuser responsibility'. One of the essential theoretical premises of 'sex offender work' is that the person who has perpetrated the abuse should be made to carry the sole responsibility for the behaviours and therefore should be made to be individually accountable in addressing this. This is an important ethical standard that underpins sexual abuse theory and practice, especially given historical mistaken attempts to conceive of a man's sexual abuse as a symptom of family or marital dysfunction. In respect of children and adolescents the picture is, perhaps, not so straightforward. This is not to suggest that children and adolescents who have sexually harmed others are not individually responsible for their behaviours, merely to stress that understanding their family experiences, and helping change aspects of their family context, is often integral to understanding and diverting them from sexually harmful or abusive patterns of behaviour. As Henggeler et al. (1998) maintain, behaviour can only be fully understood when it is viewed within its naturally occurring context.

We believe, therefore, that parents have much to offer in helping their children change. There are a range of benefits for young people themselves. Accessing parents' world view can often give clues as to the developmental challenges faced by young people. A young person's individual distortions may be mirrored or better understood in the context of family scripts, roles and views. Involving families more integrally in intervention affords a young person less opportunity to present in intervention as separate from the reality of day-to-day life. Benefits for parents themselves include feeling that they can contribute to the process of change, or as one parent put it: 'if we are part of the problem, we have to be part of the answer'. It also allows parents to demonstrate their commitment to their child and can help build parental self-esteem, create new family order and helps with relapse prevention. There is also the possibility of mutual change- not only that parents can help their child change, but that family change can flow from the progress made by the young person (Burham et al., 1999).

As can be seen by these potentially wide-ranging benefits, accepting the centrality of work with parents in this field does not require the practitioner, or indeed the wider professional system, to adopt a blame position in respect of families, whereby parents are automatically viewed as abusers themselves or as 'poor parents' who are directly responsible for their child's abusive behaviours. The evidence for involving, integrating and impacting upon family systems within the context of developmentally sensitive and holistic intervention programmes with young people who have sexually harmed others is compelling. Intervention that does not do this is, in our view, incomplete.

Why groupwork?

Whilst there is a clear argument for involving parents in intervention programmes, there has been relatively little attention given in the literature to how to do this, or descriptions of programmes or initiatives designed to work meaningfully with parents. One of us has described an integrated programme for parents whose children have sexually harmed their siblings (Hackett et al., 1998) and offered a manual for parents whose lives are affected by adolescent sexual abuse (Hackett, 2001). The work of McKeown and McGarvey in Northern Ireland and the NIAP Programme in the Republic of Ireland is notable for the emphasis placed on groupwork with parents. This chapter seeks to contribute to this developing literature by describing our own groupwork programme with parents at Kaleidoscope, which is a community-based, specialist project working with children and young people who are sexually aggressive or who have displayed sexually harmful behaviours in the North East of England. The project is operated through a partnership between NSPCC and Barnardos.

Many of the benefits associated with bringing together a group of young people who have sexually harmed others applies equally to their parents, as can be seen in the following comparative table overleaf.

One of the factors proposed as associated with the development of sexually aggressive behaviours in some young people is their experience of loneliness and isolation. Ironically, having a child who has displayed abusive or harmful sexual behaviours is one of the most isolating experiences a family can face. Community backlash, ostracism from wider family and friends, enforced secrecy and cover stories, personal guilt and loneliness, and powerlessness in the face of the professional systems that engulf their lives are the common experiences of such parents. It was on the basis of repeatedly hearing accounts of such commonly felt issues from parents that we took

Table 1:

Benefits of groupwork with young people who have sexually harmed others	Benefits of groupwork with parents whose children have sexually harmed others
Challenges isolation and models progress ('Other young people have done similar things and you can see that they are facing up to it')	Challenges isolation (e.g. 'You are not the only family in which this has happened. You can get through this')
Peer learning and peer challenging of distortions	Peer learning and challenge (e.g. 'At the beginning I felt like that but I can accept now that my child was to blame')
Opportunity to see other young people at different stages of the work	Opportunity to see how other parents have coped and have faced up to the abuse
Encourages sharing of feelings and issues which are constrained in other contexts for young people	Facilitates a unique opportunity for parents to share feelings which are not common to most parents
Increases sociability	Promotes pro-social ways of relating to other parents in similar situations

the decision to develop a parents' groupwork initiative to complement our existing emphasis on involving parents in individual work at Kaleidoscope.

Group development

Setting out to develop a groupwork programme for parents is not, in itself, a difficult task, but clearly requires considerable forethought and planning. In particular, key decisions are required about group selection in order to ensure that the group is constituted as a viable and feasible entity. In respect of groupwork with parents of children whose sexual behaviour has been harmful, there are a number of critical dynamics around group selection, as follows:

Who constitutes 'family' for the purposes of a parents' group?

One initial dilemma is who should be regarded as 'family' or 'parents' and who would therefore be appropriate to involve within the group. When developing the Kaleidoscope programme, we envisaged offering places for carers of all children who were being offered a service by the project. However, children and young people undertaking work at Kaleidoscope are variously cared for by natural parents, extended family members (such as grandparents), foster carers, residential social workers and in reconstituted families. At the point that our group was being developed, natural or step-parents and foster carers were equally

represented amongst the significant adults of children being offered a therapeutic service. Our original objective for the group was to offer a primarily educational input to help these significant adults support the young people's 'change and control' work. As such, it is clear that both natural parents and foster carers could have benefited from inclusion in such a service. However, as we discussed the development of the group, we began to see that the emotional impact of a child's behaviours in terms of guilt, loss, grief and feelings of responsibility were likely to differ significantly for parents and foster carers. The more we talked to adults involved in the lives of the children we were working with about what they would like to use the group for, the more we realised that their joint involvement in a group would radically, and unhelpfully, change the group's dynamics and limit its usefulness for longer-term carers.

We therefore decided, unlike the groupwork programme described by McKeown and McGarvey (1999), to offer the programme only to those adults, be they natural parents, step-parents or other carers, who had been responsible for the care of the child prior to the abuse being discovered. In our context, this meant that our initial group was comprised primarily of birth parents and step-parents, but with the addition of one couple who were aunt and uncle to a child and had been his de facto foster carers over a number of years preceding the emergence of the child's sexually harmful behaviours. Excluding other significant adults who play a central role in managing risk on a day-to-day basis for children was not an easy decision, but one which we would now steadfastly stand by. One characteristic of the group is the sense of commonality felt by the parents and, at times, their need to stand apart from foster carers who have become involved only in the aftermath of the abuse. For example, the issue of intense shame felt by parents for having raised a child with a conviction for a sexual offence is hardly paralleled in a residential children's home, however dedicated and empathic the residential carers are.

Should the parents in the group have ongoing contact with their child?

Further dilemmas around group selection arise in relation to the issue of the varying degrees of contact that parents and carers have with their children after the discovery of the behaviours. In our case, a number of children had remained living at home whilst others were in looked after situations, but with the prospect of a return home upon completion of the work and dependant upon family change and/or a reduction in the risk presented by a young person. In such circumstances, even though the parents concerned may have infrequent or limited contact with their child at the time, they still frequently constitute a significant influence upon the child and may have unresolved needs arising from the child's behaviour in their own right, so are able to be part of the Parents' Group.

Should parents who have abused or harmed their children be included?

As a core principle, it is our view that parents should not be held responsible for their child's sexual behaviours, but it is recognised that parents are accountable for the emotional climate within the home. Many parents of children who have sexually harmed others do have aspects of their parenting that are not optimal and some have harmed their children in some way.

When developing the Kaleidoscope group, we discussed the necessity for screening such issues and whether it would be fair or appropriate to exclude a parent who was known to have abused their child. Indeed, it is arguable that in so doing, we would have been denying the benefits of the group from the very parents who needed it the most. Therefore, we decided that the only excluding factor would be a parent who was known, or strongly suspected, to have sexually abused another person, as we felt that this could make the group process unsafe and untenable for other group members and would also distort the group content. In practice, issues of self-blame, accountability and parenting have been at the forefront of the discussion points that parents have brought with them into the group. They have used the opportunity of the group to talk with other parents about how they feel they have 'failed' their children and how they can create positive change in their own parenting behaviours in the future. The only negative experience in this respect we have had within the group has been the involvement of a father who, we now suspect, had previously been physically aggressive and abusive to his female partner. In the group, this was translated into subtle attempts to dominate, undermine and deny his partner a voice. This was challenged very strongly both by the group leaders and other group members, but we have subsequently revised our group selection criteria to exclude male carers who have perpetrated domestic abuse and have not accepted responsibility for these behaviours.

Couples, individuals and gender issues

A consistent and current theme in research about work with families is the need to engage fathers in taking an appropriate and closer role in parenting issues (Ryan, 2000). Social workers have long been criticised for putting disproportionate emphasis on mothers for ensuring the protection of their children and failing to engage with male carers in families. In relation to parenting of children in situations following sexual abuse, the demands of monitoring and risk management are such that both carers should be fully involved in this process. The Kaleidoscope group is therefore offered to both male and female carers. However, this raises a number of issues which need to be dealt with sensitively. Single carers may feel socially and emotionally disadvantaged in the group, particularly at times when the level of group cohesion is not high, for example when new members are introduced. Involving couples in the group also runs the risk of unhelpful issues from the wider relationship being played out in groupwork sessions. Some male carers in partnerships refuse to attend or, due to patterns of work shifts, cannot make arrangements to be there consistently. In such cases, our groupwork programme is offered to the available carer. Most frequently this is a woman. Although it could be argued that this reinforces the very gendered dynamics in families which we are striving to challenge, on balance this inclusive principle has worked in the interests of those women who have attended alone. Below, we further discuss our experience of working with issues of gender in the group.

Open or closed? Fixed or rolling?

Consideration also needs to be given to the degree to which group membership should be fluid; in other words the length of the programme and whether it should be open or closed. Our initial process was to interview potential group members either individually or in pairs with their partners in order to gain their perspectives on these issues. Parents articulated very quickly that their major fears were about meeting new people, whether they would get on with the others, trust them and feel part of the group. It was clear that a closed group was necessary for parents to be able to develop a sense of predictability, ownership and continuity in the group. This, however, poses a challenge to projects such as Kaleidoscope where new referrals are made on a continuous basis and where, at any one point in time, families may be at differing stages in the work and with different needs. Our view was, therefore, that we should develop a rolling programme with entry points at approximately three monthly intervals into the group. This way, the group is closed from week to week and retains its sense of safety and predictability, but allows the introduction of new group members at planned intervals, taking into account the group's functioning and any particular issues within the group, and the external lives of its members, at that particular point in time.

The rolling programme has been punctuated in our case by our realisation, very quickly, such were the issues of monitoring and supervision for the majority of group members, that it was only going to be possible to hold the group during school term time. Thus, school holidays provide natural and helpful breaks in what is an intense and focused process during term time. On balance, the major, but somewhat

unexpected, benefit of structuring the group like this is the way in which, at any time, parents who are nearing the end of their child's intervention work and those who have just discovered the abuse, can learn from, assist and support each other. Whilst this means that neatly packaged content with a discreet start and end point is not possible, this is far outweighed by the positives that flow from parents at different stages sharing their experiences of hope for the future. For new parents, this gives a sense that they can survive the immediate crisis of the sexual abuse. For more established group members, this can starkly highlight for themselves how far they have come in their own journeys since their early days in the group.

Group process and content issues

Group aims

One decision that programmes need to consider is the particular orientation of the group, for example whether it will be primarily educative or therapeutic. A major tenet for our group at its inception was to support the children and young people in their work at Kaleidoscope and therefore we envisaged that its emphasis would not be therapeutic. Nonetheless, this has been its outcome. Broadly stated, the aims of the group, as we see them are:

- To assist parents in supporting their children's assessment and 'change and control' work.
- For parents to have a safe place to share their concerns, experiences and successes.
- To help parents safely express the sense of isolation brought on by the discovery of their child's behaviour.
- To increase group members' knowledge of factors contributing to children's sexually harmful behaviours and of the social and emotional environments needed in order to support children in making appropriate changes.
- To focus on issues of safe care, consistent with the individual service offered by Kaleidoscope to the child.
- To gain emotional support from other families in a similar position with similarly isolating experiences.

Confidentiality concerns

One of the arguments sometimes used against groupwork is that it is difficult to manage issues of confidentiality and that, potentially, parents will gain information which puts them or other people at risk in their local communities. Prior to setting up the group, we were sensitive to this issue by checking addresses of potential group members and by ensuring that the parents concerned were not likely to know each other or live in close proximity to each other. We also ascertained that the children who had displayed sexually harmful behaviours did not attend the same schools. In our preparation sessions with individuals and couples, confidentiality is an issue that we discuss in great detail, asking questions such as 'what would it be like for you if you were to bump into another group member in the middle of the city?' In practice, parents are themselves highly sensitive to these issues. Many parents need reassurance from the facilitators about the management of confidentiality and parents degree of comfort about this is often the deciding factor as to whether they will participate in the group at all. We therefore have an agreed principle with all group members which states that victims should not be identified, either by name or by other details. We also considered whether we needed to have a similar clause about sharing their own personal information; for example the schools their children attend, the areas in which they live, etc. We wondered about the potential child protection issues that might be raised by parents having contact outside of the group. Would it be ethical or possible to prevent parents from sharing their telephone numbers?

Partly these dilemmas appear to revolve around professional control versus the depth of empowerment and support parents can gain through being involved in the group. For example, two mothers have routinely shared a bus journey back to the city centre after the group and another mother once gave a fellow group member who had been distressed in the group a lift in her car. For the group members concerned this was understandable and a logical extension of the group process and, as long as the group confidentiality policy is respected outside of the group, we feel that we have no right to intervene to prevent this kind of supportive contact between parents. Contact between children in these families would, of course, be entirely another matter and would necessitate a much more proactive response from workers in order to ensure an appropriate level of protection. Thus, we retain a 'no-contact between children' rule.

Group membership and issues of viability

As the group has progressed, its membership numbers have fluctuated. Indeed, maintaining a viable membership level over time has been the most significant challenge for the group leaders. At its normal level thus far, the group has had a membership of seven parents: a mixture of couples and individuals. On occasions, we have gone ahead with the group when there have been as few as two people in attendance, providing that these two are not a couple. Experience has taught us that we need to be flexible with our expectations, as many of the families we work with experience crises and problems which mean that they can be prevented from attendance at short notice. Whilst we ask parents to commit to a minimum period of eight sessions when they first enter the group, we do not feel it appropriate or desirable to have a formal process for exclusion after a stated number of absences. We do, of course, follow up non-attendance in a supportive way and check on how group members are experiencing the group in order to ensure that all group members feel enabled to participate or to withdraw if the group is not meeting their needs.

The group has consistently had more women members than men. As the overall number of members has dropped, the proportion of women has increased; in other words, one challenge has been maintaining the participation of men in the group. From feedback, we believe that this is due in part of the difficulties that some of the men have faced in gaining longer-term time off work. In part, it also appears that some men have felt that their initial needs have been met early on in the group and that they no longer need to attend. The challenge we have faced at times in sustaining men's involvement in the group may also reflect the degree to which some men feel that they have a lesser role in the family in parenting their children and in contributing to the work to prevent further sexually harmful behaviours. Being open about differences in gender perceptions and using differences in the group constructively has been an important part of responding to this challenge. For example, in one groupwork session examining group members' understanding of normal and appropriate sexual behaviours, the men and women have broken into two groups to complete the task. This has encouraged discussion of gender-related issues, but has also allowed both the men and women to share thoughts and uncertainties in their own sub-group that may have been more difficult and embarrassing to articulate in the larger group. Experience has shown that this mixture of whole group and gender-specific sub-groups works well and usually creates a helpful and appropriate level of humour and competitiveness between the two groups, with the women in particular being able to derive a sense of collective strength, empowerment and identity as a result.

The facilitator role

It is impossible for us to reflect on our role as facilitators of the parents' groupwork programme without acknowledging that this has been both an immensely rewarding and also humbling experience for us as practitioners. We have had to be flexible about our roles and prepared to give back power to the group members. At times, we have been in awe of the strength of some of the parents concerned, dismayed by their reported experiences of professional systems (of which we, of course, are also a part) and frustrated by the obstacles they face.

Consistent with many groups offering services for children and young people with sexually harmful behaviours, our groupwork programme has usually involved a mixed gender co-working pair of facilitators. The benefits of such an approach is the opportunity this affords to model appropriate ways of behaving between men and women. In total, a team of three workers, two women and one man, has been involved and, whilst only two of the workers at any one point in time have been involved in the group, all three have debriefed following group sessions and have contributed to the planning process for the next session. This is clearly a resource-intensive approach which is onerous in terms of time required within the wider project. As the group is an additional resource on top of other services offered, implementing a regular rolling programme has wide-ranging implications for the wider staff group, regardless of their direct involvement.

Balancing group process and content

As the group has developed, the balance of its educative and support function (and thereby the relative weighting of process as against content) has shifted. Our role as facilitators has also changed accordingly. Initially, in line with the group's planned educative focus, we prepared presentations and exercises to 'instruct' the group members and to 'teach' them the concepts and issues we thought they needed to have to make sense of their situation. However, we quickly realised- in fact in the first session- that this level of control and structure was neither what the group members wanted, nor would have the greatest impact upon outcomes. For example, prior to the first ever group session, we considered how difficult it would be for parents to come into a group of strangers and be expected to talk about their child's sexual behaviours. We wanted to communicate through the process of the group that those present were individual people, rather than merely the parents of a child who had a sexual behaviour problem. Therefore, we planned an initial exercise whereby parents would talk about themselves with the person sitting next to them and feed back to the rest of the group. Down to the last group member, there was a widespread refusal to undertake this exercise and a request that the group got down to the work of talking about the details of their children's sexual behaviours and the impact of these upon the wider family. This taught us an important lesson about our professional assumptions and the need to be flexible in our approach.

As the group has progressed, we retain the overall responsibility for the structuring and resourcing of the programme, but have sought to decrease the level of our own contributions. We manage the group process and provide a safety net for the group members, but are keen not to come across as the 'experts'. At the same time, when group members ask for topics to be addressed, we research and prepare information and contribute to the discussion. Each group session begins with a round of 'news'; an update from the group members about the problems they have faced in their lives and their achievements since the last group session. This frequently raises important issues relating to risk management and supervision. At times, the whole session of 1.5 to 2 hours is taken up with this process of sharing information and exchanging views. As facilitators, we were initially uncomfortable with this, feeling that we might be 'failing' the group by allowing such a full discussion on these issues and not getting round to any formally prepared topic. However, once again this issue appears to be more a reflection of professional power and control as the 'news' section often raises the central issues for parents in a real life way which is more valuable than planned exercises would be. An example of this is when a mother talked about her confusion, embarrassment and concern when she discovered semen stains on her adolescent son's bed sheets. This raised a whole debate about what acceptable and healthy sexual expression is for young people who have sexually harmed others.

As a process issue, allowing individuals to talk about the issues raised for them in a supportive and empathic environment, where other people can offer support, is hardly a complex theoretical standpoint. However, it has been life-changing for a number of the group's members. One mother was able to free herself from a long-term physically abusive relationship and commented that she could not have achieved the level of self-belief necessary to effect this change had she not been part of the group.

Programme content issues

Although we initially envisaged a more structured 'programme approach' to the group, in line with the above issues, we have moved to a more fluid approach whereby we negotiate with parents at frequent intervals the range of issues that would be helpful for them to examine in the group. This ensures that we are able to address their concerns, plan ahead but retain some flexibility and are able to deal with the frequent crises and difficulties that the group members have brought. However, some topics have proven to be core issues for our parents and we have needed to return to them at regular intervals. These include:

- Exploration of parents' attitudes and feelings about sex, sexuality, sexual abuse and sex offenders. Facing up to a child's sexual abuse has frequently forced parents to re-evaluate their own stereotypes and attributions about people who commit sexual offences. Often parents have talked about their struggle to reconcile their views of their child with their pre-existing views.
- Normal child adolescent sexual development. Group members have talked about how their child's sexually harmful behaviour has

thrown their understandings of normal sexuality into confusion.
- The impact of sexual abuse on victims, young people with sexually harmful behaviour and parents. Hearing other parents face up to the impact of their child's behaviours has helped some parents to acknowledge why others are concerned.
- Why a child or young person may sexually abuse. We have presented some of the core models used in work with children and young people, for example, Finkelhor's Four Preconditions Model (Finkelhor, 1984) and Ryan and Lane's version of the Cycle of Sexual Assault (Ryan and Lane, 1991). Parents have enthusiastically discussed these together, sharing their own views on how their child's behaviours have fitted into such models. The example of other parents addressing their children's behaviours in such an open way has helped some group members who had, up until that point, been more reluctant to see their child's behaviours as anything more than 'horseplay'.
- Reviewing the emotional and practical impact of sexual abuse on parenting and looking closely at how to monitor and supervise the child's behaviour.
- Gender issues and parenting. This has primarily concerned the need for men to take on more responsibilities for supervision in families.
- How to go about finding a safe and appropriate support network and whether and who and how to tell about the child's sexually harmful behaviours.
- Trust and forgiveness. This has involved debates between group members about how feasible and useful it is to trust their children following their sexually harmful behaviour.

Specific themes and issues brought by group members

There have been a number of consistent themes and issues raised by group members during the course of our groupwork programme. In summarising them below, we hope that these issues will be of relevance to practitioners working with other parents, regardless of whether this is in groups or individually:

Anxiety and community identification

Most parents in the group have shared an extreme sense of anxiety and nervousness that their neighbours and others in their community might find out about their child's sexually harmful behaviours. Parents have struggled with how to manage this issue; some report telling more and more elaborate 'cover stories' as time progresses. Often, children in families are repeatedly told not to tell friends at school and in the community about appointments at Kaleidoscope, or mention the project's name, in case others might be aware of the nature of the work conducted there. Parents' concern about community discovery is driven by fear of reprisals and violence towards their child and other family members. The level of anxiety felt by parents has gone beyond our prior awareness as experienced professionals in this field. For example, two parents were anxious that a letter postmarked with the name of the project might be seen by others and have talked about their increasingly elaborate cover-stories when attending appointments. These parents related how they frequently panicked when asked casual questions, for example by neighbours such as 'where are you going?' and would answer in an unconvincing way which then raised the suspicion of the neighbours. Other group members have been anxious about being recognised when entering our building and have asked for the blinds to be positioned in the group room so as to prevent their identification from outside. At times, hearing parents talk openly to each other in the group about the extent and almost paralysing impact of this issue on a day-to-day basis has been overwhelming to us as practitioners.

The extreme burden placed on parents by supervision and monitoring

There have been many instances when parents have talked about the difficulties they feel are placed upon them by the need to monitor and supervise their children's behaviours. Even parents who have been deemed to be offering 'poor' care to their children by other professionals have talked about how overwhelmed they have felt by this issue. For example, one couple talked about how they always required their son's friend to play in their home (rather than in the friend's home) so they could supervise the situation and not have to disclose information to the friend's parents. This demanded a great deal of their energies, but also made them feel guilty- were they

doing the right thing? Consistently, mothers' social lives, in some cases undeveloped before the abuse, are constrained further by the added demands of supervision placed on them. Parents have talked about how they think back to the abuse every day and how it never leaves them. Many parents appear to be experiencing secondary PTSD responses to their child's behaviours; including intrusive flashbacks and disturbing imagery relating to what they know happened or their 'worst fears' about what might have occurred. Sometimes, this relates to the pain of looking back and realising what clues to the abuse they may have missed. Feelings of intense guilt and shame have characterised the affective expressions of parents within the group. Expressions of loss often relate to the loss of self-esteem, parental role or the loss of their child from the home. Parents have also been able to use the group to reflect upon how their child's behaviours have left them with uncertainty and confusion about sexual issues or have skewed their own sexual relationships. Parents have sought guidance on how they should talk to their child about sex following the abuse or how to respond to situations where sexual material is shown on the television. Most powerfully, some parents have expressed their total inability to see how their child could and should develop healthy sexual relationships in the future. For all of these issues, the examples of other parents who have faced and worked through these painful issues, has been of vital importance.

Professional responses

A final, but consistent theme in the group has been that of professional interventions in families as a result of their child's sexually harmful behaviours. Again, as professionals working within the system, we have been shocked and dismayed by some of the accounts of poor practice we have heard. Whilst some of the parents have given specific examples of how they have been blamed or directly excluded by some professionals, the majority, even in the presence of good working relationships with individual professionals, have described a sense of overall disempowerment within the system. There has been only one notable exception to this, where the couple concerned have felt that their social worker has had time for them and has taken their concerns and views seriously.

Mostly, parents have felt that professionals hold them in suspicion and do not recognise their support needs. Many group members have related frequent and ongoing examples where they are not informed about organisational procedures and processes and are the last to hear about decisions affecting their children and families. Professionals have relied heavily on mothers for the protection and care of their children, especially when there are sibling victims, and this contributed to fathers' feelings that they were viewed as 'perpetrators'.

Conclusions: being heard, being understood

In describing our experiences of working with parents in a groupwork setting, we hope that we have done some justice to the courage of the group members who have shared their experiences within the group and that others, in turn, may consider the development of such programmes. The degree of commitment to this process demonstrated by parents, as well as their depth of reflection and willingness to examine solutions to the problems they feel they have contributed to, has been an inspiring and hopeful example of how groupwork can add another dimension to services designed to address children and young people's sexually harmful behaviours. None of the parents concerned have felt they have any other forum to discuss any of the issues which we have touched on above. Many of the parents have carried with them into the group unresolved issues and the unrecognised symptoms of secondary post-traumatic stress, despite family work already offered to them. More than anything, the group has created an overall culture of *being heard* for group members and *being understood* by others who know from first hand experience the depth of issues that individuals are facing. For some, being involved in the group has helped give them back their self respect, such that a number of group members have made significant positive changes to their own lives and relationships. In turn, as facilitators of the group, we have been inspired and privileged to be part of the process and wish to develop it further. One step we would like to take is to explore the possibility of inviting a former parent to co-facilitate the group with one of the group workers. Whilst this would require careful examination of boundaries and issues of accountability, as well as confidentiality, we are hopeful that the unique perspectives and experiences that would be added as a result would further enhance the experience of group members.

References

Allam, J. and Browne, K. (1998) Evaluating Community-based Treatment Programmes for Men Who Sexually Abuse Children. *Child Abuse Review.* 7: 13–29.

Beech, A., Fisher, D. and Beckett, R. (1999) *STEP 3: An Evaluation of the Prison Sex Offender Treatment Programme.* London: Home Office.

Bourke, M. and Donohue, B. (1996) Assessment and Treatment of Juvenile Sex Offenders: An Empirical Review. *Journal of Child Sexual Abuse.* 5:1 47–70.

Burham, J., Moss, J., Debelle, J and Jamieson, R. (1999) Working with Families of Young Sexual Abusers: Assessment and Intervention Issues. in Erooga, M. and Masson, H. (1999) *Young People Who Sexually Abuse Others. Responses to an Emerging Problem.* London: Routledge.

Chaffin, M. (2000) Family and Ecological Emphasis in Interventions: A Developmental Perspective in Working With Children, Adolescents and Adults With Sexually Abusive Behaviours. Keynote address to National Organisation for the Treatment of Abusers 10th Annual Conference, Dublin.

Cleaver, H. and Freeman, P. (1995) *Parental Perspectives in Cases of Suspected Child Abuse.* London: HMSO.

Finkelhor, D. (1984) *Child Sexual Abuse: New Theory and Research.* New York: Free Press.

Hackett, S., Print, B. and Dey, C. (1998) Brother Nature? Therapeutic Intervention With Young Men Who Sexually Abuse Their Siblings. in: Bannister, A. (Ed.) *From Hearing to Healing: Working with the Aftermath of Child Sexual Abuse.* 2nd edn. Chichester: Wiley.

Hackett, S. (2001) *Facing the Future. A Guide for Parents of Young People Who Have Sexually Abused Others.* Lyme Regis: Russell House Publishing.

Hackett, S. and O'Callaghan, D. (forthcoming) *Developmentally Sensitive Intervention With Young People who Sexually Abuse.* Dorset: Russell House Publishing.

Henggeler, S., Schoenwald, S., Bordun, C., Rowland, M. and Cunningham, P. (1998) *Multisystemic Treatment of Antisocial Behaviour in Children and Adolescents.* New York: Guilford Press.

Hird, J. and Morrison, T. (1996) Six Groupwork Interventions with Adolescent Sexual Abusers. *Journal of Sexual Aggression.* 2(1).

Masson, (1995) Children and Adolescents Who Sexually Abuse Other Children: Responses to an Emerging Problem. *Journal of Social Welfare and Family Law.* 17:3 325–36.

McKeown, L. and McGarvey, J. (1999) A Psycho-educational Support Group for a Neglected Clinical Population: Parents and Carers of Young People who Sexually Abuse Children and Others. in: Calder, M. C. (Ed.) *Working with Young People Who Sexually Abuse: New Pieces of the Jigsaw Puzzle.* Lyme Regis: Russell House Publishing.

O'Callaghan, D. and Hackett, S. (1999) Research-based Practice With Young People Who Sexually Abuse. Workshop presentation to the 9th Annual Conference of the National Organisation for the Treatment of Abusers, University of York.

Print, B. and O'Callaghan, D. (1999) Working in Groups With Young Men Who Have Sexually Abused Others. in Erooga, M. and Masson, H. (1999) *Young People Who Sexually Abuse Others. Responses to an Emerging Problem.* London: Routledge.

Rich, S. (1998) A Developmental Approach to the Treatment of Adolescent Sexual Offenders. *The Irish Journal of Psychology.* 17:1 102–18.

Ryan, G. (1999) Treatment of Sexually Abusive Youth: The Evolving Consensus. *Journal of Interpersonal Violence.* 14: 422–36.

Ryan, G. and Lane, S. (1991) *Juvenile Sexual Offending: Causes, Consequences and Corrections.* Lexington: Lexington Books.

Ryan, M. (2000) *Working with Fathers.* Abingdon: Radcliffe Medical Press.

Thoburn, J., Lewis, A. and Hemmings, D. (1995) *Paternalism or Partnership? Family Involvement in the Child Protection Process.* London: HMSO.

Trotter, J. (1998) *No-one's Listening: Mothers, Fathers, and Child Sexual Abuse.* London: Whiting and Birch.

Part 4: Assessment Issues

Chapter 11: An Integrated Systemic Approach to Intervention with Children with Sexually Abusive Behaviour Problems

Lucinda A. Rasmussen Ph.D.

Introduction

The material in this chapter was also submitted as two separate articles to the Journal of Child Sexual Abuse. One article appeared in Volume 8, Number 4 and the other has been accepted for publication.

The problem of children age twelve and younger molesting other children was first discussed in the child sexual abuse literature in the late 1980s (Cantwell, 1988; Friedrich and Luecke, 1988; Johnson, 1988, 1989). It was a full decade later before researchers completed empirical studies on this topic (Bonner, Walker, and Berliner, 2000; Gray, Busconi, Houchens, and Pithers, 1997; Gray, Pithers, Busconi, and Houchens, 1999; Pithers, Gray, Busconi, and Houchens, 1998). Until 1998, the literature on children with sexual behaviour problems was limited to a few descriptive studies (Burton, Nesmith, and Badten, 1997; Glasgow, Horne, Calam, and Fox, 1994; Hall, Mathews, and Pierce, 1998; Johnson and Berry, 1989; Ray et al., 1995). In addition, some practitioners described their treatment programmes in books (Araji, 1997; Burton, Rasmussen, Bradshaw, Christopherson, and Huke, 1998; Cunningham and MacFarlane, 1996; Gil and Johnson, 1993; Gray and Pithers, 1993; Lane, 1997; Ryan, 1997).

Recently published findings of two outcome studies funded by the National Center on Child Abuse and Neglect (NCAN) in 1991 provided the first empirical data about children with sexual behaviour problems (Bonner et al., 2000; Gray et al., 1997, 1999; Pithers et al., 1998). These studies identified subtypes of children with sexual behaviour problems and compared their responses to different treatment approaches. The researchers in one study (Gray et al., 1997; 1999; Pithers et al., 1998) sampled 127 children who were referred by the child protective service and mental health systems in Vermont

as displaying problematic sexual behaviours. The behaviours were defined as:

- repetitive
- unresponsive to adult intervention
- diverse (i.e., several types)
- pervasive across time and situations
- equivalent to a criminal violation

Cluster analysis was used to identify five subtypes of children with problematic sexual behaviour. The subtypes supported the researchers' hypothesis that children with sexual behaviour problems fit three profiles:

- non-disordered (i.e., non-symptomatic type)
- highly maltreated or traumatised (i.e., highly traumatised and sexually reactive types)
- conduct disordered or delinquent (i.e., sexually aggressive and rule breaker types)
                                        (Pithers et al., 1998)

Pithers et al. (1998) randomly assigned the children in their sample to two different treatments (i.e., a modified relapse prevention treatment based on cognitive-behavioural therapy and a 'best practice' expressive therapy approach that used 'metaphor, symbols, and creative rituals and activities' (Pithers et al., p402)). After 16 weeks in treatment, the findings showed that the cognitive-behavioural treatment was more effective for a greater percentage of children in three of the subtypes (i.e., nonsymptomatic, highly traumatised, and abuse reactive). They attained clinically significant reductions (i.e., post-treatment scores were at least two standard deviations different than pre-treatment scores) in reported sexual behaviours. The cognitive-behavioural treatment was significantly more effective than expressive therapy for the 'highly traumatised' subtype. These children:

- Had the most extensive history of sexual and physical abuse among the children in the sample.
- Were relatively young at the time they were first victimised.
- Had the highest percentage of children who received a DSM-IV diagnosis of post-traumatic stress disorder (PTSD).

The cognitive-behavioural treatment was not effective with the sexually aggressive subtype, and some of these children actually did better when receiving expressive therapy. These children:

- Had the lowest reported history of child maltreatment.
- Were older at the onset of sexual problems.
- Committed the highest percentage of penetrative sexual acts.
- Used aggression to gain victim submission.
- Had the highest percentage of children who received a DSM-IV diagnosis of Conduct Disorder.

In the other NCAN funded study, Bonner and colleagues (2000) studied 201 6 to 12-year-old children referred to mental health treatment for sexual behaviour problems in Oklahoma City, Oklahoma and Seattle, Washington. These researchers attempted to empirically define subtypes of children with sexual behaviour problems, but their cluster analyses failed to yield 'stable clusters that appeared to have clinical relevance or utility' (Bonner et al., 2000, available on-line). They then randomly assigned 110 children in the sample who agreed to participate in treatment to a structured, cognitive-behavioural group or a less structured, dynamic play therapy group. Sixty-three percent of the children completed treatment by attending at least 9 out of 12 group treatment sessions. Both treatments produced clinically significant reductions in problematic behaviour as measured by the Child Sexual Behaviour Inventory, Revised (CSBI-R) and the Child Behaviour Checklist (CBCL), with no significant differences between the two treatments.

The work of Pithers et al. (1998) and Bonner et al. (2000) demonstrated that many children with sexual behaviour problems could be treated effectively with either cognitive-behavioural therapy or expressive dynamic play therapy interventions. Furthermore, the findings

of the Pithers study supported the hypothesis that different subtypes of children with sexual behaviour problems respond differently to contrasting treatment approaches. These findings can help clinicians identify different types of children who engage in sexualised behaviours and appropriately tailor treatment goals and interventions to the needs of each type.

Integrative treatment approaches, broadly applied to different subtypes of children may be especially useful in meeting the intervention needs of children with sexual behaviour problems. This chapter presents intervention strategies from an integrated treatment model that addresses the specialised needs of children with sexual behaviour problems. It describes how the Trauma Outcome Process model (Burton et al., 1998; Rasmussen, Burton, and Christopherson, 1992; Rasmussen, 1999, 2000) can be used to guide assessment and treatment. The interventions described in this chapter are directed toward children who are engaging in abusive sexual behaviours. Some interventions may be applicable to children who display self-focused behaviours that create problems for themselves, but do not hurt others. The term 'children with sexually abusive behaviour problems' will be used throughout this chapter to refer to children who engage in sexual behaviours that are harmful to others. The term 'children with sexual behaviour problems' will be used when necessary to refer to the entire population of children under the age of 12 who engage in problematic or abusive sexual behaviours.

The Trauma Outcome Process Model

The Trauma Outcome Process (Burton et al., 1998; Rasmussen, 1999, 2000; Rasmussen et al., 1992) is a conceptual model that attempts to explain the aetiology of sexually abusive behaviour problems and offers a framework for intervention. It is an integrated model based on psychodynamic, cognitive-behavioural, and humanistic theories of practice. Like psychodynamic theory, this model views internal conflicts and unresolved feelings related to past traumatic events as important motivators of current behaviour. The Trauma Outcome Process follows cognitive-behavioural theory in emphasising the role of distorted cognitive processes in determining behaviour. It is consistent with the humanistic perspective as it stresses awareness and choice as factors influencing an individual's response to traumatic experiences.

The Trauma Outcome Process is based on the premise that individuals have three possible outcomes in response to a traumatic experience. They may:

- Internalise their emotions and become self-destructive.
- Externalise their emotions and become abusive.
- Express their emotions and come to understand and integrate the traumatic experience with their other life experiences.

The Trauma Outcome Process differentiates self-destructive and abusive patterns of behaviour and presents a recovery outcome aimed at interrupting these patterns. These three outcomes are graphically depicted as three separate pathways, or interlocking wheels. Geometric shapes (i.e., square, triangle, circle) are used to label the wheels and indicate the outcomes of Self-victimisation, Abuse, and Recovery (see Figure 1).

A second premise of the Trauma Outcome Process is that victims of abuse have a choice of three behavioural outcomes to pursue. Healthy choices depend upon the victim's level of self-awareness. Self-awareness includes awareness of physical sensations, thoughts, feelings, motivations, and actions (Miller, Nunnally, and Wackman, 1975). This 'awareness process' is depicted as the wheel in the centre of the graphic. It is labelled by a pentagon and encircled by the word 'choice' signifying that victims have choices in their response to a traumatic experience, and that each choice is the product of self-awareness (see Figure 1).

The Trauma Outcome Process model follows cognitive-behavioural theory by emphasising that victims of abuse must recognise and correct cognitive distortions and demonstrate responsible thinking in order to make healthy choices that lead to recovery from the effects of abuse. Two types of cognitive distortions are identified in the Trauma Outcome Process: thinking errors and trauma echoes. Thinking errors are distortions that people who abuse others often use to justify their hurtful behaviours and avoid taking responsibility (Araji, 1997; Burton et al., 1998). Trauma echoes are thinking errors expressed to victims by their perpetrators which victims later adopted as part

of their own thinking (Gray, 1989). For example, perpetrators often tell children that they will get in to trouble if they tell anyone about the abuse. Children who believe their perpetrator and think that they are the ones who are at fault for their abuse are experiencing a trauma echo. Trauma echoes may become deeply ingrained in a victim's thinking and persist for many years. They are destructive thinking processes that contribute to, reinforce, or trigger feelings of worthlessness and powerlessness. If trauma echoes are not corrected, these feelings may cause children to engage in or remain stuck in the maladaptive response patterns of self-victimisation or abuse.

The third premise of the Trauma Outcome Process is that the effects of traumatic experiences and efforts to recover from them are dynamic processes. The options of self-victimisation, abuse, and recovery are neither mutually exclusive nor a linear series of predictable steps. Individuals may enact self-destructive, abusive, and adaptive processes at different points in time in order to cope with the after effects of traumatic experiences.

The Trauma Outcome Process model is especially suited for addressing the unique problems of children with sexually abusive behaviour problems, who are often referred to treatment for both victimisation and perpetration issues. Many have been sexually abused themselves (Cunningham and MacFarlane, 1996; Johnson, 1988, 1989). Others may have endured other traumatic experiences (e.g., physical abuse, severe neglect, emotional abuse, or exposure to domestic violence), which may be of equal or greater importance than sexual abuse in motivating them to engage in abusive sexual behaviours (Johnson, 2000). The Trauma Outcome Process model addresses the victimisation and perpetration issues of children with sexually abusive behaviour problems by combining intervention strategies from cognitive-behavioural and psychodynamic theories. The cognitive-behavioural interventions confront the thinking errors and trauma echoes that support engaging in sexually abusive behaviour, while the psychodynamic interventions (incorporated through play therapy) encourage expression of troubling emotions associated with prior traumatic experiences. Together, both types of interventions provide a balanced treatment approach addressing the underlying

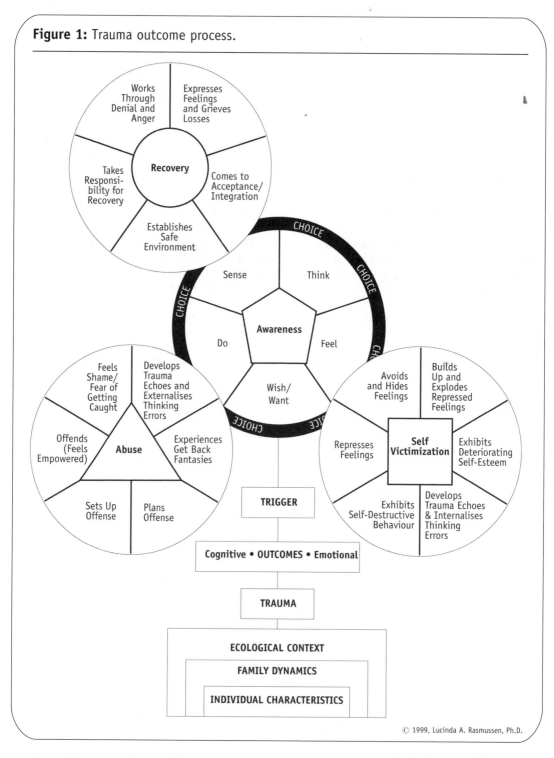

Figure 1: Trauma outcome process.

Recovery
- Works Through Denial and Anger
- Expresses Feelings and Grieves Losses
- Takes Responsibility for Recovery
- Comes to Acceptance/Integration
- Establishes Safe Environment

Awareness
- Sense
- Think
- Do
- Feel
- Wish/Want

CHOICE

Abuse
- Feels Shame/Fear of Getting Caught
- Develops Trauma Echoes and Externalises Thinking Errors
- Offends (Feels Empowered)
- Experiences Get Back Fantasies
- Sets Up Offense
- Plans Offense

Self Victimization
- Avoids and Hides Feelings
- Builds Up and Explodes Repressed Feelings
- Represses Feelings
- Exhibits Deteriorating Self-Esteem
- Exhibits Self-Destructive Behaviour
- Develops Trauma Echoes & Internalises Thinking Errors

TRIGGER

Cognitive • OUTCOMES • Emotional

TRAUMA

ECOLOGICAL CONTEXT

FAMILY DYNAMICS

INDIVIDUAL CHARACTERISTICS

issues motivating children to engage in problematic and sexually abusive behaviour. The Trauma Outcome Process model is systemic because its interventions can be applied to the individual, in small groups, and to family systems (Brown and Rasmussen, 1994; Burton et al., 1998).

Applying the trauma outcome process model in assessment

The Trauma Outcome Process model provides a framework for obtaining essential information related to the presenting problems, therapeutic issues, and family dynamics of children with sexually abusive behaviour problems. Figure 2 illustrates the Trauma Outcome Process of children with sexually abusive behaviour problems (Rasmussen, 1999). This figure shows that children with these problems are vulnerable to maladaptive responses to traumatic experiences because of child, family, and environmental risk factors. Outcomes of traumatic experiences can be emotional (distressing feelings), cognitive (thinking errors or trauma echoes), or behavioural (self-victimisation or abuse). Children who show symptoms of internalising disorders (e.g., PTSD, depression) may be enacting the self-victimisation response, while children who display behaviours indicative of externalising disorders (e.g., Oppositional Defiant Disorder, Conduct Disorder) may be enacting the abuse response. It is important to remember that some children show symptoms of both internalising and externalising disorders and may be enacting both self-destructive and abusive responses in the Trauma Outcome Process. The process of using this model to assess and treat children with sexually abusive behaviour problems is described below.

Identifying risk factors

Assessment begins by identifying child, family, and environmental risk factors that may contribute to sexually abusive behaviour. Data are collected from multiple sources: standardised measures, clinical interviews, past treatment records, and collateral contacts with other professionals who have previously seen the child. Standardised measures are an important component of the assessment as they provide objective data about the child's behaviours. The Child Sexual Behaviour Inventory (CSBI) (Friedrich, 1997) and the Child Sexual Behaviour Checklist (CSBCL) (Johnson, 1995) are the most widely used measures for assessing children's sexualised behaviours. Useful measures for assessing other aspects of the child's functioning are the Child Behaviour Checklist (Achenbach, 1991); Trauma Symptom Checklist for Children (Briere, 1996); and

Children's Impact of Traumatic Events Scale (Wolfe, Gentile, Michienzi, Sas, and Wolfe, 1991). Discussion of the use of these standardised measures is beyond the scope of this chapter.

Clinical interviews are used to gather information, observe the child's behaviour and interaction with their parents, and obtain a complete picture of the child's presenting problems, and developmental, medical, social, and family history. Several interviews may be necessary to make a thorough assessment. It is helpful to begin with a conjoint interview with the child and parents, followed by individual interviews of the child and interviews with the parents (either individually or as a couple). The practitioner must avoid taking a myopic focus of assessing *only* the presenting problems of sexualised behaviour and possible sexual abuse history, but should broadly explore, assess, and interpret all relevant issues, particularly the role of other traumatic experiences in the child's life (e.g., physical abuse, witnessing domestic violence, experiencing extreme neglect or abandonment).

Identifying risk factors can help a clinician begin to uncover a child's motivation for participating in problematic sexual behaviour. Neurobiological risk factors can inhibit a child's ability to cope effectively with traumatic experiences and can impair social functioning. For example, disorders such as Attention Deficit Hyperactivity Disorder (ADHD), learning disabilities, or developmental delay can impair the ability to respond to traumatic experiences and to implement appropriate coping strategies. Children with these disorders have cognitive and social skill deficits that limit their ability to solve problems and cope effectively with stressful situations (Fowler, 1994; Neuwirth, 1996). They may engage in sexual behaviours in response to environmental stress, or as a way to relate socially with their peers, without thinking through possible alternatives or considering the potential consequences of their actions. A holistic assessment must consider these symptoms and other problems impairing the child's functioning and how they contribute to or exacerbate the child's presenting problem of sexually abusive behaviour.

Children's sexual behaviour problems often relate directly to adversities experienced in their families. The premises of the Trauma Outcome Process model assert that sexually abusive

Figure 2: The trauma outcome process: children with sexually abusive behaviour problems.

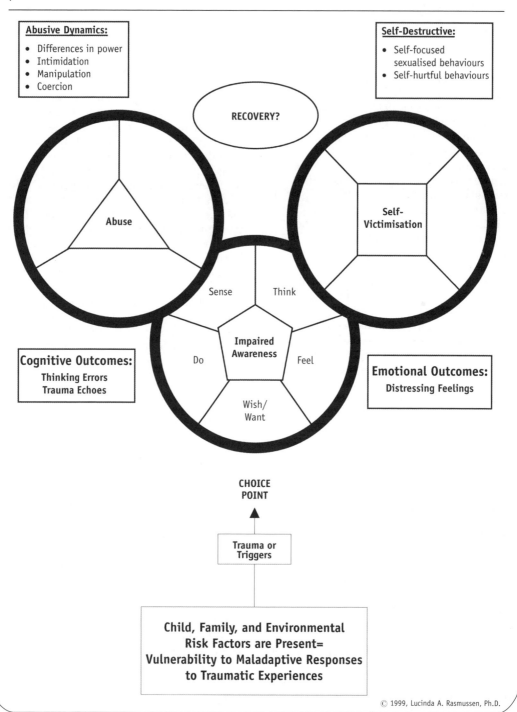

Abusive Dynamics:
- Differences in power
- Intimidation
- Manipulation
- Coercion

Self-Destructive:
- Self-focused sexualised behaviours
- Self-hurtful behaviours

RECOVERY?

Abuse

Self-Victimisation

Sense   Think

Impaired Awareness

Do   Feel

Wish/ Want

Cognitive Outcomes:
Thinking Errors
Trauma Echoes

Emotional Outcomes:
Distressing Feelings

CHOICE POINT

Trauma or Triggers

Child, Family, and Environmental Risk Factors are Present= Vulnerability to Maladaptive Responses to Traumatic Experiences

© 1999, Lucinda A. Rasmussen, Ph.D.

behaviour is a way for some children to re-enact traumatic experiences and try to master unresolved feelings (Burton et al., 1998; Rasmussen, 1999; Rasmussen et al., 1992). Some children may engage in sexualised behaviours as a reaction to their own sexual abuse (Cunningham and MacFarlane, 1996; Friedrich and Luecke, 1988; Gil, 1991). Others may have learned about sex through growing up in sexualised family environments, lacking appropriate boundaries that respect personal space and privacy (Friedrich, 1999; Gil and Johnson, 1993). These children may have witnessed the sexual activities of adults in their homes or had easy access to pornographic magazines, videos, or sexually explicit websites on the Internet. They may have been exposed to distorted values and learned to associate sexual contact with themes of degradation, manipulation, aggression, and violence (Araji, 1997; Gil and Johnson).

Children who grow up in neglectful, unsafe or violent environments are at risk for learning maladaptive coping strategies (e.g., sexual aggression). The sexual behaviour problems of some children may stem from internal conflicts associated with a history of poor attachment, neglect, or abandonment related to family factors such as divorce/separation, death of a parent, parental substance use, or parental mental illness. Other environmental stresses such as poverty, homelessness, parental unemployment, community violence, or oppression due to race or ethnicity may impair parents' abilities to provide appropriate caregiving and may negatively affect the attachment process. A review completed by Marshall, Hudson, and Hodkinson (1993) on the role of attachment in the development of sexual offending concluded that children who are securely attached to their caregivers are more empathic (Stroufe, Schork, Frosso, Lawroski, and LaFreniere, 1984, as cited in Marshall et al., 1993) and more socially competent (Stroufe, 1983, as cited in Marshall et al., 1993). In contrast, children who have grown up in a deprived environment and are insecurely attached to their caregivers may lack the skills necessary for prosocial behaviour (Marshall et al., 1993). Children whose caregivers did not provide empathic care may not learn how to relate emotionally to others and may fail to develop empathy. They may engage in sexually abusive behaviour without recognising how what they are doing hurts others.

Identifying outcomes of traumatic experiences

In the Trauma Outcome Process model, 'An experience is traumatic if it:

- Is sudden, unexpected, or non-normative.
- Exceeds the individual's perceived ability to meet its demands.
- Disrupts the individual's frame of reference and other central psychological needs and related schemas.'

(McCann and Pearlman, 1990, p10)

Therapists need to identify signs and symptoms that represent after effects of the traumatic experiences in the child's history (e.g., sexual abuse, physical abuse, emotional abuse, neglect, witnessing domestic violence, being exposed to explicit stimuli, experiencing loss of or abandonment by a significant adult), and then assess for impairment in children's cognitive, emotional, and behavioural functioning.

Therapists should assess those children who have experienced sexual abuse, physical abuse, or exposure to domestic violence to determine if they are exhibiting symptoms of PTSD or depression. Nightmares, intrusive recollections of traumatic experiences, behavioural re-enactments of traumatic events, avoidance of stimuli associated with traumatic experiences, emotional numbing, and signs of increased physiological arousal may indicate PTSD (American Psychiatric Association (APA), 1994). Abused children, as well as children who have experienced extreme neglect, major losses or abandonment, may show signs and symptoms of depression, including sad or irritable moods, tearfulness, low self-esteem, social withdrawal, excessive guilt, or suicidal ideation (APA).

Assessing self-awareness

The next step in the Trauma Outcome Process model is to assess the child's self-awareness in each of the areas of the Awareness wheel depicted in Figure 1 (Miller et al., 1975). The primary goal of treatment in the Trauma Outcome Process model is to help the child enter the 'Recovery' option of the Trauma Outcome Process. Entering Recovery requires two prerequisites: regaining a sense of personal safety and experiencing self-awareness as defined by the Awareness wheel (Rasmussen, 1999, 2000). Children living in unprotected or unsupervised environments are at risk either for continued abuse or for continuing to engage in abusive sexual behaviours. These children engage in the self-victimisation or abuse responses because they lack self-awareness and do not have the sense of safety needed to enter the Recovery outcome. Their lack of self-awareness may be seen in their thinking errors or trauma echoes, their inability to talk about their feelings or sexual sensations, and their difficulty in regulating their emotions and behaviour. Increased self-awareness is necessary before they can engage in the three stages of the recovery response:

- Clarifying responsibility for prior abuse or other traumatic experiences.
- Expressing feelings and grieving losses.
- Accepting and integrating past traumatic experiences with other life experiences.

(Burton et al., 1998; Rasmussen, 1999;
Rasmussen et al., 1992)

The conjoint interview: creating a trusting therapeutic alliance

The role of the therapist when using the Trauma Outcome Process model varies according to the stage of treatment. When beginning treatment, the therapist takes a nondirective, client-centered approach that conveys empathy and respect for the child and his or her parents and understanding of their feelings. After rapport is established, the therapist can be more direct in confronting the thinking errors and trauma echoes used by the child and the parents, and in encouraging them to take responsibility for their behaviours (Rasmussen and Cunningham, 1995).

The recovery response requires a safe and trusting environment that allows children with sexually abusive behaviour problems to begin to admit responsibility for their inappropriate sexual behaviours, discuss past traumatic experiences, and express the feelings associated with their presenting problems and prior trauma. Children with sexually abusive behaviour problems and their parents often enter therapy with deep feelings of shame and embarrassment. They feel alone with their problems and are often surprised to find that other families struggle with similar issues. The empathic responses of the therapist may be the first time that anyone has acknowledged their shame and isolation. Therapists need to assure these children and their parents that they have expertise in treating sexual behaviour problems and that other children whom they

have treated have successfully stopped engaging in abusive behaviours. Believing in their therapist's competence, as well as discovering that other families have faced and overcome similar challenges, instils hope when children and parents are struggling with the intensely painful feelings associated with the discovery of the child's sexually abusive behaviours.

It is essential that therapists directly address the presenting problem of sexually abusive behaviour as soon as possible in conjoint interviews with children and their parents. The therapist should state the reason for the assessment in clear terms (e.g., 'We're here because Michael has had a touching problem,' or 'We're here because Jennifer said that Michael touched her in ways that are not appropriate'). Bringing the sexual behaviour problems out in the open in the beginning of the conjoint interview can alleviate some of the anxiety that the child and parents may feel in coming to therapy. It also sets the stage for a therapeutic process that directly and honesty addresses the child's problems, as well as any problems of the parents that have contributed to the child's sexualised behaviours. Other tasks of the conjoint interview are for the therapist to establish a collaborative relationship with the parents and begin to formulate a treatment plan. Part of the treatment plan should be establishing a 'prevention team' consisting of concerned adults who can help the child to stop engaging in sexually abusive behaviour and prevent relapse (Gray and Pithers, 1993).

Interviewing the child

The focus of individual interviews with children with sexually abusive behaviour problems is twofold. First, therapists need to help children feel safe enough to admit their involvement in sexual behaviour problems and to begin discussing their feelings and the circumstances surrounding each incident. Second, therapists need to assess for signs and symptoms that may be after effects of prior traumatic experiences and help the child begin to talk about their feelings related to those traumas. The interviewing strategies employed in individual interviews with children with sexual behaviour problems differ from those employed in conjoint interviews with the children and their parents. Rather than immediately stating the presenting problem of sexually abusive behaviour, as in the conjoint interview, it is usually best to wait until the middle portion of the individual interview before questioning children about their sexual behaviour problems or prior traumatic experiences. Children should be somewhat comfortable with their therapists before they are asked to discuss specific details about their sexually abusive behaviour or prior abuse.

The interview should take place in a child-friendly office containing a few well-chosen toys, puppets, and art materials. Therapists can tell children that their office is a place where they can talk about their feelings and problems, including touching problems (Gil and Johnson, 1993). Suggesting that children draw while they talk is often an effective way of beginning the interview. Drawing a picture of themselves or their family can help put children at ease about talking with a strange adult and may allow them to feel less threatened (Lukas, 1993). These drawings may later provide useful diagnostic material when the observational data from the interviews are combined with data compiled from standardised measures, intake forms, and collateral contacts.

The order of topics addressed in the interview should proceed from least threatening to the most threatening (i.e., sexual behaviour problems and prior traumatic experiences). The therapist can begin the questioning by asking about the child's recreational interests. This allows the child to talk about things that he or she enjoys and facilitates development of rapport with the therapist, particularly when the therapist joins the child by pointing out interests they have in common. Next, the therapist can ask about the child's friends, both in the neighbourhood and at school. Deficits in social skills often contribute to children seeking control through engaging in sexually abusive behaviour (Burton et al., 1998; Cunningham and MacFarlane, 1996; Lane, 1997). Different types of social problems may be identified in the assessment. Some children are socially isolated and may have difficulty naming their friends when asked, or may relate experiences involving negative interactions with peers. Other children, who have experienced insecure attachments, lack empathy, and engage others in superficial ways, may name numerous friends when asked, but cannot identify any close relationships or name a 'best friend'.

The interview process often becomes more threatening to children with sexually abusive behaviour problems when therapists ask them to talk about school. Children who have academic difficulties or who get in trouble at school because of impulsive or aggressive behaviour may be reluctant to disclose their difficulties at school. The therapist's skillful use of empathic responses may be necessary to persuade the child to be forthcoming and bring up school problems. School problems, both academic and behavioural, may indicate other disorders needing assessment (e.g., learning disabilities, developmental delays, or ADHD). Acknowledging behaviour problems at school helps children begin the process of being accountable and prepares them to take responsibility for their sexually abusive behaviour.

The heart of the assessment interview explores children's relationships with their parents and other family members. Discovering that a child has sexually abused a sibling can be devastating to a family. Parents often feel torn between their children. On the one hand, they feel love for all their children, but on the other hand, they are angry with their perpetrating child and are grieving for their victimised child (Burton et al., 1998). When a child has abused children in the neighbourhood or relatives in the extended family, parents may be overwhelmed by feelings of shame and embarrassment. In either case, whether children have abused siblings or children outside the home, they may be well aware of the reactions of their parents to their sexually abusive behaviour and the family conflict it has caused. Questioning children about their relationships with parents or siblings often leads to a direct discussion of their sexually abusive behaviour problems.

Encouraging accountability for sexually abusive behaviour

A child can tolerate anxiety provoking questions after trust has been established. This may happen in the initial interview, but some children may require two or three interviews. If after two or three interviews, the child is still unwilling to talk about his or her sexual behaviours, the therapist should consider employing cognitive-behavioural interventions to directly address the child's resistance and encourage disclosure.

Confronting thinking errors is a cognitive-behavioural intervention used to increase cognitive awareness and increase accountability for self-destructive or abusive behaviours. Therapists should expect children with sexually abusive behaviour problems to initially deny, minimise, blame others, or use other thinking errors when first asked about their sexually inappropriate behaviour. A therapist using the Trauma Outcome Process model responds to denial by exploring fears that may underlie the denial, in order to increase the child's emotional and cognitive awareness. For example, the therapist might ask, 'What do you think might happen if people knew that you really did do the touching? What would your parents say and do?' A therapist might address a child's feelings of shame or embarrassment by asking, 'What would it mean about you if you did the touching? Do you think it means that you're a bad person?' If the child acknowledges feelings of worthlessness, the therapist could say, 'I've talked to other kids who had problems with touching and they felt like they were bad too.' The therapist could reassure the child, 'Touching others' private parts when they don't want you to is a very bad thing to do, but it doesn't make you a bad person.' The therapist can instill hope by saying, 'I've seen other kids stop their touching problems. Coming here (to therapy) can help you learn to do that too.'

An accurate assessment of the child's sexual behaviour problems depends upon using carefully worded questions geared toward obtaining specific details about the reported sexual behaviour and the circumstances surrounding it. Contextual factors in the relationship between the children involved in the sexual behaviour are important to assess (Johnson, 1993; Ryan, 1997). Contextual factors known as 'abusive dynamics' characterise the Abuse response in the Trauma Outcome Process model. There are four abusive dynamics:

- Power differences: using greater age, size, physical or mental ability.
- Intimidation: using implied status or authority (e.g., Babysitting).
- Manipulation: using games, tricks, or bribes.
- Coercion: using physical force or weapons.
       (Burton et al., 1998; Rasmussen, 1999)

A combination of these factors is usually needed to conclude that an interaction is abusive. An interaction can be considered abusive whenever coercion (Dynamic 4) is present, or when differences in power (Dynamic 1) or intimidation (Dynamic 2) are combined with manipulation (Dynamic 3) or coercion (Dynamic 4) (Rasmussen, 1999). The therapist should ask about the following areas when assessing abuse dynamics and the child's thinking errors (Burton et al., 1998):

- Who was involved in the sexual activity (i.e., 'Whom did you touch?')
- The type of sexual behaviour that occurred (i.e., 'How did you touch?)
- The onset and duration of the behaviour (i.e., 'When was the first time that you touched? When was the last time?)
- The severity of the behaviour: frequency and number or victims (i.e., 'How many different times did you touch? How many different kids have you touched?')
- The times of day and locations where the behaviour occurred (i.e., 'What time of day was it when you touched? Where were you?')
- Abusive dynamics in the relationship between the children who are involved:
  —Dynamic 1: 'How old is? How big is?'
  —Dynamic 2: 'How did you get to know them? Did they trust you?'
  —Dynamic 3: 'What did you say to get them to let you touch? Did you offer to give them something if they let you touch?'
  —Dynamic 4: 'Did you do anything to make them let you touch? Did you make threats? Did you use any weapons?'
- Thinking errors (i.e., 'What were you thinking about before you touched? How do you think they felt about the touching?')

Accepting accountability for sexually abusive behaviour is a primary treatment goal for children with sexually abusive behaviour problems (Burton et al., 1998). It may take several sessions to ask all the needed questions in order to obtain a complete assessment of a child's sexual behaviours. When a child uses thinking errors during assessment interviews, the therapist may intervene by confronting the child and teaching them how to correct them. For example, a child may reply to the question 'How do think the other person felt about the touching?' by saying, 'She liked it; she wanted to do it.' The therapist might ask the child, 'How do you know? Did you ask her how she felt?' and point out, 'We can't know what somebody else feels or wants to do unless we ask them first.' The therapist might say to the child, 'What I just heard you say is a thinking error. Thinking errors are ways that people think to help stay out of trouble and feel okay about doing things that hurt others. The thinking error that you just used is called 'assuming.' It means thinking you know how somebody else feels without first checking it out and asking them.' If a child says, 'It's not my fault; she started it,' the therapist might ask for an explanation of how the other child started it. If the child is unable to give a reasonable answer and if collateral information about the incident indicates that they were responsible for initiating the sexual interaction, the therapist might say to the child, 'I just heard you use a thinking error called 'blaming.' Blaming is when you say someone else is at fault for something you did.' The therapist can teach the child how to correct their thinking error by saying, 'When you correct a thinking error, you become more responsible. You can correct a 'blaming' thinking error by admitting what you did.' Therapists might post a list of common thinking errors in their offices and use it as an intervention tool. The clinician can refer children to the chart when they use thinking errors in therapy sessions. Together, the child and clinician can identify the specific thinking errors used and discuss ways to make corrections. Parents can help their children apply at home what they are learning in therapy by putting a copy of the thinking error list in a prominent place in the house (e.g., refrigerator door) and referring to it when their children use thinking errors.

The process of addressing denial can be like peeling an onion; it takes place one layer at a time. It is not reasonable to expect children with sexually abusive behaviour problems to take full responsibility for their behaviour in the initial assessment interview. Therapists should encourage children to begin to take responsibility as soon as they can in the early sessions of treatment, while recognising that achieving full accountability will be an ongoing goal. Therapists should also allow children to admit responsibility in ways that are easiest for them. Some children may not be able to verbally tell what they did, but may be able to take responsibility for their sexually abusive behaviour in less direct ways through play therapy interventions. They may draw a picture about the sexually abusive incident (Cunningham and MacFarlane, 1996; Burton et

al., 1998), write about it in a journal, or use puppets to role-play what happened. Therapists should also give permission to children to report more details about their sexually abusive behaviour in subsequent sessions. A therapist might say to a child, who admits only a few details in the initial interview, 'Kids don't usually tell me everything about their touching behaviour the first time. If there are more things that you weren't ready to tell me today, or if you remember other things that you forgot to talk about, it's okay to come back next week and tell me more about what happened.' This conveys that the therapist understands that talking about sexual touching is difficult and will allow details to be disclosed at a pace that is tolerable for the child.

Exploring and resolving feelings related to traumatic experiences

Past traumatic experiences may be disclosed by the child during the assessment interviews or uncovered by the practitioner through careful questioning. Therapists need to wait until children have trust in the therapeutic relationship before inquiring about past physical or sexual abuse or other trauma. When trust has been established, practitioners may pose questions that may elicit disclosures. Examples include: 'Where did you learn this behaviour (sexual touching)?' 'Has anyone hurt you or done things to you that made you feel uncomfortable?' 'How did they hurt you?' (Burton et al., 1998). Practitioners should proceed with caution, being careful not to ask leading questions, and take detailed notes when disclosures are given. New disclosures of abuse must be reported immediately to law enforcement or child protective services.

Identifying, exploring, and expressing one's feelings about past traumatic experiences is the essence of the Recovery response in the Trauma Outcome Process. Learning about feelings and increasing emotional awareness is an important component of treatment for children with sexually abusive behaviour problems, both in terms of addressing their unresolved issues related to traumatic experiences and learning to have empathy for others. Psychodynamically oriented play therapy strategies using various mediums (i.e., toys, puppets, sand tray, and art materials) increase self-awareness and allow children to express and begin to master their feelings. Charts with faces of children showing different feelings help children with sexually abusive behaviour problems to acquire a vocabulary to express feelings and to recognise different feelings expressed by others. Children can participate in 'feeling charades' where they guess what characters in different situations might feel (Burton et al., 1998, p152–4).

Bibliotherapy is another medium for helping children to identify their own and others' feelings and learn to have empathy. Using books and stories in therapy helps children identify and explore feelings about their abuse or sexual touching problems. They can begin 'to see their adversities in a new light' by 'finding the words' to express how they feel about their traumatic experiences (Katz, 1997, p67–8). Once children gain awareness of feelings related to their own abuse or other traumatic experiences, they are better able to develop empathy for the feelings of those whom they have hurt through their sexually abusive behaviour. Some books that facilitate exploring feelings related to abuse issues are *The Giving Tree* (Silverstein, 1964), *The Hurt* (Doleski, 1983), *The Man Who Kept His Heart in a Bucket* (Levitan, 1991), and *There's a Nightmare in my Closet* (Mayer, 1970).

Art therapy provides opportunities for traumatised children to access and express their feelings. The 'Safe Place' is an art therapy exercise in which children identify what they need to help them feel safe. In this exercise, children imagine a place in which they are free from abuse (Burton et al., p232–3), and then draw a picture of their safe place. Other art therapy exercises include:

- Drawing a picture of the perpetrator (Mandell and Damon, 1989).
- Drawing 'how you looked and how you felt' during the abuse (Burton et al., 1998, p152–4).
- Drawing pictures of one's family before and after abuse was disclosed (Burton et al., p177–8).

Children experiencing nightmares may draw pictures of the things that they are afraid of and then draw ways to deal with their fears (Cunningham and MacFarlane, 1996). Grieving losses is an important part of resolving past traumatic experiences. Children can draw a 'loss timeline' (Burton et al., p165–9; Cunningham and MacFarlane) illustrating the significant losses and traumatic experiences in their lives and how they felt about each loss/experience.

Determining the primary behavioural response

The final step of assessment using the Trauma Outcome Process model is to identify which of the options in the Trauma Outcome Process is the child's primary behavioural response. Determining the primary behavioural response establishes the initial focus of treatment (Rasmussen, 1999). Children whose primary behavioural response is self-victimisation have thinking errors and trauma echoes that they turn against themselves (e.g., blaming themselves for their own abuse). Their behaviours are self-destructive, problematic, and can include self-focused sexualised behaviours (e.g., excessive masturbation or masturbating in front of others). Sexualised behaviours involving others are limited to only one or a few incidents and are usually not coercive. These children often have salient issues related to their previous abuse. They can best benefit from treatment that primarily addresses past traumatic experiences (e.g., individual therapy focused on resolving their past trauma or a therapy group for victims).

Children whose primary behavioural response is abuse have thinking errors and trauma echoes that they turn against other people. Their behaviours, including sexual behaviours, are hurtful to others because they involve the abusive dynamics noted above (i.e., differences in power, intimidation, manipulation, and coercion; Burton et al., 1998; Rasmussen, 1999). These children are best treated with interventions that address their distorted thinking and abusive behaviours (e.g., individual therapy focused on increasing accountability and developing empathy for the feelings of others, group therapy for children with sexually abusive behaviour problems).

Summary and conclusions

Recent empirical research has demonstrated the effectiveness of two intervention strategies: cognitive-behavioural therapy and expressive therapy (Bonner et al., 2000; Pithers et al., 1998) in treating children with sexual behaviour problems. This chapter has presented a conceptual framework, the Trauma Outcome Process model, and explained how the framework can be used to create an integrated treatment approach for assessing children with sexually abusive behaviour problems and treating their perpetration and victimisation issues. Intervention strategies using the Trauma Outcome Process model involve creating safety for children who have experienced traumatic experiences and increasing their awareness of thoughts, feelings, body sensations, motivations, and actions. The chapter presented interventions that are directed toward enhancing the self-awareness and are geared toward helping children with sexually abusive behaviour problems to express and cope with their feelings in a constructive, rather than self-victimising or abusive way. The application of this integrated model can help clinicians provide a therapeutic environment that conveys empathy and respect to children with sexually abusive behaviour problems, yet confronts their sexually abusive behaviours and prevents relapse.

Acknowledgement

The author acknowledges Jan Ellen Burton, Ph.D. and Barbara J. Christopherson, LCSW for their work in the creation and development of the Trauma Outcome Process model, and Arthur H. Brown III, Ph.D., Julie Bradshaw, LCSW, and Steven C. Huke, M.S. for their helpful suggestions in later modifications to the model.

References

Achenbach, T. (1991). *Child Behaviour Checklist for Ages 4–18.* Burlington, VT: University of Vermont.

American Psychiatric Association (1994). *Diagnostic and statistical manual of mental disorders.* (4th edn.). Washington, DC: American Psychiatric Association.

Araji, S. K. (1997). *Sexually aggressive children: Coming to understand them.* Thousand Oaks, CA: Sage.

Bonner, B. L., Walker, C. E. and Berliner, L. (2000) *Children With Sexual Behaviour Problems: Assessment and Treatment.* Final report. National Center on Child Abuse and Neglect, Administration for Children, Youth, and Families, U. S. Department of Human Services. *http://www.calib.com/nccanch/pubs/childassessment/index.htm*

Briere, J. (1996). *Trauma Symptom Checklist Children.* Odessa, FL: Psychological Assessment Resources.

Brown, A. H. and Rasmussen, L. A. (1994) *Environmental Contributors to Sexually Offending Behaviour: A Family Systems Application to the Trauma Outcome Process.* Paper presented at the 13th Annual Research and Treatment Conference of the Association for the Treatment of Sexual Abusers (ATSA). San Francisco, CA.

Burton, D. L., Nesmith, A. and Badten, L. (1997). Clinician's Views on Sexually Aggressive Children and Their Families: A Theoretical Exploration. *Child Abuse and Neglect.* 21:2 157–70.

Burton, J., Rasmussen, L. A., Bradshaw, J., Christopherson, B. J. and Huke, S. C. (1998). *Treating Children With Sexually Abusive Behaviour Problems: Guidelines for Child and Parent Intervention.* New York: Haworth Press.

Cantwell, H. B. (1988) Child Sexual Abuse: Very Young Perpetrators. *Child Abuse and Neglect.* 12: 579–82.

Cunningham, C. and MacFarlane, K. (1996) *When Children Abuse: Group Treatment Strategies for Children With Impulse Control Problems.* Brandon, VT: Safer Society Press.

Doleski, T. (1983) *The Hurt.* Mahwah, NJ: Paulist Press.

Fowler, M. (1994) *Attention-deficit/hyperactivity Disorder: NICHCY Briefing Paper.* Washington, DC: National Information Center for Children with Disabilities.

Friedrich, W. N. (1997) *Child Sexual Behaviour Inventory.* Odessa, FL: Psychological Assessment Resources.

Friedrich, W. N. (1999) *The Use of Psychological Assessment With Sexually Aggressive Children: Treatment Planning and Risk Assessment.* Paper presented at the 18th Annual Research and Treatment Conference of the Association for the Treatment of Sexual Abusers.

Friedrich, W. N. and Luecke, W. J. (1988) Young School-age Sexually Aggressive Children. *Professional Psychology Research and Practice.* 19:2 155–69.

Gil, E. (1991) *The Healing Power of Play: Working With Abused Children.* New York: The Guilford Press.

Gil, E. and Johnson, T. C. (1993) *Sexualized Children: Assessment and Treatment of Sexualized Children Who Molest.* Rockville, MD: Launch Press.

Glasgow, D., Horne, L., Calam, R. and Cox, A. (1994) Evidence, Incidence, Gender, and Age in Sexual Abuse of Children Perpetrated by Children: Towards a Developmental Analysis of Child Sexual Abuse. *Child Abuse Review.* 3: 196–210.

Gray, A. S. (1989) *New Concepts in Sexual Abuse Recovery: Healing The Effects of Trauma.* Paper presented at the Fourth Annual Training Conference on the Treatment of Juvenile Sex Offenders, Salt Lake City, UT.

Gray, A., Busconi, A., Houchens, P. and Pithers, W. D. (1997) Children With Sexual Behaviour Problems and their Caregivers: Demographics, Functioning, and Clinical Patterns. *Sexual Abuse: A Journal of Research and Treatment.* 9: 267–90.

Gray, A., Pithers, W. D., Busconi, A. and Houchens, P. (1999) Developmental and Etiological Characteristics of Children with Sexual Behaviour Problems: Treatment Implications. *Child Abuse and Neglect.* 23:6 601–21.

Gray, A. S. and Pithers, W. D. (1993) Relapse Prevention With Sexually Aggressive Adolescents and Children: Expanding Treatment and Supervision. in Barbaree, H. Marshall, W. and Hudson, S. (Eds.) *The Juvenile Sexual Offender.* New York: The Guilford Press. 289–319.

Hall, D. K., Mathews, F. and Pearce, J. (1998) Factors Associated With Sexual Behaviour Problems in Young Sexually Abused Children. *Child Abuse and Neglect.* 22:10 1045–63.

Johnson, T. C. (1988). Child Perpetrators: Children Who Molest Other Children. Preliminary Findings. *Child Abuse and Neglect.* 12: 219–29.

Johnson, T. C. (1989) Female Child Perpetrators: Children Who Molest Other Children. *Child Abuse and Neglect.* 13: 571–85.

Johnson, T. C. (1993) Assessment of Sexual Behaviour Problems in Preschool-aged and Latency-aged Children. *Child and Adolescent Psychiatric Clinics of North America.* 2: 431–49.

Johnson (1995). *Treatment Exercises for Child Abuse Victims and Children With Sexual Behaviour Problems.* South Pasadena, CA: Author.

Johnson, T. C. (2000) *First do no Harm: Potential Pitfalls for Interventions With Child Sexual Abuse Victims.* Handout distributed at workshop presented at the San Diego Conference on Responding to Child Maltreatment, San Diego, CA.

Johnson, T. C. and Berry, C. (1989) Children who Molest: A treatment Program. *Journal of Interpersonal Violence* 4:2 185–203.

Katz, M. (1997). *On Playing a Poor Hand Well: Insights from the Lives of those Who Have Overcome Childhood Risks and Adversities.* New York: W. W. Norton.

Lane, S. (1997) Special Populations: Children, Females, the Developmentally Disabled, and Violent Youth. in Ryan, G. and Lane, S. (Eds.) *Juvenile Sexual Offending: Causes, Consequences, and Correction.* (Rev edn) San Francisco: Jossey-Bass. 322–59.

Levitan, S. (1991) *The Man Who Kept his Heart in a Bucket.* New York: Dial Books for Young Readers.

Lukas, S. (1993) *Where to Start and What to Ask: An Assessment Handbook.* New York: W. W. Norton.

Mandell, J. and Damon, L. (1989) *Group Therapy for Sexually Abused Children.* New York: The Guilford Press.

Marshall, W. L., Hudson, S. M. and Hodkinson, S. (1993) The Importance of Attachment Bonds in the Development of Juvenile Sexual Offending. in Barbaree, H. E. Marshall, W. L. and Hudson, S. M. (Eds.) *The Juvenile Sex Offender.* New York: The Guilford Press. 164–81.

Mayer, M. (1968) *There's a Nightmare in my Closet.* New York: Dial Books for Young Readers.

McCann, I. L. and Pearlman, L. A. (1990) *Psychological Trauma and the Adult Survivor: Theory, Therapy and Transformation.* New York: Brunner Mazel.

Miller, S., Nunnally, E. W. and Wackman, D. B. (1975) *Alive and Aware: Improving Communication in Relationships.* Minneapolis, MN: Interpersonal Communication Programs Inc.

Neuwirth, S. (1996) *Learning Disabilities.* Washington, DC: National Institute of Mental Health, U. S. Department of Health and Human Services.

Pithers, W. D., Gray, A., Busconi, A. and Houchens, P. (1998) Children With Sexual Behaviour Problems: Identification of Five Distinct Child Types and Related Treatment Considerations. *Child Maltreatment.* 34: 384–406.

Rasmussen, L. A. (1999) The Trauma Outcome Process: An Integrated Model for Guiding Clinical Practice With Children With Sexually Abusive Behaviour Problems. *Journal of Child Sexual Abuse.* 8:4 3–33.

Rasmussen, L. A. (2000) *Integrating Cognitive-behavioural and Expressive Therapy Interventions: Applying the Trauma Outcome Process in Treating Children With Sexually Abusive Behaviour Problems.* Manuscript submitted for publication.

Rasmussen, L. A., Burton, J. and Christopherson, B. J. (1992) Precursors to Offending and the Trauma Outcome Process in Sexually Reactive Children. *Journal of Child Sexual Abuse.* 1:1 33–48.

Rasmussen, L. A. and Cunningham, C. (1995) Focused Play Therapy and Non-directive Play Therapy: Can they be Integrated? *Journal of Child Sexual Abuse.* 4:1 1–20.

Ray, J., Smith, V., Peterson, T., Gray, J., Schaffner, J. and Houff, M. (1995) A Treatment Program for Children With Sexual Behaviour Problems. *Child and Adolescent Social Work Journal.* 12:5 331–43.

Ryan, G. (1997) Perpetration Prevention. in Ryan, G. and Lane, S. (Eds.) *Juvenile Sexual Offending: Causes, Consequences, and Correction.* (Rev edn) San Francisco: Jossey-Bass. 433–54.

Silverstein, S. (1964) *The Giving Tree.* New York: Harper and Row.

Wolfe, V. V., Gentile, C., Michienzi, T., Sas, L. and Wolfe, D. A. (1991) Children's Impact of Traumatic Events Scale: A Measure of Post-sexual-abuse Symptoms. *Behavioural Assessment.* 13: 359–83.

Chapter 12: The Assessment of Young Sexual Abusers

Dr Eileen Vizard

Introduction

Public and professional awareness during the last decade in the UK has certainly moved on in relation to work with children who sexually abuse other children. It is now possible for a limited public debate to occur about the nature of sexually coercive or abusive behaviour by children, although this debate may still carry rather hysterical overtones (Birkett 2000; Vizard 2000). It is important to remember that ten years ago, the possibility that children might be perpetrators was not considered by a media preoccupied with the aftermath of the Cleveland Inquiry and the unsettling emergence of adult sex offenders into the public consciousness.

This chapter will consider definitional issues, relevant findings from the research and evidence based clinical literature, will describe a systemic context for assessment of young sexual abusers including steps towards assessment and liaison issues. The rationale for a preliminary professionals meeting will be covered and a suggested approach to the assessment of children and young people will be given. Practice issues including interview techniques, producing a comprehensive report and working in multidisciplinary teams will also be described. The summary will highlight the main issues covered and will suggest areas for future research and clinical development.

The model of clinical practice with children and young people who sexually abuse which is described in this chapter is based on 10 years work with this client group, drawn from a national catchment in the UK and seen in a specialist forensic outpatient team based in a large community trust in London and managed by NSPCC. Over 300 cases have been seen in the Young Abusers Project and research into the characteristics of these children and follow up of their later progress is under way. The assessment approach described is therefore evidence based and rooted in child protection practice.

Definitional issues

A major problem in identifying this group of children has been the lack of definitional agreement about how to describe sexually

aggressive and sexually abusive behaviour in childhood (Hanks, 1997; Vizard, Monck and Misch 1995; Vizard, Wynick, Hawkes, Woods and Jenkins, 1995). This, in turn, has led to confusion and ambivalence about naming the behaviour and referring children and young people on for assessment and treatment services. Even when children and young people are identified as being sexual abusers, few sustained professional efforts are made to halt the escalation of this juvenile behaviour into adult offending patterns. In 1992, the Department of Health's research into available treatment resources noted:

> Because of ignorance and denial of others, many abusing youngsters are not being referred. If they are recognised, some are being referred as victims, with their abusing behaviour being viewed as a symptom of their own abuse. Is it more comfortable to refer a victim than an abuser?
>
> (p5)

However, since the early 1990s in the UK (NCH, 1992) and rather earlier in the USA (Davis and Leitenberg, 1987; Johnson, 1988), the existence of a group of sexually predatory adolescents has been recognised and attempts at defining the behaviour of these children have been made (Calder, 1997, 2001; Vizard et al. 1995). Furthermore, in the last 10 years, progress has been made in establishing a network of projects around the UK which offer assessment and treatment services for sexually aggressive and sexually abusive children and young people. Whilst many of these new services are run by NSPCC and other voluntary societies, some are linked to the NHS and to other agencies dealing with children including the new YOTs (Youth Offending Teams). Within the Young Abusers Project in London, the average age at referral has dropped from 17 years old in 1992 (when the Project started) to 12 years old in 2000, thus indicating that some referrers at least are aware of the need to refer cases earlier.

Despite this progress, there is persisting reluctance by some referrers to refer children and adolescents who sexually abuse for assessment and treatment. Indeed, some of the UK local authorities with whom the Young

Abusers Project deals are still able to maintain that, fortunately, they do not really have many cases in their particular area. One reason for the reluctance to refer young sexualised children for assessment may relate to professionals' fear of 'labelling' sexually aggressive children and adolescents (Araji, 1997; Department of Health, 1992; Vizard et al., 1996) and see discussion below. However, it is evident from discussion with referring colleagues that the resistance to referral also links quite directly with anxiety about how to manage the problem locally when abusive behaviour has been confirmed by a specialist assessment. Major issues including the funding of treatment by other agencies, the funding of specialist foster placements and therapeutic placements, the management of sexually aggressive behaviour in various contexts and the legally charged issue of parental responsibility for the child or young person with this problem, all combine to persuade local authorities to try to contain the escalating behaviour locally to save money and to avoid the financial and legal consequences of referral.

In relation to labelling as a factor in resistance to referral, it has been noted (Calder, 1997; Vizard et al., 1996) that a considerable number of descriptive labels have been given to sexually abusive children including sexually aggressive children, abuse-reactive children, sexual perpetrators, oversexualised children, sexually coercive children, sexual abusers and sexual offenders. Virtually all of these terms may be criticised on some basis or other, particularly when the attempt is to describe inappropriate, oversexualised or sexually coercive behaviour in very early childhood. The term 'young abuser' does at least spell out the specific professional concern about known sexually abusive behaviour, usually (but not always) in pre-pubescent or adolescent children and young people. For younger children under 10 years old, for instance, 'sexually aggressive' or 'sexually coercive' may be appropriate when their behaviour clearly involves repetitive sexual contacts with other children or adults. 'Oversexualised' may be an appropriate term for children of any age whose behaviour is compulsively sexualised, extends over a number of contexts and does not respond to ordinary social sanctions.

It should also be pointed out that in England, where the age of criminal responsibility is 10 years old, the term 'offender' does not have relevance for sexually abusive children under 10 years old who cannot be charged with a criminal offence.

It remains the case that children and adolescents under the age of 16 years old cannot be given a psychiatric diagnosis of paedophilia within ICD 10 or DSM IV classification systems since it is assumed that 'paedophile' interest in other children simply does not occur before that age. This assumption is not in line with existing criminal statistics (see Home Office, 1998) on sexual offending against children by juveniles nor is it in line with clinical experience in the Young Abusers Project with sexually abusive children under 10 years old, some of whom already fulfill several of the clinical criteria for adult paedophilia. From the perspective of psychiatric diagnosis the lack of an accepted classification system is unacceptable and the possibility of a new diagnostic category such as 'sexual arousal disorder of childhood' or sexual behaviour disorder of childhood or something along these lines has been put forward for discussion (Vizard et al., 1996).

The debate on how to describe sexually abusive children is not helped by the dearth of comparative data available on 'normal' sexuality in childhood, a subject which remains controversial and subject to various religious and cultural interpretations. Normal childhood sexuality is virtually impossible to research (Vizard et al., 1995) since there would be serious ethical implications involved in, for instance, testing reactions of normal children to sexually explicit material or allowing children to be involved in sexual behaviours which might be considered abusive, for the purposes of research observation. However, Hank's discussion of normal sexual behaviour in childhood, tabulated by age and developmental status is extremely helpful to clinicians working with sexualised young children where a key question is often 'Is this abuse or is it 'normal' childhood experimentation?' (Hanks, 1997, 2001).

Whilst it is absolutely correct that very young oversexualised children must not be needlessly 'labelled' as abusers it is still not clear what proportion of persistently sexualised children who do not receive an early assessment or treatment service will later go on to abuse. The descriptive data emerging from the Young Abusers Project (Vizard, 2001) strongly suggests that it is the presence or absence of an effective, co-ordinated agency response to oversexualised behaviour in childhood, which is likely to prevent or allow the later development of abusive behaviour patterns. For instance, perusal of the case records of children whose early oversexualised behaviour was ignored by professionals shows that this behaviour escalates over succeeding years and contributes to the worsening of existing psychiatric disorders in adolescence. In contrast, Toni Cavanagh Johnson (1988) and others working with very young oversexualised children suggest a much more hopeful outcome for such children when preventative programmes can be accessed early. Cavanagh Johnson's 1993 work attempts to demolish the myth that all oversexualised children are likely to become abusers and offers clear guidance on methods of working preventatively with very young children. However, it is still the case in the UK that many such young oversexualised children are not getting an assessment or treatment service, and are being left until their behaviour becomes too serious to ignore. There is then an urgency in relation to intervention with pre-pubescent and adolescent sexual abusers since time is literally running out for them and social exclusion, school based problems, learning disability and psychiatric disorders are all likely to worsen with the persistence of the sexually abusive behaviour.

Evidence based assessment work

One difficulty in evaluating the efficacy of many treatment intervention schemes for young sexual abusers is the wide range of theoretical models used by professionals to understand the problem and to devise treatment approaches. This wide variation in the range of theoretical models is linked to a rather limited treatment outcome literature for juvenile sexual abusers regardless of theoretical approach (Barbaree, 1993; Vizard et al., 1995). In 1991 Gail Ryan described a range of 'theories of etiology' in relation to juvenile sexual offending and these included psychosis theory, physiological theory, intrapsychic theory, learning theory, developmental theory, cognitive theory, addictive theory, family systems theory and integrative theories. Hawkes, Jenkins and Vizard, 1997, described the 'Integrated Perspectives Theory' in which a range of theoretical approaches were conceptually integrated and represented diagrammatically. More recently, Epps (1999) has provided a helpful meta-analysis of the range of theoretical

approaches drawn on in relation to work with young sexual abusers. Earlier research (National Children's Homes, 1992) looking at the range of then available treatment facilities, concluded that there was a wide variation in the type of treatment interventions being offered and that there was patchy understanding by practitioners of the real differences between the theoretical approaches which they claimed were being offered.

Practitioners working with more seriously disturbed adolescent abusers and also with much younger children have long advocated a more integrated, multifactorial theoretical approach to the work (Araji, 1986; Hawkes, Jenkins and Vizard, 1997) to ensure that all levels of sociological, systemic, dynamic, neurobiological and cognitive complexity can be addressed. However, this conceptual approach is far from simple and demands much in training of practitioners, supervision and perhaps some form of accreditation (see Hawkes in Chapter 8) for professionals to work well within such a framework.

An example of this sort of 'joined up' integrated thinking can be found in the Integrated Abuse Cycle (IAC), (Vizard et al., 1996), the use of which in assessment is described later. The IAC draws on published and well respected cognitive models such as the original sexual abuse cycle devised by Sandy Lane and colleagues in 1978 in the Closed Adolescent Treatment Centre (CATC) of the Division of Youth Services in Colorado and subsequently published (Lane and Zamora, 1984).

An orderly and structured approach to the assessment of juvenile sex offenders is favoured by most authorities working in this field (Calder, 1997, 2001; Gray and Wallace, 1992; O'Callaghan and Print, 1994; Steen and Monnette, 1989; Vizard, 1996; Will, 1999). Gray's 1992 Adolescent Sexual Offender Assessment Packet is prescriptive with clear lists of Dos and Don'ts in relation to interview technique with high risk youth. This approach to assessment is refreshingly forthright and has a clear forensic structure which may make it very appropriate for interviews with young people facing criminal charges. Gray describes an interview technique in which interviewer control of 'antisocial clients, adolescent sexual offenders, aggressive and passive-aggressive clients, clients who frequently lie and exploit and juvenile firesetters'. (p7) is harnessed to a very clear focus on the assessment issues and where the interviewer ensures that client distraction strategies, denial etc., do not result in the focus being lost. O'Callaghan and Print (1994) write from the perspective of one of the most experienced teams in the UK (G-Map) dealing with young sexual abusers. Their experience confirms the need for a thought out structured approach to assessment of this client group. Will (1999) also describes a structured approach to assessment of juvenile sex offenders. In his approach, the importance of 'establishing a common language for sexual organs and functions' (p92) and using this common language to establish the young person's masturbatory patterns before moving on to the exploration of any sexually abusive behaviour, is stressed. His assessment model also underlines the importance of an assessment of the child or young person in the context of his family or carers. Calder (1997 and 2001) reviews in detail the range of currently available structured approaches to assessment with this client group.

Systemic context for assessment

A child protection context at all times

Since the victims of juvenile sexual abusers are all children, it is essential that there is a full child protection response to any allegations or disclosures of abuse by children. This means that there should be a case conference on the abusive child as a known or alleged perpetrator of abuse and that the behaviour should not just be processed as if the child is a sexualised victim. Government guidance (Department of Health, 1999) is clear about the need to case conference abusive children as perpetrators when these children are 'considered personally to be at risk of continuing significant harm'. In those cases where it is agreed that there is no need for a conference a multiagency approach is recommended (Department of Health, 1999) to deal with the complex needs of the young abuser. Three key principles which should guide work with children and young people who abuse others are listed (Department of Health, 1999) as follows:

- 'There should be a co-ordinated approach on the part of youth justice, child welfare, education (including educational psychology) and health (including child and adolescent mental health) agencies.

- The needs of children and young people who abuse others should be considered separately from the needs of their victims.
- An assessment should be carried out in each case, appreciating that these children may have considerable unmet developmental needs, as well as specific needs arising from their behaviour.'

However, in practice, local professionals are often reluctant to take these steps. Local colleagues who have views about 'labelling' children and young people as sexual abusers may also be reluctant to offer support for any long term treatment and therefore all local colleagues need to be actively recruited into supporting any such interventions.

Ethical issues

Ethical issues arise in the general professional resistance to any form of assessment resulting in a clear formulation of the child or young person's mental state, level of risk to others or level of learning disability, if present. Is it ethical, for instance, not to allow a child or young person to undergo psychological testing on the grounds that it is 'stigmatising' subsequently to be 'labelled' as learning disabled? A contrary position would be that it is unethical to deprive the learning disabled child or client of an assessment opportunity which can identify special needs for which particular help should be given. In a similar way, some workers may fear and resist the referral to psychiatrists on the basis that they do not want the young sexual abuser or oversexualised child 'labelled' as mentally ill or disturbed. However, the other side of this argument is that failure to allow the child or young person the chance to see a psychiatrist will deprive that child of the chance to have psychiatric disorders diagnosed, treatment given and, possibly, the chance to seek compensation in the courts for any such disorders, which have failed to be recognised or treated.

Finally, the Human Rights of children who are also defendants in the criminal courts must also be remembered. Unless psychiatric and psychological assessments can be undertaken on young children facing charges of serious sexual offences in court, it will not be possible to ascertain whether or not the child is fit to plead to the charges and to stand trial in the first place. Without such assessments of his fitness to plead, the child or young person may very well wish to seek legal redress later under the Human Rights Act on the basis that his human right to participate fully in a fair trial was infringed.

It is clearly vital that work with children and young people who sexually abuse, is not undertaken in isolation from other agencies or from other workers and that communication is excellent. However, the lack of a centralised co-ordinated approach to the development of this work in the UK has meant that independent projects, clinicians and trainers working on their own without supervision or accreditation are not unusual. Referrers are often so desperate for a sexually abusive child or young person to be seen that an 'anything is better than nothing' approach may prevail and the child may be sent to the next name on the list for assessment or treatment.

However, referrers should remember that assessment and treatment projects offering single aspects of work with offenders such as 'risk assessment', 'relapse prevention' modules or 'victim empathy' modules without the active involvement of the local authority and preferably a named, allocated local authority social worker, are undertaking dangerous practice outside a proper child protection context. 'Going it alone', without the local authority, in work with juvenile sexual offenders, (no matter how young the child or experienced the worker) is not a safe option. Careful preparatory work with all members of the professional network is necessary before any assessment or treatment is offered to ensure support of local colleagues when further disclosures of abusing behaviour emerge or when re-offending occurs. Confidentiality should be on a 'need to know' basis (Vizard, 1995). At the beginning of treatment, it should be made clear to the young sexual offender that all disclosures of abuse or reports of approaches to victims etc., will be shared with the local authority and that no secrets will be kept by the specialist team.

Interagency and multidisciplinary work

Since sexually abusive children and young people have needs which cross many agency boundaries, it is clearly essential that all relevant agencies are kept involved throughout the assessment process. Calder (1999) has set out clearly both the case for working together and the barriers which may prevent this desired outcome. However, this is easier said than done and Calder (1999) has reviewed the contributions of a number of authors who have looked at the many reasons why interagency and multidisciplinary work does not often seem to work in practice. Very familiar themes emerge from Calder's (1999) review of these difficulties and issues, such as differences in background and training, status and power, different perspectives, lines of authority and decision making and communication to name a few. Many of these barriers to effective communication are identical to those pinpointed in one child abuse inquiry after another over the last twenty years or so (Reder and Duncan, 1999) and raise the, almost heretical, question in child protection practice about whether or not such interagency collaboration is actually possible.

In the Young Abusers Project one of the recurring difficulties in managing the work has been the resistance of referring professionals to continue to take case responsibility once the referral has been made. This resistance is one reason for the development of the approach described below since the fullest possible interagency collaboration is needed, in practice, to ensure that anxious, angry, denying and perhaps very disturbed young people are actually brought to the Project for assessment. However, there are sometimes much more serious consequences when further abusive or violent behaviour occurs (as it is bound to do with such a client group) and when there is then an agency rush to distance themselves from this behaviour and to find someone else within the network to carry the can. These situations can resemble a sort of professional 'pass the parcel' and in this context, the newly arrived specialist team may well find itself 'to blame' because they happened to be holding the baby at that particular point in time i.e. an assessment had just been arranged or had just occurred. Calder (1999) has pointed out some of these dynamics when he said:

> ... whilst there is an expectation of collective responsibility, the reality is that social services have the lead responsibility and any offers of help will be gratefully received. Yet unless this is agreed and understood formally and locally, a culture of blame will prevail.

Calder goes on to point out that child protection work is 'dirty work' and that this can lead to social workers redefining their roles such that they are enabled to 'ditch the dirty work on to the others'. However, in reality, professionals from all disciplines dealing with cases of sexually abusive children and young people are only too anxious to off load or close the cases or to find someone else to share the often overwhelming feelings of anxiety engendered by such cases.

How then, does the professional engaging with this work deal with and navigate these dynamics, retain a working relationship with colleagues and still manage to deliver a service to this very challenging client group?

Firstly, it is vital that the role of the professional network is acknowledged as being pivotal to the success or otherwise of any intervention within the system, particularly that of the specialist assessment team. Before any appointments for clients are made, before any decision is made about inclusion in treatment groups or in individual therapy sessions, the ground rules for the whole assessment engagement need to be agreed, and confirmed in writing, with the professional network. If this is not done, all the potentially destructive dynamics mentioned above are very likely to swing into action as soon as the first appointment letter is sent. In contrast, when a truly collaborative professional system is established around the referred child, it is often surprising how much constructive work can be done to arrange meetings, provide services, facilitate placements etc., when an atmosphere of goodwill prevails.

Secondly, an orderly approach to assessment is absolutely essential if the wide range of issues which need to be addressed are to be covered in a coherent manner. However, cases are often referred from systems which are, or appear to be, in a degree of panic or chaos with high anxiety levels, e.g. 'His placement is breaking down again, we need an assessment now to advise us where he should go next . . .' Such high levels of anxiety in the referrer can make it difficult for the specialist team to function well under stress. Therefore, it may be helpful to think about organising the external and internal systems with which we have to work such that chaos is minimised. Listed below are certain issues which need to be organised before the assessment can start.

Organising from chaotic systems

External Agency Systems:

- Absolutely solid child protection framework, i.e. an allocated social worker.
- Reject unsuitable cases or offer consultation.
- Address unrealistic expectations of assessment at outset.
- Preliminary professionals meeting.
- Invite decision makers and practitioners from each agency.
- Extensive information gathering from all agencies.
- Clear professional boundaries within and between agencies.
- Confirm agency carrying case responsibility.
- Confirm limits of team involvement (assessment only, long term work) at outset of referral. Offer follow up appointments or consultation whenever possible.
- Seek feedback from children and young people on contact with service.

Internal Team Systems:

- Very careful record keeping including notes of phone calls etc.
- Clearly written letters, reports and recommendations.
- Audit failed referrals to improve practice.
- Agreed model of team work based on evidence from practice.
- Mandatory debrief of team after each assessment and treatment session.
- Live supervision of assessment interviews and group work.
- External team consultant.
- Mutual support and mutual criticism but not blame culture.
- Awareness of 'Zone of Safety'/professional behaviour issues.
- Personal reflection about impact of work with abusers.

Finally, it should be remembered that, whatever the outcome of the assessment of sexually abusive behaviour, these findings are only one part of a complex professional system in which the assessments, opinions and reports of many others also play a vital part. This is an important consideration when the child or young person is caught up in legal proceedings, Children Act 1989 or criminal proceedings, since instructing solicitors are often prone to 'hype up' the value and relevance of any expert reports arising from the assessment as if the whole case may be decided somehow on the basis of the team's report. This is seldom the case, even in criminal proceedings when reports from other agencies such as the YOTs and probation will also be taken into account.

Steps towards assessment

1. Is this an appropriate referral?

Obvious as it may seem, not all cases referred are suitable for assessment and unsuitable cases need to be identified at the earliest opportunity to avoid wasting everyone's time. Often cases which are unsuitable (at this point) for direct assessment of the child or young person are in urgent need of consultation on case management. In such situations, preliminary consultation about the priorities for case management may be needed to inform the care plan for the child or young person and assessment should follow consultation.

2. The referral letter or letter of instruction

No child's case should be taken on, let alone seen at interview, without a clearly laid out referral letter from a local authority, health colleague or other professional referrer or a letter of instruction from a solicitor.

A referral letter should contain summary details about the present and past behaviour, an outline of relevant family history, a statement about why the assessment is required now (i.e. worries about mental state, placement, treatment needs etc.), the professional disciplines needed in the assessment, time scale for the report and an undertaking to pay fees (in income generating teams).

The general outline for a letter of instruction in the Children Act 1989, proceedings from a solicitor to an expert (of any discipline), is laid out in the Expert Witness Pack (Vizard and Harris, 1997). This is a simple, common sense format (Vizard, 1997), which can be applied perfectly well to a letter of instructions from defence solicitors in relation to a child or young person facing criminal charges on whom a report is requested. A prompt, written reply to the referral letter or letter of instruction is important to start communication rolling for the new case and also to put on record any reservations or queries about the assessment issues.

3. Consultation as an alternative or precursor to assessment

As mentioned in 1. opposite, direct assessment of the child may not be desirable or possible at the point of referral. For instance, it may emerge that seriously unethical practice is occurring with a convicted adolescent sexual abuser living in the same house as his victim or other vulnerable children. Alternatively, a referral may arrive from a health or other agency where no notification of the local authority about sexually abusive behaviour by a young person has occurred and where child protection procedures have not been followed. In these and other inappropriate situations, consultation is likely to be the best way forward. However, a word of warning (or two) about consultation! It is vital that all relevant agencies and players in the professional network are invited to attend and that they do confirm attendance at the meeting. Almost inevitably, comments will be made about third parties (i.e. the child protection practice of absent agencies) in consultation or professionals meetings. Therefore, agreement should be reached at the outset about how the meeting will be minuted and copies should be sent to absent agencies. It is also important that all present at the consultation meeting understand that case responsibility stays with the referrer and is not taken on by the agency offering consultation. Given the possibility of recidivism by this client group, issues of agency responsibility need to be clarified at the outset and experience suggests that, perhaps paradoxically, anxiety levels drop among referrers and other agencies when this is done. A concise and clear summary or report from the consultation should be made available to all who were invited to the meeting.

4. Clarifying the legal context

Ideally, the referral letter or letter of instruction should lay out the legal context clearly so that this information is available before starting the preliminary professionals meeting. However, sometimes only a partial account of the legal status of the child or young person will be given in the referral letter and further details should be urgently sought. There are several reasons for needing clarity on this issue which are laid out below:

- Parental responsibility needs to be clarified: which adult or agency will give consent (see below) for the assessment which will ask probing personal questions of the child or young person.
- Are Children Act 1989 proceedings under way in relation to the referred case or a sibling? If so, will the assessment report be used subsequently in these proceedings? If this has not been hitherto considered, the team should ask the referrer for clarification and for any further instructions about issues to be assessed, i.e. contact, placement etc.
- If Children Act '89 proceedings are under way, establish in writing from the instructing solicitor whether a 'finding of fact' in relation to sexual abuse is expected to be made by the Judge during the proceedings. If this is to occur, establish in writing about whom the finding of fact will be made, i.e. will it be a finding of fact that an adult or older child has abused the referred child or will it be a finding of fact that the referred sexualised/abusive child himself has abused another child. This information may be crucial in your decision about whether or not to accept the case before the care proceedings are completed and any judicial fact finding process has occurred. Failure to clarify this issue could lead to criticism of your teams' involvement in the case if you have proceeded to ask questions about possible abuse history and or abusive behaviour when these are the issues under consideration by the court.
- Unfortunately, requests for assessment of over sexualised behaviour and outright abusive behaviour are often made (appropriately) by referrers to help decide whether or not to proceed with legal action. Hence refusal to get involved in risk assessments for the reasons mentioned above, will need to be explained to local agencies who may, rightly, feel that there is a rather vicious circle emerging where assessment of the sexualised behaviour as a possible ground for the care proceeding cannot proceed until the Judge has first established if it has occurred.
- It seems that the established practice of making judicial findings of fact in relation to adult abusers of children who are the subject of care proceedings, has been adopted without particular reflection in relation to the recently recognised category of sexualised or abusive children who are themselves also the subject of care proceedings. At an early stage, before court proceedings, the question should be asked by the professionals concerned as to whether such a judicial fact finding exercise will actually assist the care planning for the child? Experience suggests that a negative finding of fact (no abuse victimisation or abusing behaviour occurred) will make any subsequent therapeutic work on these topics impossible. A positive finding of fact (abuse victimisation or abusing behaviour did occur) also brings with it undesirable elements of 'labelling' of the child as a victim or someone whom a court has 'found' to have committed abuse. Matters become much more complex with young sexualised children who are abused, sexually coercive but not quite in the sexually abusive category – one might ask what is the point of a fact finding exercise with these children when the very nature of their behaviour and the terms used to describe it are so unclear? It may be that a care order can be made more appropriately on other grounds in relation to significant harm so that subsequent assessment and treatment of these sexually abusive children is not jeopardised. Wider discussion of the judicial decision making process in relation to care cases involving sexually coercive or sexually abusive children would be clearly be useful for practitioners working with this client group. In the meanwhile, practitioners are advised to exercise caution when taking on cases of sexually abusive children involved in care proceedings.
- Is the child or young person facing criminal proceedings? If so, what is the purpose of the present report? Will the assessment report be used subsequently to inform sentencing and advise on disposal post court?
- Furthermore, in young children and in those where learning disability is known or suspected, has the question of assessing the child's fitness to plead to the charges been considered? If not, this issue needs to be discussed at the professionals meeting and arrangements made for a psychological assessment to test cognitive functioning.

Furthermore, subsequent specialist assessment of the child or young person should address the question of the extent to which he can understand the charges against him, instruct a defence solicitor and participate fully in the trial process (see *Ethical issues*). There are serious human rights issues involved here and workers should be aware of the implications of the Human Rights Act 2000 following the European Court Judgement involving Thompson and Venables (T. vs the UK; V. vs the UK 1999; Ashford, 2000).

Finally, if facing criminal proceedings and attending for an assessment interview, will the child or young person's solicitor be advising a 'no comment' interview for fear of jeopardising the trial? If so, preliminary discussion should occur with the defence solicitor to ensure that his client is made aware that the interview is an opportunity to determine whether or not he has problems requiring professional help, to assess his likely response to treatment and to suggest disposals to the court and that such an interview will be found most helpful to the court. Such discussions are usually effective in ensuring that the child or young person arrives ready to talk in the assessment.

5. Consent to assessment

- Informed consent to the interview itself needs to be obtained in every case and should include the signature of the parents or agency representative with parental responsibility.
- Where a child is under a full care order to a local authority, written consent to the assessment needs to be obtained from the allocated social worker and also from the parents if possible.
- When children or young people are at a sufficient age and level of understanding to give informed consent to the interview process, this consent should be sought.
- Accommodated children where parents are working in partnership with the local authority, will need the fully informed consent of their parents as well as a signature on the consent form from the allocated social worker.
- Other types of consent include:
  —Video consent forms for video recording of the assessment interview.
  —Research consent forms for the use of any client data in research.

Whatever the nature of the consent form, the need for signed, informed consent should be highlighted in the service's information pack and arrangements for signature should be finalised during the professionals meeting.

No assessment interview, with or without video recording, should take place without the informed consent of those with parental responsibility for the child or young person.

6. Issues to be assessed

As mentioned in 2. above, the referral letter or letter of instruction should clearly lay out all the issues which require assessment. If this is not the case, the worker managing the case needs to speak urgently to the author of the letter and ensure that another letter is sent with the relevant information. Starting the assessment process without the clearest possible idea of what to assess is asking for trouble and is likely to lead to subsequent challenge of any report produced. It is very poor practice, for instance, with cases involving known or alleged sexually abusive behaviour, to enter the assessment room with only a vague idea of what to ask, or perhaps in the hope of 'something' emerging somehow. An organised interview format (see below) is essential but a clear list of agreed assessment issues is also a pre-requisite for effective work.

7. Role of the referrer in the assessment process

It seems to be a fact of life in unpopular cases, such as children and young people who sexually abuse, that referrers will often attempt to 'dump and run', i.e. offload the case onto the specialist agency. This may be understandable but it is pointless in the long run since the case responsibility lies with the referrer. A key element of the systemic approach to assessment is the active involvement of the referrer in the whole process including his or her presence in the interview room (see below) to explain the reasons for the referral.

Firstly, the presence of the referrer in the early part of the assessment gives a clear mandate to the assessing team to ask questions and have discussions with the child or young person about the worrying issues which the referrer described in simple terms at the outset of the meeting.

Secondly, the physical presence of the referrer in the interview room gives a clear signal to the child or young person that this is the individual (and agency) with continuing responsibility for him or her and not the interviewers. The issue of who takes legal responsibility for the actions of the child or young person is likely to feature strongly in the subsequent assessment discussions about responsibility for offending behaviour etc., and the referrer's presence in many ways helps to spell out that containment of offending behaviour is now going to occur and that responsibility for such actions needs to be taken by both the child and the adult referrer.

Thirdly, the referrer can and should be a strong supporter of any further assessment and treatment interventions to be undertaken by the specialist team. Such strong support is much more likely to occur, so clinical experience suggests, if the referrer has been physically involved in the assessment and can remember the verbal and non-verbal reactions of the child or young person to the questions and discussion which occurred. In other words, if the referrer is actively engaged in the process of assessment, it is much more likely that he or she will make subsequent enthusiastic efforts to support treatment.

8. Preparing the child or young person for assessment

It is clearly vital that the child or young person who is going to be seen is prepared for the assessment in advance by a professional who is able to explain the reasons for the assessment and the likely format and content of the interview. Advice on how to set the scene for the interview with the young person himself is given by Morrison and Print (1995), who favour an open approach in which it is made clear that the interviewers will not be shocked and it is the behaviour which is wrong, not the person. Gray's 1992 forthright advice for interviewers dealing with high risk youth is also relevant in helping key workers to convey something to the child or young person of the tone of the subsequent assessment. The tone conveyed should be brisk, matter of fact, kind but definitely not cloyingly sympathetic and above all, professional. Key workers living closely with such children pre-assessment may become understandably involved with the victimised and deprived aspects of these clients and it may be important to underline the assessment focus on offending behaviour and the need for an objective stance at all times.

The young person needs to be told the following things:

- The length of the interview, toilet arrangements, breaks to be taken etc.

- Ground rules for the assessment, e.g. smoking allowed or not, express angry or distressed feelings in words but no physical violence, throwing of objects or carrying weapons into the interview room. It should be made clear that the young person should not have been drinking or taking drugs immediately before the assessment.
- The range of questions to be asked during the assessment. It should be explained that questions will be asked covering all of the young person's life, e.g. physical and mental health, school or employment, leisure time activities, friends and family background including any issues of own abuse in childhood etc., as well as specific questions about the sexually abusive behaviour.
- The young person should be told that they will be spoken to in clear, simple language in relation to sexually abusive matters and that clear, honest responses will be expected.
- It should be explained that the young person can interrupt or challenge the interviewers or referrer at any time should they not understand what has been said or should they not agree with statements made.
- It should be made clear that the assessing team have established anti-discriminatory practices and that issues of ethnicity, culture and sexual orientation will be dealt with sensitively.
- Should the young person be from an ethnic minority group and require a translator, this should be arranged in advance. Selection of translator's who are able to retain objectivity whilst translating highly emotive, offence specific material from a child or young person from within their own culture, is a sensitive but important issue.
- The translator should also be prepared in advance and their role spelled out before arrival at the interview premises. Training and support of such translators is an issue which should be addressed separately from the current assessment.
- The young person should be told, in advance, that they may have a variety of reactions to the questions asked, ranging from anger and distress to boredom and even relief that issues have been broached.
- It should be made clear to the young person, in advance, who will be the responsible adult to whom they can talk and debrief after the assessment.

- It should be explained in advance whether or not it is possible that the young person will see the interviewers or their colleagues again for more assessment or treatment after the assessment.
- The young person should be told that there will be a report produced with the findings and opinion of the assessing team and that they will be told the contents of the report in due course.
- If the young person is of sufficient age and emotional maturity to read the report then a careful arrangement for this should be made by the allocated social worker so that explanation and support is available for the young person. This issue requires very careful consideration since the content of such assessment reports may be both sexually explicit and, in terms of any predictions for the young person's future, may be negative or at least worrying. The possibility that an already vulnerable young person might experience significant harm on reading such a report unsupported needs to be borne in mind.
- Without anticipating the content of the assessment interview, some preliminary discussion with the young person about the pros and cons of possible therapy would be helpful and would set the scene for this issue to be raised in the interview.

9. Being prepared to deal with distressed, angry or violent behaviour

In a minority of children and young people referred for assessment, there may be a known history of extremely distressed responses to interviews with professionals or there may be a track record of angry, aggressive or violent outbursts in discussions with staff or other adults. Some of the more seriously conduct disordered children or young people may be known to carry weapons or may have injured or attacked another person with a weapon.

In all these cases, the most careful, preliminary discussion with the referrer and key workers will be essential. The ground rules for the assessment (see above) should be spelled out and conveyed in advance to the young person who should be told that the interview will terminate if the ground rules are infringed. When necessary, arrangements should be made for additional escorts to accompany the child or young person to the interview and to sit outside the room.

In the case of children or young people being brought for assessment on remand from a secure setting or from a prison setting, it may be necessary, for instance, to negotiate with the accompanying prison officers about taking off any handcuffs and whether or not the officers would be prepared to sit in the video viewing room rather than in the interview room, etc. Such negotiations should be undertaken in advance with the secure unit or the prison, if possible. Concerns about possible violent outbursts should be discussed and arrangements agreed as to who will deal with which aspects of the violent behaviour should it occur on the assessment day. Reception staff in the assessment premises should be informed that there may be a risk of angry or violent behaviour during the session.

Generally speaking, it is sensible to arrange the seating in the interview room so that the potentially violent young person is nearest to the door with a clear route of angry exit. This avoids any untoward stumbling over the interviewers' chairs, tables etc. to escape, since this will only increase the level of anger being expressed. Through prior arrangement (see above) there should be an escort waiting outside the interview door, ready to take containing and calming measures when needed. If it is not possible to recommence the interview, the escorts may need to take the young person from the premises and back to the placement.

If the young person is able to calm down and return to the interview he should be congratulated briefly on regaining control and should be told firmly that this sort of behaviour will not be tolerated and that the interview will terminate the next time it occurs. The interviewers should then move on briskly to the next issue for discussion.

In the case of very young agitated and aggressive children under 10 years old, say, the procedure should focus on keeping the child contained within the interview room rather than allowing an angry small child to charge out of the room and up and down corridors in an uncontained way etc. However, basic ground rules still apply and if the child's behaviour is not containable, then the interview should be stopped but the child should be told that another assessment will be arranged when it is hoped that they can stay calmer.

Overall Structure of Assessment of Young Sexual Abusers (Vizard et al., 1996)

1. The professionals meeting
2. The assessment interview
3. The psychological assessment
4. The comprehensive report

1. The professionals meeting

Since there is usually a great deal of information to be processed during time limited professionals meetings, an organised approach is most helpful. The following issues need to be addressed during the meeting:

- **Getting organised beforehand.** Before the meeting starts, the team members should agree who will take notes, who will chair and who will do any subsequent summary letters or reports. Coffee, tea etc. should be provided as a matter of courtesy and to encourage a sense that colleagues are welcome. Comfortable chairs should be provided since the meeting may last a couple of hours. Equipment needed for the meeting includes a flip chart or board and a selection of coloured pens, all of which should be laid out in advance.
- **Introductions.** The chair should ensure that introductions are made and names recorded in the team notes. This may seem absurd to state, but such are the high levels of anxiety around certain cases that colleagues may well launch into discussion before sitting down and some 20 minutes later, it may be remembered that several people have not met before and that the agencies represented are not yet known. It is usually helpful to circulate a sheet of paper asking for names, titles, agencies and phone numbers.
- **Explain format for meeting.** The chair should explain the format for the meeting and should explain that many queries will arise about family background, health etc., which will need subsequent liaison. The chair should emphasise that the meeting is also intended to encourage active collaboration and support for the assessment and treatment process and that it is not just an information gathering exercise. At the outset, the chair should try to engender a sense of hope that something positive can be done about the case, even if this initially only involves producing an excellent report with recommendations. The

chair should move on firmly to the next stage in the professionals meeting.
- **List of Current Concerns.** The chair should now enlist the help of colleagues to write up on a flip chart or board a list of the main current concerns which have brought professionals to today's meeting. It should be made clear that, at this point in the meeting, descriptions of the work which individuals are doing with the child or young person are not required but merely an 'off the top of the head' list of the most worrying issues facing each professional in relation to the child or young person concerned. The chair will then write up these concerns as they arise and will try to complete this task within about 20 minutes from the beginning of the meeting. The list will usually contain worries such as:
—Concerned that X will re-abuse and be sent to prison.
—Concerned that X may have serious emotional problems.
—Concerned that there are no suitable placements for X left, etc.
Often such a professionals meeting will generate between 10 and 20 pressing professional concerns which may not all be outlined in the referral letter. It is essential that the legal context (or lack of it) and the care plan are added to this list. If no-one else expresses any concern about these issues the chair and team colleague should write them up for discussion. The chair should very briefly re-cap on these written concerns and note that they will be re-visited at the end of the meeting. It is usually noticeable that the level of anxiety in the room has diminished by the time everyone has contributed to the list. However, the chair needs to be aware that this may well change as the meeting progresses and patterns of worrying behaviour begin to emerge.
- **Construct a Family Tree or Genogram.** This exercise needs to be done as collaboratively as possible with the chair asking for information about the family from each of the agencies represented at the meeting. Even if pre-existing family trees are brought the chair should not simply copy these onto the flip chart since the whole idea is to create a picture of the family afresh, as a group task. It should be pointed out that there will be many gaps at the end of the genogram exercise but colleagues will subsequently be

asked to send in missing information to complete the picture before the assessment. The chair should now start to draw the family tree or genogram from the centre of the flip chart or board, making sure that all core family, extended family members, family friends and all relevant professional agencies are included. Once individuals and agencies are on the flip chart, the chair should start to mark coloured lines on to the genogram to indicate known or suspected child sexual abuse including schedule one offences against children, physical abuse, domestic violence, convictions for violent offences, psychiatric disturbance, drug and alcohol abuse and other relevant issues. A colour coding system which has been found helpful in the Young Abusers Project is as follows:

—Dotted red line   Suspected child sexual abuse
—Solid red line   Known child sexual abuse
—Dotted green line Suspected psychiatric disorder
—Solid green line   Known psychiatric disorder
—Dotted blue line   Suspected physical violence
—Solid blue line   Known physical violence

The genograms which result from this exercise are usually complex, featuring several families interlinked in patterns of cross generation abuse of one sort or another, with many known and suspected indications of physical and sexual violence and psychiatric disturbance in children and parents. The process of struggling together, as a professional group, to co-ordinate the construction of the genogram is usually very enlightening for all concerned and is an extremely effective way of ensuring that all professionals involved in the case are interested and engaged in producing a positive outcome.

- **Make a summary of emerging themes.** Having completed the genogram, the chair should now attempt a summary of any themes arising from the exercise and should link these, where appropriate, to the list of current concerns created at the beginning of the meeting. For example, does the expressed fear that the referred child might end up in prison have any basis in terms of their past patterns of criminal behaviour? Is

there any relevant family history to explain current abusive behaviour, e.g. histories of child sexual abuse, etc.

- **Review the assessment issues.** At this point, the chair should check whether the issues for assessment have now changed, i.e. is there a serious concern about the child's mental state or capacity to use therapy and if so, should a child psychiatrist or child psychotherapist now be involved? At the same time, the role of other agencies in supporting the referral should be checked through, e.g. is it clear that funding (if appropriate) has been approved and that social work time is indeed free to support the assessment etc. If a new referral letter or letter of instruction is needed, the chair should request that this is sent before the assessment occurs.

- **Practical arrangements for the assessment.** The chair should give the allocated social worker an explanation of the exact sequence of events which will be followed in the assessment interview and if there is any written service information (Vizard et al., 1996) about the process, this can be handed over. It should be explained that the social worker will be asked at the beginning of the interview to make a clear statement about the reasons for bringing the child or young person for assessment, that they will leave the room at the first break and will then observe the interview through the video system. The chair should then go through, in some detail, the issues to be raised with the young person to prepare them for the meeting (see item 8). The need for signed consent forms to be sent to the service well in advance of the assessment to avoid last minute delays on the day should be mentioned. Arrangements for suitable escorts should also be discussed at this point and it should be established with whom the young person can debrief on completion of the interview.

- **Pre and post assessment liaison arrangements**. Although it is assumed that the local authority will take case management responsibility, it is important that this fact is again spelled out before the end of the professionals meeting. If there is a clear legal context, i.e. a care order or pending criminal proceedings, in relation to the child, then lines of communication with a named lawyer should be established. A named liaison person in each of the agencies who attended the meeting should be agreed and copies of any letter or report arising from the professionals meeting should be sent to these people and to any other key professionals who did not attend.

2. The assessment interview

Given the serious child protection concerns in every case of a sexually aggressive or sexually abusive child or young person presenting for assessment, it is strongly recommended that all interviews are live supervised by colleagues from the specialist team, either through an existing video system or through a one way screen.. There is no particular advantage, from the point of view of workers undertaking assessments, in taking a concurrent video of the interview. Concurrent video recording of assessment interviews may be useful in providing a visual record of the proceedings, and some videos may provide valuable training material for colleagues learning about this work.

However, it should be remembered that these video recordings may be brought into subsequent care proceedings and that there is always the danger of any subsequent legal pre-occupation with the content of the video overshadowing the key issue of the professional opinion expressed within the assessment report. There should be an agreed team policy about the issue of video recording, or not, which is made available to referrers and a decision about whether or not to video record the interview should be taken well in advance of the assessment occurring to allow for the consent form to be signed.

The integral role of the allocated social worker in preparing for the assessment is discussed above. However, the social worker is also a key participant in the interview itself and may have a role in providing additional information to the live supervisors and hence to the interviewers via the live supervision process whilst the interview is occurring. This means that the information being discussed with the child or young person is more likely to be accurate, can be challenged for any obvious discrepancies noted on either side of the video system and that the focus of the discussion can be altered depending on information emerging from the social worker or others observing the assessment. The semi-structured approach to this assessment interview is described in

outline elsewhere (Vizard, 1996) and will be described more fully here with bullet points to indicate the main issues.

Stage 1. Clarification and Rapport Building

- Introductions made and format for interview including video, live supervision, breaks, ground rules and ending explained.
- Child or young person encouraged to contribute to discussion and to challenge or ask for clarification.
- Drawing materials or toys on table are indicated and child or young person is encouraged to draw or play as interview progresses.
- Interviewers actively attempt to establish a rapport and engage in eye contact with the child or young person.
- Social worker gives reasons for referral using short, plain words and spelling out exact nature of known or alleged sexually coercive or abusive behaviour.
- Specialist team state nature of their involvement, i.e. to look at strengths and weaknesses, to assess any worrying behaviours and to produce a report. Emphasis on team not being shocked or judgemental about behaviour. Comment about need for child or young person to be as honest as possible.
- Child or young person invited to respond to social worker's concerns.
- Brief discussion of referral concerns between child or young person and team.
- Before the first break, team enquire whether or not child or young person believes that they have a problem and if so, what this is?
- Child or young person stays in room, has a toilet break if necessary, draws or plays with toys or has non assessment related discussion with escort who sits in room.
- Team and social worker leave the room and join live supervision team for discussion.

First Break

Stage 2. Mapping the Abuse: the Fantasies, Strategies and Behaviour

- Team return alone, escort leaves room and discussion resumes with child or young person.
- In order to establish rapport, basic questions about physical health, eating, sleeping etc. are put by one of the team and this leads on to a mental state examination in which any emotional or psychiatric problems are explored.

- Second team member picks up on any trauma related responses which emerge from earlier questions and opens discussion about child or young person's own abuse experiences. Use of drawings or enactment of events with toys or dolls is encouraged and team members may interact with younger children, e.g. using puppets, playing with toys, to encourage communication.
- Working together, team members now move the discussion on from child or young person's own abuse or trauma related issues to abusive specifics such as nature of the sexualised behaviour which is concerning professionals.
- Child or young person is first encouraged to give a verbal description of their sexualised behaviour: what did they do to whom and with what part of their body? Can child or young person say what were the thoughts, sexual and otherwise, in their head at the time of the sexualised behaviour.
- The team may now feel that the child or young person can engage in a dialogue about sexual behaviours, thoughts, feelings, strategies etc. Should this be the case, one of the team will take the lead in constructing an Integrated Abuse Cycle (IAC) (see p191 and Hawkes et al., 1997) on the flip chart with active input from the child or young person. This is a clinical decision and will be strongly affected by the earlier break discussion and by current input from the live supervisor via the ear bug.
- If the child or young person is not able or willing to engage in this level of dialogue, the team may decide to construct a family tree, or genogram, on the flip chart. This exercise is also intended to engage the interest of the child or young person in the hope of sketching out visible patterns of abusing behaviour (with their help) in the family and linking these to the current sexually coercive or abusive behaviour.
- With very young, severely learning disabled or seriously psychiatrically disturbed children or young persons who cannot or will not sit still or construct any sort of dialogue, the team should move on to the use of toys, dolls, puppets, drawings etc., in an effort to allow the child to communicate something of their inner world and anxieties. The team will need to guard against turning this sort of work into a mini therapy session and should be able to revert to verbal discussion of abusive behaviour as soon as possible.

- If the child or young person is totally unwilling to go further in any exercises of this sort, the team need to move on to attempts to construct a verbal narrative around the known or alleged abusive events. If the child or young person shows high levels of denial or resistance to talking, then a range of questioning styles such as circular questioning (see p191) should be used.
- Just before the break, the team should recap with the child or young person on the main issues which have emerged and should check that they agree with the summary. This summary should include a statement of the level of risk which the team and the child or young person now believe is posed to other children. The team should note, but not challenge, any disagreements at this point.
- The child or young person should again be asked if they feel that they have any sort of problem with which they need help and should be encouraged to explain why help is needed, if possible writing down a list of their main problems in order of importance during the next break.
- The team leave the room for the next break and the escort sits with the child or young person.

Second Break

Stage 3. The Future: Placement, Treatment and Personal Change

- The team re-enter the room and discuss any drawings, lists or relevant play sequences which the child or young person may have done in their absence.
- The team acknowledge that the interview is about to end and that a great deal has been discussed today, that the child or young person will or will not be seen again in the service and that some feedback on today's meeting will be given shortly.
- Meanwhile, the team discuss with the child or young person what their views are about relevant placement issues, what, if anything, needs to change in their behaviour and what their view is about any treatment or help for various problems.
- The team members now give a concise summary of their views about the child or young person's strengths and weaknesses, the risk of sexual abuse of others by the child or young person and the need for treatment or other intervention.

- A statement is also made by the team members about the sorts of reactions which other children and young people have had after assessment interviews, including distress, anger and considerable relief. The child or young person is encouraged to write down or draw any issues which were not raised in today's meeting and to give these to the social worker who will pass them on to the team.
- The child or young person is congratulated on having completed the assessment, even if their behaviour was poor or communication was limited.
- Paradoxically, there is often an anxiety laden increase in talk and disclosure from certain children or young people at this end point of the interview. Hence, the team need to handle closure sensitively, with regular references to the time left today and to the support person (earlier identified) with whom they can later talk. At the end of the interview, the child or young person should be in a calm state, if at all possible, and ready to leave.
- Before ending the interview, the team should ask the child or young person to name one good and one bad thing about attending today. Even with the most uncommunicative child or young person, some very telling last minute comments are made such as, good thing; 'Got it off my chest'. Bad thing; 'Getting up early to get here'.
- The child or young person should always be asked to come and meet the live supervising team and inspect the video equipment if they wish.

Interview techniques

How many assessment interviews?

The approach advocated by the Young Abusers Project, described above, involves only one assessment interview but it is the case that other specialist teams may prefer to see the child or young person on more than one occasion, perhaps for several meetings. However, clinical experience (Vizard, 1996) suggests that the bulk of relevant assessment material is elicited in one carefully conducted, semi-structured interview, as described above. Although new material will always emerge in second, third and subsequent interviews, this is not always of major importance and does not usually alter significantly the risk assessment undertaken in the first interview.

The systemic approach advocated above will elicit considerable pre-interview data. Since the assessment interview will be accompanied by a clinical psychology assessment and possibly also a child psychotherapy assessment it has been the experience of the Young Abusers Project that there is more than enough data to draw together into a holistic, multidisciplinary assessment looking at all aspects of the young person's life including the sexualised behaviour. In deciding the number of interviews to undertake, the specialist team needs to bear in mind that assessment of young sexual abusers, like the assessment of any young offender, needs to retain an overall focus on the unacceptable behaviour, it's consequences for victims, remorse, empathy, risk of further offending and future outlook, if it is to be of any use to referrers.

Overall approach to assessment interviews

In general terms, regardless of the specific structure of the interview, the early stages of the meeting should deal with factual matters, as much as possible, with the child or young person being encouraged to give their version of the sexualised behaviour or offence. Challenge of the almost inevitable discrepancies in the factual account or challenge of the child or young person's unacceptable attitudes about abusive behaviour should be left until later on in the interview.

There are two main reasons for this suggestion. Firstly, from an assessment point of view, the interviewers want as many of these discrepancies and unacceptable attitudes as possible to emerge so that the level of risk can be gauged accurately. Secondly, premature challenge on these issues will mobilise the child or young person's defences to such an extent that disclosure of any further discrepancies or attitudes will stop.

In this sense, interviewers of young sexual abusers need to retain a strategic overview of the interview and full control of the process (Gray and Wallace, 1992).

How to work with denial and resistance

There are no easy answers to this technical problem!

However, several minds from different disciplines (the multidisciplinary team) do contribute very helpful and different perspectives on the reasons for denial and resistance. Furthermore, a live supervisor or interviewers team needs to be as used to working with each other as possible so that a really free flow of ideas about questioning style and content of questions can occur. Having said this, denial and resistance need to be addressed by varying the style, content and pace of the exchanges with the child or young person as much as possible. Long, dull, exchanges of questions followed by 'I dunno . . .' type answers should be avoided at all costs. Breaking up the pace with a range of techniques will introduce a helpful element of surprise into the young person's mind and often an answer is blurted out without the young person having the chance to block off a response. Helpful techniques include the following:

- The use of circular questions, e.g. If the judge or your parent or a social worker or a schoolteacher was sitting here now (in that chair over there, look . . .) What would they say about your attitude?
- Making lists, verbal or written, to avoid pushing the young person into yes or no answers, e.g. What's top of your list of worries right now? What's bottom of the list? What worries are in the middle?
- Moving strategically between verbal and written exchanges of ideas with the young person e.g. Can you pick up the pen now, please, and write up what you think your victim might be feeling about you now?
- Using concrete examples, within circular questioning, e.g. When you are aged 25 years old, married with two children how safe will they be with you? Very safe, safe enough, not safe?
- Introducing toys, dolls, drawings and other play adjuncts into the discussion, acknowledging input from the live supervisor during the interview, giving tasks for the child or young person to do during breaks.
- Expressing puzzlement about discrepancies and resistance first of all before moving on to direct challenge of these issues later if needed.
- Getting up and moving around the room to write on flip charts, move chairs, take breaks, fetch materials at strategic points will break up a 'stuck' atmosphere and may re-introduce the element of surprise into the meeting.
- Use specific concrete exercises to involve the young person, preferably to get him or her up on their feet, writing things on the flip chart. These techniques break up

resistance, distract the young person away from entrenched defences and can also introduce a sense of achievement and involvement in the interview.

Examples of such concrete exercises used in the Young Abusers Project include the drawing of a family tree or genogram with the young person or construction of the Integrated Abuse Cycle (IAC). The IAC (Vizard, 1996) is a cognitive exercise where the external circle of two concentric circles represents sexual and other actions taken and the internal circle represents the corresponding thoughts, feelings and fantasies about the events. By drawing on a board the sequence of actions taken and engaging the young person in a dialogue about the corresponding thoughts, feelings and fantasies about their sexual behaviour, this exercise with the Integrated Abuse Cycle attempts to help the young person 'join up' their inappropriate sexual fantasies with their illegal sexual behaviours. In other words, this cognitive exercise is really a way of breaking through denial and helping a child or young person to acknowledge, perhaps for the first time, that their own mind was indeed in charge of their own body when they abused another child. This concrete and visible technique for dealing with denial in children and young people who sexually abuse has proved helpful both in the assessment interview and subsequently in the treatment phase of engagement. Most importantly, working with the IAC has proved popular with children and young people themselves and seems to be less intimidating or confusing than, for instance, predominantly verbal exchanges with adult professionals during assessment. Further examples of how to work with the Integrated Abuse Cycle in clinical practice are described in Hawkes, 1999.

3. The psychological assessment

A full psychological assessment including cognitive assessment of every child and young person referred for assessment in specialist young abuser teams should be undertaken. The reasons for this psychological assessment are that around 40 per cent of the children and young people referred to such services for assessment have a learning disability and assessment of all cases is needed to ensure that the requested risk assessment can be appropriately managed.

Secondly, in relation to children and young people facing criminal proceedings, the presence of learning disability may mean that they are not fit to plead in the current proceedings and that a psychological report needs to be sent to court to this effect.

Thirdly, psychological assessment is needed to inform any subsequent treatment, whether individual psychodynamic, individual cognitive behavioural or group treatment programmes.

Although existing educational psychology reports will cast very helpful light on patterns of school based underachievment, for the reasons mentioned above, the psychological assessment needs to be undertaken by a clinical psychologist with experience in assessing offending children and young people.

4. The comprehensive report

Whatever the format of the assessment, it is essential that a report is produced which is informative and reliable.

However, in an earlier discussion of the nature of such a comprehensive report (Vizard et al., 1996) it is emphasised that 'The report produced at the end of the assessment should be a structured, coherent account of the issues addressed in the assessment with a concise formulation of the child or young person's difficulties and a list of recommendations.' Vizard et al. (1996) also point out the importance of describing sexual arousal, sexual behaviours and future prospects for the young person in the clearest possible terms whilst at the same time being sensitive to the fact that the family, child or young person may subsequently wish to read the report. The need for professional input to be provided to explain and support any distressed or angry reactions to such a comprehensive assessment report, is also discussed (Vizard, 2001).

Multidisciplinary Teams and Young Sexual Abusers

At present in the UK most assessment of young sexual abusers is carried out by specialist social workers in NSPCC or other community based teams. Given the dearth of trained child psychiatrists, clinical psychologists, child psychotherapists and other disciplines working with children and young people, it is unlikely that this situation will change in the near future. However, for many of the reasons described in this chapter, it is highly desirable that a multidisciplinary input is sought from

local health colleagues since this population of young abusers has many developmental and health needs over and above the sexualised behaviour. The role of the YOTs in linking to health in relation to offending children may prove to be helpful in facilitating input from child psychiatry and clinical psychology to community based young abuser teams. The detection of learning disability and any emotional disturbance or mental health problems in this client group depends on input from other disciplines. Conversely, the developmental needs of young sexual abusers cannot be fairly said to be met by social work only teams any more than a fully effective child protection response can be expected from health only teams.

However, even when the desired multidisciplinary input has been achieved, the team functioning is not always so straightforward. Firstly, it is important to achieve a proper balance between contributions from different disciplines in multidisciplinary teams where child protection is concerned. This is sometimes more difficult than it may seem where assertive individuals from a range of professional backgrounds may hold opposing views!

Bell (2001) has emphasised the need for a, preferably independent, team co-ordinator to ensure that the more frequent contributions to meetings by individuals from disciplines or positions with perceived higher status are balanced by input from less assertive team members whose views may be crucial. The balance of power in multidisciplinary teams consisting of individuals from different agencies such as police, health, social work etc. may be assisted, according to Bell's (2001) study if a balance in funding from the parent agencies is achieved and if team meetings are rotated around different agencies. Although there may not be many multidisciplinary teams including police which operate in the way described by Bell (2001) in the UK involving young sexual abusers, there are clearly important lessons to be learned from this work in relation to good multidisciplinary team practice.

Gray (1992), in the list of Do's and Don'ts for interviewing high risk youth, also makes the following important 'Don't' point: 'Do not isolate yourself (do seek colleague input and support, share concerns, ideas and feelings, attend trainings and network)'.

Summary

There is a need for increased public and professional awareness of the nature of juvenile sexual offenders against children. Serious professional doubts about persistent, inappropriate sexualised behaviour in childhood should lead to a prompt referral for assessment, not to procrastination over definitions. Conclusive treatment outcome results are not yet available for juvenile sexual offenders.

However, a multi-agency approach involving all professionals working within a child protection context is most likely to ensure that treatment occurs and that the outcome is positive. An integrated theoretical treatment approach drawing on a number of theoretical models will have a better treatment outcome.

Recidivism is less during the treatment process and during follow up by professionals. Recidivism rises when follow up stops. Clinical experience strongly suggests that outcome is better when children start in treatment at a young age, preferably before puberty. However, follow up research data on these young children is not yet available.

Acknowledgments

I would like to acknowledge the support of NSPCC in providing a containing management context for this frequently uncontained and difficult work. Particular thanks are due to Madeleine Ismach for her long term support of the Young Abusers Project. I am also tremendously grateful to my colleagues Colin Hawkes, Jane Millarini, Richard Reynolds and Judith Usiskin in the Young Abusers Project for their support and clinical wisdom in dealing with this work over many years. Finally, I remain indebted to the hundreds of children and young people who have shared their thoughts and feelings with us and whom we have tried to help in the Young Abusers Project over the last 10 years.

References

Araji, S. and Finklehor, D. (1986) Abusers: A Review of the Research. in Finklehor, D. (Ed.) *A Sourcebook on Child Sexual Abuse*. London: SAGE Publications. 89–118.

Araji, S. K. (1997) Identifying, Labelling and Explaining Children's Sexually Aggressive Behaviors. in Araji, S. K. (Ed.) *Sexually Aggressive Children. Coming to Understand Them*. Thousand Oaks, Ca: Sage. 1–46.

Ashford, N. and Chard, A. (2000) *Defending Young People in the Criminal Justice System*. Legal Action Group.

Barbaree, H. and Cortoni, F. (1993) Treatment of the Juvenile Sex Offender within the Criminal and Mental Health Systems. in Barbaree, H. Marshall, W. and Hudson, S. (Eds.) *The Juvenile Sex Offender*. NY: Guilford Press.

Bell, L. (2001). Patterns of Interaction in Multidisciplinary Child Protection Teams in New Jersey. *Child Abuse and Neglect*. 25: 65–80.

Birkett, D. (2000) Why Little Boys are not Sex Offenders. *The Guardian*. Nov. 21.

Calder, M. C. (1997) *Juveniles and Children who Sexually Abuse: A Guide to Risk Assessment*. Dorset: Russell House Publishing.

Calder, M. C. (1999) A Conceptual Framework for Managing Young People who Sexually Abuse:Towards a Consortium Approach. in Calder, M. C. (Ed.) *Working with Young People who Sexually Abuse. New Pieces of the Jigsaw Puzzle*. Dorset: Russell House Publishing. 117–59.

Calder, M. C. (2001) *Juveniles and Children Who Sexually Abuse: Frameworks for Assessment*. Dorset: Russell House Publishing.

Davis, G. and Leitenber, H. (1987) Adolescent Sex Offenders. *Psychological Bulletin*. 101: 417–27.

Department of Health and National Children's Homes. (1992) *Survey of Treatment Facilities for Young Sexual Abusers*. NCH.

Department of Health, Home Office and Department of Education and Employment. (1999) *Working Together to Safeguard Children*. London: The Stationary Office.

Epps, K. (1999) Causal Explanations: Filling the Theoretical Reservoir. in Calder, M. C. (Ed.) *Working with Young People who Sexually Abuse: New Pieces of the Jigsaw Puzzle*. Dorset: Russell House Publishing.

Gray, A.S. and Wallace, R. (1992) *Adolescent Sexual Offender Assessment Packet*. Orwell, VT: The Safer Society Press.

Hanks, H. (1997) Normal Psychosexual Development, Behaviour and Knowledge. in Calder, M. C. (Ed.) *Juveniles and Children who Sexually Abuse: A Guide to Risk Assessment*. Dorset: Russell House Publishing. 16–23

Hanks, H. (2001) Children's 'normal' sexual and psychosexual development, knowledge and behaviour. in Calder, M. C., op cit, 77–85.

Hawkes, C., Jenkins, J. and Jenkins J. A., Vizard, E. (1997) Roots of Sexual Violence in Children and Adolescents. in Varma, V. (Ed.) *Violence in Children and Adolescents*. London: Jessica Kingsley Publishers.

Hawkes, C. (1999) Linking Thoughts to Actions: Using the Integrated Abuse Cycle. in Kemshall, H. and Pritchard, J. (Eds.) *Good Practice in Working with Violence*. London: Jessica Kingsley Publishers.

Home Office. (1998). Table 3. Persons Found Guilty at All Courts or Cautioned by Type of Offence, Sex and Age Group, per 100,000 Population in the age Group 1981, 1985, 1988, 1994–96. in (1996) *Aspects of Crime. Young Offenders*. Crime and Criminal Justice Unit, Research and Statistics Directorate, Home Office. 11, 22.

Johnson, T. C. (1988) Child Perpetrators: Children who Molest Other Children: Preliminary Findings. *Child Abuse and Neglect*. 12: 219–29.

Johnson, T. C. and Feldmeth, J. R. (1993) Sexual Behaviours: A Continuum. in Gil, E. and Johnson, T. C. (Eds.) *Sexualised Children: Assessment and Treatment of Sexualised Children and Children who Molest*. Rockville, MD: Launch Press. 41–52.

Lane, S. and Zamora, P. (1984) A Method for Treating the Adolescent Sex Offender. in Mathias, R., Demuro, P. and Allinson, R. (Eds.) *Violent Juvenile Offenders*. San Francisco, Ca: National Council on Crime and Delinquency.

Morrison, T. and Print, B. (1995) *Adolescent Sexual Abusers: An Overview*. Hull: Bluemoon Corporate Services/NOTA.

NCH. (1992) *Children Who Abuse Other Children*. London. National Children's Home.

O'Callaghan, D. and Print, B. (1994) Adolescent Sexual Abusers. Research, Assessment and Treatment. in Morrison, T, Erooga, M. and Beckett, R. C. (Eds.) *Sexual Offending Against Children. Assessment and Treatment of Male Abusers*. Routledge. London, 146–77.

Reder, P. and Duncan, S. (1999) *Lost Innocents: A Follow up Study of Fatal Child Abuse*. London. Routledge.

Ryan, G. (1991) Theories of Etiology. in Ryan, G. and Lane, S. (Eds.) *Juvenile Sexual Offending. Causes, Consequences and Corrections*. Lexington, Ma: Lexington Books.

Skuse, D., Bentovim, A., Hodges, J., Stevenson, J., Andreo, C., Lanyado, M., New, M., Williams, B. and McMillan, D. (1998) Risk Factors for the Development of Sexually Abusive Behaviour in Sexually Victimised Adolescent Boys: cross Sectional Study. *British Medical Journal*. 317: 175–8.

Steen, C. and Monnette, B. (1989) *Treating Adolescent Sex Offenders in the Community*. Springfield, IL. Charles C Thomas.

Vizard, E., Monck, E. and Misch, P. (1995) Child and Adolescent Sex Abuse Perpetrators: A Review of the Research Literature. *Journal of Child Psychology and Psychiatry*. 36:5 731–56.

Vizard, E., Wynick, S., Hawkes, C., Woods, J. and Jenkins, J. (1996) Juvenile Sexual Offenders. Assessment Issues. *British Journal of Psychiatry*. 168: 259–62.

Vizard, E. and Harris, P. (Eds.) (1997) The Expert Witness Pack. For Use in Children Act Proceedings. *Family Law*. Jordans.

Vizard, E. (2000) Letter to Guardian in response to Birkett's article Why Little Boys are not Sex Offenders. The *Guardian*. Nov. 23.

Vizard, E. (2001) Sexual Offending in Adolescence. in Bailey, S. and Dolan, M. (Eds.) *Textbook of Forensic Adolescent Psychiatry*. London: Blackwell Science.

Will, D. (1999) Assessment Issues. in Erooga, M. and Masson, H. (Eds.) *Children and Young People who Sexually Abuse Others. Challenges and Responses*. London: Routledge.

Case of T. vs the UK (Application no. 24724/94). Judgement of the European Court of Human Rights in Strasbourg. December 1999.

Case of V. vs the UK (Application no. 24888/94). Judgement of the European Court of Human Rights in Strasbourg. December 1999.

Chapter 13: South Asian Adolescent Sex Offenders: Effective Assessment and Intervention Work

Kamran Abassi and Shabana Jamal

Introduction

This chapter is not intended to offer a theoretical framework to practitioners but information concerning offenders' background, culture and religion that suggest possible explanations for offending behaviour and may assist in risk assessment and appropriate offence focused work. The authors' involvement with young South Asian sex offenders will be examined by way of several case studies. This chapter will seek to explore themes and issues arising at the assessment stage and when undertaking intervention work with this group of offenders.

In this chapter, South Asian is defined as those people of Indian, Pakistani, Bangladeshi, Sri Lankan and British origin with heritage with one of the above-mentioned countries.

The South Asian Offenders and Families project works in partnership with Greater Manchester Probation Service. It seeks to ensure that South Asian offenders receive a culturally appropriate service through the provision of cultural, religious and linguistic advice to probation staff from initial pre-sentence stage through to pre-release and post-sentence stage. The project aims to inform and educate both the service provider and the service users.

This chapter stems from a workshop undertaken by the authors for NOTA North West in December 1999 and related themes arising from it.

Issues

There are a number of issues that need to be discussed in relation to this group of offenders. These impact upon accurate assessment and effective intervention work.

Barriers to assessment and intervention

Offender
- Communication
- Lack of understanding of the criminal justice system
- Perceptions towards victims and offending
- Second/third generation South Asians
- Relevance of offence focused work
- Gender and race

Professional
- Communication
- Lack of understanding of cultural and religious issues
- Different value base
- Assumptions and stereotypes

Leading potentially to: Inaccurate assessment and Inappropriate intervention.

Communication

Communication is an integral part of any assessment. Where English is not the first language of the offender or their family, problems arise instantaneously.

To overcome this, professionals should use interpreters. One must be aware of a number of factors when using interpreters. Firstly, interpreters must not be other members of the family or local community. This is to ensure objectivity and confidentiality. Where possible, interpreters should hold a relevant qualification in interpreting and translation.

The interpreter needs to be fully aware of the content and the context of what they are interpreting. This is particularly important with sex offences, since sexual matters are taboo within the South Asian communities. As such, one needs to ascertain whether or not the interpreter is comfortable interpreting such material. The role of the interpreter must be clear. They are *not* consultants, their role is to accurately translate one language to another. For a detailed review of issues relating to the use of interpreters the reader is referred to Calder (1999).

The second and closely related factor is one of vocabulary. As sexual matters are not discussed, vocabulary is either very academic or perceived to be obscene. Through experience, the authors have found that use of direct or obscene language (which is widely understood) has had a greater impact upon the offender and their family, bringing reality and understanding to the offence.

Where possible, additional written information should be made available in the offenders and their families first language. This can aid the understanding of all the relevant issues and procedures.

Culture and religion

Within South Asian communities, culture and religion are a central feature in an individuals life. Offenders and families may use cultural aspects and give them religious imputation by misquoting verses of the Qur'an (or other religious books). Therefore, a lack of cultural and religious knowledge on the part of professionals can form barriers to assessment and intervention.

Within South Asian communities sex before marriage is forbidden. As such 'sex' is a taboo subject that is *never* discussed. Any form of sex offence brings extreme shame ('sharam') upon the whole family. The family honour ('izzat') is destroyed and the family standing is reduced both within the extended family and the local South Asian community. It is not surprising therefore that many offenders and their families deny the offence has occurred or try to minimise it or conceal it by not discussing it.

The notion of 'honour' and 'shame' are the foundations upon which social life is based within South Asian communities. As such, professionals must acknowledge the importance of these ideals when undertaking assessment and intervention work.

Repercussions for such offenders and their families are far reaching. The offender can find themselves ostracised and disowned by their family. Where the family support the offender, it may find itself being ostracised by its own community. Marriage proposals for both the offender and any siblings may be affected, and stigmatisation may carry through generations.

Perceptions toward victims and offending

A common feature within *all* offender groups is that of having little or no victim empathy. In almost all the cases the authors were involved in, the victims were 'white females'. Offenders held stereotypical views of 'white girls' making reference to their clothing and mannerisms. Offenders perceived their victims as easily accessible for sex, unlike girls from their own community. These perceptions were based upon media images and portrayals, TV, films, magazines, and from other peers.

A lack of formal sex education coupled with the unwillingness of parents to discuss such matters (because of the taboo nature) meant that such 'distorted thinking' went unchallenged, leading to offences being committed.

South Asian families readily blame the 'Western society' and its 'openness' to sex as the primary cause for their family members committing sexual offences. Thus, families externalise offences rather than accepting and dealing with them. This reinforces stereotypes already held by the offenders.

In the face of racism, there is a necessity for South Asian communities to maintain a 'flawless' image in which crime does not feature. Acknowledgement of such offences would add to stereotypes and discrimination already experienced, hence, another reason for denial.

Second and third generation South Asians

The issue of identity is another crucial aspect that needs to be taken into consideration when working with adolescent Asian sex offenders. Second and third generation 'British Asians' find themselves living between two diverse cultures. Many offenders come from traditional families which have strong cultural and religious beliefs and expectations. The offenders are expected to adhere to these. At the same time, offenders are living and experiencing Western culture and values which are different to the South Asian culture. Inevitably, conflict arises as offenders struggle to find their identity.

Additionally, the idea of individuality is not a readily accepted concept within South Asian communities. The individual is regarded as a member of a family rather than a person in their own right. The family's needs and expectations take priority, not individuality. Young South Asian males find themselves under immense pressure to fulfil family expectations. They are regarded as carrying the family name forward and upholding family honour.

The 'generation gap' has left second and third generation Asians unable to share their dilemmas with their parents, who in turn are unable to empathise as they have not shared this common experience. Lack of positive role models, and suffering racism, compound identity issues prevalent to second and third generation South Asians.

Relevance of offence focused work

For intervention work to be effective, it needs to be 'relevant' to the offender group which it is targeting. Sex offender material is written in the large part by white professionals from a white value base system. This does not acknowledge cultural and religious issues relevant to South Asian sex offenders. Sex offender material needs to address concepts and ideologies of shame and honour which are so important to South Asian communities. This will promote anti-discriminatory practice and relate the material to the offender.

Use of Eurocentric scenarios and characters is common place. These need to be developed when working with South Asian adolescent sex offenders. 'Culturally relevant scenarios and characters' need to be used to engage offenders and bring a sense of reality to them (An example follows, 'Way forward: Shabaz's brother remembers').

A further issue arises where English is not the first language of the offender: translating sex offending material into the relevant language of the offender may have cost and time implications. However, these must not be used as reasons for failing to undertake intervention work. Necessary arrangements should be made to overcome these barriers, with workers, interpreters and translated material being made available.

There have been exhaustive debates about inclusion of 'Black and Asian' offenders in group work programmes or individual treatment programmes. This chapter will not seek to provide a 'universal' answer to this. The experiences of the authors has been to undertake individual work rather than group work with adolescent Asian sex offenders. This has been to overcome barriers such as isolation, targeting and communication and to address culturally specific issues.

Gender and race

The gender of the professionals is a key issue to achieve accurate assessments and interventions. Due to the taboo nature of sex offences within South Asian communities, one must be aware of the possible implications of using Asian female interpreters or workers with male offenders and vice versa. Embarrassment and shame (by either offenders or professionals) may contribute to inaccurate assessments and intervention work as issues are not fully discussed or interpreted.

The race of professionals can also impact upon interaction with offenders and their families. A professionals' lack of understanding of cultural and religious issues may be exploited by offenders and go unchallenged.

The different value base of the professional to the offender can form barriers. Values and beliefs should not be imposed upon one another as this may lead to discrimination and bad practice.

All these issues need to be given due consideration when undertaking any form of assessment or intervention work with adolescent South Asian offenders and their families, as they form the basis of good practice.

Case studies

The following case studies will seek to highlight the aforementioned issues. These are real cases in which the authors have been involved at both assessment and intervention stages. The identities of the offenders and victims have been protected for reasons of confidentiality and as such, names have been omitted and ages of offenders and victims have been altered.

Initially, the background to each case will be described. Following this, common themes and issues prevalent in all the cases will be examined, after which specific issues relating to individual cases will be examined.

Case study 1
Background

Offender A was a 16-year-old Pakistani male. Following a trial in which Offender A pleaded not guilty throughout, he was convicted of an indecent assault on a 12-year-old white girl. The case was adjourned for a pre-sentence report and the authors were asked to co-work the interview with the probation officer.

Offender A lived in a closely knit Asian community with his 40-year-old mother and younger sister aged 12. His father died when he was seven years old. Social services were in the process of arranging a home visit to undertake child protection investigations regarding Offender A's 12-year-old sister and a visit by the police was imminent as Offender A was to register on the sex offender register by virtue of his Schedule 1 status.

Case study 2

Background

Offender B was a 16-year-old Pakistani male. He had been charged with the rape of an 18-year-old white female. Offender B had returned to England from Pakistan at the age of 14. His father remained in Pakistan and Offender B was living alone with his mother.

Offender B denied the offence and there was a strong belief in the family of the occult and 'jadu' (black magic) and Jinn possession. Offender B was found guilty following a trial and the judge had requested an adjournment for a pre-sentence report. The authors had been asked to co-work the interviews.

Case study 3

Background

Offender C was a 16-year-old Sikh girl who had been found guilty of indecently assaulting her seven-year-old male cousin. Offender C was sentenced to a three year probation order and registered on the Sex Offender Register.
She lived at home with her mother and father.

The authors were asked to co-work the probation order alongside the probation officer.

Common issues and themes prevalent in all three case studies

Communication and Language Barriers. In all three cases, none of the parents could speak, read or write English. These barriers were overcome by the female author acting as interpreter for the mothers, and the male author interpreting for the father (see Gender issues below). Whilst acknowledging the sensitive nature of this type of offending, the authors developed a line of using 'vulgar' terminology. This impacted significantly upon the offenders and their parents bringing reality, clarity and consistency to the situation. Use of academic or medical terminology was not understood by the offender or the family and would add to minimisations already held by them regarding the offence.

The profound lack of knowledge of all the parents' understanding of the operation of the criminal justice system (matters such as registration as a sex offender, the role of the Probation Service and Social Services to mention but a few), was evident, and the interpreting aided to overcome this.

Religion and culture. All parents talked about the 'sharam' (shame) and disgrace their children's offending had brought upon them. Their 'izzat' (honour) had been destroyed and the parents felt ashamed and embarrassed to face other relatives and members of their community for fear of ostracising and loss of standing in the community. The parents made clear reference to their respective religions (Islam in Case Study 1 and 2 and Sikhism in Case Study 3), which forbid any form of sex before marriage, thus making sex a taboo subject, never to be talked about. The 'shared' background of the authors enabled these barriers to be broken through an educative process on the relevant laws of the land in which one resides and knowledge of the concepts of Islam and Sikhism.

Perceptions of victims and offending. Offenders A and B showed no victim empathy, holding stereotypical views about 'white girls' as 'girlfriends', 'prostitutes', 'easy game', making references to mini-skirts and red lipstick. These negative stereotypes were broken down by the authors discussing both situations when the offenders had been 'labelled', and their personal experiences of racism and discrimination. All the parents reinforced these stereotypes by externalising the offences and blaming the 'Western society and culture'. The parents expressed feelings of anxiety and helplessness stating that had they been in India or Pakistan these offences would never have occurred. The authors sought to break down these stereotypes by informing parents that sex offences did in fact occur in India and Pakistan but reporting was significantly lower because of the stigma such offences had. The authors supported this by showing newspaper articles of such events.

Second and third generation South Asians. All three offenders stated that their personal identity was at a crisis. They talked about leading a double life, one 'inside' the home, viewed as acceptable by their parents as it fitted into the traditional concepts of family life. The other life was 'outside' the home amongst their peers and involved alcohol, drugs and mixing with members of the opposite sex. These would all be viewed as unacceptable to their parents, hence a need to hide such behaviour. The offenders found it extremely difficult and stressful to live between the two cultures and had no one to talk to who 'understood' their dilemma. The offences related to their experiences of racism and a feeling of confusion and unwant and not fitting in.

As second generation Asians, the authors shared congruence with the offenders and a common experience. This was useful when understanding some of the attitudes and stereotypes displayed by the offenders and constructively challenging them on these points.

Relevance of Offence Focused Work. The authors looked at current practices and models of working with adolescent sex offenders. They could not find any appropriate material that took into consideration cultural and religious issues pertinent to South Asian adolescent sex offenders. Eurocentric scenarios were in use and the offenders could not relate to these.

The authors developed the material to include concepts of honour and shame, as social life within the Asian community pivoted on these. The authors included 'culturally appropriate scenarios' which the offenders could relate to rather than the Eurocentric scenarios in use.

Lack of sex education and awareness was common with all three offenders. Parents were unwilling to discuss these issues as they were considered unacceptable religiously and culturally. Offenders stated that they gained their knowledge from peers, films, television and magazines, often leading to distorted thinking and anti-social behaviour. This was acknowledged by the authors by incorporating sex education material into the offence focused work.

Offenders A and B viewed their crimes as less serious because their victims were white. The authors addressed victim empathy issues by using hypothetical examples featuring their mothers and sisters as victims of sex offences. This had a significant impact on the offenders as they viewed females in their families with the utmost respect. The offenders talked in great detail about thoughts and feelings their female family members would have had if they had been subjected to a sex offence and related this back to their 'white victims', agreeing they were no different to females in their families.

Gender and race. The gender of the workers was essential in all three case studies due to the taboo nature of this type of offence and the stigma and shame attached to it. This was reflected in the gender balance of the authors with the male author working with the male offenders and the father of Offender C, and the female author with the female offender and all the mothers.

Sharing the same ethnic background also proved vital as the authors could constructively challenge religious and cultural issues that at times had been misinterpreted by the offenders and their parents.

Specific issues relating to individual case studies

Case study 2: Belief in the occult, 'jadu' (black magic) and jinn possession.

Both the offender and his mother shared a strong belief in this. The Qur'an (the Holy Book for the Muslims) makes specific reference to Jinn (a being created by Allah by fire not visible to the naked eye) and black magic. As such, this issue could not be overlooked by the authors at the pre-sentence stage.

The authors were also aware that Jinn possession had been used in the past by families to externalise offending behaviour and as a means to keep their standing in the community, as it was an acceptable excuse. The authors used a passage from the Holy Qur'an Surah 32 Ayah 6 which explained that 'every day problems' should be dealt with within their natural surroundings and not explained away as possession, because such people would ultimately be answerable to Allah. This proved to be a constructive method to challenge minimisations and justifications of anti-social behaviour and distorted thinking held by offenders. These issues were all mentioned in the pre-sentence report, giving the judge a broader understanding of the issues involved.

Case study 3: Female offender.

As a female offender committing a sexual crime within the family, there was an added stigma attached to this offence. Offender C's parents expressed a fear of her being unmarriageable and possible stigmatisation for future generations. Offence work was undertaken wholly by the female author and incorporated these concepts.

Way forward

- Literature and research on South Asian adolescent sex offenders is very limited. A suggested reading list is included at the end of this chapter. In-depth research is required into this group of offenders and their families, taking into account cultural and religious factors specific to them. As such, the research should be developed and managed by community groups or individuals aware of these issues.

- With the emergence of the Youth Offending Teams, developing partnerships with community groups should be high on their agenda. This will ensure equality of service provision and address culturally specific issues for Asian adolescent offenders.
- Policies, practices and treatment programmes need to be 'culturally appropriate' across the range of offences (not only for sex offences). They need to include culturally specific scenarios for offenders to identify with. An example is included below. The authors have used it with a number of offenders with a marked increase in victim awareness.

Shabaz's brother remembers

The following exercise is designed to help you become more aware of what it is like to go through a sexual abuse experience. Shabaz's brother tells about when Shabaz was abused.

You are now going to go back to when you were five years old. I want you to imagine living in a terraced house amongst an Asian community. Your mum works in the day because your dad died when you were younger. You have not yet started school and you spend a lot of time playing with your six year old brother Shabaz. You and Shabaz live alone with your mum and since the house has only two bedrooms, you and your brother share one. Imagine what your room looks like, toys on the floor and pictures on the wall.

Your mum works in a factory and sometimes has to work late into the evening. Your cousin Parveen looks after you when your mum works late. On this day, Parveen has to go to the mosque and your mum has to find another babysitter. She calls another cousin, Abdul and asks him to baby-sit. He has babysat a few times before. Abdul sometimes played cricket with the other kids in the street and even though he was sometimes mean, he was always nice to you and Shabaz.

On this night, Abdul comes over and you all have chicken and roti your mum made before she went to work. At eight o'clock Abdul sends you to bed, which you don't like because normally you and Shabaz go to bed at the same time. You miss your mum and wish she was there.

A few minutes after getting into bed you remember that you haven't used the bathroom so you get up and go to the door of your room. You hear your brother's voice asking Abdul what he is doing. You then hear Abdul saying, 'It's okay Shabaz, I'll let you watch a video if you play the game.' You creep downstairs and quietly open the door and peek into the TV room. Through the crack in the door you see Abdul sitting next to Shabaz with his arm on Shabaz's leg. This seems strange to you so you open

the door a few more inches. Abdul sees you and gets really mad and tells you to go back upstairs to bed. You look at Abdul and realise that Shabaz looks tiny compared to him. He sounds really mad so you quickly go back to your bedroom. After closing the door, you stand there to listen if Abdul is coming to check on you, your heart pounding. He doesn't and you hear Shabaz saying 'I don't want to play, Abdul!'

A few minutes later, you hear him yell 'I'm going to tell amee (mum)'. You then hear Abdul saying 'Be quiet, just do it.' When you don't hear anything else you again creep downstairs and peek in. What you see really confuses you.

Shabaz seems to be crying, Abdul is holding Shabaz's head down between his legs and moving it up and down. but you can't tell for sure. You open the door a little more to see better. Abdul raises his head and sees you looking and yells' 'Shut that door you kuta (dog)'. You quickly close the door and run upstairs and go and lie down in your bed holding in tightly to your covers.

A while later, Shabaz comes into the bedroom and you notice he has tears in his eyes. You ask 'What happened bahai (brother), did Abdul hurt you?' Shabaz tells you he's not supposed to talk about it because 'Allah will get Khafah (upset)'. You go to sleep wondering what happened in the living room and if Abdul would ever do the same thing to you.

1. List all of the feelings you think Shabaz would have had during the incident.
2. List all of the feelings you think you would have had if you had just experienced this situation.
3. Describe your gut-level reaction to reading or listening to this story.

As highlighted in all three case studies, there is an unwillingness by parents to discuss sexual matters with their children, as it is an area of religious and cultural taboo. Offenders' knowledge on sexual matters is therefore gauged from films, magazines, peers and experimentation leading to offending behaviour. Thus, any programme of work or model of treatment with this group of offenders needs to incorporate sex education at its core. This must be viewed in the wider context of honour and shame specific to this community.

Stereotypical views held by both offenders and their families regarding sex offences as a 'White phenomenon' need to be constructively challenged. This is achievable through an educative process, increasing awareness that such crimes do in fact occur in the Indian sub-continent, providing offenders and their families with evidence. An example of ascertaining parental views on offending is a

Parent Questionnaire used by B. Sheikh in her study *'Sexual Crimes and Young Asian Sex Offenders'*.

In all three case studies, offenders talked about their personal identity being in crisis. They could not identify a single positive role model of the same ethnic background. A way forward is to provide a Mentoring Scheme whereby someone with a shared background to the offender can mentor them. Providing positivety, identity and empathy and empowering offenders to make positive choices would lead to 'nipping criminality at its bud' and reduce re-offending.

References

Anwar, M. (1981) *Between Two Cultures. A Study of Relationships Between Generations in the Asian Community in Britain.* London: Commission for Racial Equality.

Baim, C. and Roberts, B. (1999) A Community-based Programme for Sex Offenders Who Deny Their Offending Behaviour. *NOTA News.* 30.

Calder, M. C. (1999) Towards Anti-oppressive Practice With Ethnic Minority Groups. in Calder, M. C. and Horwath, J. (Eds.) *Working for Children on the Child Protection Register: An Inter-agency Practice Guide.* Aldershot: Arena. 177–209.

Gahir, M. and Garrett, T. (1999) Issues in the Treatment of Asian Sexual Offenders. *The Journal of Sexual Aggression.* 4:2 94–104.

Hopkinson, J. (1995) Some thoughts on working with sex offenders and racial difference. *NOTA News.*13.

Sheikh, B. A. (1997) *Sexual Crimes and Young Asian Sex Offenders.* West Yorkshire Probation Service.

Mtezuka, M. (1990) Towards a Better Understanding of Child Sexual Abuse Among Asian Communities. *Practice.* 3 and 4: 248–60.

Chapter 14: Abused *and* Abusing: Work with Young People who Have a Dual Sexual Abuse Experience

Simon Hackett

Understanding the place of personal victimisation work in intervention with young men who sexually abuse others is a matter of importance to the field, but remains a somewhat contentious issue. As literature describing clinical populations of adolescents who have sexually abused has increased, so has the recognition that young people who abuse constitute a heterogeneous group and that distinct subgroups of young abusers may exist, each with discreet treatment needs (Worling, 2001). One such subgroup is comprised of young male abusers who themselves have experienced sexual victimisation (Cooper et al., 1996; Hummel et al., 2000; Worling, 1995).

As noted by Veneziano et al. (2000), prior sexual victimisation of sex offenders has been a consistent finding across the adult and juvenile literature, despite considerable differences in samples and data collection. Younger children with sexual behaviour problems also typically have chronic sexual victimisation histories (Burton, 2000). There remains, however, significant variance in reported own experiences of sexual abuse in different populations of young men who have sexually abused. For children under 12 with sexual behaviour problems the rate identified in studies typically ranges between 65% and 100% (Burton et al., 1997; Burton, 2000; Friedrich and Luecke, 1998; Gil and Johnson, 1994). In samples of sexually aggressive adolescents reported rates are as low as 25% (Sefarbi, 1990) but more frequently fall within a range of 40% to 65% (Becker et al., 1987; Burgess et al., 1995; Davis and Leitenberg, 1987; Vizard et al., 1995; Worling, 1995). Such variance is likely to be due to a range of factors, including the definition of sexual abuse used, the methods used to determine abuse histories and the nature of different clinical samples.

Even if the definitive proportion of young abusers with own sexual victimisation experiences could be agreed, the *meaning* of such experiences in the context of an individual young man's subsequent abusive behaviour may remain very unclear. There are some authors who suggest that the very experience of sexual victimisation puts an individual at risk of becoming an abuser (Freeman-Longo, 1986), others raise objections to such a simple cause-effect relationship (Dhawan and Marshall, 1996). If most young men who abuse have themselves been sexually abused, this reinforces the notions of cycles of intergenerational abuse; what I call the 'contagion theory' of sexual abuse. Conversely, if the proportion of young abusers who have been sexually abused themselves is not significantly greater than the rate in general populations of young men, this may lend some weight to a hypothesis that sexually abusive behaviour is more a problem of masculinity rather than a traumagenic consequence of sexual victimisation. Although I simplify both sides of this argument necessarily here, resolving this issue is clearly a key task for the sexual aggression field. It also requires us to go beyond the sex offender orthodoxy and scrutinise the research evidence from the wider sexual abuse field, in particular, studies examining the dynamics and consequences of male sexual victimisation. Thus, this chapter seeks to take an evidence-based approach to address the following key questions:

- How far is own sexual victimisation an important factor in the development of adolescent sexual aggression and what mechanisms are involved?
- How far is own sexual victimisation a significant factor in differentiating sub-groups of young abusers, and if so, what are the implications for the group with a dual sexual abuse experience?
- What can we learn from research about male victims of sexual abuse, to inform work with young men who have sexually abused others?
- How can practitioners develop an approach to the dual focus of a young person's sexual abuse experience?

How far is own sexual victimisation an important factor in the development of adolescent sexual aggression and what mechanisms are involved?

There is agreement amongst authors that the relationship between early sexual victimisation and later sexual offending is complex and, as yet, not fully understood (Veneziano et al., 2000). Nonetheless, the higher proportion of young abusers with prior experiences of sexual victimisation than in non-abuser control groups or in general population studies, despite methodological problems, suggests that processes or mechanisms may be present in some male victims which lead them towards sexually abusive behaviour. Better understanding of these mechanisms, and importantly why other abused males escape these mechanisms, is a crucial element for the field, both in terms of treatment and prevention (MacMillan, 2000). Several suggestions have been made as to the mechanisms which may be present (Veneziano et el., 2000). These include:

- The re-enactment of the abuse (Longo, 1982) and a replication of parallel dynamics of own victimisation (Veneziano et al., 2000).
- An attempt to achieve mastery over conflicts resulting from the abuse (Watkins and Bentovim, 1992).
- Subsequent conditioning of sexual arousal to assaultive fantasies (Hunter and Becker, 1994).
- A reactive or learnt behaviour response (Ryan et al., 1987).

In their empirical review of these processes in a sample of 74 adolescent male sex offenders, Veneziano et al. (2000) found close parallels between own abuse characteristics and subsequent sexually aggressive behaviours. In particular, they found that young men who were themselves abused under the age of five were twice as likely to select victims who are younger than five. Those who were abused by males were also twice as likely to abuse males themselves. More significantly, they found a close correlation between types of victimisation experience and type of abuse. Boys who were subject to anal intercourse were fifteen times more likely to anally abuse their own victims than adolescent sex offenders who had not been abused in this way themselves. Similarly, if their own abuse had involved fondling, they were seven times more likely to

abuse their victims in this way. The evidence from this study, then, goes some way to supporting the hypothesis that:

> ... for a subset of adolescent sexual offenders, the explanation of their behaviours may be seen as a re-enactment of their own experiences of sexual abuse.
>
> (Veneziano et al., 2000: 370)

There are two related implications of this finding for practitioners working with young men with a dual sexual abuse experience. The first is that, in seeking to more fully understand the nature of sexually aggressive behaviour, we should pay attention to what is known about the young man's victimisation history. Conversely, a clear pattern of sexually aggressive acts may provide clues as to victimisation history (Veneziano et al., 2000). Secondly, paying specific attention to a young abuser's victimisation history alongside his current sexually aggressive behaviours may 'provide a mechanism for defining high-risk situations' (Veneziano et al., 2000: 372) and for assisting the development of specific risk management plans.

Burton (2000) used an anonymous survey to explore the relationship between trauma and perpetration in three groups of incarcerated adolescent sex offenders. The first group were those who admitted to sexual offending before the age of 12 only, the second were those that admitted to sexual offending after the age of 12 only and the third group of continuous offenders, i.e. those admitting to sexual offending both before and after the age of 12. Whilst it was found that victimisation and subsequent perpetration were significantly correlated in all three groups, the continuous offenders had both higher trauma and perpetration scores. The conclusion is that many sexually aggressive young people are highly traumatised and suggests that this 'validates the movement in the field toward resolution of that trauma as an *important and relevant factor in treating child and adolescent sexual offenders*' (Burton, 2000, p45, *my emphasis*).

Paolucci et al. (2001) provide a helpful meta-analysis of the effects of child sexual abuse (CSA). They argue that previous studies have created confusion about the impact and severity of CSA on human development due to inconsistencies and methodological problems. Their attempt is to provide a coherent view of the impact of abuse across six key specific effects, namely PTSD, depression, suicide, poor academic achievement and, most notably for the purposes of this chapter, sexual promiscuity and the propensity for victims of abuse to perpetrate subsequent sexual abuse. Paolucci et al.'s findings are of great importance, particularly as they are based on a large number of participants (in total, 25,367) and have a high level of reliability. In contrast to other previous reports, they find no statistical difference in impact of sexual abuse according to type of abuse (i.e. contact versus non-contact), the age at which the abuse occurred, the relationship between the perpetrator and the victim, or the number of incidents of abuse. Whilst these findings contrast significantly with other previous studies, the authors conclude that:

> *It may be that the experience of CSA itself stands out as a negatively significant event, which does not discriminate across individuals but rather affects human development in a consistent manner.*
> (Paolucci et al., 2001: 31)

Importantly, whilst the authors found no statistically significant difference between male and female victims, they clearly demonstrate that individuals who were sexually victimised in their childhood appear to be at increased risk of developing a range of symptoms, including sexual promiscuity and sexual perpetration (Paolucci et al., 2001).

Nagy et al. (1994) compared the risky health behaviours of young people who are sexually active, those who have been sexually abused and adolescents who abstain from sexual behaviour. For both girls and boys they found significantly higher levels of risky behaviour and liberal sexual attitudes in the sexually abused group than in the non-abused and abstaining groups. Again, it is not possible to infer causality from these findings, but they are striking as they are based on normative and non-clinical samples. They appear to show that sexual abuse predisposes both male and female adolescents to episodes of risky health behaviours, some of which are sexual in nature (Nagy et al., 1994).

In summary, the evidence about the relationship between prior sexual victimisation and sexual aggression is complex and tentative, but nevertheless important. We should certainly not assume a simplistic mono-causal link between victimisation and subsequent sexual aggression. This is a potentially stigmatising and dangerous assumption for the vast majority of male victims of sexual abuse who survive their experiences without recourse to sexual aggression. At the same time, to fail to recognise the inter-relationship between victimisation and abusive behaviour where it exists misses an important treatment opportunity. Evidence supports the view that experiencing sexual abuse is in itself and in isolation of other factors a poor predictor of future sexual aggression. Sexual victimisation is also an inadequate single explanation of sexually abusive behaviour where it is displayed (Hummel et al., 2000). Indeed, Rutter argues that any one psychosocial risk factor in isolation of other factors shows a poor relationship to psychosocial problem behaviour (Rutter, 1995). Hummel et al. (2000) conclude that experiencing CSA is therefore 'probably only to be considered a categorical stress factor if the dimensions of such experience are intensive and long-lasting' (2000: 316). Thus, we should regard sexual victimisation as a distinct traumagenic component in a young man's pathway to sexually abusive behaviour, a factor which may have had a direct or indirect influence upon his cognitions and subsequent behavioural expression. In this sense, sexual victimisation can be especially significant in that it provides an explicit *sexual* motivation to what are often a range of distorted cognitive processes and maladaptive behavioural responses to non-sexual difficulties in a young man's life.

Are young male abusers with own sexual victimisation experiences different from those without such experiences?

Having considered the complexity of the relationship between victimisation and abusive behaviour, a second consideration is the degree to which this sub-group of young male abusers is different from non-abused adolescent sexual offenders.

Hummel et al. (2000) examined the similarities and differences in a group of 107 identified male adolescent sex offenders between those with and those without a history of sexual abuse. They found no statistical differences between the two groups in terms of IQ, physical development and intellectual ability. Nor were there significant differences in victim choice; i.e. those who had been abused were no more likely to abuse boys than they were girls. This differs from Worling's (1995) earlier study, in which he found that 75% of sexually victimised adolescents abused only boys or both boys and girls. Hummel et al. (2000) did find striking differences, however, in relation to family characteristics, with the victimised perpetrator group experiencing significantly more loss of parent due to death, separation, divorce or fostering before the age of 14. Similar findings emerge from Skuse et al. (1998). This may signify that sexually victimised perpetrators are more likely to carry with them into their adolescence more pronounced disorders of attachment. Hummel et al. (2000) also found that the non-abused group were significantly more likely to have fondled their victims, as opposed to the abused group, who tended to engage in more 'mature' genital acts, reflecting their own traumatic and precocious introduction to sexual behaviour through their abuse. They hypothesise that, for the non-abused group, sexually abusive behaviour is more likely to be **instrumental**; i.e. it serves as a means of establishing sexual contact with another person for the first time, whereas for the victimised perpetrator it is more likely to be **expressive** in nature, representing a form of sexualised violence. Whilst these hypotheses remain tentative, it is clear that the meaning of a young person's sexually abusive behaviour may be different when it occurs within the context of prior sexual victimisation. These are factors which clinicians need to consider carefully when planning interventions with sexually abusive adolescents.

What can we learn about the impact of sexual abuse on males which is of relevance to the sexual aggression field?

What differentiates boys who have been sexually abused and appear to manage this experience without displaying sexually aggressive behaviours from those who are abused and go on to victimise others? This is an important clinical question for practitioners who are working with young abuser populations. Feiring et al. (2000) examined the influence that shame and self-blame have on mediating the adolescent victim's response to sexual abuse. In particular, they noted that the way victims evaluate their own abuse experiences and the degree to which they have a self-blaming attributional style is related to subsequent psychological distress. One of the implications of this model in the victim field is that it might be possible to explain which

victims are most at risk of psychological and interpersonal problems following abuse. Research by Feiring et al. (1998) into this conceptual model found that the effects of characteristics of a victim's abuse experience (for example, the number of assaults, severity of incidents, etc.) were mediated by the victim's level of shame and attributional self-blame and that these mediators had a significant relationship to psychological distress.

This model offers a useful conceptualisation for practitioners working with adolescent sexual aggressors in that it helps to understand why some young people appear to respond so significantly to relatively transient sexual abuse experiences and others appear to have escaped relatively symptom-free from more extensive histories of sexual abuse. According to the model described by Feiring, more shame and higher levels of self-blame for the abuse are related to higher levels of depression, higher levels of post-traumatic stress and poorer self-esteem in victims (Feiring et al., 2000). Victims with higher levels of shame and more pronounced self-blame attributional styles are more likely to have smaller friendship networks, less supportive and satisfying peer relationships and feel less competent in terms of romantic relationships. These may clearly be important factors presenting within work with young abusers. Whilst these may traditionally be seen as part of a presentation of denial (e.g. 'John is always trying to adopt the victim position'), the research suggests that these factors may have had an important role in influencing the degree to which the victimisation experience has propelled the young man towards sexually aggressive behaviour. One implication for work with young men with a dual sexual abuse experience is that we should assess routinely the degree to which a young person blames himself and feels shame for his own abuse, as well as his understanding of responsibility issues for his own behaviours. For young people who exhibit higher levels, we should put early effort into enabling them to free themselves from the distortion of shame relating to victimisation and to 'de-link' blame and responsibility issues regarding their own victimisation from their abusive behaviours. This can be a long and difficult process for many such young men.

In order to identify factors that may increase the risk of development of sexually abusive behaviours in abused male adolescents, Skuse et al. (1998) compared two groups of young men who had been sexually abused. The first group had gone on to develop sexually abusive behaviours following their victimisation, the second had not. Importantly, they found that the risk of becoming an abuser in their sample did not appear to be related to the severity of the victimisation experience. However, the two groups were best distinguished by the frequency by which the adolescents who went on abuse others had experienced and witnessed intrafamilial violence. Again, this is important as it highlights that factors apparently not directly related to the sexual abuse experience itself are pertinent as mediators of the damage of the victimisation experience. The developing theory and research base in respect of resilience (see, for example, Rutter, 1999; Heller, 1999) offers the clearest perspective to date as to the mechanisms which may be involved here. Resilience has been defined variously but can be seen as 'the *process* of, *capacity* for, or *outcome* of successful adaptation despite challenging or threatening circumstances' (Masten et al. 1990, *my emphasis*). Like most other psychosocial risk factors, we now know that there is substantial individual variation in males' responses to sexual abuse. Part of this may be constitutional, but it is in part also social in origin. The damage of the sexual abuse tends to have a greater impact when it occurs in the context of other stresses or vulnerabilities. Thus, the cumulative impact of psychosocial risk factors facing a male who is being abused is important. However, examination of risk mechanisms alone cannot account for why some children appear to be resilient following abuse. There is an equal need to examine the range of protective mechanisms which may moderate a young person's response to a risk situation, in this case sexual abuse. In order to understand and promote resilience we need to try to understand how risk and protective factors or mechanisms work and how they **interact**. For the sexual abuse field, this means paying attention to the wider context within which a child experiences sexual abuse, assessing the interlinking nature of risk and protective mechanisms. It may be as important to understand the young person's developmental pathways leading to exposure to the risk factor (sexual abuse) as the pathways or processes from the victimisation experience to the pyschosocial outcome (sexual abusive behaviour). Such a theoretical model goes some

way towards explaining why some boys appear to be so significantly damaged by their sexual abuse that they are thrown towards a trajectory of sexually abusive and aggressive sexuality, whereas others escape such a trajectory.

Conceptualising and understanding male sexual abuse impact mechanisms

Understanding the wide-ranging consequences of male CSA for victims is vital for practitioners in the sexual aggression field who need to be aware of the likelihood that young male abusers who have been sexually abused will be carrying into assessment and treatment unresolved impact issues from their own abuse experience. It is necessary to understand the processes by which these come to influence a young man's presentation. For example, it would be over-simplistic to understand a young man's depictions of himself as a victim in his life purely as an offence-specific cognitive distortion used to defend himself against taking on responsibility for his abusive actions, when in fact the young man has indeed been sexually victimised. We cannot simply expect a young man to suspend this core element of his experience in order to look at his own actions. Indeed, we should not approach sexually aggressive behaviour on the basis that any emotional difficulties or victimisation-related problems are invalidated by the person's status as an 'abuser'. Understanding the litany of potential victim impact issues, and the mechanisms by which they are promoted and interact, is therefore an important feature of remaining responsive to young men who have a dual sexual abuse experience.

There may be several important factors which distinguish male sexual victimisation from female sexual abuse. This is not to suggest that one is more serious than the other, merely that the socialisation of males and females, and the respective social norms which influence their sexual identification and behaviour, vary according to gender. Duncan highlights how traditional male sexual scripts dictate how males should be the initiators of sexual interaction and be dominant, whilst female partners should be in a submissive role (Duncan, 1998). Additionally, she maintains that social norms dictate that such interaction should be agreed on. Generally in cases of sexual abuse it is the second norm which is violated, but in the case of sexual abuse of males the first norm is also transgressed, as the male is put in a submissive and victim position (Duncan, 1998).

The body of empirical research addressing the long-term impact of male sexual victimisation is small in comparison to that which examines sexual abuse of females. However, the evidence suggests that men sexually abused as children are more likely than their non-abused peers to have negative self-perceptions and low self-esteem (Browne and Finkelhor, 1986; Finkelhor, 1990; Hunter, 1991) and increased difficulties in the development and maintenance of satisfying intimate adult relationships (Briere et al., 1988; Elliott and Briere, 1992). Elliott and Briere (1992) also found that sexually abused men are more likely to masturbate compulsively and have greater difficulty in establishing sexual relationships. Duncan (1998) hypothesises that the long-term negative impact of child sexual abuse of males on heterosexual relationships may be more pronounced when the abuse is perpetrated by female care-givers than when perpetrated by males. At the same time, it is known that experiencing same sex sexual abuse does impact upon males' sexual beliefs and gender role identity (Duncan, 1998). Various studies have found a correlation between same-sex sexual abuse in boys and later homosexual behaviours (for example, Finkelhor, 1979; Johnson and Shrier, 1987) although care needs to be taken to avoid unsupported causal inferences. Seeing a young person's gay sexual identification simplistically as a response to abuse, or even worse, as an indication of risk of abusive behaviour, is greatly problematic and pathologising. Little research has been undertaken on the influence of gender of perpetrator upon impact responses to CSA. However, Duncan's (1998) follow up of 106 males who were sexually abused in childhood twenty years later found that males who had been abused by women were more likely to be adolescent sex offenders and adult sex offenders than comparison males.

Given that such a range of impact issues reported in the research and the literature is so broad, it may be useful to develop a conceptual map of potential impact issues on three interlinking levels of impact response, i.e. neurophysiological, cognitive and behavioural. Figure 1 is offered as an assessment tool for practitioners who may be encountering a range of interlinking impact responses in young men.

Clearly, we should guard against a simple checklist use of the chart, or indeed a simplistic analysis of impact issues. As we have seen above, sexual abuse is traumagenic in nature and its impact is mediated by a host of variables associated both with the abuse and other wider constitutional, familial and environmental factors. Nonetheless, the nature of male sexual abuse means that we may be able to identify a range of key presentation issues often associated with male CSA victims who go on to perpetrate sexual abuse:

Denial of vulnerability, distortions of responsibility

Some young men entering treatment as a result of their sexually abusive behaviour have difficulty acknowledging or even recognising that they have previous experiences of being sexually victimised. Young men's socialisation leaves them little room to express or experience vulnerability. If they do, they are given the implicit message that they are weak and therefore not real men. It is no wonder, then, that some young males do whatever they can to shun the identity of 'victim'. Aggressive and exaggerated attempts to retain or regain control in their interactions with other people, including sexual aggression, are common. Vulnerability exposes young men in a most humiliating and disempowering way. As a result, young men may present as stubborn and engage in power struggles, or alternatively they can present as passive and over-conforming. Although at different ends of a continuum, both responses are concerned with self-protection. It is important to encourage young men at either end of this continuum to accept their own vulnerability and lack of responsibility for their own victimisation, whilst understanding their responsibility and their victims' vulnerability in relation to the abuse they have perpetrated. At initial presentation, many young men cannot de-link these issues and the two sides of their sexual abuse experience can appear to them as an amorphous and indistinguishable mess. Assessment and intervention work should be sensitive to this and we should not simply assume that a young man's failure to see the two aspects of his sexual abuse experience as separate entities is a convenient way of denying responsibility for the harm he has perpetrated.

Figure 1: Male sexual abuse trauma impact chart.

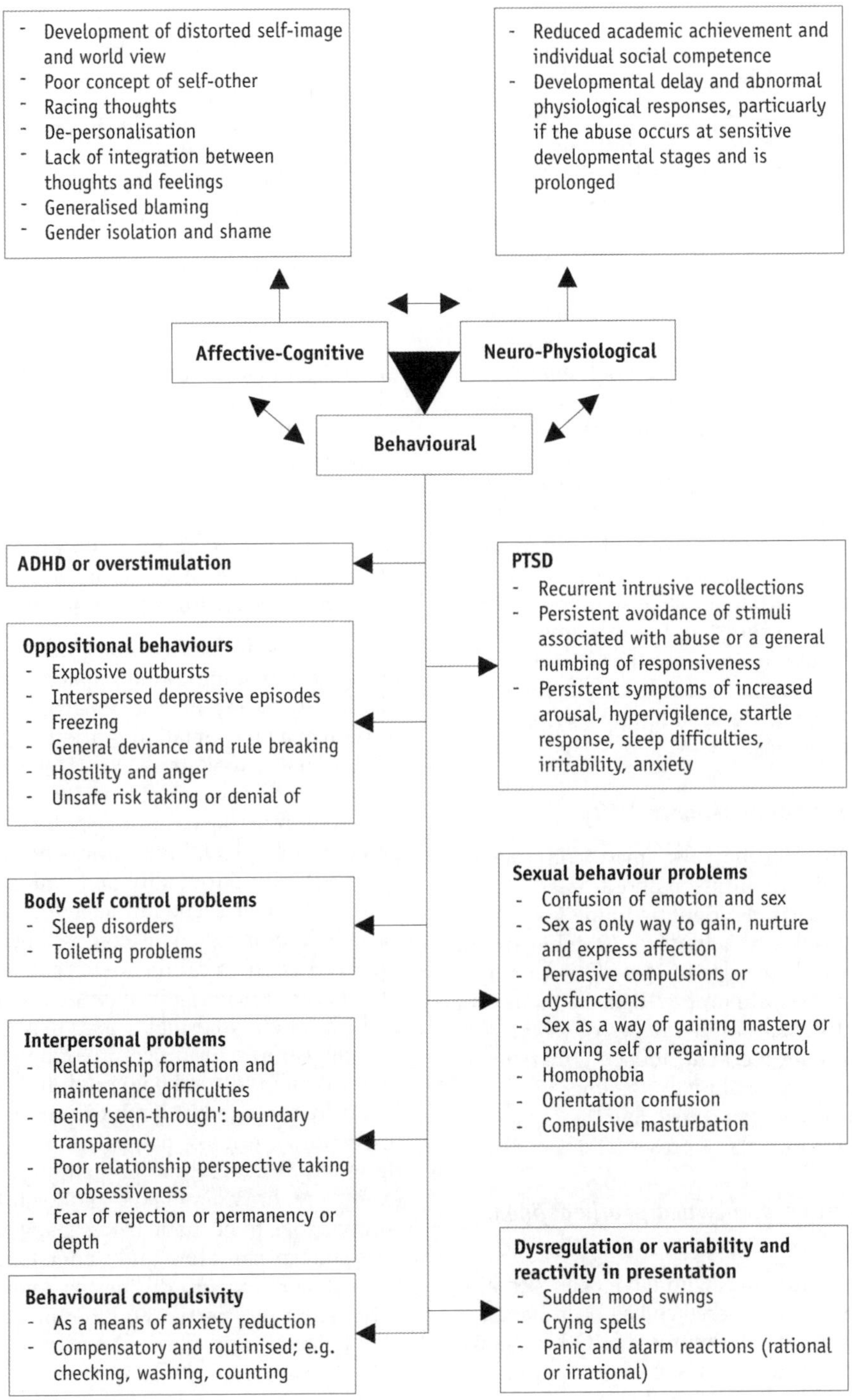

Development of distorted self-image and world view
- Development of distorted self-image and world view
- Poor concept of self-other
- Racing thoughts
- De-personalisation
- Lack of integration between thoughts and feelings
- Generalised blaming
- Gender isolation and shame

- Reduced academic achievement and individual social competence
- Developmental delay and abnormal physiological responses, particuarly if the abuse occurs at sensitive developmental stages and is prolonged

Affective-Cognitive

Neuro-Physiological

Behavioural

ADHD or overstimulation

PTSD
- Recurrent intrusive recollections
- Persistent avoidance of stimuli associated with abuse or a general numbing of responsiveness
- Persistent symptoms of increased arousal, hypervigilence, startle response, sleep difficulties, irritability, anxiety

Oppositional behaviours
- Explosive outbursts
- Interspersed depressive episodes
- Freezing
- General deviance and rule breaking
- Hostility and anger
- Unsafe risk taking or denial of

Body self control problems
- Sleep disorders
- Toileting problems

Sexual behaviour problems
- Confusion of emotion and sex
- Sex as only way to gain, nurture and express affection
- Pervasive compulsions or dysfunctions
- Sex as a way of gaining mastery or proving self or regaining control
- Homophobia
- Orientation confusion
- Compulsive masturbation

Interpersonal problems
- Relationship formation and maintenance difficulties
- Being 'seen-through': boundary transparency
- Poor relationship perspective taking or obsessiveness
- Fear of rejection or permanency or depth

Behavioural compulsivity
- As a means of anxiety reduction
- Compensatory and routinised; e.g. checking, washing, counting

Dysregulation or variability and reactivity in presentation
- Sudden mood swings
- Crying spells
- Panic and alarm reactions (rational or irrational)

Confusion regarding sex and sexual identity

Having been abused and having subsequently abused others can bring with it a profound sense of confusion about the role of sex in the context of a young man's wider interpersonal relationships. For some young men, this means that they may enter treatment without any sense or experience of non-abusive sexuality. Their degree of sexualisation through their own abuse may have left them with a distorted view that sex is the same as nurturance, with sex as the primary means of meeting their own emotional needs. Sexual identity or orientation is frequently an unresolved issue. If the young man was abused by another male and then goes on to abuse male victims, this may clearly raise questions about homosexual identity, which needs to dealt with appropriately by practitioners. Some young men respond by processing all same sex sexual interaction as abuse. The practitioner task is to help the young man to de-link abusive and healthy sexual identity and expression. Young men may also face the doubly difficult experience of traumatic flashbacks or intrusive imagery to both sides of their abuse experience. For example, Dean (14 years old) told me that he had traumatic dreams in which his own abuser was watching over him and laughing as Dean abused his victims.

Gender shame or hypermasculinity

Gender dynamics may also impact on a wider level to produce confusion and anxiety regarding masculine identity. Some young people can be extremely uncomfortable around other men and struggle to identify with male peers. They may attempt to distance themselves from negative masculine images or to avoid identifying with the male abuser. Others may present hyper-masculine traits, where aggression and violence become the predominant models of presentation.

Boundary transparency and poorly defined sense of self

For many young men who have been sexually abused, their life experience has been one of continual boundary trangression. Other people have not respected their sexual and emotional boundaries. They may fear that others can see their failures and vulnerability and experience difficulty in developing trust. Their own abusive behaviour has further compounded this, as they have learnt how to meet their own needs by trangressing others' boundaries. They may have little sense of their own worth or value of themselves as an individual with rights, needs and responsibilities. For example, Sean aged 15 abused boys aged 8-years-old in ways which reflected his own abuse at the age of eight, whilst at the same time becoming involved himself on the rent scene, where he was exploited and abused by adult men.

Chaotic relationships

Many young men, through the process of being abused and abusing, have enormous difficulties around intimacy, autonomy and relationships. They may experience extreme and intense swings in their desire for closeness and distance with others, including within a therapeutic context.

How can practitioners develop an approach to the dual focus of a young person's sexual abuse experience?

Having considered the implications of research and theory relating to the impact of male victimisation, and having reviewed a number of particular presentation issues for young men with a dual sexual abuse experience, I now turn to how such issues can be dealt with within an integrative approach. By this, I mean an approach which both positively *recognises* and *deals* with the duality of a young man's abuse experience. The rationale for such an approach, in my view, is compelling. Whatever the exact aetiological role own sexual victimisation plays *for an individual young person*, and I have stressed that it may play a different aetiological role for different young people, its presence should not be ignored. Indeed, it is my contention that it affords an excellent opportunity to make parallels in treatment designed to treat sexual perpetration. For example, there are obvious and useful comparisons to be made between a young man's own conceptualisation and understanding of himself as the victim during his abuse and his subsequent perspectives on the impact of his own behaviour on those who he has victimised.

In the past, traditional approaches to adolescent sex offender treatment have tended to steer clear of making such connections, under the assumption that addressing a young abuser's victimisation experiences may, in some way, be diverting attention away from a focus on his abusive behaviour or that it may equate to colluding with the offender. This, however, seems to be a remarkable example of a partial and disjointed therapeutic response-seeing an 'issue' (i.e. the abusive behaviour) as the key factor, rather than the person. The challenge in the field is therefore to find ways of balancing respectful and appropriate recognition of a young person's own abuse with appropriate challenges to abusive behaviour. Rather than conceptualising these two elements as incompatible, it is my view that the two are symbiotic and can be used to complement each other. Moreover, young abusers who have themselves been sexually victimised (however large that this sub-group actually is) have a right to have their victimisation acknowledged in a way which helps them resolve its impact, regardless of their own status as 'abusers'. There is growing evidence that this perspective is supported in the field. For example, Muster (1992) surveyed practitioners' attitudes in respect of treatment of victimised adolescent perpetrators. Although her sample is small, only 18 clinicians in the sexual abuse and sexual aggression fields, she found that these practitioners did not agree that offender issues must be dealt with first, rather that these issues should be dealt with flexibly and simultaneously with victimisation issues. Additionally, respondents' did not attribute significance to the idea that 'sympathetic' treatment of victimised perpetrators is likely to reinforce minimisation and denial (Muster, 1992).

Towards a model for practice – the process

It is important to state that I do not advocate that sex offender therapists should see themselves as offering the primary recovery work for a young man's own sexual victimisation. For some young men, skilled victimisation-specific therapy should be offered in isolation to and before any work on their abusive behaviour. However, I am supportive of the view that practitioners working primarily with abusive behaviours should build into their programmes opportunities to encourage the young person to explore the interconnections between the two elements of their experiences, their similarities and differences, and the young person's affective and behavioural responses

to the totality of their abuse experiences. This element of work is therefore not meant as a stand-alone model of practice, nor should it be envisaged merely as a one-off session within the course of a 'sex-offence specific' programme, but it is more a consistent theme or thread running throughout intervention designed to address a young person's abusive behaviour. Alan Jenkins' work on addressing the dual sexual abuse experience of young male abusers provides a helpful model for such an integrative approach (Jenkins, 1995). Adapting Jenkins' model slightly, we can conceive of a six-stage process in addressing victimisation experiences:

1. Acknowledge the significance of the young person's sexual abuse experience and the importance of its disclosure.
2. Help the young man reflect upon the impact of the abuse upon his development, attitudes, feelings and behaviours.
3. Encourage the young man to draw distinctions between his own abusive behaviour and his own abuse and abuser.
4. Acknowledges that facing abuse is a sign of maturity and respect (to self and others).
5. Help the young man to de-construct his experience of victimisation.
6. Help the young man to re-construct his experience of victimisation.

Table One demonstrates practitioner tasks within each of the stages, together with some suggested interventions.

A number of additional issues are highlighted in respect of the process and orientation of work on victimisation issues.

The first is the need for a non-emotive approach by the worker to the young person's own abuser. It is clearly not appropriate to 'demonise' the young person's abuser when dealing with victimisation issues. This is a relatively common approach in sexual abuse recovery work, for example the kind of techniques which encourage adolescent and adult survivors to express their anger about their abuse by beating cushions which represent their abuser. Mark, aged 15 who had abused his brother but who was offered separate work on his own victimisation experiences told me that being asked to do this by his therapist made him feel like he was 'beating himself up'. Indeed, there is evidence that highly cathartic interventions are ineffective with young men who have been abused (Gonsiorek, 1994) and, indeed, such approaches may also be

Table 1: Addressing young abusers' sexual victimisation experiences (Jenkins, 1995, adapted).

Stage	Therapist's tasks	Examples of intervention
(1) Acknowledge the significance of the young person's sexual abuse experience and its disclosure.	Stress the young person's courage in being able to address both aspects of his abuse experience. Encourage the young person to own up to and quantify the pain, distress and unfairness of his abuse experience.	• *Is this the first time that you have talked about –?* • *What did it take for you to be able to speak out?* • *How has it been to keep your abuse inside?* • *How does it affect you to recall your abuse?* • *How much (out of ten) has the abuse hurt you?* • *What are you proving (to yourself and your abuser) by speaking out?* • *What difference will speaking out make to you/to your family/to how others see you?*
(2) Reflect the impact of the abuse upon the young man	Reflect the impact of the abuse and mobilise it as a force for responsibility and behavioural change. Reflect the link between the abuse experience and the abusive behaviour.	• *Is it fair that you are expected to face up to your abuse, if no-one has tried to understand what you have been through?* • *Who knows how hard it is for you to face up to what you have done to victim?* • *How could coming to terms with your own abuse help you to face up to what you did to victim?* • *Who else is aware of how difficult it is to live with your offence when you know how it feels to be abused?*
(3) Help the young man to draw distinctions between his own abusive behaviour and his own abuse and abuser	Focus upon the abuser's lack of courage or inability to stop. Highlight the difference between the young person facing the abuse and the abuser's denial.	• *Did your abuser ever face up to his abuse of you, like you are doing now about victim?* • *Do you think that your abuser has ever taken the time to think about you and what he did?* • *How do you feel about yourself now that you have had the courage to do something he has never done?* • *By starting to make changes and be committed to an abuse-free life, do you think that you are following his ways or are you breaking free from his influence?* • *What do you think your abuser would think to hear you breaking his secrets?* • *Will being honest about the things that have happened give him or you more power?*

Table 1: *Continued.*

(4) Acknowledge that facing abuse is a sign of maturity and respect (self and others)	Acknowledge how the young person is showing self respect and respect to those he hurt. Stress the alternatives for dealing with the legacy of abuse other than to hurt others.	• *Do you know what I mean when I say that burying your hurt feelings usually ends up with you taking them out on someone else?* • *Have you ever faced your feelings of hurt and talked about them as maturely as you are doing today?* • *What ways are you learning not to take out hurt feelings on others?* • *What difference will this make?*
(5) De-construct the young person's experience of victimisation	Pick up on clues given by young person Help the young person split up the abuse experience into manageable bits Avoid the young person being overwhelmed or flooded.	• *Whose idea was it?* • *How old were you when it started?* • *How old was your abuser?* • *How did your abuser trick you/set you up for the abuse?* • *How did he try to convince you it was OK?* • *How did he try to silence you?* • *How did he make you feel like you were responsible or to blame?* • *How did he make you carry his shame?*
(6) Re-construct the young person's experience of victimisation	Chart responses and build up a picture over time; e.g. timelines. Highlight the new meanings of the abuse.	• *What difference does it make to your memories and understandings?* • *What light does this shed on your choice to abuse victim?* • *How can we understand things differently now?* • *What does this free you up to achieve now?* • *Can you handle facing up to your abuse of victim even though you still have painful memories of your own past?* • *What would it say about you if you could do this despite the pain your own abuse has caused?*

dangerous for young men who have a dual abuse experience as they can promote the kind of emotional flooding and dysregulation that accompanied their abusive behaviour. Rather than the emotional stimulation afforded by such approaches, in my experience it is often more useful for young men to be taught methods for relaxation and stress relief, rehearsing these over time.

Secondly, we should expect high levels of variability in young men's presentation; swinging between cognitive, affective and behavioural extremes as they deal with their experiences. This is often a reflection of the lack of integration of their own behaviour to their abuse experience.

Thirdly, we should be aware that these young men have often been highly sexualised and over-stimulated throughout their childhoods and adolescence. We should make sure, as a fundamental aspect of this work, that the young man is supported in his efforts to face up to his dual sexual abuse experience by reducing any external over-stimulation and sexualisation in his living environment.

Finally, when asking young men to consider perhaps the two most significant and difficult aspects of their life experience, we should make therapy (and ourselves as therapists) entirely reliable and predictable. The process and parameters of our approach need to be explained from the outset. Indeed, it is often helpful to spell out clearly to a young man with a dual sexual abuse experience the aims of the intervention (i.e. prevention of further abusive behaviour) whilst also giving him explicit permission to address issues arising from his victimisation. Without this, many young men will simply assume that their own abuse is 'off limits' and these issues will not emerge.

Towards a model for practice – the content

I have found it useful to cover the following specific content issues relating to victimisation issues within a programme of work with a young man about his sexually abusive behaviour. The relative weight and importance of these issues varies between young people and, of course, this calls for an individual rather than a blanket approach to these issues. Practitioners will need to make particular decisions about the timing of this work, in order that the 'dual focus' does not allow for collusion or avoidance of responsibility on the young person's part. As a minimum, I have found that it is important, before considering victimisation issues, for a young man to have worked on: the nature of sexual abuse, power, consent, coercion; self-disclosure work on own offending behaviour; and (if applicable) the cycle of sexual assault and the importance of planning and cognitive distortions.

1. *What is sexual abuse?* (revisited)
   I have found that it is often important for young men to review their understandings of what sexual abuse is in light of subsequent work on their own victimisation. This can help in two ways. Developing a better understanding of their own abuse can facilitate greater awareness of the unacceptability of their own abusive actions. Conversely, more general work on sexual abuse can help a young man to reappraise his own perceptions of his victimisation experiences. This work often generates important information on a young man's understandings of issues of responsibility and blame. I also consider the young man's views of masculinity and abuse, examining some of the common messages and myths surrounding abuse of males.

2. *Similarities and differences in my sexual abuse experiences*
   A relatively simple, but nonetheless effective task is to encourage the young man to consider the similarities and differences between both aspects of his sexual abuse. This often promotes a level of insight and connection for the young man which is often lacking at the beginning of intervention. (See intervention exercise one below).

3. *Fitting the pieces of my abuse together*
   Sexual abuse fragments children's development and can cause dysregulation between different developmental strands (e.g. sexual development may be out of step with emotional or social development). Young men often find it difficult to put the pieces of their past in their correct place. As well as not grasping the significance of their personal history, they may also have no sense of the order and duration of their abuse within the context of other life events. Using life lines, I encourage the young man to plot significant life events, charting the duration, frequency and intensity of his sexual experiences. Using different coloured pens to highlight his own abuse, sexually abusive and appropriate sexual experiences can help provide a visually clear map for the young man of his experiences, using conxtextual and environmental clues to build up the picture; e.g. 'who was your best friend when this started to happen?' etc.

4. *Counting the cost of your sexual abuse*
   Here I review with the young man his understanding of the impact and influence of his abuse on his thoughts, feelings and behaviours. I encourage the young man to consider the interconnections between the two sides of his abuse, then widen the focus to look at issues of loss as a result of the abuse, etc.

5. *What my abuse made me believe*
   The basis of this work is to identify how the victimisation experience may have generated distorted cognitions and attributions, some of which may have contributed to a young man's subsequent abusive thoughts and behaviours. The aim of this work is to ask the young man to identify, reconsider and correct these cognitions. (See intervention exercise two below).

6. *The impact of my abuse upon my sexuality and sexual thoughts*
   This is a more focused version of the two areas outlined in 4) and 5) above, but here

I seek to take the young man's awareness further, specifically to consider how his dual abuse experience may have influenced his sexual identification.

7. *My own experiences against those of my victim*
I am careful to avoid too early a comparison between victim related issues, however find that it is useful later in a programme to address these issues side by side. I find it more useful to ask a young man to consider his own and his victim experiences, rather than focusing on comparing affective responses.

8. *A life without abuse: developing healthy ways of coping and sexual expression*
An important part of work on dual sexual abuse experiences is the need to leave a young man with a clear sense of what healthy sexual identification is. Such young men have experienced two very powerful models of inappropriate sex, but often have no experience or examples of positive and appropriate sexual expression. Considering future sexual goals and relationship aspirations can be an important marker for the young person to see beyond abuse.

The following are two examples of intervention exercises which illustrate how practitioners can devise resources to work on the above issues. (You can download formatted versions of these and other 'dual focus' exercises from: *www.sexualaggression.com*).

Intervention exercise one: looking at the similarities and differences of your abuse

(a) Take a piece of paper and draw a line down the middle and head one column 'Similarities' and the other 'Differences'.

(b) Ask the young person to think back to both sides of his abuse experience. Use the space to record what was the same and what was different about the abuse he experienced and the abuse he committed. Aim to help the young man to write down five things that were the same and then five things that were different.

(c) Go over the points together. When he reviews the list of similarities next to each other, ask the young man what he realises about:

- why he abused?
- the choices he made about his behaviour?
- what he needs to do to avoid abuse in the future?

Intervention exercise two: distorted messages

(a) Explain to the young man how sexual abuse and sexual abusers often 'feed' their victims with distorted messages and leave the victim with incorrect thoughts and feelings well after the abuse itself has stopped. Sometimes the distorted messages come about as a result of something the abuser said during the abuse to make sure the victim felt guilty and did not speak out about the abuse: e.g. *'You've got an erection, so you must be enjoying it and want it to carry on.'* Other times the abuser does not need to say anything to the victims and the distorted message comes about as a result of the victim's own confusion about the abuse: e.g. *'I've got an erection, so that must mean that I want this to happen.'* Explain that identifying and freeing himself from the distorted messages his abuser left him with is an important step in learning to come to terms with his abuse and abusing.

(b) Divide some paper into two columns. In the left column help the young person to identify the messages from his own abuse and abuser left him with. Include:

- Things my abuser said to me about the abuse.
- Things my abuser said to me about the way I responded to the abuse.
- Things my abuser said about what would happen if I told.
- Things my abuse made me believe about sex.
- Things my abuse made me believe about myself.
- Any other messages or beliefs the young man was left with following the abuse.

(c) Ask the young person to review each message he has identified. Ask him to consider whether each message is fair or accurate. Use the column on the right to agree to any corrections to the distorted cognitions you have identified.

(d) Explain that once the young person has corrected the messages that were fed to him as a result of his own abuse, the next step is to think back to his own sexually abusive behaviour and to assess which of the messages from his own abuse he used in allowing himself to commit sexual abuse himself. Key questions include:

- How did you allow your actions to be influenced by the messages you received?
- Can you see any links between the distorted messages you received and the way you tried to put down or silence your victim?
- What were the particular messages you gave to your victims during your abusive behaviour? How far do these reflect the messages from your own abuse and how far are they different?

Conclusion

This chapter has sought to review the research evidence relating to male sexual victimisation and to present its relevance to the assessment and treatment of young men who have been both sexually abused and who go on to sexually abuse others. Several important theoretical issues and practical concerns have been reviewed. The evidence suggests that there is a link between own victimisation and subsequent sexually abusive behaviours, albeit this is complex and may involve both indirect and direct mechanisms. We need to be more sensitive to the way in which risk factors interact when working with such young people. We have seen that for a proportion of young men with a dual sexual abuse experience, there may be close parallels between characteristics of their victimisation and perpetrating behaviours. We should gain as full a victimisation history as we can as this may play an important role in risk management. I have suggested that practitioners can develop an intervention approach to victimisation issues within the context of holistic programmes of work designed to address perpetration issues. Perhaps the most salient and straightforward point is that practitioners who work with adolescent sex offenders need to be experts not only in the treatment of offending behaviours, but knowledgeable about and sensitive to victimisation issues. This requires vision outside of traditional professional polarities and approaches.

© *Simon Hackett, 2001. Exercises may be downloaded and reproduced for use in intervention work and training, provided that the author is credited.*

References

Becker, J., Cunningham-Rathner, J., Kaplan, M. (1986) Adolescent Sexual Offenders: Demographics, Criminal and Sexual Histories, and Recommendations for Reducing Future Offenses. *Journal of Interpersonal Violence.* 1: 431–45.

Briere, J., Evans, D., Runtz, M. and Wall, T. (1988) Symptomatology in Men Who Were Molested as Children: A Comparison Study. *American Journal of Ortho-psychiatry.* 58: 457–61.

Browne, A. and Finkelhor, D. (1986) The Impact of Child Sexual Abuse: A Review of the Research. *Psychological Bulletin.* 99: 66–77.

Burgess, A., Hartman, C., McCormack, A. and Grant, C. (1995) Child Victim to Juvenile Victimizer: Treatment Implications. *International Journal of Family Psychiatry.* 9: 403–16.

Burton, D. (2000) Were Adolescent Sexual Offenders Children with Sexual Behaviour Problems? *Sexual Abuse: A Journal of Research and Treatment.* 12, 1: 37–48.

Burton, D., Nesmith, A. and Badten, L. (1997) Clinicians' Views of Sexually Aggressive Children: A Theoretical Exploration. *Child Abuse and Neglect.* 21: 157–70.

Cooper, C., Murphy, W. and Haynes, M. (1996) Characteristics of Abused and Non Abused Adolescent Sexual Offenders. *Sexual Abuse: A Journal of Research and Treatment.* 8: 105–19.

Davies, G. and Leitenberg, H. (1987) Adolescent Sex Offenders. *Psychological Bulletin.* 101(3): 417–27.

Dhawan, S. and Marshall, W. (1996) Sexual Abuse Histories of Sex Offenders. *Sexual Abuse: A Journal of Research and Treatment.* 8: 7–15.

Duncan, L. (1998) Gender Role Socialisation and Male-on-Male Vs. Female-on-Male Child Sexual Abuse. *Sex Roles: A Journal of Research.* 39, 9/10: 765–85.

Elliott, D. and Briere, J. (1992) The Sexually Abused Boy: Problems in Manhood. *Medical Aspects of Human Sexuality.* 26: 68–71.

Feiring, C., Rostenthal, S. and Taska, L. (2000) Stigmatisation and the Development of Friendship and Romantic Relationships in Adolescent Victims of Sexual Abuse. *Child Maltreatment.* 5, 4: 311–22.

Finkelhor, D. (1979) *Sexually Victimised Children.* New York: The Free Press.

Finkelhor, D. (1990) Early and Long-term Effects of Child Sexual Abuse: An Update.

Professional Psychology: Research and Practice. 21: 325–30.

Friedrich, W. and Luecke, W. (1988) Young School-age Sexually Aggressive Children. *Professional Psychology: Research and Practice.* 19: 155–64.

Freeman-Longo, R. (1986) The Impact of Sexual Victimisation on Males. *Child Abuse and Neglect.* 10: 411–4.

Gil, E. and Johnson, T. (1994) *Sexualised Children: Assessment and Treatment of Sexualised Children and Children Who Molest.* Rockville: Launch.

Gonsiorek, J. (1994) Assessment of and Treatment Planning and Individual Psychotherapy for Sexually Abused Adolescent Males. in: Gonsiorek, J., Bera, W. and LeTourneau, D. *Male Sexual Abuse. A Trilogy of Intervention Strategies.* Thousand Oaks: Sage.

Heller, S. et al. (1999) Research on Resilience to Child Maltreatment: Empirical Considerations. *Child Abuse and Neglect.* 23, 4: 321–38.

Hummel, P., Thomke, V., Oldenburger, H. and Specht, F. (2000) Male Adolescent Sex Offenders Against Children: Similarities and Differences Between Those With and Those Without a History of Sexual Abuse. *Journal of Adolescence.* 23, 305–17.

Hunter, J. (1991) A Comparison of The Psychological Maladjustment of Adult Males and Females Sexually Molested as Children. *Journal of Interpersonal Violence,* 6: 205–217.

Hunter, J. and Becker, J. (1994) The Role of Deviant Sexual Arousal in Juvenile Sexual Offending. *Criminal Justice and Behavior.* 21: 132–49.

Jenkins, A. (1995) *Engaging Adolescents Who Sexually Abuse. Workshop Notes.* South Australia: Nada Consultants.

Johnson, R. L. and Shrier, D. (1987) Past Sexual Victimisation by Females of Males in an Adolescent Medicine Clinic Population. *American Journal of Psychiatry.* 144, 650–2.

Longo, R. E. (1982) Sexual Learning and Experience Among Adolescent Sexual Offenders. *International Journal of Offender Therapy and Comparative Criminology.* 26: 235–41.

MacMillan, H. (2000) Child Maltreatment: What We Know in the Year 2000. *Canadian Journal of Psychiatry.* 45, 8: 702–9.

Masten, A, Best, K. and Garmezy, N. (1990) Resilience and Development: Contributions from the Study of Children who Overcome Adversity. *Development and Psychopathology.* 2: 425–44.

Muster, N. (1992) Treating the Adolescent Victim-Turned-Offender. *Adolescence.* 27, 106: 441–50.

Nagy, S., Adcock, A. and Nagy, C. (1994) A Comparison of Risky Health Behaviours of Sexually Active, Sexually Abused, and Abstaining Adolescents. *Pediatrics.* 93, 4: 570–5.

Paolucci, E., Genuis, M. and Violato, C. (2001) A Meta-analysis of the Published Research on the Effects of Child Sexual Abuse. *The Journal of Psychology.* 135(1): 17–36.

Rutter, M. (1995) Causal Concepts and their Testing. in: Rutter, M. and Smith, D. (Eds.) *Psychosocial Disorders in Young People. Time Trends and their Causes.* Chichester: Wiley.

Rutter, M. (1999) Resilience Concepts and Findings: Implications for Family Therapy. *Journal of Family Therapy.* 21: 119–44.

Ryan, G., Lane, S., Davies, J. and Isaac, C. (1987) Juvenile Sex Offenders: Development and Correction. *Child Abuse and Neglect.* 11, 385–95.

Sefarbi, R. (1990) Admitters and Deniers Among Adolescent Sex Offenders and their Families. *American Journal of Orthopsychiatry.* 60(3).

Skuse, D., Bentovim, A, Hodges, J., New, M. J. C., Williams, B. T. R. and McMillan, D. (1998) Risk Factors for the Development of Sexually Abusive Behaviour in Sexually Victimised Adolescent Males. *British Medical Journal.* 317: 175–9.

Veneziano, C., Veneziano, L. and LeGrand, S. (2000) The Relationship Between Adolescent Sex Offender Behaviors and Victim Characteristics with Prior Victimisation. *Journal of Interpersonal Violence.* 15, 4: 363–74.

Vizard, E., Monck, E. and Misch, P. (1995) Child and Adolescent Sex Abuse Perpetrators: A Review of the Research Literature. *Journal of Child Psychological Psychiatry.* 36: 731–56.

Watkins, B. and Bentovim, A. (1992) The Sexual Abuse of Male Children and Adolescents: A Review of Current Research. *Journal of Child Psychology and Psychiatry.* 33: 197–248.

Worling, J. (1995) Sexual Abuse Histories of Adolescent Male Sex Offenders: Differences Based on the Age and Gender of Their Victims. *Journal of Abnormal Psychology.* 104: 610–3.

Worling, J. (2001) Personality-based Typology of Adolescent Male Sexual Offenders: Differences in Recidivism Rates, Victim-Selection Characteristics, and Personal Victimisation Histories. *Sexual Abuse.* 13:2, 149–66.

Chapter 15: A Holistic Approach to Treating Young People who Sexually Abuse

Robert E. Longo MRC, LPC

We teach People what they are.

Pablo Casals

Introduction

The field of assessing and treating youth with sexual behaviour problems, although not new, is still in a developmental stage. As of the writing of this paper, there is no literature that defines the 'best practice' in treating children with sexual behaviour problems (Development Services Group, 2000). In fact, the field still operates with the understanding that much of what we do in assessing and treating children with sexual behaviour problems comes from an understanding that the field operates using many assumptions (National Task Force, 1993).

The assessment and treatment of juvenile sexual offenders (youth with sexual behaviour problems) has been developing and growing over the course of the past 25 years (Burton et al., 2000). This growth has been influenced primarily by the field of treating adult sexual abusers. More often than not there has been a trickle down effect in the assessment and treatment of children with sexual behaviour problems without looking at children who sexually abuse as a separate and distinct group of patients with individual differences and treatment needs. In many cases developmental and contextual issues have been ignored in working with this population (Ryan and Associates, 1999)

In many programmes this trickle down process has resulted in:

1. The misuse of technology.
2. The lack of addressing children and their treatment needs by taking into account their developmental stage.
3. Using a language and materials that may not be easily understood by children who have learning disabilities.

4. Highly confrontational approaches that may trigger trauma in youth with histories of child abuse and neglect.

The majority of juvenile sexual offender (JSO) treatment programmes have generally adhered to traditional sex offender treatment models and strategies for treating adolescents with sexual behaviour problems. These standard treatments usually include cognitive-behavioural or relapse prevention models, and a variety of treatment modalities including teaching the sexual abuse cycle, empathy training, anger management, social and interpersonal skills training, cognitive restructuring, emotional development, teaching coping responses and interventions, assertiveness training, journalling, sex education, and communication skills (Burton et al., 2000; Freeman-Longo et al.,1995; Knopp et al., 1993).

Recently, some of the more traditional approaches to treating sexual abusers have come under criticism, including relapse prevention (RP) the most widely used treatment model by programmes treating both juvenile and adult sexual abusers (Ward and Hudson, 1996; Laws et al., 2000). First, they have noted the limited ways to account for offence behaviour, second, the presentation of the offence chain is overly rigid and leaves no room for individual differences in behaviour (there is no flexibility in the chain of behaviours and events leading to sexual assault), the model is very academic (it intellectualises sex offending) with abstract concepts and complex terms and language, and it relies on coping strategies that are not positive goal oriented i.e., avoidance and escape. Although the model has many limitations, it is a viable model that when modified can be used in conjunction with a holistic approach.

Another criticism of sex offender treatment includes the use of the sexual abuse cycles, a traditional method of teaching the sexual abuse process, which has also come under fire in recent times, Maletzky (1998). Maletzky notes, 'If sexual offenders operated in cycles of behaviour, they would be perpetually seeking deviant gratification; however, that does not match the reality of most sex offenders.' What Maletzky fails to realise, however, is that cycles are not timed in any special way. For some the cycle can take minutes, for others, hours or days, and yet for others weeks, or months. Unhealthy cycles can be broken and new healthy behaviours learned. Furthermore, the concept of cycles goes well beyond the field of sexual abuse treatment. From early times to the present many cultures including those of aboriginal peoples have used the concept of cycles, life cycles, cycles of life, etc. to describe human behaviour and the progression through the varied stages of human life. Cycles are not absolute nor limited. Cycles can have sub-cycles that can develop and build up over time. As Carich (1999) notes in response to Maletzky, 'The definition of a cycle used by Maletzky is very limited when applied to sexual offenders.'

Teaching clients about relapse prevention and the cycle of sexual abuse can be readily blended into a holistic model (Freeman-Longo, 2000). The relapse prevention model has already been adapted to teaching the sexual abuse cycle for many years (Freeman-Longo and Pithers, 1992). Recent modifications to this model enable the blending of the four universal needs, the four aspects of self, and the use of core values and beliefs (Figure 1) to teaching clients about cycles of abuse (Figure 2). By developing a four phase cycle, the four universal needs and the four aspects of self can be readily adapted.

The 'pretends-to-be-normal' phase of the cycle represents the universal need for belonging and the spiritual self. When a client is in this phase of the cycle, basic life areas are not being managed and problems are ongoing. He/she is likely to be withdrawn from others, and the spiritual self not developed.

In the 'build-up' phase of the cycle, the client is engaging in a variety of risk factors, lapses, and maladaptive coping responses. The emotional self is not healthy and the client mismanages emotions often leaving him or her with feelings of anger, rejection, low self-esteem, etc. The universal need for mastery is malfunctioning as the client continues to lose control of his life, thoughts, feelings and behaviours.

The 'acting out' phase of the cycle is the sexual abuse behaviour. The universal need for independence is not met as the client needs a victim in order to act out his feelings and problems. The physical self is acting irresponsibly.

The 'justification phase' of the cycle or the 'downward spiral' represents the universal need for generosity and the mental self. During this phase the client is engaging in denial and other defence mechanisms and the mental self is filled with unhealthy thoughts and cognitive distortions. The need for generosity is replaced with a selfish impulse to protect the self and the client takes from others if he engages others at all and he or she does not give or share.

This chapter will promote the use of a holistic model in the assessment and treatment of sexual abuse and its application to youth with sexual behaviour problems. The holistic model described takes into account the fact that:

1. Children progress through various stages of development.
2. That these stages are often arrested as a result of trauma, child abuse and neglect, attachment and bonding disorders.
3. Humanistic approaches and a focus on developing a therapeutic relationship with these clients is essential to the healing and recovery process.
4. Children learn and work with a variety of learning styles and multiple intelligences.
5. Many traditional assessment and treatment approaches in working with sexual abusers can be modified if necessary.

Traditional sex offender models and treatment modalities can be blended into a holistic model that addresses the wide variety of problems these children have when entering treatment in addition to the sexual behaviour problems for which they are referred to programmes.

Holistic treatment and wellness

What is holistic treatment? Although many often think otherwise, holistic treatment is not a new age fad, but rather a traditional approach to healing and wellness. In regard to the treatment of youth with sexual behaviour problems, holistic treatment is a model that incorporates and modifies, yet moves beyond, the traditional cognitive-behavioural and relapse prevention models used by the majority of programmes. It uses both a variety of

Figure 1: Holistic Treatment.

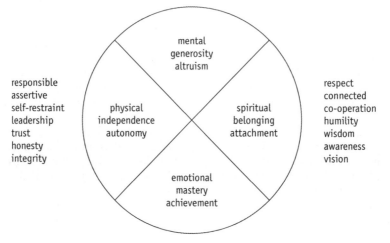

motivation, giving, sharing, compassion, caring, empathy, creativity, forgiveness

mental
generosity
altruism

responsible
assertive
self-restraint
leadership
trust
honesty
integrity

physical
independence
autonomy

spiritual
belonging
attachment

respect
connected
co-operation
humility
wisdom
awareness
vision

emotional
mastery
achievement

confidence, self-control, persistence, achievement, zeal, self-awareness, self-motivation,
self-determination, courage, faith, perseverance, strength

© Robert E. Longo, 2000

Figure 2: The acting out or abuse cycle.

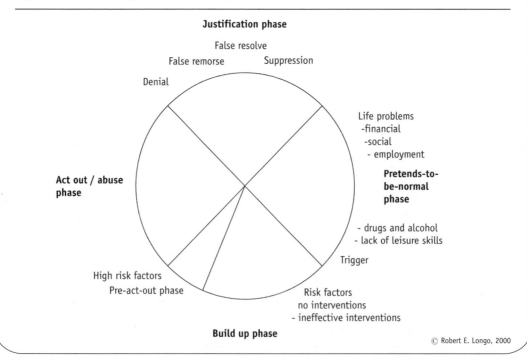

Justification phase

False resolve

False remorse   Suppression

Denial

Life problems
-financial
-social
- employment

**Act out / abuse
phase**

**Pretends-to-
be-normal
phase**

- drugs and alcohol
- lack of leisure skills

Trigger

High risk factors
Pre-act-out phase

Risk factors
no interventions
- ineffective interventions

Build up phase

© Robert E. Longo, 2000

traditional and alternative treatment methods and techniques that explore and incorporate a variety of models to improve ones overall mental and physical health and recovery. In addition, it uses a balance of theoretical and humanistic knowledge that embraces the concept that the therapeutic relationship is the focal point of treatment and essential to the treatment process if it is going to impact the client.

Holistic treatment focuses on wellness. When we label others by the behaviour or with a particular diagnosis, we potentially brand them for life. We see this most clearly with psychiatric diagnosis. People become known as bi-polar, paedophiles, mentally ill, etc. The clearest example I can think of in regard to the field of treating sexual abusers is the saying 'shooting one's self in the foot.' In the field of sexual abuse I use a similar analogy that I refer to as 'the double barrel shot to the feet.' Back in the late 1970s when I entered this work I heard two statements that I found problematic. The first was, 'all victims of sexual abuse are damaged for life,' and the second, 'sex offenders cannot be cured.' Unfortunately, we continue to hear these statements today even in the midst of scientific literature that tells us otherwise.

We know from the literature that as many as 20–25 per cent of child victims of sexual abuse who enter treatment emerge into adulthood with little or no residual trauma. We meet adults who have been sexually abused that are thriving today and have happy, healthy and productive lives. If we work in this field long enough we are blessed with the opportunities to meet women and men who have been brutally raped as children or adults and have not only worked through the horrific trauma of these experiences but also celebrate life.

We know from our experience and the experience of other professionals that many sexual abusers go on to lead productive happy lives after going through treatment. There are literally hundreds of thousands of sexual offenders who have been through specialised treatment programmes and live productively and happily in our communities. Yet when we treat youth with sexual behaviour problems, how often are we guilty of making statements to them that victims are damaged for life and sex offenders cannot be cured? In fact, youth with sexual behaviour problems are more likely

to re-offend in non-sexual offences (Calder, 2001).

As most youth with sexual behaviours have experienced childhood abuse or neglect, what messages are we giving them when we talk about life long damage, and no cure? These powerful statements are debilitating and do not give clients a sense of hope and potential for recovery any more than the statements we give people in medicine that they have a terminal illness. Holistic treatment has a focus on wellness with messages of hope. It gives clients a clear message that they can heal, that they can go forward, and that they are human beings worthy of respect and dignity.

A return to basics

Holistic treatment, in the simplest of terms is a return to basics; looking at the four domains or aspects of self; mind, body, spirit and the emotional self (see Figure 1). In addition, a holistic model addresses the four universal needs for generosity, belonging, mastery, and independence (Brendtro, L., Brokenleg, M., and Van Bockern, S., 1990). The need for generosity is the need for people to give and share of themselves. This is not a giving of materialistic goods, but rather a giving and sharing of time, of one's feelings and one's self.

The need for belonging transcends all cultures and societies. Human beings are social animals with a need to belong to a family, a community, a society, and the need to feel connected to the universe. The lack of belonging leaves one feeling isolated, lonely, and intimacy suffers. Our spiritual self begins to die.

The need for mastery is essential for personal growth and learning. Each of us has a need to feel we have the courage and strength to master tasks from the simple to the more complex. We need to feel in control of ourselves and assured that we can master the tasks that will take us through life.

Finally, the need for independence is that need to operate our lives in a fashion in which we are free from dependence upon others. This is not to say that we don't need or depend on others from time to time, we all do. However, to depend upon others consistently especially in co-dependent ways is unhealthy. A healthy independent self is being responsible for ourselves and assertive in getting our needs met.

The teaching focus of a holistic approach takes into account several core values and beliefs that address the four aspects of self and the four universal needs. These concepts also fit nicely with four leading theories in psychology; altruism, autonomy, attachment, and achievement (see Figure 1).

The core values

Within the holistic model of treating youth with sexual behaviour problems, there is a component that teaches clients about core values and beliefs. Children enter treatment programmes because they have been damaged and need to heal. The damage, often the result of abuse and neglect, leaves these clients lacking in a sense of self. They often do not identify strengths, but generally are able to recite the many weaknesses they see in themselves. Thus, part of the therapeutic journey entails them learning to recognise their strengths and build upon them as well as teaching them healthy values common to cultures and societies and belief systems that reject the notion that they are worthless, that no one cares, that the world is evil and not a safe place.

In Figure 1, the characteristics in the outside of the circle are values and beliefs that coincide with the four universal needs and the four aspects of self. Of course, they are not exclusive to each area but represent areas of learning and development to make up the 'whole' person. They are not unique to a holistic model and many are concepts taught in programmes which treat youth with sexual behaviour problems. For example, in as much as trust and honesty are essential for one to develop a healthy sense of independence, these two values are equally important in developing relationships that foster a sense of belonging and connection to others as well as a belief in one's self.

Each value and belief can be used to develop and enhance the client's potential to use the multiple intelligences that help the client learn and grow personally. In most cases, the professional is stuck with the resistance of clients to adopt these values and beliefs while letting go of the destructive ones they have harboured, in many cases for years and even from shortly after birth.

Labelling

Of importance when looking at a holistic model, is that treatment helps engage clients by being sensitive to the individual's culture, race, and spirituality. A holistic model addresses and includes all life issues and strives for balance and harmony. Holistic treatment sees each person as unique, yet does not label. In the field of treating sexual abusers, clients are often called and labelled as 'sex offenders.' Many programmes often require clients to open group sessions by taking turns saying, 'My name is and I'm a sex offender. I . . .' similar to addictions models such as Alcoholics Anonymous. Negative labels do not help people heal but rather reinforce them staying in the unhealthy state such as 'sex offender' for life. A holistic model does not view people as their label or their behaviour but rather sees people as humans first with a particular problem.

Integration of models and theories

Holistic treatment seeks to bring a variety of theories and models into the treatment process to enhance a person's potential. For example, Howard Gardner (1983), noted for his work on multiple intelligences, teaches us that children have a variety of learning styles and abilities and suggests there are seven learning styles common to children:

- intrapersonal intelligence
- interpersonal intelligence
- visual or spacial intelligence
- verbal or linguistic intelligence
- logical mathematical intelligence
- musical or rhythmic intelligence
- body or kinesthetic intelligence.

Intrapersonal intelligence involves knowledge of the internal aspects of the self, such as knowledge of feelings, the range of emotional responses, thinking processes, self-reflection and metacognition (a sense of our intuition and awareness of spiritual realities). It allows us to step back from ourselves and watch ourselves as an outside observer. It involves our capacity to experience wholeness and unity, to discern patterns of connection with the larger order of things, to perceive higher states of consciousness, to experience the lure of the future, and to dream of and actualise the possible. In working with youth with behavioural problems it is not likely that this intelligence has been developed and one facet of treatment will be to develop this intelligence in order to promote the client's ability to develop relationships, empathy, and work with unhealthy thinking patterns. If this intelligence is not developed as a part of treatment, there is less likelihood that cognitive restructuring and emotional development will realise its fullest potential as part of the treatment process. Most certainly, the lack of developing this intelligence will affect attachment and the ability to form meaningful relationships. Examples of methods to develop this intelligence include teaching silent meditation or reflection, thinking strategies, emotional processing, focusing or concentration skills, complex guided imagery.

Interpersonal intelligence involves the ability to work co-operatively with others in a group as well as the ability to communicate verbally and non-verbally with other people. This intelligence builds on the capacity to notice distinctions among others; for example, contrasts in moods and temperament. Thus, interpersonal intelligence operates primarily through person-to-person relationships and communication. When this intelligence is used, the therapeutic relationship can be extremely powerful in teaching clients and supporting them through the treatment process. Examples of methods to develop this intelligence include giving and receiving feedback, intuiting other's feelings, co-operative learning strategies, practising empathy, collaboration skills, group projects.

Visual or spatial intelligence deals with such things as visual arts (including painting, drawing, and sculpture), and games which require the ability to visualise objects from different perspectives and angles such as chess. Visual or spatial intelligence relies on the sense of sight and being able to form mental images or pictures in the mind and to visualise objects. For children who do not work well with verbal/linguistic intelligences, this intelligence can be a primary mode of learning and assimilating information. Experiential therapies are useful in working with those who use this form of intelligence. Examples of methods to develop this intelligence include guided imagery, working with colour schemes, patterns and designs, art therapies, and working with pictures.

Verbal or linguistic intelligence is related to the use of words and language, both written and spoken. The use of and reliance upon this intelligence dominates most western educational systems and includes poetry, humour, story-telling, use of metaphors, symbolic thinking, abstract reasoning, and reading and writing. This is the intelligence most treatment programmes for youth with sexual behaviour problems rely upon, as they incorporate a variety of reading and writing assignments. Use of this intelligence is also used in sit down individual and group therapies, psycho-educational classes, and the like. For children who do not learn well with this intelligence it is likely the client will not do well in treatment or may even drop out of or fail in treatment. Examples of methods to develop this intelligence include reading, vocabulary development, journal/diary keeping, creative writing, use of humour, impromptu speaking, and storytelling.

Logical mathematical intelligence is most often associated with what is known as 'scientific thinking,' or inductive reasoning. It requires the capacity to recognise patterns, work with abstract symbols, and see connections between separate and distinct pieces of information. Many clients who suffer developmental delays and learning disabilities will often not rely upon this form of intelligence for learning. Examples of methods to develop this intelligence include outlining, number sequences, calculation, problem solving, and pattern games.

Musical or rhythmic intelligence includes such capacities as the recognition of rhythmic and tonal patterns, including sensitivity to various environmental sounds, the human voice, and musical instruments. Of all forms of intelligence, the 'consciousness altering' effect of music and rhythm on the brain is probably the greatest. Examples of methods to develop this intelligence include teaching rhythmic patterns, vocal sounds and tones, music composition, percussion vibrations, humming, singing, and music performance.

Body or kinesthetic intelligence is related to physical movement and the knowing/wisdom of the body, including the brain's motor cortex which controls bodily motion. This intelligence relies on the ability to use the body to express emotions, to play a game, and to create new products. It is 'learning by doing.' Examples of methods to develop this intelligence include folk/creative dance, martial arts, physical exercise, mime, and experiential therapies such as drama therapy and role playing.

In addition, Daniel Goleman (1995) in his book on emotional intelligence teaches us that EQ (emotional quotient) plays an equal if not greater role than IQ (intelligence quotient) in the way people relate to and treat each other.

Wellness as a whole

Holistic treatment uses a 'Wellness' approach, and looks at the 'whole' person, not at damaged parts. It pushes personal growth while noting that one's problems are a 'part' of the whole, not the whole person. Holistic treatment is a strengths based model, and seeks to find out what one can do, as in 'approach goals', as against looking at the person's weaknesses alone, a deficit-based model, that addresses only what one should not do by 'avoidance and escape goals' which comes from the criminal justice or forensic model, and which is often focused on punishment.

While looking at the whole person, the holistic model works with all parts of humans. There is a focus on the physical part of self instead of viewing the client as a sex offender and focusing on just the genitals. It sees the connection between a healthy physical self and a balanced whole person including a healthy mental, emotional and spiritual self.

Unlike most sex offender treatment programmes in existence today, a holistic model incorporates spirituality into the treatment process. Incorporating spirituality into treatment does not mean engaging clients in organised religious activities, although that may be the path in which many clients choose to develop their spiritual self. In a more global sense, addressing the client's spiritually means as professionals we need to address the client's need for 'belonging,' his yearning, sadness, etc., which is a part of one's spirituality.

The holistic model recognises that to be healthy and keep a balanced life, the client must also work on developing his mental self and emotional self. These two parts of the whole can only be healthy when the physical self is healthy and the two combined make up a healthy spiritual self. The mental self feeds denial systems, and when unhealthy supports the client's cognitive distortions and unhealthy thinking processes. While most programmes for youth who sexually abuse address thinking errors, they must also be sure to develop and enhance the client's healthy thinking process.

The emotional self is probably one of the most difficult aspects of self to heal and make healthy. Most programmes have a treatment component that addresses teaching empathy, but there is more to healthy emotions than the ability to have empathy. In fact, to have empathy for others means one must first have empathy for one's self, an aspect of treatment often overlooked by sex-offender specific treatment programmes. A holistic model teaches clients about feelings, how to recognise feelings in one's self and others, how to express one's feelings, and utilises a variety of modalities to help clients explore their feeling self.

Power

We live in a world that is based upon personal power, and this is often the power and control over others, a dynamic that is apparent in the majority of sex offences committed by clients. It is a world that at times appears to be divided into two core groups of people, the 'oppressor' and the 'oppressed.' Holistic treatment avoids the 'oppressor' and 'oppressed' dichotomy. As children who sexually abuse, our clients experience both sides of this dichotomy. At the time before offending, they often feel powerless, out of control, and in some cases controlled by others, or as the oppressed. During the commission of a sexual offence, the client often feels a sense of being powerful and in control, or the oppressor. Upon entering treatment, the client is now placed in a position of being the oppressed once again. The holistic model attempts to level the playing field or relationship between the client, programme and programme staff by seeing the client as an equal partner in the treatment process.

Holistic treatment does not ignore societal influences that perpetuate sexual abuse, but helps the client understand and manage ways to live with them. Again, our cultures and societies look down upon those who commit these crimes and sees them as bad and evil persons deserving of punishment and to not have the rights of others. Holistic treatment is non-judgmental and non-punitive. It teaches that respect and empathy are critical components. Empathy in the therapeutic relationship is critical and continues to hold the client accountable and responsible for their behaviour and choices in life. However, it does so with respect for the client and seeing them as a human being first and as a person with an unhealthy lifestyle in need of repair. It teaches clients they are healthiest when they have power and control over their own lives, not the lives of others.

The therapeutic relationship

Holistic treatment sees a healthy therapeutic relationship as the foundation of good treatment and essential to the healing process. It supports a mutual relationship of give and take and learning. According to Blanchard (1998) a healthy therapeutic relationship consists of the following components; trust, compassion, self-disclosure, humour, respect, congruence, equality, authenticity, vulnerability, warmth, and a willingness to attempt to understand the client's emotional condition and life situation with a concern for his/her growth and happiness.

We live in a world that abhors violence. It is a society that sees others as their behaviour, their image. Even in the field of mental health we can become calloused to the point of losing respect for the people we treat and this is more likely to occur when we work with those who are violent and harm others. As professionals we must monitor our own values, beliefs and biases. We must be vigilant in keeping ourselves free of biased and angry thoughts about those we treat. This is not to say we accept the behaviour of our clients, but rather that while we may despise their behaviour, we respect the person and offer understanding and compassion while holding them accountable for their behaviour.

In order to facilitate the therapeutic relationship and maximise the potential for both therapist and client to learn and grow there must be an element of trust, compassion, and respect for the client. The client must experience the professional as genuine and caring, and supportive yet challenging of unhealthy ways. We must be authentic in the relationship while being one's self so that warmth and understanding comes across. When there is an act of kindness true healing will occur.

Holistic treatment as a process

Holistic treatment is process oriented and looks at the Gestalt. It is interactive and experiential, not something we do to clients but rather a process of change, growth and healing we experience with clients. It facilitates change while including goals, and the process/journey is equally as important. It recognises the client's need for a connection to others and the community. It incorporates a Wellness plan focused on wellness activities in each of the four aspects of self, mental, spiritual, emotional and physical. Traditional sex offender treatment is very structured and directive, focuses on target goals and thus is very goal oriented. This type of treatment has the potential to isolate the client. Prevention plans are focused on avoidance and managing risk factors.

Wellness plans utilise approach goals with a focus on healing and self-improvement. While wellness plans may suggest avoidance of certain behaviours or activities, these restrictions are always followed by what the client should do in order to change the behaviour into a healthy one. For example, a wellness plan may incorporate the following:

How to maintain **Emotional** health and balance to stay well and manage risk:

- Be more aware of how you experience feelings, both yours and what you observe in others.
- Explore your feelings so you can better understand them and where they are coming from.
- Avoid overreacting to situations. Learn to respond with appropriate assertiveness.

How to maintain **Mental** health and balance to stay well and manage risk:

- Challenge irrational thoughts.
- Try to keep in harmony with your head, heart, gut, and environment.
- Avoid 'all or nothing' thinking, be flexible.

How to maintain **Spiritual** health and balance to stay well and manage risk:

- Participate in spiritually related activity (meditation, church, meetings, etc.) regularly.
- Take time for yourself.
- Realise what you can control and what you cannot control. Give what you can't control to God or a higher power.

How to maintain **Physical** health and balance to stay well and manage risk:

- Continue on medications you are taking.
- Don't isolate or withdraw, seek others for companionship and activities.
- Keep active, spend leisure time wisely, exercise regularly and take care of your physical health.
- Eat on a regular and healthy basis.

(Adapted from Lawrence Ellerby. A Holistic Approach to Treating Sexual Abusers/ Workshop. ATSA 18th Annual Conference 9/24/99. Lake Buena Vista, Florida.)

It must be noted however that holistic treatment recognises that some individuals are damaged to the point that the holistic method may be difficult for them to use or they may not be willing to use it. Like any other model in mental health, some client's will offer resistence or an unwillingness to engage in any type of therapy, or in the case of persons assessed and determined to be psychopathic personalities, the model will not work.

Aetiology of sexual aggression and the use of holistic treatment

There are various theories regarding the aetiology of sexual aggression, some more plausible than others but each with their case examples. What we do know is that there is no identifiable single cause for sexual aggression and thus no simple solutions for prevention. Sexual abuse is a complex issue that requires a multi modality approach to treatment. To simply treat youth with sexual behaviour problems by addressing their sexual behaviour only will not be effective in addressing the plethora of problems they have which lead to their problematic behaviour.

Some of the more widely cited theories regarding the aetiology of sexual abuse include:

- addiction theory
- attachment disorders
- cognitive theory
- development contextual
- family systems theory
- learning theory
- dysfunction family theory
- physiological neurological/hormonal
- psychosis

(Ryan and Lane, 1997)

Addiction theory suggests that sexually abusive behaviour is the result of one developing a sexual addiction. There continues to be a debate regarding whether or not there is such a disorder as sexual addiction. The ability for juveniles to become sexually addicted, if sexual addiction is in fact a disorder, has not been determined. We do know that compulsive and impulsive behaviours are commonly found in various addictions, and that youth can be diagnosed with such disorders.

Attachment disorders theory suggests that the lack of appropriate attachment resulting from abuse and neglect may lead to sexually aggressive behaviours and other behavioural

problems. A lack of attachment or unhealthy bonding during early stages of development can lead to loneliness, isolation from others, and withdrawal from others. These are widely cited risk factors in the literature on sexually abusive behaviour.

Cognitive theory suggests that sexual abusers develop cognitive distortions based upon a variety of life experiences or in some instances may be born with a criminal personality. The combination of thinking errors, cognitive distortions, and emotional mismanagement are all a part of the cycle of sexual abuse and the relapse process.

The developmental or contextual theory suggests that abuse and neglect lead to various risk factors that may be associated with sexually abusive behaviour. The literature is replete with examples of abuse cycles. There is much scientific evidence that when parents abuse children, the chances are they too were abused as children although there is less evidence of this with sexual abuse. Domestic violence is another example. The majority of men who batter their wives and partners report witnessing violence against women in their families. While statistics vary, the majority of youth who sexually abuse come from homes in which physical and psychological abuse are common. There is more discrepancy about the numbers of youth who are sexually abused. Clearly, the majority of youth, with sexual behaviour problems in specialised programmes, report histories of sexual abuse including not only hands on sexual abuse, but witnessing sexual behaviour between adults, exposure to pornography, or other sexualised experiences in the early stages of their development.

Family systems theory implies that life experiences within the context of the family generate sexual misconduct. For example there are several case studies that demonstrate generations of incestuous relationships and/or other sexual behaviour problems within the family. The sexual behaviour problems within the family, similar to the developmental/contextual theory, may include exposure to sexual materials, witnessing sexual behaviour between adults or between adults and children, and the like.

Within the field of sexual abuse the most widely cited theory is learning theory. Learning theory suggests that sexual abuse is a learned behaviour. Like other theories noted above the learning may be from direct experiences of being sexually abused, through exposure to sexual materials, or being raised in highly sexualised environments.

Although a smaller number of cases, there are documented cases of physiological neurological/hormonal problems within sexual abusers to suggest that individual physiology may be the cause of sexually aggressive behaviour. Within this theory there are those who suggest that some offenders are born with a proclivity to be sexually aggressive. Current research is looking at biological and genetic factors, including possible brain anomalies as a possible cause of sexually aggressive behaviour.

Finally, there are many documented cases of mentally ill sexual abusers. Diagnosable mental illness, psychosis, may generate sexual aggression. However, it is believed that less than eight per cent of sexual abusers suffer from mental illness, and that the clear majority are emotionally disturbed individuals who are knowingly responsible for their behaviour. When a sexual abuser is diagnosed with a major psychiatric disorder, the disorder is often readily controlled through medication.

As there are multiple theories regarding the aetiology of sexually aggressive behaviour and the likelihood in many cases that the aetiology is multi-determined, we must be willing to not only look at multiple causes but be willing to address them within the context of treatment. A holistic approach looks at all possible factors and causes and addresses them within the context of treatment. A holistic model recognises that traditional sex offender treatment strategies may not, in and of themselves, address the multitude of problems determined in individual cases. Holistic treatment readily acknowledges that adjunctive therapies and alternative treatments may be necessary to work with the whole person and the various parts that make up that whole.

Using a holistic treatment approach with youth who sexually abuse

In addition to the above areas discussed thus far, the following are suggested areas to address in the treatment process. The first step in treatment is to give the client a general orientation to the treatment programme and review what is expected of the client while in treatment. Programme rules, homework expectations, general conduct, writing of an autobiography, etc. are all reviewed.

A major component of working with youth with sexual behaviour problems is family work. While some clients may have families who are unavailable or unwilling to participate, whenever possible the family should be included in the treatment process and family treatment conducted routinely.

Sexual abuse results from a variety of problems which include cognitive distortions and unhealthy thinking. Cognitive restructuring is essential to the treatment process to counter those thoughts that feed low self-esteem, violent impulses, anger, denial, and the many problems with which the client is faced. Cognitive restructuring is critical in the development of empathy. This work should also address dispelling family and other myths.

Most youth entering treatment programmes suffer from a lack of or deficit of healthy emotions. Like unhealthy thinking, unhealthy emotions serve as a block to developing empathy. Helping clients develop a healthy emotional self should include learning about feelings and how to recognise them in one's self and in others, emotional expression, and empathy training and development.

Personal victimisation work is a necessary component of any treatment programme for youth with sexual behaviour problems. As noted above, the majority of youth entering such programmes have experienced childhood abuse that may be psychological, verbal, physical, sexual, or a combination of abuses. More often than not these abusive incidents and periods of a child's life play a direct role in the abuse they do to others. Programmes should provide clients with the opportunity to work on personal abuse issues with the hope of achieving some level of resolution.

No child with sexual behaviour problems comes into treatment without anger problems. If one examines the cycle of abuse (Figure 2) it is evident that anger is occurring in the pretends-to-be-normal phase of the cycle and continues to be prevalent throughout the cycle. Anger management and positive assertiveness are critical to developing a healthy self. Anger management should include work with developing self-esteem, teaching situation perception training, and involve teaching clients relaxation techniques.

Youth with sexual behaviour problems need to learn a variety of techniques that help them cope with problems and intervene in destructive cycles of behaviour. This part of treatment should focus on positive goal setting, managing risk factors, and opportunities made available to youth to practice the coping responses and interventions they are learning. Interventions and coping responses should be both realistic (able to address the problem at hand) and there should be a likeliness that the client will use them.

The fact that youth with sexual behaviour problems have committed sexually abusive acts is reason to address healthy sexual behaviour during the course of treatment. Teaching clients about human sexuality is a more detailed and laborious process than simply providing them with a class in sex education. Healthy sexuality curriculums should include information on sexual anatomy of both men and women, sexually transmitted diseases, contraception and disease prevention, male and female roles in sexual relationships, what constitutes consent (including legal age requirements), what constitutes healthy sexual practices (including foreplay, various forms of intercourse, and the variety of sexual practices in which people engage), deviant sexual practices, fantasy work, and dating skills. The information taught should be age appropriate.

As noted above, a holistic model includes working with clients to develop healthy values and belief systems that parallel those of society in general.

The majority of programmes treating youth with sexual behaviour problems teach clients about cycles of abuse or relapse prevention. These models help clients integrate knowledge that sexual abuse is not only about behaviour management but also includes emotional and intellectual processes that contribute to the cycle of abuse and the relapse process.

When treating clients in a residential setting, transition planning and community living strategies are essential to the clients eventual success. Transition planning should begin the first day of treatment, and include where the client will live, aftercare treatment, family work, working with the client's school, establishing healthy peer relations, and developing a community support system. Many programmes require clients to develop a community living plan and wellness plan (Freeman-Longo, 2000).

Because holistic treatment includes a variety of treatments and integrates them within the context of treatment while taking into account individual client differences in development and learning style, the use of a variety of experiential therapies should be used in the treatment process. The use of experiential treatments and therapies is too extensive to address here, given the limited scope of this chapter, however, they deserve mention and endorsement regarding their use in working with youth. It should be noted that only trained and experienced clinicians should engage clients in such therapies and that they can be power interventions that generate extreme cathartic experiences. Therefore caution must be exercised when using these therapies especially when used in out-patient programmes where follow-up care can not be readily given to clients who are emotionally engaged, or traumas re-experienced during the course of participating in experiential treatments.

There are a variety of experiential treatments that can be used with sexually abusive youth. The more common ones used include role plays, drama therapy, art therapy, music therapy, and exercises used to build trust and explore family issues. In addition to using experiential therapies, professionals and programme staff must also be aware that they perform a variety of roles and functions when they are working with youth. These include a recognition and understanding that as professionals we are role models. While having contact with clients we are both serving as role models as well as engaging in re-parenting.

The use of touch is controversial within the field, with many programmes having policies regarding the nature and extent of touch between clients and between clients and staff. Some programmes have strict written policies prohibiting any form of touch between clients and very limited touch between staff and clients, i.e., handshakes. We must keep in mind that healthy touch is a part of the human experience and that these clients have come to us with a lack of understanding about what constitutes healthy touch. For some clients, all touch leads to sexualised thoughts, feelings, and behaviours. Lack of attachment or inappropriate attachment may result in children fearing touch, not having clear boundaries about touch (what is sexual and what is not), and as a result of personal trauma clients may fear any type of touch.

A holistic model suggests that when touch is a problem, this problem needs to be addressed in the context of treatment. After all, if programmes and professionals do not teach children about healthy touch, personal boundaries, and what constitutes unhealthy or sexualised touch, who will?

Closing comments

Holistic treatment with youth who have sexual behaviour problems is quickly growing in its acceptance within the field. We have come to recognise that the trickle down of adult sex-offender based treatment methods and models have serious shortcomings and potentially negative implications in regard to their application to youth with sexual behaviour problems.

Youth are resilient and have a tremendous capacity to recover from trauma and childhood experiences and problems that have resulted in serious behavioural problems. In working with youth we must take into account that they are *not* miniature adults and our work with them must take into account developmental and contextual issues as well as learning differences and learning disabilities.

Holistic treatment means treating the whole person not just a particular problem. All too often programmes treating youth with sexual behaviour problems view the client in the context of the referring problem. They see the child as a sex offender instead of the child as a person with many parts, of which sexually abusive behaviour is only one aspect. Visualise a circle cut into sections much like a pie. If we were to look at the person solely as a sex offender, the circle would have no slices. A holistic approach sees the person as a circle with many parts or slices (such as a pie would have) and one of those slices is the sex offending part of that whole person. The other parts or slices of the pie would include the many other parts of the clients life such as family, peers, community, school, hobbies and leisure time interests, sports, dating, and so forth.

When we see the whole person as a person with many facets, many of which are damaged parts, then we are better able to understand the nature of what we must treat and the complexities of doing so. Each part that is damaged needs to be repaired and given the time and opportunity to heal. A holistic approach works toward healing the whole person.

Treat patients, clients, and work personnel as they 'could be': so that they will become that (if only treated as they currently are, they will stay that way).

(Goethe)

References

Brendtro, L., Brokenleg, M., and Van Bockern, S. (1990) *Reclaiming Youth at Risk: Our Hope for the Future.* Bloomington, Indiana: National Education Service.

Burton, D., Freeman-Longo, R., Fiske, J., Levins, J. and Smith-Darden, J. (2000). *1996 Nationwide Survey of Treatment Programs and Models: Serving Abuse Reactive Children and Adolescent and Adult Sexual Offenders.* Brandon, VT: Safer Society Press.

Calder, M. C. (2001) *Juveniles and Children Who Sexually Abuse: Frameworks for Assessment.* (2nd edition). Dorset: Russell House Publishing.

Carich, M. S. (1999) In Defence of the Assault Cycle: A Commentary. *Sexual Abuse: A Journal of Research and Treatment.* 11:3 249–51.

Development Services Group (2000) *Understanding Treatment and Accountability in Juvenile Sex Offending: Results and Recommendations From an OJJDP Focus Group.* Prepared for: Office of Juvenile Justice and Delinquency Prevention Training and Technical Assistance Division.

Freeman-Longo, R. E. (2000) *Paths to Wellness.* Holyoke, MA: NEARI Press.

Freeman-Longo, R. E., Bird, S., Stevenson, W. F. and Fiske, J. A. (1995). *1994 Nationwide Survey of Treatment Programs and Models: Serving Abuse Reactive Children and Adolescent and Adult Sexual Offenders.* Brandon, VT: Safer Society Press.

Freeman-Longo, R. E. and Pithers, W. D. (1992). *A Structured Approach to Preventing Relapse: A Guide for Sex Offenders.* Brandon, VT: The Safer Society Press.

Gardner, H. (1983) *Frames of Mind: The Theory of Multiple Intelligences.* New York: Basic Books.

Goleman, D. (1995) *Emotional Intelligence: Why it Can Matter More Than IQ.* New York: Bantam Books.

Knopp, F. H., Freeman-Longo, R. E. and Stevenson, W. F. (1993). *Nationwide Survey of Juvenile and Adult Sex Offender Treatment Programs and Models, 1992.* Orwell, VT: Safer Society Press.

Laws, D. R., Hudson, S. M. and Ward, T. (Eds.) (2000) *Remaking Relapse Prevention with Sex Offenders: A Sourcebook.* Thousand Oaks, CA: Sage Publications.

Maletzky, B. M. (1998). Defining our Field II: Cycles, Chains, and Assorted Misnomers. *Sexual Abuse: A Journal of Research and Treatment.* 10:2 1–3.

National Adolescent Perpetrator Network (1993) The Revised Report from the National Task Force on Juvenile Sexual Offending. *Juvenile and Family Court Journal*. 44(4): 1–121.

Ryan, G. and Associates (1999) *Web of Meaning: A Developmental-contextual Approach in Sexual Abuse Treatment*. Brandon, VT: Safer Society Press.

Ryan, G. and Lane, S. (Eds.) (1997) *Juvenile Sexual Offending: Cause, Consequences, and Correction*. San Francisco, CA: Jossey-Bass Inc. Publishers.

Ward, T. and Hudson, S. M. (1996). Relapse Prevention: A Critical Analysis. *Sexual Abuse: A Journal of Research and Treatment*. 8:3 177–200.

Chapter 16: Family Work with Adolescent Sex Offenders

Carol Barnes and Gareth Hughes

Introduction

It's the Government's fault that he's in here. They shouldn't allow such filth on TV.

The Home Office Sex Offender Treatment Programme (SOTP) is a validated programme (Beech, Fisher, and Beckett, 1999) based on an extensive literature (e.g., Hanson and Bussiere, 1998; Lipsey and Wilson, 1993) that has described and evaluated a number of cognitive-behavioural programmes for adult sex offenders implemented throughout North America. The SOTP is now being used in Young Offender Institutions in England. Treatment of adolescent sex offenders is clearly a priority given that a recent study by Veneziano et al. (2000) estimated that adolescents are responsible for approximately twenty per cent of rapes and from thirty to fifty per cent of child sexual abuse.

While there has been little evaluation of how suitable the programme is for adolescents, there are no a priori reasons to assume that the programme is not suitable. However, unlike most adult offenders, the influence of families of origin could well have a significant impact on those adolescent sex offenders taking part. The majority of the young sex offenders undertaking the programme had been living at home with their families prior to incarceration and continued to maintain close contact throughout their sentence. There are a number of reasons to believe that the family systems of adolescent sex offenders are an important factor in the aetiology of their sexually abusive behaviour. Additionally, families could offer a source of support in motivating the offender to successfully engage in the SOTP, desist from future offending, and play a part in any relapse prevention programme that might be implemented following release. Indeed, there is evidence to suggest that involving families in the treatment of adult sex offenders may be an important and effective adjunct that increases understanding and implementation of effective relapse prevention plans by offenders (Eher et al., 1997).

Several research studies into the aetiology of violent offending in young adults have included a large variety of family variables that may impact on offending behaviour and reliably predict delinquency. For example, a paper from the Family Studies Centre in 1993 notes several studies that include family factors (Utting et al., 1993). One such study is the Newcastle 1000 study, 1947–1979 (Kolvin et al., 1990) that compared backgrounds of children who became delinquent with those who did not. Using a number of indices of family functioning, those who were identified as having backgrounds of family deprivation accounted for the majority of criminal behaviour, while those who avoided a criminal record, were recorded as having good parental care and supervision. These researchers concluded that '. . . good parenting protects against the acquisition of a criminal record'.

The Cambridge Study of Delinquent Development (West and Farrington, 1982) looked at a range of factors which might predict a delinquent lifestyle. They observed that social deprivation on its own is not sufficient for delinquency to develop, and that a good care giving environment can modify other negative influences, such as economic deprivation. Wilson (1980) concluded that poor parental supervision increased the rate of delinquency by seven times more than that seen in families assessed as being 'strict'. A six-year follow-up study confirmed that poor supervision is akin to parental abandonment that, in turn, opens the door to negative peer group influences.

Also clear from previous research (e.g., Ryan, 1991; Thomas, 1991) is the idea that the family influences and shapes the offender's patterns of behaviours, attitudes, beliefs, and values. While there is no evidence demonstrating that family factors such as poor communication, blurred role boundaries, or breakdown in relationships are specific causal factors in sexually abusive behaviour, they may contribute to a family climate which increases vulnerability to all types of offending behaviour (Bentovim, 1992 and 1995). Loeber and Stouthamer (1986) constructed four interlocking models, which exemplify the influence that malfunctioning families, can exert on children:

Neglect; Conflict; Deviant behaviour and attitudes, and Disruption. A paper by Farrington and West (1990) called for action to tackle poor child-rearing behaviour by parents, stating: *'It is clear from our research that problem children grow into problem adults, and that problem adults tend to reproduce problem children. Sooner or later, serious efforts, firmly grounded on empirical research results, must be made to break this cycle'*.

There is certainly evidence (e.g., Saunders and Awad, 1988; Shields and Jordan, 1995) that severe family problems are associated with adolescent sex offending. Manocha and Mezey (1998) note that in their sample of 51 adolescent sex offenders, over half came from dysfunctional families. Of particular note were histories of abuse and victimisation, family violence, lack of sexual boundaries and a lack of parental protection. Sappington (2000) notes that childhood histories of physical, sexual, and psychological abuse, as well as children witnessing parents abuse one another, are all associated with later problems of violence in general.

Fletcher (1999) reports data on 263 adolescent sex offenders in which 43 per cent had experienced sexual problems in earlier childhood. Ryan (1991) reports a study of juvenile sex offenders in which the family functioning of most of their families was rated as 'below average', 'inappropriate', or 'dysfunctional'. Such offenders are often exposed to a lack of consistent, empathic care, early parental loss, substance abuse and parental violence. Additionally they tend to hold offence-sustaining attitudes towards women, sexuality, and relationships. Ryan (1991) suggests that the child's role has often been to act as a receptacle for the negative feelings in the family, and that sexual abuse may be part of acting out behaviour. Bentovim (1991) describes this as 'pathology of the family'. The majority of the research suggests that sex offenders do not come from functional healthy families, and several theories (e.g. Marshall and Barbaree, 1990) suggest that many risk factors converge within the child's early life experiences.

Rex (2000), in a reflective paper on the use of cognitive-behavioural programmes in the prison system, argues that it is imperative that such programmes '. . . take account of the social environments in which offenders are taking decisions . . .' While there have been studies demonstrating that some offenders do desist on the basis of a rational costs-benefits analysis, Farrall and Bowling (1999) suggest that there is often a failure to acknowledge that social and family functioning may constrain the offender from making a rational decision. Citing a long term study of Youth Treatment Centres by Bullock and Associates, Bailey (1995) notes that a key factor in good outcomes is 'the ability to enable the young person to look at the dynamics of their own family life, and wherever possible to involve the family in treatment' (p6).

Because of the importance of families in the aetiology and maintenance of criminal behaviour, families are likely to play a significant role in post treatment when young offenders are released back into the community. There is now a developing literature (e.g., Blechman and Vryan, 2000; Gordon, Graves, and Arbuthnot, 1995) demonstrating that the provision of family therapy significantly reduces recidivism rates in young offenders. The family's inclusion in the treatment process, in our opinion, is paramount to a relapse prevention approach to working with adolescent sex offenders. By being uninvolved in the wider therapeutic process, there is the possibility that they could be encouraging the offender's resistance to an offending behaviour programme, thus compromising programme integrity (Hollin, 1995).

Systemic family therapy

His dad is not facing up to it. He's not very respectful towards women.

Systemic family therapy applies systems theory to family constellations. The systems therapist sees all behaviour as a communication about relationships, and therefore can be better understood within the context in which it occurs, and is influenced. In applying systems theory it may be necessary to deal with others in the system, in order to eliminate pathological behaviour. Once actions are seen as being connected to other relationships, it makes sense to involve others in the therapeutic process.

Many approaches to delinquency focus solely on the offender. This assumes that the perpetrator, not the family, has a problem. Systemic theories hold that, as families function as a 'system', change in one member can bring about changes in others. It is therefore important to understand the belief and value systems within the families of young violent sex offenders, as youthful antisocial beliefs and attitudes may go unchallenged, if they are shared and accepted as 'normal' within a family. Pennell and Browne (1999) state, 'The role of the parent in the development of anti-social behaviour by young people should not be underestimated'.

Parents who model caring, nurturing, the value of education, and the delay of immediate gratification can offset other family and social predictors of delinquency, such as criminality and poverty. Rutter (1987) asserts that good role models, or interpersonal relationships, act as protective mechanisms against life's stresses. He argues that the concept of psychosocial resilience helps young people to select positive peers. Attachment theory holds that this ability to choose rewarding relationships is facilitated by a pattern of responsive care (Bowlby,1988). Marshall et al. (1993) found that there is evidence to suggest a relationship between poor attachment bonds in early childhood, and the later development of antisocial behaviour, and more specifically, of sexual offending.

A number of studies, e.g. Kolvin et al. (1990); West and Farrington (1982); Wilson (1980) have concluded that the determining factor in whether tendencies towards aggressive and antisocial behaviour are inhibited or allowed to develop is the quality of the relationship between parent and child. Most of these studies observed that parenting styles exert a direct influence over their children and their attitude towards anti-social and abusive behaviours. Parental knowledge of, and attitudes towards, their child's social lifestyle are particularly relevant when working with young sex offenders, many of whom refer to peer influence when committing antisocial behaviours.

The work initiated with the families of the young prisoners at HMYOI Feltham was not based on any single model of systemic theory. This group of families came from widely differing cultures, which had to be respected in therapeutic conversations, for example different hierarchical and gender family boundaries. One way of helping families articulate their own experiences is through the technique of Narrative Therapy, White and Epson (1998). This method provides access to aspects of family processes, which help the therapist to discover the different realities of each family member concerning the pathways, which led to the abusive behaviour. Attitudinal

shifts can be detected by the way that significant themes are described, developed and changed. Often, new information emerges about previously unrecorded sexually abusive behaviour.

The programme

What's this 'treatment programme' about? I won't allow needles to be stuck in him.

The families of eight offenders attending the core SOTP were contacted by letter and telephone, requesting them to make an appointment committing them initially to an introductory session with the Family Therapist. Consequent to this the average number of sessions attended by each family was between four and five, and ranged from one to fifteen. The few families who were unable to attend usually replied with apologies claiming difficulties with childcare or illness. As good practice dictates in Systemic Therapy, each session was videotaped with the participants' written consent.

There appeared to be little resistance on the part of any family member invited to attend Family Therapy sessions. On the contrary, further family members were often invited at the prisoner's request, and several families travelled some considerable distance, taking time off from work and staying locally overnight. The ninety-minute sessions were arranged at intervals averaging between three and four weeks. It was noticeable that, in spite of the distance and work commitments, those family members who were invited rarely missed any appointments.

One of the aims of this intervention was to encourage those families who attended, to become an integral part of the offender's treatment plan. Once a 'therapeutic alliance' has been established, there is a great potential for families to help in identifying problems and develop strategies for dealing with them. It is also possible to use Finkelhor's (1984) 'Four Factor Model' to explore the offender's development with his family: emotional congruence; sexual arousal; blockages, and disinhibition. This model is included in the prisoner's group offending behaviour programme, and may serve as a useful opportunity to engage families with a view to explaining and supporting Relapse Prevention Plans.

To summarise, the family involvement might be described as a way of identifying individual

Table 1: Pertinent historical variables relating to the sample of adolescent sex offenders whose families accepted at least one family session

Reported physical abuse as a child	40%
Social Services involvement with the family	27%
History of inconsistent carers	67%
History of some form of maladaptive relationship with, or absence of, a father or step-father	77%
History of truancy from school	71%
History of non-sexual offending	63%
History of prior sexual offending	27%
Sexual offence committed alone (versus with peers)	68%
Victim age appropriate	49%
Victim under age 13	27%

and family processes that impact on the relationships and sexually abusive behaviour of the young offender.

The offenders and their families

We thought he was innocent, because he told us that someone else was wearing his hat.

During the twenty-four month period that family therapy was offered to adolescent sex offenders, fifty-three were identified as potential candidates, following referral to the Institution's SOTP. Of this total, 37 offenders' families responded positively to attending at least one session of family therapy. Composition of families varied both in number and relationship. They included a family of father and uncle and a family of a grandmother and sister. Eighteen of the families attending included both mother and father (or partner) and a further thirteen included at least one parent.

The average age of the offenders at the start of the SOTP was 17 years 10 months, with a range of 15 to 20 years. The average sentence length was approximately five years and six months, with a range of 18 months to 12 years. From social histories and other file information, a number of pertinent background factors were noted. Table 1 details these factors where the information was available for at least sixty percent of the sample. The overall impression is that of disturbed and maladaptive families and prior behavioural difficulties on the part of the young offenders.

Two measures of family process were obtained from self-report of the offenders and one observational-rating measure of family functioning was made from the initial family session. The Parental Bonding Instrument (PBI) (Parker et al., 1988) is a self-rating questionnaire

that provides an estimate of perceived parental care and protection throughout childhood. The 'care' scale assesses affection, emotional warmth, and closeness versus emotional coldness, indifference, and neglect. The 'over-protection' scale assesses control, domination, and intrusion versus autonomy and encouragement of independence. Each parent is assessed and can be assigned to one of four quadrants:

- optimal bonding
- affectionless control
- weak bonding
- affectionate constraint

The Family Forgiveness Scale (FFS) (Pollard et al., 1998) is a measure of a concept of communication and relationships within the family that includes five sub constructs or important elements of 'forgiveness'. The five sub-scales are:

1. Realisation (expression of feelings).
2. Recognition (perspective taking).
3. Reparation (apologising and accepting responsibility).
4. Restitution (making amends).
5. Resolution (burying the hatchet).

Hargrave and Sells (1997) suggest that the concept of 'Family Forgiveness' is a useful measure of change in family dynamics following family therapy. Unfortunately, for practical and operational reasons, we did not obtain a second measure.

The observational measure used was the Circumplex Model of Marital and Family Systems (CM) (Olson, 1988). The CM is a tool for assessing family functioning and attempts to bridge family theory, research, and practice. The model integrates three central dimensions

Table 2: Means of age, sentence length, and self-report measures of adolescent sex offenders who engaged in family work and control sample of violent young offenders

	Sex offence N=37	Violent offence N=42	Difference
Age	17.81 (1.17)	16.71 (0.83)	***
Sentence	5.63 (2.51)	3.01 (1.75)	***
PBI			
Care (Mother)	26.59 (7.52)	28.18 (5.72)	
Care (Father)	21.23 (9.61)	22.45 (8.27)	
Protection (Mother)	15.68 (8.92)	11.88 (5.07)	*
Protection (Father)	11.32 (5.98)	11.52 (7.31)	
Total	57.73 (8.09)	57.24 (7.33)	

*p<0.05, ***p<0.001

of family behaviour, cohesion, adaptability, and communication. Family cohesion is defined as the emotional bonding that families have toward one another. Family adaptability is defined as the ability of a family system to change its power structure. Family communication is the facility of the family to keep cohesion and adaptability in balance.

Both the self-report measures as well as sentence length were obtained from a sample of forty-two consecutively admitted violent but non-sexual offenders. This information was also available from those adolescent sex offenders who, for operational reasons, were not offered a family session. A comparison of sex offenders who attended family sessions with those sex offenders who did not, revealed no significant differences on any of the measures available. Thus, there was little reason to believe that our sample of sex offenders who undertook family work was biased. Table 2 compares the means of age, sentence, and self-report measures for sex offenders receiving family intervention with the sample of violent offenders. Tests of significance indicated that the violent non-sexual offenders were serving significantly shorter sentences (average sentence length of three years) than the sex offenders (average sentence length of five and a half years). The violent offenders were significantly younger, by about one year. However, this may have been an artefact of their age at admission compared with the age at which the sex offenders began treatment, i.e., not necessarily at the beginning of sentence. The violent non-sexual offenders also self-reported significantly lower levels of maternal protection on the PBI.

Assessments of parental bonding by our sex offender sample indicated that the majority (80 per cent) perceived themselves as having experienced 'optimal bonding' (i.e. low overprotection and high care) with their mothers and that approximately 60 per cent perceived themselves as having experienced 'optimal' bonding with their fathers. The average scores for the sample did not look remarkably different to those reported for a normative sample of Australian adolescents by Cubis et al. (1989). Clearly this sample of offenders did not view their parenting as particularly dysfunctional.

The observational measure of family functioning also suggested a high level (65 per cent) of balance between cohesion and adaptability. There was, however, a noticeable trend towards 'structured' and 'separated' communication, with only one family being rated as 'connected' and 'flexible'. Once again, there is a sense in which these families are not overtly dysfunctional as assessed by our measures, rather they function very effectively to maintain what we might consider anti-social attitudes.

Family observation

It's not fair to put him away for what he's done.

Many questions may be asked about the families' motivation to attend, as there was an observable resistance from family members to engage in any discourse about the offender's sexually abusive behaviour. Typically, they sought to avoid mentioning the offence, and expressed no particular interest in the SOTP. They preferred instead to discuss the problems that have arisen for them as a result of the notoriety resulting from the conviction, which had caused extensive public comment, neighbourhood condemnation, and adverse publicity. Most families expressed relief at having the opportunity to air their concerns in this forum.

Denial in its many shapes and forms was the frequent (87 per cent) response to offence related dialogue. Typically they minimised and tried to justify the offending behaviour, mentioning peer group pressure, victim blame etc. Comments such as:

> *Everyone does it in Streatham.*
> *When he gets out he'll be old enough to get married, so he won't need to do it again.*
> *He only did what was done to him by some pervert.*
> *Well, she was only a prostitute or something.*

. . . were typical of the minimisations offered by parents. The offender was often a minor contributor to this family discourse, as he usually allowed the parental dialogue to support the *poor me* image that he presented.

Perhaps this denial should be understood within the context of the shock and shame of the aftermath of the Court proceedings. Thomas (1997) identifies the initial shock of a conviction as 'The crisis of disclosure', and states that this recognises the parents' feelings of failure, causing resentment and resistance. As offence related behaviours are central to the therapeutic discourse, it is important to find ways of helping the family to talk about the 'untellable'. A trans-generational approach was possible with families who disclosed sexual abuse within the family. The concept of the family ledger (Bozormenyi-Nagy et al., 1991) provided a useful model of working through sensitive issues by encouraging the parents to talk about their own upbringing, and how this affects the way they themselves parent their child.

The young offenders in this study were often in denial because of fear of family rejection if they admitted the offence. Two recent studies on denial in sex offenders in prison support this conclusion. Kalsy (1997), in a study of 40 young sex offenders at Feltham YOI found that 62.5 per cent were in denial to their families for fear of losing emotional support, and 20 per cent of these felt the need to be reassured that, once they admitted, they would continue to receive support. Lord and Willmot (submitted) in their study of 60 'deniers' (41

adults and 19 young Offenders), found that, in interview, 67 per cent showed that the clearest single reason for denying a sexual offence was the fear of losing the support of family and friends. They also found that 67 per cent of the respondents said that their families had accepted their original denial. This would support our findings that denial is present in families, and help to explain the collusiveness of this denial. Although the fear of negative evaluation was present in our young offender cohort, their families had their own agendas for supporting denial.

The term 'seemingly irrelevant disclosure', borrowed from relapse prevention literature, could be used to describe the previously unrecorded information that family members disclosed about abusive behaviour in their own past. These disclosures were often made in a casual, incidental manner, but significantly covered issues not known to the treatment team. Various parents noted unusual childhood behaviour such as habitual dishonesty, bizarre games and bullying behaviour. Some went surprisingly far in revealing accusations of sexual misconduct that had not been proceeded with due to lack of evidence, or to protect child witnesses. Some parents admitted that they had caught their son with 'hard core' pornography in the form of magazines and videos. The most frequent disclosure was from mothers who spoke of their own abuse. Some chose to share their trauma with their son, others preferred to disclose such sensitive information privately to the therapist. Previous research has found that maternal own abuse was not uncommon amongst mothers of young sexual abusers (Bentovim,1998).

It is not unusual for families to 'close ranks' when confronted with unpalatable situations. These families adopted a defensive strategy of denial as a protection against the numerous negative consequences they revealed including deterioration in physical or mental health, abuse from neighbours forcing relocation, rifts within the extended family, etc. They expressed anxiety and overprotection towards their other children. Smith and Trepper (1992) suggest that parental reactions to their son sexually offending may follow a common pattern, not unlike the stages of bereavement: pervasiveness of the problem; helplessness; active involvement (often in the 'appeal' process), and return to relative normality. Another similarity with the grieving process is the 'intimate loneliness':

isolated; awkward conversations; embarrassment, and fear of triggering emotions.

It may be that the feelings of shame associated with own abuse contributed to the difficulty of accepting the abusive behaviour of their son. This *shame* might also explain many of the mothers' seeming inability to display any victim empathy.

Qualitative evidence suggested that families were especially unaware or reluctant to discuss victim consequences. When victims were mentioned, empathy was low and they were often blamed in some way for the offence's occurrence. This took the form of a discourse about power ratios, usually eliciting such statements as *'these girls throw themselves at boys'*, or *'she was known as the village bike'*.

Offence minimisation by families often included the rationalisation that the offence was an expression of sexual experimentation. One set of parents thought that their son had 'tried out' his fear of being a homosexual by seeing what it was like to rape a young boy. Another couple insisted that their son had 'proved' his heterosexuality by changing his victim abuse from his young brother in preference to his young sister. Parents of rapists rationalised the offence as the product of promiscuity, drug abuse, lack of sexual education, video violence and negative peer influences.

Accepting that denial and distortions are pervasive, expectations for change should be realistic. Families may try to deny that the offence took place, or try to rationalise its impact on the victim. It was frequently suggested by parents that the abusive behaviour was an isolated incident, and the offender had now been 'cured'.

Gray and Pithers (1993) refer to 'initial shock or numbness'. The crucial therapeutic challenge is managing the transition from this shock, through disbelief, uncertainty and minimisation, to an acceptance that the offence occurred, and that they have a part to play in supporting relapse prevention.

It was apparent to the therapist that the parents in this study knew very little about their son's peer group activities, social habits and their active criminal lifestyle. This contrasts with a study by Graham and Bowling (1995) who found that 32 per cent of male adolescent offenders reported 'high parental' supervision, measured in terms of parents knowledge of who they were with and where they were going,

when out with friends. The awareness of an active criminal lifestyle by the majority of the young sex offenders appeared to come as a surprise to their families. Studies which identified 'neglectful parenting' (Kolvin et al., 1990; Wilson, 1980 and 1987) concluded that lax supervision was tantamount to abandonment, allowing the children to become vulnerable to negative peer group influences. In our study the 'gang rape' offenders all admitted to other non sexual group criminal activities, such as street robberies.

Conclusion

He didn't do it. The police are such liars.

On the observational measure of family functioning (Circumplex Model), these families did not present as 'enmeshed' or 'disengaged' on the extreme opposite poles, thus disallowing the classification of 'dysfunctional', by these criteria. The majority of families fell within the 'mid-range of the 'rigidly separated' quartile. Structural Theorists, e.g. Minuchin (1974), and other systemic approaches maintain that rigid patterns of relating play an important part in triggering and maintaining destructive behavioural patterns. While the family structure may not appear to be dysfunctional, in terms of present day family functioning, there are nevertheless, individual relationships within the family, impacting on offending behaviour, and which appear to be dysfunctional, and possibly sometimes destructive.

Family members had varying degrees of knowledge about the offence and judicial process that had brought about their son's conviction. Clearly, the families of the young sex offenders in this study hold distortions about the offences. This has implications for those working with these families about issues concerning the offending behaviour of their son. There appears to be a sub-cultural support system for sexually offending behaviour, as defined by their acceptance of deviant attitudes towards the behaviour. This normalisation of criminality has been described as 'defining deviancy down', Rieber (1997) and shows an acceptance of greater tolerance towards a criminal lifestyle. This acceptance was evidenced in comments such as 'we knew he was doing other things, but we didn't think it would come to this'. If families are not aware of the belief systems that may support the sexually abusive behaviour, then the changes that have been made by the prisoner on the SOTP will be negated when he returns into an unchanged family system.

'Specialist' sex offenders were rare in our study as the offenders tended to lead a more deviant lifestyle generally. The families shared a different reality concerning sexually abusive behaviour, to that which the Courts hold, and this is in line with current research that concludes that there is no impact on future abusive behaviour by imposing more severe penalties. As Hoffman (1993) states: 'sending child molesters to gaol does not alter the recipe for abuse, handed down to the next generation'. Clinical evidence showed that there were no discernable shifts away from denial by family members, during the period that the prisoners were attending the SOTP. This has clear implications for offending behaviour programmes for young offenders, who are not yet ready to break free from childhood bonds. The notion of support from families for relapse prevention must similarly be treated with caution.

It is clear from clinical observation that the abusive behaviour is central to the present functioning of the family system, and that by discussing the offence and surrounding circumstances, changes could be brought about by better understanding. The intrusive nature of sexual abuse is based on long standing patterns of behaviour that have developed over time, and cannot be addressed in isolation.

One of the questions frequently asked by families was: 'why should we change, we've done nothing wrong?' It is time that offending behaviour programmes for young sexual abusers took up the challenge of finding methods to help families look at ways in which their beliefs and values have influenced the offender's beliefs, behaviour and relationships, which in turn led to the abusive behaviour.

While the effectiveness of standard treatment modalities such as the SOTP can be measured, empirical evidence has not yet been developed for evaluating the family work. New Labour's political statement of intent, 'what counts is what works', may suffice to explain the gratitude that families expressed for being supported and informed about the offender's treatment programme, but it is not definable. Statistical measures may record a set of risk factors, but as family response has not been evaluated, we do not know if supportive families shorten the odds of reconviction, or whether motivation to attend family sessions

plays any part. This study sought to explore effective measures for shifts in parental perceptions of providing a 'safe enough' home environment for the offender's return, and to identify factors in therapeutic processes which measure family change, in order to evaluate 'what works'.

References

Bailey, S. (1995) Young Offenders, Serious Crimes. *British Journal of Psychiatry.* 167: 5–7.

Beech, A., Fisher, D. and Beckett, R. (1999) *Step 3: An Evaluation of the Prison Sex Offender Treatment Programme.* London: Home Office.

Bentovim, A. (1991) Clinical Work With Families in Which Sexual Abuse Has Occurred. in Hollin, C. R. and Howells K. (Eds.) *Clinical Approaches to Sex Offenders and Their Victims.* Chichester John Wiley and Sons.

Bentovim, A. (1995). *Trauma Organized Systems* (revised). London: Karnac.

Bentovim, A. and Williams, B. (1998) Children and Adolescents: Victims Who Become Perpetrators. *Advances in Psychiatric Treatment.* 4: 101–7.

Blechman, E. A. and Vryan, K. D. (2000) Prosocial Family Therapy: A Manualized Preventive Intervention for Juvenile Offenders. *Journal of Aggression and Violent Behaviour.* 5:4 343–78.

Bozormenyi-Nagy, I., Grunebaum, J. and Ulrich, D. (1991) Contextual therapy. in Gurman, A. S. and Kniskern, D. S. (Eds.) *Handbook of Family Therapy (Vol. 11).* New York: Brunner/Mazel.

Bowlby, J., (1988). *A Secure Base: Parent-child Attachment and Healthy Human Development.* New York: Basic Books.

Cubis, J., Lewin, T. and Dawes, F. (1989) Australian Adolescents' Perception of their Parents. *Australian and New Zealand Journal of Psychiatry.* 23: 35–47.

Eher, R., Dwyer, M. Prinoth, S., Wagner, E. Fruhwald, S., and Gutierrez, K. (1997) Sexualstraftater im Massregelvollzug und deren Angehorige: Ergebnisse gemeinsamer Therapiesitzungen. *Psychiatrische Praxis.* 24: 190–5.

Farrall, S. and Bowling, B. (1999) Structuration, Human Development and Desistance from Crime. *British Journal of Criminology.* 253–68.

Farrington, D. P. and West, D. J. (1990) The Cambridge Study in Delinquent Development: A Long-term Follow-up of 411

London Males. in Kerner, H. J. and Kaiser, G. (Eds.) *Criminalitat: Personlichkeit, Lebensgeschichte und Verhalten.* Berlin: Springer-Verlag.

Finkelhor, D. (1984) *Child Sexual Abuse: New Theory and Research.* New York: Free Press.

Fletcher, R. (1999) Early Intervention for Sexual Behaviour Problems among Young Offenders. *Forum on Corrections research.* 11:2 30–3.

Gal, M. and Hoge, R. D. (1999) A Profile of the Adolescent Sex Offender. *Forum on Corrections Research.* 11:2 7–11.

Gordon, Graves, and Arbuthnot, (1995) The Effects of Functional Family Therapy for Delinquents. *Criminal Justice and Behaviour.* 22: 60–73.

Graham, J. and Bowling, B. (1995). Young People and Crime. *Home Office Research Study 145.* London. Home Office.

Gray, A. S. and Pithers, W. D. (1993) Relapse Prevention with Sexually Aggressive Adolescents and Children: Expanding Treatment and Supervision. in Barbaree, H. E., Marshall, W. L. and Hudson S. M. (Eds.) *The Juvenile Sex Offender.* NY: Guilford Press.

Hanson, R. K. and Bussiere, M. T. (1998). Predicting Relapse: A Meta-analysis of Sexual Offender Recidivision Studies. *Journal of Consulting and Clinical Psychology.* 66:2 348–62.

Hargrave, T. D. and Sells, J. N. (1997). The Development of a Forgiveness Scale. *Journal of Marital and Family Therapy.* 23:1 41–62.

Hoffman, L. (1993) *Exchanging Voices.* London: Karnac.

Hollin, C. R. (1995) The Meaning and Implications of 'Programme Integrity'. in McGuire, J. (Ed.) *What Works: Effective Methods to Reduce Reoffending.* Chichester: Wiley.

Kalsy, S. (1997) A Study of Denial Behaviours in Incarcerated Juvenile Sex Offenders. *Unpublished Paper.*

Lipsey, M. W. and Wilson, D. B. (1993) The Efficacy of Psychological, Educational, and Behavioral Treatment: Confirmation from Meta-analysis. *American.* 48: 1181–209.

Loeber, R. and Stouthamer-Loeber, M. (1986) Family Factors as Correlates and Predictors of Juvenile Conduct Problems and Delinquency. in Tonry, M. and Morris, N. (Eds.) *Crime and Justice: An Annual Review of Research. Volume 7.* Chicago: University of Chicago Press.

Lord, A. and Willmot, P. (submitted) *The Process of Overcoming Denial in Sex Offenders.* Paper submitted for publication to *Sexual Abuse.*

Manocha, K. F. and Mezey, G. (1998) British Adolescents Who Sexually Abuse: A Descriptive Study. *Journal of Forensic Psychiatry.* 9:3 588–608.

Marshall, W. L. and Barbaree, H. E. (1990) An Integrated Theory of the Aetiology of Sexual Offending. in Marshall, W. L., Laws, D. R. and Barbaree, H. E. (Eds.) *Handbook of Sexual Assault: Issues, Theories and Treatment of the Offender.* NY: Plenum. 257–75.

Marshall, W. L., Hudson, S. M. and Hodkinson, S. (1993) The Importance of Attachment Bonds in the Development of Juvenile Sex Offending. in Barbaree, H. E., Marshall, W. L. and Hudson S. M. (Eds.) *The Juvenile Sex Offender.* London: Guilford Press.

Minuchin, S. (1974). *Families and Family Therapy.* Cambridge: Harvard University Press.

Olson, D. H. (1988) *Clinical Rating Scale (CRS) for the Circumplex Model of Marital and Family Systems (revised).* St. Paul, MN: Family Social Science, University of Minnesota.

Parker, G. Tupling, H. and Brown, L. B. (1979) Parental Bonding Instrument. *British Journal of Medical Psychology.* 52: 1–10.

Pennell, A. E. and Browne, K. D. (1999) Film Violence and Young Offenders. *Journal of Aggression and Violent Behaviour.* 4:1 13–28.

Pollard, M. W., Anderson, R. R., Anderson, W. T. and Jennings, G. (1998) The Development of a Family Forgiveness Scale (FFS). *Journal of Family Therapy.* 20: 95–109.

Rex, S. A. (2000) *Beyond Cognitive-behaviouralism? Reflections on the Effectiveness Literature.* Paper presented to the 24th Cropwood Conference, Cambridge, Jun.

Rieber, R. W. (1997) *Manufacturing Social Distress: Psychopathy in Everyday Life.* New York: Plenum Press.

Rutter, M. (1987) Psychosocial Resilience and Protective Mechanisms. *American Journal of Orthopsychiatry.* 57: 3–15.

Ryan, G. D. (1991) The Juvenile Sex Offender's Family. in Ryan, G. D. and Lane, S. L. (Eds.) *Juvenile Sex Offending: Causes, Consequences, and Correction.* Lexington, MA: Lexington Books.

Sappington, A. A. (2000) Childhood Abuse as a Possible Locus for Early Intervention into Problems of Violence and Psychopathology. *Aggressive and Violent Behavior.* 5:3 255–66.

Saunders, E. B. and Awad, G. A. (1988) Assessment, Management, and Treatment Planning for Male Adolescent Sexual Offenders. *American Journal of Orthopsychiatry.* 58:4 571–9.

Seghorn, T. L., Pretky, R. A. and Boucher, R. J. (1987) Child Sexual Abuse in the Lives of Sexually Aggressive Offenders. *Journal of the American Academy of Child and Adolescent Psychiatry.* 26: 262–7.

Shields, I. W. and Jordan, S. A. (1995) Young Sex Offenders: A Comparison With a Control Group of Non-sex Offenders. *Forum on Corrections Research.* 7:1 17–9.

Smith, B. J., and Trepper, T. S. (1992) Parents' Experience When their Sons Sexually Offend: A Qualitive Analysis. *Journal of Sex Education and Therapy.* 18:2 93–103.

Thomas, J. (1991) The Adolescent Sex Offender's Family in Treatment. in Ryan, G. D. and Lane, S. L. (Eds.) *Juvenile Sexual Offending: Causes, Consequences, and Corrections.* Lexington, M.A: Lexington Books.

Utting, D., Bright, J. and Henricson, C. (1993) Crime and the Family: Improving Child-rearing and Preventing Delinquency. Occasional paper. Family Policy Studies Centre.

Veneziano, C., Veneziano, L. and LeGrand, S. (2000) The Relationship Between Adolescent Sex Offender Behaviour and Victim Characteristics with Prior Victimisation. *Journal of Interpersonal Violence.* 15:4 363–74.

West, D. and Farrington, D. (1982) The Cambridge Study in Delinquent Development. in Utting, D. Bright, J. and Henricson, C. (1993) *Crime and the Family: Improving Child-rearing and Preventing Delinquency.* Occasional paper: Family Policies Study Centre.

White, M. and Epston, D. (1990) *Narrative Means to Therapeutic Ends.* New York: WW Norton.

Wilson, H. (1980) Parental Supervision: A Neglected Aspect of Delinquency. *British Journal of Criminology.* 20:3 203–35.

Wilson, H. (1987) Parental Supervision: A Neglected Aspect of Delinquency, Re-examined. *British Journal of Criminology.* 27:3 275–301.

Chapter 17: Management of Programme Pitfalls in Juvenile Sex Offender Treatment

Edward Wieckowski, Curtis R. Grant and Charles E. Hodges, *Jnr*

Introduction

All juvenile sex offender treatment programmes are dynamic, and fluctuate in relation to their strengths and weaknesses. The degree and direction of the fluctuation has a direct relationship to overall programme quality. During any given time, programme staff address issues based on the immediate needs of the programme. Issues critical during the development and implementation phase of a programme may become secondary in an established programme. Out of necessity, staff constantly prioritise their focus of attention. Problems arise when staff lose sight of the big picture. They focus on one area of a treatment programme, and are blinded to other areas. This narrow vision opens the doors for pitfalls to develop and interfere with treatment. Pitfalls are defined as the unknown or not easily recognised hazards that encumber treatment services. They are a common, but frequently unexpected occurrence, which can significantly distract the unprepared professional and jeopardise the effectiveness of a programme.

Professionals working with juvenile sexual offenders can be taught to prepare for programme pitfalls, avoid them when possible, or deal with them in an expedient manner. Unfortunately, many professionals find themselves under pressure to provide timely, comprehensive services to juvenile sexual offenders, and are unexpectedly forced to deal with pitfalls. They are not prepared to deal with these unexpected digressions from treatment, and spend valuable time looking for possible solutions.

The treatment of juvenile sexual offenders is a relatively new field compared to other treatment disciplines, and professionals are just starting to identify common pitfalls they experience during their delivery of services. The literature has alluded to potential programme pitfalls, but there is no exclusive work addressing this critical issue. This chapter provides a concise and systematic four-step model to identify and manage the following 10 common pitfalls:

1. one-size-fits-all treatment approach
2. compartmentalisation
3. under-utilisation of front line staff
4. countertransference
5. complacency among staff
6. over-sexualising juvenile offender behaviours, thoughts and feelings
7. inadequate screening and selection of juveniles
8. insufficient measurement
9. external controls at the expense of self-management
10. staff burnout

The conceptual problem-solving model

Programmes that consistently monitor key problem areas obtain ongoing critical information about their effectiveness. The better the monitoring, the greater the probability that potential pitfalls will be noticed and addressed. The Conceptual Problem-Solving Model, a programme evaluation tool, is a systematic approach for helping professionals identify and manage pitfalls that occur in treating juvenile sexual offenders. The model helps professionals detect, alleviate or avoid pitfalls, so that programme effectiveness is maintained.

This model assumes problem-solving is the ongoing process of monitoring potential problem areas, identifying pitfalls, implementing intervention strategies, and modifying the strategies to meet the needs of a fluctuating sex offender treatment programme. Ideally, it occurs in a team environment with several trained professionals offering input.

This model can be applied to new or existing programmes, in both residential and community based settings, during their development, implementation, and maintenance phases. It can address a wide range of juvenile sex offender treatment areas, including general programmatic issues, specific treatment objectives, and staff/juvenile issues.

The steps of the conceptual problem-solving model

1. Monitoring with Awareness
   Staff realise program pitfalls occur. They continually remain aware of the programme goals and potential pitfalls that may interfere with these goals. Communication among staff is critical to help identify early signs of problems. Staff continually monitor potential problem areas, and utilise a pro-active rather than a reactive approach. They understand unexpected pitfalls usually cause the most problems.
2. Identification of the Pitfall
   Staff determine the type, frequency and severity of the programme pitfall that is emerging. They identify factors that generate and support the pitfall. They realise the potential for the pitfall to escalate, and do not down-play its potential consequences.
3. Application of Intervention Strategies
   Staff problem-solve and select potential intervention strategies. They embrace change, and look at a wide scope of intervention possibilities beyond those with predictive qualities. They may look at other fields or disciplines for input. They remain flexible and creative in their ideas. They set a clear course of action with specific goals and target dates. They keep staff and juveniles accountable for meeting goals and dates.
4. Modification of Intervention Strategies
   Staff assess the course of action at set intervals to determine effectiveness of the intervention strategies. They look at bottom-line results, and modify the course of action as needed. This important step is frequently omitted because staff convince themselves the problem has been addressed, and they focus their efforts elsewhere. Just because a series of intervention strategies were implemented does not signify they are effective.

Application of Warning Signs and Intervention Strategies to 10 Common Pitfalls

Pitfall 1: one-size-fits-all treatment approach: 'It worked for one, it'll work for all'

Most sex offender treatment programmes use a relapse prevention treatment protocol. Relapse prevention has relatively standardised treatment objectives with a strong psychoeducational thrust. This standardised treatment approach predisposes it as a treatment template that is applied in a one-size-fits-all manner.

A potential programme pitfall is professionals 'one-sizing' treatment. They use a sex offender treatment template, and do not take into account the individual differences of the offender. One-sizing may occur for various reasons based on the professional and their work experience. Professionals new to the field may lack confidence and apply treatment in a cookbook style. Some may 'play it safe' because they fear modifying the techniques will cause them to omit a critical piece of treatment and alter treatment results in a negative manner. Others may be under time constraints and not have the time to consider the best way to modify treatment to meet the needs of the offender. Some professionals may be assigned just one piece within a larger treatment programme, and discouraged from thinking beyond their assignment. On the positive side, one-sizing ensures every professional provides, and every offender receives, the same services. This may be beneficial for professionals new to the field, but constraining for experienced professionals. One-sizing ignores the individual etiology of deviant sexual behaviour and the heterogeneity of juvenile sexual offenders. Etiology significantly varies among juvenile sexual offenders, and they are seen as a heterogeneous population, coming from various cultural, racial, geographic, and socio-economic backgrounds (Knight and Prentky, 1993: Ryan, 1997). These theories, and subsequent treatment approaches, work best when integrated in such a way as to match the juvenile's specific background and pattern of offending. One-sizing also assumes each professional has a similar therapeutic style or the same comfort level and effectiveness with each treatment technique. What works well for one professional may not work as well for another. Professionals who know their strengths and weaknesses may achieve similar results with different techniques.

Warning signs of a 'one-size-fits-all' approach

- Treatment plans for all offenders look very similar.
- Juveniles address issues that are not significant to their offence dynamics.
- Professionals find themselves superficially addressing certain treatment issues just

because they believe it is part of the standard treatment protocol for all offenders.

- Professionals feel they cannot use a combination of sound clinical judgement and creativity in developing treatment plans.
- Professionals find themselves using treatment techniques that they are not comfortable with, or are not in their area of expertise.

Intervention strategies

- Assess the strengths and weakness of the juvenile.
- Have a good understanding of the juvenile's individual offence dynamics.
- Examine the juvenile's relevant cultural and racial issues.
- Prioritise the treatment issues based on the juvenile's needs.
- Be creative in determining methods that can be used to help him attain treatment goals. Ask for feedback from the treating team, colleagues not working with sexual offenders, and the juvenile himself. You may be surprised where you get the best ideas.
- When you have a 'gut feel' that a certain treatment issue is not applicable, consult with colleagues or skip it, you can always come back to it later.

Pitfall 2: compartmentalising treatment components: *'Each treatment piece is a separate unit, no reason for the juvenile to know how it all fits together'*

Many issues addressed in sex offender treatment address specific and distinct areas of sexual offending, such as life story, cycle of abuse, cognitive distortions, victim empathy, arousal issues, and relapse prevention. Compartmentalisation is the division of sex offender treatment into specific compartments for the ease of the professional and the offender. It is advantageous for offenders who are either young, intellectually low-functioning, concrete thinkers, resistant, immature or impulsive. It breaks down treatment into smaller understandable pieces.

A common programme pitfall is professionals not integrating the various treatment components into one overall treatment strategy prior to the offender completing treatment. Professionals can accomplish integration by taking the treatment components and combining them, seeing their interaction, and having the offender understand how they fit

together. Some offenders can integrate their treatment work throughout treatment, while others need compartmentalisation and then integration. Integration confirms they thoroughly know the information, how it fits together, and how to use it as one piece of a comprehensive relapse prevention strategy. It also increases the likelihood that juveniles can generalise and apply the information they learned in treatment to various real life situations, both sexual and non-sexual.

Warning signs of compartmentalisation

- Offenders have a limited understanding of how to apply the information they learned in treatment to interrupt their offence cycle.
- Offenders and professionals have difficulty seeing how the treatment issues relate to, and impact one another.
- Offenders have difficulty generalising the information to other sexual and non-sexual situations.
- Juveniles recite back information, but have difficulty conceptualising how it fits into a comprehensive relapse prevention strategy.

Intervention strategies

- Relate treatment objectives to each other. For example, the autobiography helps the juvenile identify possible factors in his offence cycle, and cognitive distortions help alter the juveniles belief patterns, which prepare him for victim empathy.
- Have the juvenile apply each treatment issue to both sexual and non-sexual situations.
- Have the juvenile find similarities among objectives.
- Instruct the juvenile to identify ways each treatment issue impacts the other treatment issues.

Pitfall 3: under-utilisation of front line staff: *'Who needs them anyway!'*

Front line staff can 'make or break' a treatment programme. Properly trained, they are the 'eyes and ears' of a programme. They are key professionals in the delivery of treatment services, providing important information to clinical and administrative professionals. They monitor juveniles' behaviours, thoughts and feelings outside formal treatment sessions, encourage them to work on treatment, and observe their application of the material to everyday situations. Many juveniles can feign treatment compliance for a few hours a week in the presence of their therapists, but find it significantly more difficult in constant presence of front line staff.

A programme pitfall is when properly trained front line staff are not utilised to their full potential. The frequent cause for this is a disruption in clear and meaningful communication between front line staff and other professionals working with the juvenile. Clinical and administrative professionals may fail to provide front line staff critical information about the juvenile's treatment or they may disregard or ignore the input from front line staff, based solely on their perceived hierarchical position.

Warning signs of under-utilisation of front line staff

- Front line staff do not feel they are part of the programme.
- They are not asked for input on programme issues.
- Clinical and administrative staff do not involve front-line staff in the decision making process.
- Communication between clinical and front line staff is minimal.
- Juveniles are able to easily 'split' clinical and front line staff.
- Evidence of passive aggression between front line staff and other professionals in the programme.
- Lack of enthusiasm among front-line staff.
- Front-line staff are late or do not show up for meetings.
- They are apathetic and believe they cannot make a difference.

Intervention strategies

- Remind front line staff they are an integral component of the treatment program.
- Ask them for feedback and input on a regular basis.
- Involve front line staff in decision making processes.
- Train them about each treatment component so they can help monitor the juveniles' progress in treatment.
- Share general information about each juvenile's offence dynamics with front line staff, so they can help the juvenile identify lapses he experiences in treatment.

- Take seriously the concerns of front line staff, and do not sweep them under the table.
- Involve senior front line staff in providing training for new employees.
- Invite them to attend conferences to increase knowledge base and as a break from daily work routines.
- Reward them for their work, and ask them to participate in conference presentations to share their experience with others.

Pitfall 4: countertransference: *'I hate that kid'*

Juveniles may inadvertently or deliberately detect a sensitive area or weakness in a professional that triggers a strong emotional reaction from the professional. Counter-transference can be a powerful tool in treatment, if the professional is able to remain objective. In countertransference, the juvenile sends a significant amount of information about his personal interaction style. It also provides the professional with much information about the way this juvenile interacts with other individuals, thus giving clues about his offence dynamics. The key for professionals is to remain objective, consult with others, and be aware of their own 'baggage' that interferes with the intended objectivity.

A programme pitfall occurs when professionals allow their emotions to interfere with their objectivity in providing services, which significantly compromises treatment. Professionals who are able to emotionally disengage and examine the interaction from a cognitive perspective are able to objectively gather and examine the information. If the professional becomes emotionally over involved, critical information may be lost because the juvenile is unconsciously revealing something about himself that the professional is ignoring. For example, a disparaging comment from the juvenile can elicit strong feelings of anger and put the professional on the defensive. As a result, the professional focuses more on their reaction and less on why the juvenile acted out. They get bogged down in details and overlook their part in the treatment process.

Warning signs of counter-transference

- Difficulty remaining objective toward the juvenile.
- Evidence of a strong attraction or dislike for the juvenile.

- The juvenile reminds the professional of someone in their past.
- The professional spends less or more time with the juvenile compared to other juveniles.
- Strong feelings, either positive or negative, toward the juvenile.
- Obsessing about the juvenile.
- The juvenile is able to 'push your buttons.'
- Difficulty engaging or disengaging in a therapeutic relationship with the juvenile.

Intervention strategies

- Examine your 'baggage' and how it interferes with the therapeutic relationship.
- Assess your own emotions, and what they are telling you. If he elicits certain feelings or reactions from you, he likely did this to other individuals in his past. What is he getting out of it? Is it a defensive manoeuvre, is he attaining a sense of power, or is he trying to push you away?
- Switch from emotional reactions to cognitive reactions. Momentarily, emotionally disengage from the juvenile, and attempt to determine what the juvenile is attaining from this interaction. You are likely seeing first-hand how he interacted with significant others in his life, which is a very important piece of therapeutic information.
- In some cases, share feelings and thoughts that were elicited by the juvenile, and examine them with him.
- Discuss your thoughts and feelings with colleagues, as a way of addressing the countertransference objectively.
- Refer the juvenile to another professional if the countertransference is strong and interferes with the therapeutic relationship.

Pitfall 5: complacency among staff: *'We're pretty good, no reason to change anything'*

Most programmes reach a level where the professionals charged with developing and implementing the programme have attained their intended goals. The programme is effective, it has a good reputation in the community, and juveniles are successfully completing it. Staff are content with the programme, and may focus their energies elsewhere.

A programme pitfall is when staff, almost subconsciously, say to themselves 'We've done well enough,' 'Don't fix it if it's not broken,' or 'We've come a long way, nothing can bring

us down.' They assume everything is okay, and may not realise that potential problems may be developing around the corner. The danger is minimising or not attending to minor problems. Professionals may not check the offenders' written work as closely as before, minor behavioural outbursts are ignored, and therapy sessions may be missed or are less effective.

Warning signs of complacency

- An escalation in significant programmatic problems.
- Lack of enthusiasm at work.
- Group sessions are missed or shortened.
- Paperwork is late or only met minimal standards.
- Professionals do not attend local and national conferences.
- Professionals are not aware of current trends in research and practice.
- The programme structure has not significantly changed to keep up with research and literature.

Intervention strategies

- Develop a programme review committee, composed of internal and outside professionals, to provide objective opinions and analysis.
- Regularly talk to other professionals in the field.
- Attend conferences related to juvenile sexual offending.
- Be aware of recent developments in research and treatment.
- Address minor problems as they develop within the treatment programme.
- Invigorate the professionals. Increase morale, motivation, and enthusiasm among staff, so they are mentally ready and eager to look for potential pitfalls.

Pitfall 6: sexualising all juvenile offender behaviours, thoughts and feelings: *'Sometime a cigar is just a cigar'*

Professionals working with juvenile sexual offenders are taught to closely monitor the juvenile's sexual behaviours, thoughts and feelings. Frequent areas of concern include: behaviours that suggest sexual deviance, deviant sexual fantasies, oversexualisation, and obsessions about sexuality. Monitoring these areas is good practice with juvenile sexual offenders because some of the primary goals of treatment are to decrease deviant sexual fantasies and behaviours, increase appropriate sexual fantasies and behaviours, and help the juvenile develop interests beyond his initial sexualised world-view.

A programme pitfall for professionals working with juvenile sexual offenders is to interpret inappropriate or deviant motives or tendencies behind all sexual behaviours, thoughts, and feelings. It is prudent to always rule out the possibility of a sexual slant to what an offender might do, think, or feel, but the action should be considered in the context of the offender's age, patterns and preferences.

Programmes that are ultraconservative in all interpretations of offender behaviour run the risk of 'shutting down' what the offender is actually experiencing in exchange for parroting what he perceives the treating professionals want to hear. An example is the use of grooming by an offender. Many offenders do not actually know how to be friends with same age peers. Some of their attempts to step out of their social isolation and low self-concept might be misinterpreted as grooming another person for future sexual abuse. It is true offenders often groom their victims to put them in a position to be sexually offended upon. However, there are other times when the offender might actually be seeking attention, trying to develop non-sexual friendships with same age peers, or becoming involved in some other non-sexual activity. While safety is critical, treatment requires a certain element of calculated risk and earned trust in the offender so that the offender can eventually test and practice the new skills.

Warning signs of sexualising the juvenile's behaviours, thoughts and feelings

- Staff focus only on the 'sexual offender' role of the juvenile, and fail to perceive his other roles in the context of a 'whole person,' such as a brother, son, student, friend, or neighbour.
- The juvenile decreases his disclosure of personal information, especially related to sexuality, as a defensive stance towards staff's over hypervigilance of his behaviours, thoughts and feelings.
- There is an increase in the juvenile parroting what professionals want to hear, but being

unable to integrate the information into daily living.
- The juvenile has difficulty explaining 'normal' sexual behaviour.
- The juvenile presents himself as asexual, and reports having little or no sexual thoughts or urges.

Intervention strategies

- Assess how other treating professionals view the juvenile's same actions, thoughts and feelings.
- Determine the similarity between the juvenile's questionable behaviour, thoughts, or feelings, and his offending pattern and known distorted world-view.
- Examine the juvenile's progress in treatment, and whether he has demonstrated improved and appropriate internal monitoring skills.
- Determine whether this is a high-risk situation for the offender.
- Look at evidence that the offender's behaviour is offence oriented.
- Have a safety net in place if the calculated course of action is incorrect.

Pitfall 7: inadequate screening and selection of juveniles: *'Sure, we'll take him into the programme'*

In recent years, there has been a significant increase in both juveniles identified as 'sexual offenders' and the number of programmes treating them (Burton, Fiske, Freeman-Longo, and Levins, 2000). Juvenile offenders vary in etiology, offence type, and treatment needs, and programmes differ in the type of service they provide, and the type of offender they can successfully treat. A sex offender treatment programme cannot meet the needs of all sexual offenders. A critical task for programme staff is to ensure a good match between a juvenile sexual offender and the treatment services offered in the programme.

Effective programmes use a three-step system of screening, selecting, and maintaining appropriate candidates. The first step is establishing initial *screening criteria*, which clearly identify those juveniles that would be good referral candidates for a specific programme. These criteria are critical to screen-out juveniles who are obviously not appropriate for the programme, and reduce the pool of potential candidates to a reasonable number. They tend to be objective criteria, such as gender, age range, offence-type, mental-health status, intelligence, and recent behavioural compliance. The second step is developing *selection criteria*, which determine what juveniles should be placed in the programme. Staff use these criteria to fine-tune their initial screening of juveniles to ensure a significantly better probability of a good match. These criteria tend to be more subjective, and may include the juvenile's personality functioning, match to other juveniles in the programme, amenability to treatment, compliance during the interview, risk of re-offending, and motivation to participate in treatment. The third step is establishing *maintenance criteria*, which determine the minimal requirements juveniles need to attain to remain in the programme. These criteria identify juveniles who are no longer a good match. These are a combination of objective and subjective criteria, which measure factors such as lack of progress in treatment, behavioural problems, negative influence on peers, and sabotaging treatment for self or others.

Warning signs of inadequate screening, selection and maintenance of juveniles

- The range of juveniles is too broad (i.e. age, offence type, IQ, etc.).
- The treatment services do not match the existent population.
- Decreased trust and teamwork among juveniles.
- Excessive acting out among juveniles toward staff or peers.
- Programme staff consistently giving in to outside pressure from the community to admit inappropriate candidates.
- Selection of juveniles only guided by monetary considerations.

Intervention strategies

- Consistently examine and refine criteria to match the changing needs of the programme, juveniles and community.
- Clearly state programme criteria to referring agencies, court officials and community professionals.
- Do not be afraid to say 'no' to inappropriate referrals.
- Examine what is guiding selection procedure. Focus on ensuring a good fit rather than conceding to community, political or monetary pressures.

Pitfall 8: insufficient measurement: 'Who needs data anyway!'

Effective programmes are guided by data. Experience has shown that a complete database consists of at least four components: demographics; treatment; testing; and follow-up. *Demographics* include basic information about the juvenile, family, school, medical, and mental health. *Treatment* includes information about the specifics of the juvenile's offences, and his step-by-step progress in treatment. *Testing* reflects the results of the juvenile's general psychological and sex offender specific tests and scales, which can be used as pre and post measures. *Follow-up* is data measuring the juvenile's adjustment to the community and recidivism rate. These data are indispensable when programme staff desire to:

- obtain an objective opinion of programme effectiveness.
- conduct research
- compare their programme to other programmes
- determine what treatment components work
- refine selection criteria
- conduct recidivism studies

A programme pitfall for many juvenile sexual offender treatment programmes is the difficulty for professionals to objectively measure programme effectiveness. The main focus for treatment programmes is providing direct services to juveniles. Data collection is secondary to treatment. Although data bases are frequently created at the start of a programme, data collection is usually the first component of a programme to be overlooked. Lack of data collection is often blamed on time constraints, outdated computer hardware and software, shortsightedness about the benefits of data, and staff shortages. Another significant problem is data may be entered into the computer, but staff do not know how to analyse or properly interpret it.

Warning signs of insufficient programme measurement

- Basic data is not available upon request.
- Staff do not engage in research efforts.
- Data is stored on hard copies, but not entered into a computer.
- Measurement system is too complicated to be used effectively, which encumbers data entry, access, and interpretation.

Intervention strategies

- Block out time in staffs' schedule to collect, enter, and analyse data.
- Train staff to use testing materials that produce useful data.
- Train staff to accurately interpret and analyse data.
- Employ college interns to assist in objective periodic analysis.
- If state-of-the-art testing instruments are purchased, ensure staff are properly trained to use and interpret them.

Pitfall 9: external controls at the expense of self-management: *'We gotta keep him in handcuffs all the time!'*

Treating professionals stabilise external behaviours of juvenile sexual offenders before establishing the foundation for self-management. Juveniles in treatment are initially placed under strict supervision and taught strategies to reduce their probability of re-offending. They learn the treatment material with the expectation of retaining it. However, to stop here is to miss a critical part of the necessary work required to ameliorate the predatory actions of many offenders.

A programme pitfall is mistaking changes in the juvenile's external behaviours for substantive progress in treatment. This often results from lack of comprehensive treatment planning, poor staff training, public ignorance, inadequate programme implementation, and limited resources. Some juveniles that heavily rely on external controls may change for the better if they have adequate community and family support. But, many more will offend again or manifest their abusive actions in other forms, even though they may be able to recite treatment principles when 'tested.' Treatment programmes that focus too much on external controls are more likely to equate the juvenile following rules and completing homework assignments with substantial long-lasting treatment outcomes. They lose sight of the more important 'process,' rather than the content aspect of treatment.

Once the juveniles' external behaviours are stabilised, programme staff should support the transition from external control to cultivating behavioural self-management. A programme's structure is a type of *containment field* that can provide the opportunity for offenders to experiment in a safe way with new behaviours, gain insights, and make real changes to avoid future victimisation. Juveniles need to be given the opportunity to practice and apply the newly learned material and skills in successively less restrictive environments. When offenders become comfortable with their newly acquired skill of healthy behavioural self-management, they have a greater chance of remaining offence-free.

Warning signs of external controls at the expense self-management

- Juveniles only parrot treatment information, but have difficulty explaining it in their own words.
- Their behaviours regress when they believe no one is monitoring them.
- They become overly dependent upon staff.
- They become 'institutionalised,' and find it difficult to function without a high level of supervision and structure.
- They lack self-confidence when staff are not constantly encouraging them.
- They have difficulty making decisions.
- Their ability for establishing short and long term goals is limited.

Intervention strategies

- Create a treatment environment whereby the real world is safely approximated in daily living through controlled treatment experiments.
- Increase the juvenile's self-esteem and confidence level for becoming more self-reliant in their application of the material they learned in treatment.
- Train treatment professionals to avoid *chasing behaviours* that unrealistically exaggerate the juvenile's lapses, and prematurely increasing external controls beyond a reasonable level.
- During the early stages of treatment, programme staff, family, and community professionals avoid doing the treatment work for the offender in the hope he will become more motivated at a later date.
- Assist the juvenile to develop a support group of mature adults, parents, therapists, group home staff, and court personnel to act as a safety-net and a resource as he practices his newly learned skills.

Pitfall 10: staff burnout: *'I'm fine, I'm *#@anding fine!'*

Staff burnout is a serious problem in the field of sex offender treatment. Juvenile sexual offenders are not the ideal clients. They are frequently forced into treatment, and many are highly defensive, deceptive, impulsive and manipulative. Treatment has a confrontive bent, and professionals always have to be on their toes. Professionals frequently experience pressure from agencies, society, and from within, to unrealistically 'cure' the offender. The stakes are high. Failures in treatment represent the potential for more victims in the community. The topics addressed in treatment range from 'not normal' to bizarre and abhorrent, and can be very emotionally unsettling to the professional. Other professionals, friends, or family members may question their choice to work with sex offenders. Some professionals work in isolation, without colleagues to discuss cases or problems, which exacerbates the problem of burnout.

The programme pitfall is not noticing the early signs of burnout until it's too late. Although most professionals are aware of the potential for burnout, most do not realise they are experiencing burnout until it has taken a toll on their private and professional life. They avoid the warning signs, and slowly the quality of their work, mental health and overall life has significantly been diminished.

Warning signs of burnout

- The professionals place an unrealistically high burden for treatment success on self.
- Expectations are too high, and include 'the need to cure' the offenders.
- Blame recidivism on self.
- Obsessively question own sexual behaviours, thoughts and feelings.
- Experience frequent reminders of own unresolved abuse issues.
- Ally with the juvenile's beliefs or cognitive distortions.
- Frequently feel angry and frustrated.
- Feel sad or depressed.
- Blunt their emotions.
- Avoid meeting with offenders.
- Avoid work, and do non-work related business in the office.
- Frequently absent from work.
- Decrease in enthusiasm and motivation at work.
- Work interfering with home life.
- Skewed definition of normal sex.
- Unrealistically hyper-vigilant about sexual abuse.

Intervention factors

- Set realistic expectations for treatment outcome.
- Place responsibility for treatment progress onto the juvenile.
- Limit number of sex offender clients.
- Rotate case assignments to work with non-sex offender populations.
- Talk with colleagues who work with sexual offenders.
- Participate in study groups with colleagues in the same field.
- Participate in conferences to revitalise self with new treatment methodology.
- Use relaxation and stress management techniques.
- Do not take work home.
- Take vacations.
- Use humour with self and co-worker.

The 10 programme pitfalls identified in this chapter represent recurrent problems experienced by the authors in their work with juvenile sexual offenders. Other programme pitfalls exist, and may prove to be significant obstacles to treatment as well. In most cases, unexpected pitfalls pose the greatest risks to treatment programmes. The key to managing programme pitfalls is early identification and intervention through the use of the Conceptual Problems Solving Model presented in this chapter. Professionals that apply this model will be prepared to manage and/or avoid most of the pitfalls that surface in the treatment. The model helps professionals meet the needs of a dynamic treatment programme without jeopardising its effectiveness.

References

Association for the Treatment of Sexual Abusers (ATSA) (1997) *Ethical Standards and Principles for the Management of Sexual Abusers*. Beaverton, Oregon: ATSA.

Barbaree, H. E., Marshall, W. L. and Hudson, S. M. (1993) *The Juvenile Sex Offender*. New York: The Guilford Press.

Blanchard, G. T. (1995). *The Difficult Connection: The Therapeutic Relationship in Sex Offender Treatment*. Brandon, VT: Safer Society Press.

Bukowski, W. M., Sippola, L. and Brender, W. (1993) Where Does Sexuality Come From?: Normative Sexuality From a Developmental Perspective. in Barbaree, H. E. Marshall,

W. L. and Hudson, S. M. *The Juvenile Sex Offender*. New York: The Guilford Press.

Burton, D., Fiske, J. A., Freeman-Longo, R. E. and Levins, J. (2000). *The 1996 Nationwide Survey of Sexual Abuse Treatment Providers and Programs*. Brandon, VT: Safer Society Press.

Camp, B. and Tyler, B. (1993) Treatment of Adolescent Sexual Offenders: A Review of Empirical Research. *The Journal of Applied Social Sciences*. 17: 191–206.

Freeman-Longo, R. E. and Pithers, W. D. (1992) *A Structured Approach to Preventing Relapse: A Guide for Sex Offenders*. Brandon, VT: The Safer Society Press.

Knight, R. A., and Prentky, R. A. (1993) Exploring Characteristics Foe Classifying Juveniles Sex Offenders. in Barbaree, H. E. Marshall, W. L. and Hudson, S. M. *The Juvenile Sex Offender*. New York: The Guilford Press.

Lab, S. P., Shields, G. and Schondel, C. (1993) Research Note: An Evaluation of Juvenile Sexual Offender Treatment. *Crime and Delinquency*. 39: 543–53.

Laws D. R. (Ed.) (1989) *Relapse Prevention With Sex Offenders*. New York: The Guilford Press.

Marshall, W., Laws, D. and Barbaree, H. (1990) *Handbook Of Sexual Assault*. New York, NY: Plenum Press.

National Adolescent Perpetrator Network (1993) The Revised Report from the National Task Force on Juvenile Sexual Offending. *Juvenile and Family Court Journal*. 44: 4.

Pithers, W. D. (1990) Relapse Prevention With Sexual Aggressors: A Method for Maintaining Therapeutic Gain and Enhancing External Supervision. in: Marshall, W., Laws, D. and Barbaree, H.E. (1990) *Handbook of Sexual Assault*. New York, NY: Plenum Press.

Ryan, G. (1997) Theories of Etiology. in Ryan, G. and Lane, S. (Eds.) *Juvenile Sexual Offending: Causes, Consequences and Correction*. San Francisco: Jossey-Bass Inc. 19–35.

Ryan, G. and Lane, S. (1997) The Impact of Sexual Abuse on the Interventionist. in Ryan, G. and Lane, S. (Eds.) *Juvenile Sexual Offending: Causes, Consequences and Correction*. San Francisco: Jossey-Bass Inc. 457–74.

Chapter 18: A Proposal for Comprehensive Community-based Treatment of Female Juvenile Sex Offenders

Dr Darlene Williams and Mark Buehler CSW

Introduction: The Prevalence of the Female Juvenile Sexual Offender Phenomenon and the Need for More Research

Although it has long been assumed that males are the primary perpetrators of sexual abuse, there is a need for more research on female sexual offenders. Fehrenbach (1988) points out that much of the literature is *male-centred*. Finkelhor's (1984) data helps dispel the myth that females are not sexual perpetrators, showing that 34 per cent of sexually abused males and 13 per cent of sexually abused females had been *victimised by females*. Scott (1994) writes, *'Male and female offenders in therapy frequently describe instances of childhood sexual exploitation by mothers, baby-sitters, older sisters, and other caretakers,'* suggesting that instances of *female* (italics added) abuse have long gone unreported and unresolved. Mathews (1997) adds, *'More is needed on adolescent female abusers . . . because . . . as the male victims' movement grows and more men and boys name their abusers, more female sex offenders are starting to be identified.'*

Additionally, information on juvenile offenders, *as compared to adults*, is rather lacking and more is needed. This need is evidenced by Brown et al. (1984), and Matsuda et al., (1989), showing that 20 per cent of sexual assaults and between 30 per cent and 50 per cent of all child sexual abuse can be attributed to *adolescent* perpetrators.

Knight and Prentky (1993) state in their review of several studies, that when sex offenders are assured complete confidentiality, as many as 50 per cent report their first sexual assault occurred during *adolescence*. Clearly, this indicates a need for more *juvenile* sex offender research and for more juvenile sex offender treatment programmes.

Frequently, researchers point out that there is a paucity of literature on female sexual offenders and, in particular, on *female juvenile* offenders (Lane and Lobanov-Rostovsky, in Ryan and Lane, 1997). Charles and McDonald (1997) point out; *'Slightly more is known about adult female offenders, but not enough is known about either (adult female or adolescent female) age group to be able to generalise between these two populations.'* Additionally, Mathews et al. (1997) point out; *'In contrast to a growing body of literature on juvenile male sexual perpetrators, relatively few studies have been published on sexually assaultive juvenile females'* (p. 187).

For example, Ryan and Lane, (1997), wrote a five-hundred page book on the treatment of juvenile sexual offenders, and although the entire text was on the aetiology and treatment of juvenile offenders, *less than twenty pages* were dedicated to juvenile female offenders.

Under-reporting of female sexual offenders

A key point to keep in mind when researching the dynamics of female juvenile sexual offenders is that presently, only the 'worst case' female offenders are usually brought to the attention of the courts or to departments of social services in the US (Fehrenbach, 1988). Under-reporting of offences, *and especially the less aggressive offences*, occurs for a variety of reasons.

Primarily, sexual abuse across the board is a *'silent malignancy'* (Mathews, 1997). For example, Russell (1984, in Salter, 1995) found that only 5 per cent of sexual offences were ever even reported to the police; and, Abel et al. (1987, as cited in Salter, 1995) claims that the likelihood of detection is overall 3 per cent. Additionally, societies generally accept *and encourage* the expression of female sexuality. This sexualisation of females causes the tolerance level to be higher for *almost any* sexual behaviour that females engage in. For example, how common is it for a woman to be arrested for showing her breasts at a public event? Yet, at the same event, in the US, a man who is relieving himself in a dark corner is subject to arrest for indecent exposure. What message does this send to young women? As Fehrenbach (1988) points out, exhibitionism, peeping, or indecent phone calling has been treated less harshly with females than with males:

> It is more likely that teenage girls are brought to the attention of authorities and referred to programmes ... if they have committed more 'serious' offences, such as rape or indecent liberties, than if they are involved in such 'hands-off' offences as exhibitionism. Clearly our society tolerates, or even encourages, nudity more among females than males. Exhibitionism in a female teenager might, for example, more readily be labelled 'promiscuity' than viewed as a legal offence such as indecent exposure.
> (p150)

Conversely, societies are generally in denial, as they comfortably view females as being *nurturers*; and, therefore, are not able to see females (as they do males), as behaving in a sexually aggressive manner. Thus, despite research findings that females may represent a percentage larger than once thought of all adolescent perpetrators in general, under-reporting has resulted due in large part to society's tolerance for expression of female sexuality and denial about female sexual aggression. Consequently, *female juvenile research and treatment has lagged significantly behind that for adults and for male juveniles*. It is paramount that a longitudinal study of female juvenile sexual offenders be conducted. Research, treatment guidelines, and programme evaluations are sorely needed in this emerging field, which, traditionally, has been bypassed.

Etiological Issues and Comparison of Female to Male Perpetrators

Perpetrators' own history of sexual victimisation as a major contributing factor to subsequent perpetration

Researchers and psychotherapists have long known of the fairly common relationship between having a childhood history of being sexually abused and the subsequent manifestation of sexual perpetration performed by that former victim. In studying aetiology, researchers are attempting to understand how significant it is that having a prior (before offending) history of being sexually abused contributes to one becoming a sexual perpetrator. This is because the percentage of all non-victimised people becoming perpetrators is significantly lower than the percentage of all former victims becoming perpetrators. The data clearly show that a significant proportion of child molesters *do* have

a prior history of their own victimisation; conversely though, a significant proportion of the data show that many molesters *do not* have that prior victimisation history. Aetiological research must look beyond this 'causal factor,' albeit a critical factor, and identify and measure other powerful, contributing variables, as well.

Not only is having a history of sexual victimisation a strong aetiological factor for perpetration, but it is apparent from the research findings that this psychosexual variable *has even more startling implications for female juveniles*. That is, female juveniles, compared to male juveniles, accumulate even more extensive biopsychosocial trauma before they manifest a perpetrator response to that trauma (See Table 1).

This is significant in that treatment programmes for female juvenile offenders, as opposed to males, need to include a larger component of victim trauma work as a primary treatment intervention or, at minimum, as a significant adjunct to traditional cognitive-behavioural perpetrator treatment (Turner and Turner, 1994).

Female juvenile sexual offenders have more sexual victimisation compared to male counterparts

A survey from The Safer Society Program (Knopp and Lackey, 1987) reported on 346 programmes that treated female juvenile sexual offenders. Out of four programmes reporting on female juvenile sexual offenders below the age of eleven, 33 youths (100 per cent), were sexually abused prior to becoming an offender. For the age range of 11 to 17, (with 14 programmes reporting a total sample of 130 female youth), 100 per cent were sexually abused prior to offending. In the age range of 18 and over, 11 out of 19 programmes (with a sample of 313 female perpetrators), reported that 100 per cent of their clients were sexually abused prior to offending.

Table 1 illustrates how female juvenile sexual offenders have a much more chronic sexual victimisation-trauma history than their male counterparts.

Female juvenile sexual offenders have more etiological trauma in other areas compared to male counterparts

Mathews et al. (1997) report their findings that 'relative to the juvenile males, the histories of

Table 1: The percentage of female and male juvenile sexual offenders who have a childhood history of sexual victimisation.

Researcher	Juvenile females	Juvenile males
Finkelhor et al., 1986 (Review of the Literature)	Between 6% and 62%	Between 3% and 31%
Fehrenbach and Monatersky, 1988	46.4%	18.0%
Mathews et al., 1997	77%	44%
Knopp and Lackey, 1987 Safer Society Ss = All Female	Majority of Programmes Report 100%	N/A
Rasmussen, 1999 Ss = All Male N = 170	N/A	Less than 40%

the studied females reflected even more extensive and pervasive childhood maltreatment . . .' (p187). Other researchers have found similar results (See Table 2).

Blues et al. (1999) present their observations regarding physical abuse and how female juvenile sexual offenders differ from their male counterparts. They point out the difference in that:

> For most girls, the physical abuse has been directly related to their levels of compliance or otherwise within their own experiences of sexual abuse. This is in contrast to the boys whose experiences of physical abuse tend to be responses to non-compliance to male caregivers or older brothers although not necessarily in a sexually abusive relationship.
>
> (p173)

Female anger dynamics compared to males

Turner and Turner (1994) provide two psychodynamic assessments of female sexual offenders who have a prior history of sexual abuse victimisation. First, they stress that females differ from males in regard to dealing with anger and, in particular, in dealing with anger stemming from victimisation. That is,

females are more likely to internalise anger, whereas males are more likely to externalise their anger. They point out that anger is 'a masculine phenomenon.' When profound and chronic, anger is turned inward, *against* oneself, and it may then be manifested by depression, guilt, and, ultimately self-abuse, as well as by continued sexual victimisation or perpetration. They explain:

> By denying women the expression of anger, society denies them a valuable mobilising tool for action and change. When the anger that comes from sexual abuse is not given expression, the female victim is likely to feel disempowered and depressed, and may either submit to additional victimisation or go to extreme lengths to regain a sense of power, perhaps by committing sexual offences against others.
>
> (p15)

Another psychodynamic interpretation these authors present is that, in general, women are taught to be caretakers and, also, are 'driven by the need and desire for relationship.' Therefore, when victimised, the female may:

- Avoid tearing the family (relationship) apart and (unconsciously) continue to manifest a victim role (p16).

Table 2: A comparison of trauma history between juvenile female and male offenders.

Trauma	Juvenile females	Juvenile males
Mean number of molesters[1]	4.5	1.4
Having >1 molester[1]	74.5%	9.7%
Those who were 5 years old or younger at their first victimisation[1]	64%	26%
Physical abuse[1]	60%	45%
Force used by their molester[1]	72.5%	45.2%
Incidence of rape[2]	53.6%	22.9%

[1]Mathews et al., 1997.
[2]Fehrenbach and Monatersky, 1988.

- In order to maintain the family relationship, may 'identify with the aggressor,' thereby 'normalising' (unconsciously accepting) the behaviour and not severing that relationship.

Conversely, the authors explain that the female victim may perpetrate, as opposed to unconsciously continuing the victim role, for one of three possible reasons:

1. To differentiate themselves from enmeshed, victim-identified mothers.
2. To 'act out' rage at their mothers, who failed to protect them from their own victimisation experiences.
3. Spiralling onward, with her internalised aggressor, she may then perpetrate herself, as a learned means of conducting and maintaining relationships with people younger and weaker than herself.

In these dynamics, it seems that females would be expressing their profound anger externally, similar to males.

Non-etiological perpetrator characteristics of the female juvenile sexual offender

Other aetiological characteristics have been studied that increase our understanding of this population. While the data on most of these categories is limited, the information provided calls our attention to specific areas for continued research.

Female juvenile frequency of perpetration compared to males

There is conflicting evidence regarding the percentage of female juvenile sexual offences to male juvenile sexual offenders. Mathews et al. (1997) reports that 'The juvenile female perpetrators engaged in offending behaviours comparable in frequency and magnitude to their male counterparts.' In their sample of 67 females and 70 males, the females had a mean of 2.3 victims while the males had a mean of 1.8 victims. In contrast, however, most other researchers' findings show that female juvenile sex offenders usually account for *far less* cases of perpetration than do male juveniles. Camp's et al. (1993) review of ten studies from 1983 to 1990, found that less than 5 per cent of all reported adolescent sex offenders were

female. In a study in Finland, with 11,000 same-age adolescents in the general population, Rantakallio et al. (1995) report that there were zero female juvenile sexual offenders and 12 male juvenile sexual offenders. Additionally, Lane et al., in Ryan et al. (1997) did a review of research and concluded that females only account for a quarter of the adolescent sexual offender population.

Female juveniles and the influence of co-perpetrators

The issue of whether offenders included a co-perpetrator has been found frequently in the adult female population, but extremely rarely in the adult male population. Fehrenbach and Monastersky (1988) studied 28 female juvenile sexual offenders, finding that all of the offenders committed their offences independently. Whereas, they point out two studies that show that '77 per cent' and, 'half' of female adult sexual offenders had been accompanied or coerced by a male offender (McCarthy, 1986, and Wolfe, 1985, in Fehrenbach et al., 1988.) Fehrenbach et al., 1988 adds; *'These findings are in contrast to those on both adolescent and adult male sexual offenders, who most frequently act independently and without coercion by co-offenders.'*

Female juveniles and the use of manipulation and coercion compared to males

As shown in the above section, female juvenile sex offenders are not as influenced by male coercion to perpetrate, as are their adult female counterparts, Fehrenbach and Monatersky (1988). However, female juveniles are more likely to use coercion in order to manipulate their victim to remain quiet about the perpetration, whereas male juveniles are more likely to use force to do so (Blues et al., 1999, in Erooga and Masson, Eds., p174).

Age of onset

Blues et al., 1999 review of the literature describes how the few studies that report on age-of-onset are somewhat conflictual with one another. Generally speaking, they indicate that females have a later age-of-onset (16–17 years) than males (14–16 years or younger) and point out that this coincides with the female's entry into babysitting roles. Confusing these

Table 3: Generalised comparison of characteristics of female juveniles to male juveniles.

	Female juvenile	Male juvenile
Trauma	Higher rate of being sexually victimised[1]	Significant history of being victim of sexual assault, yet noticeably lower rate as compared to females
Trauma	Victimised at an earlier age, compared to males[1]	Victimisation began at a later age, compared to females[1]
Physical abuse	Physical abuse experienced more likely within the victimisation[2]	Physical abuse more likely occurs from older males not necessarily within the victimisation[2]
Anger	More likely express victim-related anger inward. Leads to increased victimisation role; more self-injurious[3]	More likely to express victim-related anger outward. Leads to increased perpetrator role; decreased victimisation role[3]
Anger and perpetration	If prior victimisation, may perpetrate out of anger to distance self from victim-identified mother, or regain a sense of power, or to act out rage against mother's failure to protect[3]	Same as above
Defence mechanism	Identify with the aggressor in order to 'normalise' behaviour and perpetrate out of a need to maintain relationship[3]	Identify with the aggressor, and may normalise being a perpetrator out of the need to express anger externally[3]
Co-perpetrator	Usually commit offences independently[4]	No studies have been found by these authors that show co-perpetration
Keeping the secret	More likely to use coercion to make their victim 'keep the secret.'[2]	More likely to use force or intimidation to make their victim 'keep the secret.'[2]
Perpetrations	May have more perpetrations than males[1] yet most studies report it is much less than males	Most studies show more perpetrations than females
Treatment	Current treatment becoming more likely to focus on the perpetrators' own victimisation prior to, or concurrently, with dealing with perpetration issues; expressive therapies[3]	Treatment historically more likely to focus on perpetration and criminal point of reference.[5] Cognitive-behavioural[6]

[1]Mathews et al., 1997. [2]Blues et al., in Erooga and Masson, Eds., 1999. [3]Turner and Turner, 1994. [4]Fehrenbach and Monastersky, 1988. [5]Knopp, in Otey and Ryan, Eds., 1985. [6]Charles and McDonald, 1997.

statistics is that many children younger than these age groups are seen in treatment. If, indeed, females do perpetrate at a later age than males, then this adds to the theory that females internalise their prior victimisation, either sexual, physical, or other, and do not manifest the 'externalised response' of perpetration as readily as do males. This has implications for treatment.

The Need for Female Juvenile-Centered Research and Treatment

Implications for treatment

Since there has been too little research on the female juvenile sexual offender, it is difficult to provide consistent data on this population as well as on the comparisons between female to male juvenile offenders. Even when juvenile sexual offender research *does* include females, it often tends to blend the females in with the males and merely reports on overall percentages and characteristics of juvenile offenders. Clearly, more female-oriented research is needed.

However, with the female juvenile research that we have found, it is apparent that female juveniles do have some clear distinctions compared to male juvenile sexual offenders. These female juveniles may have a more profound history of victimisation and other abuses than do the male juveniles. In combination with that, the coping skills that females tend to use may, in fact, exacerbate their victim role (as opposed to males, who may externalise their anger, and thus manifest control and rage via their own conduct as perpetrators.) Treatment programmes for females, then, must include an anger component aimed at enlightening them to their 'internalisation of anger' and 'continued victimisation' dynamics. With this enlightenment, female victim perpetrators can then begin the task of learning new, healthy coping skills and stop both their continued victimisation and their perpetration response. They can learn that although their childhood coping mechanisms – identification with the aggressor, maintaining 'relationships' at all costs, displaced anger or control and perpetration – once served them a psychodynamic purpose (survival), they can now shed these maladaptive coping mechanisms, with comprehensive treatment and on-going support, and can learn newer, healthy, coping mechanisms.

Program design and components

The programme described in this chapter is designed for clients aged 12 to 16, and is intended to last approximately eighteen months. Clients are placed in groups according to their age, (i.e., 12–14, 14–16) taking into account the maturity level of individuals in respective groups. Juveniles aged seventeen and up are referred to adult programmes; those under twelve, to child programmes). The last six months of the programme is a maintenance phase whereupon clients attend a multifamily group at least once per month with their families. (Due to individual differences, some families may finish the programme significantly later or somewhat earlier.) Individual and family sessions of course, may extend beyond

'programme' completion. As long as 'programme' treatment goals have been accomplished, juveniles are still able to successfully complete the programme, despite continued participation in other modalities of treatment. To date, too few clients have successfully completed this programme to allow for outcome data (due in part to extinguished referrals because of budget cuts) however, outcome data collection and analysis remain the goals of these researchers.

Program goals

Successful completion of this proposed treatment programme is based upon, but not limited to, six general treatment goals. In addition, each juvenile participant will have individualised family or personal goals that need to be completed for graduation from the programme. These goals will be determined during treatment team meetings on a case-by-case basis. General programme goals include the following:

- Juvenile participants must assume complete responsibility for their offences. That is, rationalisation, denial, minimisation, and victim blaming must be completely eliminated in order to successfully complete the programme.
- Participants will develop accurate empathy for primary, secondary, and tertiary victims of their sexual offences. Their own victimisation will be addressed in terms of properly assigning blame for their abuse, such that they may, likewise, take full responsibility for *their* perpetrations. Part of this process will include dissipating the intense, debilitating guilt that impedes progress, by illuminating additional symptoms that must be addressed (Travin et al., 1990).
- Participants will demonstrate a fact-based understanding of sexuality and sexual development. As a result, they will develop healthy sexual behaviour and relationship patterns.
- Participants will evidence general improvement in peer relationships and in personal empowerment through skill attainment in areas such as assertiveness, conflict negotiation, and especially anger awareness and expressiveness.
- Participants will achieve a heightened self-awareness of their offence cycle and ways to intervene when certain (client-specific) 'triggers' are activated, in order to prevent relapse.

- Observable improvement will be evidenced in participants' family systems around the issues of cohesion, support, and responsiveness, as well as in awareness of the juveniles' triggers for re-offence, *and* improvement in behavioral monitoring skills (offence related behaviours) by parents. The attainment of these goals will better facilitate appropriate supervision of these juveniles in the community by utilising 'trained parents' to assist in relapse prevention and in the maintenance of the juveniles' treatment gains.

Programme structure

Before commencing treatment, each juvenile is given a comprehensive sexual abuse evaluation by a licensed psychologist. As a result, some of the juveniles may be removed from their home environments until they are further along in treatment, due to their level of dangerousness to other family members. The family is also assessed at this time with respect to their level of functioning on several variables. This information is used as baseline data, which will be compared with post-treatment data at various time intervals to provide information regarding treatment gains and maintenance thereof. Polygraph tests are utilised on an as needed, case by case basis for clients over the age of fourteen. This treatment programme utilises an 'open' format, such that referrals can enter treatment at any time; groups are always ongoing.

The programme is comprised of five levels, each level building upon the prior. The interventions utilised represent a variety of treatment modalities and theories, as will become clear.

Certificates are given to each participant as she is promoted to the next level of treatment throughout the programme. Ideally, when there are enough juveniles in the programme to warrant separate groups, each will be formally moved to the next level group when promoted in order to more fully realise the concept of moving forward in a healthy direction.

Level One: accepting full responsibility

Characteristics

The first level of treatment consists of establishing group cohesiveness, and requires that participants take full responsibility for their offences. In order to establish these goals,

various interventions and treatment tools are utilised. Some examples are ice-breaking exercises on both an experiential and cognitive level, such as *The Thinking, Feeling and Doing Game, Ungame*, exercises from LeFevre, (1988) *New Games for the Whole Family*, and body murals. (Clients lie on butcher paper, their form is traced, and then filled in with pictures or drawings of things that describe their unique personalities). The cognitive piece of Level One requires that the juveniles comprehensively verbally address specific categories with respect to their alleged offence. For example, method of operation, deviant thinking, etc.

A parents' group meets simultaneously to the juveniles' group at all times. At times, the parents' group becomes multifamily, depending on the process of this group at a given time. At other times, this group solely involves the parents.

For Level One in the parents' group, participants will be working on similar issues as in the juvenile group, i.e., building cohesion between families such that they can be an effective support system for each other, and accepting the reality of the offence their daughters have committed. Parents address behaviour and school problems of their juvenile participant at this time, and share regarding common family treatment issues. The concept of behavioural monitoring is introduced at this time to the parents; that is, parents are taught to closely monitor their juvenile's behaviour, and to identify and correct behaviour that runs counter to programme goals. Journalling begins in Level One for both the juveniles and the parents on a weekly basis. Common myths about sexual offenders are dispelled in Level One in both groups.

Ancillary treatment

At this point in the programme, juveniles as well as parents who were identified at intake as needing individual treatment to address unresolved victimisation issues are referred for their own individual treatment with another therapist involved with the programme. Any parent couples who were identified as having issues which would interfere with the treatment process are referred at this time for couple's counselling as well. Depending on the particular participants in the juveniles' group at any given time, a brief social skills module might need to be introduced in Level One to assist with effective communication, and with comfort in interacting with their peers in the group. This module would additionally help the juveniles to express themselves in an effective, appropriate manner. These skills would be further honed in individual sessions, and through observations and interventions in the home environments via behavioural monitoring.

Goals

Examples of treatment goals to be attained by the juveniles at this level include increased self-expressiveness, assertiveness, decreased behavioural acting out, and increased cognitive analysis of their offence. In individual sessions at this time, assertiveness skills would be addressed, with a focus on needs awareness and assertion, which assists in building personal responsibility skills in both the juveniles and their family members.

Interventions

Interventions not previously mentioned but that are often utilised at this level across groups include, but are not limited to, the following:

1. Introducing 'character' types that individuals assume which enable them to avoid taking responsibility for their negative behaviour in general. The group fully analyses how each juvenile or family member plays this 'character' at a given time, after a specific event has occurred. (For example, playing 'the clown' to minimise or distract others from the impact of a verbally abusive interaction that occurred recently in the home or group).
2. Showing the Arts and Entertainment Network video on the Mary Kay Laturnio case, and processing how she and the country were in denial about her level of sexual deviance, and how this denial contributes to the problem of female sexual offending in societies.
3. Table top family sculpting to illuminate communication styles and roles within the families, as well as to show perceived alliances or enmeshments, and their impact on family members.

Promotion criteria

After each juvenile has cognitively analysed her offence in detail by talking in group about specific, required categories (individualised thinking errors, etc.), *and* has demonstrated

consistent, improved responsibility taking in the home and school settings, she is promoted to Level Two.

Level Two: empathy development

Characteristics

As research has consistently indicated that the most important component of relapse prevention for sexual offenders across populations is empathy development, Level Two is the most therapy intensive level in the proposed programme. Whereas Level One is primarily focused on cognitive and cognitive-behavioural concepts and interventions, Level Two is insight oriented and experiential in nature. In contrast with adult male offenders' treatment, for the female juvenile offenders, empathy development, both self and other, is the centrepiece of treatment. Likewise, it is the most intensive level of treatment for this population, and most of the work required for successful programme completion occurs at this level.

In the multifamily group at this time, parents are introduced to psycho-educational modules explaining the relationship between empathy and moral development, which includes ways to monitor and enhance empathy in their daughter, and information about Post-traumatic Stress Disorder. Additionally, family members learn ways to develop empathy towards their daughter, through psychodrama exercises in the group, and via homework assignments. These homework assignments are shared in group. In these ways, the group 'community' assists each family, including the juvenile, in internalising empathy.

Ancillary treatment

A common theme indicating regression that tends to recur with a vengeance in Level Two (although previously addressed in Level One) is what is referred to by Wright and Schneider (1999) as 'motivated self-deception' regarding the perceived 'consent' of the victim. When this is present in the juveniles or any of their family members (commonly seen in previously untreated, victimised mothers), it is an indication that further work needs to be done with the 'perceiver' regarding their victimisation issues. Examples of some unresolved feelings that may presently be relieved by this self-deception are extreme guilt for the offence behaviour, shame, and self-abhorrence. This usually occurs due to the perceiver's identification with their aggressor. Clearly, these issues need to be resolved (AKA 'self empathy') before the juvenile or their respective family member can move on to victim empathy.

Goals

Attachment theory reminds us that 'self empathy' is missing in those who victimise others. Thus, affect awareness and expression become important goals for the juveniles who are in individual treatment at this time. Also the crux of survivors' issues is addressed at this level; Level Two is where most survivor work will be done. A helpful tool at this level for the juveniles as well as the parents and teachers is Lee (1995) *The Survivor's Guide*.

Interventions

Most interventions utilised in Level Two are expressive. Examples are movement therapy, psychodrama, art therapy, and poetry writing. These interventions are aimed at releasing negative emotions, and creating a new identity based on self-empowerment. Many of the expressive exercises of Level Two are modifiable for use in the multifamily groups as well (such as creating a 'poetry book' that contains art and poetry submitted by any and all participants in the programme at a given time, and given as a termination gift to all participants).

Promotion criteria

Once the juveniles have demonstrated self and victim empathy, and the depth of victim impact is realised as evidenced through role plays, and feedback from parents, the juveniles then progress to Level Three. Level Three addresses relationship issues, assertiveness training, anger expressiveness, emotion management, sexual education, and cycle awareness, all essential tools for healthy self-empowerment.

Level Three: self-empowerment

Characteristics and goals

Since research has shown that juvenile sexual offenders in general tend to have some specific social incompetencies, Level Three is skill based (i.e. behavioural). Successful completion of

Level Three requires participants to become comfortable and proficient with social skills, and consistently show application of these skills in their group, home, and school environments. For female juvenile offenders in particular, learning to properly balance self versus relationship needs is a major focus, as is anger awareness and expressiveness. As mentioned previously, on occasion, this module may need to be done first, in Level One, depending on the extremity of social skills deficits in a given group.

In Level Three, participants must also demonstrate sufficient knowledge about sexuality. Finally, awareness of individualised triggers, as well as 'offence cycles' is required for completion of Level Three. Basically, each individual's cycle of offending is uncovered in this level of the treatment programme.

Interventions

To facilitate the goals of Level Three, approximately six sessions are devoted to an assertiveness/anger expressiveness skills training module. This part of the treatment programme is probably the most structured in that specific skills and certain information about managing anger and conflict negotiation are presented in more of a didactic type format.

A lot of homework and journalling occurs in Level Three. Role-playing is heavily utilised in this portion of the programme, especially when addressing assertiveness skills. One especially favourite intervention of these authors is to do before and after videos of assertive situations. That is, group members write scenarios that they are having difficulty with on index cards. The group leader picks some of these scenarios that could be easily demonstrated and videotaped. The scenarios are enacted by group members and directed by the person who submitted the particular entry. The scenarios are enacted as the individual presently handles the situation; an assertiveness training module is then introduced in the group and several weeks later, the same scenario is enacted and directed by the same individual and actors. However, this time, the scenario is enacted as the person handles it in the present time; i.e., after the individual has had the benefit of the assertiveness training module. This intervention has been found to be especially effective in demonstrating to all group members how they have made progress. This, in turn, has a very positive effect on group cohesiveness, on self-esteem of the individual participant, and on the self-esteem of the group as a whole, as everyone becomes aware of everyone else's progress. This intervention also further enhances motivation for further treatment gains and positive feelings towards the programme itself, as well as towards the facilitators of the programme.

This exercise can be used in the parents' group to attain the same goals and build cohesion across the families involved in the treatment programme, which has the added benefit of creating a therapeutic community for these young women and their families. Finally, this intervention is helpful in illustrating to the therapist skills retention on the part of the juveniles, which helps to assess individuals' readiness to move on to the next level in the programme.

Another module introduced in Level Three is a sexual education module. Multimedia resources are utilised including pamphlets, videos, and role-plays. Educational videos are also presented in the multifamily group at this time to open lines of communication within families regarding delicate issues, and to clarify any myths about sexual information. The results of the latter intervention make it easier for the juveniles to speak to their parents about sexual issues, thereby ideally decreasing incidences of sexually acting-out in any manner. Retention of information presented in this module is best tested in a light-hearted manner through, for example, a game devised for the juveniles' group similar to 'Jeopardy' (whereupon small, perhaps dollar-store items are offered as 'prizes' for correct answers given regarding the sexual information previously presented in this module).

Finally, in order to facilitate offence cycle awareness and interruption, after a brief didactic presentation on the topic, group participants develop potential scenarios that trigger their offence cycles, and identify 'blocks' (individualised interventions), that they can utilise to interrupt their cycles. This part of Level Three is actually preparation and practice for relapse prevention skills, which are the focus of Level Four.

Ancillary treatment

As in all levels of the programme, in Level Three, individual and family sessions are ongoing for clients and families as needed to help generalise the skills presented thus far. These sessions will also be made available to address any residual PTSD symptoms that may be currently impacting progress either on an individual level, or in the family systems. In multifamily groups in this level, the juveniles have another opportunity to demonstrate and practice their newly acquired skills, which provides a safe avenue for skill mastery.

Promotion criteria

Skill retention and application is tested via role-plays in the groups, where individuals share scenarios that represent triggers for them, and role-play how they would apply an intervention at a particular point in time which would interrupt their usual cycle and prevent them from making an inappropriate behavioural response. Additionally, a lot of behavioural monitoring is going on at this time between the therapists and the probation officers, the therapists and the parents, and the therapists and the teachers, in order to further assess progress and skill retention in this arena. Therefore, unified decisions can be made regarding readiness for progression to the next level in the programme.

Level Four: relapse prevention

Characteristics and goals

The centrepiece of Level Four is developing and refining individualised relapse plans. Level Four accomplishes this by focusing on the mastery of specific skills and digestion of information that will assist the juveniles in avoiding behaviours that could lead to re-offending. Vocational assessment and career counselling is also an essential focus of Level Four, to orient the juveniles to goal directed behaviour and life planning. Termination from the juveniles' group is fully experienced and processed through structured interventions as each client completes this level of treatment.

Interventions

One skill that is addressed in this level is stress identification, inoculation and management. In this module, clients devise and fine tune individualised stress-management plans. Individuals are introduced to and practice various methods of relaxation and stress reduction until each member has designed a specific plan to manage the stress in their lives, a plan that they have tested, and that actually works for them. These plans, of course, are shared with the family members during family sessions such that family members become aware of specific ways to assist the juveniles in managing their stress appropriately, and are able to help the juveniles choose appropriate behaviours for expressing their stress. Thus, family members become monitors as well as facilitators for healthy responses to stress.

As mentioned previously, the centrepiece of Level Four is developing and refining individual relapse plans. It is here where individuals actually restructure their lifestyles, which includes incorporating proper support systems and exploring personal interests that are incorporated into their lives, and future directions. Some interventions utilised during the development of relapse plans are an in-depth analysis of, for example, the 'trustworthiness' of individuals being considered for inclusiveness in the juvenile's support system, identifying risky thoughts and behaviours, as well as identifying realistic consequences for same, and identifying apparently 'irrelevant decisions' (per Salter, 1988). Other homework assignments revolve around 'apparently irrelevant decisions' to improve self-monitoring skills. Appropriate outside activities for each individual are identified, and with the support of the family, as possible, are incorporated into the juveniles' weekly schedules. Depending on personality and age, *The Secret Way of the Peaceful Warrior* (Millman, 1991) or Disney's *Mulan* may be presented in group, or assigned as homework and later processed in group, to further illustrate programme concepts and facilitate treatment closure.

Approximately three sessions are set aside in Level Four per participant for career and vocational planning. This includes comprehensive vocational testing.

In the multifamily group, a psycho-educational component is presented addressing 'apparently irrelevant decisions', as well as academic concepts regarding relapse prevention, to prepare the families to support and guide the juveniles with their own relapse prevention plans and career/vocational pursuits.

As each client winds down and finishes up her requirements of Level Four in the juveniles' group, each participates in a termination process. This involves finding her own way to say goodbye to the group, saying goodbye to each individual group member, and reviewing progress made (perhaps reviewing a video clip demonstrating particular progress made with a specific skill). All potential graduates make a transitional termination object as well. This object involves each group member contributing or adding something to the object. Some examples are a piece of jewellery, a tee-shirt, a poetry book or a decorated stuffed animal that serves as a positive reminder of the experience and of the individuals who were involved in the person's life in a supportive fashion during such a challenging, and life-altering journey.

Ancillary treatment

Individual and family sessions convene at this time on an as-needed basis to help solidify relapse plans and address any obstacles that may be occurring on a systems level. In Level Four, intensive family systems work may need to be done to avoid sabotage as the juveniles are changing their lifestyles. The juveniles' role in their family is commonly drastically altered as they become empowered in healthy ways, which often causes much family turmoil and thus requires additional intervention in Level Four.

Promotion criteria

Demonstration of skill competencies, lifestyle changes, and appropriate goal-directed behaviours are the behavioural indices of readiness for promotion to Level Five.

Level Five: maintenance

The maintenance level for each of the juvenile participants begins immediately following their termination from the juvenile group. 'Maintenance' requires that each family, including the juvenile client, attends the multifamily group at least once a month for six months. Here, clients problem solve, solidify gains made throughout the treatment programme, and obtain additional support as needed from the other families.

Role-plays are utilised as needed to process difficulties with implementing interventions/skills learned throughout the programme. During maintenance, individual and family sessions are held on an as-needed basis for each family to address any problematic situations that may arise that require individualised

Table 4: Programme levels and corresponding goals and group dynamics.

Level	General programme goal	Focus of individual or family work	Multi-family group focus
1.	Accepting full responsibility	Increased self-awareness. Decreased behavioural acting out. Increased cognitive analysis of the offense. (Assertiveness module: Only if treatment-indicated prior to Level 3.)	Establishing group cohesiveness. Ice-breaking exercises. Address characteristics of offense. (Social skills module: Only if treatment-indicated prior to Level 2.)
2.	Empathy development	Self-empathy development. Victim-empathy development.	Psychodrama and trauma work. Psycho-educational modules and empathy building for their daughter.
3.	Self-empowerment	Social skills development. Assertiveness skills. Anger expressive skills (role play, etc.) Increased awareness of individualised triggers. Increased awareness of individualised offence cycle. Developing coping skills to counteract triggers. Explore 'relationship-driven aetiology.'	Skill-based, behavioural treatment. Highlight on clients' strengths. Assertiveness and anger expressive module. Homework more predominately used in this level. Sexual education module. Open communication with family and youth regarding youth's sexuality myths.
4.	Relapse prevention	Develop relaxation and stress reduction skills. Refining individual relapse plans. Incorporate proper support systems. Cultivate personal interests.	Stress management module. About three sessions devoted to career module. Termination issues.
5.	Maintenance	Problem-solving. Implementing skills.	No longer participating in the on-going juvenile group. Maintain treatment gains via multi-family groups.

attention, and for crisis management. Each family has their own 'termination' session from the multifamily group as they successfully complete the programme. Continued contact between the families and other families that remain participants in the multifamily group is encouraged to provide continual support for these families, as they face inevitable challenges in today's world.

To start a database and to evaluate programme effectiveness, families graduating the programme are given post-treatment family and individual assessments. Additionally, at intervals of six months, one year, five years, and ten years post-treatment, these families are tracked as best as possible through follow-up questionnaires to assess progress, maintenance, and programme effectiveness.

Conclusions

Female juvenile sexual offenders remain greatly misunderstood, and thus have been generally overlooked to date. It is unknown how many female survivors in treatment are also perpetrators. In order to identify and properly treat the juvenile female offenders, therapists need to rethink the way they help their clients to reconceptualise their own victimisation and victimisers. Also, public education seminars regarding sexual abuse are greatly needed to raise awareness and perhaps fiscal, as well as community, support for treatment efforts, which will also serve as encouragement for participation in treatment. As is said, 'It takes a community to raise a child'. It also takes a 'community' to heal such deep and reverberating wounds as those associated with sexual abuse.

References

Blues, A., Moffat, C. and Telford, P. (1999) Work with Adolescent Females Who Sexually Abuse. in Erooga, M. and Masson, H. (Eds.) *Children and Young People Who Sexually Abuse Others*. London: Routledge. 168–82.

Brown, E. J., Flanagan, T. J. and McLeod, M. (Eds.) (1984). *Sourcebook of Criminal Justice Statistics: 1983*. Washington, DC: Bureau of Justice Statistics.

Camp, B. H. and Thyer, B. A. (1993) Treatment of Adolescent Sex Offenders: A Review of Empirical Research. *The Journal of Applied Social Sciences*. 17: 191–206.

Charles, G. and McDonald, M. (1997) Adolescent Sexual Offenders. *Journal of Child and Youth Care*. 11: 15–25.

Elliott, M. (Ed.) (1993) *Female Sexual Abuse of Children*. London: John Wiley and Sons.

Fehrenbach, P. A. and Monastersky, C. (1988) Characteristics of Female Adolescent Sexual Offenders. *American Journal of Orthopsychiatry*. 58: 148–51.

Finkelhor, D. (1984). *Child Sexual Abuse: New Theory and Research*. New York: Free Press.

Knight, R. A. and Prentky, R. A. (1993) Exploring Characteristics for Classifying Juvenile Sex Offenders. in Barbaree, H. E., Marshall, W. L. and Hudson, S. M. (Eds.) *The Juvenile Sex Offender*. New York: The Guilford Press. 45–83.

Knopp, F. H. (1985) Recent Developments in the Treatment of Adolescent Sex Offenders. in Otey, E. M. and Ryan, G. D. (Eds.) *Adolescent Sex Offenders Issues in Research and Treatment*. U.S. Department of Health and Human Services. 1–108.

Knopp, F. H. and Lackey, L. B. (1987) *Female Sexual Abusers: A Summary of Data from 44 Treatment Providers*. Orwell, VT: The Safer Society Program.

Lane, S. and Lobanov-Rostovsky, C. (1997) Children, Females, the Developmentally Disabled, and Violent Youth. in Ryan, G. and Lane, S. (Eds.) *Juvenile Sexual Offending*. San Francisco: Jossey-Bass Publishers. 322–59.

Lee, S. A. (1995) *The Survivors Guide*. Thousand Oaks, CA: Sage Publications, Inc.

LeFevre, D. N. (1988) *New Games for The Whole Family*. New York: The Putnam Publishing Group.

Mathews, F. (1997) The Adolescent Sex Offender Field in Canada: Old Problems, Current Issues, and Emerging Controversies. *Journal of Child and Youth Care*. 11: 55–62.

Mathews, R., Hunter, J. A. and Vuz, J. (1997) Juvenile Female Sexual Offenders: Clinical Characteristics and Treatment Issues. *Sexual Abuse: A Journal of Research and Treatment*. 9: 187–99.

Matsuda, B., Rasmussen, L. A. and Dibble, A. (1989) *The Utah Report on Juvenile Sex Offenders*. Salt Lake City, UT: The Utah Task Force of the Utah Network on Juveniles Offending Sexually.

McCarthy, L. M. (1986) Mother-child Incest: Characteristics of the Offender. *Child Welfare*. 65: 447–58.

Millman, D. (1991) *The Secret of the Peaceful Warrior*. Tiburon, CA: Starseed Press.

Rantakallio, P., Myhrman, A. and Koiranen, M. (1995) Juvenile Offenders, With Special Reference to Sex Differences. *Social Psychiatry and Psychiatric Epidemiology*. 30: 113–20.

Rasmussen, L. A. (1999) Factors Related to Recidivism Among Juvenile Sexual Offenders. *Sexual Abuse: A Journal of Research and Treatment*. 11: 69–85.

Salter, A. C. (1988) *Treating child sex offenders and victims*. Newbury Park, CA: Sage Publications.

Salter, A. C. (1995) *Transforming Trauma: A Guide to Understanding and Treating Adult Survivors of Child Sexual Abuse*. Thousand Oaks, CA: Sage Publications.

Scott, L. K. (1994) Sex Offenders, Prevalence, Trends, Model Programs, and Costs. in Roberts, A. R. (Ed.) *Critical Issues in Crime and Justice*. Thousand Oaks: Sage Publications. 51–76).

Travin, S., Cullen, K. and Protter, B. (1990) Female Sex Offenders: Severe Victims and Victimisers. *Journal of Forensic Sciences*. 35: 140–50.

Turner, M. T. and Turner, T. N. (1994) *Female Adolescent Sexual Abusers: An Exploratory Study of Mother-daughter Dynamics With Implications for Treatment.* Brandon, VT: The Safer Society Press.

Weisinger, H. (1985) *Dr Weisinger's Anger Work-Out Book.* NY: Quill.

Wolfe, F. A. (1985) *Twelve Female Sexual Offenders.* in Fehrenbach, P. A. and Monastersky, C. (1988) Characteristics of Female Adolescent Sexual Offenders. *American Journal of Orthopsychiatry.* 58: 148–51.

Wright, R. C. and Schneider, S. L. (1999) Motivated Self-deception in Child Molesters. *Journal of Child Sexual Abuse.* 8: 89–111.

Part 6: Management Issues

Chapter 19: Structural Changes in the Management of Young People who Sexually Abuse in the UK

Martin C. Calder

Introduction

This chapter will chart the evolution of the structural response to the problem of young people who sexually abuse in the UK. In doing so, the principal focus will be on the recent guidance and legislation issued by central government and the reality that it has potentially set our work back with this group at least ten years (Calder, 2001). I will then look at some potential mechanisms for remedying this unsatisfactory state of affairs at a local level.

The Origins of the Response

Structurally

Working Together (DoH, 1991) clearly identified young people who sexually abuse as a child protection issue and stated that official responses and interventions should take place within child protection procedures. It recommended that Area Child Protection Committees should co-ordinate the development of a strategic plan for dealing with this group, bring them into the child protection system, and devote a section of their annual report to outlining progress.

Working Together pointed to the need for the appropriate child protection procedures to be followed in respect of both the abuser as well as the victim (paragraph 5.24.1). This is to 'ensure that such behaviour is treated seriously and is always subject to a referral to child protection agencies' (paragraph 5.24.2). It then indicates that a child protection conference in relation to the abuser should be held to consider the current knowledge about the alleged abuser, their family circumstances, the offence committed, their level of understanding they have about it, and the need for further work. This should include consideration of possible arrangements of accommodation, education (where applicable) and supervision in the short-term pending the compilation of a comprehensive assessment (paragraph 5.24.4).

The child protection conference, including initial plans, should be as prescribed for the standard conference and should 'reconvene following the completion of the comprehensive assessment, to review the plan in the light of the information obtained and to co-ordinate the interventions designed to dissuade the abuser from committing further abusive acts' (paragraph 5.24.5).

Operationally

Each ACPC went off to develop their responses in isolation from one another, unnecessarily allowing the same wheel to be re-invented. Whilst there is a range of responses noted (see Masson, 1996 for a review) there are some common elements worthy of note.

In the face of the increased constraints against working together in the child protection field (see Calder, 1999 for a review), a significant amount of progress was made in unifying the child protection and the criminal justice camps responsible for the management of the young person who sexually abuses (see Calder, 1997a and b for a review). This integration occurred at a number of levels. Firstly, there was an attempt to construct local procedures that tried to clarify the respective professional roles and responsibilities, and this was accompanied by inter-agency child protection training. Secondly, there was a move towards the provision of detailed practice guidance that aimed to equip workers with accessible operational tools to undertake the initial and core assessments asked of them (see Calder, 1998). Thirdly there was a move towards auditing the emerging programme responses given that there was the potential for a fragmented proliferation of services that would leave frontline workers unsure about what to do and who to approach (NOTA North-West Branch). Finally, there were discussions about consortium approaches to ensure that there was an integrated cross-boundary response that maximised the use of precious resources (especially access to psychological and psychiatric services).

The following description presents an overview of the local frameworks that developed within the context set out above. As we are talking about sexual abuse, a joint police-social services response was promoted to avoid unnecessary duplication of task. Their remit was:

- To determine whether the alleged perpetrator has himself been the victim of abuse and is in need of protection.
- To determine whether protective action is necessary in respect of any other children with whom the alleged perpetrator may be in contact.
- To identify the need for services to the alleged perpetrator and their family.

The procedures for managing this group did however differ in a number of key respects from traditional child protection procedures:

- There was no differentiation between intra and extra-familial sexual abuse given the concern about crossover (see Calder, 1997 and 2001 for a detailed discussion on this point).
- There was no discretion extended as to whether an initial child protection conference should be held.
- There was rarely any discussion about registration, as the system was designed to deal with victims rather than abusers. Many areas developed a separate category for registration although this has led to problems in some areas. For example, where a young person has been registered because of the sexual risk, but no subsequent services were provided to try to reduce that risk, this has left authorities vulnerable to prosecution if he went on to offend and this is attributed to a failed or non-existent intervention. As you can imagine, this led to the withdrawal of the separate category in many authorities.

The process of professional involvement differed depending on whether the young person admitted or denied the alleged sexual abuse.

Admission

Where the young person admitted the alleged abuse, the police would refer the matter to the Juvenile Diversionary Panel who would often adjourn the case for a period of up to eight weeks to allow an initial assessment to be undertaken to evaluate the circumstances of the case, to consider the level of risk and any necessary work, and make recommendations as to what the most appropriate disposal might be. The police could only charge the young person immediately if the offence was of a serious nature (such as rape or buggery) or where the circumstances of the offence required it (such as kidnapping).

The initial assessment was charged with several key tasks:

- To collect information to inform the decision making process about immediate management. For example, to consider the safety of the children the young person has ongoing contact with (home, school, community, extended family, etc.); and to consider where the young person should live (e.g., foster or residential care, extended family, or remain at home).
- Collect details about the nature of the abuse and the particular situational contexts in which it has occurred (such as in the house, at school, babysitting) and consider how the abuse was developed, i.e. grooming behaviours (game playing, use of bribes, threats).
- Consider any predisposing (e.g., family attitudes, friends, a history of abuse) or precipitating (opportunity) factors for the abuse.
- Consider the likelihood of repeat behaviours, (bearing in mind there are no predictive indicators from research).
- To identify the potential for the development of an appropriate 'treatment' programme.
- Future risk management based on a more comprehensive assessment.
- Consider whether a legal mandate is necessary for the work, or whether it is possible to engage the young person and their family or carers on a voluntary basis. It is important not to mistake compliance for co-operation in making these decisions (adapted from Calder, 1999b).

In most cases, the initial assessment would be undertaken by a field social worker and a youth justice worker. In order to provide a practical framework for these workers to translate the tasks into operational reality, Calder (1998 and 1999b) constructed the following framework for initial assessments:

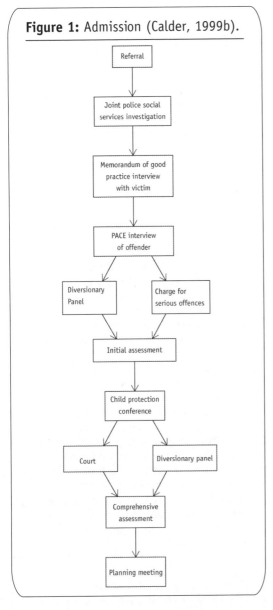

Figure 1: Admission (Calder, 1999b).

The field social worker would use the following framework to undertake their tasks:

Areas to be covered

Who has made the complaint: the victim or someone acting on their behalf?

How was the activity revealed?

Was the victim a sibling, friend or stranger? What are the implications for where the abuser lives? Are there contact implications?

The Young Person

Social history: serves three purposes: to gather developmental information that may help to explain their abusing behaviour; details of their recent history will help to identify contemporary factors which may have contributed to the current cycle of offending; and it unravels their personality style, their ability to recount events and their general willingness to disclose. It should include educational history, peer relationships, anger, assertiveness, self-esteem and self-contempt, social competence, health and medical history. The area of social skills is central to understanding the origins of the abusive behaviour, and the younger the child, the more important this becomes.

Patterns of their behaviour, or familial patterns of abuse.

Willingness to co-operate with the agencies involved? Reluctance should increase concern and may be an indicator that a prosecution is necessary.

Risk to the Child Exhibiting the Behaviour

Dangerous networks.

Neighbourhood response to the behaviour: on behalf of the victims as well as the abuser.

Legal consequences.

Exclusion from home, school or community?

Future life consequences.

Risk of suicide or self-harm?

Psychological or psychiatric assessment indicated?

View of parents or carers of the victims.

Family Assessment

Full details of all members of the relevant present or past household?

What do the parents believe happened?

What are the family reactions to the behaviour? How supportive are the family? Do they deny or minimise the abuse or try to shift the blame? Will they support or hinder the comprehensive assessment of the young person? Is a prosecution necessary to ensure this happens? It is important to remember that the parents can be the biggest motivating factor for the young abuser facing up to their responsibilities for the abuse.

Family dynamics: interaction and differences.

Management of intra-familial abuse: balancing protection of victim and siblings with support to the abuser and the need for the abuser to undertake assessment work and face up to their responsibilities.

Family history: particularly any previous suspicion of abuse or reports of inappropriate behaviour?

What observations have they made of the young person's sexual attitudes and behaviour?

Care and control strategies: particularly any management strategies suggested or deployed.

Sexual attitudes and practices within the family, interaction, knowledge, etc.

Parental stress: environmental and employment.

Parental and sibling victim experiences.

The following framework utilises the skills of the youth justice workers and guides them through the information required to look at the offence(s) and the likelihood of repeat behaviours. The timing of this work is dependent on client admission or denial.

Dangerousness

Nature of behaviour: e.g. any evidence of planning? Evidence of targeting vulnerable children (e.g. handicapped) or those with distinguishing characteristics (e.g. blond hair)? What, if anything, did the young person do to gain access to the other children (e.g. create opportunities)?

The act itself: How did the sexual contact take place? Is it through mutual agreement and negotiation, or is there covert aggression, coercion or bribery? If so, this usually indicates an abusive relationship, and may indicate that the abuser knew that their behaviour was wrong. The circumstances of the offence may give some clear indications of the degree of fear, humiliation and intimidation experienced by the victim.

What is the age difference between the persons involved? The greater the age difference, the more inappropriate the sexual activity. There could be a difference in functioning as well as chronological age: either emotional immaturity or intellectual functioning. The social relationship is therefore important, particularly if there are clear power differentials or if the abuser is in a position of authority over the victim, e.g. babysitting.

Consent needs careful examination, as consenting to sexual activity means giving informed consent, e.g. consent is freely given and implies a full understanding and a freedom to say no. Consent is different to co-operation or compliance. The lack of resistance does not imply that informed consent has been given.

Escalation: Has the young person committed previous sexual offences? Examine their previous record to determine any pattern or change in pattern. Has the abuse become more frequent or elaborate? Any increase in aggressions should increase concern.

Risk to the child exhibiting the behaviour: Dangerous networks. Neighbourhood response to the behaviour: on behalf of the victim as well as the abuser. Legal consequences. Exclusion from home, school or community? Future life consequences.

Denial: Does the young person admit or deny the offence? How honest have they been regarding the details? What levels of responsibility are they accepting for what has happened? What distorted explanations are they presenting to justify their behaviour? Attempts to minimise or deny the offence or shift the blame should increase concern.

Level of empathy with the victim: How do they think their behaviour has affected the victim? Where is the victim now? How do they feel about that? Do they think about their victim now? Do they think about them often? Do they think they hurt their victim? If yes, in what ways? Do they think the victim was partly to blame? Why? Describe their feelings for the victim before, during and after the abusive incident. Get them to describe how they think the victim felt during and just after they had abused them.

Risk of repeat behaviour: Previous criminal history. Frequency: How persistent is the sexual activity? Has the frequency increased? Frequency is an important indicator of repeat behaviours. Patterns. Willingness to co-operate with the agencies involved? Reluctance should increase concern and may be an indicator that a prosecution is necessary. Sexual knowledge, experience, fantasy, attitudes, beliefs and behaviour. Consequences of their abusive behaviour versus benefits of continuing their behaviour.

At the end of the information-gathering process, the workers would integrate their findings and present them to an initial child protection conference. The initial child protection conference would address the following areas:

- Whether there are any outstanding child protection issues with regard to any children with whom the alleged perpetrator is in contact.
- Whether there is any reason to suspect that the alleged perpetrator has been the victim of abuse and is in need of protection.
- Whether there is any need to provide any immediate services to the alleged perpetrator and their family.
- What method of disposal is to be recommended in respect of the alleged offences.

The conference recommendation on disposal would go back to the police who would either administer a caution or charge the young person. That decision remained the province of the police alone and there were tensions on occasions about the perceived pressure of conference recommendations on their territory. The conference would also consider the need for a comprehensive assessment in respect of the alleged perpetrator and the form that such an assessment should take. The conference would also look at where the young person should live whilst the identified work was carried out, contact with other children and young people, particularly in the school environment, and whether any specialist intervention should be commissioned.

Denial

Where the young person denied the abuse, the police would have to take a decision about whether a charge should be brought or whether there should be no further action. This was clearly dependent on the available evidence at that stage in the investigative process. There was a need still to consider any child protection

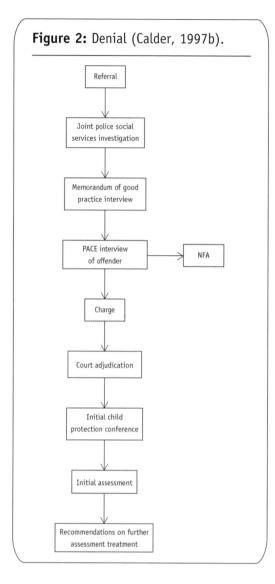

Figure 2: Denial (Calder, 1997b).

an early stage without the criminal process having been concluded, then the police would seek to disclose their information confidentially without the family present, and this can have an alienating effect in the longer-term. It proved more fruitful to await the court finding and then pursue an initial assessment that would inform any disposal, although the possibility of further work if acquitted was limited.

There appeared to be an acceptance that an assessment was needed in order to inform the disposal, and this led to systems where recommendations from conference were made to the police or the Diversionary panel. The child protection conference stood centre stage in the process, and assembled information from disparate sources, weighing up the issues that needed to be addressed, such as placement and legal options, and then trying to provide a structure for the way forward.

It would be wrong to portray the system as always efficient or faultless, and Masson (1995) found that whilst child protection procedures regarding young people who sexually abuse others have become common there is considerable variation in local arrangements. She noted that staff within agencies, involved at some level with young abusers, identified a set of concerns relating to systems, co-operation and communication between agencies. These concerns included:

- Lack of clarity as to responsibility.
- Lack of specialist services for assessment and treatment.
- Problems in the placement of young abusers.
- Inadequate training, supervision and managerial support.

Masson also found that unless the local arrangement was delivered via a dedicated project then practitioners reported a relatively low degree of time allocated and a limited amount of clinical experience gained.

Calder (1999) has formulated a conceptual framework in an attempt to provide a unifying approach for Area Child Protection Committees (see Figure 3).

He argued that each ACPC needs to develop shared aims and purposes about the work, which needs to be set in a local mandate, standards, structures and resources. This is essential because of the conflicting views held by the childcare and youth justice systems. Once a corporate baseline is established, a philosophy

implications from the allegations: for the young person themselves and for other children whom they might have continuing contact with. This was especially true when there were siblings at home. The matter would often come to child protection conference to explore such issues, although the timing of this was important. It is often impossible to consider what to do in the absence of initial assessment information, and so this was often delayed until the court had adjudicated, although preliminary decisions on risk would have been made in relation to siblings, who might have been processed through the child protection system in their own right as potential (or actual) victims. Where a conference was convened at

Figure 3: A conceptual framework for responding to young people who sexually abuse (Calder, 1999).

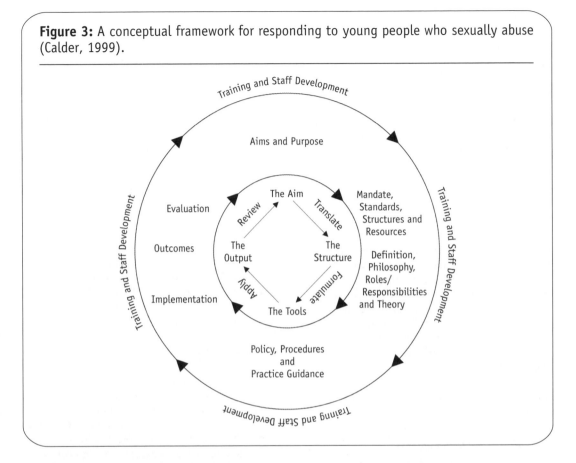

of intervention is required as well as clarity about respective roles and responsibilities. The next stage is to develop local policy, procedures and practical guidance. These areas are discussed in great detail in the original chapter.

Recent Guidance and Legislation

It is often only when something is taken away from you that you realise how valuable it was (Calder, 2000b and c). This is true in the case of young people who sexually abuse. There have been tremendous changes in the central government approach to youth crime and justice systems, views as to who should manage young people who sexually abuse, coupled with significant developments in theory governing young people who sexually abuse and risk analysis. I will look at each of these changes individually before exploring the collective challenges for us to tackle. This can be done under the headings of criminal justice and child protection.

Criminal justice directives

The Sex Offenders Act 1997

Hampson (1999) has produced the following overview of the The Sex Offenders Act 1997, which came into force on the 1st September 1997. It requires those who have convictions for certain specified offences to register with the police in the area in which they live, and to provide and keep up to date information about their whereabouts.

The Act's stated purpose is to ensure the accuracy of the information on sex offenders recorded on the police national computer. Prior to the introduction of the Act, this information was often limited to the address of the offender at the time of his conviction, and was therefore very often out of date.

Guidance issued in support of the Act has made it clear, however, that the purpose is not simply to record the information but to use it proactively to undertake risk assessments of all convicted sex offenders living in the community and to monitor the activities of those who are considered to represent a significant risk.

The Act is not retrospective. It applies only to persons convicted after the 1st September 1997 and those who, on the date of implementation, were serving community or custodial sentences for relevant offences (in this respect it could be said in a limited way to be retrospective).

The Home Office estimated that there were around 4,000 offenders in prison on the 1st September 1997 to whom the provisions of the Act would apply.

Qualifying offences

Qualifying offences include rape, buggery and indecent assaults on adult men or women and incest, rape indecent assault and other indecency offences involving children. A complete list of all the qualifying offences is set out in Schedule 1 of the Act. Schedule 1 of the Sex Offenders Act is substantially different from Schedule 1 of the Children and Young Persons Act 1933 in that, among other differences, it includes sexual offences against adults and excludes offences involving physical assaults on children.

Administrative arrangements

Those convicted of a qualifying offence after the 1st September, 1997 will be issued with a certificate by the Court in which they are convicted. This certificate provides confirmation of the conviction or finding and contains a summary of the registration requirements with which the offender must comply. A copy of the certificate is sent to the police criminal records unit (in the area in which the offender normally resides) and, where a prison sentence is imposed, to the relevant custodial establishment. The custodial establishment will inform the police of the prisoner's release date.

All those who are liable to register must, within 14 days of conviction or release:

- Inform the local police of their name, date of birth and current address.
- Report any subsequent change of address within 14 days of the change.
- Notify the police of any other address at which they stay or are resident for 14 days or longer in any 12-month period.

Notification may be provided in writing or by going in person to any police station in the area where the offender is living.

Responsibility for registration lies with the offender himself. Supervising probation officers are expected to ensure that the offender is aware of the requirements but are not directly responsible for ensuring compliance. However, agency procedures generally require confirmation of the advice given to the offender to be provided to him in writing with a copy to the local police.

The offender must register within 14 days of sentence or release. Failure to register is a criminal offence punishable by a fine and up to six months' imprisonment.

Offenders under 18 years cannot be sent to prison for failing to comply with the registration requirements. However, the court in which the juvenile offender is convicted can impose the notification requirement on the offender's parent or guardian. In the case of young people who are looked after, the local authority can, by order of the court imposing sentence, be made responsible for discharging the registration requirements.

The length of time for which the registration requirements apply depends upon the length of the sentence imposed for the qualifying offence or offences. In the case of young people under the age of 18 years, the period of registration is half that which would apply if an adult had received a similar sentence.

Length of sentence	Adults	Juveniles
Life imprisonment	Indefinite	Indefinite
Hospital (restriction order)	Indefinite	Indefinite
>30 months prison	Indefinite	Indefinite
6 months to 30 months	10 years	5 years
<6 months prison	7 years	3 and a half years
Hospital (no restriction order)	7 years	3 and a half years
Non custodial sentence or caution	5 years	2 and a half years

The notification period starts from the date of caution, conviction or release from sentence. When a court convicts a person of one of the qualifying offences it will issue a certificate to the offender and send a copy to the police. The police will issue a similar certificate where the offender receives a caution.

Local arrangements for responding to the act

Home Office Circular 39/97 directs the police to undertake a risk assessment in respect of each offender in order to determine:

- Generally, the potential threat to the community.
- Specifically, the immediate threat to any persons with whom the offender may be having contact (including members of the same household).

The police will receive notification of an individual's requirement to register from a number of sources e.g. from courts following sentence, and from prisons prior to the offender's release. Whilst specific local arrangements may vary, it is likely that most will follow a procedure similar to that operating in Greater Manchester and described below.

Within two weeks of notification (and regardless of actual registration) the local Crime Management Unit (CMU) must complete an initial intelligence check and risk assessment which will include:

- Details of all previous sex offences including sentences.
- Details of all offences involving violence.
- The method and pattern of the individual's offending.
- Details of any treatment received.
- Attitude towards victims/offences.
- Any significant relationships with other sex offenders.

In gathering information and undertaking the assessment of risk the CMU is expected to liase with other police units and with other agencies who may have a contribution to make. In particular, the local probation service will be contacted in order to establish whether the offender is currently under supervision or has been known to them in the past. The probation service is itself required to undertake an assessment of the potential for harm and the risk of re-offending for all clients with whom they are involved or on whom they have prepared a pre-sentence report (PSR).

Following the completion of the initial intelligence check and risk assessment each offender will be provisionally assigned to one of the following categories:

1. Screened out: low or moderate risk.
2. Screened in: offender in custody, high risk.
3. Screened in: offender in community, high risk.

Where an offender is screened out this decision will be reported to other agencies and the case will be reviewed in 6–12 months. Where an offender is screened in, i.e. assessed as high risk, consideration will need to be given to the development of a strategy for managing the risk. This will include consideration of whether the criteria for referral to a Multi-Agency Risk Panel (MARP) are met. All cases where there is thought to be a need for disclosure to a third party must be referred to the MARP.

Home visits by the police are considered to be an important source of information in undertaking the risk assessment and in verifying the information provided to the register by the offender.

Multi-Agency Risk Panels (MARPS)

Multi-Agency Risk Panels were originally developed in West Yorkshire in response to concerns about difficulties in protecting the public from those known to represent a risk to the community. Lead responsibility is shared between the police and probation services with other agencies, particularly health, housing and social services also playing an important role.

The purpose of the Multi-Agency Risk Panel is to provide a forum for sharing information on potentially dangerous offenders and for developing strategies for managing the risks that they pose to individuals and to the community. The panels do not deal exclusively with sex offenders, the sole criteria for referral being that there is believed to be a high likelihood of re-offending and that the nature of the offences that are likely constitute a serious risk of harm.

The administration of the panels is managed by the probation service at district level and all referrals are routed through a panel manager. Meetings are usually held at six weekly intervals but there is provision for meetings to be convened at very short notice in special cases.

In addition to the core membership, attendance is usually restricted to those who have a significant contribution to make. Issues of confidentiality are given a high priority in order to facilitate the free exchange of information within the meeting. There is an expectation that offenders who are the subject of a panel will be told of the meeting unless this would be likely to put someone's safety at risk.

The objectives for the panel in each individual case are:

- To share information at critical stages of an agency's contact with the offender e.g. prior to his release from a custodial sentence.
- To assess the level of risk to individuals and/or the community.
- To devise strategies for managing and minimising the risks involved.
- To decide whether to include the offender's name on the MARP register.
- To agree arrangements for monitoring and review.

The MARP register operates in a similar way to the child protection register in that it includes only those who are considered to represent a continuing risk of significant harm to the community. Registration is supported by the development of a formal multi-agency plan to address the main areas of risk and these arrangements are reviewed at regular intervals to ensure that they are appropriate to the needs of the case and that registration continues to be justified.

There is a range of options available in seeking to address the concerns that may arise. These may include:

- Preventing or delaying the offender's release.
- Imposing conditions on release.
- Arranging accommodation.
- Surveillance/monitoring.
- Intelligence/information sharing.
- Victim preparation and protection.
- Contingency planning.

Wherever possible the co-operation of the offender will be sought, but unless there is the power to include conditions in an order or licence, compliance is voluntary.

Issues when applying the requirements to young people who sexually abuse

Schwartz et al. (1993) found that the majority of American citizens favour trying juveniles as adults for serious crimes. Such a view is associated with an increased public fear of victimisation, particularly in older citizens.

There are growing concerns about the register overall, and there are some issues particular to the juvenile population. Brown (1998) has argued that they need to be treated differently from their adult counterparts both because of their age and maturity and because of the nature of their offending behaviour. In addition, the low rate of disclosure, the high rate of denial among young people and their families and the variation across the country in the type of offence pursued by the courts or through a caution means that young people in different parts of the country are treated in a very different way.

Brown identified four potential difficulties for adolescents, which I have added to and expanded upon:

- Disclosure and investigation: whilst we do not want to ignore sexual behaviour of concern, there is no national uniformity around how to deal with particular presenting situations. This leads to a huge inconsistency in how adolescents are dealt with. There is a case to be made which allows us to address the behaviour but outside the criminalisation of the activity. There should be an assessment pre-disposal in order to filter out those cases where a repetition of the sexual behaviour is considered unlikely. The standards and timescales accompanying the Crime and Disorder Act 1998 are making this almost impossible and where they are taking place, within unrealistically short timescales. At the other extreme, there is evidence of serious sexual abuse being diverted from the legal system, thus giving the message out that their behaviour is OK.
- The need for a register: Registration of adults who commit sexual offences is based on a need to monitor those who may re-offend so that there is some protection for the public. Adults who have developed a pattern of offending are likely to find opportunities to re-offend. However, most adolescents have not been offending for long enough to develop a clear pattern of abusing and many are still very immature. With appropriate intervention, the risk of long-term offending is low for the majority of young people. Those young people who are assessed as high-risk do need to be registered as they become adults.

- Issues of denial: This is a feature of most adolescents, largely because of fear and a lack of understanding of what is likely to happen to them as a result of their behaviour which they have not fully understood. They know what they did was sexual but they often lack the maturity to fully recognise the consequences and effects of their behaviour on others and on themselves. They are not aware of the processes, which lead to patterns of offending because no one has ever looked with them at exactly what is going on. They do not usually have any sense of their own motives and may not make any links with their own experiences as victims or have a real understanding of their own values about sexual issues. They may have been brought up with a skewed understanding about the reasons for sex and its meaning and never have had an opportunity to clarify this. There is a real need to have time to overcome denial, working through the fears and enabling the young person to become motivated to change.
- Risks to the young person: one of the difficulties young people who have been involved in abusing behaviour often face is the reaction of their local community. Because of the variations in how young people are expected to report, there are still circumstances where they go to the police station, wait in a queue and announce the reason for their visit. It is hardly surprising that this information may leak out locally and cause problems. This may penalise them inappropriately and they may run the continuing risk of ostracism or actual physical violence. Retreat into isolation can serve to trigger repeat sexually abusive behaviour (Calder, 2001).

There has to be some genuine concern that registration, in itself, is neither helpful to the young person or the community at large. Because we are often uncomfortable with their sexuality and the ways in which it finds expression, we are at risk of treating them all like 'little adults' and ascribing to them motivations and understanding, which they have not yet developed. In doing so, we label and subscribe their behaviour so that they, their families and the other agencies involved with them, think that there is no possibility of change.

Clearly, if the registration system serves to increase the apprehensions and resistance of parents to engage in treatment work, then the potential gains will have been more than outweighed by the alienation of the group most critical to the monitoring and management of juveniles, the parents.

The workings of the Act may also increase the potential tensions between the criminal justice and social work philosophies of intervention. Since the Sex Offenders Act (1997) came into force, a further conflict has emerged between the police and social services relating to the implications of cautioning and the link to sex offender registration. There is now evidence that the police are struggling to accept the need to caution a young person because of the implications of this in statute. This has resulted in differences in how to deal with abusers, with the knock on effect being a polarisation of views between the agencies. This has the potential to detract us from the task in hand.

This polarisation has been identified elsewhere in an inverted way. Sanders and Ladwa-Thomas's (1997) study involving the survey of perspectives on child sexual abuse and practice issues of working with young people who sexually abuse, found that on the issue of whether young people who sexually abuse should primarily be seen as victims or abusers, they found that child protection specialists felt that they should be seen as victims whereas juvenile justice workers and the police felt that they should be seen as sex offenders. The police were also much less inclined to see young abusers as 'children in need' than child protection workers were. This seems to suggest a change across camps, with the youth justice favouring a strong inclusive approach compared to a diversionary approach from child protection workers.

NACRO guidelines (1999)

There needs to be a way of addressing the concerns raised by the sexually abusive behaviour in a constructive and agreed way without reverting to complete diversion that arguably avoids the presenting problem. One suggestion for achieving this emanated from NACRO in 1999 and recommends that systems are in place not to divert young people from the system, but to review the need for continuing registration after the necessary work has been completed. The following section draws extensively from this paper.

They note that implications of being classified as a Schedule One Offender are potentially far reaching:

- Schedule One status is for life.
- Most Local Authorities maintain a register of Schedule One Offenders.
- Where a Schedule One Offender is known to be living with children a child protection investigation is likely to ensue.
- Schedule One status will severely restrict access to certain forms of employment particularly those involving contact with children and other vulnerable groups.
- Serving prisoners attracting Schedule One classification are usually precluded from having visits from children and may often be at risk from other inmates if their status becomes known.

While protection of children is obviously of paramount importance, conviction for a Schedule One Offence may not, on its own, reliably distinguish those offenders who represent a continuing risk to children from others who may not. This is particularly true where the offender is also aged under 18 and in such circumstances there will often not be any ongoing child protection implications. For example, unlawful sexual intercourse, which was consensual and between parties of a similar age may not imply a continuing risk to children.

Historically, whether a young person who committed a Schedule One Offence was classified as a Schedule One Offender was a relatively arbitrary process. While procedures varied extensively from one area to another, it is possible to give a general account of the circumstances in which Social Services were notified of a young person alleged to have committed a Schedule One Offence:

- Where an offence is one that merits the involvement of the local police child protection team, the Social Services Department will always be involved. Offences of violence would however rarely be covered by this arrangement.
- Youth Justice Services have seldom had any procedures in place for notification at any stage in the process (for either violent or sexual offences).
- The Probation Service is required to notify Social Services prior to release from custody of a Schedule One Offender although some

areas also consider notification following the passing of a community sentence particularly where the offender is residing with children.
- Prior to 1994, the Prison Service notified the Local Authority only where the offence was committed within the home.

In 1994, prisons were issued with guidance that required them to notify the Local Authority and the Probation Service at commencement of a custodial sentence and towards the end of the period of detention of all offenders who are convicted of a Schedule One Offence. Significantly, notification is required both:

- Where the offender is sentenced to custody as a result of an offence against a child or young person.
- Where an offender in custody for an offence of another type, has a previous conviction for any Schedule One Offence irrespective of the sentence imposed. For example, a young person imprisoned for burglary who has a previous conviction for an offence of assault on a young person of his own age some years ago, will trigger a notification on the basis of that previous conviction.

As a result, for the first time, significant numbers of young people are now being classified as Schedule One Offenders. Inevitably, this group will include those who attain that status on the basis of offences which are not of a sexual nature, which did not result in a custodial sentence (indeed there are examples where the 'trigger' offence was disposed of by way of conditional discharge) and do not give rise to concerns of a continuing risk to children.

There is, within the guidance notes, provision for a local authority Social Services Department to decide not to apply the arrangements on rare occasions and it is clear that the purpose of this provision is to allow discretion in cases where there is not thought to be child protection implications.

Where the Prison Service receives a letter signed by an officer at not below the level of Assistant Director of Social Services, indicating that the usual arrangements should not apply and setting out reasons for the decision, then references to Schedule One status will be deleted from prison records and the Local Authority and Probation Service will be informed in writing that the previous notification papers should be destroyed. The actual criminal conection remains but they become free of the consequences associated with having a schedule one status. In practice, however, this rarely happens as the papers referring to the offence and the work completed are often destroyed, the workers involved have frequently moved on and all that is left is the offender's version of what happened.

NACRO has argued that few Social Services Departments are taking advantage of the opportunity that exists for them to exercise their discretion not to apply the usual arrangements for Schedule One Offenders. As a result there are increasing numbers of young people attracting Schedule One status who ought to be excluded. They argued that there is an urgent need to develop agreed local mechanisms which ensure that proper consideration is given to waiving the usual procedures in all cases where the offender is under 18 years of age. Good practice suggests that such mechanisms should be proactive rather than responsive to Prison Service information and that decisions should be made at the point of conviction or sentence. Youth Offending Teams ought to be centrally involved in that decision making process.

A possible model for good practice

The implications of being classified as a Schedule One Offender are such that a young person should only be so classified following a clear decision that his or her behaviour is such as to engender child protection concerns. In these circumstances, every Local Authority ought to have a clear locally agreed procedure for ensuring that full consideration is given to whether to waive the usual arrangements for Schedule One Offences in all cases where the offender is also a child or young person. While arrangements are likely to differ from one area to another to take account of local circumstances and existing child protection procedures, it is nonetheless possible to give an outline of the elements, which such a procedure might contain. Elements of what follows are drawn from the procedures currently in operation in Luton and Kent.

As indicated above, current Social Services practice tends to be responsive to notification from other agencies and, in particular, the Prison Service. Insofar as young offenders are concerned, procedures should be proactive so that a decision as to classification is made as soon as possible after conviction or sentence. There are a number of advantages to such an approach. First, where notification is subsequently received from the Prison Service, either because the Schedule One Offence results in a custodial disposal or because the young person is later detained in relation to another matter and notification is based on a previous conviction, the Local Authority will already have considered the case. Where the usual arrangements are not to be applied, the Social Services Department will be able to make an immediate and informed response. Secondly, where Schedule One status is considered appropriate, classification shortly after conviction or sentence will enhance the protection of children. Thirdly, rapid decision-making eliminates the possibility, which currently exists, of a young person attaining Schedule One status some considerable period after the offence has been disposed of: where for instance the young person subsequently receives a custodial sentence for a different offence. It is therefore also in the best interests of the young offender and his or her family. Finally, such a system ensures an equitable treatment of all young people who commit Schedule One offences irrespective of which other agencies are involved.

Court staff within the Youth Offending Team (YOT), or Local Authority Youth Justice Team prior to the establishment of a YOT, will be best placed to monitor convictions of young people for Schedule One Offences. Such staff should, in liaison with their line manager, be responsible for monitoring the progress through court of any offences listed in the schedule from the point of first appearance. At point of conviction or sentence, the Youth Offending Team Manager should notify in writing a designated officer within the Social Services Department with responsibility for child protection and maintaining the Schedule One Register. Notification should be in an agreed format and include, as a minimum, details of the offender and the victim, the nature of the offence and the Court disposal. In every case, the Youth Offending Team Manager should also make a recommendation as to whether the young person should be treated as a Schedule One Offender. Detailed reasons for the recommendations should be provided.

Although each case should be judged on its individual merits, Youth Offending Teams should develop written guidance outlining the circumstances in which it will be appropriate for a young offender to be excluded from

Schedule One status. Ideally, the Area Child Protection Committee should agree such guidelines.

On receipt of the notification and recommendation from the Youth Offending Team, the designated officer within the Social Services Department will make an initial decision as to Schedule One status. Where that initial decision is in conflict with the Youth Offending Team's recommendation, a multi-agency panel consisting of a senior member of the Police Child Protection Team, a Senior Probation Officer, a Senior Social Worker with child protection responsibility and a senior member of the Youth Offending Team should review the case and make a final decision as to classification.

Responsibility for informing relevant parties of the decision (including a decision not to apply Schedule One status) should be agreed locally. Inevitably, most of that responsibility will fall to the Social Services Department but it may, for example, be sensible for the Youth Offending Team to ensure that the young offender and their family understand the implications of any decision.

Given the potential for future notifications from other agencies in relation to the same offence, it will be important to maintain a clear record of all decisions and the reasons for them even where it is agreed that the circumstances are not such as to warrant Schedule One classification.

Factors to be considered in the decision making process

Each case should be judged on its own merits and on the basis of the fullest available information. At the same time it is possible to identify a number of factors which will be relevant to every decision and consistent approach will be assisted by the production of locally agreed guidelines to underpin the decision making process. As indicated above, the Area Child Protection Committee would ideally agree such guidance. The Youth Offending Team, given its central role in the model outlined above, may be best placed to formulate such guidance in the first instance in conjunction with child protection specialists from the Social Services Department.

Relevant factors might be thought to include: seriousness of the offence; offence type; relative age of the victim and offender; and evidence

of targeting. The distinction between these factors is not, of course, an absolute one: thus relative age of the victim or evidence of targeting will impinge on the seriousness of the offence. Any informed decision will, of necessity, take into account the totality of the circumstances. It is nonetheless possible to outline some of the relevant considerations in relation to each of the factors in turn, which might then form the basis of more detailed written guidance.

Seriousness of the offence

Generally speaking, the sentence imposed by the Court for an individual offence is an indicator of its overall seriousness and may therefore provide a backdrop against which decisions can be made. This has changed significantly over time. More specifically, where the offence did not result in either a community penalty or a custodial sentence (that is, the Court imposed a discharge, financial penalty or a reparation order), it is unlikely that Schedule One status is appropriate in the absence of any contraindications.

Where the Schedule One offence resulted in a community penalty, it may be helpful to distinguish further between:

- Those cases where custody was not available due to the age or previous convictions of the defendant.
- Those cases where custody was available but the Court elected not to impose it.

Where custody was available but not imposed, it may be that the Court has taken a particular view of the seriousness of the offence in which case there may be grounds for supposing that Schedule One status should be applied only where there are other indicators of risk. On the other hand, it may be that the offence was serious and a community penalty was imposed on the basis of strong personal mitigation or in order to allow the offender to participate in a programme of supervision (including, for instance, treatment for a sex offender), which might better reduce the risk of re-offending. Further information will therefore be required before a view can be taken as to seriousness.

Where custody was not available for technical reasons, it will be important to approach the issue of seriousness independently of the Court's disposal. A custodial sentence on the other hand, gives a clear indication of the seriousness of the offence and may give a prima facie indication that registration should be considered. As indicated below, however, seriousness on its own may not be sufficient to justify Schedule One status.

Offence type

Schedule One effectively encompasses two broad categories of offences against children and young people: those involving violence and those which are sexually motivated or involve abusive behaviour. In general terms, the former offences, even if quite serious, are less likely to generate child protection concerns where both victim and offender are under 18 years of age. Thus an assault on another young person of a similar age may be sufficiently serious to justify a custodial outcome but depending on the context may not be thought to indicate a continuing risk to children. Unless the offence is particularly vicious, sadistic or targeted, therefore, it will generally not be appropriate to apply Schedule One status.

Even where the offence is of a sexual nature, it should not be assumed that Schedule One status would automatically follow. It is important to distinguish genuinely abusive behaviour from adolescent experimentation, which is consensual. The fact that an action is against the law and prosecution has resulted may not itself be the best guide. For instance, the decision to prosecute may be based on factors unrelated to the issue of whether there are child protection concerns such as the wishes of the victim's parents or previous offending which may be of a totally different nature. In these circumstances, while a sexual offence will often make registration more likely, it may be possible to specify a number of specific circumstances where Schedule One status would be inappropriate. An example of such circumstances might be consensual unlawful intercourse where there is not more than a two-year age difference between victim and offender.

Relative age of victim and offender

Where the offender is older than the victim, child protection concerns will obviously be greater especially, though not exclusively, where the offence is of a sexual nature. Conversely, where the age differential is reversed, that may constitute a factor weighing against registration. In both circumstances, the extent of the age gap is a significant consideration but other factors such as level of intellectual functioning are very important as to abuse of power etc. Moreover, wherever possible, it will be important to weigh the emotional maturity or vulnerability of both parties rather than rely solely on chronological age.

Absolute age may also be a consideration. It might be thought, for instance, that a 17-year-old offender might be classified as a Schedule One offender in circumstances where a 10-year-old ought to be excluded. On the other hand, it might be possible to reach a consensus that any sexual offence against a victim under a specified age (perhaps 10 or 12 years) would generally warrant Schedule One status.

Evidence of targeting

Child protection concerns will also be highlighted where there is evidence that the choice of victim was, in part, motivated by the fact that she or he is a child or young person. While there may occasionally be such evidence arising from the circumstances of an individual case, it will more commonly be the case that repeat offending is suggestive of such targeting.

It is, however, important to recognise that repeat offending may not demonstrate targeting. For instance, a number of assaults where the victim is under 18 years may simply represent the fact that the offender is more likely to have contact with young people of his or her age. (It may also of course demonstrate a problem with anger management but that may not, of itself, warrant Schedule One status.) In such circumstances, were the violent behaviour to continue, one might expect the age of the victim to rise with that of the offender.

By the same token, targeted offending may not in itself be conclusive as to the requirement for registration. Thus a series of offences against young victims may be targeted but may represent a pattern of offending associated with youth offending culture in a particular area. Instances of such offending might be behaviour of a type associated with bullying or with gang rivalry. In such circumstances, the choice of victim may in part be determined by age but one would not necessarily expect such victimisation to be continued into adulthood.

Conversely, repeat sexualised offending may well be indicative that the behaviour is more than adolescent experimentation and might therefore favour classification of the young person as a Schedule One offender.

In the absence of guidance from central Government on the application of Schedule One procedures to offenders under 18 years of age, it is incumbent on local authorities to develop local procedures. A proactive decision making mechanism underpinned by detailed guidance can both improve protection of children while avoiding unnecessary registration of young people who do not generate child protection concerns. Youth offending teams, given their key role within the youth justice system, are well placed, where there are not adequate existing procedures, to take the initiative to ensure that this important issue is given the attention which it merits.

The Crime and Disorder Act 1998

This Act had its origins in research by the Audit Commission on youth crime and its management (Audit Commission, 1998). The White Paper *No more excuses* recommended the development of a clear strategy to prevent offending and re-offending; that offenders and parents face up to their offending behaviour; and its effects on families, victims and communities; that offenders take responsibility for their behaviour; that earlier, more effective intervention when young people first offend should be developed, with the aim of helping young people develop a sense of personal responsibility; faster, and more efficient procedures from arrest to sentence; and partnerships between all youth justice agencies to deliver a better, faster system. The thrust is thus on interventionist and not diversionary approaches. The Act included reprimands and final warnings that replace cautions and the Diversionary panel, but which should trigger services from the new Youth Offending teams. There is also an accompanying range of new sentencing provisions.

The reprimand replaces the basic caution. A young offender can only receive one reprimand. In certain circumstances where the cautioning officer believes an intervention is required, the offender can be referred to the YOT as a result of a reprimand. The Final Warning is introduced as the equivalent of a second caution. It will trigger an automatic referral to the YOT. A young offender will normally only receive one final warning unless two years have elapsed since the previous final warning

was administered. A young offender can receive no more than two final warnings. The final warning scheme contributes toward the delivery of the aim to prevent re-offending by:

- Ending repeat cautioning and providing a progressive response to offending behaviour.
- Ensuring appropriate and effective action when a young person starts to offend to help prevent re-offending.
- Ensuring that juveniles who re-offend after a final warning are dealt with quickly and effectively within the court system.

In order to safeguard the offender's interests, the following conditions must be met before a reprimand or final warning can be administered:

- There must be sufficient evidence of the offender's guilt to give a realistic prospect of conviction.
- The offender must make a clear and reliable admission of the offence.
- The young offender has not previously been convicted of an offence.
- It is not in the public interest for the young offender to be prosecuted.

There is no longer a requirement for parental consent.

A first time offender should normally receive a reprimand, unless the gravity factors indicate that the offence is so serious that the offender should be given a final warning or be charged. A second time offender who has previously been reprimanded cannot receive a second reprimand and should normally receive a final warning. A second time offender who has previously received a final warning should not normally receive a further final warning and should be charged. If two years have elapsed since the last final warning was given a second final warning can then be given. A third time offender should normally be charged, unless two years have elapsed since the last final warning was administered. If this is the case, a reprimand cannot be given and a second final warning should be administered. Any young offender committing a fourth or subsequent offence *must* be charged. When considering an offender's previous history, one previous caution counts as a previous reprimand and two or more cautions count as a previous final warning.

One of the problems of integrating this new approach into the management of young people who sexually abuse is not the interventionist philosophy alone, but the time scales and prescriptive formula for determining what outcome should be attributed to which offence. In many areas, the police have responded to the Act by setting strict timescales for the processing of a case from arrest to disposal. This started off as little as four hours and clearly challenged the procedure of allowing an initial assessment to be undertaken by the social services and youth justice workers before making an informed recommendation on the way forward. There was also no replacement mechanism for the Diversionary Panel that had considered the information collected before recommending a particular disposal to the Police to process.

In the Greater Manchester region the police have developed a gravity matrix (based on Home Office Guidance) to guide the custody sergeant in the disposal of a case, within the required four-hour period. The gravity matrix is presented as Figure 4. All offences are given a gravity score to aid the decision-making process on whether to reprimand, warn or charge. The scores range from 1 (minimum response) to 4 (always charge). Aggravating and mitigating factors are listed which could increase or decrease a gravity score, taking into consideration the circumstances of the offence. You can only increase or decrease the baseline gravity factor by one point, no matter how many of the aggravating or mitigating factors may be present.

There is a major concern that you cannot address the complexity of sexually abusive behaviour by the allocation of points, as there is increasing evidence that it is the non-sexual dimensions that have contributed to the evolution of their sexual behaviour and which may also provide sustenance for it over time (see Calder, 2001 for a review of the theoretical terrain with this group).

Youth Offending Teams (YOTs) and the Youth Justice Board

The development of YOTs is one of the major consequences of the Crime and Disorder Act at a local level. They are responsible to the local authority's chief executive and comprise a manager, police, social work, probation, education and health staff. Together their task is to *prevent* re-offending by children and young people. This is *unlikely* given that agencies

have often provided one staff member each rather than a greater number. The consequence of this is that the YOTS will have to set the threshold for their service at a level, which their resources allow, leaving a potentially large level of unmet need (see Figure 5).

This is important, in terms of the joint management of children and young people who sexually abuse, with social services, who have themselves been forced to articulate and implement strict thresholds for the provision of a social work service (see Calder, forthcoming for a detailed discussion on this point). This parallel process of restricting service provision has implications for the previously developed joint approach at a number of different levels. Firstly, a criminal charge cannot be brought in England for a child under 10. This is likely to remove the involvement of YOTs who may be dealing with a large number of offenders brought through the criminal system. Secondly, social services may not be in a position to provide a worker for the cases being dealt with primarily by YOTs unless there are clear child protection issues that require the conduct of a section 47 investigation. This point will be clearer to the reader once they have read the next section on child protection directives.

The Youth Justice Board is a national innovation with a remit to: establish national standards; maintain a rolling programme of inspections; initiate training; and identify and disseminate good practice. It also allocates monies from a pot of £85 million over the next three years (same time scale as the Quality Protects monies) to assist YOTs locally. This is a significant development for young people who sexually abuse given the resistance centrally to setting national standards and practice for this group.

ASSET

The Youth Justice Board have developed and disseminated a series of ASSET documents (core assessment profile, risk of serious harm form, self-assessment form) that the youth offending teams should have been using since April 1st 2000 (reproduced in Calder, 2001). These forms *must* be completed by a YOT member and the core ASSET profile should be completed *before* any intervention is undertaken by the YOT with the young person: either pre or post sentence, or post final warning. It should then

Figure 4: The Gravity Matrix.

Offence	Gravity score	Aggravating factors	Mitigating factors
Gross indecency	2	Group action Genuine possibility of the public witnessing the offence Youth victim	Consenting victim but under the legal age of consent
Indecent exposure	2	Victim put in fear Repeat performances	
Rape	4		
Procuration of woman for sex by threat or drugs	4		
Buggery (without consent)	4		
Buggery (consensual with an adult)	2	Observable by persons other than the participants	Victim under 16 consents but is technically under age of consent
Assault with intent to commit buggery	4		
Incest	3	Victim did not wholly consent Element of coercion	Offender and victim are youths close in age Brother and sister both mature: further offences unlikely Both parties over age of consent and no element of coercion or seduction
Unlawful sexual intercourse with mental defective	4		
Unlawful sexual intercourse with a girl under 13	4	Facilitated by drugs or alcohol	Offender and victim of similar age and no element of coercion or corruption present
Unlawful sexual intercourse with a girl under 16	2	Element of coercion Element of corruption Considerable age gap Facilitated by drugs or alcohol	No coercion No corruption Relationship in place
Indecent assault (on male or female)	3	Force used Elderly or youth victim	

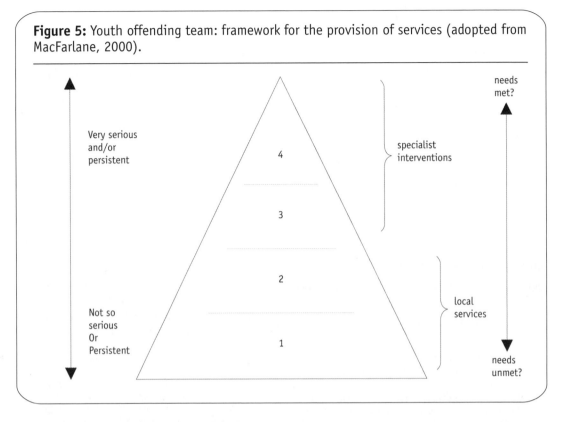

Figure 5: Youth offending team: framework for the provision of services (adopted from MacFarlane, 2000).

be redone post intervention to assess the progress that has been made. These documents appear to have been developed independently of the Department of Health work on developing their assessment framework for *all* children in need and their families. There is certainly no integration in the two sets of documents and some may argue they contradict each other. The official line appears to be that they had different needs, purposes, and time scales and thus they will look at the pairing as the pilot periods continue. This is not a good example of joined-up government and it most certainly does not model partnerships across departments or agencies. The timescale for completing the ASSET is three days maximum and this is unrealistic when you look at the complexity of the areas to be covered and which extend significantly beyond the offence itself.

Home Office guidance to the Probation Service on work with sex offenders (March, 1999)

The teams will deliver, or co-ordinate the delivery of, the full range of work with young offenders, and will ensure that this is properly integrated with any wider

activity related to youth crime or the probation service and other agencies ... the youth offending teams will take lead responsibility for intervention with children and young people who are sex offenders. Setting the Boundaries (Home Office, 2000) (p5)

Setting the Boundaries (Home Office, 2000)

This consultation paper on the law governing sexual offences acknowledges that young people do sexually abuse as well as experiment and it defines the criminal law as providing '*a remedy that can be used to deal with those children who do abuse*' (p58). They went on to note that '*a variety of suggestions have been made as to the best way to treat young abusers*' and included '*that wherever possible they should be removed from the criminal justice system, and civil remedies, together with welfare support, should be used to tackle abusive behaviour*'. They declined to process this further, arguing that '*the principles of the punishment or treatment of young offenders is beyond our remit, but we did consider that whatever approach was adopted needed to reflect the basic principles of protecting the community and the individual and preventing re-offending*' (p59).

In their recommendations, they argued that it is

> 'important that these young offenders are given appropriate sentences and disposals to ensure that they do not continue to pose a risk to others, and they receive appropriate treatment. Baseline assessment of these children was important for the courts in sentencing them appropriately, and we thought it was essential that courts had available a detailed specialist assessment of the child, to inform the judges' decision on sentencing and disposal. This would need to take into account the perceived risk that the young offender presents, which should also include situational factors such as family perceptions; collusion; denial etc, and any kind of abuse suffered by the offender . . .'

(p59)

Child protection directives

Working together to safeguard children (DoH, 1998; 1999)

The initial consultation paper (1998) argued that:

> . . . handling juvenile sexual abuse cases within ACPC procedures will continue to provide the most effective way of tackling the problem. Young abusers should be the subjects of inter-agency consideration and a written case plan should be drawn up. As part of the plan, it will be important to ensure that abusers are held accountable for their abusive behaviour and are left in no doubt that it is unacceptable. Views are invited on the circumstances in which juvenile abusers should be the subject of child protection conferences and their names placed on the child protection register.

(Paragraph 5.29)

> New guidance will need to address the inter-relationship between child protection procedures and the criminal justice process which is triggered by the arrest of the alleged abuser. This guidance will take account of proposals for new powers to set statutory time limits for cases involving young defendants, and a range of new disposals for under-18s for use by the courts. It will also need to reflect, in the longer term, proposals for further reform of the Youth Court which were set up in a government White Paper 'No More Excuses: A new approach to tackling youth crime in England and Wales' published in November 1997.

(Paragraph 5.30)

When the consultation draft was issued in August 1999, there had been quite a shift in thinking, and this was endorsed in the final document (DoH, 1999). They noted that

> such children and young people are likely to be children in need and some will in addition be suffering or at risk of suffering significant harm, and may themselves be in need of protection

(Paragraph 6.30)

> Children and young people who abuse others should be held responsible for their abusive behaviour, whilst being identified and responded to in a way, which meets their needs as well as protecting the public

(Paragraph 6.31)

Three key principles should guide work with children and young people who abuse others:

- There should be a co-ordinated approach on the part of youth justice and child welfare agencies.
- The needs of children and young people who abuse others should be considered separately from the needs of their victims.
- An assessment should be carried out in each case, appreciating that these children may have considerable unmet developmental needs, as well as specific needs arising from their behaviour.

(Paragraph 6.32)

> ACPCs and Youth Offending Teams should ensure that there is a clear operational framework in place within which assessment, decision-making and case management takes place. Neither child welfare, nor criminal justice agencies should embark upon a course of action that has implications for the other without appropriate consultation

(Paragraph 6.33)

Decisions for local agencies, according to the responsibilities of each, include:

- The most appropriate course of action within the criminal justice system, if the child is above the age of criminal responsibility.
- Whether the young abuser should be the subject of a child protection conference.
- What plan of action should be put in place to address the needs of the young abuser, detailing the involvement of all relevant agencies.

(Paragraph 6.35)

> A young abuser should not be the subject of a child protection conference unless he or she is considered personally to be at continuing risk of significant harm. Where there is no reason to hold a child protection conference, there may still be a need for a multi-agency approach if the young abusers needs are complex. Issues regarding suitable educational and accommodation arrangements often require skilled and careful consideration

(Paragraph 6.36)

In the same document, it states explicitly that the Area Child Protection Committee should retain the *lead responsibility* for the management of young people who sexually abuse, even though the above guidance clearly exits the majority from the child protection system. This means that these cases will fall into the 'children in need' umbrella advocated in the new assessment framework (DoH, 2000), although this will again rely on the capacity of social services to deliver on all their duties given the resource constraints (see Calder, forthcoming).

The assessment framework (AF) (DoH, 2000)

The new assessment framework has emerged in order to provide a standardised procedure and framework for children in need, and not just those in need of protection. It was designed to redress the problems created by both the earlier 'orange book' (DoH, 1988) and the findings from '*Messages from Research*' (DoH, 1995) and various critical inspection reports. It is built on theory and research and there can be some, but not overwhelming challenge to its origins. Where it does fail most acutely is when it comes to its application to sexual abuse, and in relation to young people who sexually abuse (see Calder, 2000 for a detailed critique). There is only one chapter of 3000 words to guide the worker in the right direction and to furnish us with the current evidence base (Print and Erooga, 2000). This is dangerous and overly simplistic. Calder (forthcoming) is attempting to redress this in a very practical way and equip workers with operational tools.

The timescale set down for the process of involvement when a referral is made (see Figure 6) is unhelpful in many ways, ranging from un-necessary focus on process rather than engaging the professionals and the family, to lacking any evidence-base and being blind to the resource constraints on the local authority. There is also no fit with the significant delays experienced in the care proceedings taken.

Conflicts and confusions

Where do you start? There are a number of conclusions that can and should be reached from the information shared to date:

- The Home Office, The Youth Justice Board and the Department of Health have clearly not communicated in developing their materials. As such, the lead responsibility is given to both the ACPC and YOTs by different branches of government. They have also developed core assessment documents independently of each other that are not compatible or congruent. They have different tracks.
- There has been a shift of position between the criminal justice and child protection camps, with youth justice being forced to adopt an interventionist approach as compared to a diversionary approach within child protection.
- There are numerous obstacles to inter-agency working with young people who sexually abuse (explored in detail in Calder, 1999) and which did not require these additional hurdles. The prescriptive interventionist approach will potentially lead to a new system that will determine disposal before any kind of assessment has been done; will result in a police decision being inherited by YOTs and social services who are then required to pick up any pieces and undo any damage done; and which will then fall outside the formal child protection system.
- By leaving responsibilities duplicated and unclear allows services to formulate their own eligibility criteria and screen in cases according to resource availability and priorities rather than identified need. There is thus a potential for many cases to fall outside the various systems, and this will leave the path for escalating abusiveness open to some abusers.
- The outcome will remain a fragmented system with ad hoc responses, and one has only to refer back to the state of our work in 1992 (as set out in NCH, 1992) to reach the conclusion that we are no further forward. This is unfortunate since we had a system with huge potential before these fragmented changes were introduced. These new initiatives are certainly not integrated or helpful in the work we need to do.

Parallel developments of significance

It would be unhelpful to view the struggle facing ACPCs and YOTs as being located within the central guidance, although the points I will make in this section are driven by central government also.

The assessment framework and deletion of risk

The government appears to be jettisoning the concept of risk and risk assessment in their

Figure 6: Maximum Timescales for Analysing the Needs of Child and Parenting Capacity (DoH, 1999).

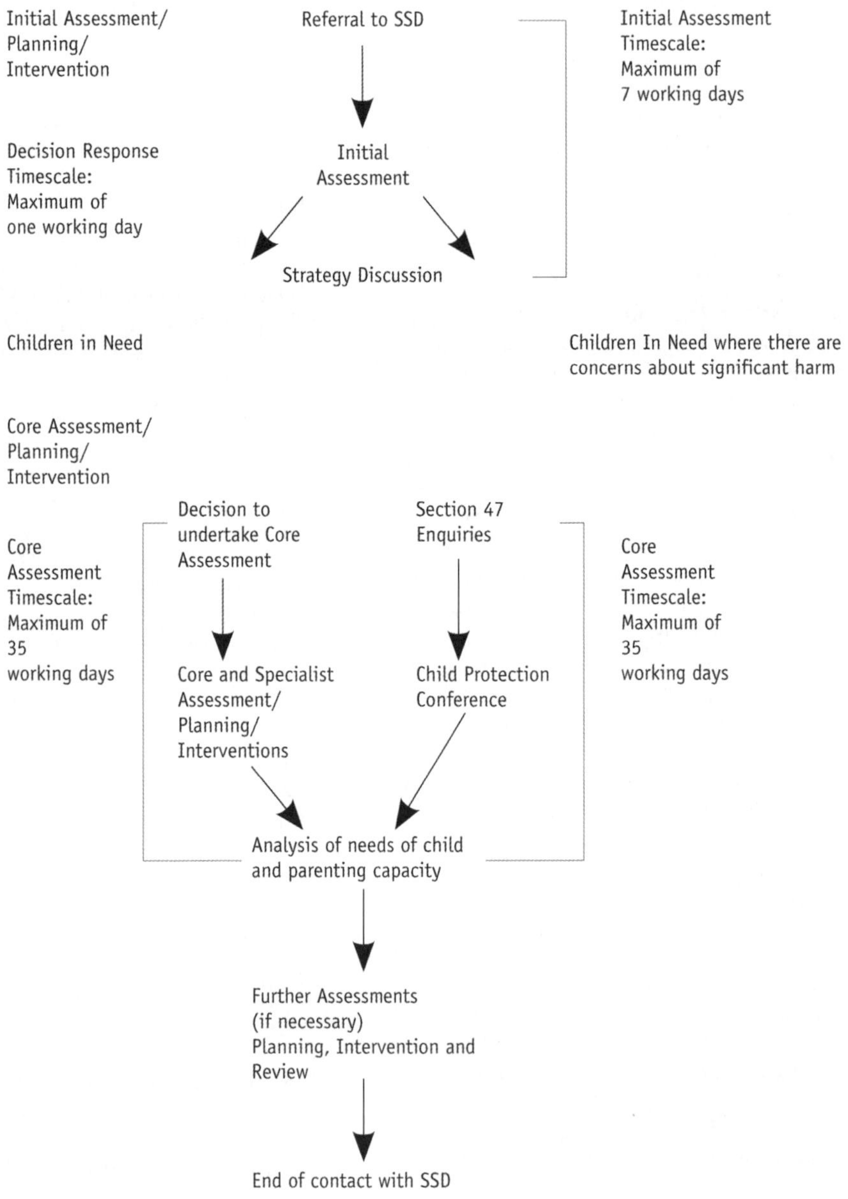

Initial Assessment/
Planning/
Intervention

Referral to SSD

Initial Assessment
Timescale:
Maximum of
7 working days

Decision Response
Timescale:
Maximum of
one working day

Initial
Assessment

Strategy Discussion

Children in Need

Children In Need where there are
concerns about significant harm

Core Assessment/
Planning/
Intervention

Decision to
undertake Core
Assessment

Section 47
Enquiries

Core
Assessment
Timescale:
Maximum of
35
working days

Core and Specialist
Assessment/
Planning/
Interventions

Child Protection
Conference

Core
Assessment
Timescale:
Maximum of
35
working days

Analysis of needs of child
and parenting capacity

Further Assessments
(if necessary)
Planning, Intervention and
Review

End of contact with SSD

latest guidance in favour of a needs-led assessment. The DoH assessment guidance of 1988 was built almost entirely on the notions of risk and dangerousness yet these do not appear to have been satisfactorily defined or applied in practice. This may be because it is a term which is often misused in social work because it focuses exclusively on the risk of harm, whereas in any other enterprise a risk equation also includes a chance of benefit resulting (Carson, 1994). Any risk assessment, should, therefore, be concerned with weighing up the pros and cons of a child's circumstances in order to inform decision-making as to what should happen with regard to intervention and protection. It involves examining the child and family situation to identify and weigh various risk factors (such as parents, family or other influences that increase the likelihood that a child will be harmed in a certain way), family strengths, family resources, and available agency services. This assessment information can then be used to determine if a child is safe, what agency resources are needed to keep the child safe, and under what circumstances a child should be removed from the family. The government thus appears to be redefining risk by utilising the component parts and framing them in the context of need. This is not convincing when there is repeated backtracking from needs-led assessments to a reminder that the child's safety is the primary objective of professional intervention.

One of the most confusing issues is that at a time in which the government is moving away from notions of risk, there are huge developments in risk assessments emerging in the field of sexual abuse. This is unfortunate for several reasons:

- Identifying risk is a central part of our work in sexually abusing families.
- It is an extremely difficult task for any professional, particularly given the lack of scientific evidence regarding predictions of human behaviour.
- There is a need to ensure that we construct our risk estimations based on theory and research in each sub category of sexual abuse and not rely on a transfer of knowledge from adult male sex offenders.
- There is a need to move from general risk estimations (high, medium or low risk) to the nature of the risk and the particular situations/contexts in which they apply.
- In the absence of a quantification of risk, then it is difficult to construct a plan to manage it. For a detailed resume of risk assessments, see Calder (in press).

Hanson (1998; 1999) argued that risk assessments consider two distinct concepts: enduring propensities, or potentials to re-offend; and factors that indicate the onset of new offences. These offence triggers are not random, but can be expected to be organised into predictable patterns (offence cycles), some unique to the individual and some common to most sexual offenders.

Different evaluation questions require the consideration of different types of risk factors.

Static, historical variables (e.g. prior offences, childhood maladjustment) can indicate deviant developmental trajectories and, as such, enduring propensities to sexually offend. Evaluating changes in risk levels (e.g. treatment outcome), however, requires the consideration of dynamic, changeable risk factors (e.g. co-operation with supervision, deviant sexual preferences). The relatively low recidivism rates of sexual offenders' makes it difficult to detect dynamic risk factors. Over a 4–5 year period, approximately 10–15 per cent of sexual offenders will be detected committing a new sexual offence (Hanson and Bussiere, 1998). Although age is sometimes considered a dynamic factor, the most important dynamic factors are those that respond to treatment. Dynamic factors can further be classified as stable or acute. Stable factors have the potential to change, but typically endure for months or years (e.g. personality disorder) and, as such, represent ongoing risk potential. In contrast, acute factors (e.g. negative mood) may be present for a short duration (minutes, days) and can signal the timing of offending. Most risk decisions require consideration of both static and dynamic risk factors.

Development of actuarial risk tools

In an attempt to move away from the unvalidated instruments of risk assessment used extensively with both adult and young people who sexually abuse, there has been a move towards actuarial risk tools. Since no single factor is sufficient to determine whether offenders will or will not re-offend, practitioners need to consider a range of relevant risk factors. There are three plausible methods by which risk factors can be combined into overall evaluations of risk:

- Empirically guided clinical evaluations: which begins with the overall recidivism base rate, and then adjusts the risk level by considering factors that have been empirically associated with recidivism risk. The risk factors to be considered are explicit, but the method for weighting the importance of the risk factors is left to the judgement of the worker.
- Pure actuarial predictions: in contrast, explicitly state not only the variables to be considered, but also the precise procedure through which ratings of these variables will be translated into a risk level. In the pure

actuarial sense, risk levels are estimated through mechanical, arithmetic procedures requiring a minimum of judgement.

- Clinically adjusted actuarial predictions: begins with a pure actuarial prediction, but then raises or lowers the risk level based on consideration of relevant factors that were not included in the actuarial method (see Quinsey et al., 1995). As research develops, actuarial methods can be expected to consistently outperform clinical predictions. With the current state of knowledge, however, both actuarial and guided clinical approaches can be expected to provide risk assessments with moderate levels of accuracy.

There has been considerable work done in the development of such tools in the adult sex offender field by Karl Hanson and his materials are reviewed in detail in Calder (2000). There has been some debate as to the viability of developing similar tools with young people who sexually abuse. There are those who argue the young person is too young to have enough relevant history to use in dynamic risk assessments, whilst others such as Gail Ryan believe there is some mileage in testing the matter out in practice. Several prototype actuarial risk models for young people are starting to emerge, such as the J-SOAP (Prentky et al., 2000), ERASOR (Worling and Curwen, 2001) and AIM. These are all produced and discussed in detail in Calder (2001).

What is important is that the development of more sophisticated risk tools is not undertaken in isolation from the need to assess client strengths (Calder, Peake and Rose, 2001). Jane Gilgun (1999) has developed an actuarial

model for assessing risks and assets in children who sexually abuse (called CASPARS) reproduced in Calder (2001). This includes an excellent matrix for balancing risks and assets to help us determine the most appropriate way forward.

Type 1 children

Children who are high on assets and low on risks are Type 1 children who, along with their families, require some education, supportive counselling, and limit setting, but not intense, long-term interventions. These children and their families will be fairly 'easy' to deal with in treatment and are likely to do well in the long term.

Type 2 children

Children high on assets and high on risks are Type 2 children. These children and families require intense and long-term intervention and education to decrease risks and to maintain and increase assets. Sometimes families are functioning fairly well, but the social environment is full of risks. Conversely, families might be struggling with substantial issues but reside in a resource-rich community and have strong positive relationships with extended family, community groups and work. Children from families that have difficult issues may have important supports outside their family. These children and their families will be challenging and are likely to do well in treatment.

Type 3 children

Children who are low on assets and low on risks are Type 3 children and require education and long-term intervention to increase assets and to deal with risk factors. Important are interventions to increase their links to supportive systems outside of their families and to increase supportive interactions within their families. These children and families may be difficult to reach and may appear uninterested or unmotivated for change. If they do well as a result of intervention it will be because the worker has succeeded in engaging them in changing the situation.

Type 4 children

Children who are classified as low on assets and high on risks are Type 4 children. They would require intensive, long-term interventions focused not only on strengthening

Figure 7: A classification by risks and assets (Gilgun, 1999).

Type 1	Type 2
High assets	**High risks**
Low risks	**High assets**
Type 3	Type 4
Low assets	**Low assets**
Low risks	**High risks**

connections and interactions among family members but also in developing supportive connections with individuals and social institutions outside their families. Some Type 4 children will not have the support of their families and may be in foster or residential care. Chemical abuse and dependency issues, chronic neglect, and severe disorganisation are often found in Type 4 children.

The aim of treatment is to move children to Type 1: high asset/low risk.

Theory

To date there is generally no accepted theory about why young people sexually abuse. A number of factors have received empirical attention, including maltreatment experiences, exposure to pornography, substance abuse, and exposure to aggressive role models. Weinrott (1996) has argued that most explanations of juvenile sexual crimes are too simplistic or are applied universally. He recommended improved integration of findings from typology research and aetiological studies, noting that different types of juvenile sex offender should be focused on individually. Developmental models should be broadened to include larger social variables such as exposure to sexually violent media and characteristics of social ecologies. Marshall and Eccles (1993) have even suggested that a comprehensive theory of young sex abusers may not be possible, and they propose that specific theories are needed for different types of sexual offence, each emphasising different processes.

The absence of a clear understanding of the aetiologies of juveniles who sexually abuse has hampered the development of early identification and intervention programmes; has complicated the tasks of ascertaining amenability to treatment, determining type and level of service required, and defining risk of recidivism and made them less scientific endeavours (Becker et al., 1996). Because of the complex nature of adolescent work generally, working with adolescent sexual offenders can be particularly problematic and fraught with difficulties (Connolly and Wolf, 1995). It is for these reasons that a considerable amount of time and energy has been expended on trying to understand the origins of sexually abusive behaviour in young people. There has also been considerable time spent on trying to understand the differences between adults and young people who sexually abuse and what theories and materials are transferable between the two groups (see Calder, 2001 for a detailed review of these issues). There is also a need to look at issues for females who sexually abuse.

One of the most important issues to take from the emerging literature is that we should only concentrate on the offence in a small number of cases as the social history holds the key to most presenting cases. The younger the child, the more important this consideration becomes (Calder, 1997). This is reflected in the emerging frameworks for the conduct of core assessments with young people who sexually abuse (see Calder, 2001 and Figure 8)

The young person should be seen holistically. It is unhelpful to single out and target their sexually abusive behaviour in isolation from other key developmental areas, such as life experiences and communication and relationships skills, etc. Such an approach will only lead to partial assessments and will potentially alienate the young person. It is their behaviour and not their identity that needs to be addressed and labelled. If we target their sexual abuse behaviours at the exclusion of all else then we will be unlikely to repair any damaged self from their own past and thus have not effected change that is likely to be sustained. History of child abuse/witnessing domestic violence

Procedures for the Management of Children and Young People who Sexually Abuse (Salford Area Child Protection Committee)

1. Introduction

1.1 These new procedures are intended to provide workers with a guide to the steps to be taken in dealing with children and young people who sexually abuse. They incorporate recent changes in the law and in national and local guidance concerning this group of young people.

1.2 The revised edition of *Working Together* continues to allocate lead responsibility for the management of children and young people who sexually abuse to the ACPC. However, they are now to be dealt with outside of the child protection system unless there is clear evidence that they are themselves the victims of abuse and they continue to be at risk.

Figure 8: The core assessment schedule (Calder, 2001).

Individual history

- Demographic data
- Educational occupational history
- Peer relationships
- Interpersonal relationships or Intimacy
- Attachment history
- Assertiveness
- Aggression
- Anger
- Self-esteem and self-concept
- Social competence
- Social skills
- Health and medical history
- Non-sexual offending
- Drug and alcohol abuse

Family composition and functioning

- Perceptions of family life
- Family problems, secrets and conflicts
- Family interactions
- Support issues
- Coping strategies
- Marital relationship and violence
- History of child abuse or witnessing domestic violence
- Family strengths and functioning
- Protective features

Sexual history, knowledge and attitudes

- Sex education and knowledge
- Sexual experiences
- Masturbation history
- Sexual fantasies
- Cognitive distortions
- Sexual attitudes: to men, women and children
- Sexual beliefs
- Sexual values
- Sexual self-concept
- Attachment and intimacy
- Sexual interests and preferences
- Sexual arousal
- Understanding of consent
- Sexual dysfunction
- Sexual orientation
- Effects of drugs and alcohol on sexual behaviour

The alleged abuse

- Aspects of preparation
- Selection of victim
- Level of consent and power relationships
- Creation of abusive situations
- What they did to the victim
- What they required the victim to do
- The use of coercion
- Evidence of co-abusers?

Denial and excuses

- What is the source of their denial?
- Is it a shifting denial?
- Consequences of addressing their abusive behaviour
- Where are they on the continuum of denial?

Victim empathy and awareness

- How aware are any young people of victim empathy?
- How might the young person's own experiences influence their thoughts and behaviour?
- Are we happy that re-abuse or victim retaliation is not a current issue for the young person?

Motivation to change

- Where are they on the continuum of motivation?
- Do they know why it is important for them to change?
- Do they have the ability to change?
- Who do they want to support them in their efforts to change?

Feedback and report

- To the young person
- Their parents
- The commissioning body
- Should address an appraisal of the assessment, with recommendations on treatment, disposal or mandate needed, risk, etc.

1.3 Quite separately, the Crime and Disorder Act led to the establishment of Youth Offending Teams (YOTs) with a remit to prevent youth crime and to take lead responsibility for co-ordinating treatment programmes.

1.4 There are two recently introduced models which are relevant to the assessment of children and young people who sexually abuse. These are the *Framework for the Assessment of Children in Need* issued by the Department of Health and ASSET, which is more offence- orientated, issued by the Home Office.

1.5 The purpose of these procedures is to provide a clear operational framework within which the processes of assessment, decision-making and case management can take place. This requires a collaborative approach between child welfare and criminal justice agencies which ensures that no one agency will embark upon a course of action that has implications for others without appropriate consultation.

1.6 In order to facilitate this collaborative approach there needs to be some consensus on the philosophy of intervention. Research has shown that children and young people who sexually abuse have considerable needs themselves as well as potentially posing a significant risk of harm to other children. They may have experienced considerable disruption in their lives, been exposed to violence within the family, have witnessed or been subject to physical or sexual abuse, have problems in their educational development, and may have committed other offences. There is often huge potential for change and thus it is essential that a system is in place that identifies those at highest risk of re-offending in order to target limited resources effectively.

2. Principles

2.1 The complex nature of the problem requires a co-ordinated multidisciplinary approach, which addresses both child protection and criminal justice issues.

2.2 The needs of the children and young people who sexually abuse should be considered separately from the needs of their victims.

2.3 Children and young people who abuse others are in need of help and are entitled to appropriate services.

2.4 The reasons why young people sexually abuse are multi-faceted and to explore this further a full risk assessment and an assessment of need must be carried out in every case.

2.5 The primary objectives of intervention must remain at all times the protection of victims and potential victims and the avoidance of any repetition of the abusive behaviour.

2.6 The young person will be held accountable for his or her behaviour.

2.7 Wherever possible, young people who sexually abuse have a right to be consulted and involved in all matters and decisions which affect their lives. Their parents have a right to information, respect and participation in matters that concern their family.

3. Procedure

3.1 Separate routes will be taken by those children and young people who are referred through the child protection and criminal justice systems and also for children who are below the age of criminal responsibility (10 years).

Criminal Justice Route

3.2 For those young people who are the subject of an allegation of sexual abuse and who are admitting the offence, the investigating police officer will inform the young person and their parents or carers that they are to be bailed for 20 working days to allow for an assessment to be undertaken. Leaflets will be available in police stations to explain the assessment process in more detail to the young person and their parents or carers. The Youth Offending Teams will also hold copies of these leaflets for distribution.

3.3 The investigating police officer will then contact the Youth Offending Team with the young person's details and initiate the assessment process outlined in Appendix 1.

3.4 In cases originating within the criminal justice system the Youth Offending Team worker will take lead responsibility for arranging a multi-disciplinary strategy meeting to consider the conduct of the assessment and then the actual outcomes. They may contact either the Social Services Department, NSPCC or CAMHS to identify a co-worker, but the YOT will retain lead responsibility for the completion of the assessment.

3.5   The strategy meeting will be chaired by an officer from the Child Protection and Reviewing Unit and should ensure that both the child protection and criminal justice issues have been adequately addressed.

3.6   In all cases it is important that an assessment is carried out. The young person and their parent/carer will be asked by the assessors to sign a consent form agreeing to participate in the process (see Appendix 2).

3.7   If consent is refused, but concerns remain, an assessment should still be undertaken but will take the form of a paper exercise, drawing on all available information.

3.8   For those young people who go straight to charge, the assessment will be triggered by their first appearance in court. At this point a request for a 20 day adjournment should be made in order to carry out the assessment, which will inform the recommendations in the pre-sentence report.

3.9   In those cases where a young person commits a further offence whilst on bail, their bail status will need to be reviewed.

3.10   Young people who are denying the offence will not go through the assessment process at this stage unless there are obvious outstanding child protection issues which need to be addressed. However, those who are subsequently convicted should be subject to an assessment in order to inform the recommendations in the pre-sentence report.

3.11   In those situations where there is an immediate decision to charge the young person, the Youth Offending Team worker who undertakes the assessment will also complete the subsequent reports.

3.12   It is not appropriate for a Youth Offending Team worker who has acted as the appropriate adult in a PACE interview of the young person to subsequently be responsible for undertaking the assessment.

3.13   If there is an identified social worker for the victim they should not be directly involved in the assessment of the young person who is the alleged perpetrator.

3.14   The final report will make a recommendation to the police regarding disposal for the young person. However, having fully considered the assessment team's recommendation and any other relevant information which has been collated regarding mitigating and aggravating factors, the police maintain the right to make a final decision.

Child Protection Route

3.15   Allegations or suspicions of sexually abusive behaviour by children and young people, regardless of their age, should always be treated seriously and should always be the subject of a referral to the relevant Community Social Work Team.

3.16   Upon receipt of such a referral child protection enquiries should be initiated in the same way as for all allegations or disclosures of abuse and a decision taken within one working day about the required response.

3.17   In addition to those cases where the alleged or suspected perpetrator is known to the victim or is a member of the same household, a formal investigation will also normally be indicated in those cases where the alleged perpetrator is not previously known to the child. These procedures will also apply in cases where the abuse involves children in foster care, children's homes or other residential settings. Where there is any doubt about the inclusion of an incident within these procedures, advice should be sought from the Child Protection Unit.

3.18   The child protection investigation will need to consider the details of the incident and the circumstances of both the alleged perpetrator and the victim in order to determine whether the incident should be regarded as constituting abuse (see Appendix 3 for guidance). An initial evaluation of risk to self and others, and the need for any immediate protective action will also be required. The investigation into the circumstances of the alleged perpetrator will need to focus on the abusive behaviour, including any pattern that may have developed; and the alleged perpetrator as a child in need, who might have been, or continues to be the subject of abuse.

3.19 The investigation will also need to determine whether a child protection conference or an inter-agency planning meeting will be held. An initial child protection conference in respect of an alleged or suspected perpetrator should only be held if he or she is considered personally to be at risk of continuing significant harm.

3.20 Where there is no reason to hold an initial child protection conference, there may still be a need for a co-ordinated multi-agency approach if the young person's needs are complex. In these circumstances the social worker should convene an inter-agency planning meeting, the purpose of which is to assess the needs of the child/young person and to agree a plan of action.

3.21 Any meeting convened in relation to the alleged perpetrator will need to consider:

- The nature of the concerns.
- The degree to which responsibility for the behaviour has been accepted by the young person.
- The need to share relevant information with the wider community e.g. schools, on a confidential basis to ensure the continued safety of the young person and that of others from them.
- The level of risk or dangerousness posed to themselves and others.
- The family background.
- The family's attitude to the concerns including their level of co-operation.
- An agreed intervention strategy and what appropriate services are available.
- The likelihood of the child or young person engaging in the assessment process including an exploration of strategies to ensure co-operation.
- The management of any potential risk to the community.
- Whether an assessment (as outlined in Appendix 1) is required and if so, who should undertake this piece of work e.g. social worker and a representative from YOT, NSPCC or CAMHS.
- Whether the assessment framework or ASSET documentation should be used to record the work undertaken.

3.22 The assessment as set out in Appendix 1 should be conducted in any of the following circumstances:

- Young people who admit the offence but whose behaviour is deemed so serious at the outset that the police make an immediate decision to charge.
- Young people who admit the offence but who have previous offences and are therefore not eligible for the Final Warning and Reprimand scheme and are immediately charged.
- Young people who admit the offence and are likely to receive a Reprimand or a Final Warning.

3.23 Other routes into the assessment process may be triggered by Social Services, NSPCC, Education or Health.

3.24 Once the assessment has been completed, the social worker will take responsibility for setting a date for a multi-disciplinary meeting to consider the assessment outcomes. The parents/carers and the young person should be invited to attend the meeting at the discretion of the agencies involved.

3.25 The meeting should be attended by the workers who undertook the assessment and any other relevant professionals e.g. Education, Health.

3.26 Written reports from relevant professionals should be forwarded to the social worker prior to the meeting. If any agency that is invited to attend is unable to send a representative they should still receive a copy of the minutes of the meeting.

3.27 The meeting should produce a shared multi-disciplinary plan, which addresses:

- Any outstanding child protection concerns in respect of the young person.
- The safety of potential victims and other relevant victim issues.
- Risk management issues at home, in school and in the wider community.
- Immediate living arrangements for the young person.
- School attendance and related education issues.
- Support for the young person and their family.
- The wider developmental needs of the young person.
- Intervention/treatment issues.

- An outline of roles, tasks and expectations for different professionals/agencies.
- Any need for further assessment or therapeutic work.
- The date for any subsequent review.

3.28 The assessment informs the proposed intervention options that are organised utilising the AIM matrix (see appendix 4 for details) (Print et al., 2001).

3.29 The assessors will share the report with the young person and their parents and note any areas of disagreement.

4. Placement considerations

4.1 There are a number of important factors that need to be taken into account by workers when considering the placement for young abusers outside the home. Given the research evidence that suggests that it is wise to assume a significant level of ongoing risk unless it is specifically contra-indicated or can be effectively managed within a given situation, workers must consider the potential risks to other children in the placement. In all situations where there has been an allegation of sexual abuse against a young person, all relevant information (the allegation and any assessment findings/treatment recommendations) must be shared with the potential carers in order to enable them to make an informed decision about whether to accept the placement.

4.2 When the Family Placement Team or the Residential Team Leaders are approached about a child needing a placement, they need to elicit details about the young person and consider the risk they might pose to others, as well as considering whether there are any children already in the placement that might pose a risk to them. Where there are a number of children potentially affected, discussions should take place between workers to weigh up the pros and cons of the situation. This should be carefully recorded on a risk assessment pro forma (see Appendix 5).

It is important that the divisions of responsibility between the YOT and the Community Social Work Teams is clear for young people who are also 'looked after'.

5. Exempting the young person from the continuing consequences of his Schedule 1 Status

5.1 A Schedule 1 status may not, on its own, reliably distinguish those offenders who represent a continuing risk to children from others who may not. This is particularly important for young offenders (under 18 years) in those circumstances where the assessment is that there are no ongoing child protection concerns. This section provides some guidelines for ensuring that young people are not included in the notification arrangements for Schedule 1 Offenders unnecessarily. Local Authorities do have discretion not to apply the usual arrangements for Schedule 1 Offenders, but often lack the relevant, often historical information in order to do so safely.

5.2 By adopting the following procedure (from NACRO, 1999), the Social Services Directorate should be able to make an informed decision about whether or not to waive the usual arrangements. The YOT are well placed to monitor convictions of young people for Schedule 1 convictions. At the conclusion of the YOT intervention, the YOT Team Manager should notify the Custodian of the Child Protection Register, in writing (using the pro forma in Appendix 6), of the details of the offender and victim, the nature of the offence, the court disposal, and they should always make a recommendation as to whether the young person should continue to be subject to the Schedule 1 Offender notification arrangements, accompanied by detailed reasons. The receiving Principal Manager will make a preliminary decision as to Schedule 1 status. Where there is disagreement, the matter will be refered to the Assistant Director (Social Services) who will make a final decision as to classification. There should be a review of the decision at the conclusion of the order and/or the end of the treatment programme.

5.3 In reaching a decision, certain factors remain key and include:

- The seriousness of the offence as reflected in the court order made. For example, it may not be appropriate to maintain a Schedule 1 status where a financial penalty was imposed, although the potential impact of plea-bargaining should be considered. Where a high tariff community sentence or a period of imprisonment has been imposed then it is likely that serious concerns will remain that justify the maintenance of the Schedule 1 status.

- Offence type is important and where there is evidence of coercion or violence or serious charges such as rape are brought, then no consideration should be given to exclusion.
- The relative ages of victim and offender and the extent of the age gap may be a key factor (see Appendix 1), as are factors such as power and size differentials.

Evidence of targeting is a critical factor. Where there is evidence of targeting of children and there is a history of repeat offences, then exemption should be discounted.

Conclusions and recommendations

In some respects we have taken one step forward through the local initiatives that responded to the Department of Health introduction of this group into the child protection system in 1991, yet have been forced to take two steps back due to the worrying lack of inter-governmental consultation and guidance issued recently. This has set us back considerably and unless we are careful and collate our responses to avoid the unnecessary duplication of tasks as evidenced in the last decade (Calder and Horwath, 1999), the focus of our work will be on procedure rather than work with the young people themselves.

We should try and move away from categorising someone as generally being high, medium, or low risk, as this is principally labelling for the purposes of worker self-protection rather than being a valuable aid to worker intervention. If we label someone high-risk then we are covered if they re-offend. If we label them low-risk and they re-offend then the workers may be held responsible for this. It is more helpful to try and identify broad risk bands but which split this down into a context. For example, offence characteristics, their history or background, behavioural features, and attitudes, thoughts and fantasies. The focus should then be one of risk management. The development of more sophisticated risk tools should allow us to more effectively screen in and screen out cases according to the anticipated risk coupled with

the potential for change (see Print et al., 2001 for the AIM materials). Decisions then have to be reached as to whether to target the high risk group where the outcomes may be average or poor or target the middle group where the risk might not be so acute but where the projected outcomes are probably significantly better. That choice is probably being made for us by the public and the politicians: who want certainty in controlling the young person exhibiting sexually abusive behaviour.

Appendix 1: Assessment Practice Guidelines for Assessors

Introduction

The purpose of these guidelines is to provide a frame of reference and structure for decision making; for assessors undertaking an assessment with young people aged 10 to 18 years who have displayed sexually abusive behaviour.

The model adopts a partnership approach and incorporates the concepts of the Department of Health Framework for Assessment and the ASSET frameworks as employed by the Youth Offending Teams. As such it attempts to use language and terminology that is not specific to a particular discipline. It is also intended to be useable within the timescales operated by the criminal justice and child protection systems.

It is designed to assist all professionals in opening a dialogue between the assessors, the young person and their family. It can provide an opportunity to engage the young person and their family with the necessary issues, identify need, motivate change and it is key to the planning of services that will best ensure the young persons future safe behaviour. It is the first stage in gathering and analysing information. It is not so self contained as to suggest that you have 'done it all'. It can be a means opening other doors if required, to appropriate further assessments and interventions.

The model recognises that family dynamics and responses to the abuse are key in the assessment as the family and carers will play an integral role or not, in supporting the young person through assessment and treatment. Indeed, it may be inappropriate for the young person to remain within their family and the assessment may indicate an alternative placement is required. This may be because the young person is a risk to other children within the family or because the young person themselves is considered to be at risk if they remain in their family.

In assessing the distinction between behaviour that is experimental in nature and behaviour that is abusive the notions of consent, power, equality and authority need to be ever present in the assessors thinking.

Ultimately, the model does not make decisions for assessors but can support decision-making. It is drawn on current evidence, understanding and thinking which will inform and influence good practice.

Four domains of the assessment model (Print et al., 2001)

The model is based on four domains of assessment.

The questions presented are not exhaustive or to be used as a checklist. They are suggested guidelines for gathering the necessary information that needs to be collated and understood by the assessors in order to inform the assessment model's continuum indicators of strengths and concerns, which will in turn inform where the young person should be placed in the matrix.

In writing your findings into a report it is suggested that the headings below be used to organise your thinking and analysis. They should be preceded by the young person's personal details and concluded with a summary and recommendation section.

1. Offence specific

- *Offending History*
  Has the young person committed previous offences (sexual or non-sexual)? If yes, did this result in a conviction, caution, reprimand or final warning?
- *Nature of the Sexual Offence*
  Was the offence an isolated incident or part of a series of offending?
  Did the behaviour escalate over time?
  Did the offence involve penetration?
  Was the offence of an experimental or peer influenced nature?
- *Attitude to Victim*
  Did the young person know their victim?
  Does the young person show any feelings or remorse or guilt?
  Does the young person accept any responsibility for the offence?

- *Offence Planning*
  Did the offence involve detailed and careful planning?
  Did the young person prepare (groom) the victims over time?
  Did the young person have persistent thoughts about the offence before it occurred?
- *Violence*
  Has the young person a history of violence or aggressive behaviours?
  Did the offence involve violence or sadistic behaviours?
- *Previous Professional Involvement*
  Has the young person received help for previous sexual behaviour in the past?
  If Yes:
  —What were the outcomes of previous assessments or treatment?
  —Did the young person complete or drop out of treatment?
  —If they dropped out of treatment, at what stage and for what reason?
- *Motivation to Engage with Professionals*
  Does the young person consider that they have a problem?
  Is the young person worried that the problem may impact on their future?
  Does the young person believe that they might benefit from professional intervention?
  Is the young person willing to accept professional help?
  Does the young person have a history of absconding, failing appointments or non-compliance?

2. Development

- *Resilience Factors*
  How isolated or sociable is the young person?
  Does the young person have personal goals and ambitions?
  Is the young person involved in social activities and hobbies?
  Can the young person express their feelings adequately?
  Does the young person communicate reasonably?
  Does the young person have positive reports from school or employers?
  Is the young person able to understand the possible consequences of their behaviour?
- *Health Issues*
  Does the young person have any history of serious physical ill-health?

Has the young person ever suffered depression or any other form of mental ill-health?

Have they ever been diagnosed as suffering a psychiatric illness?

Does the young person have any difficulties in concentrating, learning or communication?

- *Experienced Physical, Sexual or Emotional Abuse or Neglect*

Has the young person been subjected to any form of abuse?

If Yes:

—What was the nature of this abuse?

—How long did it continue?

—Who perpetrated the abuse?

—How old was the young person when the abuse began?

—What impact did the abuse appear to have on the young person?

—Has the young person suffered abuse due to racial, cultural, religious reasons or because of a disability?

- *Witnessed Domestic Violence*

If the young person has witnessed domestic violence within the home:

—Who was involved?

—What was the nature of the violence?

—How long did it continue for?

—How frequently did it occur?

—How old was the young person when the violence commenced?

—Does the violence still occur?

- *Quality of the Young Person's Early Life Experiences*

What attachments did the young person form with carers?

Has the young person experienced consistent 'good enough' care?

Has the young person experienced harsh or inconsistent care?

Has the young person been in substitute care? If so, why, when and for how long?

Has the young person experienced a supportive community environment?

- *Behaviour Problems*

Does the young person exhibit a range of problem behaviours?

What was or is the nature of the behaviours?

When did they commence or desist?

Where did they occur?

How were they dealt with?

Has the young person ever been diagnosed with a conduct order?

Does the young person exhibit impulsive or compulsive behaviour traits?

Does the young person regularly engage in substance abuse?

- *Sexuality*

Has the young person's sexual development been appropriate (including sexual education, puberty and sexual experiences)?

Is the young person confused about their sexual identity?

Does the young person have persistent thoughts about abusive sexual behaviours?

3. Family and carers

- *Level of Functioning*

Does the family function in a positive, caring manner or is it chaotic with high levels of dysfunction?

Is there a history of abuse in the family or extended family?

Can parents or carers demonstrate appropriate support for the young person?

Do the parents have a positive social network?

- *Attitudes and Beliefs*

Do parents or carers accept that the offence occurred?

Do they accept that the young person was responsible for the offence?

Do they express a degree of concern for the victim?

Do they have positive attitudes?

Do they believe that professional intervention may benefit the young person?

Do they accept they have a role to play in further intervention?

- *Sexual Boundaries*

Are parental and carers attitudes towards sexual abuse reasonable?

Do they employ appropriate boundaries in the home (e.g. regarding privacy)?

Can they communicate positively about sexual matters?

Are their attitudes towards sex and sexuality reasonable or rigid?

- *Parental Competence*

Do parents or carers generally display empathic, reasonable and responsible attitudes?

Do they display abilities in supervising and managing the family appropriately?

Do family members display feelings appropriately?

Are there additional or frequent periods of crisis or trauma in the family?

Appendix 2: Parent or Carer Consent Form

I/We the parents/carers of _____

Agree to participate in an assessment process which will address both concerns and strengths in the following areas:

Offence specific

Developmental issues

Family issues

Environmental and community issues

I/We understand that we will have access to the report and the opportunity to write an addendum addressing any areas of disagreement.

Signed _____

Signed _____

Signed _____

Witnessed _____

Dated _____

---

4. Environment

- *Opportunity for Further Offending*
  How easily will the young person gain access to the victim or other potential victims?
  Are plans for the supervision of the young person reasonable and responsible?
  Are those who will act in a supervisory capacity able to appropriately exercise this role?
  Is the young person willing to comply with supervision/management plans?
- *Community Support*
  Are those in the community who 'need to know' aware of the offence and management plans (e.g. teachers)?
  Is there support for the young person in the community (e.g. teachers, friends etc)?
  Is there support from parents in the community?
  Is the young person or family likely to be at risk of aggressive or retributive actions?

Appendix 3: Criteria for Differentiating 'Normal' from Abusive Behaviour: A Framework (Calder, 1997)

Young people

What is the age relationship between participants?

Most would agree that a five-year age difference is abusive, although it would be unwise to see this as the sole difference between normal and abusive behaviour. We would also consider issues of size, power, ability and authority in the judgement. The narrower the age difference, the more difficult it becomes to make the judgement. We have to remember that it is not always the older child who is the initiator of sexual behaviours, particularly where the child is dis-empowered in some way.

What is the social relationship? In what context did the abuse occur? Are they related?

The symbolic meaning of the sexual activity is important, particularly where it involves an abuse of power or authority. A very frequent scenario for sexual abuse is the baby-sitting arrangement where they are abusing an assumed authority and position of trust. We need to assess what part power differences play in the activity or generally in the relationship – are they bigger? Stronger? More assertive? Where difference exists, abuse should be considered. We then need to consider what purpose the behaviour serves for the abuser. Where no power difference is evident, the context should be considered.

What type of sexual behaviour is exhibited?

Is it consistent with the juvenile's intellectual, emotional and social functioning? Are these developmental levels below chronological age? If they are, we need to consider what part the sexual behaviour is as a function of any immaturity. We also need to consider what other functions the behaviour may serve e.g. anxiety reduction. Does the incident involve acts which have sexual implications through physical assaults involving sexual parts of the body, or the use of sexual language, which is offensive or which make explicit sexual suggestions? Is the behaviour age-appropriate? How sophisticated is the activity? Was the behaviour planned or spontaneous? Is there any aspect of victimisation in the behaviour? Are they imitating something they have seen? What is the purpose of the behaviour? Have they been confronted about their behaviour in the past? How often, and for how long did the activity happen?

What is the experience of the victim?

Do they see them as abusive? Do they blame themselves? Are they able to consent in the activity even if they have expressed no concerns? How did the victim feel about what happened? What was the victim's contribution to what happened? Have there been any attempts to secure secrecy by any of the individuals involved? Why?

How does sexual contact take place?

There needs to be an assessment of whether the sexual contact has occurred by mutual agreement, deception, enticement, intimidation, threat, physical force or violence. All sexual activity that is not based on mutuality, reciprocity and consent is considered abusive.

How was the sexual activity revealed?

Was it discovered taking place in an appropriate place? Or in public? Did the victim disclose with the hope they would be helped? Is there an indication that they are feeling uncomfortable about what happened? Abusers rarely self-disclose.

How persistent is the sexual behaviour?

Repetitive inappropriate behaviour may indicate a preoccupation with sexually abusive activity, and may imply the development of abusive sexual preferences. How often and how long has the behaviour been occurring? What preceded the behaviour? Whilst one incident may be abusive, the more frequent or persistent the activity, the more there should be concern that it is inappropriate.

Evidence of escalation

Is there any evidence of escalation in the nature or frequency of sexual behaviour under consideration? Has the pattern of activity changed over time? e.g. the victims are getting younger. A changing pattern of behaviour can indicate that the young person is developing a pattern to the behaviour. Has there been any escalation in the use of actual or threatened physical force or violence? Are there any discernible patterns in the type of behaviour or choice of victims? Is the behaviour ritualistic in nature?

Sexual fantasies

What is the nature of the sexual fantasies that precede, accompany or follow the sexual behaviour? These may indicate problems with sexual identity and preferences, or highlight inappropriate sexual interests, for example in children. Those who fantasise about these scenarios may be more likely to enact these in abusive situations. Fantasies can indicate the way in which the abuser views themselves, sex and sexual behaviour.

What are the characteristics of the victims?

These may include: age, sex and social relationship to the abuser, some sort of physical or intellectual handicap or some other form of vulnerability. Discernible preferences for particular victims may indicate developing sexual interests, motives, underlying the sexual behaviour, or reflect the abuser's own experiences of abuse. They may also target particular geographical areas to find victims.

Children

Sexual activity compared to developmental level

Concerns exist where the sexual activity exceeds the developmental level of the child, e.g. oral sex is beyond the behaviours expected from children under five years, whilst anal and vaginal penetration in children aged 6–10 years suggests a sexual behaviour problem. Any child aged 10–12 years, who engages in sex play with much younger children, or who forces someone to engage in sex, has a sexual behaviour problem. Children tend to obtain sexual information progressively; firstly, interest in themselves, followed by an interest in experimentation with others. This may be accelerated by explicit sexual information from family or peers, pictures or videos, observation of sexual activity between parents or among siblings or others, and direct sexual experiences. We clearly need to look at the kind of presenting sexual behaviour alongside the age of the child, before considering the family context, how or where the behaviour has been learned, and possible access to sexually explicit material.

Inappropriate sexual behaviour may not always involve other children: persistent masturbation (particularly in public), excessive sexual interest in sexual matters, a sexualisation of non-sexual situations and a sexualised content in their play, art or conversation indicates the need for a fuller assessment. Where other children are involved, we also need to ask ourselves whether the behaviour of the other participants is commensurate with their developmental level.

Relative power of children

If one child participating in a sexual activity has more power than another, it is more likely that the sexual behaviour is a problem. This is sometimes referred to as social coercion and reflects the power imbalances. Power can be measured along several dimensions:

- **Age difference**: where it is greater than two years the situation warrants further investigation. The younger the child the more questionable it is for them to give informed consent. We clearly need to differentiate consent from compliance to acquiescence.
- **Size difference**: is crucial where two children of similar ages are engaged in sexual play, as issues of power, dominance or the misuse of authority need to be considered, and
- **Difference in status**: needs to be considered, particularly where one child is acting as a baby-sitter or temporary caretaker, and has more authority which compromises the other child's ability to make choices, even where no threat or force is used. Any child with higher status or authority can use the

inequality to coerce co-operation in another child. Even where two children appear to be about the same size and age, they do not necessarily share equal power, as there may be an inequality in their developmental sophistication. The workers need to be clear about the relative power positions of the participants, e.g. It is an obvious or a less obvious power imbalance, or were they peers where one child was taken by surprise and thus placed at a disadvantage? Or where one is always 'the leader' and the other is always 'the follower'? If one child has a severe learning disability and another has not, a clear difference in power exists.

Complaint status

Where a complaint of sexual abuse has been made either by the victim or someone acting on their behalf, we can assume that someone has already objected to sexual behaviour initiated by a child and deemed it questionable, inappropriate, or abusive.

Behavioural indicators of sexual abuse

The presence of any behavioural indicators in either of the child participants may be significant as it will help add weight to the diagnosis, although it clearly should never be considered in isolation.

Coercive sexual behaviours

This involves intimidation, force, trickery or bribes, and may involve the use of a weapon or threat of a weapon to obtain submission. We clearly need to establish whether the presenting behaviour involved any of these features. If it did, there is a problem requiring further assessment. What did the victim believe would be the result of non-compliance with the sexual behaviour?

Compulsive or obsessive behaviours

Features of either compulsive (seeing as if the child cannot control it) or obsessive (something the child thinks about continually) behaviour are indicative of some kind of sexual behaviour problem, and a further assessment is indicated.

Ritualistic and sadistic behaviours

Any element of bondage, sacrifice, torture or other sadomasochistic elements within the sexual behaviour is an indicator that something is wrong.

Secrecy

The workers need to assess whether the sexual behaviour was initiated openly or furtively, with concerns about discovery or disregard for being detected, and whether the participants were bribed or threatened? There is a need to distinguish a child's natural sense of privacy or embarrassment about sexual feelings from the secrecy that allows abusive sexuality to continue.

Appendix 4: AIM Matrix Guidance: Using the Model (Print et al., 2001)

(a) Using the concern continuum, Fig. 1

Any factors that apply to the abusive behaviour, the young person, their family or environment should be checked on the continuum and the number of factors in each column calculated. If items 1, 2 or 3 in the high concern column (A) are identified then the young person should be considered high concern regardless of other items that are checked.

If two or more items in medium concern column (B) are identified then the total for the high concern column should be increased by one. Similarly if more than three items in the medium column (C) are identified then the total of the high concern column should be further increased by one.

Once the above adjustments have been made, consideration is given to whether the young person's overall scores fall predominantly in the high or low concern columns.

(b) Using the strength continuum, Fig. 2

Any relevant information gained from all sources regarding the young person should be marked on the continuum.

If two or more items in medium strength column (B) are identified then the total for the high strength column should be increased by one.

Once the above adjustments have been made the total number of factors in the high and low columns are plotted on the outcome grid below and the quadrant into which most of the factors fall is identified.

(c) The outcome matrix, Fig. 3

The following matrix provides an indication of the needs the young person and the type of further interventions that may be helpful. The matrix acts as the second stage of analysis in which the picture gained by use of the continuums is further refined by using the outcome matrix to consider case management options. The text in italics in the grid identifies the most likely recommendation for those involved in the criminal justice system, although each case should be viewed individually and recommendation made primarily on the basis of the needs of the individual, known victims and community safety.

Figure 1: Continuum of indicators of concerns. (© Print et al., 2001)

High concerns A	Medium concerns B	C	Low concerns D
1. *Young person has previous convictions for sexual offences or evidence of previous sexual offending	1. Young person has been suspected of previous sexual assaults	1. Young person has poor capacity for empathy	1. First known assault or one off assault
2. *Formal diagnosis of Conduct Disorder or a history of interpersonal aggression	2. Early onset of severe behavioural problems	2. Young person denies responsibility for assault	2. Non-penetrative (including attempts) assault
3. *Very poor social skills or deficits in intimacy skills	3. Young person diagnosed with ADHD	3. Has difficulties in coping with negative feelings	3. No history of significant trauma or abuse
4. *Use of violence or threats of violence during assault	4. Cold callous attitude in commission of assault	4. Has poor sexual boundaries	4. Demonstrates remorse or empathy
5. *Self-reported sexual interest in children	5. Young person diagnosed with depression or other significant mental health problems	5. Parents express anger or no empathic concern towards victim	5. Assault appears to be experimental or peer influenced
6. *Young person blames victim	6. Young person has significant distorted thoughts about sexual behaviours	6. High level of parental, carer and family denial	6. No significant history of non-sexual assaults
7. Persistently threatens to commit abusive acts	7. Obsessive pre-occupation with sexual thoughts or pornography	7. Social group is predominantly pro-criminal	7. Healthy peer relationships
8. Has persistent aggressive or sadistic sexual thoughts about others	8. Copes with negative emotions by use of sexual thoughts, behaviours or use of pornography or graffiti	8. Family members include Schedule 1 offenders	8. No documented school problems
9. Has history of cruelty towards animals	9. Targets specific victims because of perceived vulnerability		9. No history of behavioural or emotional problems
10. Little concern about being caught	10. *Pattern of discontinuity of care or poor attachments		
11. *High levels of trauma e.g. physical, emotional, sexual abuse, neglect or witnessing domestic violence	11. Unsupervised access to potential victims		
12. *High levels of family dysfunction or abusive or harsh child rearing regime	12. Young person regularly engaged in significant substance abuse		
13. *Evidence of detailed planning			
14. *Early drop out from treatment programme			
15. *Highly compulsive or impulsive behaviours			

Note: Those items marked with * are research informed indicators of risk. Those without such mark are based on a consensus of clinical judgments.

Figure 2: Continuum of indicators of strengths. (© Print et al., 2001)

High strengths A	Medium strengths B	Low strengths (High need) C
1. Young person has ability to reflect and understand consequences of offence behaviour	1. Young person has at least one parent or carer who supports and is able to supervise	1. Young person appears to not care what happens
2. Young person is willing to engage in treatment to address abusive behaviour	2. Young person demonstrates remorse for offence (even if not accepting responsibility)	2. Young person has poor communication skills
3. Young person has positive plans or goals	3. Parents carers are healthy and there is no other family trauma or crisis	3. Young person has no support or is rejected by parents or carers
4. Young person has positive talents and interests	4. Parents demonstrate responsible attitudes and skills in family management	4. Young person has been excluded from school or is unemployed
5. Young person has good problem solving and negotiation skills	5. Parents carers have no history of own abuse or abusive experiences are resolved	5. Isolated family
6. Young person has at least one emotional confidant	6. Family has positive social network	6. Absence of supportive structured living environment
7. Young person has positive relationships with school or employers	7. Community is neutral towards young person and their family	7. Parents or carers unable to supervise
8. Young person has experienced consistent positive care		8. Family is enmeshed in unhealthy social network
9. Parents demonstrate good protective attitudes and behaviours		9. Family has high levels of stress
10. Family has clear, positive boundaries in place		10. History of unresolved significant abuse in family
11. Family demonstrate good communications		11. Family refuses to engage with professionals
12. Family demonstrate ability to positively process emotional issues		12. Domestic violence in family
13. Family is positive about receiving help		13. Community is hostile towards young person and their family
14. Young person lives in supportive environment		
15. Network of support and supervision available to young person		

Figure 3: The outcome matrix. (© Print et al., 2001)

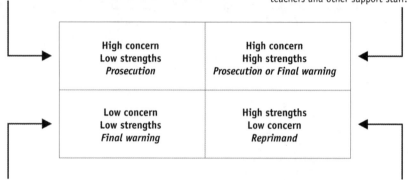

These young people are likely to need a more detailed specialist, comprehensive assessment

Individuals in this category are likely to include the most worrying of young people. They are likely to have significant needs across a range of areas. They are likely to need high levels of specialist intensive treatment and high needs for management and supervision.

Young people in this category may have high levels of need but may be managed safely in the community. They may require placement away from home. Their needs are likely to require the involvement of a range of disciplines, including specialist workers, carers, family workers, teachers and other support staff.

High concern **Low strengths** *Prosecution*	**High concern** **High strengths** *Prosecution or Final warning*
Low concern **Low strengths** *Final warning*	**High strengths** **Low concern** *Reprimand*

Young people in this category are likely to require help in meeting a range of needs and may require a full needs-led assessment. Intervention may include involvement in a brief programme of education regarding healthy sexual behaviours. Parents or carers are likely to require support. Emphasis may need to be placed on increasing resilience factors, family work and family support.

Young people in this category may require limited intervention. They can usually remain at home and parents or carers are often the best people to help the young person with any information, advice or behavioural change required. Parents may need professional support and information. Review after three months.

Appendix 5: Service User Risk Assessment

Name	Risk assessor
Address	Date
DOB	Review date
SOSCIS no	Manager

(1) The perceived or known risks the service user presents to third parties

(2) The perceived or known risks the service user presents to themselves

(3) Any perceived or known risks to the service user or provider from the environment they are placed in

(4) How will the perceived or known risks be managed?

Appendix 6: Review of Schedule One Status

Name of young person   DOB:

Home address

Current address

Family Composition

Details of the alleged abuse with conviction and sentence details

Details of the victims including names, dates of birth and address

Details of any previous relevant convictions

Recommendation from YOT Manager on Schedule One Status (should include detailed reasons for the recommendation)

SIGNED: _____   DATE: _____

References

Becker, J. V., Johnson, B. R. and Hunter, J. A. (1996) Adolescent Sex Offenders. in Hollin, C. R. and Howells, K. (Eds.) Clinical Approaches to Working With Young Offenders. Chichester: John Wiley, 183–95.

Brown, A. (1998) The Sex Offenders Act Part 1: Issues Relating to Adolescents Convicted of a Sexual Offence. *NOTA News*. 27: 21–7.

Calder, M. C. (1997) *Juveniles and Children Who Sexually Abuse: A Guide to Risk Assessment*. Dorset: Russell House Publishing.

Calder, M. C. (1997b) Young People Who Sexually Abuse: Towards International Consensus. *Social Work in Europe* 4:1 36–9.

Calder, M. C. (1998) *Young People Who Sexually Abuse: Assessment and Practice Guidance*. Salford: Salford ACPC.

Calder, M. C. (1999) A Conceptual Framework for Managing Young People Who Sexually Abuse: Towards a Consortium Approach. in Calder, M. C. (Ed.) *Working With Young People Who Sexually Abuse: New Pieces of the Jigsaw Puzzle*. Dorset: Russell House Publishing, 117–59.

Calder, M. C. (1999b) Young People Who Sexually Abuse: A Framework for Initial Assessment. *Child Care in Practice*. 5:3 262–80.

Calder, M. C. (2000) *The Complete Guide to Sexual Abuse Assessments*. Dorset: Russell House Publishing.

Calder, M. C. (2000b) The Evolving Management Of Young People Who Sexually Abuse: Towards Critical And Evidence Based Practice. Keynote presentation to a national conference 'Working with adolescent sex offenders: towards a therapeutic approach within a judicial context', Ort House, London, 6th Nov.

Calder, M. C. (2000c) Young People Who Sexually Abuse: A Framework for Assessment. Workshop presented at the Millennium BASPCAN Congress, 'Meeting children's needs: The opportunity for change in child protection, University of York, 17–20 Sep.

Calder, M. C. (2001) *Juveniles and Children Who Sexually Abuse: Frameworks for Assessment*. (2nd edn). Dorset: Russell House Publishing.

Calder, M. C. (forthcoming) The Assessment Framework: A Critique and Reformulation. in Calder, M. C. and Hackett, S. (Eds.) *Assessments in Child Care: A Comprehensive Guide to Frameworks and Their Use*. Dorset: Russell House Publishing.

Calder, M. C. (in press) A Framework for Conducting Risk Assessments. *Child Care In Practice*.

Calder. M. C. and Horwath. J. (1999) Policies and Procedures: Developing a Framework for Working Together. in Calder, M. C. and Horwath, J. (Eds.) *Working for Children on the Child Protection Register: An Inter-agency Practice Guide*. Aldershot: Arena. 45–80.

Calder, M. C., Peake A and Rose K (2001) *Mothers of Sexually Abused Children: A Framework for Assessment. Understanding and Support*. Dorset: Russell House Publishing.

Carson, D. (1994) Dangerous People: Through a Broader Concept of 'Risk' and 'Danger' to Better Decisions. *Expert Evidence*. 3:2 21–69.

Connolly, M. and Wolf, S. C. (1995) Services for Juvenile Sex Offenders: Issues in Establishing Programs. *Australian Social Work*. 48:3 3–10.

DoH. (1988) *Protecting Children: A Guide for Social Workers Undertaking a Comprehensive Assessment*. London: HMSO.

DoH. (1991) *Working Together Under The Children Act 1989: A Guide to Arrangements for Inter-agency Co-operation for the Protection of Children from Abuse*. London: HMSO.

DoH. (1995) *Child Protection: Messages from Research*. London: HMSO.

DoH. (1998) *Working Together to Safeguard Children: New Government Proposals for Inter-agency Co-operation*. London: HMSO.

DoH. (1999) *Working Together to Safeguard Children: A Guide to Inter-agency Working to Safeguard and Promote the Welfare of Children*. London: HMSO.

DoH. (2000) *Framework for the Assessment of Children in Need and their Familes*. London: HMSO.

Gilgun, J. F. (1999) CASPARS: Clinical Assessment Instruments that Measure Strengths and Risks in Children and Families. in Calder, M. C. (Ed.) *Working With Young People Who Sexually Abuse: New Pieces of the Jigsaw Puzzle*. Dorset: Russell house Publishing. 49–58.

Hampson, A. (1999) The Management of Sex Offenders in the Community. in Calder, M. C. *Assessing Risk in Adult Males Who Sexually Abuse Children: A Practitioner's Guide*. Dorset: Russell House Publishing.

Hanson, R. K. (1998) *Using Research to Improve Sex Offender Risk Assessment*. Keynote presentation to the NOTA National Conference, University of Glasgow, Sep.

Hanson, R. K. (1999) Sex Offender Risk Assessment. in Hollin, C. R. (Ed.) *Handbook of Offender Assessment and Treatment.* Chichester: John Wiley and Sons Ltd.

Hanson, R. K. and Bussiere, M. T. (1998) Predicting Relapse: A Meta-analysis of Sexual Offender Recidivism Studies. *Journal of Consulting and Clinical Psychology.* 66:2 348–62.

Hanson, R. K. and Harris, A. (1998) *Dynamic Predictors of Sexual Recidivism.* Ottawa: Department of the Solicitor General of Canada.

Hanson, R. K. and Harris, A. (2000) *The Sex Offender Need Assessment Rating (SONAR): A Method for Measuring Change in Risk Levels.* Ottawa: Department of the Solicitor General of Canada.

Hanson, R. K. and Harris, A. (2000b) Where Should we Intervene? Dynamic Predictors of Sexual Abuse Recidivism. *Criminal Justice and Behaviour.* 27:1 6–35.

Hanson, R. K. and Thornton, D. (1999) *Static 99: Improving Actuarial Risk Assessments for Sex Offenders.* Ottawa: Department of the Solicitor General of Canada.

Hanson, R. K. and Thornton, D. (2000) Improving Risk Assessments for Sex Offenders: A Comparison of Three Actuarial Scales. *Law and Human Behaviour.* 24:1 119–36.

Home Office. (2000) *Setting the Boundaries: Reforming the Law on Sex Offenders.* London: Home Office.

HM Inspector of Probation. (1998) *Exercising Constant Vigilance: The Role of the Probation Service in Protecting the Public from Sex Offenders.* London: Home Office.

Marshall, W. L. and Eccles, A. (1993) Pavlovian Characteristics for Classifying Juvenile Sex Offenders. in Barbaree, H. E., Marshall, W. L. and Hudson, S. M. (Eds.) *The Juvenile Sex Offender.* New York: Guilford Press, 118–42.

Masson, H. (1995) Children and Adolescents Who Sexually Abuse Other Children: Responses to an Emerging Problem. *Journal of Social Welfare and Family Law.* 17:3 325–36.

Masson, H. (1996) *Children and Young People Who Sexually Abuse Other Children: An Emerging Problem.* School of Human and Health Services: University of Huddersfield.

NACRO. (1999) *Young People Who Commit Schedule One Offences.* Briefing paper. Feb. London: NACRO.

National Children's Homes. (1992) *Report of the Committee of Enquiry into Children and Young People Who Sexually Abuse Other Children.* London: NCH.

Prentky, R., Harris, A., Frizzell, K. and Righthand, R. (2000) An Actuarial Procedure for Assessing Risk With Juvenile Sex Offenders. *Sexual Abuse: A Journal of Research and Treatment.* 12:2 71–93.

Print, B. and Erooga, M. (2000) Young People Who Sexually Abuse: Implications for Assessment. in Horwath, J. (Ed.) *The Child's World: Assessing Children in Need.* Reader. London: NSPCC, 249–61.

Print, B., Morrison, T. and Henniker, J. (2001) An inter-agency assessment framework for young people who sexually abuse: Principles, processes and practicalities. In Calder, M. C. *Juveniles and Children Who Sexually Abuse: Frameworks for Assessment* (2nd edition). Lyme Regis, Dorset: Russell House Publishing, 271–81.

Quinsey, V. L., Rice, M. E. and Harris, G. T. (1995) Actuarial Prediction of Sexual Recidivism. *Journal of Interpersonal Violence.* 10:1 85–105.

Sanders, R. and Ladwa-Thomas, U. (1997) Interagency Perspectives on Child Sexual Abuse Perpetrated by Juveniles. *Child Maltreatment.* 2:3 264–71.

Schwartz, I. M., Guo, S. and Kerbs, J. J. (1993) The Impact Of Demographic Variables On Public Opinion Regarding Juvenile Justice. *Crime and Delinquency.* 39: 5–28.

Weinrott, M. R. (1996) *Juvenile Sexual Aggression: A Critical Review.* Colorado: Institute of Behavioural Science.

Worling, J. R. and Curwen, T. (2001) *The 'ERASOR': Estimate of Risk of Adolescent Sexual Offence Recidivism.* Ontario: SAFE-T Program. This also appears in Calder, M. C. (2001) *Juveniles and Children Who Sexually Abuse: Frameworks for Assessment.* (2nd edition). Dorset: Russell House Publishing.

Chapter 20: Forensic Foster Care for Young People Who Sexually Abuse: Lessons from Treatment

James Yokley and Sarah Boettner

Introduction

The present chapter reviews lessons learned from seven years of treatment at the Treatment for Appropriate Social Control (TASC) Forensic Foster Care programme for youth with a history of sexually abusive behaviour. Programme development, treatment issues, foster parent selection and foster parent retention are discussed. This mode of treatment provides another level in the continuum of care where youth abusers can progress through a step down treatment supervision process, from residential to forensic foster care and finally into the traditional outpatient setting during family reunification or an independent living placement.

What is forensic foster care?

Forensic medicine applies medical knowledge to legal problems. Forensic Foster Care applies treatment knowledge to foster youth whose externalising, abusive behaviour can or has resulted in legal problems. Forensic Foster Care offers a less restrictive environment than residential treatment for youth abusers who are not candidates to complete treatment in the outpatient setting due to problems with placement in their family of origin. Forensic Foster Care offers another level in the continuum of care between residential and outpatient treatment for youth abusers whose behaviour management needs require gradual re-entry back into the community under supervised conditions. In addition, there is some evidence that Forensic Foster Care offers a functional family treatment setting that is most conducive to helping youth with a history of abusive, delinquent behaviour. For example, incarcerated boys who were randomly assigned to a forensic foster care programme designed to address that population (referred to as Multidimensional Treatment Foster Care) had significantly fewer criminal referrals and returned to live with relatives more often than those who received group home care (Chamberlain and Reid, 1998). In contrast to traditional therapeutic foster care where treatment is typically conducted by mental health professionals during weekly community mental health centre visits, TASC forensic foster parents are an integral part of a multidisciplinary treatment team of abuse specialists that implement a therapeutic community treatment approach throughout the week. TASC Forensic Foster Care utilises Social Responsibility Therapy in a cluster placement model to teach youth pro-social skills and values that compete with antisocial abusive behaviour.

Who are These People? Demographic Characteristics of Foster Youth in General and of Those Who Sexually Abuse

Demographic characteristics of foster care youth

One third of foster youth in the United States are between the ages of 13 and 18, the remaining two thirds are elementary school age or younger (Benton Foundation, 2000). The most prevalent intervention used in cases of identified child sexual abuse is temporary or permanent placement of children into foster homes (Cooper, Peterson, and Meier, 1987) and at least half have experienced some form of reportable child abuse (Dubner and Motta, 1999). Children in foster care exhibit consistently high rates of mental health problems (e.g., Clausen et. al., 1998). Traditional foster care like other social service systems must focus on meeting the needs of the majority of its consumers. A large proportion of these consumers are elementary school aged victims of abuse or neglect.

Demographic characteristics of sexually abusive foster youth

Economic rule 1: Since returning youth abusers to the natural home for outpatient treatment is the least expensive treatment option, all who are able, go home. Thus, abusers placed in forensic foster care have either failed multiple

Table 1: Multiple abuse behaviour in the population of youth who sexually abuse.

Study	Sexual abuse	Physical abuse	Property abuse	Substance abuse
Awad et. al., 1984	100%		44%	8%
Becker et. al., 1986	100%		41%	9%
Ferenbach et. al., 1986	100%	36% (also robbery)	38%	
Van Ness, 1984	100%	86%		52%

times in their natural home placement or have no appropriate family placement. By definition this means that they are lacking in family adjustment ability and are in need of a treatment that teaches pro-social, family values if a family based placement is to be preserved.

Sexually abusive youth referred for treatment in Forensic Foster Care tend to be multiple abusers, i.e., sexual abusers who exhibit more than one type of abuse requiring treatment. Recent demographic data from the Treatment for Appropriate Social Control (TASC) Forensic Foster Care programme revealed that the average age was 16, 97 per cent were male and 72 per cent were Caucasian. The average number of different types of abuse exhibited was 4.5 and 59 per cent exhibited problems at admission with five types of abuse (i.e., sexual abuse, physical abuse, property abuse, substance abuse and trust abuse). Fifty three percent were on probation or parole (Yokley and Boettner, 1999a). This is consistent with many other youth sex abusers who are also multiple abusers (see Table 1 above).

Each type of abuse exhibited by these youth (i.e., sexual, physical, property, substance and trust) involves a maladaptive way to assert power, get what they want, meet their needs and make themselves happy, often at the expense of others. Each type of abuse also involves a pathological level of social-emotional immaturity.

Many youth who sexually abuse suffer from 'pan immaturity' in emotional/social adjustment (Fehrenbach et al., 1986; Shoor, Speed and Bartelt, 1966) and character disorder. This social-emotional immaturity and character disorder is conceptualised as 'pathological social immaturity' (Yokley, 1996). This form of developmental delay involves:

• Immature, maladaptive social maturity in the form of a pro-social values deficit (e.g., a lack of honesty, trust, loyalty, concern and

responsibility) that impairs the ability to develop positive, healthy relationships.
• Immature, maladaptive emotional maturity manifest as:
—Inadequately developed self-control (e.g., a lack of appropriate social behaviour control, emotional control problems including low frustration tolerance, an emotional awareness deficit and 'justifying actions based on feelings').
—Maladaptive self-image and needs (e.g., low self-efficacy, a Control and Power Obsession, a sick need for acceptance, a sick need for excitement or sensation seeking, authority problem and criminal pride for 'getting over' on others, winning by intimidation or other opportunistic exploitation that demonstrates a lack of empathy).

What to expect: behaviour norms for foster youth who sexually abuse – 'the few, the proud, the resistant'

Behaviour norm research on youth referred for sex abuser treatment in forensic foster care (Yokley and Boettner, 1999a) has revealed that it is not unusual for these multiple abuser youth to receive about six behaviour incident reports per month fairly equally divided between problems in the home (45 per cent) and community. An evaluation of TASC Forensic Foster Care programme incident reports revealed that on the average a problem in the area of oppositional immaturity can be expected for each youth every week while an episode of more serious conduct problem acting out occurs about every other week. Despite the fact that the sexual abuse incident reports included a broad encompassing range of behaviours related to that problem, staff ratings indicate that the most frequent problem behaviour is in the area of trust abuse (e.g., lying, deceiving). The second most frequent behaviour problem was in the area of property abuse (i.e., stealing and borrowing without permission). On average, youth violate their programme rules about once a week and their probation/parole or legal statutes about once a month. The vast majority of behaviour incidents related to social maturity problems are in the areas of responsibility (44 per cent) and concern (20 per cent). Although not as frequent as the problem behaviours, pro-social behaviour accomplishment awards can be expected once per month during active treatment. There was a significant treatment completion difference in mean number of incident reports per quarter. Specifically, multiple abuser youth that completed treatment had an average of nine behaviour incident reports per quarter compared to 20 incident reports for those who did not complete treatment. Preparing forensic foster parents for what to expect in terms of these ongoing externalising behaviours is considered to be an important stress inoculation procedure.

What about treatment? 'No violence, no threats of violence and stay in your seat at all times'

Given the nature of the treatment population, effective Forensic Foster Care requires a treatment approach that addresses the pathological social-emotional immaturity thought to support multiple types of abusive behaviour while preserving placement in the foster family setting by teaching pro-social, family values. The treatment selected needs to be easily integrated into ongoing foster care with techniques that can be administered by foster parents who have the maximum contact and opportunity to implement behaviour change procedures. The treatment applied needs to be accepted and thus should be consistent with existing parent intervention skills and foster family values. The treatment approach employed needs to use effective behaviour change tools that can be implemented by foster parents with specialised training but that do not require a mental health professional license for foster parents to administer.

Social Responsibility Therapy is used in the Forensic Foster Care of multiple abuser youth referred for sexual abuse treatment as it addresses the aforementioned treatment needs. Social Responsibility Therapy targets five basic types of abusive behaviour (i.e., sexual abuse,

physical abuse, property abuse, substance abuse and trust abuse). A primary goal of this treatment approach is to block abuse by teaching pro-social alternatives to antisocial, abusive behaviour. Another important goal of Social Responsibility Therapy is to help the youth and their foster parents understand The Abuse Development Triad to aid the youth in relapse prevention. This model helps explain how the abuse behaviour was acquired, what maintained it and how it generalised into other problem areas (Yokley, 1995). A brief case example illustrating The Abuse Behaviour Triad is provided in Appendix A. A third important goal of Social Responsibility Therapy is to demonstrate social responsibility through emotional restitution to abuse victims and their families (e.g., Yokley, 1990). Thus far in the TASC Forensic Foster Care programme the use of Social Responsibility Therapy has eliminated the need for seclusion and restraint through ongoing proactive intervention that relieves stress build-up.

Social Responsibility Therapy utilises a therapeutic community approach that teaches cross-cultural values and integrates professional and paraprofessional staff making foster parents equal partners with psychologists, counsellors and social workers in the treatment process. The therapeutic community social learning experiences used in Social Responsibility Therapy foster pro-social behaviours, decrease abusive behaviours in multiple abuser youth and can be effectively implemented by forensic foster parents (Yokley, 1999a, 1999b). Although originally developed for multiple abusers referred for substance abuse treatment, therapeutic community learning experiences have been demonstrated to be effective with multiple abusers referred for youth sex abuser treatment (Yokley, 1999a). These learning experiences help get the abuser in touch with the feelings of others, provide role reversal experiences and develop emotional expression responding which satisfies the three-component model of empathy (Feshbach and Feshbach, 1982). This is critical to the treatment goal of making genuine emotional restitution to victims in the Victim Responsibility Training portion of Social Responsibility Therapy (Yokley, 1990; Yokley and McGuire, 1990; 1991). A brief case example illustrating emotional restitution to victims during Victim Responsibility Training is provided in Appendix B.

Treatment truth in advertising: the labelling issue

Multiple abuse behaviour treatment in Social Responsibility Therapy has a number of advantages for youth who have been sexually abusive. In addition to targeting other forms of abuse that can cause adverse impact on the community, result in re-arrest or trigger sex offence relapse, multiple abuser treatment buffers the potentially damaging effects of labelling. While not as much of an issue for adults, recent labelling concerns for 'youth sex offenders' have already resulted in changes for the youngest of this population. To avoid unnecessary labelling or stigmatising of young children, at least one author now refers to 'preteen sex offenders' as 'abuse reactive children' (Cunningham and MacFarlane, 1996). Offering treatment to 'multiple abuser youth' recognises that the referral type of abuse may not be the only type of abuse and does not label youth with a specific abuse behaviour pattern, which they may not retain in their later adult years.

Treatment Programme Issues with Multiple Abuser Youth

Forensic foster care programme development

The first programme development task is to locate and implement a treatment approach that addresses the needs of the treatment programme population. Existing client-centred, support focused therapeutic foster parent training does not adequately address the serious externalising problems of multiple abuser youth. Thus, the first order of business for an effective Forensic Foster Care programme is to incorporate behavioural interventions and learning experiences designed to address the externalising abuser population. While there are a number of good cognitive-behavioural treatment approaches for abusive behaviour, the therapeutic community approach is a well established method that integrates paraprofessional and professional staff in an abuse treatment setting where accountability is programme wide and everyone is responsible, i.e., 'You are your brothers keeper'. In this approach, interventions are built directly into foster parenting to increase the impact by providing treatment intervention 24 hours a day, 7 days a week. This is easily done in foster parent training sessions. A detailed discussion

of this approach in provided in Yokley (1999a; 1999b).

Secondly, from a practical standpoint it is important to remember that 'The best behaviour intervention is one that all the staff will use'. All of the behavioural interventions that are developed and implemented must be as inconvenient on the youth as possible and as convenient on the staff and foster parents as possible. If this is not the case, the interventions are not likely to be implemented consistently. Inconsistency is extremely dangerous because it sets up a variable ratio reinforcement schedule, which is most resistant to behaviour extinction. This is particularly important in Forensic Foster Care where treatment is continuous through constant foster parent contact.

A third important programme development point is to implement a behaviour monitoring system that will allow objective progress reporting on periodic reviews to referral sources. The TASC Forensic Foster Care programme has established a computer-assisted behaviour tracking system that allows an objective treatment plan review based on behaviour incident reports.

Behaviour norms for treatment intervention decisions were constructed based on 2110 behaviour reports in the TASC computer database. The results of this computer-assisted behaviour tracking provide objective data for comparison to past progress and support for treatment plan review decisions. In addition to providing an overall number of incident reports per quarter, this system generates behaviour data on the type of abuse, severity, social maturity problem, area where the incidents primarily occur and intervention impact. An excerpt of this computer-assisted progress report is provided on Table 2 (overleaf).

Effective supervision: the therapists best liability insurance

Social Responsibility Therapy includes twelve basic home safeguards and twelve basic community safety procedures that involve innovative uses of available communication, behaviour tracking and monitoring technology. Since people do not consistently follow plans they do not agree with, the first safeguard procedure for both the home and community is to get everyone involved to agree on the supervision plans and procedures. Lack of agreement on the supervision plan enables the

Table 2: Excerpt from a progress report on Greg (Incident report section).

Individual Service Plan Summary: Second Quarter

Behaviour Report Summary. Total number of incident reports in past 90 days=33

Number of learning experiences or behaviour consequences that had to be increased in order to contain problem behaviour: None.

Summary of learning experience benefit: The majority (45%) of behaviour reports indicated a very strong level of benefit from the learning experience.

Location or environment where the majority of behaviour problems occurred: 25 (76%) of the behaviour incidents occurred in the community.

Behaviour Incident Report Breakdown

Type of Abuse		Problem Severity		Problem Area	
Sexual	0	Program rule violation	19	Honesty	0
Physical	0	Probation or Parole violation	7	Trust	3*
Property	0	Legal violation	7	Loyalty	7
Substance	7			Concern	5
Trust/verbal	26			Responsibility	18

*=Decrease from previous 90 day review.

Incident Report Summary:

- The majority (79% n= 26) of behaviour incidents were in the area of problems with trust or verbal behaviour control.
- The average behaviour incident severity level was 1.6 (1= low; 2= moderate; 3= high).
- The majority (58% n= 19) of behaviour incidents were program rule violations.
- The majority (55% n= 18) of behaviour incidents related to problems with responsibility.

Epilogue: Greg went AWOL seventeen days after this report. This illustrates the practical utility of the research finding that having above 20 incident reports per quarter is a risk factor for not completing treatment (Yokley and Boettner, 1999a).

youth to sabotage supervision efforts by appealing to a team member who does not agree. Thus, all individuals involved with the youth (e.g., youth, therapist, foster parents, caseworker, parole or probation officer) must sign both the home and community behaviour contracts.

Forensic foster home safeguards include youth observation and evaluation procedures, room monitoring, direct communication links with professional staff and emergency removal procedures. Evaluation procedures include use of polygraph examination to verify victim lists, monitor compliance with safety contracts and serve as a child protective service. The TASC forensic foster care programme has found consistent increases in disclosure of abuse behaviour problems with the implementation of polygraph examinations. A summary of the basic TASC programme Forensic Foster Home safeguards is provided in Table 3. A brief case example illustrating lessons learned from

one of these procedures (i.e., random room search) is provided in Appendix C. Forensic Foster Care community safety procedures include direct communication links with community youth contacts, viable abuse cycle interruption methods and containment procedures that limit community access. A summary of the basic TASC Forensic Foster Care community safety and security procedures is provided in Table 4. A brief case example illustrating lessons learned relating to one of these procedures (i.e., community safeguards in church) is provided in Appendix D.

Crisis behaviour management

An effective abuse cycle interruption method must be selected and foster parent training implemented prior to the foster home placement of any multiple abuser youth. In addition to teaching the abuse cycle and basic relapse prevention techniques, the TASC Forensic

Table 3: Twelve basic TASC programme forensic foster home safeguards.

1. A treatment behaviour contract signed by the youth, their guardian, treatment providers and probation or parole officer which details programme rules agreed upon by all parties. The contract outlines what is expected of the youth in the home and treatment setting regarding appropriate social behaviour control (e.g., No violence, no threats of violence and stay in control at all times). This includes not abusing others (sexually, physically, verbally), self (using drugs, porno, AWOL) or treatment (through denial, negative contracts, hole punching, splitting, assignment refusal). It also includes not entering home or treatment situations that are high risk for abuse (such as unsupervised access to potential victims). Consequences for contract violation are specified and an advanced directive request by the youth to contact authorities to help contain their behaviour if they become a danger to others.

2. Incident report behaviour maintenance system. Foster parents give the youth the choice of changing their behaviour or completing an incident report on themselves. Foster parents give the incident reports to staff who administer therapeutic community learning experiences and behaviour consequences based on those reports. This achieves a balance where foster parents have control over problem behaviour but are not the target of revenge for discipline decisions.

3. Video or audio tape of abuser treatment sessions for behaviour management and youth, foster parent and probation or parole officer feedback.

4. Abuse behaviour pattern and arousal assessment. Includes gathering complete records of youth behaviour problems in their home and community environments.

5. Regular and random polygraph examination – prevents unnecessary home moves due to false accusations; promotes child protection in high-risk situations and reverses past false abuse admissions for secondary gain (e.g. to end interrogation or look 'honest' in treatment).

6. Random drug or alcohol screening. Deters relapse from substance induced impaired judgement (e.g., Alcohol impairs judgement, increases the probability of aggression and disinhibits sexual behaviour, Dermen and Cooper, 1994).

7. Door alarm. During orientation and as needed when relapse signs are exhibited.

8. Room baby monitor. During orientation, when more than one abuser shares a room and as needed when relapse signs are exhibited.

9. Random room search to check for abuse related items. A brief case example illustrating lessons learned about this issue is provided in Appendix C.

10. Initial and PRN Psychological and Psychiatric evaluations to evaluate emotional stability and help maintain behaviour control by providing medical treatment when needed.

11. Ability to contact staff at all times (wallet contact card with all pager, cell phone, e-mail, FAX numbers). Daily contact from staff includes reports on abuser behaviours to monitor. E-mail feedback after treatment sessions includes learning experiences to implement for behaviour management.

12. Ability to remove youth from the foster home immediately (respite system with group home transfer as a back up procedure to respite).

Foster Care programme inhibits falling back into an abuse cycle by holding the abuser's emotional attention with therapeutic community learning experiences. These learning experiences include a large and creative array of natural and logical consequences, which address the socially immature, irresponsible, acting out involved in multiple forms of abuse/crime. In general, therapeutic community learning experience research with the multiple abuser youth population (Yokley, 1999a) produce clinically significant improvements in abuser:

- Behaviour management (i.e., less incident reports, less serious types of violations and less serious types of abuse).
- Treatment participation (i.e., treatment homework completion, helping self or others in group therapy and higher group grades).

Table 4: Twelve basic TASC forensic foster care community safety and security procedures.

1. A community behaviour contract signed by the youth, their guardian, treatment providers and probation/parole officer which details programme rules agreed upon by all parties including permission to monitor the youth's behaviour in the community and consequences for contract violation. For example, twenty-four hour line of sight supervision on orientation, total hands off policy, do not enter community high risk situations, no contact with victims or potential victims, no baby-sitting, approved associates list, room monitoring, sleep alone, obey the law, respect others rights of privacy and no negative contracts.

2. A clear list of responsibilities and privileges which limits community access based on behaviour (five pages). TASC utilises a three-phase social maturity level system.Orientation/Evaluation: Restricted to home, room monitor, door alarm, no visitors, uniform.
Phase 1: Approved school related supervised activities. Approved associates can visit.
Phase 2: Activities with approved associates added, office visits with appropriate family, office telephone privileges, get a job, no regular room monitor.
Phase 3: Overnight visits with appropriate family. Foster home telephone use. No door alarm.

3. Abuse plan (or cycle) interruption methods to use when detention centre is full and hospitalisation is not possible (e.g., House Arrest, Shadowing, Abbreviated boot camp).

4. Three-step community safety notification system (Green light: no notification or disclosure of abuser problems to those in contact with the abuser, yellow light: partial disclosure, red light: full disclosure) and meetings on a risk level basis with teachers, employers, clergy or others with youth contact.

5. A Clergy Opinion Survey on Sex Offenders Attending Religious Services to determine appropriate type of supervision and relapse prevention. A brief case example illustrating lessons learned about this issue is provided in Appendix D.

6. Pager Supervision (only staff/foster parents have pager number, youth has 15 minutes to call when paged).

7. Shadowing (escort by adult who is aware of his problem) at all times when in the community.

8. Alternative schooling (as needed given risk), e.g., home instruction, Internet school, day treatment, adult GED classes.

9. Computer-Assisted behaviour incident report tracking system for behaviourally objective progress reporting and behaviour pattern 'profiling'.

10. Gradual supervised community re-entry with negative peer screening- 24 hour line of sight supervision on Orientation/Evaluation; Strength buddy system on Phase 1; Approved associates list on Phases 2 and 3.

11. AWOL precautions (e.g., pyjamas and slippers only).

12. AWOL notification plan (e.g., digital photographs and descriptions of dangerousness made up in advance and e-mailed directly to police station upon AWOL).

- Treatment satisfaction (i.e., by both abusers and staff) without an adverse impact on abuser emotional wellbeing as measured by psychological testing.

Since 'The wheels of justice turn slowly', effective methods to create a 'holding environment', block destructive acting out and halt progression of the relapse cycle while waiting for the legal system to act are needed (e.g., Yokley, Laraway and Clough, 1997). Every family based community abuser treatment programme must have at least one effective cycle interruption method in place. If the programme placement policy adopts the philosophy of 'It takes a village to raise a child' and implements a cluster placement approach where the youth is accepted by multiple foster homes, immediate emergency home changes are possible. As a back up, a working relationship with a local group home with adequate staff coverage and supervision is recommended. Abbreviated boot camp appears to be one effective in-home cycle interruption method but it may be important to keep the duration short for positive effects. Initial research on this approach (Yokley, Laraway, and Clough, 1997) has revealed the following:

- Psychological test results indicated significant emotional benefits to the abusers (i.e., decreases in symptoms of depression and anger) with no adverse impact on the community or those in close contact with them.
- Emotional and social maturity impact ratings on the abuser indicated that abbreviated boot camp held the abusers emotional attention while improving self-control, frustration tolerance and responsibility acceptance.
- Consumer satisfaction data indicated that youth abusers prefer the abbreviated boot camp over other typical interventions employed when youth begin to lose behaviour control.

The majority of multiple abusers are diagnosed with conduct disorder. Conduct disorder commonly co-occurs with depression (Angold and Costello, 1992; Cole and Carpentieri, 1990) and regular exercise is a viable treatment for mild to moderate depression (Tkachuk and Martin, 1999). Thus, the positive abbreviated boot camp outcome may in part relate to the impact of exercise on the dependent measure of emotional states, particularly depression. Other less favourable boot camp research has not evaluated the impact on emotional state and has used longer boot camps.

Medical treatment for sex drive reduction is a crisis management option for sexually abusive youth whose community placement is in question as a result of their problems with deviant fantasy and behaviour control. There is some evidence for positive impact in terms of keeping youth in the community using this approach (e.g., Gottesman, Yokley and Bobek, 1994). However, anti-androgen medication needs to be used in addition to group and individual therapy and close supervision must be maintained as well. It is recommended that the benefits and possible side effects (e.g., possible impact on the developing hypothalamic pituitary axis, Becker and Kavoussi, 1989) of anti-androgen medication be discussed in a meeting with the youth, their physician and guardian and an informed consent document be signed. In addition, traditional child psychiatrists may want to address underlying causes such as depression,

anxiety or impulsivity as opposed to treating the deviant arousal level directly through anti-androgen medication. In this regard, although anti-androgen medication has been the mainstay in [adult] sex abuser treatment, the use of antidepressant medications, specifically selective serotonin re-uptake inhibitors is another option that may be considered [for youth] (Greenberg and Bradford, 1997). Medical treatment of deviant sexual behaviour may be helpful for those whose intellectual ability or impulse control problems inhibits cognitive-behavioural relapse prevention methods or who have resistant deviant masturbatory fantasy. This approach is an option when community safety standards are not being followed, polygraph exams on relevant safety issues are failed, the abuser is asking for help to contain his behaviour and medication has not been forced by court order without medical examination and recommendation (Miller, 1998). Medical treatment to reduce deviant arousal level helps provide community safety and security for others while preserving the least restrictive placement for the abuser.

Forensic foster care treatment sabotage

In any abuse treatment setting there are always abuse enablers and abuser rescuers. 'Parentectomy' via foster placement is not the cure. Multiple abuser youth who have successfully manipulated destructive parent alliances in the home will find new ones after placement in forensic foster care. Different types of enabling require different interventions. Two basic types of abuser enabling are professional conflict and abuser enmeshment. Professional conflict enabling can occur when human service caseworkers with expertise in working with young victims in therapeutic foster care are assigned to monitor the progress of a teen-aged offender in forensic foster care. When those trained in the supportive client centred therapy and unconditional positive regard (Rogers, 1957) necessary to develop victim trust, become involved with adolescent abusers there is the risk that they may initially apply victim advocate techniques to offenders. A brief case example illustrating lessons learned about this issue is provided in Appendix E.

Abuser enmeshment enabling occurs when abusers are successful in manipulating friends, relatives or professionals to feel sorry for them and become enmeshed or emotionally over involved to the point of believing the abuser and taking their side against the treatment program staff. A brief case example illustrating lessons learned about this issue is provided in Appendix F.

Issues With Multiple Abuser Youth

Behaviour problem binges: two common causes

Extinction burst and successful manipulation are two common causes of behaviour problem binges. Behaviour problem binges due to extinction burst simply involve a flurry or burst of the problem behaviour (that was previously reinforced) before that behaviour extinguishes. In extinction burst, 'Things always get worse before they get better.' When abusers who in the past have been good at getting 'my way' encounter foster parents who are good at being consistent with discipline, abusers exhibit a flurry of emotional button pushing prior to abandoning their efforts at getting 'my way'. When addressing extinction burst, since we are dealing with abusers whose actions present a danger to self and others, it is important to stop the abusive behaviour first and uncover motives later. As it turns out, stopping the behaviour can sometimes help uncover the underlying motivation. A brief case example illustrating lessons learned about this issue is provided in Appendix G.

Behaviour problem binges due to successful manipulation start out with the abuser testing the limits of inconsistent discipline, trying to get away with things in the treatment setting, foster home or school and gradually pushing back the line until they are in an unruly state. Successful splitting (i.e., manipulating people against each other) gives abusers the confidence they need to test the limits of programme rules and the continuity of staff-foster parent communication.

When addressing behaviour binges due to successful manipulation, foster parents and staff must agree on whatever discipline is implemented to prevent abuser manipulation and splitting. Since successful manipulation requires discipline inconsistency and communication breakdown, discipline consensus gets priority over discipline content. While intervention methods are important, staff need to be flexible. The consistency of discipline can be as important as the type of discipline. Manipulation outbursts are inhibited if foster parents adopt the 'My Way' rule of thumb. Whenever youth abusers ask one parent for something that parent needs to assume that they were already turned down by the other parent and are simply trying to get 'my way'. The 'My Way' rule of thumb requires that forensic foster parents respond to all youth requests by asking the youth what the other parent said and then verifying the youth's statement.

Parenting the impossible: 'you're damned if you show emotions and you're damned if you don't'

The self-fulfilling prophesy of the neglected and rejected: 'Why they have to push your buttons'

Concerning the rejected, the fields of psychotherapy and forensic foster parenting have some differences and what would be considered counter transference in psychotherapy can be considered emotional involvement in forensic foster care. Pushing emotional buttons can be a behaviour test of foster parent concern. The goal of this can be to determine if foster parents care enough to show patience and restraint instead of venting their feelings on the youth with rejecting comments about them as a person, as opposed to their irritating behaviour. On the other hand some youth abusers will feel like foster parents don't care unless they are emotionally involved enough to raise their voice. This is a judgement call, foster parents must make a decision and realise that there is no such thing as a perfectly managed case.

Rejection prevention is relapse prevention

Youth in out-of-home placements are often from homes of neglect, abuse or dysfunctional chaos (Cates, 1991; Heap, 1991; Tjaden and Thoennes, 1992). As might be expected, their parents often exhibit emotional problems (Bath, Richey and Haapala, 1992) and evidence of substance abuse (Gabel and Shindledecker, 1990). Youth abusers in forensic foster care have often been rejected and disappointed by significant others in their dysfunctional families. As a result many have adopted a belief that negative attention is better than no attention at all. From this point of view, it is better to be wanted by the police than not wanted at all. Thus, the 'goal' of a youngster's rule-violating behaviours could involve a means of obtaining predictable (albeit aversive) social feedback (Wahler, 1990).

The letter policy: a behaviour test of family rejection or investment

Despite feelings of rejection and disappointment, multiple abuser youth either continue to express desire for family contact or do not tell their Human Services caseworkers that family visits are deeply upsetting. Their pathological social-emotional immaturity prevents them from letting go of naïve hopes and seeing that they are setting themselves up for failure. Thus, they continue upsetting, unrewarding family contact and repeatedly displace feelings from poor contacts on their staff and foster parents afterwards. Actually this is a complement because it demonstrates that they trust their staff/foster parents enough to express their feelings even inappropriately. When confronted about this some openly admit that they would never respond to their family in that manner for fear of physical violence. A second consequence of contact with a rejecting, dysfunctional family is in an increase in their sick need for acceptance by negative peers to compensate for rejection by family. This often results in further legal problems. Unlike telephone contact, writing and mailing a letter requires considerable more planning, time and effort. Letter writing effort indicates at least some investment in the relationship. The 'Letter Policy' prohibits any contact with anyone who does not care enough to invest the same energy and time by answering several letters that are written by the youth.

No eject, no reject policy

Providers concerned with community safety need to be aware that treatment termination can result in the abuser being placed in a less supervised environment. Much of sexual abuse treatment has been modelled after substance abuse treatment (e.g., relapse prevention and 12 step concepts). Although it is routine for contemporary substance abuse programmes to eject failing residents, this is counter to theory which indicates that 'addictive behaviour is more likely to ensue when a person is cast out of the group of origin for the outcast will find a compatible, but possibly substance abusing, subculture with which to attach' (Houts,1995, p.26). Traditional Therapeutic

Communities did not reject those who arrived for treatment under the influence and did not eject those who used during treatment. Those who came in under the influence were de-toxed 'cold turkey' (i.e., total abstinence without gradual decreases in substance dose) and those who relapsed during treatment were given an opportunity to reintegrate themselves into treatment through a commitment contract that demonstrated serious self-discipline and treatment motivation.

In traditional foster care after an initial interview or trial visit, the foster parents have the option of rejecting the youth. The TASC Forensic Foster Care policy of admitting youth into a foster cluster of homes inherently blocks rejection of appropriate youth since admission involves the majority vote of the foster cluster as opposed to one family. In addition, since more than one family has accepted the youth, ejection from the TASC Forensic Foster Care programme does not occur when youth behaviour problems require a home move. Finally, in Forensic Foster Care the youth has had ongoing involvement with the other families in the cluster where parents watch each others youth and weekend visits to other cluster family homes are common. This form of shared parenting environment reduces the possibility of any mutual youth-caretaker rejection or alienation that has in theory been expected from home moves (Proch and Taber, 1985).

Frustration tolerance and attachment issues: 'they're not my kids', 'I'm not your son'

One powerful foster parent frustration with youth abusers is not understanding their seemingly senseless behaviour which can lead to just giving up and stating, 'They're not my kids'. Given their expected attachment issues and hypersensitivity to anticipated rejection, foster parents need to let the youth grow up and reject them (Lowenstein, 1985). Exaggerated real world preparation speeches can trigger treatment sabotage. Given this situation it is important to know what not to say. No matter how much the youth complain about being held back from advancement and discharge, it is important not to remind them of any placement or programme time limits. State prisoners or involuntary psychiatric patients may warmly receive statements such as 'We like you but you can't stay here forever' but this approach with multiple abuser youth is likely to result in running away. The hypersensitivity of these youth lead them to combat their rejection anticipation, helplessness and loss of control by rejecting their caretakers before they are rejected.

'I'm not your son' is expressed by immature youth who take every opportunity to state 'you don't understand me' and then fail to give any logical explanation for their behaviour. In addition to displaying aggression, drug use and manipulation, the destructive behaviour of therapeutic community youth may include refusing to develop anything but a superficial relationship with adults (Lowenstein, 1985). This actually makes sense from a developmental prospective because there is no explanation for pathologically socially immature behaviour except being totally unsocialised as the result of never learning to adapt to a functional family setting. Their lack of supervision has left them with no sense of appropriate social behaviour control boundaries and the omnipotent attitude of 'What I want to do is right and the reason it's right is because I want to do it' (aka Dysfunctional Family Law). This dysfunctional family logic explains why these adolescents typically frustrate adults by responding with 'I don't know' when asked why they did something. The reason they did it is simple. They are pathologically socially immature babies functioning under Dysfunctional Family Law and are following the aforementioned one statute which can be applied to all their interactions. It is important to teach foster parents the 'Simple Man' concept for understanding the behaviour of pathologically socially immature youth. In this conceptualisation, the simplest, most immature and embarrassing motive for the behaviour has the highest probability of being accurate and is often confirmed through overt emotional, defensive, denial.

Limits of forensic foster parent involvement: the second shift analogy

Experienced foster parents will comment that they treat their foster children like their natural children in terms of responsibilities and consequences but not privileges, which require earning trust. This can be a problem for foster youth who are being placed because they have done things wrong and therefore must earn the trust of their foster parents. Their

history of past abuse and neglect has left them preoccupied with injustices. As a result, they may feel entitled to trust at the onset in a sort of 'innocent until proven guilty' mentality and resent having to prove themselves to foster parents because they have abused the trust of others. This is an example of a first shift problem as it relates to how the youth was treated in a prior setting (i.e., earlier shift).

In cases where the foster parent has made an emotional connection or developed a trust bond with the youth, some feelings of disappointment or responsibility can be expected when youth display resistance or rejection. However, an important difference between forensic foster parenting and natural parenting exists which foster parents must be made aware of to help buffer these feelings. Unlike natural parenting, the responsibility for seriously abusive youth is somewhat like factory work divided across three shifts. The first shift is usually the responsibility of institution staff in the facility where the youth is incarcerated, receiving treatment and awaiting parole to a community setting. In cases where the youth was never incarcerated for their abusive behaviour, the first shift was the parenting they received in their family of origin. Forensic foster parents, treatment staff and a probation/parole officer or human services worker typically assume the responsibility for the second shift when the youth is placed in Forensic Foster Care treatment and is gradually exposed to increasing privileges and responsibilities. The youth's probation or parole officer or human services worker staffs the third shift typically with the assistance of an individual outpatient therapist at a community mental health centre. Foster parents need to keep their focus on their shift. Getting preoccupied with what already happened to the youth on the first shift or worried about what may happen to them on the third shift distracts from the important supervision and corrective parenting that is required on the second shift.

Systems Issues that Effect Forensic Foster Care

Systems issues that affect Forensic Foster Care include conflicts in professional training, professional roles and agency policies. With respect to professional training conflicts, there is a fair possibility that multiple abuser treatment programme staff may have more accountability based cognitive behavioural training with adolescent abusers while guardian or case workers may have more support based client-centred training with elementary school aged victims. Caseworkers may view programme staff as responding to their client with confrontation but no appropriate concern. Programme staff may view caseworkers as responding to the multiple abuser youth with concern but no appropriate confrontation. These training perspectives can clash even without the different professional roles of forensic treatment staff and human services caseworkers.

The basic professional role conflict that can occur between human services caseworkers who place the youth multiple abuser and the forensic programme staff who treat them can be summed up as 'client advocacy versus community protection'. Caseworkers caught up in a client advocate role can view the Forensic Foster Care placement evaluation as a job interview by their client where projecting favourable attributes is the goal. This can conflict with the programme staff role to gather as much detailed information as possible about the youth abuser's behaviour that could pose a danger to others for the purpose of constructing a sound community treatment and safety plan. It is important not to let these roles conflict to the point where the youth mistakes the interview as their familiar dysfunctional family situation and feel caught in the middle between one parent putting them down and the other taking up for them.

Agency policy conflicts in Forensic Foster Care vary but one common conflict that may occur can be stated as 'family reunification versus child protection'. Human services policies for natural family visitation may conflict with parole/probation rules, which protect youth abusers by prohibiting them from associating with known criminal parents. Visitation between youth who have been abused and abuser parents triggers more deviant fantasies by abuser parents, which increases the risk of re-victimisation. Sex abusers with family visitation where victims are present have significantly more deviant fantasies about victims than those who do not have family visitation (Davis, Yokley and Williams, 1996). In addition to triggering deviant thoughts in criminal parents, visitation can also conflict with the need for a bonding period between abuser youth and their forensic foster parents as well

as trigger past traumatic thoughts on the part of the youth. Since youth placed out of the home often experienced neglect, abuse or dysfunctional chaos (Cates, 1991 ; Heap, 1991; Tjaden and Thoennes, 1992) from parents with emotional problems (Bath, Richey and Haapala, 1992), behaviour de-compensation can occur after mandated natural parent visitation. Given this situation, treatment programme staff may view the human service family visitation policies as interfering with treatment while human services staff may view the programme orientation period where no visitors are allowed as interfering with their family reunification policy.

A second agency policy conflict that may occur in Forensic Foster Care can be viewed as 'foster placement preservation versus community safety preservation'. Different variations of human services policies, which basically discourage home moves are based on the needs of elementary school aged victims for home environment consistency. One example of a placement preservation policy would be requiring a waiting period after a move has been requested so that caseworkers have time to try interventions to preserve the placement before making the move. In addition to placement preservation policy, clinical interventions have also been aimed at preventing the disruption of foster care placements for quite some time (e.g., Aldgate and Hawley, 1986). Under placement preservation policies, all home moves are negatively labelled as 'placement disruptions' despite the lack of conclusive research evidence regarding harm from home moves (Proch and Taber, 1985) and there is no 'placement accommodation' label for positive home moves. Given the estimates that nearly one third of the children in foster care experience three or more placements and that this number is substantially higher for adolescents (i.e. 7–10 placements) in foster care (Fanshel, Finch, and Grundy, 1989), it seems unlikely that all of these moves were negative 'placement disruptions'. It is more likely that some home moves are in fact positive 'placement accommodations' to meet the special environmental needs of the youth or safety needs of the community.

Broad enforcement of home 'disruption' policies for all age groups and diagnostic categories of foster youth (i.e., adolescent offenders as well as the child victims) do not address the needs of the community for safety and security. In Forensic Foster Care, human services policies that provide incentives to preserve placements (or disincentives for disrupting them) basically encourage keeping seriously dangerous multiple abuser youth in situations that are high-risk for community harm. Treatment programme staff may feel that a human services placement preservation policy waiver for multiple abuser youth is needed in order to remove them from the difficult position of having to undermine human services policies to preserve community safety and security. Human services policy makers may feel that any placement preservation policy waiver for multiple abuser youth (i.e. which would remove incentives for placement preservation or sanctions for placement disruption) could destabilise the foster care system and may be open to abuses. From this viewpoint, providing placement preservation policy waivers could open the floodgates to moves of many irritating youth by labelling them as multiple abusers just for the purpose of getting them moved without delay and not because they pose any real danger to the community.

Foster Parent Selection: 'Beggars Can't Always be Choosers'

Recruiting foster parents to take youth who have committed sexually abusive behaviour into their homes is predictably difficult. However, some forensic foster family selection characteristics can be offered.

Two heads are better than one: four eyes are better than two

When considering appropriate learning experiences for abuser behaviour problems 'two heads are better than one'. With respect to providing an appropriate level of community supervision for youth abusers, four eyes are better than two. With youth abusers quantity time is more important than quality time. With these youth the most important thing for foster parents to do is be there and be consistent. While this is certainly possible with retired single parents with established, stable relationships, it is not always possible for single parents who are still working and trying to establish relationships. Many youth abusers have already failed in homes where a single parent had to work and was not available to provide them with attention, guidance and

supervision. However, extended family and relatives can help considerably with supervision. The importance of supervision by as many adults and extended family as possible can not be over emphasised for this population with respect to the issue of community safety and security. Given their history of serious family problems (e.g. Awad, Saunders and Levene, 1984), lack of supervision and structure in the past, these youth have often had 24 hours a day, 7 days a week of pathologically socially immature, 'my way' indulgence.

Foster parent characteristics: tenacity is job 1

Forensic foster parents need to stick with the youth and stick with their decisions. Good forensic foster parent characteristics include tenacity, assertiveness, stability and experience. Tenacity and endurance are important forensic foster parent characteristics. By embroiling the family in conflict, seriously delinquent behaviour itself wears down the socialisation forces (e.g., supervision, setting limits) that could direct youth into more pro-social patterns of adjustment (Chamberlain and Reid, 1998). Thus, multiple abuser youth need forensic foster parents who model tenacity and endurance while teaching youth to 'never give up' and 'always finish what you start'. A good forensic foster parent attitude to convey to youth is 'If you're not working on the solution, you're part of the problem'.

Assertiveness, decisiveness and enthusiasm are valuable commodities to own when trading verbal exchanges with resistant multiple abuser youth. Forensic foster parents must be able to make difficult decisions without delay, be firm in their convictions and enthusiastic about behaviour maintenance or progress. A sense of value-based commitment is important in selection. If forensic treatment staff want multiple abuser youth to learn pro-social values and not compromise them, they need to select foster parents who stick by what they believe to be right even if the treatment staff do not agree with all of the foster parent's values or methods. In selection, tenacity is more important than technique, which can be modified through training. Youth abusers don't need friends, they need parents and parents don't always agree with their children. Peer associates always agree, friends agree most of the time but parents are only supposed to agree when it's good for their children. Being able to tolerate criticism helps since in forensic foster care there is no such thing as a perfectly managed case and complaints about parenting decisions are common. Multiple abuser youth can be expected to take the victim stance with their human services guardians if they receive firm, consistent discipline. In summary, good forensic foster parents can handle the fact that 'Not to make a decision is to make a decision'. The personality profile (i.e. 16PF) of successful therapeutic foster mothers suggests that self-discipline, maturity, ability to face reality, and enthusiasm, combined with ability to make decisions based on logic, were related to better foster parent functioning (Ray and Horner, 1990).

Emotional stability and being well balanced are cornerstones in parenting multiple abuser youth. Forensic foster parents don't have to be young, strong, rich or physically healthy, just mentally healthy and socially mature. Pathologically socially immature multiple abuser youth need foster parents who are honest, trustworthy, loyal, concerned and responsible. This doesn't mean easy going in style. Since socially immature youth with authority problems have needs to act those problems out on some one, easy going foster parents make it hard going for treatment staff who the youth are more likely to target for authority conflicts. Likewise, easy going treatment staff make it hard going for foster parents who then become the likely targets of authority conflicts. Both foster parents and staff have to provide mature objection to immature behaviour. Part of developing social maturity and appropriate social behaviour control is learning to function with rules that set limits on externalising behaviour. This is where father figures with strong leadership traits like bearing, courage and dependability can help with authority problems. In this respect, the personality profile (i.e. 16PF) of successful therapeutic foster fathers suggests that they are likely to be somewhat more conservative than the norm (Ray and Horner, 1990).

Experience is important in forensic foster parent selection but also isn't everything. Sometimes retraining therapeutic foster parents to be forensic foster parents is more difficult than starting from scratch. This is because traditional foster parents usually have received training by a Human Services system whose primary population is elementary school aged

victims not adolescent abusers. A shift from traditional therapeutic foster parenting emphasis on reflective listening, unconditional positive regard, trust and support mode to forensic foster parenting investigative questioning, 'trust but verify' and 'confrontation with concern' is needed. Forensic foster parents need to adopt the 'Kite Analogy of Social Maturity Development'. In this analogy, if you provide appropriate, positive resistance and pull against the kite, it rises to its maximum potential. If you stand still and don't pull against it but also don't give in, the kite maintains its present level. If you give in, go the direction the kite is pulling or run after the kite, it crashes.

Foster Parent Retention

Keep them through empowerment policies and procedures

The TASC Forensic Foster Care programme includes policies and procedures that are associated with foster parent retention. These empowerment procedures include highly specialised forensic foster parent training and a team approach where foster parents are integrated into all aspects of youth treatment as well as communication. A cluster placement model to maximise foster parent support while respecting their family diversity and minimising any adverse impact that could be associated with home moves is an additional empowerment procedure.

Forensic foster care empowerment policy 1: relevant, quality foster parent training: 'It's not just a job, it's an adventure'

Specific, frequent, quality training with relevant content has been identified as a foster parent retention factor (Chamberlain, Moreland and Reid, 1992; Denby and Rindfleisch, 1996; Urquhart, 1989). In addition to the mandated sessions for all regular foster parents and on the job training during home visits, TASC Forensic Foster parents receive 30 hours of annual training on topics relating specifically to multiple abusers. Lecture topics include: characteristics of abusive youth; understanding how abusive behaviour was acquired, maintained and generalised; maladaptive thinking of abusive youth; socially responsible parenting of abusive youth and the foster parent role in relapse prevention; community supervision, safety and security; victim impact and; stress management for forensic foster parents.

Forensic foster care empowerment policy 2: an inclusive treatment team: 'One for all and all for one'

The therapeutic community approach used in the TASC Forensic Foster Care programme blends paraprofessional and professional staff together in a unified treatment team where the specialised training and forensic parenting experience of TASC foster parents is respected as a critical aspect of treatment. Since 'the best behaviour programme is one that everyone uses', the basic TASC programme rules and consequences (including therapeutic community learning experiences) were established by consensus of the treatment team (i.e. foster parents, social worker and psychologist). Even the intake or placement selection process is inclusive of foster parents. Youth abusers have an intake interview during a treatment group where all of the treatment staff (i.e. including foster parents) are present and admission requires a majority staff vote. This team approach effectively addresses the lack of foster parent involvement in types of children placed with them (Denby and Rindfleisch, 1996) as well as service planning (Sanchirico et al.1998), both of which have been identified as retention factors commonly responsible for foster parent dissatisfaction.

Forensic foster care empowerment policy 3: communication continuity: 'A team is only as effective as it's least informed member'

As an integral part of the treatment team, TASC Forensic Foster parents are directly connected into the treatment feedback loop through centralised and as needed in home treatment services, daily communication with on call staff (pagers, cellular telephones and e-mail), weekly home visits and brief meetings before or after individual sessions. In addition, they typically sit in during the first 10-15 minutes of treatment group sessions to disclose behaviour problems and issues that have occurred. E-mail feedback to foster parents on treatment group content, process as well as therapeutic community learning experiences that were implemented is provided. The

continuity of the TASC Forensic Foster Care programme addresses the foster parent retention factor concerning the quantity and quality of agency-foster parent interaction (Urquhart,1989).

Forensic foster care empowerment policy 4: the foster cluster model: 'It takes a village to raise a child'

In the TASC Forensic Foster Care programme youth abusers are admitted into a foster cluster of several homes, which increases support through shared parenting responsibility and facilitates providing respite visits (i.e. a relationship vacation) during trying times. The foster cluster placement approach makes immediate emergency placement from one home to another easy to accomplish if needed and reduces foster parent burnout associated with keeping a stressful youth simply because there is no other placement for them. If possible, having the youth accepted into several families at once maximises the probability of getting the basic treatment messages through to them in a different family if they didn't get it the first time around. The cluster approach enhances foster parent retention by addressing their expressed need for mutual support among themselves (Urquhart,1989).

Forensic foster care empowerment policy 5: respect for family diversity: 'When in Rome, do as the Romans do'

Supporting foster parent discipline decisions and their own house rules with a programme policy that respects individual family differences is important. Since teenagers compare responsibilities and privileges at school, they are aware of the diverse differences in family rules. Thus, the rules of the foster homes in the cluster are not standardised. The TASC Forensic Foster Care policy that 'Every house has it's own rules' establishes a basic set of treatment programme rules that all professional staff and foster parents agree on while supporting the foster parents individual house rules. The TASC programme requires that youth pass a quiz on the foster parent's individual house rules. This family diversity policy mirrors the real world environment by teaching the youth that each setting is different and they must learn to adapt to the rules of each setting (i.e. home, school, work and treatment) they encounter as 'Every house has it's own rules'.

Conclusion

Forensic Foster Care offers a less restrictive and more cost-effective alternative than continued residential treatment for multiple abuser youth who are not candidates for outpatient treatment in their family of origin. The present chapter described lessons learned along with procedures developed, evaluated and refined in the TASC Forensic Foster Care programme over the past seven years.

The level of pathological social-emotional immaturity that these multiple abuser youth exhibit at treatment admission prevents them from reaching out to their foster parents and staff for advice, help or even basic support. Although some are overt while others are covert, resistance, rebellion and rejection are the prominent avoidance responses that they display towards their caretakers. If foster parents and staff have made any emotional connection with these externalising, multiple abuser youth, that connection should survive discharge. Approximately 76 per cent of TASC forensic foster youth contact foster parents or staff after discharge (Yokley and Boettner, 1999b). Reaching out to foster parents and staff to stay connected after leaving treatment is an indicator that these youth have started to learn the value of positive human relationships which is an important part of their social maturity development.

Note

[1] Portions of the present paper were presented at the 18th Annual Research and Treatment Conference of the Association for the Treatment of Sexual Abusers in Lake Buena Vista, Florida (Yokley and Boettner, 1999b). Portions were reproduced from 'The Social Responsibility Therapy Work Book: Understanding Abuse Behaviour' (Yokley, 1995) and 'The TASC Program Manual' (Yokley, 1993) with permission from the author.

Appendix A
Case example illustrating the abuse behaviour triad: how abuse behaviour was acquired, maintained and generalized

Greg was a 15-year-old African American male admitted with five types of abuse including 13

sex offence victims, homicide threats during rape, gang involvement and physical assault. He had four prior foster home failures (six sex offences in two foster homes, theft in one) and prior residential sex offender treatment where physical restraint was required to contain his aggressive behaviour. Greg progressed through the other phases of treatment, learning pro-social behaviour skills and arousal management. The following is a summary of his work on developing an understanding of how his abuse behaviour was acquired, maintained and generalised.

1. Chain of events (how abuse behaviour was acquired)

The first link in the chain of events that leads up to the initial abuse behaviour is **Past Permanent Problems**. These problems consist of bio-psychosocial disadvantages, trauma and other predisposing historical factors that could not be controlled by the youth. Greg's past permanent problems included being a victim of sexual abuse, physical abuse and neglect. He lists his mother's death due to drugs as the most intense, followed by being physically and emotionally abused by his mother and her boyfriends. He was told numerous times in his life that he was a worthless nothing and was 'shit for a son' by his mother. His father was absent from his life.

These past permanent problems involving abuse and rejection led to **Low self-efficacy and Social-emotional immaturity** (i.e. the second link in the chain of events that leads to abuse). He stated 'I would feel as though no one really cared and there was nothing else to be positive about so I acted immature in order to feel better'. His lack of self-efficacy and social-emotional immaturity was exemplified by a phrase that he repeated during treatment, 'why even try if you know you're gonna die.' The need to artificially build up his low self-efficacy along with his social-emotional immaturity gravitated him towards **High Risk Situations** for committing abusive behaviour. Greg handled his feelings of rejection and worthlessness in a socially and emotionally immature manner by gang membership and using drugs to build himself up, make him feel powerful and in control.

While in High Risk Situations such as being with the gang, Greg would experience **Maladaptive Thinking** such as 'I want what I want, when I want it', 'They shouldn't be fucking with me,' and believing that his actions didn't affect others or matter. This combination of high risk peer group and maladaptive thinking resulted in an **Initial Abuse** problem of assault and drugs. In Greg's words, 'I would use drugs to ease the pain, I would physically abuse people who I thought were stupid. I would sell drugs and I would do crimes for the thrill.' Greg's participation in gang wars would leave him feeling high on power, and 'looking for victims'. His inability to cope with these feelings led him into a Stress-Abuse Cycle that set the occasion for expanding his acting out into repeated sexual abuse.

2. Stress-abuse cycle (how abuse behaviour was maintained)

Greg's **Negative Coping** after his abusive behaviour involved minimising the extent of his behaviour, blaming others along with justifying his physical and sexual abuse because his victims 'made me angry'. Greg repeated these thoughts until he successfully cycled himself into a **Cover-up** phase where he would act like everything was all right, focus on other things and tell himself that 'everything is under control'. If anyone questioned his behaviour, Greg would lie, e.g., 'That was then, this is now.' Lying and trying to maintain the consistency of a series of lies that cover up abusive behaviour creates a **Stress Build-up** which was exacerbated by Greg 'stuffing' his feelings and getting in verbal conflicts with authority figures. After a period of Stress Build-up, Greg would **Slip or Lapse** into minor rule violations with criminal friends to see how far he could push back the line before being stopped. When caught he would create a crisis by running away (approximately 12–15 times) and **Fall or Relapse** through the Abstinence Violation Effect where he would seek out his negative peers, use drugs, sell drugs, get violent, get sexually abusive and generally go on a 'my way' gratification binge. After the relapse, Greg would use the aforementioned negative coping and re-enter the Stress-Abuse Cycle.

3. Anatomy [model] of social-emotional maturity problems that support multiple forms of abuse (how abuse behaviour was generalised to other problem areas)

The Chain of Events that Greg experienced helped develop his initial pathologically socially and emotionally immature way of venting his feelings through abusive acting out. Repeated iterations of the Stress-Abuse Cycle not only maintained his abusive behaviour but acted to further develop his pathological social-emotional immaturity which in turn supports multiple forms of abuse. Other social-emotional maturity problems that supported his multiple abuser behaviour included: a control and power problem (sensation seeking and authority problem); dishonesty (usually telling people what they want to hear); unhealthy pride (not asking for help); grandiosity (mostly selfishness and entitlement); perfectionism (you're either a hero or a zero); self-defeating habits (creating a crisis as opposed to dealing with feelings and issues) and; maladaptive values or self-image (a man is tough. He didn't even cry at his mother's funeral).

Epilogue

Although Greg was able to accept enough Social Responsibility Therapy to help him stop his interpersonal abuse (i.e. he had no need for physical restraint and no sexual or physical re-offence), his problems with substance abuse required a transfer to a residential facility for drug and alcohol treatment. He graduated from his drug treatment programme and was recently in the local newspaper for his positive volunteer work as a speaker and role model for other youth abusers.

Appendix B
Case example of emotional restitution to victims during victim responsibility training

Keith was a 17-year-old Caucasian male admitted with five types of abuse including 11 child sex offense victims, physical restraint during vaginal rape and frequent fights. He was a learning disability student with borderline intellectual functioning who failed prior treatment and sexually re-offended while on parole. Keith progressed through the other phases of treatment, learning pro-social behaviour skills, arousal management and understanding how his abuse behaviour developed. The following is a summary of his work in Victim Responsibility Training designed to help him develop empathy and demonstrate responsibility towards his sexual offense victims.

Intervention 1 (victim news articles on abuse impact)

The first intervention requires a bibliotherapy assignment of reading newspaper articles on the impact of the sexual assault. After reading the articles and answering the review questions, his responses revealed having learned some of the thoughts and feelings of victims as being, 'dirty and extremely sensitive,' and feelings of 'anger, depression, powerlessness.' He was able to discuss the hesitancy of victims to disclose feelings to other people and the lasting, often lifelong, repercussions of their sexual assault. Keith was also able to describe some of the possible stages of coping that a victim may experience and stated that the intervention 'made me think about how my offences hurt the victim in ways I never knew they could.'

Intervention 2 (letters written by victims on abuse impact)

After reading letters by unrelated victims of sexual abuse and answering the review questions, Keith was able to list 'Loss of dignity, no trust of others' as some short-term consequences of sexual abuse and again recognised feelings of anger, guilt and hurt. He listed some sexual abuse recovery steps as 'not go into denial of problem, vent their feelings . . . to keep them from leaking out on others.' Keith also acknowledged that 'this person may adjust physically, yet mentally and emotionally they may never adjust' to the sexual molestation.

Intervention 3 (victim videotape on abuse impact)

In this intervention, Keith watched a videotape documenting the impact of sexual abuse on victims. Four real-life victim survivors of sexual abuse (two males and two females) discussed the actual abuse events, their thoughts, feelings and coping mechanisms employed. After viewing the videotape, Keith's thoughts and self-reported benefit increased from an average of 'quite a bit' in the previous two interventions to 'a great deal' in this intervention. Regarding what affected him the most, he wrote 'How the fact that even today they blame themselves for the offence when it was the offenders fault, not theirs.'

Intervention 4 (victim impact group)

In the victim-impact group an unrelated sexual abuse victim (or victims) discloses the impact sexual abuse on their life in a face-to-face session with the sexual abusers while sitting between the victim and abuser therapists. Psychological testing (i.e. Beck Depression Inventory, Beck Anxiety Inventory) is administered pre- and post-session to all survivors who attended to ensure that there was no adverse impact that requires intervention.

Keith participated in a victim-impact group with Jane, an adult survivor of sexual abuse and six other youth from his sexual abuser programme. Keith sat diagonally from Jane in the circle. Jane disclosed the specific details of her repeated sexual abuse and the resulting consequences on her life and those close to her. She discussed her struggle with obesity, depression, suicide attempts and daily fear. Jane confronted Keith on his offending behaviour and he was honest about his behaviour with her. On completing his learning experience questionnaire, he responded that this intervention held his emotional attention and he experienced anxiety, self-disgust, guilt, anger, and fear during the session. Keith also indicated that he was able to look at his behaviour from Jane's point of view and stated that excuses he told himself during his sexually abusive behaviour gave him no right to commit that behaviour.

Jane's psychological testing revealed that both her levels of depression and anxiety which were clinically elevated before the impact group, dropped to within normal limits after the session and further decreased at a two-month follow-up. Thus not only was there no adverse impact on Jane, there appeared to be some therapeutic benefit from the structured intervention with the youth abusers.

Intervention 5 (apology/clarification letter to indirect abuse victim)

In intervention 5, Keith had to use what he learned about the impact of sexual abuse and victim empathy in the previous four interventions to write an apology letter clarifying his problem and responsibility to an indirect victim of his sexual abuse. Keith chose to write to his grandmother who was the guardian of him and his two sisters at the time of the offences. He had several sessions of revising and reviewing his letter with his treatment group and therapists for critiques and approval. His letter included the following, 'I am writing to apologise for the pain I have caused you by offending your granddaughters Denise and Debbie, people that I should have cared about more, yet I did not . . . what I did was my fault and no one else's . . . I was extremely jealous and made a plan to hurt them . . . That is why I chose to sexually offend. I want to again apologise for my sick, selfish behaviour. Sincerely, Keith.' Keith's grandmother indicated that she was willing to receive his personal apology and a session was scheduled.

Intervention 6 (apology/clarification session for indirect abuse victim)

Keith met with his grandmother with his therapist present. He apologised again, clarified how he developed his sexually abusive behaviour, took responsibility and answered all of her questions to the best of his ability. In a follow-up questionnaire, Keith's grandmother said that the apology session helped her to accept what he had done to be able to discuss the abuse more openly. She also expressed that her feelings and thoughts of guilt, anxiety, and anger decreased after receiving the apology letter and even more so after the apology session.

Intervention 7 (apology/clarification letter to direct abuse victim)

With the approval of his grandmother, Keith wrote an apology letter to his direct victims, Denise and Debbie, his sisters, which was mailed to their therapist to process with them in a session. Again, his letter was read, discussed and revised with the help of his treatment group. Keith's letter apologised to Denise and Debbie for his 'sick, disgusting and inhumane behaviour for abusing you both.' He clarified that as an older brother he should have been looking out for his little sisters, not taking advantage of them and he owned responsibility for his behaviour. He clarified that 'my behaviour was an abuse of power and control. It was a violation of privacy' and explained that he let his 'anger build into a rage . . . if I hurt you physically it would leave scars . . . this is one of the reasons I chose to sexually offend you.' Keith's letter ended with 'I know that I didn't care for you both as a brother should

and would like to start by showing you I care by apologising to you both. Sincerely, Your brother Keith'. Keith's sister Denise and her therapist indicated that they wanted to meet with him in an apology/clarification session.

Intervention 8 (apology/clarification session for indirect abuse victim)

In the final intervention, Keith met with Denise and who sat between her therapist and Kevin's therapist. As a victim safeguard, Denise received psychological testing (i.e. Beck Depression Inventory, Beck Anxiety Inventory, State-Trait Anger Expression Inventory) before and after the apology session. On the post session questionnaire, Denise indicated that the session helped her 'know that he cares about me . . . and that he's sorry for what he did.' She also stated that such sessions would be helpful for all victims 'so they can understand about the feelings of themselves and to open up'. . . Denise's psychological testing showed no adverse effects from the session with a decrease in anxiety. Her therapist's response included 'it is helpful and therapeutic for the victim to be placed in a position of being in control' and that Denise is 'more positive as a result' of the apology/clarification session. Keith's responses indicated a pronounced benefit in understanding the impact of his actions upon his sister. He disclosed feelings of self-disgust as well as empathy. He concluded with, 'When my sister cried, I wanted to take the pain away yet I could not,' indicating a genuine connection and desire to make emotional restitution.

Epilogue

Keith completed his treatment at the TASC Forensic Foster Care programme for multiple abuser youth and was discharged to regular foster care after 15 months. During his treatment he had one incident of indecency in his home but no sexual re-offence and no further fights.

Appendix C
Random room search vignette

During treatment, a random room search was conducted on Chip, a 15-year-old, white male abuser with a history of seven child and peer sexual abuse victims. Chip also had a history of alcohol abuse, physical assault, pornography use and five placement failures over the past seven years. The search revealed a pair of panties and a written log with people and times listed on it. Investigation revealed Chip had broken into the home of Tracy, a 14-year-old female by climbing through her window and had stolen her panties. He had been masturbating to rape fantasies of her to the point that a rape plan was fully formed. Chip had been watching Tracy through her window for some time and the log he constructed had a list of all of the other family members living in the home along with the times that they came and left except for Tracy's brother. After Chip figured out her brother's schedule, his plan was to climb in Tracy's window at a time that he knew there was no one home but her and hide until she returned to her room. At that point Chip admitted he planned to assault Tracy, tie her up with her own panty hose and rape her. He also disclosed thoughts of strangling her afterwards. Chip was placed in detention to protect Tracy. The room search interrupted Chip's re-offence plan and saved Tracy from a traumatic sexual assault.

Epilogue

The important lesson learned from this case is that supervision in Forensic Foster Care with multiple abusers must extend beyond the boundaries of traditional psychotherapy and beyond the boundaries of traditional parenting in order to protect the boundaries of potential victims.

Appendix D
Vignette on sex abusers at religious services: the need for community safeguards in church

Mack was a 17-year-old learning disabled white male referred for youth sex abuser treatment as the result of a history of molesting male children. He was given community safety standards requiring 24-hour line of sight supervision by an adult who is aware of his problem and excluding him from all child access including Sunday school. Mack's mother filed a grievance against his treatment providers on the grounds that the treatment programme rules violated his constitutional rights to freedom of religion. She also expressed a strong belief that 'spiritual counselling' was best for her son and was pressing the local authorities to transfer him from sex abuser specific

treatment to general counselling in a Christian children's home. An informal compromise of treatment rules was reached where the abuser would not attend Sunday School but would attend church and sit between his parents who would provide his supervision. Mack had no reported behaviour problems in church for three weeks. Shortly thereafter, the church youth pastor contacted the treatment programme with complaints that Mack had made sexual advances towards two children in his Sunday school and had exposed his penis to them in a church stair well. His parents stated that he was with them at all times 'except when he excused himself to use the rest room'.

Epilogue

Church can be an easy victim target area for sex abusers especially since most in attendance do not feel that they have to keep their guard up against crime in this setting. The important lesson learned from this case is to develop an effective religious service risk reduction plan for sexual abusers. This plan needs to protect the religious rights of sexual abusers as well as the rights of potential victims by including their clergy opinion. This can be done by sending a clergy opinion survey (Roberson, Yokley and Zuzik, 1995). When clergy were surveyed on what type of sex abuser programme support they would like, their first church supervision preference was that abusers sit next to their treatment programme staff. With respect to relapse prevention methods, the first preference of clergy is that abusers take careful notes to keep their minds on the service and away from potential victims (Roberson, Yokley and Zuzik,1995).

Appendix E
Professional conflict enabling vignette

Greg, a 14-year-old African American male had failed in four different foster homes but was admitted to the TASC forensic foster care programme after completing residential sex abuser treatment. At admission Greg disclosed a history of sexual abuse (rape and molestation of 15 male and female children as well as fondling adults), physical abuse (fights and gang involvement), property abuse (theft, burglary, vandalism), substance abuse (marijuana, alcohol abuse and drug dealing) and trust/verbal abuse (violent threats, constant lying). Greg's Human Services caseworker refused to sign his consent form for regular polygraph examination, a procedure that from her humanistic victim treatment prospective did not show unconditional positive regard or basic client trust. After learning this, Greg's behaviour began to deteriorate. He became involved with negative peers doing drugs while stating that he was following the programme rules. Eventually he got out of control to the point where a return to residential treatment was necessary.

Upon admission to residential treatment, his caseworker refused to sign consent for urinalysis in keeping with her client-centered position. Greg's consequent substance abuse relapse resulted in another placement failure. He was referred back to TASC Forensic Foster Care where the relationship between his caseworker enabling him to avoid abuse-monitoring procedures (i.e., polygraph and urinalysis) and his continued placement failure was taken up with the Human Services authorities. Upon case review by the authorities, Greg received regular polygraph examination, random urinalysis and a new caseworker.

Epilogue

I believe it was Fritz Perls who said 'If your only tool is a hammer, all of your clients look like nails'. This makes sense but it is also important to remember that if your only tool is glue, all of your clients look like they can bond. In summary, there are problems with applying the cold steel confrontation approach to victims and the warm gooey compassion approach to abusers. This case teaches us two important treatment lessons. First, since many multiple abusers have been victims as well (e.g., Fehrenbach et al., 1986), a treatment toolbox, which includes tools for both populations is needed and second, intake interviews should include the caseworker as well as the youth.

Appendix F
Abuser enmeshment enabling vignette

Jesse was a 16-year-old, white male, referred to the TASC forensic foster care programme. At admission he disclosed a history of sexual abuse (fondling the penis of a four-year-old foster brother and deviant sexual contact with males at two group homes), physical abuse (fighting in school), property abuse (theft and vandalism), substance abuse (alcohol) and along with trust and verbal abuse (constant lying and manipulation). Jesse urinated all over his room and claimed urinary incontinence as a medical necessity to have his night door alarm removed, after which he ran away six times and filed false police reports of being physically abused in his foster home on several occasions when he was caught.

After finally getting arrested for his delinquency, Jessie successfully identified a vulnerable institution social worker and manipulated her into becoming enmeshed with him. He then told his worker that TASC programme staff had abused him, and used another incarcerated sex abuser that he was having oral and anal intercourse with to corroborate his story. She filed a police report stating that Jesse was a victim of abuse by TASC programme staff.

Following a short sympathetic incarceration, Jessie was discharged to a group home setting where he failed to follow the rules or even maintain his basic hygiene and was referred back to the TASC programme after his group home placement was terminated. His parole officer, placement co-ordinator and programme staff were present at his first group when Jesse openly admitted that he lied about being abused by TASC staff. It was not considered necessary to provide this feedback to his institutional social worker as she had been transferred to an all-female institution after becoming enmeshed with another young male client and allegations of an inappropriate relationship.

Epilogue

This case teaches us the importance of upholding the 'No eject, no reject policy' even in cases where the staff are angry at the abuser for committing trust abuse on them. If the treatment staff had let their feelings about this youth block his readmission, the abuser would not have had to face the staff whose trust he had abused and the issue may have never been resolved.

Appendix G
Addressing extinction burst vignette

Harley was a 15-year-old, white male perpetrator of both sexual (molestation of two elementary school aged female cousins) and physical abuse (repeated assault). His extreme violent assaults at school were always on male peers and always after minor perceived injustices. The beatings he administered to others were severe to the point of being alarming and traditional therapeutic intervention focusing on uncovering possible reasons for his behaviour was unproductive. He only seemed to value his free time outside of school. He seemed to live for the weekends when he had control and could do what he wanted to do when he wanted to do it.

After his last vicious assault in school, a recommendation was made to the court that he receive 30 days detention spread across 15 weekends without informing Harley of any time limit on his weekend detention. He was under the impression that every week he was out of control and assaultive in school, he would spend the weekend in juvenile detention. Since the local detention centre policy was to spend the first two days in solitary confinement including meals in your cell, this actually meant total and complete time out on the weekends for abusive behaviour during the week. During the course of his extinction burst, he spent the first, second, third, fourth, fifth and sixth weekends in a row in detention. After that there were no further detentions during the following year of his therapy. He was discharged without further episode of violent abusive behaviour.

Epilogue

This case teaches two valuable lessons. First, jail can be therapeutic. Only after being forced to stop the abusive behaviour did Harley admit in therapy that around age five his father repeatedly beat and anally raped him. He disclosed memories of regularly crawling into bed bleeding from the rectum and crying himself to sleep. This trauma was experienced as a learned helplessness depression that was relieved by Harley re-enacting the successful defence of his past victimisation through the violent assault of those who acted unjustly towards him. Since the abusive behaviour itself acted as relief from adverse emotions, Harley had no motivation to find another way to cope until that maladaptive behaviour was prevented. The second lesson learned from this case is not to expect an immediate drop in abusive behaviour just because you have implemented an intervention that uses consequences known to affect the youth.

References

Aldgate, J. and Hawley, D. (1986) Preventing Disruption in Long-term Fostercare. *Adoption and Fostering.* 10:3 23–30.

Angold, A., and Costello, E. J. (1993) Depressive Co-morbidity in Children and Adolescents: Empirical, Theoretical, and Methodological Issues. *American Journal of Psychiatry.* 150: 1779–91.

Awad, G., Saunders, E. and Levene, J. (1984) A Clinical Study of Male Adolescent Sexual Abusers. *International Journal of Abuser Therapy and Comparative Criminology.* 28: 105–15.

Bath, H., Richey, C. and Haapala, D. (1992) Child Age and Outcome Correlates in Intensive Family Preservation Services. *Children and Youth Services Review.* 14: 389–406.

Becker, J. and Kavoussi, R. (1989) Diagnosis and Treatment of Juvenile Sex Offenders. in Schwartz, H. I. and Rosner, R. (Eds.) *Juvenile Psychiatry and the Law.* New York: Plenum. 133–43.

Benton Foundation. (2000) *What you may not know about foster care.* Children and Foster Care Feature Article. Available: www.connectforkids.org.

Cates, J. A. (1991) Residential Treatment in the 1980s: I. Characteristics of Children Served. *Residential Treatment for Children and Youth.* 9: 75–84.

Chamberlain, P., Moreland, S. and Reid, K. (1992) Enhanced Services and Stipends for Foster Parents: Effects on Retention Rates and Outcomes for Children. *Child Welfare.* 71:5 387–401.

Chamberlain, P. and Reid, J. (1998) Comparison of Two Community Alternatives to Incarceration for Chronic Juvenile Abusers. *Journal of Consulting and Clinical Psychology.* 66:4 624–33.

Clausen, J. M., Landsverk, J. Ganger, W. Chadwick, D. and Litrownik, A. (1998) Mental Health Problems of Children in Foster Care. *Journal of Child and Family Studies.* 7:3 283–96.

Cole, D. A. and Carpentieri, S. (1990) Social Status and the Co-morbidity of Child Depression and Conduct Disorder. *Journal of Consulting and Clinical Psychology.* 58,:748–57.

Cooper, C. C., Peterson, N. L. and Meier, J. H. (1987) Variables Associated With Disrupted Placement in a Select Sample of Abused and Neglected Children. *Child Abuse and Neglect.* 11: 75–86.

Cunningham, C. and MacFarlane, K. (1996)
When Children Abuse. Brandon, Vermont:
The Safer Society Press.

Davis, G., Yokley, J. and Williams, L. (1996) *An
Evaluation of Court-ordered Contact Between
Child Molesters and Children: Polygraph
Examination as a Child Protective Service.* 15th
Annual Research and Treatment Conference
of the Association for the Treatment of Sexual
Abusers, Chicago, Illinois.

Denby, R. and Rindfleisch, N. (1996) African
Americans' Foster Parenting Experiences:
Research Findings and Implications for Policy
and Practice. *Children and Youth Services
Review.* 18:6 523–52.

Dubner, A. and Motta, R. (1999) Sexually and
Physically Abused Foster Care Children and
Posttraumatic Stress Disorder. *Journal of
Consulting and Clinical Psychology.* 67:3 367–73.

Fanshel, D., Finch, S. and Grundy, J. (1989)
Foster Children in Life-course Perspective:
The Casey Family Program Experience. *Child
Welfare.* 68:5 467–78.

Fehrenbach, P., Smith, W., Monastersky, C. and
Deisher, R. (1986) Adolescent Sexual Abusers:
Abuser and Offence Characteristics. *American
Journal of Orthopsychiatry.* 56: 225–33.

Feshbach, N. and Feshbach, S. (1982) Empathy
Training and the Regulation of Aggression:
Potentialities and Limitations. *Academic
Psychology Bulletin.* 4: 399–413.

Gabel, S. and Shindledecker, R. (1990) Parental
Substance Abuse and Suspected Child
Abuse/Maltreatment Predict Outcome in
Children's Inpatient Treatment. *Journal of the
American Academy of Child and Adolescent
Psychiatry.* 29: 919–24.

Gottesman, H., Yokley, J. and Bobek, A. (1994)
*The Use of Oral Medroxyprogesterone Acetate
in Adolescent Sex Abuser Treatment: A Case
Study of Risk-benefit Factors.* 13th Annual
Research and Treatment Conference of the
Association for the Treatment of Sexual
Abusers, San Francisco, California.

Greenberg, D. and Bradford, J. (1997) Treatment
of the Paraphilic Disorders: A Review of the
Role of the Selective Serotonin Re-uptake
Inhibitors. *Sexual Abuse: A Journal of Research
and Treatment.* 9: 4 351–59.

Heap, K. K. (1991) A Predictive and Follow-up
Study of Abusive and Neglectful Families
by Case Analysis. *Child Abuse and Neglect.*
15: 261–73.

Houts, S. (1995) Explaining Alcoholism
Treatment Efficacy With the Theory of

Reintegrative Shaming. Alcoholism Treatment
Quarterly. 13:4 25–38.

Lowenstein, L. (1985) Let Them do the Rejecting:
The Treating of Physically and
Psychologically Abused Children.
Contemporary Review. 247:1439 304–10.

Miller, D. (1998) Forced Administration of Sex-
drive Reducing Medications to Sex Abusers:
Treatment or Punishment. *Psychology, Public
Policy and Law.* 4:1/2 175–99.

Proch, K. and Taber, M. (1985) Placement
Disruption: A Review of Research. *Children
and Youth Services Review.* 7:4 309–20.

Ray, J. and Horner, W. (1990) Correlates of
Effective Therapeutic Foster Parenting.
Residential Treatment for Children and Youth.
7:4 57–69.

Roberson, G., Yokley, J. and Zuzik, J. (1995)
Developing Treatment Guidelines for Sex
Offender Attendence at Religious Services:
A Clergy Opinion Survey. 14th Annual
Research and Treatment Conference of the
Association for the Treatment of Sexual
Abusers, New Orleans, Louisiana.

Rogers, C. (1957). The Necessary and Sufficient
Conditions of Personality Change. *Journal of
Consulting Psychology.* 21: 95–103.

Sanchirico, A., Lau, W. J., Jablonka, K. and
Russell, S. J. (1998) Foster Parent Involvement
in Service Planning: Does it Increase Job
Satisfaction? *Children and Youth Services
Review.* 20:4 325–46.

Shoor, M., Speed, M. and Bartelt, C. (1966)
Syndrome of the Adolescent Child Molester.
American Journal of Psychiatry. 122:, 783–9.

Tkachuk, G. and Martin, G. (1999) Exercise
Therapy for Patients with Psychiatric
Disorders: Research and Clinical Implications.
Professional Psychology: Research and Practice.
30:3 275–82.

Tjaden, P. G. and Thoennes, N. (1992).
Predictors of Legal Intervention in Child
Maltreatment Cases. *Child Abuse and Neglect.*
16: 807–21.

Urquhart, L. (1989) Separation and Loss:
Assessing the Impacts on Foster Parent
Retention. *Child and Adolescent Social Work
Journal.* 6:3 193–209.

Wahler, R. (1990) Who Is Driving the
Interactions? A Commentary on 'Child and
Parent Effects in Boys' Conduct Disorder'.
Developmental Psychology. 26:5 702–4.

Yokley, J. (1990) The Clinical Trials Model:
Victim Responsibility Training. in Yokley J.
(Ed.) *The Use of Victim-abuser Communication*

in *The Treatment of Sexual Abuse: Three intervention Models.* Orwell, Vermont: The Safer Society Press. 69–110).

Yokley, J. (1993) *Treatment for Appropriate Social Control (TASC) Program Manual.* Revised 1997. Ohio: Clinical and Research Resources.

Yokley, J. (1995) *Social Responsibility Therapy Work Book: Understanding Abuse Behaviour.* Revised 1997. Ohio: Clinical and Research Resources.

Yokley, J. (1996) *The Development of Abuse in Youth Sex Abusers: A Conceptual Model with Treatment Implications.* The 12th Annual Conference of the National Adolescent Perpetrator Network, Minneapolis, Minnesota.

Yokley, J. (1999a) Using Therapeutic Community Learning Experiences with Youth Sex Abusers. in Schwartz, B. (Ed.) *The Sex Abuser: Theoretical Advances Treating Special Populations and Legal Developments.* Kingston, NJ: Civic Research institute. 3: 19.

Yokley, J. (1999b) The Application of Therapeutic Community Learning Experiences to Adult Abusers. in Schwartz, B. (Ed.) *The Sex Abuser: Theoretical Advances Treating Special Populations and Legal Developments.* Kingston, NJ: Civic Research institute. 3:25.

Yokley, J. and Boettner, S. (1999a) *Behaviour Norms for Outpatient Youth Sex Abusers: Constructing A Database for Treatment Intervention Decisions.* Association for the Treatment of Sexual Abusers 18th Annual Research and Treatment Conference, Lake Buena Vista, Florida.

Yokley, J. and Boettner, S. (1999b) *Youth Sex offender Treatment in Therapeutic Foster Care: Lessons from Five Years of Treatment Program Experience.* 18th Annual Research and Treatment Conference of the Association for the Treatment of Sexual Abusers, Lake Buena Vista, Florida.

Yokley, J., Laraway, C. and Clough, A. (1997) *Behaviour Therapy and Criminal Justice: The Controversy over Boot Camp Treatments.* 31st Annual Convention of the Association for the Advancement of Behaviour Therapy, Miami Beach, Florida.

Yokley, J. and McGuire, D. (1990) introduction to the therapeutic use of victim-abuser communication. in Yokley, J. (Ed.) *The Use of Victim-abuser Communication in The Treatment of Sexual Abuse: Three Intervention Models.* Orwell, Vermont: The Safer Society Press. 7–22.

Yokley, J. and McGuire, D. (1991) *Emotional Restitution: The Therapeutic use of Sex Abuser Communication with Victims.* Association for the Treatment of Sexual Abusers 10th Annual Research and Treatment Conference, Fort Worth, Texas.

Chapter 21: The Community Management of Young People who Sexually Abuse

Dr Tony Baker

Introduction

In this chapter the concepts underpinning a community based therapeutic service for young people who have committed sexually abusive acts with other children will be described. In addition there will be an account of how those concepts have been applied in the therapeutic programme at Ashwood Centre in Surrey in conjunction with the committed involvement of parents/carers and professionals from social services and education.

Ryan (1991) and Hawkes et al. (1997) have considered the various theoretical approaches to aetiology. The experience at Ashwood Centre has confirmed our view that the combination of a broad developmental approach and family systems theory is the most useful in formulating a view about aetiology in any particular case. The *Four Antecedents Model* described by Finkelhor (1986) still provides a helpful way of considering the stages of abuse development and the attribution of responsibility. The disinhibiting factors for children who abuse will be qualitatively different in pattern as they develop into adulthood. It is also useful to apply the abuse-cycle model (Lane and Zamora 1984) to the understanding of repeated acts of abuse by children and it would be important to establish to what extent the abusive behaviour fits a pattern of compulsive or addictive behaviour. In addition, the constitutional, learning ability and mental health issues should not be overlooked as this may significantly alter the basis for the understanding of specific sexually abusive contexts.

The focus of this chapter will be on post-pubertal adolescent males (under eighteen years) who engage in sexual activity with other young people or children, such activity being coercive, exploitative or inappropriate to the other young person's own personal development or situation. There is a distinction to be made between younger and older children who abuse. The issues in the community management of pre-pubertal boys revolve around the differences in the meaning and function of the abuse. While the statutes confer criminal responsibility on children of ten years and above, this delineation does not take into account the development of individual children.

The conceptual overview

Sexually abusive behaviour always has a history to its evolution and occurs in a developmental context to the extent that a number of parallel developmental factors may be significant. The genesis of these priming factors can usually be discovered as developmental inhibition, precocity or distortion. It is helpful to consider the physical, cognitive, social, emotional and sexual development of the individual as part of the assessment and formulation of the problem. Epps (1999) highlights that this area of theoretical development (social-emotional) has to date been relatively neglected and has yet to be pulled into a useful theoretical framework. To widen this theoretical field it is useful to consider that the sexual (abuse) behaviour serves a maladaptive function in relation to broad developmental needs and should not be seen as a primary disorder of sexual development.

The physical and sexual development in terms of puberty and circulating hormone levels is a useful marker to distinguish between two distinct groups of young abusers. The differences in cognitive and social development are often very marked from both the young person's and other children's subjective views and from the objective adults' views. There needs to be a difference in the way these different age groups are approached in the community in terms of assessment, risk management and therapy. The family and school environments are quite different in terms of social activity and interests, expectations, structure, mobility and supervision. Similarly, if the child is placed in a foster home or residential placement, his peer group is likely to be younger and the carers will have a different approach to the care task and will be dealing with quite distinct risk factors.

The philosophy and practice we have developed at Ashwood Centre excludes group-work with pre-pubertal children whether they are the victims or perpetrators of sexual abuse. For the younger child, the family or care setting provides the most important influences for growth and change. The therapeutic options of individual (non-directive or focused play therapy), dyadic or family therapy in combination with consultation to parents/carers, social workers and teachers offer the safest therapeutic environment. In our view, group-work with this younger group exposes them to the risk of contamination with information about a range of novel sexual acts that may arouse their interest and increase their risk. While family or carer influences will also be important for the older group, the influence of the peer group as a context for growth offers a distinct advantage as it reinforces the socially appropriate sexual boundary between teenagers and their parents. As the older group are regarded as being more responsible for their choices and actions, it is not such a risk to expose them to managed information about other abusers' history of offending.

The assessment and treatment activities concerning sexual abuse are very significant experiences for the abusive young person and their family or carers, usually in the aftermath of an allegation, disclosure or admission of such incidents. The young individual to be assessed may himself be a minor and the issues of informed consent need to be addressed with those who have parental responsibility for him. The consent for assessment will be distinct from consent for therapy. Best practice demands that therapy is informed by a formulation with recommendations that address the structure, process and content of a proposed therapeutic plan.

Sexual abuse has come to imply the inappropriate use of power in the abusive relationship combined with transgression of usual behavioural and privacy (sexual) boundaries. Institutional placements are used to detain and contain those who are deemed to be unmanageable or unplaceable in the community because the risk is judged to be unmanageable. However, there are hazards to institutional containment because the peer group may contaminate each other, with a resultant increase in interest, excitement and preoccupation with the gratifying aspects of abusive fantasy, which may even be acted out if inadequate supervision allows. The prospect of a residential facility, which specialises in working with such a client group, may present a social work team with a 'solution' in which problems may actually become compounded rather than resolved.

Inevitably, such collections of young people sharing an environment at close quarters will be challenged or excited by the power dynamics of such group living, especially if there are opportunities for sexual acting out. Non-specialised community placements, including residential care, fostering and placement in the extended family if the young person cannot remain in their family home, may offer a context in which the individual's broader developmental needs can be addressed. Specialist resources can then engage the abuser, their carers and their statutory workers in parallel processes to address the abusive behaviour, risk appreciation and management, child protection network support, liaison and consultation. There is a danger that those with responsibility for the abuser may be able to content themselves that a specialist residential unit will take over all their responsibilities in a way that allows the problem (which nobody actually wants to own) to disappear from mind. A well-managed community resource leaves ownership of the responsibility where it belongs.

If families, carers and professional workers in social services and education are excluded from involvement in the processes of assessment and treatment, the successful outcome of an intervention is seriously jeopardised. The tasks of this network of people include providing containment, facilitating engagement, supporting attendance and compliance, understanding the requirements of risk management and implementing strategies to minimise risk. It is also their role to play a part in protecting actual and potential victims who may continue to be targeted by the young sexual abuser. It is crucial that the young person experiences this group of adults as being interested and prepared to be involved in his process, notwithstanding the fact that some of those adults will feel and even express a strong revulsion for the offences he has committed.

The child or young person who sexually abuses may himself be at risk from sexual victimisation. The source of this may not be evident from the outset. However, it should also be recognised that, whenever a young person acts in this way towards another, they are also damaged in some profound respect by their own conduct. The child protection issue is therefore wider than may be generally realised.

Risk management is an inexact science. It is impossible to achieve a state of comfortable certainty. It is recognised that during a treatment process the risk of re-offending is reduced (but not abolished) statistically. Once services are withdrawn, the risk of recidivism increases. The concept of safe-enough uncertainty is useful in considering the limitations of risk management and risk reduction. There will be general and specific items of information that will need to be accessible, shared and understood in each case as part of the risk monitoring strategy of the young person's network. What informs that checklist will be: – the fullest possible understanding of the past behaviour; the nature of the chosen victims and the quality of relationship that gave rise to the opportunity to offend; the fantasy of abusing; the strength of compulsions and addiction and other disinhibiting factors; the capacity for openness; the developmental deficits and responses to intervention; and, the motivation to change and reform.

Assessment in the community

Assessment is a process that, in this context, is intended to inform about risk, risk management, therapeutic potential and strategic planning. Where the development of an individual and his relationships (including abusive relationships) are concerned, no assessment can be said to reflect a final position; no absolutes can be established. Assessment is better regarded as a continuous process and any initial assessment will be subject to review, especially where there is an intervention that is directed towards change.

An assessment is commissioned by a referrer who may need help, through a stage of prior consultation, to define the purpose and the possibility of realising their objectives. Some situations can only be described as very high risk at this initial stage and there may need to be a structural change or a motivational shift in the people most closely involved in the situation

before an assessment can be conducted that is likely to meet the referrer's objectives.

Sexual abuse is highly emotive, not the least because of the common assumptions and myths that can cloud thinking. There is often a high level of anxiety or even fear, which may be manifest with obvious resistance as aggression or denial, not only in the abuser but also in their families and victims, in their school setting and in their peer groups. This anxiety may be compounded by anger in the stakeholders which may be quite understandable and even justified but it can serve to deepen the trenches of resistance both in the person to be assessed and also some key members of the family if they are fully supportive of the denial.

The first step in engagement in the assessment may be to work with the denial by exploring the myths, assumptions and meanings of the alleged sexual abuse for the family that are driven to contain their young abuser's fear by joining them in their denial. Additionally, it has to be said that the resistance of key adults may be self-serving if they have had a direct or indirect role in the causation of the abusive behaviour. Families may also experience corporate guilt and shame that may have the effect of silencing family members and suppressing answers to important questions.

The Developmental History

The parents can provide essential information about the young person's development. The topics to be covered will necessarily include the following:

- **Physical development,** i.e. growth, health, sensory and motor competence, constitutional factors e.g. attentional problems and speech or articulation ability.
- **Cognitive development,** i.e. academic progress and learning ability, memory competence, reasoning ability and capacity for abstract thinking and the formation of an understanding of 'the way the world works' (or internal working model of culturally accepted social constructs). The educational history will also assist.
- **Social development,** i.e. attachment and belonging, trust, communication skills, power repertoire, responsibility, self-care and self-protection skills (including awareness of danger), capacity to share, experience empathy, hold personal values, show respect, capacity to hold and share beliefs and

capacity to work towards a personal or shared goal.

- **Emotional development,** i.e. the capacity to experience, express, manage and resolve feelings in response to internal or external events, in particular **anxiety** (re: physical or social survival), **guilt** (re: sense of responsibility), **anger** (re: sense of injustice) and **grief** (re: sense of irrevocable loss). In addition it may be helpful to discover the young person's capacity to manage positive arousal states of anticipation and excitement, to use humour appropriately and to respond to expressed affection. There is often a disconnection between verbal expression and feelings that amounts to a dissociation that is evidenced by the 'cut-off' presentation of the young abuser.
- **Sexual development,** i.e. gender identity, gender-appropriate activities and choices, distorting experiences (if known), preoccupations or obsessions, sexual awareness and knowledge base (including the sources of information available to the individual), precocity, attitudes and interests, access to and use of pornography. This material may not be available from family members, but there will be information to elicit about family attitudes and customs in relation to sexual or privacy boundaries.

By using this approach, the parents may begin to perceive the assessors as professionals who are interested in the person as much as the abuse history. This may be important in gaining their full co-operation in the work to be undertaken.

The purpose of gathering the information about the individual's development is to set the known facts about the sexual abuse into a context to inform a working hypothesis about the function of the abuse to the perpetrator. Any divergence from the normal range of developmental capacities noted above might have significance for our understanding of how the abusive attitude and behaviour has arisen.

To exemplify this, it can be seen that a child who has grown up feeling alienated because of a constitutional difficulty and where there is a poor model of power dynamics in family relationships combined with a distorted understanding of social relationships and premature exposure to poorly understood sexual experiences, may develop an interest in secretive sexualised 'power-play' with other children. Similarly, younger children who have been sexually abused and eroticised within that sexual contact may be driven to act out or repeat the experience in their own terms with a younger and less assertive child. The permutations are seemingly endless, but experienced practitioners will recognise important patterns in the complex interaction between the respective developmental drives of the abuser.

There are three less common specific situations that require further discussion:

- A significant number of young sexual abusers are shown to have learning difficulties or even learning disability (O'Callaghan, 1999). The meaning of sexualised behaviour in this context may be found in the cognitive distortions and sub-cultural norms of the individual. The young person may be able to give a history of premature or poorly understood sexual incidents when they witnessed or experienced violation of sexual boundaries. They may then have integrated coercive sexual acts into their understanding of 'the way the world works' and then acted this out in response to their own arousal.
- Children and teenagers with Autistic Spectrum Disorders such as Asperger's Syndrome (Haracoupos and Pederson, 1992; Birtwell and Bowly, 1999) may develop a fixated interest or obsession with aspects of sexuality. Their peer relationships may be very limited and they may have access to younger children. The self-serving persistent young person may repeatedly seek to act out sexually with others in particularly idiosyncratic, sometimes mechanistic, ways that will probably be related to an iniating incident when they were exposed to sexual information either as an observer or as a victim or participant.
- Considerable work has been undertaken to explore the links between *attachment disorders* and sexual offending (Santry and McCarthy, 1999). Some children develop an attachment disorder that can be described as an *erotic attachment*. Such a disorder is characterised by the confusion a child has about its own sexual interest and arousal with a perception of intimacy (real or fantasised) with a key attachment figure. This situation can arise when a very young child is invited into an incident or series of events when they and the key adults are aroused, out

of control, frightened or frightening and where the hiatus is resolved by a sexual act or intimacy which either involves the child directly or indirectly as a witness. This would include situations of domestic violence between the adults, which include sexual violence. The child's 'role' may be that of mother's comforter in such scenes, but an element of the child's experience is that they enjoy the closeness and intimacy, which contributes to their own genital arousal in combination with their own fear and relief responses. Such children will be more likely to seek to sexualise affectionate contacts with adults, carers and authority figures than to sexually abuse younger children, but when this is frustrated it can lead to the transgression of other boundaries of real or imagined intimacy.

After the background information is elicited it will be more possible to generate an operational understanding of the abusive behaviour in terms of the function that the abusive behaviour had for the individual when they began on their pathway to abuse and then to arrive at another level of understanding in terms of the persistence or development of abusive behaviour. Using a developmental model of assessment is the first logical step towards exploring how the abuse came about.

Meeting the Young Person who Abused

In the first contact it is necessary that the referring worker, who will have statutory responsibility for his case, accompany the young person. Inclusion of the referrer at this stage allows the responsibility for the assessment to be actively owned in a way that is clear to the individual. It is a shared responsibility to help the young person understand the relevance, purpose, scope and limitations of the assessment. The legal context may provide another basis for the discussion of the potential implications of the assessment. To this end, the referrer will be asked to summarise the history of concern with details of any statements or allegations that have been made. An immature young person will be likely to feel safer if they have a parent or carer on hand, in another room, while they are being met for the first time in case they become distressed and need active support and comfort.

This early assessment process provides an infrastructure for receiving the subject of the assessment as a *person* who has abused, for a first interview. Too close a focus on the abusive behaviour at the outset can increase resistance and can be experienced as dehumanising, as if we are only interested in the offensive conduct and not the person himself. Various techniques can be used to engage the young person in this process including creating a genogram or eco-map. With younger children, the interviewer may need to use other skills and techniques of facilitating communication and rapport.

By broadening the horizons of our interest through a developmental focus we may even encourage the young person to think that there will be a reason or way of understanding what they have done that is so wrong or shameful. Too often the abuser does not actually think about their actions as they follow their impulses to create and act on opportunities to pursue sexual contact with younger children. Addictive behavioural cycles may be established at an early stage within their distorted development. Shame and fear of discovery may act as factors to suppress any process of reflection, as well as ensuring that victims are effectively silenced. By demonstrating that we are prepared to think about them as people who have come to make choices that have damaged others and got themselves into serious trouble, we may be making first steps in engagement of the young person in their own analysis of what they have done.

Such a context may make it easier for all concerned to have a conversation of enquiry about the history of sexual abusing, the evolution of a *modus operandi* and the abuser's motives in pursuing their victims. In the early stages of this work, 'don't know' is a very common defensive response to relevant or searching questions. Avoidance of eye contact, aggressive and abusive attitudes are all indicators that the young person's fear of judgement and punishment, fear of loss of key relationships or even loss of civil freedom may be playing a great part in their resistance to engagement in the pursuit of understanding. There is a danger that the assessment becomes another process that the young person perceives that they have to survive. The use of historical data about developmental issues and family background may be instrumental in bringing back the focus and purpose of the assessment as relevant to the young person's agenda.

It is also important that the assessors do not lose sight of the victims, and it is necessary to widen the discussion to include consideration of the victim's responses to the abuse. What can the young person say about that from his perception?

Once there has been a satisfactory discussion with the individual, it is helpful to have a forum discussion, in his presence, with parents and other key adults, including the referring social worker, probation officer or mental health worker. The purpose is to give feedback about any new understanding or information about the abuse that has been elicited. It is an opportunity to clarify the history and corroborate significant data.

Establishing a Safety Net

Wherever the young person is living, there will need to be adults who are working in partnership with the statutory services. If he remains in the family home, the parents will be required to demonstrate a capacity to think in a detailed way about risk as well as show the authority to manage and implement the decisions of a wider network on a day-to-day basis. Open communication will be the key to working together. The selection of an alternative placement will depend upon the fulfilment of these criteria as a first step. The home setting will be the place where the most pertinent questions may need to be asked and the viability of this arrangement will depend on the young person's ability to develop effective communication around the issues of risk and safety.

When advising on risk management, the assessors will need to meet with the key adults who form the day-to-day protective network. This will include representatives from the school or college setting who will play a crucial role in determining what strategies can realistically be implemented. The protective network may be quite unfamiliar with such a task in a focused way and the knowledge gap will need to be bridged through the processes of liaison and consultation to increase awareness and inculcate a new sub-culture that is enabled to always *think risk*.

When attempting to achieve a state of *safe-enough uncertainty*, it is clearly essential to identify as closely as possible the context in which risk may be heightened. The young person will need to adapt to a new environment in which they have to accept that those caring for them and supporting them do not trust them. This will lead to the young person needing to be more visible and audible than may be the norm for their age and maturity. This can be experienced as quite intrusive, but it is a fact that the young person who has the freedom to hide and close down communication is the young person who is at high risk.

The abuse of power that is inherent in the abuse dynamic has demonstrated that the abuser cannot be trusted with ordinary freedoms where they would have the power to choose secret gratification. The abuser who is motivated will accept and tolerate the need for adult presence and adult awareness of his plans and movements. The ideal state is one where the adults and professional workers experience the young person as fully co-operating rather than merely complying resentfully.

If the physical and emotional environments of the young abuser offer *safety, containment and opportunities for secure attachment,* it is possible to consider offering the individual inclusion in a therapeutic process. If those factors are not operating, it should be the objective of the network of adults to work towards achieving them as the first therapeutic task. This will be seen as work that is aimed more at the adult network than necessarily involving the young abuser directly. It requires commitment of time and energy and a focus on the relationships that the young person can enjoy in their ordinary world. There may be a role for a family therapist or systems consultant to enable fulfilment of this goal. Indeed, it can be seen that the lack of safety, containment or healthy attachments in the abuser's world creates the conditions for abuse to arise and continue. The impossibility of meeting these criteria in any given placement context may inform the interim care plan in pursuit of suitable alternatives.

Therapeutic Programme

The therapeutic alliance

The therapeutic alliance is the establishment of a relationship between the abuser, his family/carers, the referrer, the funding authority and the therapeutic agency. In some instances the Court may be part of the therapeutic alliance and may have an active role in the reviewing process. The relationship depends on an understanding of the purpose and objectives of intervention and agreement that is based upon a formulation of the presenting problem. The assessment process will have delivered a coherent formulation that includes the following:

- A description of the presenting problem and its consequences.
- The history and developmental context of the problem.
- The prognosis if there is no intervention, including current risk factors.
- An understanding of the problem that also identifies issues yet to be clarified.
- The prospects of therapeutic engagement, including perceived obstacles.

The formulation is the keystone to the therapeutic alliance and provides a foundation for discussion about the therapeutic objectives, the therapeutic strategies, the processes to be agreed, the time scale, reviewing processes and outcome assessment.

The young abuser will need to understand what is being offered, but his age and maturity may preclude him from giving fully informed consent. For minors, it will be necessary in any event for those with parental responsibility to give their informed consent. It will be essential to convey an understanding of the therapeutic agency's policy on confidentiality within the therapeutic process. In general, it is acceptable for the agency's representative to report into the professional network any information that arises concerning increased risk, and indeed such an issue will be expected to lead to a consultation/discussion about any necessary changes to the risk management strategies that have been agreed. Similarly, if information arises that identifies any other actual victims, that information should be shared with the relevant statutory authorities. The most helpful approach is to consider therapy as a process that is open to the professional network in this instance.

The young person and his carers will be given a set of rules and expectations governing his attendance, his conduct within the therapeutic programme and the requirements concerning his boundaries within the community. This will include any specific measures agreed with the school or college authorities, and may involve prohibitions or special supervision in respect of certain places or activities. There may be other specific limits set on his freedom, involving Internet access, use of pornography

and unstructured/unsupervised settings (e.g. play areas, swimming pools etc.).

The question then arises as to how the agreed boundaries will be policed and compliance or co-operation assessed. The social worker is in a key role within the professional system and all those with contact, including the parents/carers will need to agree to a method of communicating about any failure to comply. The young person will need to be informed of who knows about his situation and the rules in any given setting where risk needs to be managed. He can be encouraged to liaise with a nominated person in the event of any difficulties he has had in achieving compliance.

Consulting to the safety net

The network of parents, carers and professional workers will be required to commit to supporting the work of the therapeutic agency by attending for regular meetings which can be scheduled at the outset. These meetings provide an ongoing opportunity for those stakeholders to obtain progress reports, to provide reports on compliance and any incidents of concern, to discuss revisions and to work with the therapeutic agency to resolve any problems. In our experience there are always problems that require attention!

The safety net is the mechanism by which the maintenance of safety, containment and attachment can be achieved. The very fact that a dedicated group of people are meeting regularly to support the young person in therapy is a powerful message to him that he does not have to address the problems alone, that there are no more secrets and that he cannot play interested parties off against each other. Failure of the safety net will undermine the success of the outcome.

Funding issues need to be clearly established with the funding authority who will require a contractual arrangement. While this may be agreed for a core programme, in our experience it is prudent for the agency to identify any anticipated contingencies that might lead to additional requirement for funding, for instance family therapy.

Therapeutic approaches

The core programme is run on a group-work model. The size of group envisaged is a maximum of nine participants with three therapists working as a team. It was decided that at least one of the therapists in the therapy team would be a female because of the difficulties that some of the young people have had in relating to women.

The group meet weekly for three terms of ten weeks, following the school term structure. Each session lasts for three hours, with breaks. The components of each session allow for a social activity, individual or small groups working on set exercises, which prepare the members for a group discussion and art therapy.

The set exercises will be supervised by one of the therapy team for each small group and will usually be focused around an aspect of sexual abuse. The programme is designed to help each member work through the following steps:

- Admit to what you have done wrong, and in doing so describe the steps you took in carrying out the abuse. Explain how you first thought of doing this and how you justified it to yourself. Describe the pattern of abusing, how you forced or persuaded the other children to comply with your wishes and how you made sure that it was kept secret. Tell us about your thoughts and feelings between each time you carried out the sexual acts.
- Prepare an apology to all those people who have been affected by what you have done. Identify each person and think about how your actions have offended or upset him or her. Explain how you think they feel towards you now.
- Think about how you might help those people to feel better, especially the victims and their parents and your own parents or carers.
- Show that you are prepared to accept restrictions on your freedom until you can be trusted again or until you can act responsibly. Explain your understanding of the restrictions on you at present and what they are supposed to achieve.
- Promise not to abuse again and when you make the promise, say what you think you need to do that will help you to keep the promise.
- Keep the promise, but remember that other people have the right to ask you questions to be sure that you are keeping safe. Decide whom you can talk to if you feel you are close to breaking the promise. Work on an action plan for now and the future.

- Forgiveness may be important to you but saying sorry is not enough to achieve it. When you are forgiven it means that the person forgiving you does not feel they have to keep taking your past actions into account. People are likely to forgive you when they feel that they love you or care for you and they understand why you went astray. To be able to understand you, they will need you to talk to them in ways that help them to feel that you and they understand what went wrong and that you are doing all you can to be a safe person.
- Remember that when you do wrong, you are one of the people that are harmed by your actions. Show how you think you have harmed yourself by what you did wrong.

One of the first steps in this group-work is to establish a safe environment that is containing and that allows for secure attachment. Within the group context, the safety is established by the rules that each group member will sign up to. Those rules will establish boundaries around the work, like *confidentiality about the other group members, no alcohol, drugs or weapons, no swearing, no bullying, no violence, no mocking, listening to each other respectfully, no travelling together, no contact outside the group (either by meeting, telephone, text messages or e-mail), no pornography to be used at any time nor to be brought to the group, no sexual behaviour in the group and no judgements or insults about each others families.* The first group discussion will focus on the rules and why they are important. Exclusion and other sanctions will be discussed. None of the written material will be taken home but members will have a folder and writing materials provided for them to use at the sessions.

It is important to consider the mix of young people that are accepted for inclusion into any particular group. For instance, young people with low ability will perform better in the group if they are not alone in this respect. It is also not advisable to include two young people from the same residential or educational setting in a group, as this will compromise safety in a number of ways.

Before convening the group, each member that is accepted for the programme will be introduced to one of the therapy team who will have six individual sessions to establish a relationship that will allow a rapport to develop. Various aspects of the individual's daily life, relationships, important past events, interests and hobbies will form the content of these six hour-long meetings. By establishing the personal relationship with a key worker in this way, the young person may find it easier to manage their anxiety about being in a group. There is always reluctance, in our experience, and experience has shown that the young person identifies the key worker as someone who can meet their needs in the context of the group. The therapy team also obtain confidence in their relationship with the individuals before having to meet their needs as a group.

This introductory phase does seem to have the effect of limiting the initial acting out and avoids the perils of the young people attaching to each other for support in a maladaptive way that organises resistance to the feared therapeutic process.

Within the weekly sessions, the structure we have found most helpful that has evolved over a series of group-work programmes is as follows:

- Fifteen minutes: weekly news round-up.
- Five minutes: task setting for small groups or individuals.
- Thirty minutes: on task.
- Twenty minutes: one small group prepares a food item under supervision that will be shared by the whole group during the break while the two other groups work together on an art therapy project (related to the small group exercise).
- Thirty minutes: 'social break' to have a drink and eat the pancakes, cakes, biscuits etc. that have been made. The art therapy group share their work and talk it through with the rest of the group. This may be followed by a group physical activity.
- One hour: group presentation and discussion on the set task from the small groups.
- Fifteen minutes: writing up their personal journals on that day's group and what has been learned. This is a time when personal reflection is supported individually by the key-workers who will spend a few minutes with each young person.
- Five minutes: to be together as a group before departing. This gives an opportunity to remind the group about the agreed rules and keeping safe.

The therapy team will need to spend time together before and after each group session. Planning and co-working are essential in this work. The reason for employing three workers is that such a group cannot be run by one person alone and in the event of unplanned absence, there will usually be two workers remaining who can run the group session. It has been found to be helpful for the supervision sessions to take place after the group sessions. The therapy team attend seven supervision sessions for every ten-week term. Additional time may be required for planning and modifying the programme elements to address particular issues that arise in the group dynamics.

The professional or parents network are invited to commit to two meetings per term. The consultant to the network who is the programme co-ordinator manages liaison in the meantime. At the end of each term, the group member is required to attend a review with the programme director, their social worker and therapy key worker also being present for this meeting. Parents/carers will also play a part in the termly review process.

Working with specific relationships

The assessment may have revealed significant pathology in the relationships that the young person has with their family or a particular family member. If appropriate, at some point therapy sessions to address particular issues will be arranged in addition to the other elements of the programme. This may be deferred until after the group sessions have been completed. Such work may be focused towards the young abuser returning to the family home where there are younger siblings who may be deemed to be at risk. If the young person is in alternative care, there may be specific issues in the placement that require facilitated discussions between the carer and the young person to address safety and risk.

Addressing developmental issues

The initial assessment will have shown developmental deviance of some form. Some difficulties preclude group working, but if the young person is suitable for group work, it is based on the premise that they are likely to benefit from inclusion in the group. Within the combined individual, small group and larger group work, part of the key therapist's role will be to ensure that specific issues of social development are addressed. The social aspects of group-work are designed to have a social skills training component. Clearly, the session content will be aimed at addressing cognitive distortions and abuse promoting beliefs and attitudes. The individual work and the art therapy are aimed at facilitating the development of emotional articulacy. The parents and carers will be asked to focus on safety and developmental issues in the network consultations.

Assessing Outcomes and Reviewing Risk Management

Sources of information and distribution

Information on progress will be available from those who have regular contact with the young person including the therapy team, the parents/carers and the designated professional workers in social services and education. The young abuser will also provide information about himself. This information can be collated into the review reports that will be made available to child protection case conferences, statutory service managers, funding authorities and others on a need to know basis (e.g. parents and carers).

Measures

It is impossible to know the details of thoughts and fantasies that another has. A simple measure of known re-offending is unreliable if the young abuser has been able to establish a secret abusing relationship. If an opinion about outcome is to be given, it can only be based on an appraisal of observations of the young person's actions, attitudes, openness, co-operation, emotional responses (especially congruity), relationships, communication skills and willingness to address significant issues.

Other measures are comprehensively discussed by Carich and Lampley (1999), who use a fifteen-factor assessment model to address 'recovery' issues with young people who sexually abuse.

Therapy team report

A useful structure for the therapy team report is as follows:

- attendance and punctuality
- participation in discussions
- honesty

- openness and congruity of emotions
- sensitivity to target victims
- sensitivity to other victims
- attitude to group and behaviour during sessions
- self-centredness
- asking questions
- attitude to offence
- developmental profile (including areas of growth and change)
- relationships with other group members
- relationship with key therapist and attitude to female therapist
- progress in therapeutic objectives

The therapy team will also be asked to rate current level of risk (high, medium or low) and to comment on specific risk factors that have come to light during the individual or group discussions.

A wider perspective will be obtained from the safety net. Of special importance will be the following:

- general reliability and honesty
- attitudes to key relatives, carers and authority figures
- willingness to discuss his involvement in the group and to share spontaneously what he has learned
- compliance and co-operation with restrictions
- attitude to risk related questions
- performance and integration in education and social contexts
- peer relationships
- observed interests and hobbies and general activity levels
- observed risk taking behaviour
- observed progress in therapeutic objectives
- developmental changes perceived
- ambition and investment in his future
- resolution of his history of victimisation
- mental health issues
- outcome of legal proceedings

Risk management

One of the main objectives of the review process is to estimate level of risk. The levels can be defined operationally as:

- **High Risk:** The young person is in denial about his offending in terms of whether he did it in the face of incontrovertible evidence or in terms of the significance or implications for those affected by it. Blanket denial of perceived future risk will also undermine compliance with risk reduction strategies. Young people who are generally out of control, anti-authoritarian, involved in parallel delinquency or other socially unacceptable behaviour or who express ideas that promote sexual deviance would also be included in this category as would those who report high levels of abuse fantasy with masturbation. Any evidence of attempting to associate with younger children or especially vulnerable young people should also raise concern. Similarly the use of disinhibiting intoxicants or any out-of-control addictive or compulsive patterns of behaviour would warrant inclusion in this group. Mental health issues like depression, despair and self-harming behaviour should alert the assessors to suicidal risk.

- **Medium Risk:** The young person is ambivalent about the programme, unreliable in compliance with restrictions, a poor communicator and is cut-off or incongruent emotionally. Unreliable attendance and punctuality is a clear indicator of resistance to engagement, as are under-performance in any of the areas listed above in the review format. Of particular concern would be dishonesty, disrespect, cognitive distortion, unresolved conflicts about abusing, resistance or hostility to questions and lack of sensitivity to victims.
- **Low Risk:** Sustained progress in all of the areas for review with clear evidence of improvement in the developmental profile will encourage assessors to include the young person in this category. Good motivation for reform will need to be observed in all the individual's living, social, educational and therapeutic contexts. It should be remembered that young people may achieve this status but if restrictions are relaxed too soon or without a graduated testing of response they can easily shift into medium or high risk states.

When assessing risk, it is important to evaluate the performance of the safety net. Failure to sustain commitment and involvement will influence the young person's risk assessment and in deciding on risk management strategies, it may be necessary to review the young person's living or educational arrangements so that a proper level of commitment can be obtained. The safety net may need to include adolescent mental health services, for instance, if there are significant mental health issues. The child protection case conference may be a suitable forum in which to address such issues and the therapeutic agency will need to consider a report to the local child protection co-ordinator if there is a failure on the part of the statutory agencies to fulfil the initial agreements of the therapeutic alliance.

At the conclusion of the group programme the young person's therapeutic needs will be re-assessed. There may be value in continuing with individual therapy plans that might also include dyadic or family therapy, especially if there is a plan to reintegrate the young person into a setting where the abuse occurred. The therapeutic agency may have a continuing role in consulting to the safety net and monitoring progress after the therapeutic involvement is ended.

Follow up

Follow up serves to assess the performance of the programme and the individuals. An ideal framework uses a five-year time scale during which periodic review meetings are held with the young person and their parents or carers. Reports can be obtained from statutory agencies indicating their current involvement and any information on the young person's legal status or reported recidivism. The difficulties in pursuing this are self-evident as young people may move on without a forwarding address and key personnel may move.

Conclusion

Work with this group of young people is very challenging. To embrace all the facets that are inherent in child sexual abuse work is daunting and no single agency can assume all the roles that emerge. The achievement of a dedicated network of adults that includes family, professionals and therapy team is a task in its own right. The work should be seen as a long-term investment in child protection that warrants the commitment of adequate resources. The human resource implications should not be ignored in terms of support and supervision. The workers also need *safety, containment and attachment* if they are to be maximally effective with their vulnerable and potentially dangerous clients.

References

Birtwell, G. and Bowly, A. (1999) The Young Person with an Autistic Spectrum Disorder and Sexually Abusive Behaviour. in Calder, M. C. (Ed.) *Working with Young People Who Sexually Abuse: New Pieces of the Jigsaw Puzzle.* Dorset: Russell House Publishing.

Carich, M. S. and Lampley, M. C. (1999) Recovery Assessments with Young People who Sexually Abuse. in Calder, M. C. (Ed.) *Working with Young People Who Sexually Abuse: New Pieces of the Jigsaw Puzzle.* Dorset: Russell House Publishing.

Epps, K. J. (1999) Causal Explanations: Filling The Theoretical Reservoir. in Calder, M. C. (Ed.) *Working With Young People Who Sexually Abuse: New Pieces of The Jigsaw Puzzle.* Dorset: Russell House Publishing.

Finkelhor, D. (1986) Abusers: Special Topics. in Finkelhor, D. and Associates. *A Sourcebook on Child Sexual Abuse.* California: Sage Publications.

Haracoupos, D., and Pederson, L. (1992) *Sexuality and Autism.*

Hawkes, C., Jenkins, J. A. and Vizard, E. (1997) Roots of Sexual Violence in Children and Adolescents. in Varma, V. (Ed.) *Violence in Children and Adolescents.* London: Jessica Kingsley.

Lane, S. and Zamora, P. (1984) A Method For Treating The Sexual Offender. in Mathias, R., Demuro, P. and Allinson, R. (Eds.) *Violent Juvenile Offenders. National Council on Crime and Delinquency.* San Francisco, California.

O' Callaghan, D. (1999) Young Abusers with Learning Disabilities: Towards Better Understanding and Positive Interventions. in Calder, M. C. (Ed.) *Working with Young People Who Sexually Abuse: New Pieces of the Jigsaw Puzzle.* Dorset: Russell House Publishing.

Ryan, G. (1991) Theories of Etiology. in Ryan, G. and Lane, S. (Eds.) *Juvenile Sexual Offending. Causes, Consequences and Corrections.* Lexington, Massachusetts: Lexington Books.

Santry, S. and McCarthy, G. (1999) Attachment and Intimacy in Young people who Sexually Abuse. in Calder, M. C. (Ed.) *Working with Young People Who Sexually Abuse: New Pieces of the Jigsaw Puzzle.* Dorset: Russell House Publishing.

Part 7: Outcomes

Chapter 22: Research on the Development of Sexually Abusive Behaviour in Sexually Abused Males: The Implications for Clinical Practice

Dr Arnon Bentovim

Introduction

A controversial issue in the treatment of young people who are sexually offending is of how best to treat their experience of victimisation, whether sexual or physical. There are concerns that if victimisation experiences are the focus of therapeutic work, then offending behaviour will not be adequately addressed. Victimisation experiences may be used as a justification, and a minimisation of offending behaviour. At the same time young people who abuse other children sexually are often close to their own experiences of victimisation. Indeed many may still be living in family contexts where they remain at risk even if their own behaviour has also become abusive. In working with adults who abuse sexually there is a consensus that the focus of work needs to be on offending behaviour, in work with young people there is less clarity and this chapter will explore these issues.

There is agreement that young people who abuse sexually often have extensive experience of victimisation themselves. It seems reasonable therefore to suppose that young people who have been abused sexually represent a high risk population and will contain a significant number of young people who will become abusers in turn. This was the premise which influenced research at the Institute of Child Health linked with Great Ormond Street Children's Hospital. The aim of the research was to understand what were the risk factors for the development of sexually abusive behaviour in boys who themselves had been sexually victimised. This was examined in cross-sectional and prospective research. The basic findings will be reported in detail. In summary the key issue which appeared to be responsible for the development of sexually abusive behaviour in young people was that in addition to being sexually abused they had been subject to a cumulative set of traumatic and stressful experiences during their development. It is hypothesised these experiences result in attitudes and behaviours which contribute significantly to abusive action perpetrated against other young people. These findings have implications for the treatment of young people who are offending. Therapeutic work needs to address both the offending patterns which have been initiated, and also the long-term effects of living in a context where there has been extensive violence perpetrated against them, with persisting effects. This chapter will:

- Provide a brief review of the history of maltreatment in young people who go on to offend.
- Give a summary of the research conducted at the Institute of Child Health.
- Discuss the implications for therapeutic work which follows.

Brief Review of Relevant Research on Maltreatment

Becker (1998) in reviewing current knowledge of sex offending adolescents noted that adolescent sex offenders reported more histories of maltreatment, both physical and sexual, compared to generally conduct disordered young people. Findings from adult sex offenders again compliment what is described with young people who abuse. Rates vary considerably from study to study. Groth and Burgess (1979) reported 32 per cent of their sample of child molesters had reported some

The support of the Department of Health for the cross-sectional and prospective research described here is gratefully acknowledged.

form of sexual trauma. Faller (1988) reported 27 per cent, Pithers et al. (1988) 56 per cent. Freeman-Longo (1986) argued that abuse involving multiple abusers, or repeated abuse of long duration is more influential, indicating that it was not just the fact of abuse itself that was of relevance. It would appear therefore that the sexual abuse of boys in childhood was an important contributory, but not a necessary factor in the development of a perpetrator (Watkins and Bentovim 2000).

Current approaches to research are refining such notions. It is beginning to be possible to devise a more sophisticated pathway approach to understand what are the risks of an abused individual abusing others, and what are the protective factors which will mitigate against such repeating patterns, and what other sort of interventions may help prevent such a process.

Cross-sectional and Longitudinal Exploration of the Factors Which Lead to the Onset of Sexually Abusive Behaviour in Males who are Sexually Abused in Childhood

Cross sectional study (Skuse et al., 1998)

This took the form of an intensive hypothesis generating study on a relatively small number of young people. A series of young people and their families were studied intensively. There were four groups recruited including:

1. Boys between 11 and 16 who had been victims of sexual abuse who showed no evidence of perpetrating abuse against others, that is there was no evidence of the victim to offender cycle being evident.
2. Boys who had been victims of sexual abuse who were showing evidence of having begun to perpetrate against other children, that is a group who were showing the victim to offender cycle.
3. A group of boys with no evidence of sexual abuse, but who nevertheless were offending against other children, therefore a group of young people with no evidence of having been sexual abused, yet they were offending against other children.
4. A group of young people who were showing antisocial behavioural problems, but with no evidence of sexual abuse in their history, nor of abuse of others. This group acted as a control population.

It was therefore possible to carry out a variety of assessments on each group of these young people, to understand what were the specific factors which increased the risk of a young person who had been abused in childhood beginning to offend against other children. Awareness of such factors form the focus for prevention of the victim to offender cycle.

In total 78 boys were referred to the study, of whom 32 had abused other children and young people.

In the first stage of the assessment information was collected on intelligence, behaviour, pubertal status, socio-economic circumstances, and friendships. A socio-metric study was carried out in the schools the young people attended to understand peers perceptions of the boys.

The second stage consisted of three months of individual weekly psychoanalytic psychotherapy sessions. Sessions were both semi-structured with a variety of standardised instruments including measures of attachment, and hostility, and analysed using a grounded theory approach to derive childhood themes relating to history of care and maltreatment.

There were also less structured sessions covering the boys life history, their pattern of sexually abusive behaviour, and sexual fantasies. There was verification from independent sources. Birth mothers were interviewed about their own life history, their experience of maltreatment and aspects of family life. It was therefore possible to carry out a variety of comparisons and derive hypothesises to assist in understanding the processes which could lead from victim to offender cycles. The important factors which emerged from the analyses were as follows:

1. There were no differences found between the groups who suffered abuse in terms of their experience of sexual victimisation, based on personal accounts and contemporaneous records. Severity of abuse was ascertained from evidence of penetration, whether there were a number of perpetrators involved, or whether abuse was within or outside the family. This lack of difference was unexpected because there is a clinical impression that those boys who go on to abuse others appear to have been more severely abused over longer periods, by a number of perpetrators. The numbers assessed were small, therefore there may

have been a referral bias. However selecting young people to intervene on the basis of more serious abuse may not be the sole factor in terms of preventing the victim to offender cycle.

2. A number of other factors were looked at which seemed to be relevant during the assessment process. These included:

- experiencing intrafamilial violence
- witnessing intrafamilial violence
- rejection by the family
- discontinuity of care
- rejection by peers
- experiencing a generalised sense of grievance
- poor identification with father figures
- absence of a non-abusive male attachment figure
- having a mother who was sexually abused in childhood
- maternal depression
- poor sibling relationships
- having a mother who was physically abused in childhood
- low levels of guilt concerning abusive action

Many of these are factors which emerge when working with young people who have abused sexually, and therefore may well seem to be a natural focus of concern in preventing the victim to offender cycle. In this cross-sectional study the most significant factors however were those relating to:

- experiencing intrafamilial violence
- witnessing intrafamilial violence
- discontinuity of care

These experiences preceded the sexually abusive behaviour which led to referral. Other factors were present in other young peoples lives who did not go on to abuse other children and young people. We conceptualised the factors which differentiated this group as living in a climate of intrafamilial violence which may or may not have directly involved the boys as a victim. It was felt that discontinuity of care and rejection amplified the effects of witnessing and being subject to violence, through disrupting attachments and negatively affecting their emotional lives.

There were many similarities in the lives of boys who abused sexually, but who had no history of sexual abuse themselves, indicating that sexual abuse may be a risk factor amongst others. They also grew up in a family context where they were exposed to a climate of violence in the home. In addition the mothers of boys who abused other children had themselves been subject to extensive sexual and physical abuse not only in their own childhood, but in adult life. So that these boys were exposed not only to a climate of physical violence, but also to sexual violence to a key figure in their lives which may have had a similar effect to being sexually abused themselves.

Although this cross-sectional study could not look at mechanisms, we hypothesised that experiencing physical violence directly or being exposed to a climate of violence subjects a child to prolonged fear, stress, often for long periods of childhood development. This will adversely affect key developmental tasks and personality development through early childhood, middle childhood, adolescence and adult life (Pynoos et al. 1996).

Discontinuity of care, living in turn with various parents and step-parents, or being in Local Authority care could lead to a profound feeling of rejection. This had a bearing on the formation of attachments, and may result in the lack of a secure relationship with an adult. Severe, unpredictable stresses have links with psychopathology in both adolescence and adulthood. We felt that these boys were having the worst of both worlds, suffering both disruption of care and violence. They were missing confiding relationships which could have protective effect.

We also felt that directly traumatic, and traumagenic effects of pervasive violence lead to subjected helplessness, the evacuation of defensive aggressive fantasises and traumatic visualisation of abusive experiences. Later sexualisation of aggressive fantasies led to the 'eroticisation' of aggression, which leads in turn to abusive behaviour. We felt that such aggressive behaviour may well be a fight response, taking the form of revenge fantasises acted out in adolescence to reverse a sense of powerlessness and project such feelings on other young people as a way of feeling less burdened themselves.

Prospective study (Skuse et al., 1999)

These findings were further tested in a prospective manner. All males referred to Great Ormond Street for reasons relating to sexual abuse from 1980 were studied. A sample of 284 male subjects were studied, with a subset of

107 subjects who were subjected to more intensive studies. Demographic data and information about sexual victimisation of the sample was collected from Clinic, and Social Services files when these were available. Evidence of the victim to offender cycle was obtained by further scrutiny of Social Services files when they were available in the years which followed original victimisation. In addition criminal record data were studied from a range of sources, national police conviction records, and local police caution records to ascertain which of the young people had gone on to abuse.

We were therefore able to address the following questions:

- What proportion of sexually victimised subjects would become sexual perpetrators in later life? What is the risk of victims following the victim to offender cycle?
- What proportion of such victims are dealt with subsequently through criminal procedures?
- What proportion of those individuals who perpetrated during adolescence continue to offend in later life?
- The more intensive study directly addressed the issues concerned with prevention of the victim to offender cycle, by asking what experiences would increase the risk of a sexually victimised young person becoming a perpetrator, and what experiences would decrease this risk. Which risk factors should alert professionals to the danger of a young person going on to abuse others, and what are the factors which can be brought into play to prevent this process occurring?

Young people who had been abused sexually were investigated intensively by both Social Services Department and at Great Ormond Street who referred young people for treatment. There was considerable information available which throws light on any subsequent perpetration which became evident through tracking the young person's subsequent history. 37 of the 284 boys originally referred as victims subsequently became sexual perpetrators, that is 12 per cent of the original sample of victims. About a third of these received either a caution or conviction for a sexual offence. It was noted that a greater proportion of those young people who had been abused and went on to abuse other children also committed crimes of violence, indicating that the relevant factors which lead to the sexual abuse of others

may also lead to other forms of violence against others, suggesting a generally antisocial picture.

Looking at the group of young people who perpetrated during adolescence, a further 12 per cent of them continued beyond the age of 16 into adult life.

Risk factors

There was confirmation that the originally defined risk factors which distinguished those young people who had been victims of sexual abuse who went on to become offenders were operating in the longitudinal study, i.e. they experienced physical abuse, witnessed family violence, and experienced disruption of care.

The prospective design has clarified the importance, not only of a climate of violence, but also a climate of neglect, failure of care, supervision, a female care figure who sexualises and the mother child relationship as well as a paternal figure who provides a violent role model for identification. (Detailed results on this are due to be published shortly.)

Protective factors

A number of protective factors were tested to see whether the above risk effects could be modified:

- Having one good relationship with an adult in the child's life.
- Having a good relationship with a sibling.
- Having a good relationship with a peer.
- Spending a significant period of years in foster care, with non-abusive male carers and non-abusive female carers.
- Having a significant period of time cared for by the same carer.
- Receiving therapeutic help.

The importance of potential for positive attachments and adequate care, neutralising the impact of living in a climate of violence, and the cumulative effects of abuse and neglect was demonstrated.

A Clinical Example

To illustrate how the risk and protective factors appear in a clinical case, a young person referred to a therapeutic community to which the author consults will be described. He was 14 years of age when he was referred and he completed his treatment over a three year period and was followed-up some three years after discharge.

He reported that his parents separated when he was 18 months of age. His mother remarried, the relationships with John's step-father was turbulent, there was domestic violence and John was scapegoated, blamed for his parents' conflicts and punished severely.

Between the ages of five and eight he was abused by his step-father sexually, there was both contact and non-contact abuse. He was made to watch his step-father masturbate, there was mutual masturbation, and forced oral sex. John attempted to tell his mother on a number of occasions, but he was disbelieved and blamed for the continuing turmoil in the relationships between herself and the step-father. He made a number of allegations within the school context which were investigated, and he was taken into care between the ages of 8 and 10. He then went to live with his father and step-mother between the ages of 10 and 14. The one positive relationship he made was with his step-mother but the relationship between John and his father continued to be negative, punitive and rejecting.

John was an intellectually able young person but because of his image and behaviour he tended to be rejected by peers and drifted to younger children. He made a relationship with one of the children in his class who had been placed in a normal class with special assistance. She was the same age but had a learning disability. He presented himself to her family as a caring and responsible young person, and was invited to spend time with her family. He was warned against making a sexual relationship, because of her immaturity and developmental vulnerability. However, he later revealed that he developed extensive sexual thoughts and masturbatory activity about her. He made sexual approaches, and eventually abused her anally to avoid pregnancy.

Subsequent investigation indicated that the young person had no sexual interest in him and felt abused by him which triggered extreme guilt and shame when it was discovered. John's family rejected him, he was physically beaten by his father, and placed once more in foster care. He spent some months building up a positive relationship with his foster carer, but he began to remove underwear from his foster mother, later found in his room. He was using them to masturbate. He was also exposing himself to other young people.

Looking at the various risk factors which were identified in the research of the key factors:

- He experienced extensive intrafamilial violence, not only the extensive sexual abuse by a step-father but also punitive care by his mother, step-father and his father.
- He witnessed intrafamilial violence between his mother and step-father and indeed was blamed for causing conflict between his mother and step-father.
- There was considerable rejection within the family context, his mother disbelieved his statements of abuse by his step-father, and refused to act when he spoke to her about his abuse. He had to leave the family home after the abuse was discovered, even though his step-father was convicted for his abuse.
- He therefore experienced discontinuity of care, being rejected by his mother, placed in care for a period and then eventually placed with his father and step-mother. His father continued to be generally rejecting towards him, he was inadequately supervised seeking refuge in an alternative family where he eventually abused a vulnerable young person.
- Although not one of the key factors identified in the research, he conformed to other general factors which were noted initially, particularly the rejection by peers. The original research demonstrated that boys who had been sexually abused, and those who had been abused and had gone on to abuse others were rejected by peers, so it may well be that John's rejection was a more generalised factor relating to his abuse rather than being a factor which could be seen to lead to a pathway of abusing behaviour.
- He experienced a general sense of grievance as a result of the experiences. Although this was not a key aspect of the basic findings in the research, again it was one of the general clinical findings that we noted and a characteristic of John's attitude.
- A further factor which we felt was important on clinical grounds was poor identification with father figures. Given the extensive abuse by his step-father and his physical abuse and general rejection by his father, he would certainly appear to have poor identification with a father figure.
- Associated with this was another factor which is the absence of non-abusive male attachment figures.

It is not possible to comment on other factors which we noted: maternal depression, having a mother who was sexually or physically abused in childhood. By the time John was referred there was no ongoing contact with his family and we were not able to make these assessments.

Protective factors

We noted that having a reasonable set of protective factors may be sufficient to prevent a young person with moderate levels of risk from abusing. John appeared to have a high level of risk factors, e.g. witnessing domestic violence, experiencing violence, primary disruption of care, rejection, so that it may well be that even though some protective factors were present, they may not have been sufficient to counteract the force and effects of the risk factors. Looking at the protective factors as noted earlier:

- **Having one good relationship with an adult.** He did have one good relationship with an adult in his life, which paradoxically was his step-mother rather than any biological parent. It may be important to note this because although such protective factors did not appear to be sufficient to negate the force towards abusive behaviour, nevertheless during the therapeutic phase of work this was a factor which seemed to assist John in developing an abuse-free lifestyle. He made particularly good relationships with female therapists, female staff members.
- **Having a good relationship with a sibling**. John did not have any current relationships with a sibling but he was close to a sibling who had died.
- **Having a good relationship with a peer**. John had poor relationships with his peers because of his immature, arrogant, defensive style of relating and he was perceived as unpopular. During the therapeutic process of work he established more positive relationships with peers and again it may well be an important aim of therapeutic work to strengthen the protective factors which can negate an abusive potential and neutralise them to maintain an abuse free life.
- **Spending a significant period of years in foster care, with non-abusive male carers and non-abusive female carers.** Although John had a period in care following the abuse by his step-father, he then went to live with his father and step-mother. Although his step-mother was a positive influence in his life, the overall context was not one which

could lessen the impact of the original abuse by his step-father, given the rejection by his father. Again it is of interest to note that one of the advantages for John of having a period in a therapeutic community subsequent to the discovery of his serious offending has given him a significant period of care which has offered him a reparenting experience. He maintained a positive relationship with his latest foster carer despite having erotised the relationship which meant it was inappropriate to continue his placement.

- **A significant period of time cared for by the same carer**. The nature of John's care during his early life was disruptive, and there was a limited period of time of care by the same carer, and particularly one which was not abusive.
- **Receiving therapeutic help.** There is no record of John receiving focussed therapeutic help for his abusive experiences once the abuse by his step-father was revealed. A number of recent studies, e.g. Monck et al., 1996, Finkelhor and Berliner, 1995, Jones and Ramchandani, 1999, has revealed the effectiveness of focussed therapeutic work for children who have been sexually abused. John did not receive such therapeutic work and therefore the absence of therapeutic intervention meant that this protective factor was not available or present to help counter abusive forces.

Focus on Offending Behaviour and Experiences of Victimisation During the Therapeutic Process

To further examine the issues of focussing on offending behaviour and victimisation experiences, the process of therapy will be tracked for John. The advantage for him attending a therapeutic community rather than participating in an out-patient rolling programme of therapeutic work is that it is possible to follow John's responses in a variety of different contexts, and to examine the focus of therapeutic work:

1. Pre-therapy assessment

What was striking about John's initial assessment as well as revealing the set of factors which has already been commented on was the extensiveness of his cognitive distortions. He stated that the young person was attracted to him, that she could have stopped the abuse easily if she had wanted to, she felt good and excited by the abuse, she led him on. He was uncertain whether he was responsible or not for his extensive abusive action, and found it extremely difficult to confront these beliefs.

He did not own responsibility for his behaviour in the foster carer's home, with his interest in her underwear, or exposing himself to younger children. It was these activities which made the initial assessment team feel he needed a specialist residential setting as he would potentially be a continuing risk living in the community other than in a closely supervised context.

Whatever the original factors were which had led him to develop an abusive orientation, his pattern of thinking was now highly dangerous. He had developed a set of beliefs which justified and rationalised his abusive behaviour, and he took very little responsibility for the abusive action he had perpetrated and had continued to perpetrate within the foster home. Measures used to assess adolescent offenders typically focus on such issues as cognitive distortions; the congruence with a child as a sexual object; the minimisation and sanitisation of abusive behaviour; the degree of openness; and motivation for treatment and perceived need to change. These were also limited.

2. Individual therapy: early stages

An individual cognitive behavioural approach to therapeutic work requires the young person to accept responsibility for his offending, to develop a greater understanding of how he planned, set up and carried out the offence, to perceive his victim as a person rather than an object of sexual interest, and to gain insight into the victim's experience of abuse and to develop a relapse prevention plan.

His initial response to this approach was to be highly resistant to addressing his offending behaviour. He spoke extensively of his experiences of abuse and he talked in considerable detail about the fact that his experience of victimisation formed the basis of masturbatory activity and abusive action. He described a considerable sense of grievance associated with flashbacks of his own abuse, both of his step-father's sexual abuse, and his father's physical abuse. Thus he focussed on his sense of cumulative grievance, and the weight of his own abusive experiences rather than

face the abusive action which followed. Such a response may be a defence against addressing abusive action, or it may be necessary to focus on such issues as a preliminary for him to be able to address abusive action. There was intense resistance to the therapist confronting him with the fact that Kay could not have given consent, and he had very considerable difficulties thinking about how she might feel herself. Given a greater sense of trust with his female therapist he was able to describe an increasing sense of disgust with himself. In parallel he continued to address the extensiveness of his own victimisation which occurred over a number of years, associated with rejection, and his mother's not being able to listen and understand what was happening to him. Giving the growing trust and attachment to his therapist, he seemed to be able to confront the nature of his abusing behaviour and victimisation.

3. Subsequent work with individual therapist

He then changed to a male therapist which led to considerable regression, a repeat of the sanitation and minimisation of his actions. He once more began to blame Kay for making him respond to her in a sexual way, rather than him taking responsibility for his actions. He sulked, showed considerable grievance, and went on hunger strike. It was hypothesised that the withdrawal of a caring supportive female figure in his life after a 12 month period reinforced by the change of therapists triggered a regressive response and return to a previous mode of response.

A dynamic interpretation of the meaning of the change to a male therapist was given to John. His male therapist wondered whether he not only felt the loss, anger and grievance at losing the therapist he valued, but he was faced with having a male therapist with all the re-awakening of his feelings of having been victimised by men. He might feel anxious about what might happen with the re-awakening of fears and anxieties associated with his earlier abuse. John was able to acknowledge the truth of these observations, and the therapist felt that he was able to move forward to confronting John with his offending behaviour.

He wondered whether John was ready to confront his offending behaviour by reading the statements made by his victim, or whether John needed to continue to focus on his own sense of victimisation. John responded to the challenge and reread his victim's statements. He responded with a good deal of distress, he became aware once more of the degree of distress that she expressed both during his abusive action itself, and subsequently. He also became re-aware of the struggle she had in being able to report the nature of his actions against her. He faced the degree to which he silenced her, and the fear he induced which prevented her being able to speak to her parents, which he had used to be able to exert control over her.

It is striking that at this point in the therapeutic process John was able to fully confront the actual detailed aspect of the way in which he silenced Kay, the way in which he induced fear, the fact that she was extensively distressed, all of which he had basically put out of his mind and had replaced with a set of distorted thinking, enabling him to perceive her as the perpetrator, the one who evoked sexual feelings in him (Bentovim, 1995). Actions perpetrated against a young person, e.g. as John described in his own earlier life, can have a traumatic effect leading to avoidance, re-enactment through flashbacks, or arousal. But actions perpetrated *against* another child, because of the impact on the victim, can also have a traumatic effect, and can lead to avoidance, as well as excitement leading to re-enactment, arousal and addictive responses. Finding a non-abusive attachment to a male therapist as part of the attachment to the community, reducing the effects of victimisation, may assist a young person in being able to confront their abusive action rather than perpetrating avoidance, and a cycle of arousal, further avoidance and dissociation. The notion that young people need courage to confront their abusive self is meaningful in this context.

He accepted that he set the situation up, that he was motivated by anger, and that there was a direct temporal link with the humiliation he felt at his father's physical punishment of him. This led to his desire to revenge himself and to project such feelings on someone else, justifying the enactment of his sexualised erotic feelings towards Kay. In turn the cycle of abuse was fuelled with continuing abusive action.

This pattern conformed to the model which suggested itself as a result of the original research, pervasive powerlessness during the first years of life being associated with

aggressive fantasies. If such fantasies become sexualised in middle childhood, e.g. by sexual abuse or exposure to extensive sexualisation of relationships, then in adolescence highly erotised fantasies of an aggressive nature become enacted, a pattern to which John appeared to conform. Having created a coherent picture of his abusive behaviour which connected his victimisation experiences to his abusive action, he was able to take far greater responsibility for his behaviour, and an increasingly responsible, sensitive young person emerged in his work in groups and in the community.

Responses in group and in the community

John found it extremely difficult initially to accept that other people who had been longer in the community were more open about their experiences than he was prepared to be. He continued to use what was essentially a victimisation mode to justify his aversive cutting off stance. He sulked, and when he felt powerlessness and responded with anger, his grievance sparked off anger in others which he then justified to leave the group. He described the way in which in the initial phases there was a continuing triggering of re-experiencing phenomena associated with his own abuse, physical abuse, emotional abuse, sexual abuse, through confrontation with other young people and with carers. He related better to women staff at first, evoking a maternal need, not taking responsibility for his own room, and curling up in a regressed state. He gradually presented in a far more responsible way, managed to complete his education, responding well to the intensive educational input, and was able to move into the community and involve himself in both further education and work.

There was a striking change in areas such as his cognitive distortions, his taking responsibility for abuse, and in his emotional congruence with children as sexual objects. He was able to begin to relate sexually to other young females when he moved into the community, and maintained links with one of the other young people with whom he struck up a close friendship. At follow-up he continued to describe the continuation of traumatic memories of his own abuse in his family context. He was following a non-abusive lifestyle, both in his interests, his work and his general activities. He had made some contact with his foster carer with whom he kept in touch, regarding her as a positive factor in his life, as well as his step-mother. There was occasional contact with his mother but not his father or step-father.

General implications for therapeutic work

In general terms the model of risk and protective factors which emerged during research on the exploration of risk for development of sexually abusive behaviour in sexually victimised males can be tracked in a young person such as John who develops abusive behaviour. In planning therapeutic work as well as making an assessment of the degree of risk and protection which a young person has experienced, it is essential to gain an understanding of the abusive patterns which have been triggered and the way in which they become reinforced, and are perpetuated. These include the development of distorted thinking, fixation on children, thoughts about children's sexuality, the level of denial of the impact abuse has had on their victims, level of accountability for these actions, and the issue of how extensive denial and need for social desirability that is present. These are the factors which are perceived as the prime focus for therapeutic work with young sex offenders.

The examination of a case such as John's, representing a young person with a severe disorder, illustrates that his presentation can be understood in this way. Yet at the same time it is evident in his presentation in therapeutic work that he is preoccupied with his own victimisation experiences. Although it could be argued that this is a response to his avoidance of taking responsibility for his actions, nevertheless the extensiveness of his victimisation responses as noted in the therapeutic setting, and in individual and group work indicates that he is being significantly affected by the longer-term impact of the risk factors which were identified in the research – exposure to physical violence perpetrated against himself, rejection, emotional abuse, neglect of care. His response both to his therapist, to his group and in the community can be seen as his adaptation to the way in which these forces have impacted on his life, and have disrupted his attachments, his emotional life and his sense of self. Placement in the therapeutic community, or with alternative carers, act as a protective factor which, as in

boys who have been abused less seriously and extensively, can neutralise risk factors and provide support to ensure that a relapse plan can be put in place to interrupt the cycle of powerlessness, grievance and abusive action.

Disrupted attachments were helped by providing consistency, non-abusive care and re-parenting. Emotional distress linked with extensive abuse was helped by processing, allowing the young person to share his experiences extensively. He was helped to develop a more positive sense of himself as survivor, rather than as a powerless, angry, resentful young person (Deblinger et al. 1996). This enabled John to confront his offending behaviour. It was necessary for him:

- To understand the link with the abuse perpetrated against himself.
- To create a coherent account of what led him to abuse: from victim to perpetrator.
- To give a detailed account of his abusive action, the cycle of abusive action, and the way that it operated in considerable detail.
- To understand and appreciate that not only was he extensively abused himself, but that he extensively abused and hurt a young person who he should have respected because of that powerlessness and her learning disability.
- He was supported to confront his actions, to take responsibility for them, and to adopt an abuse free life himself through a meaningful relapse prevention plan.

Conclusion

It is essential that careful note is taken of the risk factors which a young person who has abused others has experienced. The impact on their lives needs to be assessed and the therapeutic process adjusted, ensuring protective factors are put in place for the repair of attachments, to deal with the extensive negative emotional effects of cumulative abuse, and to repair the sense of self. Only by dealing with such victimisation experiences, and strengthening protection factors, will it be possible to address the detailed addictive abusive cycle which has been enacted as a way of coping with, and projecting a personal sense of victimisation. In turn such actions have developed a way of dealing with an extensive sense of powerlessness, stigmatisation and sexualisation. The traumagenic dynamic effects described by Finklehor can manifest themselves either through internalising processes seen in those young people who are not abused so severely and so demonstrate victim responses, or through the externalising responses of those young people who are abused so extensively and whose response is to enact their experiences with others, and to create a 'Trauma Organised System' (Bentovim, 1995) where victims are blamed for provoking abusive action, thinking is distorted to feeling 'powerless' in the face of overwhelming impulses which cannot be controlled. Those who should protect are recruited to blame the victim, and support the perpetrator.

References

Becker, J. (1998) What We Know About the Characteristics and Treatment of Adolescents Who Have Committed Sexual Offenses. *Child Maltreatment.* 3: 317–29.

Bentovim, A. (1995) *Trauma Organised Systems: Physical and Sexual Abuse in Families.* London and New York: Karnac.

Bentovim, A., Elton, A., Hildebrand, J., Tranter, M. and Vizard, E. (Eds.) (1988) *Child Sexual Abuse within the Family.* London: Wright and Sons.

Deblinger, E., Lippman, J., Steer, (1996) Sexually Abused Children suffering Post Traumatic Stress Symptoms: Initial Treatment Outcome Findings. *Child Maltreatment.* 1: 310–21.

Faller, K. C. (1989) Why Sexual Abuse? An Exploration of the Intergenerational Hypothosis. *Child Abuse and Neglect.* 13: 543–8.

Finkelhor, D. and Berliner, L. (1995) Research on Review of Treatment of Sexually Abused Children. *Journal American Academy of Child Psychiatry* 34: 1408–23.

Finkelhor, D. (1987) The Trauma of Child Sexual Abuse, Two Models. *Journal of Interpersonal Violence.* 2: 348–66.

Freeman-Longo, R. (1986) The Impact of Sexual Victimisation on Males. *Child Abuse and Neglect.* 10: 411–4.

Groth, N. and Burgess, A. (1979) *Sexual Trauma in the Life Histories of Rapists and Child Molesters.* New York: Whiley.

Jones, D. and Ramchandani, P. (1999) *Child Sexual Abuse: Informing Practice from Research.* Oxford: Ratcliffe Press.

Monck, E., Bentovim, A., Goodall, G., Hyde, C., Lewin, R., Sharland, E. and Elton, A. (1996) *Child Sexual Abuse: A Descriptive and Treatment Study.* London: HMSO.

Pithers, W. D., Kashima, K. M., Cumming, G. F. and Beal, L.S. (1988) Relapse Prevention: A Method of Enhancing Maintenance of Change in Sex Offenders. in Salter, A. (Ed.) *Treating Child Sex Offenders and Victims: A Practical Guide.* Beverly Hills: Sage Publications.

Pynoos, R. S., Sorensen, S. B. and Steinberg, A. M. (1993) Interpersonal Violence and Traumatic Stress Reactions. in Goldberger, L. and Breznitz (Eds.) *Handbook of Stress: Theoretic and Clinical Aspects.* 2nd edn. New York: Free Press. 573–90.

Skuse, D., Bentovim, A., Hodges, J., Stevenson, J., Andreou, C., Lanyardo, M., New, M., Williams, B. and McMillan, D. (1998) Risk Factors for Development of Sexually Abusive Behaviour in Sexually Victimised Adolescent Boys: Cross Sectional Study. *British Medical Journal.* 317: 175–9.

Skuse, D., Stevenson, J., Hodges, J., Bentovim, A., Richards, M., McMillan, D., Salter, D. and Moore, T. (1999) *Risk Factors for the Development of Sexually Abusive Behaviour in Sexually Victimised Males.* Submitted to the Department of Health. London: Institute of Child Health.

Watkins, B. and Bentovim, A. (2000) Male Children and Adolescents as Victims: A Review of Current Knowledge. in Mezey, G. (Ed.) *Male Victims of Sexual Assault.* 2nd edn. Oxford: Oxford University Press.

Chapter 23: Factors Associated with Recidivism in Juvenile Sexual Offenders: A Study of Serious Offenders

Michael Miner

Introduction

Adolescents perpetrate at least 15 per cent of all sex crimes reported in the United States (FBI, 1994), and specialised treatment programmes for juvenile sex offenders have proliferated over the last 10 years, yet little empirical research has been conducted on factors related to juvenile sex offender recidivism (Weinrott, 1996) Those studies that have been conducted have, for the most part, used convenience samples and idiosyncratic measures. This chapter will review the relevant literature on risk prediction in juvenile sex offenders, adult sex offenders and non-sexual juvenile delinquents. Using the findings from these populations, a study will be presented that extends the available literature by testing the applicability of identified risk factors for recidivism in the adult and non-sex juvenile delinquency literature to a sample of adolescent sex offenders. The goal is to inform the reader on the available knowledge for predicting re-offence risk in juvenile sex offenders, and help to inform the practice of forensic evaluation of adolescents convicted or adjudicated for sexual crimes.

Findings from studies of juvenile sex offenders

As stated by Weinrott (1996), there has been little research on the factors related to recidivism risk in adolescent sex offenders. While a few studies were identified, they tended to be poorly designed and use convenience samples and readily available clinical measures. A comparison of juvenile sex offenders who recidivated with sex crimes, those who recidivated with non-sexual crimes and those who did not recidivate found that those committing new sex offences showed less depression and denial than the other two groups. They also appeared less aware of the expoitativeness of their behaviour, were more likely to have victimised older persons, more likely to have victimised strangers, and more likely to have had a history of sexual or

physical abuse (Smith and Monastersky, 1986). A retrospective study of juvenile sex offenders found those with functional deficits such as poor sex knowledge and social skills were at decreased risk for total re-offence (that is any type of new criminal behaviour). However, school problems such as behavioural problems and truancy, and having a sibling with a history of sexual abuse were related to increased risk for total re-offence. Sexual recidivism was found in this study to be associated with behaviours specific to the subjects' index sex offence, that is using verbal threats, blaming victims for their offences, and denial of offences (Kahn and Chambers, 1991). The outcomes from these two studies are difficult to compare largely because different variables were studied, and because the same variables were operationalised differently. Even more troubling in both these studies is the use of chi-square procedures to determine the association between variables and different offence types. This procedure, while providing the significance of an association between variables, is very sensitive to sample size and does not provide any indication of the strength of the association between variables. In addition, using bivariate chi-square procedures provides no indication of the relative importance of various variables in predicting re-offending. The design used by Smith and Monastersky (1986) provides us with indications about how the studied variables are differentially associated with the three study groups, but provide no information about the predictive nature of any of the variables. In order to gain an understanding to the predictors of re-offending, it would be necessary to follow a sample of sex offenders over time.

A study that followed a sample of juvenile sex offenders into adulthood found that those who committed sex crimes as juveniles were more likely to commit sex crimes as adults than were those adjudicated as delinquents for other crimes (Sipe, Jensen, and Everett, 1998). Interestingly, multiple adjudication for sex crimes did not increase the chance of committing a sex crime over the effect of having at least one prior sex offence. However, even in the sex offender sample, the rate of adult sex crimes was only 9.7 per cent, indicating that most adolescents who commit sex crimes do not go on to become adult sex offenders. The authors did not indicate what characteristics were associated with juvenile sex offenders progressing to adult sex crimes.

In another study, Rasmussen (1999) used event history analysis (Yamaguchi, 1991) to explore the predictors of recidivism in a sample of 170 adolescent boys convicted in 1989 of sex offences in Utah. While bivariate analyses indicated a number of variables significantly associated with re-offending, multivariate Cox Regression analysis indicated that increased risk for sex offending recidivism was associated with the number of female victims, whereas increased risk for non-sexual recidivism was related to the number of prior non-sexual offences and failure to complete sex offender specific treatment (p80). The predictors of sex offences are inconsistent with the adult literature, which finds that the presence of male, not female victims increases the risk of re-offending. The risk factors derived for non-sex re-offending, however, are consistent with the adult literature, in that prior criminal behaviour predicts subsequent criminal behaviour. Also consistent with the adult literature is the finding that failure to complete treatment increases the risk for re-offending. Rasmussen (1999) made no attempt to replicate her findings in an independent sample. Thus, there is no indication if the associations found are generalisable to other populations of juvenile sex offenders, nor whether they are stable associations.

Another recent exploration of the predictors of re-offending in adolescent populations found too few re-offenders in their sample (n = 8, 3 sex offenders), to allow for statistical exploration of predictors (Prentky, Harris, Frizzell, and Righthand, 2000). The authors did compare the levels of scores on four scales they derived from file reviews, and found that those who re-offended had higher scores on a scale that measured impulsive, anti-social behaviour than those who had not re-offended.

The literature on juvenile sex offenders is unclear as to the predictors of re-offending in this population. In general, the research is difficult to compare because of differential predictor variables across studies, non-standardised operationalisation of constructs, and in some cases, poor statistical power. For example, the studies that have found that certain offence characteristics predict future offences have sometimes used objective characteristics such as number of victims, characteristics of victims (e.g., gender, age), or use of threats (Kahn and Chambers, 1991; Rasmussen, 1999; Smith and Monastersky, 1986), while others have described offender attitudes and beliefs, such as blaming victims or denial of offences (Kahn and Chambers, 1991). These differences appear less related to theoretic considerations and more related to the types of data that were available to the investigators. What is clear from the available literature on juvenile sex offenders is that further studies are needed to clarify the factors that relate to re-offending, especially those related to development of an adult criminal pattern.

Research with adult sex offenders

On the other hand, a number of significant advances have been made in the prediction of re-offending in adult sex offenders. Parallel investigations of the predictors of re-offending in sex offender populations were conducted in a maximum-security forensic hospital in Canada (Quinsey, Harris, Rice, and Cormier, 1998) and in a state prison system in the United States (Epperson, Kaul, Huot, Hesselton, Alexander, and Goldman, 1999). These lines of investigation resulted in the development of three risk assessment tools that will be described below.

Quinsey and his colleagues at the Penetanguishene Mental Health Centre in Ontario, Canada, studied the predictors of sex offender recidivism over the last 25 years with samples of maximum security psychiatric patients (Quinsey, Harris, Rice, and Cormier, 1998). Their work has resulted in the development of two risk assessment tools, the Violence Risk Appraisal Guide (VRAG: Rice and Harris, 1995), and the Sex Offender Risk Appraisal Guide (SORAG: Rice and Harris, 1997). The VRAG and SORAG are substantially the same, although the SORAG includes variables specific to sex offences, such as number of prior sex offence convictions, phallometric test results, and if offender had only female victims under age 14 years. These tools provide methods for predicting the likelihood of violent re-offending, including sex offences, in samples of adult sex offenders.

A group of researchers at the Minnesota Department of Corrections have also been working on predictors of sex offender recidivism. Their tool, the Minnesota Sex Offender Screening Tool – Revised (MnSOST-R) includes many offence description variables, as well as individual history variables included in the SORAG (Epperson et al., 1999). In addition to those variables included in the VRAG and SORAG, this instrument includes indications of attendance and completion of substance abuse and sex offender treatment while incarcerated. These variables appear related to re-offending. The MnSOST-R has shown reasonable predictive validity (Epperson, et al., 1999), although it has not been as well studied as the VRAG.

Prentky, Knight, and Lee (1997) studied the predictors of recidivism in a more select sample including only adult child molesters. This study explored factors related to sex, non-sex violent, and any recidivism in subjects released from the Massachusetts Treatment Center, a maximum-security institution serving forensically commitment patients, including sex offenders. The data was collected in a systematic manner, using a detailed chart review protocol, from the Treatment Center records of subjects. Prentky, et al. (1997) found that the predictors of sexual recidivism differed from those of non-sexual recidivism, with sex offences related to the degree of sexual preoccupation with children, the presence of multiple paraphilias, and the number of prior sex offences. Non-sexual recidivism, on the other hand, was related negatively to amount of contact with children, and positively with presence of multiple paraphilias, juvenile anti-social behaviour, and adult anti-social behaviour.

Hanson and his colleagues conducted a meta-analysis of the available literature on risk prediction, which included the above lines of research. In their published report, Hanson and Bussière (1998) concluded that predictor variables for sex offenders differed depending on the type of offences used as criteria. Specifically, their findings indicated that general re-offending (similar to Prentky, et al.'s non-sexual re-offending) was related to variables such as being under age 25 at time of release from incarceration or treatment, never having been legally married, being of minority race, and having either a DSM diagnosed anti-social personality disorder or scoring high

on the Hare Psychopathy Checklist (Hare, 1991). Sex offences, on the other hand, were predicted by sexual interest in children, prior sex offences, victimisation of strangers, extra-familial and male victims, sex offending beginning at an early age, and perpetration of different types of sex offences. This meta-analysis led to the development of two further risk assessment tools, the Rapid Risk Assessment for Sexual Offence Recidivism (RRASOR) which includes four variables, prior sex offences, age at release (current age), victim gender (for sex offences), and relationship to victim (for sex offences) and the STATIC-99 (Hanson and Thornton, 1999) which includes the four items in the RRASOR, and convictions for non-contact sex offences, non-sex violent offences (both current and prior), any stranger victims, prior criminal sentences, and marital status. The RRASOR was cross validated in a number of populations and found to be comparable to the VRAG and SORAG in terms of predictive ability (Hanson, 1997), while the STATIC-99 was developed because of its superior predictive ability to the RRASOR (Hanson and Thornton, 1999).

The results of the above research indicate that re-offending in adult sex offenders can be predicted by a consistent set of factors. However, these factors are not necessarily those that have been studied with juveniles, and in most cases, even when studied, the constructs have been operationalised in different ways. Thus, it is unclear whether the risk assessment tools and the variables found as predictors for adults can be applied to juvenile sex offender populations.

Research on general delinquent populations

The final body of research, which has implications for understanding re-offence prediction in juvenile sex offenders, is the work on juvenile delinquency. The most consistent finding in the juvenile delinquency literature is that recidivism can be predicted by age at first adjudication or arrest (Ashford and LeCroy, 1988; Ashford and LeCroy, 1990; Myner, Santman, Cappelletty, and Perlmutter, 1998; Wierson and Forehand, 1995). That is, the younger the offender was when first identified, the more likely they would continue to engage in delinquent behaviour. The number of prior offences has also consistently been found related to recidivism after incarceration or treatment in juvenile populations (Funk, 1999; Moore, Pauker, and Moore, 1984; Tollett and Benda, 1999). Poor behaviour and achievement in school (Funk, 1999; Moore, et al., 1984); and unstable family environments (Funk, 1999; Moore, et al., 1984; Putnins, 1984) have been found associated with re-offending in some samples. However, these findings are not consistent.

The juvenile delinquency literature shows some similarities to the findings from the adult sex offender literature, for example, age of first offence is related to re-offence in both bodies of research, as is number of prior offences. The inconsistent finding with respect to school achievement and problems is consistent with the juvenile sex offender literature.

Current investigation

Clearly, the data on predictors of re-offending in juvenile populations are few and provide conflicting results. Additionally, in general, the factors studied are not those found to predict re-offence in adult samples, thus provide no method for comparing with the adult literature. In the remainder of this chapter, I will present data from a study designed to explore the predictors of recidivism in a juvenile sex offender population. This study uses data collection methodology and variable definitions consistent with Prentky, et al. (1997) and includes those predictors found associated with sex offender recidivism in adult samples, as well as the two consistent predictors from juvenile delinquency research, age at first arrest and number of prior juvenile offences.

The data were collected as part of an evaluation of a juvenile sex offender program (see Miner, Petersen-Seikert, and Ackland, 1997). Detailed review of institutional charts were conducted using a protocol adapted from the Massachusetts Treatment Center Coding Guide (Knight, Carter, and Prentky, 1989), the same instrumentation used by Prentky, et al. (1997). Two analyses were conducted using Cox Regression procedures. One to predict sexual re-offending and one to predict any re-offending. These analyses were designed to test three hypotheses:

- Sexual re-offending and any re-offending will be predicted by different factors.
- Sexual re-offending will be predicted by preoccupation with children, the presence of multiple paraphilias, and the number of prior sex offences.

- Any recidivism will be predicted by anti-social behaviour, age of first criminal offence, and number of prior non-sex offences.

Subjects

The subjects are 86 of 121 residents of a corrections-based juvenile sex offender programme in Minnesota, for whom complete file review information was available for abstraction. Thirty-five subjects had been released from treatment and parole prior to the implementation of the evaluation project, and thus complete file information was not available. The treatment programme was implemented by the Minnesota Department of Corrections to meet the needs of those juvenile sex offenders who could not be served by community-based outpatient and/or inpatient programmes. In order to be admitted to the programme, youths had to be adjudicated delinquent for some type of sexual offence and either failed a community-based residential sex offender specific treatment programme or been found to be unsuitable for such a programme. All individuals found to meet these criteria were admitted. Individuals were released from the programme after completion of their commitment time, or upon reaching the age of 19 years. The programme had no mechanism for declining to admit an individual, for premature termination of non-involved individuals, or for youths to drop out of treatment. Thus, the 86 subjects included in this study do not reflect a selection of youths admitted to treatment; they reflect all youths for which both chart review and re-offending information was available. The average age of the sample at admission to the treatment programme was 17.2 years, with a range from 14 to 19 years of age. The sample was predominantly Caucasian (72 per cent Caucasian, 14 per cent African American, 8 per cent Hispanic, 3 per cent Native American, and 1 per cent Asian). The median full scale IQ was 88, with 54 per cent of the sample having been in special education classes. Eighty-three percent of the sample had one or more prior penal commitments. The average age at first criminal offence was 13.7 years.

The subjects were predominantly offenders who molested children. The average age of their victims was 8.8 years; 64 per cent offended against children under 11 years old. Forty-one percent of the sample had at least one male victim.

Procedures
Chart reviews

Data were abstracted from institutional charts using a detailed protocol adapted from the Massachusetts Treatment Center Coding Guide, the instrument developed by Knight and his colleagues for their sex offender typology work (Knight, et al., 1989). The institutional records, which were abstracted within two months of the subjects' admission to the treatment programme, contained the results of all assessments conducted, either within the corrections system or by other sources, reports of institutional adjustment, police reports, court transcripts, and other legal information.

Data abstracting was done by five trained research assistants. To insure comparable results across raters, all raters were trained using standard files and required to have at least 80 per cent agreement on all variables before coding study charts. Each file required approximately four hours to code.

Description of risk assessment variables

In order to be consistent with the earlier research, data was combined using the same scales and variables as Prentky, et al. (1997)

Preoccupation with children. This variable is a measure of the degree to which children are a major source of sexual interest for the subject. It was defined as high if one or more of the following behaviours were present:

- Three or more sexual encounters with children over a time period that is greater than six months.
- Evidence that the offender has had enduring relationships with children, including sexual and nonsexual contact.
- Offender initiated contact with children in numerous situations over his lifetime.

Social competence. This variable is a measure of the ability of subjects to develop and maintain interpersonal relationships. It is the sum of three items that include:

- quality of peer relations outside the institution
- quality of peer relations inside of the institution
- level of heterosexual attachments

Quality of peer relationships were rated on a four point scale, which ranged from 'virtually no peer interaction or friends' (1) to 'rarely alone, most often involved with many friends, frequently went to parties or other social events' (4) Level of heterosexual attachments measured the highest level of dating or relationship experience attained by the subject. It was a six point rating scale ranging from no dating experience (1) to having lived with a female partner (6)

Anti-social behaviour. This variable was constructed to conform to Prentky, et al's. (1997) juvenile anti-social behaviour. Thus, it is the sum of two dichotomous variables rated as either present or absent: (1) instigation and involvement in fights, and (2) vandalism and destruction of property.

Impulsivity. This variable is a measure of impulsive lifestyles. It is the sum of four dichotomous items rated as either present or absent:

- financial irresponsibility
- reckless behaviour
- repeated aggressive or destructive responses to frustration
- subject experience of acting on irresistible impulses

Any male victim. This variable was a dichotomous variable constructed from descriptions of all serious (victim involved) sex offences in subjects' histories. It was coded as present if the offender had ever had a male victim in any of his current or prior serious sex offences.

Number of prior sex offences. This variable was the total number of charges for serious (victim involved) sexual offences committed by the subject prior to the current offence.

Frequency of alcohol use. This variable was a four point rating that assessed the highest level of reported drinking behaviour during the subjects' lifetime. The levels included:

- Virtually never drank alcohol.
- Drank on occasion moderately or occasionally became intoxicated.
- Drank regularly and became intoxicated on a regular basis.
- Drank frequently and was intoxicated more often than was sober.

Paraphilias. This variable is the sum of three dichotomous variables: the presence of fetishism, transvestitism, and/or promiscuity. Promiscuity was defined as having many sexual partners, a general obsession with having sex and/or having been involved in prostitution.

Age of first arrest or adjudication. This variable is the age, in years, at which the subject was first arrested for a crime, not just sexual crime, or was adjudicated delinquent for criminal activity.

Number of prior non-sexual offences. This variable was the total number of arrests or adjudications for property or violent, non-sex crimes.

Sources of re-offence data

Data were collected from three sources, one maintained by the Minnesota State Bureau of Criminal Apprehension (BCA) and two maintained by the Minnesota Department of Corrections (MnDOC). These data sources were chosen to provide the most detailed descriptions possible for each criminal activity, as well as to insure that data were available for criminal activities outside of Minnesota. Even with the addition of the direct chart review, re-offence remains a rather insensitive measure of recidivism, since it does not measure behaviour, but behaviour that is identified and reported.

Bureau of Criminal Apprehension (BCA) Automated Database. This is an automated database that includes arrests and dispositions for felonies and gross misdemeanors for adults apprehended in the State of Minnesota. This database provided information on the date of arrest, the charges for which an individual was arrested and the disposition for each charge. This database is also linked to the United States Federal Bureau of Investigation's Uniform Crime Reporting System, which provides similar data for most States, thus allowing for identification of offences that occur outside the State of Minnesota.

Minnesota Department of Corrections (MnDOC) Automated Database. This is an automated database of admissions to Minnesota correctional facilities and assignments to probation in non-Community Corrections counties. This database provided data on re-admissions to correctional facilities for new crimes and technical violations of parole. It was not possible to define the nature of the crimes from these data. This database includes re-admissions to both adult and juvenile facilities.

Office of Juvenile Release Files. The Minnesota Department of Corrections, Office of Juvenile Release maintains central probation/parole files of all youths released from MnDOC facilities. These files include a range of information, including the setting into which a youth was released, the discharge plan, adjustment reports, and reports of any adverse actions. In our review, we were interested in the adjustment reports, which are completed by each youth's parole agent every six months, and the reports of any parole violations or new charges. These files allowed us to identify offences that did not appear on the automated databases, and to clarify offences identified in the automated searches that were either unclear or for which insufficient data were present. For example, re-incarceration identified from the MnDOC database did not provide sufficient information to determine what type of crime had been committed, and sometimes, whether it was, in fact a new crime. Also, automated files did not characterise the details of a probation violation, which could be better described after review of the probation or parole records.

Data Aggregation. Data were aggregated across our three sources of information. Initially, all incidents reported were cross-referenced to insure that duplicate data were removed and thus only discrete events were included in our analysis. Additionally, information available from the Office of Juvenile Release files was used to supplement the automated data by adding incidents that failed to show up on either automated database and to clarify the nature of offences that were identified through the MnDOC database, which only reports return to custody.

The analyses presented in this report are based on unique events, that is we tried to insure that we are not double counting recidivism incidents. We acknowledge that the reported data may underestimate recidivism because of our reliance on officially reported behaviour.

Results and conclusions

Two definitions of recidivism will be used for the analyses presented in this chapter: (1) an arrest, conviction, or parole violation for any new crime (n=47), and (2) an arrest, conviction or parole violation for a new sex offence (n=7) The average time at risk for the sample was 4.29 years.

The model for predicting any criminal behaviour was significant, $\chi^2 = 20.2$ (4, N=86), p⟧.0005, and contained four variables: any male victim and paraphilias were associated with decreased risk of recidivism, and preoccupation with children and impulsivity were related to increased risk of recidivism. The resultant model for predicting sex offences was also significant, $\chi^2 = 20.2$ (4, N = 86), p⟧.0004. As with the above analysis, any male victim was associated with decreased risk of recidivism and impulsivity was associated with increased risk. Two new variables were retained in the model for sex offending: frequency of alcohol use and anti-social behaviour. Interestingly, both of these variables were associated with decreased risk for recidivism.

Our results suggest several differences in how risk factors impact youths versus adults. Overall, in our juvenile sample we did not find sex offence recidivism to be solely related to sexual factors; rather, a mix of sexual and non-sexual factors was retained in the model. Second, contrary to the adult literature, the predictors of sexual and non-sexual recidivism were similar. In the first analysis, non-sexual recidivism was predicted by four factors, two of which (any male victim and impulsivity) were also predictors of sexual re-offending. The most robust predictor of sexual re-offending in our sample was impulsivity, which increased the risk of re-offending about 11 times for each unit of change in the scale. This finding is consistent with some of the work in juvenile delinquency, where self-restraint is found related to positive outcomes following treatment (Feldman and Weinberger, 1994; Tinklenberg, Steiner, Huckaby, and Tinklenberg, 1996). Impulsivity, which was defined in this study as being reckless, aggressive and acting on irresistible impulses, would appear to be the opposite of self-restraint.

Another important difference between these results and the adult literature is the association between sexual re-offending and having previously molested a boy. The consistent finding in the adult literature is that those who molested boys are at higher risk for sexual re-offending than those who have not (Hanson and Bussière, 1998). Our data, however, indicate that juveniles who molest boys are at considerably less risk of re-offending (0.01 times the risk) than those whose only victims were female. This is somewhat consistent with Rasmussen (1999) who found that the number of female victims, not male victims, was related to increased risk for re-offending in a juvenile population. The fact that the presence of

male victims decreases, rather than increases, the risk for re-offence in this sample seems to suggest that victim gender selection in adolescent sex offenders has very different dynamics than victim gender selection in adult offenders. This conclusion, however, must be made with caution, since the analysis was based on only seven sexual re-offences.

The use of alcohol, along with anti-social behaviour, was a significant indicator of decreased risk for new sexual offending. This finding is consistent with some of the literature on juvenile delinquent recidivism (Wierson and Forehand, 1995; Wooldredge, Hartman, Latessa, and Holmes, 1994), while contradicting other results with juvenile delinquents (Dembo et al., 1991; Loeber and Dishion, 1983). A recent study of juvenile sex offenders also found a similar pattern of results, with higher frequency of alcohol use and anti-social behaviour associated with decreased risk of recidivism (Auslander, 1999). It may be that these behaviours reflect involvement in exploratory and acting out behaviour, which decrease the risk of future sexual offending behaviour either because such individuals gain access to delinquent peer groups where sexual exploration is accepted and willing partners are available, or because they 'burn out' on delinquent behaviour as they mature (Moffitt, 1993), or because adult sex offending is less related to general anti-social behaviour and more a sexual issue (Hanson and Bussière, 1998; Prentky et al., 1997; Quinsey, Lalumière, Rice, and Harris, 1995).

Paraphilias were significant predictors of non-sexual offences in the Prentky, et al. (1997) study, however the direction of the association was different. In their study, paraphilias increased the risk of committing a new non-sex crime, whereas in this study, the presence of some type of paraphilia decreased the risk of re-offending by about 40 per cent. Since sexuality is not likely to have been fully formulated in this sample, it may be that the identified paraphilias are reflections of exploratory and acting out behaviour, and do not reflect a paraphilic sexual orientation. Thus, the presence of such behaviours may reflect a youth that is willing to explore non-conventional behaviour across any number of domains, and may be another indication of sensation seeking, rather than an established pattern of sexual interest in unconventional behaviour, as found in adults.

Implications

These data suggest that the factors that have been found to predict re-offending in adults may not be useful with adolescent populations, thus calling into question the use of the actuarial assessment tools that have been developed with adult samples. Additionally, these data lead to questions about the differences between juvenile sex offenders and juvenile delinquents. In this study, the factors most associated with re-offending in delinquent populations, age of first arrest and prior offences, were not associated with recidivism, either sexual or non-sexual. Additionally, the measures of delinquent behaviour, such as anti-social behaviour and alcohol use, were actually related to decreased risk of offending, rather than increased risk.

The most robust predictor of sexual re-offending was impulsivity, which also was associated with increased risk for any re-offending. This finding may provide some support for a Relapse Prevention conceptualisation of the recidivism process since if one conceptualises sex offending as an indulgent behaviour, a behaviour motivated by short-term gain without consideration of the long-term consequences, (Nelson, Miner, Marques, Russell, and Achterkirchen, 1988), it is obvious that those with impulse control problems would be most at risk. Thus, these data provide some empirical evidence that the overwhelming reliance on Relapse Prevention interventions by sex offender specific treatment programmes for juveniles (Freeman-Longo, Bird, Stevensen, and Fiske, 1995) may be warranted.

Finally, there may be little offence specificity in juveniles, thus the issue of future risk may be more related to general personality characteristics, such as impulsivity, than to any particular set of delinquent behaviours. This certainly calls into question the policy, in many states, of including juveniles in community notification and sex offender registry requirements. Certainly these data indicate that sex offence characteristics that would lead to a higher 'risk' rating are either unrelated to re-offence potential or decrease such potential.

There are a number of important methodological factors that limit the generalisability of our findings and the stability of the associations identified. First, our sample of serious juvenile sex offenders is not representative of the population of juvenile sex offenders. In fact, this sample can be viewed as the most treatment resistant and conduct disordered of those identified in Minnesota. In terms of sex offence recidivism, however, they do not appear different from other samples (Hall, 1995). They do, however, have a higher level of overall recidivism than found in most samples of adolescent sex offenders, although it is lower than other youths released from the same facility in which this study was conducted (OLA, 1995). While this limits the populations to which we can generalise our results, it does provide information on a population of juvenile offenders that would be of most concern. Another limitation of this study is the small sample size. Of the 121 subjects who had been released from sex offender treatment, only 86 had sufficient data to be included in this study. As a result, our sex offence analysis was based on only seven re-offenders, and any recidivism analysis on 47 re-offenders. This lack of statistical power would lead to questions about the stability of the associations found in this study. Of particular concern are those found for sex offences. Giving some confidence in the identified associations is the extent to which they are consistent with other research using juvenile populations. In sum, our results and review of the literature point to a need for more research on adolescent sex offenders. Currently, there are no consistent data for predicting dangerousness in this population, thus it is premature to develop systematic prediction tools such as the Juvenile Sex Offender Risk for Re-Offending Assessment (Stetson School, 2000), which has recently received a great deal of discussion on the Association for the Treatment of Sexual Abusers listserv.

References

Ashford, J. B. and LeCroy, C. W. (1988) Predicting Recidivism: An Evaluation Of The Wisconsin Juvenile Probation And Aftercare Risk Instrument. *Criminal Justice and Behaviour.* 15: 141–51.

Ashford, J. B. and LeCroy, C. W. (1990) Juvenile Recidivism: A Comparison of Three Prediction Instruments. *Adolescence.* 25: 441–50.

Auslander, B. A. (1999) *An Exploratory Study Investigating Variables in Relation to Juvenile Sexual Offender Re-offending. Dissertation Abstracts International.* 59: 9–B 5069.

Baird, S. C. (1982) *Classification of Juveniles in Corrections: A Model Systems Approach.* Madison, WI: National Council on Crime and Delinquency.

Dembo, R., Williams, L., Schmeidler, J. Getreau, A., Berry, E., Genung, L., Wish, E.D. and Christensen, C. (1991) Recidivism Among High-risk Youths: A 2-½ Year Follow-up of a Cohort of Juvenile Detainees. *International Journal of the Addictions.* 26: 197–221.

Epperson, D. L., Kaul, J. D., Huot, S. J., Hesselton, D., Alexander, W. and Goldman, R. (1999) *Minnesota Sex Offender Screening Tool Revised (MnSOST-R)* St. Paul, MN: Minnesota Department of Corrections.

Federal Bureau of Investigation (1994) *Age-specific Arrests Rates and Race-specific Arrest Rates for Selected Offences. 1965–1992.* Washington, DC: U.S. Government Printing Office.

Feldman, S. S. and Weinberger, D. A. (1994) Self-restraint as a Mediator of Family Influences on Boy's Delinquent Behaviour: A Longitudinal Study. *Child Development.* 66: 195–211.

Freeman-Longo, R., Bird, S., Stevenson, W. and Fisk, J. (1995) *1994 Nationwide Survey of Treatment Programs and Models.* Brandon, VT: Safer Society Press.

Funk, S. J. (1999) Risk Assessment For Juveniles On Probation: A Focus On Gender. *Criminal Justice and Behaviour.* 26: 44–68.

Hall, G. C. N. (1995) Sexual Offender Recidivism Revisited: A Meta-analysis of Recent Treatment Studies. *Journal of Consulting and Clinical Psychology.* 63: 802–9.

Hanson, R. K. (1997) *The Development of a Brief Actuarial Risk Scale for Sexual Offence Recidivism. User Report 1997-04.* Ottawa: Ontario: Department of the Solicitor General of Canada.

Hanson, R. K. and Bussière, M. T. (1998) Predicting Relapse: A Meta-analysis of Sexual Offender Recidivism Studies. *Journal of Consulting and Clinical Psychology.* 66: 348–62.

Hanson, R. K. and Harris, A. (2000) *The Sex Offender Needs Assessment Rating (SONAR): A Method for Measuring Change in Risk Levels. User Report 2000–1.* Ottawa, Ontario: Department of the Solicitor General of Canada.

Hanson, R. K. and Thornton, D. (1999) *Static-99: Improving Actuarial Risk Assessments for Sex Offenders. User Report 99-02.* Ottawa, Ontario: Department of the Solicitor General of Canada.

Hare, R. D. (1991) The Hare Psychopathy Checklist – Revised. Toronto: Multi-Health Systems.

Kahn, T. J. and Chambers, H. J. (1991) Assessing Re-offence Risk With Juvenile Sexual Offenders. *Child Welfare.* 19: 333–45.

Knight, R. A., Carter, D. L. and Prentky, R. A. (1989) A System for the Classification of Child Molesters: Reliability and Application. *Journal of Interpersonal Violence.* 4: 3–23.

Loeber, R. and Dishion, T. J. (1983) Early Predictors of Male Delinquency: A Review. *Psychological Bulletin.* 94: 68–99.

Miner, M. H., Petersen-Seikert, G. and Ackland, M. (1997) *Evaluation, Juvenile Sex Offender Treatment Program. Minnesota Correctional Facility, Sauk Centre (Final Report, 1995–1997 Biennium).* Minneapolis, MN: Program in Human Sexuality, University of Minnesota.

Moffitt, T. E. (1993) Adolescence-limited and Life-course-Persistent Antisocial Behaviour: A Developmental Taxonomy. *Psychological Review.* 100: 674–701.

Moore, R., Pauker, J. D. and Moore, T. E. (1984) Delinquent Recidivists: Vulnerable Children. *Journal of Youth and Adolescence.* 13: 451–7.

Myner, J., Santman, J., Cappelletty, G. G. and Perlmutter, B. F. (1998) Variables Related to Recidivism Among Juvenile Offenders. *International Journal of Offender Therapy and Comparative Criminology.* 42: 65–80.

Nelson, C., Miner, M., Marques, J., Russell, K. and Achterkirchen, J. (1989) Relapse Prevention: A Cognitive-behavioural Model for Treatment of the Rapist and Child Molester. *Journal of Social Work and Human Sexuality.* 7: 125–43.

Prentky, R. A., Knight, R. A. and Lee, A. F. S. (1997) Risk Factors Associated With Recidivism Among Extrafamilial Child Molesters. *Journal of Consulting and Clinical Psychology.* 65: 141–9.

Prentky, R., Harris, B., Frizzell, K., and Righthand, S. (2000) An Actuarial Procedure for Assessing Risk With Juvenile Sex Offenders. *Sexual Abuse: A Journal of Research and Treatment.* 12: 71–93.

Putnins, A. L. (1984) Family Structure and Juvenile Recidivism. *Family Therapy.* 11: 61–4.

Quinsey, V. L., Harris, G. T., Rice, M. E. and Cormier, C. A. (1998) *Violent Offenders. Appraising and Managing Risk.* Washington, DC: American Psychological Association.

Quinsey, V. L., Lalumière, M. L., Rice, M. E. and Harris, G. T. (1995) Predicting Sexual Offences. in Campbell, J. C. (Ed.) *Assessing Dangerousness: Violence by Sexual Offenders, Batterers, and Child Abusers*, Thousand Oaks, CA: Sage Publications. 114–37.

Rasmussen, L. A. (1999) Factors Related to Recidivism Among Juvenile Sexual Offenders. *Sexual Abuse: A Journal of Research and Treatment*. 11: 69–85.

Rice, M. E. and Harris, G. T. (1995) Violent Recidivism: Assessing Predictive Validity. *Journal of Consulting and Clinical Psychology*. 63: 737–48.

Rice, M. E. and Harris, G. T. (1997) Cross-validation and Extension of the Violence Risk Appraisal Guide for Child Molesters and Rapists. *Law and Human Behaviour*. 21: 231–41.

Sipe, R., Jensen, E. L. and Everett, R. S. (1998) *Adolescent Sexual Offenders Grown up: Recidivism in Young Adulthood. Criminal Justice and Behaviour*. 25: 109–24.

Smith, W. R. and Monastersky, C. (1986) Assessing Juvenile Sexual Offenders' Risk for Re-offending. *Criminal Justice and Behaviour*. 13: 115–40.

Stetson School (2000) Juvenile Sex Offender Risk for Re-offending Assessment. Barre, MA: Stetson School.

Tinklenberg, J. A., Steiner, H., Huckaby, W. J. and Tinklenberg, J. R. (1996) Criminal Recidivism Predicted from Narratives of Violent Juvenile Delinquents. *Child Psychiatry and Human Development*. 27: 69–79.

Tollett, C. L. and Benda, B. B. (1999) Predicting 'Survival' in the Community Among Persistent and Serious Juvenile Offenders: A 12-Month Follow-up Study. *Journal of Offender Rehabilitation*. 28: 49–76.

Weinrott, M. R. (1996) *Juvenile Sexual Aggression: A Critical Review (Center Paper 005)*. Boulder, CO: Center for the Study and Prevention of Violence, Institute of Behavioural Science, University of Colorado.

Wierson, M. and Forehand, R. (1995) Predicting Recidivism in Juvenile Delinquents: The Role of Mental Health Diagnoses and the Qualification of Conclusions by Race. *Behaviour Research and Therapy*. 33: 63–7.

Wooldredge, J., Hartman, J., Latessa, E. and Holmes, S. (1994) Effectiveness of Culturally Specific Community Treatment for African American Juvenile Felons. *Crime and Delinquency*. 40: 589–98.

Yamaguchi, K. (1991) *Event History Analysis*. Newbury Park, CA: Sage.

Chapter 24: Assessing Risk of Sexual Assault Recidivism with Adolescent Sexual Offenders

Dr James Worling

Introduction

One of the most important goals of a comprehensive assessment for an adolescent sexual offender is to make some determination regarding the risk of future sexual offences. Estimates of risk are used by legal and treatment professionals for a variety of reasons such as to determine the appropriate criminal sentence, to assess the impact of treatment, to time family reunification interventions, to determine the level of unrestricted access in the community, and to decide the appropriate intensity and modality of treatment.

Of course, there are many risks that should be considered in addition to the risk of further sexual violence. Depending on the characteristics in each case, one should also consider the adolescent's risk of self-harm, the risk of school failure, the risk of non-sexual violence, the risk of being re-victimised sexually by older peers/adults, and the risk of substance abuse, for example. The focus of this chapter will be limited to a discussion regarding the prediction of risk of subsequent sexual assaults as this has been an area of considerable interest and controversy in the field; particularly with the recent availability of a number of actuarial scales for the prediction of *adult* sexual re-offending.

Approaches to risk assessment

Boer, Hart, Kropp, and Webster (1997) and Grubin (1999) point out that there are two traditional approaches to the prediction of future sexual violence: unstructured clinical prediction and actuarial assessment. In forming unstructured clinical predictions, clinicians use the accumulation of their anecdotal experiences to make a determination of risk level. Although there is evidence that unstructured clinical judgements are, on average, just slightly better than chance when predicting adult sexual recidivism (Hanson and Bussière, 1998), there are a number of serious concerns with this approach (see Monahan, 1995, for a complete critique). For example, it is often very difficult to

ascertain just how clinical risk ratings are made and, as such, these predictions are difficult to question, challenge, or support. The most serious concern, of course, is the poor level of accuracy, and this is a considerable problem given that clinicians risk assessments are used to determine the level of an offender's freedom in the community.

In actuarial risk assessments, on the other hand, a fixed number of risk factors are evaluated using a structured and objective rating system. Scores for each risk factor are summed, and this typically yields an overall risk score that can be linked to a probabilistic statement of risk (e.g., 30 per cent chance of a sexual re-offence within the next 5 years). The development of most actuarial risk assessment tools is based on research that links recidivism to the variables of interest. Some of the benefits to actuarial risk assessment include a high degree of agreement between different raters, ease of administration and scoring, retrospective empirical support for each risk factor considered, and the ability to test the accuracy, or predictive validity, of the numerical algorithms that are proposed to predict risk. Despite the many advantages of the actuarial method, however, there are some drawbacks. For instance, no actuarial instrument could possibly include *all* potential risk indicators (Hanson, 2000). Another criticism is that many of the variables included in actuarial systems are static, or 'fixed' (such as gender), and are of limited use to those who are devising a treatment programme to manage risk of sexual re-offending by targeting changeable, or dynamic, factors. Once deemed 'high risk' using such static factors, an offender will necessarily always remain at high risk.

Hanson (2000) pointed out that 'the optimal approach to risk assessment depends, to large extent, on the quality of the available research' (p5). In the case of adult sexual offenders, for example, many retrospective follow-up studies are available for researchers to 'distil' risk factors with established relationships to criminal recidivism. Therefore, there are several actuarial risk prediction tools for adult sexual offenders that have been found to be predictive of sexual re-offence risk.

There have only been a handful of follow-up studies with adolescent sexual offenders; therefore, there has not yet been sufficient research to conduct meta-analyses to derive reliable risk factors. Hunter and Lexier (1998) recently pointed out that clinicians making risk predictions for adolescent sexual offenders must rely on 'unproved theoretical assumptions about factors that increase risk of dangerousness' (p344). Although there are a number of published risk-prediction checklists or guidelines for adolescent sexual offenders that are popular in clinical practice (Bremer, 1998; Calder, Hanks, and Epps, 1997; Epps, 1997; Lane, 1997; Perry and Orchard, 1992; Ross and Loss, 1991; Steen and Monnette, 1989; Wenet and Clark, 1986), there are no empirical data regarding their reliability or validity.

Prentky, Harris, Frizzell, and Righthand (2000) recently published an actuarial scale for assessing risk with juvenile sexual offenders. For their analyses, they used 12-month follow-up data from a group of 75 offenders, aged 9-20 years. The authors noted that the number of sexual recidivists was too low (likely due to the brevity of the follow-up period) to warrant any statistical comparisons between sexual re-offenders and sexual non-re-offenders. Therefore, there is currently no empirical support regarding the use of this measure to predict sexual recidivism for adolescents. Prentky et al. (2000) acknowledged that this scale represents an initial contribution to the field of risk prediction for juvenile sexual offenders, and that further refinement and data collection is necessary to develop a valid scale.

A recent development in the prediction of sexual recidivism is a third method of estimation that Hanson (1998) has called the empirically-guided clinical judgement. In this approach, assessors base their predictions on a fixed list of risk factors that have been suggested by existing research and professional opinion. Hanson (2000) pointed out that 'in the murky, initial stages, simply identifying relevant risk factors is a significant advance' (p5). The advantage of the empirically guided clinical judgement in comparison to clinical prediction is that there is the promise of higher accuracy given the scientific evidence to support the risk factors being evaluated. Furthermore, the empirically guided approach is more

systematic than unstructured clinical prediction and should lead to better agreement among professionals. The most significant drawback, of course, is that the final determination of risk remains a clinical estimate.

We (Worling and Curwen, 2000b) recently developed an empirically guided, clinical risk-prediction tool called the Estimate of Risk of Adolescent Sexual Offence Recidivism, The ERASOR Instrument, available from the authors. The first step in developing this instrument was to examine the available research and expert opinion regarding potential risk factors. Our risk assessment instrument is based, in part, on the following analysis.

Risk factors

It is important to stress that although we are attempting to predict the risk of sexual re-offending, the research that is used to support or refute each risk factor is based on the offender's subsequent involvement of the criminal justice system. Although some researchers discuss recidivism statistics as if they are actually equivalent to re-offending, each entry in a researcher's recidivism database is contingent on the victim's willingness to report the crime, the ability of the police or child protection agency to investigate the complaint (if the report is made to them), the decision of police to lay charges that reflect the sexual nature of the crime, and the accurate and timely entry of the charge into a computerised database. Of course, when criminal conviction is used as the estimate of re-offending, the database entry is additionally dependent on charges not being dropped or altered to a non-sexual charge through plea bargaining or on the outcome of the trial. It is important to be mindful of the distinction between re-offending and recidivism, as we are predicting re-offending based on recidivism research.

The risk factors have been divided into 4 groups based on the degree of support. The first group of risk factors are the most likely to be shown to be reliable and valid as there is at least some supporting research with adolescent sexual offenders, there is some consensus in expert clinical opinion, and there is also support from research with adult sexual offenders. The second cluster of factors are labelled 'promising'. Although there is no empirical support for these factors with adolescents at this point, there is some agreement in professional opinion and supporting research with adult sexual offenders. The third group of risk factors are possibly predictive of risk; however, they remain highly speculative given the current lack of support. The fourth and final group of risk factors are those least likely to be predictive of risk for adolescent sexual offenders given the lack of empirical support and/or highly contradictory evidence.

1. Well Supported Risk Factors

This group of risk factors are those that are supported by some published, follow-up research with adolescents, by general consensus in professional opinion (i.e., published risk prediction checklists or guidelines), and by follow-up research with adult male sexual offenders. Relative to any other factors, these presently have the most defensible support and should, therefore, be relied upon most when forming predictions of future risk.

Deviant sexual interests

Adolescents who are sexually aroused by prepubescent children and/or by sexual violence are more likely to be at risk of committing subsequent sexual offences. In a recent retrospective study of adolescent sexual offenders, Worling and Curwen (2000a) found that self-reported sexual interest in children, including past or present sexual fantasies of children, child-victim grooming behaviours, and intrusive sexual assault activities with children, was a significant predictor of sexual re-offending after a mean follow-up of six years. Schram, Malloy, and Rowe (1992) also found that those adolescent offenders rated by clinicians as most likely to have deviant sexual interests were significantly more likely to re-offend sexually. Authors of existing risk-prediction checklists and guidelines for adolescents have commented that those adolescent sexual offenders who display sexual interest in young children or in sexual violence are at higher risk for sexual recidivism (Calder et al., 1997; Epps, 1997; Lane, 1997; Ross and Loss, 1991).

Deviant sexual arousal can be assessed by self-report (questionnaires or interview data) or inferred by patterns in recent behaviours (e.g., several assaults against prepubescent children could be evidence of deviant sexual interest in children). Given the scientific and ethical concerns regarding the use of penile plethysmography (PPG) with adolescents

(Hunter and Lexier, 1998; Worling, 1998), there is little support at present to recommend the use of PPG with this population.

Turning to research with adult sexual offenders, deviant sexual interest, particularly sexual interest in children, was found to be the variable most related to subsequent sexual re-offending in a recent meta-analysis of retrospective studies of adult male sexual offenders (Hanson and Bussière, 1998). The presence of deviant sexual arousal has also been listed as a high-risk factor for adult male sexual offenders in actuarial risk-prediction tools such as the Sex Offender Risk Appraisal Guide (SORAG; Quinsey, Harris, Rice, and Cormier, 1998) and the Minnesota Sex Offender Screening Tool: Revised (MnSOST-R; Epperson, Kaul, and Hesselton, 1998).

Attitudes supportive of sexual offending

Adolescents who believe that sexual assaults are 'invited', 'educational', 'desired', 'harmless' or otherwise 'welcomed' by victims are most likely to be at higher risk to continue committing sexual assaults. Although there are few empirical data regarding this factor at present, this may be a result of the fact that it has rarely been studied in research. In one study, Kahn and Chambers (1991) found that those adolescents who blamed their victims were significantly more likely to have subsequent convictions for sexual assault after an average of 20 months. Authors of existing risk-assessment checklists/guidelines for adolescent sexual offenders note that assault-supportive attitudes such as victim blame and the belief that sexual assaults are not wrong or harmful are indicators of higher risk (Calder et al., 1997; Epps, 1997; Perry and Orchard, 1992; Prentky et al., 2000).

Hanson and Harris (1998) found that attitudes supportive of sexual offending were significantly related to sexual recidivism in a study of adult male sexual offenders, and this variable is included in the SONAR (Hanson and Harris, 2000).

Numerous past sexual offences

Adolescents who have committed a number of sexual offences are most likely at higher risk of re-offending. This is likely the case whether there have been numerous offences against the same victim or single offences against numerous victims. It is important to note, however, that research support with adolescent is presently limited to the offender having more than one past victim. Rasmussen (1999), for instance, found that the number of female victims was significantly related to subsequent sexual offences five years post release. Schram et al. (1992) found that adolescents with at least one prior conviction for a sexual assault were significantly more likely to re-offend sexually. After a mean follow-up period of five years, Långström and Grann (2000) found that offenders aged 15–20 who offended against two or more victims were four times more likely to be re-convicted of a sexual crime than offenders with one known victim. Although we (Worling and Curwen, 2000a) originally found no correlation between subsequent sexual offending and the total number of victims, a re-analysis of these data revealed that, in comparison to offenders with one known victim, adolescents with two or more victims were more than twice as likely to have been charged with a subsequent sexual offence.

Authors of available risk-prediction checklists and guidelines also suggest that the presence of frequent past sexual offences is a high-risk marker (Bremer, 1998; Epps, 1997; Lane, 1997; Perry and Orchard, 1992; Prentky et al., 2000; Ross and Loss, 1991; Steen and Monnette, 1989; Wenet and Clark, 1986).

In retrospective studies with adult male sexual offenders, a history of previous sexual offences is highly related to later sexual re-offending (Hanson and Bussière, 1998). Actuarial risk-prediction tools for adult male sexual offenders include some assessment of the number of previous sexual offences (Epperson et al., 1998; Hanson, 1997; Hanson and Thornton, 1999; Quinsey et al., 1998).

Selection of a stranger victim

Adolescents who have ever targeted a stranger for a sexual assault are most likely at greater risk of continued sexual offending. This may be partly attributable to the fact that lengthy grooming behaviours are unlikely, and offences can occur quickly once a victim has been identified. Furthermore, the availability of strangers is certainly substantial.

In their list of potential risk factors, Ross and Loss (1991) suggest that adolescents who consistently target strangers are at a higher risk of sexual re-offence. Thus far, research with adolescents for this factor is consistent. Both

Smith and Monastersky (1986) and Långström and Grann (2000) found that the selection of stranger victims was associated with sexual re-offending.

Results of retrospective research with adult male sexual offenders have indicated that the selection of victims who are strangers is significantly related to sexual re-offending (Hanson and Bussière, 1998). Actuarial systems of risk prediction for adult male sexual offenders include the selection of stranger victims as an indicator of higher risk (Epperson et al., 1998; Hanson and Thornton, 1999).

Lack of intimate peer relationships or social isolation.

Adolescent sexual offenders who are unable to form emotionally intimate peer relationships or who are socially isolated are likely to be at higher risk to commit further sexual offences. Without intimate peer relationships, adolescents are likely to feel lonely and isolated, and they may turn to children or forced sex with peers or adults when they desire sexual interactions. Although there is no evidence for a link between broadly-defined social skills deficits and sexual recidivism (Kahn and Chambers, 1991; Worling and Curwen, 2000a), it is likely that the more specific social deficit, inability to form and maintain an emotionally intimate relationship with a peer, is related to risk of further sexual assaults.

In a recent meta-analysis of research with violent adolescents (including sexual offenders), Lipsey and Derzon (1998) noted that the most robust predictor of violent re-offending was peer unpopularity and lack of social activities. Långström and Grann (2000) found that adolescents with limited social contacts were more than three times more likely to be re-convicted for a sexual crime after a follow-up period of five years. Social isolation is listed as a high-risk indicator in previous checklists and guidelines for adolescents (Bremer, 1998; Lane, 1997; Perry and Orchard, 1992; Prentky et al., 2000; Ross and Loss, 1991), and Epps (1997) listed chronic peer relationship difficulties as an indicator of increased risk.

Grubin (1999) suggested that a long-standing history of social isolation is an indicator of higher risk for adult sexual recidivism. Hanson (2000) stated that intimacy deficits could be one of the more promising dynamic (potentially changeable) factors for predicting risk of sexual recidivism for adults.

High-stress family environment

An adolescent who is a member of a family that is currently characterised by an elevated level of distress is likely to be at an increased risk of re-offending sexually. High levels of family distress will undoubtedly impact on the adolescent in a variety of ways: depending on the particular source of stress. For example, heightened marital discord may contribute to feelings of insecurity for the adolescent, or the adolescent may blame themselves for the marital conflict. Alternatively, violent family relationships could serve to contribute to feelings of low self-worth, depression, and rejection. A high-stress family environment may also serve to heighten the adolescent's negative emotional states that preceded the sexual offences, such as anger, abandonment, depression, or loneliness.

In their recent meta-analysis of recidivism research regarding violent (including sexual) juvenile offenders, Lipsey and Derzon (1998) found that a high level of family distress was a significant predictor of subsequent criminal re-offending. Available risk-prediction checklists and guidelines include extreme family dysfunction or distress as an indicator of high risk for adolescent sexual re-offending (Bremer, 1998; Lane, 1997; Perry and Orchard, 1992; Ross and Loss, 1991; Steen and Monnette, 1989; Wenet and Clark, 1986).

Problematic parent-offender relationships or parental rejection

Adolescent sexual offenders who currently have highly problematic relationships with a parent, or who feel rejected by a parent are likely to be at greater risk of further sexual assaults. A problematic parent-child relationship or parental rejection is likely to contribute to negative affect such as anger, depression, hopelessness, rejection, and abandonment; feelings that could heighten the risk for the adolescent to choose to re-offend.

Presently, empirical support for the inclusion of this factor for adolescent sexual offenders is limited. We (Worling and Curwen, 2000a) recently found a moderate correlation between the offenders' feelings of parental rejection and subsequent sexual recidivism. In their meta-analysis of recidivism research, Lipsey and Derzon (1998) found that poor parent-child relations (characterised by such attributes as

low warmth, low parental involvement, punitive discipline, and negative attitude toward the child) were significantly related to subsequent violent (including sexual) re-offending.

In their checklist of risk factors, Ross and Loss (1991) suggest that offender-parent relationships that are marked by role reversal, emotional unavailability, and abuse are indicators of higher risk to re-offend sexually. Similarly, Lane (1997) suggested that adolescents who have a close relationship with a parent are at a lower risk for sexual re-offending.

Parent-child relationships are not often examined in research with adult sexual offenders. However, Hanson and Bussière (1998) found that adult males who described negative relationships with their mothers were more likely to re-offend sexually.

Incomplete offence-specific treatment

Adolescent sexual offenders who have yet to complete sexual offence specific treatment are likely to be at higher risk to re-offend sexually than are those offenders who have completed treatment. Although there are very few published studies with both treatment and comparison groups, recent research has demonstrated that those adolescent sexual offenders who participated in comprehensive treatment that combines a strong family-relationship component along with offence-specific interventions are less likely to commit further sexual and non-sexual offences (Borduin, Henggeler, Blaske, and Stein, 1990; Worling and Curwen, 2000a). Most available risk-prediction checklists and guidelines for adolescent sexual recidivism list unwillingness to engage in treatment as a high-risk factor (Epps, 1997; Lane, 1997; Perry and Orchard,1992; Ross and Loss, 1991; Steen and Monnette, 1989).

There is certainly much debate regarding treatment efficacy with adult sexual offenders. It should be pointed out, however, that in their recent meta-analysis, Hanson and Bussière (1998) found that those adult males who completed sexual offender treatment were significantly less likely to re-offend sexually.

2. Promising Risk Factors

The following factors have been found to be predictive of adult male sexual re-offending.

Furthermore, authors of existing checklists for adolescent sexual offenders have stressed the importance of assessing these variables. To date, there are no published data regarding the validity of these variables with respect to adolescent sexual recidivism. This is likely because these factors have yet to be examined in research with young offenders. When formulating risk estimates, these factors should be considered; however, it is important to be aware of the fact that there are currently no published data to support their predictive value with adolescents.

Obsessive sexual interests

Adolescent offenders who are preoccupied with sexual thoughts or gestures are likely to be at greater risk of further sexual assaults. Authors of existing risk-assessment checklists and guidelines for adolescent sexual offenders have noted the need to assess the presence of sexual preoccupation (Epps, 1997; Lane, 1997; Prentky et al, 2000; Steen and Monnette, 1989), compulsive ideation regarding past offences (Perry and Orchard, 1992), and compulsive, deviant masturbatory fantasies (Ross and Loss, 1991; Wenet and Clark, 1986).

Sexual preoccupation has been shown to be related to subsequent sexual recidivism for adult males; therefore, this variable is included in the Sex Offender Need Assessment Rating (SONAR; Hanson and Harris, 2000), an actuarial risk-prediction tool for adult sexual offenders.

Impulsivity

Adolescent sexual offenders who are highly impulsive, and who have difficulty regulating their behaviours and their affective expression are likely to be at greater risk of continued sexual offending. In recent discussions of risk-prediction factors for adolescent sexual offenders, Bremer (1998), Epps (1997), Lane (1997), and Prentky et al. (2000) noted that offenders who are generally impulsive are at greater risk to re-offend sexually.

With respect to adult sexual offenders, Hanson (2000) suggested that general self-regulation is one of the more promising dynamic factors for predicting risk of sexual recidivism for adults, and Hanson and Harris (2000) have included general self-regulation as a high-risk marker on the SONAR.

Environment supporting an opportunity to re-offend

Adolescent sexual offenders who spend considerable periods of time in environments supporting opportunities to re-offend sexually are likely to be at higher risk to commit subsequent sexual offences. For example, adolescent offenders who are provided with unsupervised access to potential victims, who often 'test' themselves by purposely entering high-risk environments, or who reside with adults who deny the presence of high-risk indicators are more likely to commit further sexual offences.

Despite the intuitive logic of this argument, there is surprisingly little research available at present with either adolescent or adult sexual offenders. In a recent investigation of adult male sexual offenders, however, Hanson and Harris (1998) found that sexual recidivists were more likely to place themselves in situations providing greater access to victims. The SONAR (Hanson and Harris, 2000) includes access to victims as a high-risk indicator for adult male sexual offenders. Epps (1997) and Ross and Loss (1991) suggested that adolescent offenders who are provided unsupervised access to potential victims are at a greater risk to re-offend sexually. Prentky et al. (2000) suggested that a highly unstable environment characterised by such factors as abuse, substance use, poor boundaries, and pornography are likely related to higher risk of recidivism for the adolescent.

3. Possible Risk Factors

The third group of risk factors are those that are presently viewed by some as likely; however, they are highly speculative given the current state of empirical support and expert clinical opinion. One should use considerable caution when basing risk assessments on these factors. Subsequent research will be helpful in determining whether these factors should be further supported or deleted altogether.

Selection of a male child victim

Adolescent males who have purposely selected a male child victim may be at higher risk to re-offend sexually. Although the research supporting the use of this factor with adults is clear (see below), the findings are mixed for adolescents. Smith and Monastersky (1986) found that adolescent males who selected male victims were significantly more likely to have committed a subsequent sexual offence. Similarly, Långström and Grann (2000) reported that adolescent male offenders who selected male victims were almost four times more likely to be convicted of a subsequent sexual offence after an average of five years. On the other hand, we (Worling and Curwen, 2000a) found that victim gender was unrelated to subsequent sexual offending. Similarly, Rasmussen (1999) found that the number of male victims was unrelated to sexual recidivism for adolescent male offenders.

With respect to adult sexual offenders, men who have ever offended against male children are rated as higher risk when using the Rapid Risk Assessment for Sexual Offence Recidivism (RRASOR) (Hanson, 1997), the Static-99 (Hanson and Thornton, 1999), and the SORAG (Quinsey et al., 1998). In their meta-analysis of retrospective studies of primarily adult males, Hanson and Bussière (1998) found that sexual recidivism was significantly related to the selection of male victims.

Threats of, or use of, excessive violence/ weapons during sexual offence

Adolescents who have used excessive violence and/or weapons during the commission of their sexual assault are more likely to be at greater risk to commit further sexual assaults. The use of violence/weapons may be indicative of sexual arousal to violence or may reflect attitudes supportive of sexual violence. Authors of existing risk-prediction checklists and guidelines have commented that those adolescents at higher risk to re-offend sexually are those who have used violence or weapons during their sexual assaults (Bremer, 1998; Epps, 1997; Lane, 1997; Perry and Orchard, 1992; Ross and Loss, 1991; Steen and Monnette, 1989; Wenet and Clark, 1986). The limited research for this factor is mixed. Kahn and Chambers (1991) found that those adolescents who made verbal threats during the commission of their sexual assaults were more likely to have subsequent sexual assault convictions. On the other hand, Långström and Grann (2000) found that the use of weapons or death threats was not related to subsequent sexual assaults. Perhaps this finding is a result of the focus on death threats in particular and not other threats of violence. Further research will be necessary

to determine whether this factor can be supported consistently for adolescents.

Research regarding this variable with adults is also mixed. Authors of the MnSOST, an actuarial risk-estimation tool for adult male sexual offenders, note the importance of assessing the use of force when predicting risk of sexual re-offending for adults (Epperson et al., 1998). However, in their recent meta-analysis, Hanson and Bussière (1998) found that the offender's use of force and the presence of injury to the victim were not related to sexual recidivism.

Interpersonal aggression

Adolescent sexual offenders who have demonstrated a pattern of interpersonal aggression, in addition to their sexual offence, may be at higher risk of committing further sexual offences. Adolescents who are aggressive and hurtful towards others may demonstrate a callous and remorseless attitude towards others, or they may have learned to cope with personal difficulties by relying on aggressive behaviours.

Available risk-prediction checklists for adolescent sexual offenders suggest that a history of interpersonal aggression is an indicator of risk for continued sexual offending (Bremer, 1998; Epps, 1997; Perry and Orchard, 1992; Prentky et al., 2000; Ross and Loss, 1991; Wenet and Clark, 1986).

In their recent meta-analysis of studies of adult sexual offenders, Hanson and Bussière (1998) found a small correlation between sexual recidivism and anger problems. History of non-sexual violence is also coded as a high risk factor on the Static-99 (Hanson and Thornton, 1999).

4. Unlikely Risk Factors

The factors addressed here should not be used when formulating risk estimates for adolescents, at least at present, given the lack of empirical support. Perhaps with the collection of additional data in the future, and/or better measurement techniques, these factors will be demonstrated to be related to subsequent risk. Of course, it is also likely that subsequent research will demonstrate that these factors are not predictive of adolescent sexual re-offending.

Denial of the sexual offence

It is almost an article of faith that offenders who deny their sexual crimes are at higher risk to re-offend sexually. Adolescents who deny that they were present at the time of the assault, or who deny that the interaction was at all sexual, or who deny that the sexual interaction was assaultive (i.e. maintain it was consensual between peers) are often judged to be high risk until they can begin to acknowledge their offences in some capacity. Indeed, *all* of the available risk prediction checklists and guidelines list denial of the sexual offence as a high risk marker (Bremer, 1998; Epps, 1997; Perry and Orchard, 1992; Prentky et al., 2000; Ross and Loss, 1991; Steen and Monnette, 1989; Wenet and Clark, 1986). The available research indicates that, on the contrary, adolescent sexual offenders who deny their sexual crimes are *not* more likely to re-offend sexually (Kahn and Chambers, 1991; Långström and Grann 2000). Kahn and Chambers (1991) actually noted that none of the adolescents who denied their offences were re-convicted of sexual crimes after a mean of 20 months of follow-up. When I analysed the available file data from our recent study (Worling and Curwen, 2000a), I also found that those adolescents who denied their sexual assaults were significantly *less* likely to re-offend sexually. Specifically, deniers were 30 times less likely to have been charged with a sexual crime after a mean follow-up of six years. In their recent meta-analysis of studies of adult sexual offenders, Hanson and Bussière (1998) found that there was no relation between denial of sexual offence and sexual recidivism.

Lack of victim empathy

As in the case of denial, almost all published checklists and guidelines include the lack of remorse or empathy as evidence of heightened risk for adolescent sexual offenders (Epps, 1997; Perry and Orchard, 1992; Prentky et al., 2000; Ross and Loss, 1991; Steen and Monnette, 1989; Wenet and Clark, 1986). It is widely assumed that offenders who are unable to appreciate the harm that they have caused, or who have difficulty empathising with the feelings of others, are likely to repeat their sexual assaults. Despite the strength of this clinical assumption, however, there are currently no data supporting the use of this factor. For example, Smith and Monastersky (1986) found that there was no significant relation between sexual recidivism after a mean of 28 months and the offender's inability to understand the exploitiveness of their sexual offences. Similarly, Långström and Grann (2000)

found that offenders with low general empathy were no more at risk of being re-convicted for a sexual crime. In their review of the adult sexual research, Hanson and Bussière (1998) found that there was no relation between sexual recidivism and low empathy for victims. Perhaps if researchers devise different measures of victim empathy or remorse, support for the use of this variable will be found.

History of non-sexual crimes

A history of non-sexual crimes is noted as a risk factor for adolescent sexual recidivism in several published checklists/guidelines (Bremer, 1998; Epps, 1997; Perry and Orchard, 1992; Prentky et al., 2000; Ross and Loss, 1991; Wenet and Clark, 1986). Although it is certainly true that a history of non-sexual criminal charges is related to sexual recidivism for *adult* male sexual offenders (Hanson and Bussière, 1998), there is a consensus in research completed to date that this factor is *not* related to subsequent sexual offences for adolescent sexual offenders (Kahn and Chambers, 1991; Lab, Shields, and Schondel, 1993; Långström and Grann, 2000; Sipe, Jensen, and Everett, 1998; Rasmussen, 1999; Worling and Curwen, 2000). As expected, however, most researchers have found that a history of non-sexual crimes is predictive of subsequent *non*-sexual crimes.

Penetrative sexual assaults

Authors of available checklists and guidelines suggest that adolescents who engage in penetrative (anal, vaginal, or oral) sexual assaults are at higher risk for re-offending sexually (Epps, 1997; Ross and Loss, 1991; Steen and Monnette, 1989). In the only study of this factor with adolescents, however, Långström and Grann (2000) found that victim penetration was unrelated to subsequent convictions for sexual offences. Indeed, the data reported by these authors suggest that offenders who engage in non-contact offences are, on average, three times more likely to be re-convicted for a sexual offence. Interestingly, a history of non-contact offences is counted as a high risk factor for adult sexual offenders on the Static-99 (Hanson and Thornton, 1999).

Offender's own history of child sexual abuse

It is assumed by some authors that those adolescents who are victims of child sexual abuse are at greater risk for re-offending sexually (Perry and Orchard, 1992; Steen and Monnette, 1989; Wenet and Clark, 1986). It is not clear why this assumption is so popular; however, the available data indicate that adolescent sexual offenders who acknowledge a history of child sexual abuse are at no greater risk of sexual recidivism (Hagan and Cho, 1996; Rasmussen, 1999; Worling and Curwen, 2000a). With respect to adult sexual offenders, Hanson and Bussière (1998) found that there was no relation between sexual offence recidivism and an offender's childhood sexual victimisation history.

Conducting Risk Assessments

At the present time, there is no research to support an actuarial system that involves tallying the number of high-risk factors and making a determination of risk for adolescent sexual offenders. It is possible, for example, that an offender with only one or two high-risk factors, such as sexual interest in children and unwillingness to alter deviant arousal, will be rated as 'high' risk. Furthermore, there may be some case-specific factors not addressed above, such as the offender's stated intention to re-offend sexually, that would be critical to include. With further research, an actuarial scale will hopefully be developed that will assist in the formulation of more precise risk determinations. Until then, the following general guidelines are offered for evaluators of future risk, and these are based, in part, on those made by Boer et al. (1997):

- Evaluators should assess multiple domains of the offender's functioning, including sexual (e.g. sexual arousal, sexual attitudes), intra-personal (e.g. affective expression, impulsivity), interpersonal (e.g. social involvement, aggression), familial (e.g. parent-child relationships, family distress), and biological (e.g. physical health).
- Evaluators should use multiple methods of data collection to form opinions regarding risk. Methods could include clinical interviews, psychological tests, behavioural observation, and reviews of previous case records and reports.
- Evaluators should collect information from multiple sources such as the offender, reports from the victims, the police, family, friends, and other mental health professionals who are familiar with the offender and their

family. Of course, risk predictions based on information collected solely from the offender should be interpreted with significant caution.
- Evaluators should collect information regarding both static (historic and unchangeable) and dynamic (variable and potentially changeable) factors. Although research with adult sexual offenders has demonstrated that static factors are often the best predictors over lengthy time intervals, there is promise that a number of dynamic factors will be supported in future research (Hanson, 2000). Furthermore, information regarding dynamic factors will assist in treatment planning.
- Evaluators should have sufficient training regarding the assessment of adolescent sexual offenders and should have a good working knowledge of the research regarding etiology, assessment, treatment, and recidivism. In particular, evaluators responsible for making risk predictions should be sufficiently familiar with the follow-up research cited in this chapter to make determinations regarding the limitations of their decisions.

Communicating Risk Estimates

Any prediction of future sexual recidivism risk should be limited and qualified. All too often, risk estimates are made without reference to the quality of the information gathered, the scientific basis for the judgements, and the need to re-evaluate risk. The following guidelines are suggested regarding the communication of risk estimates:

- Evaluators should inform their audiences of the scientific limitations of their risk predictions. For instance, it is essential to inform others that, although risk predictions are based on the best available research and consensus in expert opinion, there are currently no empirical data to support precise predictions of risk for adolescent sexual offenders. Furthermore, many of the factors discussed in this chapter are included because of research with *adult* male sexual offenders.
- Evaluators should note that their estimates of risk of sexual recidivism are time limited. Most of the retrospective research regarding risk factors is based on follow-up data of three years or less, and no study used a mean follow-up period beyond six years. Given this fact, plus the rapid developmental changes (i.e. social, physical, familial, sexual, cognitive, etc.) during adolescence, it will be

important to note that any risk predictions are strictly time limited and should be repeated after a fixed time interval (such as one year) or following significant change in one or more of the risk factors.

- Evaluators should justify risk estimates by referring to the presence and absence of specific high-risk factors. It would be helpful to comment specifically on the reasons why an offender is at a particular level (i.e. 'low', 'moderate', or 'high') of risk.
- Evaluators should make recidivism estimates as specific as possible. For example, if it is determined that an adolescent presents a high degree of risk for continued sexual assaults against younger males, this should be noted in the communication of findings.
- Evaluators should list circumstances that might exacerbate the offender's risk of re-offending sexually in the short-term. It would be helpful, wherever possible, to describe situations that could be warning signs for those working with the offender. For example, proximity to young females, cancelled family visits, or availability of pornography may be issues that could be noted if they were anticipated to increase risk for a particular offender.
- Evaluators should list strategies that they believe would be helpful in managing the offender's risk. In addition to possible therapeutic interventions, this may include recommendations regarding issues such as place of residence, community supervision, and timing of family reunification interventions.

Summary

Estimating the risk of a sexual re-offence for an adolescent sexual offender is a complex task, and the evaluator's accuracy has significant implications for both the offender and the community. Although there is currently insufficient research to warrant precise estimates, there is considerable support for a number of risk factors such that evaluators can make informed and defensible decisions. Once risk estimates have been formulated, it is important for evaluators to qualify and limit their conclusions with respect to such things as the quality of the data, the degree of certainty, and the need for reassessment.

Acknowledgements

This chapter is based, in part, on the Estimate of Risk of Adolescent Sexual Offence Recidivism (The ERASOR), by Worling and Curwen (2000b). I thank Sabrina Ramdeholl for her valuable editorial suggestions on a previous draft, and I thank Tracey Curwen for her tremendous research assistance. I am also grateful for the operational support of the Thistletown Regional Centre and the SAFE-T Program.

References

Borduin, C. M., Henggeler, S. W., Blaske, D. M. and Stein, R. J. (1990) Multisystemic Treatment of Adolescent Sexual Offenders. *International Journal of Offender Therapy and Comparative Criminology*. 34, 105–13.

Bremer, J. F. (1998) Challenges in the Assessment and Treatment of Sexually Abusive Adolescents. *Irish Journal of Psychology*. 19, 82–92.

Boer, D. P., Hart, S. D., Kropp, P. R. and Webster, C. D. (1997) *Manual for the Sexual Violence Risk-20*. Burnaby, British Columbia: The Mental Health, Law, and Policy Institute, Simon Fraser University.

Calder, M. C .with Hanks, H. and Epps, K. J. (1997) *Juveniles and Children Who Sexually Abuse: A Guide To Risk Assessment*. Lyme Regis: Russell House Publishing.

Epperson, D. L., Kaul, J. D. and Hesselton, D. (1998) *Final Report On the Development of the Minnesota Sex Offender Screening Tool (MNSOST)* Paper presented at the 17th annual meeting of the Association for the Treatment of Sexual Abusers, Vancouver, British Columbia.

Epps, K. J. (1997) Managing Risk. in Hoghughi, M. S., Bhate, S. R. and Graham, F. (Eds.) *Working With Sexually Abusive Adolescents*. London: Sage. 35–51.

Grubin, D. (1999) Actuarial and clinical Assessment of Risk in Sex Offenders. *Journal of Interpersonal Violence*. 14, 331–43.

Hagan, M. P. and Cho, M. E. (1996) A Comparison of Treatment Outcomes Between Adolescent Rapists and Child Sexual Offenders. *International Journal of Offender Therapy and Comparative Criminology*. 40, 113–22.

Hanson, R. K. (2000) *Risk Assessment*. Beaverton, OR: Association for the Treatment of Sexual Abusers.

Hanson, R. K. (1998) What do we Know About Sex Offender Risk Assessment? *Psychology, Public Policy and Law*. 4, 50–72.

Hanson, R. K. (1997) *The Development of a Brief Actuarial Risk Scale or Sexual Offence Recidivism*

(User Report 97-04). Ottawa, Canada: Department of the Solicitor General of Canada.

Hanson, R. K. and Bussière, M. T. (1998) Predicting Relapse: A Meta-analysis of Sexual Offender Recidivism Studies. *Journal of Consulting and Clinical Psychology.* 66, 348–62.

Hanson, R. K. and Harris, A. J. R. (2000) *The Sex Offender Need Assessment Rating (SONAR): A Method for Measuring Change in Risk Levels (User Report 2000–1).* Ottawa, Ontario, Canada: Department of the Solicitor General of Canada.

Hanson, R. K. and Harris, A. J. R. (1998) *Dynamic Predictors of Sexual Recidivism (User Report 1998-01).* Ottawa, Ontario, Canada: Department of the Solicitor General of Canada.

Hanson, R. K. and Thornton, D. (1999) Static-99 Improving Actuarial Risk Assessments for Sex Offenders. Ottawa: Department of the Solicitor General of Canada.

Hunter, J. A. and Lexier, L. J. (1998) Ethical and Legal Issues in the Assessment and Treatment of Juvenile Sex Offenders. *Child Maltreatment.* 3, 339–48.

Kahn, T. J. and Chambers, H. J. (1991) Assessing Re-offence Risk With Juvenile Sexual Offenders. *Child Welfare.* 70, 333–45.

Lab, S. P., Shields, G. and Schondel, C. (1993) Research Note: An Evaluation of Juvenile Sexual Offender Treatment. *Crime and Delinquency.* 39, 543–53.

Lane, S. (1997) Assessment of Sexually Abusive Youth. in Ryan, G.and Lane, S. (Eds.) *Juvenile Sexual Offending: Causes, Consequences, and Correction.* (Rev. edn.) San Francisco: Jossey-Bass. 219–63.

Långström, N. and Grann, M. (2000) Risk for Criminal Recidivism Among Young Sex Offenders. *Journal of Interpersonal Violence.* 15, 855–71.

Lipsey, M. W. and Derzon, J. H. (1998) Predictors of Violent or Serious Delinquency in Adolescence and Early Adulthood: A Synthesis of Longitudinal Research. in Loeber, R. and Farrington, D. P. (Eds.) *Serious and Violent Juvenile Offenders: Risk Factors and Successful Interventions.* London: Sage Publications. 86–105.

Monahan, J. (1995) *The Clinical Prediction of Violent Behavior.* Northvale, NJ: Jason Aronson.

Perry, G. P. and Orchard, J. (1992) *Assessment and Treatment of Adolescent Sex Offenders.*

Sarasota, FL: Professional Resource Exchange, Inc.

Prentky, R., Harris, B., Frizzell, K. and Righthand, S. (2000) An Actuarial Procedure for Assessing Risk With Juvenile Sex Offenders. *Sexual Abuse: A Journal of Research and Treatment.* 12, 71–93.

Quinsey, V. L., Harris, G. T., Rice, M. E. and Cormier, C. A. (1998) *Violent Offenders: Appraising and Managing Risk.* Washington, DC: American Psychological Association.

Rasmussen, L. A. (1999) Factors Related to Recidivism Among Juvenile Sexual Offenders. *Sexual Abuse: A Journal of Research and Treatment.* 11, 69–85.

Ross, J. and Loss, P. (1991) Assessment of the Juvenile Sex Offender. in Ryan, G. D. and Lane, S. L. (Eds.) *Juvenile Sexual Offending: Causes, Consequences, and Correction.* Lexington, MA: Lexington Books. 199–251.

Schram, D. D., Malloy, C. D. and Rowe, W. E. (1992) Juvenile Sex Offenders: A Follow-up Study of Reoffence Behavior. *Interchange.* Jul. 1–3.

Sipe, R., Jensen, E. L. and Everett, R. S. (1998) Adolescent Sexual Offenders Grown up: Recidivism in Young Adulthood. *Criminal Justice and Behavior.* 25, 109–24.

Smith, W. R. and Monastersky, C. (1986) Assessing Juvenile Sexual Offenders' Risk for Re-offending. *Criminal Justice and Behaviour.* 13, 115–40.

Steen, C. and Monnette, B. (1989) *Treating Adolescent Sex Offenders in the Community.* Springfield, IL: Charles C. Thomas.

Wenet, G. A. and Clark, T. F. (1986) *The Oregon Report On Juvenile Sexual Offenders.* Salem, OR: Children Services Division, Department of Human Resources, State of Oregon.

Worling, J. R. (1998) Adolescent Sexual Offender Treatment at The SAFE-T Program. in Marshall, W. L. Fernandez, Y. M. Hudson, S. M. and Ward, T. (Eds.) *Sourcebook of Treatment Programs for Sexual Offenders.* New York: Plenum Press. 353–65.

Worling, J. R. and Curwen, T. (2000a) Adolescent Sexual Offender Recidivism: Success of Specialized Treatment and Implications for Risk Prediction. *Child Abuse and Neglect.* 24, 965–82.

Worling, J. R. and Curwen, T. (2000b) *Estimate of Risk of Adolescent Sexual Offence Recidivism (The ERASOR).* Toronto, Canada: Ontario Ministry of Community and Social Services.

Chapter 25: A 5-Step Family Therapy Protocol to Treat Sibling on Sibling Sexual Abuse

Charles E. Hodges, Jnr M.Div., M.S.W.

The destructive nature of *sibling on sibling sexual abuse* presents grave consequences for the victim, offender, and other family members if not properly addressed in the context of family therapy (Hodges and Young, 1999). It presents unique clinical challenges that differ from sexual offences committed on family members by non-family members (Harris and Campbell, 1998; Meinig, 1996; Werrbach, 1993; Wiehe, 1997). Parental figures who are entangled in sibling on sibling sexual abuse frequently express conflicting feelings toward the siblings. Victims report intense anger at parents for not having protected them or rejecting the offender when the abuse was discovered (Stroud, 1999). Decisions surrounding whether to remove the offending sibling from the home have to be made. There are issues of shame and guilt on the part of the parental figures. The family system frequently exhibits formidable levels of denial and minimisation in an unconscious effort to protect the family image. Offenders experience feelings of anger at the victim and rejection by the family. Managing retaliatory impulses by stepparents toward offenders can be volatile and laden with safety concerns. And, the victim may experience guilt for having the offender removed from the home and subtle family pressure to prematurely reconcile with the offender 'for the good of the family.' Families, however, who have a member sexually abused by a non-family member are in a position of concentrating a greater level of family energy and emotional support for the victim with fewer distractions surrounding loyalty. Feelings of anger and outrage can more singularly be focused upon the perpetrator. Concerns surrounding safety considerations and treatment of the victim are clearer. The decision-making process surrounding the interpretation of the abuse and decisions about how to view the attacker is less diffused. And, the potential obstacles for reaching closure surrounding the past egregious event are different when the offender is not a family member.

The purpose of this chapter is to examine a 5-Step Family Therapy Protocol that can be used to guide the clinician's work toward healthy family reunification in families that have experienced sibling on sibling sexual abuse. The use of the presented 5-Step Family Therapy Protocol is designed to augment clinical training and experience. It is a dynamic process that is more than a mindless checklist. Family therapy sessions typically begin with non-victim family members and may culminate in specialised sessions between the offending sibling and the victimised sibling(s) prior to treatment termination. Without clear guidelines and signposts to assess progress in the sessions, the well-meaning clinician can unwittingly do substantial harm by reinforcing distorted family thinking or emotionally re-traumatising the victim. Therefore, the presented five steps were developed to promote family healing by encouraging victim recovery, enhancing offender treatment, and developing a new paradigm for future family interactions, Madanes, (1990).

The presented steps have equal application in community and residential juvenile sexual offender treatment settings (Prendergast, 1991: Steen and Monnette, 1989), although one must be aware of the differences each setting provides. The residential treatment setting provides built-in safety measures that have added victim protection, increased treatment intensity, behavioural controls, and emotional respite between family sessions that a community setting cannot as easily deliver. Designing safeguards and attentiveness to treatment details are increasingly critical when the sibling offender remains in the home or community with the sibling victim. Additionally, the demand for careful monitoring of safety plans, parental supervision, family denial, treatment progress, pressure on victims, and warning signs are especially intense in a community treatment setting.

Considerations before using the 5-step family therapy protocol

Important Terms

The following terms are presented in this chapter to establish a baseline of general understanding among readers as they implement the prescribed steps in family therapy.

Sexual Offending is a sexual act that is considered 'deviant' if it meets either or both of the following prongs of the following definition: (Wieckowski and Hodges, 2000)

1. Any sexual act that is performed without full informed consent of the other person.
2. Any sexual act that is performed on a vulnerable person.

Family includes those who are tied together through their common biological, legal, cultural, and emotional history and their implied future together (McGoldrick, Gerson and Shellenbergeret,1999, p7). Family in our context could therefore include extended family members who are living in the home, non-family members who are regularly living in the home, as well as quasi-parental figures that have significant connections to the core family members.

Sibling extends beyond the traditional lines of blood relations or legal confines to include children who live in the same home setting and function as relatives for a significant amount of time with shared parental controls, family rules, and shared resources.

Parental Figure is viewed as a biological parent, guardian, or adult who is responsible for the supervision, care, and well-being of siblings in a family unit.

Family Reunification is seen as the clinical process of cautiously bringing parental figures, sibling offender, and sibling victims together through the use of the described 5-Step Family Therapy Protocol in this chapter.

Safety Plan is a written plan developed collaboratively by sibling victims, parental figures, therapists, and supervising professionals which define family member roles, boundaries, victim safety supports, detail rules of contact allowed between victims and offender, and offender consequences if plan expectations are violated. The plan is reviewed with and given to the sibling victims and offender. It is then strictly enforced.

Clinical tasks

The clinician using the 5-Step Family Therapy Protocol has a number of broad clinical tasks to manage at all times while working with the family who has experienced sibling on sibling sexual abuse. All of the tasks emphasise the clinician's responsibility to protect the victim, strengthen the family system, and hold the offender accountable for the abusive actions:

- Ensure the physical and emotional safety of all family members during treatment and transitions to a less structured treatment environment by establishing a collaborative safety plan and enforcement protocol with offender, parental figures, victim, and community resources.
- Create a non-judgmental atmosphere for the parental figures to assist them in understanding their family's individualised victim and offender dynamics and develop strengthened parental skills.
- Work with the victim's therapist to co-ordinate reunification sessions, support victim treatment, and establish post-session monitoring and follow-up.
- Educate the family about sexual offending dynamics in general and the offender's specific abuse dynamics.
- Restructure the family unit to strengthen boundaries, clarify roles, and improve communication and interaction patterns.

Family therapy treatment differences

Working with families in this context is similar in some ways to working with other family therapy populations. The therapist will utilise family assessment tools, facilitate the development of family therapy goals, examine communication and interaction patterns, clarify and strengthen family member roles and boundaries, use therapy experiments, teach parenting skills, initiate termination and transitional steps, etc. Many standard family therapy theoretical models that teach healthier coping skills, hold people accountable, clarify thinking, support family growth, and change unsafe behaviours will prove helpful in the hands of properly trained and supervised clinicians as they work with this family population (Czech, 1988; Madanes, 1995).

Some of the general differences to be considered in work with this specialised family treatment population lie in the *timing* of an intervention; managing the significant *risk of harm* to others; the *emphasis* of one intervention versus another; the *degree and pervasiveness* of the individual family member's unhealthy coping behaviours, thoughts, and feeling states; and a *shift in thinking* from a more traditional therapy approach to one of modified roles, techniques, and goals (Wieckowski and Hodges, 2000). Specifically, clinicians using the 5-Step Family Therapy Protocol find there are *limits of confidentiality* of material examined in family session due to the need for treatment co-ordination among multiple treating professionals and mandatory reporting requirements. The family work must always consider at the forefront *the level of risk* posed by any member's actions to the initial victim and other vulnerable persons available to the offender. Unlike many families that seek-out help to manage a family crisis, these families often find themselves as *involuntary clients* forced by legal and social pressures to enter treatment. *The nature of the work* itself involves uncomfortable and often embarrassing details surrounding sexual contact, parental responsibility, and family secrets. This work requires *a higher level of supportive and constructive confrontation* to modifying each family member's distorted world-view surrounding the abuse to ensure future safety, to accurately interpret the abuse itself, and as a means to encourage positive treatment outcomes. Inevitably, the family work often brings about the disclosures of *other family members' abuse*. And, there is increased *legal liability* and involvement in the rigors of an adversarial legal system as family members challenge decisions or try to quash unwanted information or actions generated by the collective treatment process.

The 5-step family therapy protocol

Each family is different in response to sibling on sibling sexual abuse and member composition. In all cases the sexual abuse must be reported and properly evaluated. At the point of entry into the sibling on sibling abuse, the family clinician evaluates what parts of the steps in the 5-Step Family Therapy Protocol may have already taken place, builds upon previous efforts, and moves forward in the family work. Parental figures, the sibling victim, and sibling perpetrator are typically the core participants initially involved in the family work. During the course of the work other

participants may also include some combination of other sibling victims and non-victims, the victim's therapist, healthy extended family members, the offender's therapist, and referral sources.

When using the 5-Step Family Therapy Protocol there are a number of significant family member dynamics possible that are seen repeatedly across many families that can be found to reoccur during the course of treatment (Sexual Assault Center, 1996). Effectively assessing, monitoring, and confronting these possible responses require close treatment co-ordination and collective monitoring between the family therapist and other professionals treating family members (Breer, 1996; Ryan and Lane, 1997). Some of the most significant dynamics include the following:

Parental figures may:

- *Deny or minimize* the abuse details or its seriousness.
- *Blame the other parent* for allowing the abuse to have taken place.
- *Express anger and a desire for retaliation* against the offending sibling.
- *Abandon* one of the siblings.
- *Practice poor boundaries.*
- *Send mixed messages* concerning the abuse.
- *Exhibit emotional ambivalence* toward either of the siblings.
- *Feel a sense of failure* as a parental figure.
- *Be reminded of personal abuse.*
- *Be too unhealthy to participate in family therapy.*
- *Learn to protect and maintain a healthy balance* in interactions with each sibling.

Sibling victims may:

- *Feel responsible* for the abuse experienced.
- *Voice anger at parental figures* for not providing protection from the abuse.
- *Feel guilt* for reporting the offending sibling.
- *Fear retaliation* by the offending sibling or family members.
- *Imagine rejection* by parental figures.
- *Exhibit shame* concerning the abuse.
- *Express ambivalent feelings* toward the abuser.
- *Feel responsible* for the family intrusion from outside professionals.
- *Hold the offender responsible* for the abuse.
- *Experience jealousy toward other siblings* who have been able to work through their sibling on sibling abuse at a quicker pace.
- *Be too unhealthy to participate in family therapy.*
- *Reach healthy closure* surrounding the abuse.

Sibling offenders may:

- *Deny or minimise the abuse itself.*
- *Continue the abuse or turn to a new victim.*
- *Try to speed through treatment.*
- *View self as different from other juvenile offenders.*
- *Express anger at the reporting sibling.*
- *Blame the victim for the abuse.*
- *Seek revenge against the victim.*
- *Fear rejection by parental figures and others.*
- *Voice jealousy over real or imagined attention the victim is receiving.*
- *Exhibit outrage at having to leave the home.*
- *Be too unhealthy to participate in family therapy.*
- *Experience shame and remorse for the offending.*

Step One: report the abuse and separate the sibling victim and sibling offender

When the abuse is discovered it is desirable to immediately have the offender separated from the victim or removed from the home to a living situation in which there is no access to other potential victims and close supervision is possible. Report the abuse to appropriate authorities and access needed resources. It is important to have all contact between the sibling victim and sibling offender suspended until the depth of the problem is known and safeguards are put in place by the family and professionals. It is prudent to consider all vulnerable family members as either victims or potential victims until a thorough sexual offender investigation has been completed. Typically it is a grave mistake to have the victim removed from the home. To remove the victim may send a signal of rejection to the abused sibling, empower the abusing sibling, and complicate future family therapy efforts.

Goal: prevent further abuse and barriers to future treatment efforts

A positive sign for future family therapy outcomes during this initial step in treatment includes: the alleged abuse has been reported, family members are protected, the offender is being held accountable, the abuse is taken seriously, initial safety plans are developed and are being followed, family members are co-operating with outside agencies, and professionals are properly trained to manage the presented dynamics.

Participants may include healthy parental figures, sibling victims, sibling offender, other healthy family members who can provide support, legal representatives, and outside agencies.

Treatment focus: Provide support for all family members. Assist the victim in feeling emotionally and physically safe and protected. Secure needed medical attention. Hold the offender accountable and encourage taking responsibility for his actions. Monitor for suicidal or homicidal ideation among family members. Support the parental figures in developing a framework to understand the abuse and offending. Develop an initial safety plan and share with family members. Establish with the parental figures short-term goals, community resources, and empower them to begin to feel in charge of the crisis.

Warning signs that could prevent movement to the next step or complicate future treatment efforts until resolved may include:

- Family member exhibits actions that may raise safety issues.
- Actions that serve to cover-up, minimise, or deny the abuse.
- Indications of non-compliance with initially established safety plan.
- Resistance to outside resources.
- Family members are not taking the abuse seriously.
- The victim is being blamed.
- The offender is not removed from the house.
- The victim is removed from the house.
- Other family secrets are being protected.
- Professionals involved are not properly trained to understand and manage the dynamics presented in this type of family case.

Proceed to next step: Take measures to resolve the warning signs that raise safety concerns and confront presented denial and minimisation of the abuse. Proceed to the next step when abuse, offender, and family system evaluations are begun.

Step Two: complete evaluations of family members

Once the sibling victim is safe and the sibling offender is being properly supervised the evaluation process can begin (Perry and Orchard, 1992). Evaluations of the abuse and family during this step may include a police investigation, medical assessment and structured abuse interview of victim, sexual offender assessment, psychological tests, and a structured parental interview. It is important family members are initially informed of the limits of confidentiality due to the need for co-ordination of treating services of all family members and legal reporting requirements that may have possible consequences. It is critical the evaluations are conducted by trained professionals who understand sexual abuse and offending dynamics, the law, and family responses to sibling on sibling abuse.

Goal: determine the appropriateness, treatment amenability, and capacity of each family member to engage in constructive individual and family therapy

Ideally all family members will be able to engage in constructive family therapy surrounding the abuse to some degree during the course of family reunification. In some cases the evaluation conclusions may indicate a family member may not be ready or ever able to participate in the family therapy. They may be emotionally toxic, dangerous, not available, unwilling to participate, deny the abuse took place, are too young, or have other significant factors that prevent involvement in the family work. The collective evaluations should provide a family picture that outlines the depth of individual needs, barriers to treatment, level of motivation to change, and special needs of each family member to facilitate healing. Based on the conclusions of the evaluations and family member treatment readiness, develop an overall plan of treatment with family members and their treating professionals to meet the individual and collective family needs.

Participants may include healthy parental figures, sibling victims, sibling offender, evaluating or treating professionals, and outside agencies.

Treatment focus: Educate family members about the necessity of the evaluations and the benefits of treatment. Support the family in not feeling this crisis is unique to them alone. Validate family members' feelings. Note how each family member is responding to and managing the abuse. Consider family strengths and weaknesses, communication and interaction patterns, roles and boundaries, and capacity to respond to available supports. Encourage honesty and a willingness to face the situation. Establish yourself as a competent treating professional with the necessary experience and

training to facilitate the family therapy. Begin to develop a working relationship with the family members and other treating professionals. Review evaluation results with parental figures and other treating professionals. Make necessary referrals. Set initial family therapy appointment.

Warning signs that could prevent movement to the next step or complicate future treatment efforts until resolved may include:

- Family members do not co-operate with the evaluation process.
- There are family secrets.
- The safety plan is not being followed.
- Denial and minimisation of the abuse continues.
- The victim begins to show signs of isolation and depression.
- The parental figures spend their time fighting among themselves rather than focusing attention on the siblings' needs.
- Parental figure begins to express retaliatory intent toward the offender.
- Abuse details significantly change and conflict in important details.
- The offending or victim sibling is ostracised from the family.
- The offender becomes physically and verbally assaultive.
- A family member is too unhealthy to participate in constructive treatment.

Proceed to next step: Take measures to resolve the warning signs that raise safety concerns, confront presented denial and minimisation of the abuse, focus family attention on the benefits of treatment, and provide a road map of what to expect during the course of treatment. Proceed to the next step when the sibling offender has begun treatment, a referral has been made for the abused sibling to begin treatment, and the parental figures have committed to the first family therapy session.

Step Three: begin family therapy

The focus of this family work step in the 5-Step Family Therapy Protocol is to bring the family members together where possible as part of a healing process and support the parallel treatment processes of individual family members outside of the family therapy setting. It is not designed to exclusively meet all the complex needs of each individual member. The family therapy setting functions as a laboratory, in which new skills learned in individual and family therapies are tested, understanding about abuse and offending information is acquired, family dynamics are restructured, old relationships are redefined, and new family directions are mapped. This is accomplished through the co-ordination of the family reunification process and close co-ordination of services with other treatment providers. The family therapy sessions usually take place every two weeks until the sibling offender has completed treatment. This allows the family members time between sessions to work in their own individual therapy on intensely charged material generated in the family session prior to returning to the next family session. When both siblings remain in the home, it will be necessary to have the offender sibling removed if this third step in the protocol is not satisfactorily completed, the safety plan is not followed, the sibling victim is adversely affected, or the offender's treatment is not going well.

Goal: Bring parental figures and offending sibling together in family therapy

A positive outcome would mean the parental figures begin to feel acceptance and support, understand the offender's offending dynamics, the extent of the sibling abuse, support the offender in treatment, and hold him accountable.

Participants may include parental figures and sibling offender. There is no sibling victim involvement at this time. The initial work is with the parental figures and the offending sibling. Other older healthy family members may be brought into the session to support the process after the parental figures have completed the foundational work with the sibling offender.

Treatment focus: This step will typically span over many sessions. The essential foundational work of this step has to do with the on-going use of a safety plan, the ability of the parental figures to develop an understanding of the presented sexual abuse and offending dynamics and clearly hold the offender responsible, exhibit healthy boundaries and role definitions with the siblings, the offender is engaged in productive treatment, and the abused sibling is moving forward in individual treatment. During this step the offender will disclose his detailed offending actions, thoughts,

and feelings. He will map out his cycle of offending by discussing with his parental figures his means of planning the abuse, maintaining compliance, and covering it up. The parental figures have to be emotionally prepared for the chilling details of the abuse events. The clinician must be prepared to work with the intense family member emotions that are sure to come. Ensuring for the physical safety of all in attendance is essential. It is critical the offending sibling be able to progress in treatment where he is able to understand the depth of the destructive nature of the abuse on the abused sibling and the rest of the family. Maintain close contact with the abused sibling's therapist during this time to exchange disclosed details surrounding the abuse, adequacy and compliance with the safety plan, and the timing of moving to the next step in the family work. Begin to prepare for the next step of sibling contact by educating the parental figures on what to expect. Additional older family members may be brought into the process near the end of this step to show support for the family members and encourage the sibling offender in his treatment.

Warning signs that could prevent movement to the next step or complicate future treatment efforts until resolved may include:

- Family members want to 'speed-up the treatment process'.
- Appointments are missed.
- Safety plan is not being followed.
- Offender is threatening the victim or having unsupervised contact.
- Offender is not engaging in productive treatment.
- Offender is complaining about the treatment.
- Offender is trying to make deals to avoid further treatment.
- Victim is having difficulties in individual treatment.
- Victim is having nightmares or demonstrating regressive behaviours.
- Parental figures minimise the abuse.
- Parental figures have poor boundaries and role definition with the siblings.
- Parental figures do not understand the important abuse and offender dynamics present in their family crisis.

Proceed to next step: Take measures to resolve the warning signs that raise safety concerns and confront presented denial and minimisation of the abuse. Proceed to the next step only when the sibling victim and offender have made sufficient progress to be able to tolerate the contact in the family sessions and the parental figures are able to provide the needed support and supervision to each. Closely co-ordinate the move with other treating professionals.

Step Four: bring sibling victim(s) and sibling offender together in family work

This step should not be attempted if step three has not been successfully completed. This is the most critical part of the family reunification work and has the highest level of risk of revictimising the victim if not managed properly. In some cases the offender may be able to be reintegrated back into the home with the victim where family members have had positive treatment outcomes, parental figures are able to maintain proper levels of support and protection for all members, the offender demonstrates genuine remorse, and the victim acknowledges it was not their fault. Reunification in this step may not be possible or desirable if parental figures are in denial about the abuse, prove toxic to the well-being of the victim or offender, treatment steps are skipped or rushed for the sake of 'going through the motions', or if either the victim or offender demonstrate a poor response to their treatment (Counseling and Consultation Services, 1999).

Goal: safely bring the sibling victim into the family reunification process

Look for the parental figures to develop and practice the skill of protecting the victim while supporting each sibling in treatment, taking charge of managing family interactions, the family reunification supports the treatment of both siblings, and the family members develop healthier interaction patterns.

Participants may include parental figures, sibling victim(s), sibling offender, older supporting family members, and individuals' therapists.

Treatment focus: The function of this step is to begin to bring the victim and offender siblings together in a safe manner that allows for each to practice what they have been learning in their own individual treatment, and to develop over time a new paradigm of how the family members will interact in the future. Consult with each sibling's therapist and the parental figures prior to and following each contact to establish session goals and

evaluate progress. Empower the sibling victim by talking about the process of the contact prior to and following each session. Develop pre-session signals for the sibling victim to give if they are feeling uncomfortable and want the sibling offender removed from the session. The work is designed to increase the role of the parental figures in the sessions. The therapist encourages and supports the parental figures in developing increased confidence in their ability to protect the siblings, establish guidelines, enforce rules, and anticipate dynamics that may be presented by each sibling. The sibling victim uses the session to express feelings and thoughts about the offender and the abuse, clearly stating future abuse will not be allowed to happen again, it was not their fault, and there is a safety plan that will be followed. The sibling offender is given the opportunity to take full responsibility for the abuse, acknowledge the sibling victim's feelings, explain what he has learned in treatment, the changes that can be expected in the future, support the safety plan, and encourage reporting if the safety plan details are not followed. The parental figures clearly state support for both siblings, outline knowledge of the sibling offender's cycle, warning signs, high risk situations, expectations surrounding future sibling contacts, and full support for future consequences if the safety plan is violated.

Warning signs that could prevent movement to the next step or complicate future treatment efforts until resolved may include:

- Safety plan details are not being enforced.
- Family members may intellectualise the abuse and avoid feelings.
- Offender may try to take control of the sessions.
- Offender attempts to blame the victim.
- Offender becomes sexually aroused.
- Offender distorts the sessions or minimises the abuse impact.
- Victim could avoid confronting the offender with their true feelings.
- Victim has nightmares.
- Victim exhibits regressive behaviours.
- Victim becomes hostile and threatening.
- Parental figures send mixed signals surrounding their feelings and future expectations.

Proceed to next step: Take measures to resolve the warning signs that raise safety concerns, look for parental figures ability and willingness to safely supervise sibling contacts, sibling's treating therapists to indicate they have each proceeded far enough in their individual work to discontinue family sessions. Sibling victim feels safe with parental figures and knows the safety plan details. The abusing sibling knows their cycle, can interrupt their cycle, can identify high-risk situations and avoid them, know and demonstrate a willingness to use relapse prevention skills, and follows the safety plan.

Step Five: family therapy termination

Begin laying the early groundwork for this step at the very beginning of the 5-Step Family Therapy Protocol process. Make referrals as necessary for follow-up services to take over after the completion of the family work. This step in the protocol is the final part of the family reunification effort to promote family healing of sibling on sibling sexual abuse by encouraging victim recovery, enhancing offender treatment, and developing a new paradigm for future family interactions. When possible have the transitional team members that will follow the family participate in a family session to allow each family member to outline the work they have accomplished, high risk situations, their interpretation of the abuse, and the details of the safety plan. Work with the family and the transitional professionals in developing future working goals and expectations.

Goal: Review treatment successes, evaluate depth of treatment integration among members, and prepare the family members for family therapy transitioning and termination

A positive outcome in this step would be for the family to follow the safety plan, the victim feels safe and empowered to protect him/herself, the offender is able to avoid high-risk situations and prevent relapse, and the parental figures take the lead in managing their family safely during the termination and transitioning phase of family treatment (National Adolescent Perpetrator Network, 1993).

Participants may include parental figures, sibling victims, sibling offender, older supportive family members, individuals' therapists, and after care professionals.

Treatment focus: Review treatment successes and transitional issues. Explore the fears of each family member. Be aware of and gently confront

regressive thinking, feelings, or behaviours. Explore family therapy termination readiness with each family member. Review progress made on initial family treatment goals. Establish new transitional goals.

Discuss offender relapse prevention follow-up services. Co-ordinate final session with other treating professionals supporting the family. Gain commitment to a three-month follow-up family session.

Warning signs that could compromise transition efforts include:

- Complaining about transitional expectations.
- Family members are not aware of regressive behaviours, thinking, or feelings.
- Feeling treatment is over and everything is back to normal.
- Not following the safety plan.
- Not showing up for final family therapy appointments.
- Family members are unable to note high-risk situations to avoid.
- Family members did not successfully complete their individual therapy.

Proceed to next step: Take measures to resolve the warning signs that raise safety concerns, confront treatment regression, ensure the family has a realistic plan to meet anticipated concerns surrounding the termination, the follow-up professionals understand the case, and services are in place.

Special areas of concern

In the course of using the 5-Step Family Therapy Protocol there are an unpredictable number of special situations that might arise. Approaches taken to manage these special challenges should always consider victim safety, parental ability to understand how and be willing to protect family members, and holding the offender responsible. A few of the more unsettling commonly seen special challenges are noted as follows:

What if there is more than one sibling victim?

This is too often the case. Several guiding principals to follow when working with this family presentation include:

- Treat each sibling victim as an individual who has a common offender and allow them to work at their own pace in individual and family work.

- Consider the different treatment needs based on age, development, gender differences, and abuse characteristics.
- Never compromise the safety of either sibling victim.
- Be aware of differing parental responses toward each sibling victim.
- Support the parental figures in understanding and appreciating the different emerging responses to the abuse by each sibling.
- Help parental figures and the sibling victims to avoid making destructive comparisons or value judgements concerning each of the victim sibling's responses to the abuse and treatment.
- Support the family in understanding that inconsistencies in abuse stories may be a function of actual fact, perception of events, or developmental levels.
- Include each sibling victim in the family therapy process and contact with the offender at their own individual pace and when cleared by their individual therapist.

What if one of the parental figures has also suffered physical or sexual abuse by the offender?

In these cases it is important for the parental figure to also be labelled a victim and be in victim treatment. The parental figure may be able to participate in the family therapy from the beginning if they are safe, willing to talk about their feelings with the offender, can protect themselves, have a safety plan in place for them also, and are not being adversely affected by the family work. In such cases the offender needs to be out of the house.

What if one of the parental figures is also abusive physically or sexually toward siblings?

Unfortunately this type of family work too often uncovers the reality that one of the parental figures might also be a physical or sexual offender against a family member in the immediate family. When this is discovered it is to be reported, investigated, and steps taken to ensure the safety of all family members. Parental offenders are not to participate in the family therapy process until they have progressed far enough in their own treatment that they are safe and not toxic to the family reunification process. Final clearance to enter sessions is up to the victims' and the offender's therapists.

Conclusion

The presented 5-Step Family Therapy Protocol provides a guide for clinicians to constructively manage the destructive nature of *sibling on sibling sexual abuse* in the context of family therapy. The presented framework can be used to augment individual clinical training and experience as decisions have to be made about how to best proceed, family member dynamics to consider, clinical tasks, and cues as to when to discontinue the reunification process or move closer to successful termination. There should always be an emphasis placed on the emotional and physical safety of all family members, especially victims or those who are vulnerable. While family reunification and healing is not always possible in cases of sibling on sibling sexual abuse, following the presented 5-Step Family Therapy Protocol increases the likelihood of positive family reunification outcomes.

Acknowledgments

It is with great appreciation I acknowledge Adam Young, MSW intern who participated in the development of the initial work from which this chapter grew and give thanks to the clinical teams at Hanover Juvenile Correctional Center Behavioural Services Unit and The Daybreak Sexual Offender Prevention Program at Poplar Springs Hospital for their support, suggestions, and encouragement as we look together for effective techniques to work with families who are the victims of sexual abuse.

References

Breer, W. (1996) *The Adolescent Molester.* Springfield, Illinois: Charles C. Thomas Publishing.

Counseling and Consultation Services, Inc. (1999) *Protocol for Therapeutically Tolerated Visitation With Sex Offenders and Children.* Johnson City, TN.

Czech, N. (1988) Family Therapy With Adolescent Sex Offenders. New York: Brunner/Mazel Inc.

Harris, B. and Campbell, J. (1998) *Face to Face: A Model for Therapists to Assess Readiness for and Provide Reunification Treatment to Juvenile Sex Offenders and their Victims.* ATSA presentation.

Hodges, C. and Young, A. (1999) *Healing the Juvenile Sex Offender's Family Through Family Reunification.* ATSA Presentation.

Madanes, C. (1990) *Sex, Love, and Violence: Strategies for Transformation.* New York: W.W. Norton and Company.

Madanes, C., Keim, J. and Smelser, D. (1995) *The Violence of Men: New Techniques for Working With Abusive Families: A Therapy of Social Action.* San Francisco: Jossey Bass Inc.

McGoldrick, M., Gerson, R. and Shellenbergeret, S. (1999) *Genograms; Assessment and Intervention.* NY: WW Norton and Company.

Meinig, M. (1996) *Family Therapy Protocol.* ATSA presentation.

National Adolescent Perpetrator Network. (1993) The Revised Report from The National Task Force on Juvenile Sexual Offending. *Juvenile and Family Court Journal.* 44: 4.

Perry, G. and Orchard, J. (1992) *Assessment and Treatment of Adolescent Sex Offenders.* Sarasota, FL: Professional Resources Press.

Prendergast, W. E. (1991) *Treating Sex Offenders in Correctional Institutions and Outpatient Clinics.* New York: Haworth Press.

Ryan, G. and Lane, S. (Eds.) (1997) *Juvenile Sexual Offending: Causes, Consequences and Correction.* San Francisco: Jossey-Bass Inc.

Sexual Assault Center (1999) *Child Sexual Abuse.* Knoxville, TN.

Steen, C. and Monnette, B. (1989) *Treating Adolescent Sexual Offenders In The Community.* Springfield, Illinois: Charles C. Thomas.

Stroud, D. (1999) Familial Support as Perceived by Adult Victims of Childhood Sexual Abuse. *Sexual Abuse: A Journal of Research and Treatment.* 11:2 159–75.

Werrbach, G. (1993) The Family Reunification Role-play. *Child Welfare.* 22:6 555–67.

Wieckowski, E. and Hodges, C. (2000) *Juvenile Sexual Offender Treatment In Community and Residential Settings: A Practical Guide for Clinicians, Administrators, Court Personnel and Direct Care Staff.* Unpublished.

Wiehe, V. (1997) *Sibling Abuse: Hidden Physical, Emotional, and Sexual Trauma.* London: Sage Publications.